# Edmund Burke

*Reflections on the Revolution in France*

# Edmund Burke

REFLECTIONS
ON THE
REVOLUTION IN FRANCE

*Edited by*

J. C. D. Clark

Stanford University Press
Stanford, California

Stanford University Press
Stanford, California
© 2001 J. C. D. Clark
Printed in the United States of America

Library of Congress Cataloging-in-Publication Data

Burke, Edmund, 1730–1797
    Reflections on the Revolution in France / Edmund Burke ; edited by J. C. D.
Clark.
            p.      cm.
    Includes bibliographical references and index.
    ISBN 0-8047-3923-4 (alk. paper) —
    ISBN 0-8047-4205-7 (paper : alk. paper)
    1. Burke, Edmund, 1729–1797—Correspondence.   2. France—History—
Revolution, 1789–1799—Foreign public opinion—British.   3. Public
opinion—Great Britain—History—18th century.   4. Burke, Edmund, 1730–
1797. Reflections on the Revolution in France.   I. Clark, J. C. D.   II. Title.

DC150.B9 B85      2001
944.04—dc21                                                      00-063732

This book is printed on acid-free, archival-quality paper.

Original printing 2001
Last figure below indicates year of this printing:
10   09

Designed and typeset by John Feneron in 10/13 Sabon

# Contents

REFLECTIONS ON THE REVOLUTION IN FRANCE — 141

[Burke provided no sub-division of his work into sections or chapters:
it began as a letter, and remained a single undivided body of prose.
What follows is the suggestion of the editor in order to make Burke's
text more easily accessible.]

# Preface

Edmund Burke's *Reflections on the Revolution in France* is an undoubted classic of political writing. That statement means, however, several things, for the work has been reinterpreted within a succession of genres from the polemical pamphlets of the 1790s to the modern canon of political texts. It has served a succession of ever-changing practical purposes: from Burke's attempt to retrieve his former influence within the Foxite Whig opposition and the defence of England's Whig, patrician and monarchical order against the French Revolution, through Victorian Conservative rearguard actions against advancing democracy, to American neo-conservative arguments during the Cold War, Irish nationalist politics and present-day environmentalist campaigns. Burke's continued currency establishes the importance of his text, but creates a hazard for its editors: many modern commentators on Burke (as on Paine) still feel the need either to eulogise, or to denigrate, their author. This edition may contribute to an emancipation from partisanship, since I have throughout sought neither to bury Burke nor to praise him, but to explain him historically.

In preparing this edition, I have incurred many debts. For their comments on drafts and for conversations on this field over many years, I am grateful to Tim Blanning, Gail Bossenga, Colin Lucas and John Pocock. Florence Boulerie, Anna Cienciala, William Doyle, Vivian Gruder, Frederick Holmes, Rene Marion, Jim McCue, Allan Pasco, Jeremy Popkin and James Sack provided references. F. P. Lock kindly read the typescript of this edition, and made many suggestions: I have profited from our discussions, which took place after the publication of the first volume of his important life of Burke and during the composition of the second. I owe most to

François Furet, whose untimely death cut short our exchanges on revolution and democracy, and deprives English historiography of one of its greatest allies. More generally, I am indebted to all those Burke scholars who have contributed to the cumulative and co-operative process of historical exegesis.

CALLALY CASTLE
NORTHUMBERLAND

# Abbreviations

| | |
|---|---|
| Blackstone, *Commentaries* | William Blackstone, *Commentaries on the Laws of England* (4 vols., Oxford, 1765–9) |
| [Burke], *Appeal* | [Edmund Burke], *An Appeal from the New to the Old Whigs, in consequence of some late Discussions in Parliament, relative to the Reflections on the French Revolution* (London, 1791) |
| Burke, *Correspondence* | Thomas W. Copeland (et al., eds.), *The Correspondence of Edmund Burke* (10 vols., Cambridge, 1958–78) |
| Burke, *LC* | *Catalogue of the Library of the Late Right Hon. Edmund Burke, The Library of the Late Sir M. B. Clare, M.D. Some Articles from Gibbon's Library, &c. &c. ... which will be sold by auction by Mr. Evans ...* ([London], 1833) |
| Burke, *LC MS* | Catalogue of Burke's library dated August 17, 1813, Bodleian MS Eng Misc d 722 |
| Burke, *Letter to a Member* | *A Letter from Mr. Burke, to a Member of the National Assembly; In Answer to some Objections to his Book on French Affairs* (Paris; reprinted London, 1791) |
| Burke, *Letter to a Noble Lord* | *A Letter from the Right Honourable Edmund Burke to a Noble Lord, on the Attacks made upon Him and His Pension, in The House of Lords, by The Duke of Bedford and the Earl of Lauderdale, Early in the present Sessions of Parliament* (London, 1796) |
| Burke, *Representation ... 1784* | *A Representation to His Majesty, Moved in the House of Commons, by the Right Honourable Edmund Burke, and Seconded by the Right Honourable William Windham, On Monday, June 14, 1784, and negatived. With a Preface and Notes* (London, 1784); often known by its second title, *Motion, relative to the Speech from the Throne* |

| | |
|---|---|
| Burke, *Speech ...* Feb. 28, 1785 | *Mr. Burke's Speech, on the Motion made for Papers relative to the Directions for Charging the Nabob of Arcot's Private Debts to Europeans, on the Revenues of the Carnatic. February 28th, 1785* (London, 1785) |
| Burke, *Speech ...* 9 Feb. 1790 | *Substance of the Speech of the Right Honourable Edmund Burke, in the Debate on the Army Estimates, in the House of Commons, On Tuesday, the 9th Day of February, 1790. Comprehending a Discussion of the Present Situation of Affairs in France* (London, 1790) |
| [Burke], *Thoughts* | [Edmund Burke], *Thoughts on the Cause of the Present Discontents* (London, 1770) |
| Burke, *Two Letters ... on the Proposals for Peace* | Edmund Burke, *Two Letters addressed to a Member of the Present Parliament, on the Proposals for Peace with the Regicide Directory of France* (London, 1796) |
| Burke, *Works* | [W. King and F. Lawrence, eds.], *The Works of the Right Honourable Edmund Burke* (16 vols., London: F. C. and J. Rivington, 1803–27) |
| Cone, *Burke* | Carl B. Cone, *Burke and the Nature of Politics* (2 vols., Lexington, Kentucky, 1957, 1964) |
| Doyle, *Origins* | William Doyle, *The Origins of the French Revolution* (Oxford, 1980) |
| Egret, *French Prerevolution* | Jean Egret, *The French Prerevolution 1787–1788* (trans. Wesley D. Camp, Chicago, 1977) |
| Fierro and Liébert | Edmund Burke, *Réflexions sur la révolution de France*, présentation de Philippe Raynaud, annotation d'Alfred Fierro et Georges Liébert (Paris: Hachette, 1989) |
| Furet and Ozouf, *Critical Dictionary* | François Furet and Mona Ozouf (eds.), *A Critical Dictionary of the French Revolution* (1988; trans. Arthur Goldhammer, Cambridge, Mass., 1989). |
| Hampson, *Prelude* | Norman Hampson, *Prelude to Terror: The Constituent Assembly and the Failure of Consensus, 1789–1791* (Oxford, 1988) |
| Lock, *Burke* | F. P. Lock, *Edmund Burke. Volume I, 1730–1784* (Oxford, 1998) |
| Mercier, *New Picture of Paris* | Louis Sébastien Mercier, *New Picture of Paris* (2 vols., London, 1800) |
| Le Moniteur | *Gazette Nationale, ou le Moniteur Universel* (Paris, 1789– ) |
| Montesquieu, *The Spirit of the Laws* | *The Spirit of Laws. Translated from the French of M. De Secondat, Baron de Montesquieu* (2 vols., London, 1750) |
| OED | *Oxford English Dictionary* |

| | |
|---|---|
| Paine, *Rights of Man* | Thomas Paine, *Rights of Man: being an Answer to Mr. Burke's Attack on the French Revolution* (London: J. S. Jordan, 1791) |
| *Parl Hist* | William Cobbett (ed.), *The Parliamentary History of England from the Earliest Period to the Year 1806* (36 vols., London, 1806–20) |
| Price, *Correspondence* | W. Bernard Peach and D. O. Thomas (eds.), *The Correspondence of Richard Price* (3 vols., Cardiff, 1983–94) |
| Price, *Discourse* | *A Discourse on the Love of our Country, Delivered on Nov. 4, 1789, at the Meeting-House in the Old Jewry, to the Society for Commemorating the Revolution in Great Britain. With an Appendix, containing the Report of the Committee of the Society; an Account of the Population of France; and the Declaration of Rights by the National Assembly of France. Third Edition, with Additions to the Appendix, Containing Communications from France occasioned by the Congratulatory Address of the Revolution Society to the National Assembly of France, with the Answers to them. By Richard Price, D.D. LL.D. F.R.S. and Fellow of the American Philosophical Societies at Philadelphia and Boston* (London, 1790) |
| Priestley, *Letters to Burke* | Joseph Priestley, *Letters to the Right Honourable Edmund Burke, occasioned by his Reflections on the Revolution in France, &c* (Birmingham, 1791) |
| Prior, *Memoir of Burke* | Sir James Prior, *Memoir of the Life and Character of the Right Hon. Edmund Burke* (2nd edn., 2 vols., London, 1826) |
| Roberts (ed.), *Documents* | J. M. Roberts (ed.), *French Revolution Documents*, vol. 1 (Oxford, 1966) |
| *Statutes at Large* | Danby Pickering (ed.), *The Statutes at Large, from Magna Charta to the end of the eleventh Parliament of Great Britain, Anno 1761* (46 vols., Cambridge, 1762–1807) |
| Thomas, *Price* | D. O. Thomas, *The Honest Mind: The Thought and Work of Richard Price* (Oxford, 1977) |
| Tocqueville, *Old Regime* | Alexis de Tocqueville, *The Old Regime and the French Revolution*, trans. Alan S. Kahan, intro. François Furet and Françoise Mélonio (Chicago, 1998) |
| Young, *Travels in France* | Arthur Young, *Travels, During The Years 1787, 1788, and 1789. Undertaken more particularly with a View of ascertaining the Cultivation, Wealth, Resources, and National Prosperity, of the Kingdom of France* (Bury St. Edmunds, 1792). |

# Chronological Table

### 1730
January 12 (NS): (year uncertain) Edmund Burke born in Dublin

### 1744
14 April: entered Trinity College, Dublin; graduated BA 1748

### 1747
23 April: name enrolled at Middle Temple, London

### 1750
? April : Burke moved to London to read for the bar

### 1756
18 May: Burke's *A Vindication of Natural Society* published

### 1757
12 March: married Jane Nugent, probably in London
21 April: Burke's *A Philosophical Enquiry into the Origin of our Ideas of the Sublime and Beautiful* published

### 1760
25 October: accession of George III

### 1765
11 July: became private secretary to 2nd marquis of Rockingham (1730–82)
23 December: elected MP for Wendover

### 1770
23 April: Burke's *Thoughts on the Cause of the Present Discontents* published

### 1773
12 January–1 March: visited France

### 1774
3 November: elected MP for Bristol

### 1775
10 January: Burke's *Speech on American Taxation* (of 19 April 1774) published
22 May: Burke's *Speech on Conciliation with America* (of 22 March 1775) published

### 1776
4 July: American Declaration of Independence

### 1777
5 May: Burke's *Letter to the Sheriffs of Bristol* published

### 1780
23 September: lost seat at Bristol
7 December: elected MP for Malton, Rockingham's pocket borough

### 1782
27 March: Lord North resigned; Rockingham became First Lord of the Treasury; Burke became Paymaster General
1 July: Rockingham died; Shelburne succeeded him; Burke resigned on 10 July

### 1783
2 April: Shelburne resigned; Fox-North coalition succeeded; Burke again became Paymaster General
3 September: Peace of Versailles ended American War
19 December: Fox-North Coalition dismissed; William Pitt succeeded; Burke resigned

### 1784
March: general election: major defeat for Foxite Whigs

### 1787
28 March: Beaufoy's motion for repeal of Test and Corporation Acts defeated in House of Commons
3 April: House of Commons voted for impeachment of Warren Hastings

### 1788
13 February: Warren Hastings's trial began
8 May: attempted French royal *coup* against the *parlements*
8 August: Louis XVI agreed to summoning of Estates General
16 August: suspension of payments from French treasury
25 September: Paris *parlement* reconvened
4 November: first meeting of the revitalised Revolution Society in London
8 November: George III's illness diagnosed; Regency Crisis began
27 December: numbers of Third Estate doubled in forthcoming Estates General

## 1789

February: Abbé Sieyès's *Qu'est-ce que le tiers état?* published

19 February: recovery of George III notified to Parliament; Foxite Whigs' hopes of office dashed

23 April: service of thanksgiving in St Paul's Cathedral

5 May: opening session of French Estates-General

8 May: Beaufoy's second motion for repeal of Test and Corporation Acts defeated

17 June: Third Estate claimed title of National Assembly

9 July: National Assembly adopted title 'National Constituent Assembly'

14 July: fall of the Bastille

17 July: Louis XVI's visit to Paris

22 July: murders of Foulon and Bertier de Sauvigny

July–August: *la Grande Peur*

4 August: National Assembly abolished many privileges of nobility and Church

26 August: National Assembly completed its vote of the *Déclaration des droits de l'homme et du citoyen*

10 September: National Assembly voted for a unicameral legislature in the forthcoming constitution

11 September: National Assembly voted the king a suspensive veto only

24 September: Necker's report to National Assembly on finances of France

29 September: Committee of the Constitution reported to the National Assembly including plan for French local government

1 October: National Assembly voted to demand *contributions patriotiques*

5–6 October: Paris mob marched on Versailles and compelled Louis XVI to return to the capital

10 October: Louis XVI's title changed to 'King of the French'

12 October: National Assembly voted to follow king to Paris

2 November: National Assembly voted that the property of French church was 'at the disposal of the nation'

3 November: National Assembly suspended the *parlements*

4 November: Richard Price's sermon to the London Revolution Society at the Old Jewry meeting house

7 November: National Assembly disqualified ministers from sitting in the legislature

8 November: Chénier's play *Charles IX* opened in Paris

17 November: Mounier's *Exposé de la conduite de M. Mounier, dans l'Assemblée nationale, Et des motifs de son retour en Dauphiné* published

19 December: National Assembly voted to begin the auction of French Church property and to issue *assignats*

24 December: National Assembly decreed toleration of non-Catholics

## 1790

January: Lally-Tollendal's *Mémoire de m. le comte de Lally-Tollendal, ou seconde lettre A ses Commettans* published

2 January: Bailly reported to National Assembly

21 January: Westminster Parliament reassembled

9 February: Burke's first public attack on the French Revolution in his speech on the army estimates

13 February: National Assembly voted to withdraw recognition of monastic vows
20 February: Burke's *Speech on the Army Estimates* (of 9 Feb. 1790) published
16 February: National Assembly voted to establish a new system of local government
20 February: Burke's *Speech on the Army Estimates* (of 9 Feb. 1790) published
16 February: National Assembly voted to establish a new system of local government
ment
28 February: National Assembly decreed a reorganised army
2 March: Fox's Bill to repeal the Test and Corporation Acts defeated, Burke speaking against
15 March: National Assembly declared feudal regime abolished
30 April: National Guard at Marseilles seized the city's royal fortresses
22 May: National Assembly voted to abolish king's prerogative over declarations of war and peace
29 May: Necker reported to National Assembly on French finances
4 June: La Tour Du Pin reported to National Assembly on state of the French army
20 June: National Assembly abolished titles of nobility
10 July: National Assembly decree on pensions
12 July: National Assembly voted the Civil Constitution of the Clergy
14 July: *Fête de la féderation* held in the *champ de Mars*
13 August: Bailly reported to National Assembly
4 September: Necker resigned
6 September: National Assembly abolished *parlements*
21 September: National Assembly decreed a partially elective system of promotion for the army
29 September: National Assembly voted issue of 800 million *livres* of *assignats*
October: Calonne's *De l'état de la France* published
1 November: Burke's *Reflections on the Revolution in France* published
27 November: National Assembly imposed loyalty oath on clergy

### 1791

13 March: Paine's *Rights of Man* [part I] published
19 April: Richard Price died
May: Mackintosh's *Vindiciae Gallicae* published
6 May: Burke's speech in Commons renouncing his friendship with Fox
21 May: Burke's *A Letter to a Member of the National Assembly* published in London
20 June: Louis XVI's 'flight to Varennes'
25 June: National Assembly suspended Louis XVI from his functions as king
3 August: Burke's *An Appeal from the New to the Old Whigs* published
3 September: National Assembly adopted French constitution
30 September: National Constituent Assembly dissolved
1 October: National Legislative Assembly met

### 1792

9 February: property of *émigrés* declared forfeit to the nation
16 February: Paine's *Rights of Man. Part the Second* published
18 February: Burke's *Letter to Sir Hercules Langrishe* published
20 April: France declared war on Austria; Prussia joined against France in the First Coalition
10 August: French royal family imprisoned

2–6 September: the 'September Massacres' in Paris
21 September: Legislative Assembly replaced by the Convention
22 September: French republic proclaimed
19 November: decree of Convention offering fraternal aid to promote revolutions abroad
18 December: Paine tried in London *in absentia*

### 1793

21 January: Louis XVI executed
1 February: France declared war on Britain and Dutch Republic
13 February: formation of the First Coalition against France
28 February: Burke and others resigned from the Whig Club
11 March: beginning of the rising in the Vendée against the Revolution
August: desecration of the tombs of French kings at Saint-Denis
5 September: beginning of the Terror
16 October: Marie-Antoinette executed
November: campaign of de-Christianization at its peak

### 1794

21 June: Burke resigned from Parliament
17 July: Burke's son Richard elected MP for Malton
28 July: Robespierre executed; end of the Terror
2 August: Richard Burke died

### 1795

17 February: armistice in the Vendée
23 April: Warren Hastings acquitted
22 September: Burke received pension from the Crown
2 November: French Directory established

### 1796

24 February: Burke's *Letter to a Noble Lord* published
19 October: Burke's *Thoughts on the Prospect of a Regicide Peace* published

### 1797

9 July: Edmund Burke died on his estate at Beaconsfield

### 1799

9 November (18 Brumaire): Napoleon Bonaparte's *coup d'état* established a military dictatorship in France

# Introduction

## (i) The identity of Edmund Burke

Edmund Burke was a Whig in politics, an Anglican latitudinarian in religion: although both his religious and his political positions were complex, and developed with time, this brief summary does no injustice to either at any stage of his career. The term 'Whig' was clearly intelligible in early eighteenth-century England and Ireland, for the political world into which Burke was born in 1730 was still locked fast in that older ideological antithesis which saw the birth of 'Whig' and 'Tory' doctrine. It was a world which had been debating the fundamental principles of authority and allegiance with bitter intensity and in recognisably similar terms since the Exclusion Crisis of the 1670s.[1] That foundational event of the Whig ascendancy, the Glorious Revolution of 1688, had also defined the relations between the two kingdoms in which Burke's career was set. This framework did not quickly fade: on the contrary, the ideological conflicts of the reign of Queen Anne, including the trial of Dr. Sacheverell and the accession of the House of Hanover in 1714, were current politics into the 1750s.[2]

Burke inevitably acknowledged the continuing relevance of these landmarks of Whig history. In 1765, he launched his parliamentary career when he 'entered into a connexion' with the second marquis of Rockingham. As he explained this decision in 1791,

[1]This edition takes as its starting point the account of Burke's intellectual setting given in J. C. D. Clark, *English Society 1660–1832: Religion, ideology and politics during the ancien regime* (Cambridge, 2000). For Burke's date of birth see Lock, *Burke*, pp. 16–17.

[2]For surveys of Whig doctrine, see Bibliography, B iii.

When he entered into the Whig party, he did not conceive that they pretended to any discoveries. They did not affect to be better Whigs, than those were who lived in the days in which principle was put to the test. Some of the Whigs of those days were then living. They were what the Whigs had been at the Revolution; what they had been during the reign of queen Anne; what they had been at the accession of the present royal family.[3]

He had perfectly understood what he was doing, he wrote; he 'was at that time as likely as most men to know what were Whig and what were Tory principles'. Burke aligned himself with a Whig grandee, and remained with the Rockinghams in opposition despite the prospect of ministerial office. He would not have done this 'for principles which he did not truly embrace, or did not perfectly understand'.[4] Political life was nevertheless evolving: although it was still polarised when Burke moved to England in 1750, the vicissitudes of that decade led to the breakup of the Tory party at Westminster and its substantial absorption by other Whig groups in the early 1760s.[5] Thereafter the term 'Tory' was used less and less, surviving as a term of abuse in the local politics of a few constituencies, and most often in the political vocabulary of Dissenters.[6] Burke had never been a Tory, although, like other Whigs in the 1750s including David Hume, he had explored on paper ways of reconciling the ancient controversy (p. [30] n).[7] After the publication of the *Reflections*, Burke was rightly indignant that Dissenting propagandists tried to pin the label 'Tory' on himself. He well knew its older, literal, meanings.

So did others of his contemporaries: Samuel Johnson, whose mind had been formed in the world of early-Hanoverian Tory-Jacobitism, regarded Burke as a man near the opposite end of the spectrum: although Johnson admired Burke's abilities, he was seldom in sympathy with Burke's politics.[8] Burke himself, by contrast, and especially in the face of the French Revolution, saw himself defending a middle ground, a 'third option' between the 'depotism of the monarch' and the 'despotism of the multitude'. He identified

---

[3][Burke], *Appeal*, p. 54.

[4][Burke], *Appeal*, pp. 53–4.

[5]J. C. D. Clark, *The Dynamics of Change: The Crisis of the 1750s and English Party Systems* (Cambridge, 1982).

[6]In the American colonies, 'Tory' was revived in the 1770s as a synonym for 'loyalist'. The term had little such renewed currency in England.

[7]References in this form are to page numbers of the first edition of the *Reflections*, given in the text below.

[8]In no sense were Johnson and Burke within a single 'conservative' camp: J. C. D. Clark, 'Religious Affiliation and Dynastic Allegiance in Eighteenth-Century England: Edmund Burke, Thomas Paine and Samuel Johnson', *English Literary History* 64 (1997), pp. 1029–67.

that middle ground emphatically with the Whiggish constitution vindicated by the revolution of 1688: 'a monarchy directed by laws, controlled and balanced by the great hereditary wealth and hereditary dignity of a nation; and both again controlled by a judicious check from the reason and feeling of the people at large acting by a suitable and permanent organ', the House of Commons. Burke was indignant at the slur that 'all those who disapprove of [the revolutionaries'] new abuses, must of course be partizans of the old' (p. [184]).

Edmund Burke was an Irishman, born in Dublin but in an age before 'Celtic nationalism' had been constructed to make Irishness and Englishness incompatible: he was therefore free also to describe himself, without misrepresentation, as 'an Englishman' to denote his membership of the wider polity.[9] He never attempted to disguise his Irishness (as some ambitious Scots in eighteenth-century England tried to anglicise their accents), did what he could in the Commons to promote the interests of his native country and was bitterly opposed to the Penal Laws against Irish Catholics. Yet Burke's personal ambition from the 1750s or 1760s was to assimilate to the English landed elite, not to return in triumph to Ireland as its political deliverer. After 1766 he visited that country only once, 'a rapid and unpremeditated journey'[10] in 1786.[11] His Irishness had its limits: he was no Jonathan Swift, no Wolfe Tone, no Daniel O'Connell.

※ Burke's deep and lasting concern for Irish interests has often been wrongly attributed to a concealed allegiance to the Roman Catholicism of his mother and of his wider family. Catholicism was a major political handicap in post-Revolution England, and Burke had constantly to defend himself from charges of crypto-Popery. Yet he was truthful in what he told the society hostess Mrs. Crewe, evidently in the 1790s:

> Mr. Burke's Enemies often endeavoured to convince the World that he had been bred up in the Catholic Faith, & that his Family were of it, & that he himself had been educated at St. Omer—but this was false, as his father was a regular practitioner of the Law at Dublin, which he could not be unless of the Established Church: & it so happened that though Mr. B— was twice at Paris, he never happened to go through the Town of St. Omer.[12]

[9]Burke to Adrien-Jean-François Duport, [post 29 March 1790]: Burke, *Correspondence*, VI, pp. 104–9, at 106.

[10]Prior, *Memoir of Burke*, II, p. 68.

[11]Burke's relations with his native country are definitively explored in the introductory material to R. B. McDowell (ed.), *The Writings and Speeches of Edmund Burke* IX, I: *The Revolutionary War 1794–1797 II: Ireland* (Oxford, 1991).

[12]'Extracts from Mr. Burke's Table-Talk', *Miscellanies of the Philobiblon Society 7*

An MP once elected, in order to take his seat at Westminster, had to take the oaths of allegiance and abjuration, the oath of supremacy, and subscribe a declaration against transubstantiation. No Roman Catholics are known to have done so in the eighteenth century. Burke consistently distanced himself from the Roman church, and did not (as Catholic rumour later claimed) receive the ministrations of a Roman priest on his death bed.[13]

Even Burke's comments on the desperate plight of the French church in the Revolution were not those of a co-religionist. His defence of its hierarchy in the *Reflections* was pragmatic; he said almost nothing about the Civil Constitution of the Clergy, a reorganisation imposed by the new government and which he presumably thought was within the state's powers; his outrage at the seizure of the goods of the French church was outrage at theft, not sacrilege.[14] It was exactly because Burke believed that church property and lay property were held by the same legal right that he inferred that the invasion of the first imperiled the second also. In the *Reflections*, he argued (p. [223]) that 'it is in the principle of injustice [i.e. theft] that the danger lies, and not in the description of persons [i.e. clergy] on whom it is first exercised'. Such views divided him beyond question from Rome, and in the *Reflections* he expressed his dissent from the Papacy's temporal claims. Burke wrote of the Papacy as 'The proudest domination that ever was endured on earth' (p. [40]); the English rightly 'refused to change their law in remote ages, from respect to the infallibility of popes' (p. [132]). He condemned the papal claim to a power of deposing civil magistrates (p. [17]). For Burke, French monks were merely 'per-

---

(1862–3), pp. 52–3. St. Omer, a town between Calais and Lille, was the site of the English Jesuit college, founded in 1592, where the sons of many British and Irish Catholic recusant families were sent to be educated. For Burke's denials 'at his own table more than once' of ever having even visited St. Omer, see Prior, *Memoir of Burke*, I, p. 46.

[13]Elizabeth Lambert, 'Edmund Burke's Religion', *English Language Notes* 32 (1994), pp. 19–28. In 1765 Burke exonerated himself to Rockingham from allegations of crypto-Catholicism, but disclosed that his mother and sister remained Catholics. There is no evidence that his father or his wife remained in that denomination, or that Burke himself was covertly a member of it. It is sometimes claimed that his father was the Richard Burke who is listed as having conformed to the Church of Ireland as recently as 1722, but this is in doubt: Lock, *Burke*, pp. 3–15.

[14]Burke occasionally used the word 'sacrilege' (*Reflections*, pp. [80, 156, 182, 222]), but it seems that he meant it rhetorically rather than technically. Elsewhere he called it 'pillage' or 'robbery': Burke, *Correspondence*, VI, pp. 36, 39, 413). All his public pronouncements up to that date told against any special sanctity in church property. For his defence of the legitimacy in principle of the reform of the monasteries by the state, see *Reflections*, pp. [239–40].

sons, whom the fictions of a pious imagination raises to dignity by construing in the service of God' (p. [239]). While not 'violently condemning ... the Roman system of religion, we prefer the Protestant' [pp. [134–5]). Burke did not violently condemn Rome, but did respectfully criticise that church. Nevertheless, he saw 'The Protestant Church' in all its denominations as an offshoot of the Catholic, and defined only by 'what is negative', i.e. against Catholicism: 'Therefore, those who wish for the overthrow of the Catholic Religion know not how dangerous a wish they make! it is as if they wished to make a Bondfire of a house in which they [sc. their] own goods were contained.'[15]

Whatever Burke's family sympathies, his principled support for Catholics derived from a position which led to his lasting support of Protestant Dissenters also: his churchmanship can be identified as latitudinarian,[16] orthodox in its Trinitarian theology and dependent on revealed as well as natural religion, but committed against the view that any one denomination possessed either the sole authority to determine doctrine, or the only divinely ordained form of ecclesiastical polity.[17] Early in his career, he endorsed Locke's view of a church as a 'voluntary society'; he regarded the established status of the Church of England as a legal creation, open to legal modification, but subject to conditions and tests for membership set by lawful civil authority. Even priesthood he treated as a human institution, not a divine one confined by the Apostolic succession.[18] Attempts to depict Burke as a lifelong crypto-Catholic on the grounds that many of his ancestors and kin were of that denomination are

[15]"Extracts from Mr. Burke's Table-Talk', p. 8 (n.d. but evidently after 1789).

[16]The term 'latitudinarian' should be used with caution: it was not synonymous with Erastianism, did not indicate membership of one of the three 'parties' into which the Church was divided by the 1850s (the late eighteenth-century Church was not so divided) and was not defined by the anti-Trinitarian theology which began to revive from the 1760s. As used in this edition it is a term of historical art, not an attempt to depict Burke as a member of a self-aware group. Certainly, he had no allegiance to anti-Trinitarians like Francis Blackburne and Edmund Law. The term is used here in the sense outlined by R. L. Emerson, 'Latitudinarianism and the English Deists' in J. A. Leo Lemay (ed.), *Deism, Masonry and the Enlightenment* (Newark, N.J., 1987), John Spurr, '"Latitudinarianism" and the Restoration Church', *Historical Journal* 31 (1988), pp. 61–82, Richard Ashcraft, 'Latitudinarianism and Toleration: Historical Myth versus Political History', in Richard Kroll, Richard Ashcraft and Perez Zagorin (eds.), *Philosophy, Science and Religion in England 1640–1700* (Cambridge, 1992), pp. 151–77, and W. M. Spellman, *The Latitudinarians and the Church of England, 1660–1700* (Athens, GA., 1993). A reconsideration of the late eighteenth century is entailed by this work, but is not yet available in the scholarly literature.

[17]Frederick Dreyer, 'Burke's Religion', *Studies in Burke and His Time* 17 (1976), pp. 199–212.

[18]Speech on the Feathers Tavern petition, 1772, in Burke, *Works* X, pp. 3–21.

misconceived, but his views were equally distinct from the moderate High Churchmanship which was the norm in the late-Hanoverian Church of England:[19] apostolic authority, primitive doctrine and liturgy, episcopacy and the identity of Church and State were not the grounds on which Burke initially defended that body.

He explained his position in 1791: 'I have been baptised and educated in the Church of England; and have seen no cause to abandon that communion ... I think that Church harmonises with our civil constitution, with the frame and fashion of our Society, and with the general Temper of the people ... I am attached to Christianity at large; much from conviction: more from affection.'[20] This statement was evidence not for Burke's covert or unconscious preference for another church, but for his principled belief that church establishments were rightly created by legal institution, and did not exist independently by divine right. 'We are protestants', he claimed, 'not from indifference but from zeal' (p. [135]). Burke was an active politician and initially had few close clerical friends. Almost wholly absent from his library[21] were the writings of the Caroline divines, the Nonjurors, or the eighteenth-century High Churchmen; missing entirely were works of Catholic devotion. Until the late influence of the High Church Bishop Samuel Horsley, Burke's reading was in English Protestant authors of the churchmanship of Chillingworth, Cudworth, Locke, Tillotson, Hoadly, Warburton and Paley.

Remarkably, his library also included more undisguisedly freethinking or anti-Establishment works like Arthur Ashley Sykes's *The Authority of the Clergy and the Liberties of the Laity Stated and Vindicated* (1720), William Wollaston's *The Religion of Nature Delineated* (1725), Michael Foster's *An Examination of the Scheme of Church-Power laid down in the Codex Juris Ecclesiastici Anglicani* (1735), Thomas Gordon's *The Independent Whig* (1743), Conyers Middleton's *Miscellaneous Works* (1752), Richard Baron's *The Pillars of Priestcraft and Orthodoxy Shaken* (1752), Francis Blackburne's *The Confessional* (1770) and Blackburne's *Memoirs of Thomas Hollis* (1780): these were not the favourite texts of any fervent devotee of the churches of England or Rome. There is no evidence that Burke himself ever inclined to theological heterodoxy, but he was well aware of the doctrinal is-

---

[19]Peter Benedict Nockles, *The Oxford Movement in Context: Anglican High Churchmanship 1760–1857* (Cambridge, 1994).

[20]Burke to unknown, 26 January 1791: Burke, *Correspondence*, VI, p. 214.

[21]Two catalogues of Burke's library exist (see abbreviations). Both are posthumous, and cannot be a certain guide to his books; but their close agreement, and their inclusion of very few titles published after his death, are evidence for their substantial reliability.

sues that the freethinkers had raised. Burke saw the political earthquakes of his age as occurring along a fault line dividing not Canterbury and Rome, but Anglican latitudinarianism and Deism. From *A Vindication of Natural Society* (1756) and *A Philosophical Enquiry into the Origin of our Ideas of the Sublime and Beautiful* (1757), Burke had constructed a coherent intellectual position that identified God's design of human inequality, demonstrated by revelation, as a necessary condition for the progress of civil society, and defined Deism as the chief intellectual threat to that principle of providential hierarchy.[22] Deism, which died with Bolingbroke in the 1750s, was resuscitated by Paine in the 1790s. *— interesting pt.*

Politicians opposed to early-Hanoverian Toryism, and to Lord Bute's attempt to assert a supra-party monarchy in the early years of George III's reign, would often target the protean genius of Henry St John, viscount Bolingbroke (1678–1751). His book *The Idea of a Patriot King* had enjoyed considerable currency from its appearance in 1749, but he presented a vulnerable target with the posthumous publication in 1754 of his collected works. These included, for the first time, his openly freethinking writings on religion. Burke's executors, presumably on his authority, claimed that the principles which led him to condemn the French Revolution could be traced in Burke's *A Vindication of Natural Society* (1756), an 'ironical exposure of Lord Bolingbroke's false philosophy' which, in Burke's words, 'sapped the foundation of every virtue, and all government, while he attacked every mode of religion'. The executors quoted Burke's aim: 'to shew that without the exertion of any considerable forces, the same engines which were employed for the destruction of religion, might be employed with equal success for the subversion of Government'. Burke, they claimed, 'in his last labours, was only waging with more serious vigour the same war, in which, with lighter weapons, he made the first essay of his juvenile strength'.[23] Burke's differences from the Dissenting intellectual Richard Price began equally early. Price's *A Review of the Principal Questions and Difficulties in Morals* (1758) assumed that the objects of understanding possessed metaphysical essences which were apprehended by human reason, a view that launched him on a career of political speculation built around abstract analysis and *a priori* ideas; by contrast, Burke's *A Philo-*

[22]Ian Harris, 'Paine and Burke: God, nature and politics', in Michael Bentley (ed.), *Public and Private Doctrine* (Cambridge, 1993), pp. 34–62. Why Burke did not respond to Paine's Deist *Common Sense* (1776) as he did to *Rights of Man* (1791) is an unanswered question.

[23][French Laurence and Walker King, eds.], Edmund Burke, *Two Letters on the Conduct of our Domestick Parties, with regard to French Politicks* (London, 1797), pp. xxxiii–xxxv.

*sophical Enquiry into the Origin of Our Ideas of the Sublime and Beautiful*
(1757) adopted the position of Lockeian empiricism to argue for the importance of experience, a view which led him to identify morality with natural
feelings rather than abstract reason. It was an early divergence that was to issue in a spectacular conflict between Burke and Price in 1789–90.[24]

In the *Reflections*, Burke wrote passages about religion which are clearly
autobiographical. He must have included himself among the men in England
who

> tolerate in the true spirit of toleration. They think the dogmas of religion,
> though in different degrees, are all of moment ... They would reverently and af-
> fectionately protect all religions, because they love and venerate the great princi-
> ple upon which they all agree, and the great object to which they are all directed
> (pp. [221–2]).

Burke condemned 'superstition', but tolerated it: 'Superstition is the religion
of feeble minds; and they must be tolerated in an intermixture of it, in some
trifling or some enthusiastic shape or other, or else you will deprive weak
minds of a resource found necessary to the strongest.' In latitudinarian fashion, Burke could sum up his own position: 'The body of all true religion consists, to be sure, in obedience to the will of the sovereign of the world; in a confidence in his declarations; and an imitation of his perfections. The rest is our
own' (p. [234]). His contention that politics should not be discussed in the
pulpit (p. [14]) perhaps showed no liking for the Anglican convention of
preaching learned polemical sermons at the state services of 30 January, 29
May and 5 November, a genre particularly valued by High Churchmen.
Burke challenged only the last three of the five 'rights' claimed in Richard
Price's sermon, and never questioned Price's 'right to liberty of conscience in
religious matters' (p. [20]).

Burke's religious belief was profoundly held, distancing him from many of
his Foxite allies, but this was a consistent theme throughout his career: his
claim in the *Reflections* that man is 'a religious animal' (p. [135]) repeated the
same phrase that he had used in his speech of 17 March 1773 on a Toleration
Bill. Nor was it a contradiction of his latitudinarianism that Burke in the *Reflections* should mount a powerful defence of the religious basis of social life.
What made this defence so usable in later ages was that he did not confine
himself to that preoccupation of the 1790s, 'Church and State', on the sole

---

[24]Frederick Dreyer, 'The Genesis of Burke's *Reflections*', *Journal of Modern History* 50 (1978), pp. 462–79, at 469–76. Dreyer shows Burke's affinity in these respects
with Francis Hutcheson, David Hume and Adam Smith: such a Burke cannot be depicted as a proto-Romantic in revolt against the eighteenth century.

basis of High Churchmen's expositions of the Church's claim to religious truth. Paine even argued that Burke defended the social role of religion in so general a way as to call in question the specific form of the Anglican establishment, and although Paine exaggerated he was not wholly wrong.[25] When Burke wrote of 'the Church' without qualification, he meant a universal Church whose division into Roman, Anglican and Dissenter he regretted. It was from this latitudinarian starting point that Burke moved closer to the High Church position as the French Revolution unfolded.

Burke's political world was born in ideological conflict, but it had its consensual features too. Assimilation and patronage, not class antagonism, were English society's keynotes; the assimilation of those subscribing to elite values rather than the career open to objectively-tested 'merit'. Burke's own career revolved around his relations with his patrons, in turn Lord Verney, William Gerard Hamilton and Rockingham. After Rockingham's death in 1782, no-one really took his place: Charles James Fox, the leading representative in the Commons of the Whig patricians, never gave Burke the support he thought he deserved. It was an affirmation of his ambitions rather than a mark of already achieved success which led Burke to buy in 1768 the estate of Gregories at Beaconsfield in Buckinghamshire;[26] here he could be the (somewhat intellectualised) English country gentleman, reading Virgil's *Georgics*, with Columella's *De Re Rustica*, the classical world's leading treatise on husbandry, in his library.[27] Yet the mortgage meant that he was financially embarrassed for the rest of his life: because he could not afford his estate, it did not give him independence. When he bought his estate he was representing not his shire but a patron's pocket borough.[28] Burke remained caught in the tension between the patrician ethic he sought to uphold and the claims of talent, which were his title to assimilation. Even in the *Reflections*, Burke remained equivocal be-

[25]Burke, *Reflections*, pp. [147–8]; Paine, *Rights of Man*, p. 76. The correct title of Paine's work should be noted; *The Rights of Man* or *The Rights of Man. Part One* are solecisms.

[26]Lock, *Burke*, pp. 249–58 gives the financial details: Burke paid significantly more than the market price.

[27]As *The Times* wrote satirically on 27 August 1790, 'EDMUND BURKE whiles away his summer at Beaconsfield, in experimental husbandry.—He sits upon a plough tail, and translates Virgil's Bucolics to the Farmers,—but they do not understand the Gentleman.' He was, in fact, busy writing the *Reflections*, in which Virgil was to supply some key images.

[28]Burke sat for Wendover, Buckinghamshire, from 1765 to 1774, the pocket borough of Lord Verney, a follower of the marquis of Rockingham. From 1774 to 1780 Burke represented a populous urban constituency, Bristol, and from 1780 to 1794 Rockingham's pocket borough of Malton, Yorkshire.

tween the claims of aristocracy by birth and aristocracy by talent, as he termed it 'a *natural* aristocracy'.[29] In this dilemma, his enemy was not 'the people' (although he was sceptical of their political wisdom) but the reforming members of the Whig nobility, like Shelburne, Richmond and Grafton, busy sawing off the branch on which Burke had only recently managed to sit.

No other figures within the modern canon of English political thought trod this patrician path to assimilation, and none provided such an agitated defence of the whole social order. Defences could indeed be found of specific aspects of it. Thomas Whately rationalised the unreformed electoral system with an off-the-cuff idea, virtual representation, for which he was later castigated: it was a minor aspect of the system. Thomas Gisborne urged the members of the middle and upper ranks to live up to their moral duties as a way of preserving the stability of a hierarchical society. Defences of Anglican hegemony against the claims of Roman Catholic and Protestant Dissenters were legion, scholarly and sophisticated. No-one, however, wrote a defence of the system that was as broad in its range and profound in its sympathies as Burke's.

Burke remained a Whig. His Whig assumptions were publicly expressed even in his first speech against the French Revolution. This posed a threat to England, he argued, in the same way that the absolutism of Louis XIV had done. Louis had established 'a perfect despotism':

> Though that despotism was proudly arrayed in manners, gallantry, splendor, magnificence, and even covered over with the imposing robes of science, literature, and arts, it was, in government, nothing better than a painted and gilded tyranny; in religion, an hard stern intolerance, the fit companion and auxiliary to the despotic tyranny which prevailed in its government. The same character of despotism insinuated itself into every court of Europe—the same spirit of disproportioned magnificence—the same love of standing armies, above the ability of the people. In particular, our then Sovereigns, King Charles and King James, fell in love with the government of their neighbour, so flattering to the pride of Kings. A similarity of sentiments brought on connections equally dangerous to the interests and liberties of their country.

In 1790, 'The disease is altered; but the vicinity of the two countries remains.'[30] These were not the words of a friend of monarchy.

---

[29][Burke], *Appeal*, pp. 129–30. In this famous passage, 'To be bred in a place of estimation; To see nothing low and sordid from one's infancy ...' Burke offered an account of patrician qualities which equally fitted nobility created either by nature or by nurture.

[30]Burke, *Speech ... 9 Feb 1790*, pp. 9–11.

The theoretical assumptions with which Burke began the *Reflections* expressed the same Whig doctrine (it is still debated to what extent he departed from such doctrine as the work progressed). Civil society could hardly be constructed on God's blueprint if it was 'the offspring of convention' (p. [87]); government was 'a contrivance of human wisdom to provide for human *wants*' (p. [88]). Where early eighteenth-century Tories had argued that the state was as much of a divine creation as the Church, Burke initially assumed, in normal Whig fashion, that man existed prior to civil society, and surrendered certain natural rights on entering it in return for certain advantages, this surrender taking the form of a contract.[31] 'By this each person has at once divested himself of the first fundamental right of unconvenanted man, that is, to judge for himself, and to assert his own cause' (p. [88]). In Burke's view, 'At some time or other, all the beginners of dynasties were chosen by those who called them to govern. There is ground enough for the opinion that all the kingdoms of Europe were, at a remote period, elective' (p. [19]). This was not an accidental slip, as Paine claimed, but a deliberately held part of Burke's Whig position. The King of Great Britain's title was secure 'whilst the legal conditions of the compact of sovereignty are performed by him (as they are performed)' (p. [19]). The king was bound by 'the engagement and pact of society, which generally goes by the name of the constitution' (p. [28]); this was, moreover, 'the common agreement and original compact of the state', which was 'equally binding on king, and people too, as long as the terms are observed' (pp. [28–9]). By the time of the publication of the *Appeal from the New to the Old Whigs* in 1791, Burke more clearly confined the term 'original contract' to the secondary contract which created the government and constitution.[32] Yet although Burke may have modified his contractarian understanding of the first formation of civil society itself, he adhered to a contractarian account of that second stage in which men created government by a contract between the people and their rulers.

Monarchy has no 'more of a divine sanction than any other mode of government' (p. [37]), Burke insisted; 'I reprobate no form of government merely upon abstract principles' (p. [185]). It was not an enthusiast for monarchy who wrote: 'The punishment of real tyrants is a noble and awful act of justice' (p. [123]). At his most Whig, Burke seemed to imply that the only legitimate

[31]This remains a contentious area in the interpretation of Burke. It seems likely that the *Reflections* marked a stage in the progressive Whig renunciation of any natural rights remaining to men after entering civil society, a renunciation which paved the way for a more utilitarian and pragmatic attitude to entitlements in later decades.

[32]See below, nn. 51, 54.

title to a throne was a Whig title, like those created in England in 1688 and
1714, and that only England had a free but effective constitution.[33] Burke did
not defend monarchy as such, but 'a mixed and tempered government' like
England's. Monarchy and democracy, by contrast with this mixed Whig constitution, were both 'extremes' (p. [184]). A 'jealous, ever-waking vigilance'
was necessary to guard 'our liberty, not only from invasion, but from decay
and corruption' (p. [79]), which these two extremes threatened. The ancients
had observed that democracy was 'rather the corruption and degeneracy,
than the sound constitution of a republic' (p. [185]). Burke boasted of his admiration not of monarchy or democracy but of 'national representative assemblies' (p. [102]). The Whig doctrine of the mixed and balanced constitution reappeared as that 'opposition of interests', that 'action and counteraction which, in the natural and in the political world, from the reciprocal
struggle of the discordant powers, draws out the harmony of the universe'
(pp. [50–1]; cf. p. [76]). It was this mechanical Whig system of checks and
balances which metamorphosed into a creation of cosmic wisdom as the *Reflections* and the Revolution progressed.

Burke explained 1660 and 1688 in similar terms, as regenerations of the
constitution 'when England found itself without a king' (p. [29]): an early
eighteenth-century Tory would not have used such a phrase, implying that the
throne was vacant, to be filled anew. Burke's view of Charles II was exceed-
ingly low:

> The person given to us by Monk was a man without any sense of his duty as a
> prince; without any regard to the dignity of his crown; without any love to his
> people; dissolute, false, venal, and destitute of any positive good quality whatso-
> ever, except a pleasant temper, and the manners of a gentleman. Yet the restora-
> tion of our monarchy, even in the person of such a prince, was every thing to us;
> for without monarchy in England, most certainly we never can enjoy either peace
> or liberty.[34]

The Revolution of 1688 was even 'obtained by a just war' (p. [43]). Burke
placed himself unequivocally in the Whig tradition with his claim: 'I never desire to be thought a better Whig than Lord Somers' (p. [27]), or, presumably, a
worse one: Burke aligned himself both with the common law tradition and
with the leading Whig jurist, the architect of the Revolution settlement.[35] He

---

[33]Burke to Charles-Jean-François Depont, November 1789: Burke, *Correspondence*, VI, pp. 39–50, at 46.

[34]Burke, *Letter to a Member*, pp. 48–9.

[35]For Burke's debt to the common law tradition, see especially J. G. A. Pocock,
'Burke and the Ancient Constitution: A Problem in the History of Ideas' (1960), in Pocock, *Politics, Language and Time* (London, 1972), pp. 202–32.

protested indignantly that his opponents argued as if they were disputing with
'some of those exploded fanatics of slavery, who formerly maintained, what I
believe no creature now maintains, "that the crown is held by divine, hereditary, and indefeasible right"' (p. [37]). He protested against himself and his
allies having been 'slighted, as much better than tories' by republicans
turned courtiers (p. [93]).

Nor was Burke an uncritical admirer of nobility as such. 'You do not
imagine, that I wish to confine power, authority, and distinction to blood, and
names, and titles. No, Sir' (p. [73]). On the contrary, 'hereditary wealth, and
the rank which goes with it, are too much idolized by creeping sycophants,
and the blind abject admirers of power'. Burke contended only for 'Some decent regulated pre-eminence' (p. [76]). Even his famous apostrophe of the nobility as 'the Corinthian capital of polished society' was supported by a classical tag (p. [205]), not by reference to eighteenth-century French defences of
nobility as a separate caste identified by 'blood'. Burke's defence of religion
was similarly qualified by Whiggery. He supported 'an established church, an
established monarchy, an established aristocracy, and an established democracy, each in the degree it exists, and in no greater' (p. [136]): this was not a
formula for reaction.

These were not merely chance echoes of Whig cliches heard by Burke in the
House of Commons, or attempts to conceal his position in 1790 against hostile
critique: they accurately reflected his position throughout his career. Burke was
a Whig, but not merely a Whig; he was on the most highly principled wing of the
political spectrum at Westminster, attracted to its most anxious purists in the
1760s, the Rockinghams.[36] On the great issue of his age, Burke instinctively
sided with the American colonists until 1775, and even thereafter failed to acknowledge the exceptional character of the American Revolution, a social cata-     — *interesting*
clysm eclipsed only by 1789. English Dissenters and Irish Catholics thought him
their friend. His programme of 'economical reform' was aimed at cleansing
what he saw as an Augean stable. Over India he pursued a tireless crusade
against what he claimed were injustice and exploitation. Only at parliamentary
reform had he drawn the line, preferring (like the Rockinghams) civic virtue to
democracy, but this was not then the defining issue that it later became.

Burke's academic and political education was largely complete by 1760;
he was from the first a zealous Whig of the reign of George II. Among conti-

[36]Burke's commitment was to reforming Whiggism within the parliamentary tradition. He had no personal dealings with the small and specialised group of extra-parlia-
mentary intellectuals now termed 'Commonwealthmen', like Thomas Hollis. It was
the younger Pitt, not Burke, who had links with such circles.

nental authors, he was influenced most by men like Montesquieu[37] and the
French Roman lawyer Domat; Burke rejected Rousseau and other *philo-*
*sophes* whose hour came in the later eighteenth century. Educated as he was
under George II, he fell into the error shared by others in the 1760s of seeing
something sinister (indeed redolent of early eighteenth-century Toryism) in
the policies pursued by the ministries of George III.[38] Until the French Revolution, his obsession was that the growing power of the English executive, insuf-
ficiently checked by a corrupt and unprincipled political elite, would end in a
*coup d'état* and royal despotism (as indeed occurred in Sweden in 1772).[39] In
his draft speech against the motion for parliamentary reform moved on 7 May
1782, Burke looked back to his youth: 'This Constitution in former days used to
be the admiration and the envy of the world.' England alone had discovered the
'grand secret' of government, he instructed Depont in 1789.[40] Burke still sought
to defend the Whig achievement of 1688, as praised by French commentators in
the first half of the eighteenth century, against the challenges and problems that
arose after 1760.

Burke's early eighteenth-century preoccupations were prominent as late as
1770, when he still thought it relevant to launch into invective against 'the
zealots of hereditary right' and extol by contrast 'the name of Whig, dear to
the majority of the people'. The 'principles and policies of the Whigs' were
simply 'the cause of liberty'. Old dangers identified the need for power to be
held in 'intermediate situations' as a barrier against 'absolute monarchy', by
implication a threat even in England. Aside from that function, wrote Burke
in 1770, 'I am no friend to aristocracy'. Kings, lords and judges were merely
'trustees for the people, as well as the Commons; because no power is given
for the sole sake of the holder'.[41] Within this scenario, Burke praised the
Rockingham Whigs: 'The Liberty they pursued was a Liberty inseparable
from order, from virtue, from morals, and from religion, and was neither

[37]C. P. Courtney, *Montesquieu and Burke* (Oxford, 1963); cf. R. J. Smith, *The Gothic Bequest: Medieval Institutions in British Thought, 1688–1863* (Cambridge, 1987), pp. 88–90. For praise of Montesquieu, see [Burke], *Appeal*, p. 115.

[38]This historical scenario was decisively refuted by Ian R. Christie, 'Was there a New Toryism in the Earlier Part of George III's Reign?' (1965), reprinted in Christie, *Myth and Reality in Late Eighteenth Century British Politics* (London, 1970), pp. 196–213. Its power in the 1760s and 70s should not, however, be underestimated.

[39]Lock, *Burke*, pp. 340–2.

[40]Burke, *Works*, X, p. 107; Burke to Depont, November 1789: Burke, *Correspondence*, VI, p. 46.

[41][Burke], *Thoughts*, pp. 6, 10, 15, 20, 35. This doctrine co-existed ambiguously with a recognition of the 'high and sacred character' of kingship (p. 32), but Whigs after 1689 had often boasted of the sanction that God gave to Whig monarchs.

hypocritically nor fanatically followed.' One such model of virtue, according to Burke, was his ally Admiral Lord Keppel:

> he felt, that no great Commonwealth could by any possibility long subsist, without a body of some kind or other of nobility, decorated with honour, and fortified by privilege. This nobility forms the chain that connects the ages of a nation, which otherwise (with Mr. Paine) would soon be taught that no one generation can bind another. He felt that no political fabrick could be well made without some such order of things as might, through a series of time afford a rational hope of securing unity, coherence, consistency, and stability to the state.[42]

A virtuous nobility made reform safe; shielded by noble patronage, Burke was a lifelong reformer. Joseph Priestley, replying to the *Reflections*, recorded his 'very sensible regret' that he could no longer class Burke

> among the friends of what I deem to be *the cause of liberty, civil* or *religious*, after having, in a pleasing intercourse of many years, considered him in this respectable light. In the course of his public life, he has been greatly befriended by the Dissenters, many of whom were enthusiastically attached to him; and we always imagined that he was one on whom we could depend, especially as he spoke in our favour in the business of subscription,[43] and he made a common cause with us in zealously patronizing the liberty of America.

Burke, claimed Priestley in 1790, had reversed his position: 'That an avowed friend of the American revolution should be an enemy to that of the French, which arose from the same general principles, and in a great measure sprung from it, is to me unaccountable.'[44]

Priestley and his allies felt Burke's defection all the more keenly because Burke had been an instinctive ally. They saw that the *Reflections* was not written by a simple enthusiast for monarchy in general or George III in person; had it been, it would have been easier for them to combat. The book continually restated Rockinghamite doctrine that the tendency of monarchical power to decline into tyranny made necessary the interposition of a virtuous nobility to safeguard popular liberties. The *Reflections* contained a vivid passage about Marie-Antoinette,[45] but said little about Louis XVI, despite his reforming record,[46] and nothing personal in praise of George III. Burke plainly

[42]Burke, *Letter to a Noble Lord*, pp. 15, 73–4.
[43]Evidently in his speech on 10 March 1773, discussed below.
[44]Priestley, *Letters to Burke*, pp. iii–iv.
[45]Burke's famous apostrophe of the Queen (pp. [112–3]) was a piece of carefully-judged public rhetoric. In private, he was often highly critical: Burke, *Correspondence*, VI, pp. 340, 348, 361; so was Richard Burke: ibid., p. 389.
[46]For rare praise of Louis XVI see Burke, *Reflections*, p. [122]. In private, he was often candidly critical of that monarch: Burke, *Correspondence*, VI, pp. 36, 241–2.

deplored France's absolute monarchy and was not displeased to see it collapse
in 1788. He did not dispraise France's democracy in 1789–90 by contrasting
it with some more authoritarian English system: to him, the monarchy of
George III was valuable not in itself but only as a guarantor of the social hierarchy and of law, tradition, precedent, prescription and all that was venerable. The new element in Burke's thought was not praise of the monarchy (on
which he was still cool), nor praise of the nobility (which dated back to his
political adoption by Rockingham in the 1760s) but his heightened emphasis
on the role of established religion. Burke had sympathised with every major
act of political resistance he had encountered in his political career[47] until
those in the United Provinces in 1787[48] and France in 1789. It was this last
which raised in a most spectacular form the issue of consistency. Burke's attempt to keep faith with his lifelong principles, while drawing an apparently
opposite conclusion from them, created the agonizing tension which made the
*Reflections* a classic of political writing.

### (ii) The Revolution of 1688

Burke wrote first about England, and we must understand why he chose to
do so. The *Reflections* might more obviously have been structured as a critique of the French *Déclaration des droits de l'homme et du citoyen*, approved
by the National Assembly on 26 August 1789 and re-published by Richard
Price as an appendix to his sermon *A Discourse on the Love of Our Country*,
the immediate catalyst of Burke's engagement; but Whigs did not deny that
men possessed natural rights, and Burke did not focus on what became the
most famous document of 1789. Nor was Burke debating with Thomas Paine:
he might have chosen to argue against the principles set out in Paine's ahistorical tract *Common Sense* (1776) or other writings on the American Revolution, which were still circulating in England, but Burke did not do so. The
*Reflections* instead began with an argument about the meaning of the events
of 1688–9 in England, and about the practicalities of the Revolution of 1789
by analogy with what had occurred in England a century before. This was essential, for two reasons: many French revolutionaries were pressing forward
while claiming that they were merely imitating England's Revolution; many

---

[47]'The Glorious Revolution of 1688, the American War of Independence, the
struggle of the Corsicans for freedom, the attempt of the Poles to preserve their national independence, and the various revolts against the minions of Warren Hastings in
India': Alfred Cobban, *Edmund Burke and the Revolt against the Eighteenth Century*
(2nd edn., London, 1960), p. 100.

[48]For which, see T. C. W. Blanning, *The French Revolutionary Wars 1787–1802*
(London, 1996).

English reformers, who had long placed an extensive interpretation on the meaning of 1688, now invited their countrymen to copy the French on the same grounds that the French had merely acted on English principles. Burke was therefore driven to defend what he saw as the middle ground of 1688–9: a state which was both stable and libertarian, with a strong executive but also law-bound, learning from experience yet open to innovation, not claiming sole access to religious truth yet enjoying a divine sanction.

Burke's tone was one of proprietorial integrity: he was obliged to vindicate 'the whole course of my public conduct' in supporting 'the principles of the glorious Revolution'. Price and his friends had merely a 'pretext of zeal' for that event (pp. [2, 7]). The Glorious Revolution was so inescapable that Burke turned to it in his first public pronouncement on the French Revolution, his speech on the Army Estimates. 1688, he argued, had not seen a social revolution:

> What we did was in truth and substance, and in a constitutional light, a revolution, not made, but prevented. We took solid securities; we settled doubtful questions; we corrected anomalies in our law. In the stable fundamental parts of our constitution we made no revolution; no, nor any alteration at all. We did not impair the monarchy. Perhaps it might be shewn that we strengthened it very considerably. The nation kept the same ranks, the same orders, the same privileges, the same franchises, the same rules for property, the same subordinations, the same order in the law, in the revenue, and in the magistracy; the same lords, the same commons, the same corporations, the same electors.[49]

This preoccupation with 1688 was neither novel nor antiquated: all English Whigs, from the moment of James II's forced departure, through the Allegiance Controversy of the 1690s, the trial of Dr. Henry Sacheverell in 1710, the Bangorian Controversy of the 1720s, the successive Jacobite attempts at a restoration, the American Revolution, the Regency Crisis of 1788 and the successive attempts by Dissenters to obtain the repeal of the Test and Corporation Acts, were obliged to take a position on just what had been implied by the exile of James and the accession of William and Mary. Although Burke promised a comparison of 1688 with the civil war of the 1640s (p. [21]), in the twentieth century to be designated England's real revolution, he did not find it necessary to perform that promise (and, remarkably, was not challenged by Price, Priestley or Paine to do so): for all of them, the crucial moment in English political argument was 1688, not civil war in 1642 or even the execution of the king in 1649. Burke's Whiggism must have entailed support for the reforming initiatives of 1640–1, and this should have implied support

[49]Burke, *Speech ... 9 Feb 1790*, pp. 28–9.

for the French reforms of 1787–8; yet this comparison was presumably too delicate to be explored.

A reliance on 1688 did not mean that Burke was principally indebted to John Locke, and although he naturally read him he ignored Locke in the *Reflections*. Burke also owned two copies of that practical compendium of Whig political theory, *The Tryal of Dr. Henry Sacheverell* (London, 1710): texts like this, and the achievements of Whig lawyers like Lord Somers, rather than Locke's *Two Treatises of Government*, described and defined Whiggery for most of the subjects of George I and George II. Burke knew that 'It rarely happens to a party to have the opportunity of a clear, authentic, recorded, declaration of their political tenets upon the subject of a great constitutional event like that of the Revolution': the impeachment of Sacheverell was such an opportunity.[50] In 1791, Burke, adopting the third person, clarified his position:

> I assert, that the foundations laid down by the Commons, on the trial of Doctor Sacheverel, for justifying the revolution of 1688, are the very same laid down in Mr. Burke's Reflections; that is to say,—a breach of the *original contract*, implied and expressed in the constitution of this country, as a scheme of government fundamentally and inviolably fixed in King, Lords and Commons.—That the fundamental subversion of this antient constitution, by one of its parts, having been attempted, and in effect accomplished, justified the Revolution. That it was justified *only* upon the *necessity* of the case; as the *only* means left for the recovery of that *antient* constitution, formed by the *original contract* of the British state; as well as for the future preservation of the *same* government. These are the points to be proved.[51]

For Burke, the 'original contract' was now the contract that determined the form of the government, not a contract that created civil society: this last, as his writing during the French Revolution was to make clear, increasingly seemed to him to be a work of God.

It was, then, the Revolution of 1688 which had provided the intellectual foundations for the Whig regime in the decades to 1789. Yet those foundations were profoundly flawed, as Sacheverell (and many others) had shown in an earlier period, and as Paine (and many others) were to show, in new ways, in the 1790s. Burke argued that James II and George I had equally good titles, since each 'came in according to the law, as it stood at his accession to the crown' (p. [32]); in Whig fashion, he ignored the fact that William III's title could be denied on just those grounds. A lasting puzzle has been to explain the remarkable rhetorical force of the *Reflections*. One source of its emotional intensity was Burke's attempt to hold together a regime whose old intellectual

---

[50][Burke], *Appeal*, pp. 54–5.
[51][Burke], *Appeal*, p. 57.

weaknesses were once more being exploited. So it was that Burke produced his agonised official defence of 1688 and the Protestant succession in the house of Hanover where Paine, in *Rights of Man*, could be openly sceptical of both in passages of remarkably candid denunciation that seem to echo early eighteenth-century Jacobite critiques.[52] But for Paine, the debate had moved on to the territory which he thought he shared with the *Déclaration des droits de l'homme.*

Burke therefore chose to defend the episode which was open to political dispute in England: 1688, not 1660. At the Restoration, the reign of Charles II was officially deemed to have begun in 1649, and the uninterrupted nature of *—interesting.* monarchy maintained; by the trial and execution of the regicides, Charles I's death was redefined as a crime, not as the assertion of an alternative theory of sovereignty. Yet if it was now impossible for the disaffected to argue for the continued existence of a popular right to execute an English monarch, it was very possible for extreme Whigs and Dissenters to argue about the Glorious Revolution; to reconcile Whig loyalties with the claim that in 1688 'the people' had exercised a right to dismiss James II and appoint William and Mary as his successors on conditions. This challenge was reactivated in the context of 1789 by the argument that England's Convention Parliament of 1689 had acted as a Constituent Assembly, just the role which France's Estates-General was claiming for itself with the new name of the National Assembly, and just the role which English revolutionaries urged that a parallel body in England should assume.

It thus became urgently necessary to reassert the orthodox Whig interpretation: James II had constructively abdicated; the Convention Parliament had acted strictly in accordance with the ancient constitution in making the minimum changes necessary to keep the government within its ancient channels, so vindicating rather than violating precedent, the rule of law and the religious underpinnings of the state. Although Burke's Whig orthodoxy was obscured by the polarization of debate during the 1790s, in the *Reflections* he presented a mainstream Whig reading of 1688. He did not argue, as some Tories had done under Queen Anne, that nothing had changed, and that the title to the crown was still as indefeasibly hereditary as it had been. Burke equally rejected the extreme Whig idea that James II had been dismissed. He argued instead that James had constructively abdicated (p. [32]), and although Burke believed that the House of Commons had officially declared that James II *had* broken the original contract this was proof of James's 'virtual abdication', not his dismissal (p. [38]). Burke wrote of 1660 and 1688 as moments when

[52]Paine, *Rights of Man*, pp. 22–3, 33, 82, 124–5, 133–5.

'England found itself without a king' (p. [29]), a choice of words implying an accident rather than the deliberate result of political actions. 'The throne was not effectively vacant for an hour' in 1688, wrote Burke, only because Whigs had acted 'instantly'[53] and wisely to fill it; by implication, Burke rejected the Tory argument that indefeasible linear succession at once filled the throne on the demise of each incumbent.

Burke conceded that something fundamental had been done in 1688; to explain it, he stressed the Whig notion of an original contract, not in the sense in which it had had been discussed but dropped by the House of Commons in its deliberations between 28 January and 13 February 1689 (a contract between free individuals which created civil society itself) but in the sense of a contract between already-existing civil society and a monarch, a contract synonymous with the coronation oath.[54] To defuse the more extensive implications of this contractarian argument, Burke argued that the Revolution had been made through necessity, that what was done was justified only because it was unique, and that contracts once entered into were permanently binding. Having proved this point to his satisfaction, Burke did not need to extend his historical horizon back to the civil war of the 1640s. He omitted the long historical retrospect to the Anglo-Saxons that he had provided in his *Abridgement of the History of England* in the 1750s to disprove the Tory/Jacobite claim that the crown of England had always descended by unbroken hereditary right (p. [30]). Burke was not now arguing against Tories, but against Dissenters who had become yet more Whig than himself.

Burke's conception of a contract was very different from that of the Nonconformists. Burke believed in contract as the title of government, and asserted that, in England, contract had established the descent of the crown by hereditary right. A contract, once made, was permanent:

> Neither the few nor the many have a right to act merely by their will, in any matter connected with duty, trust, engagement, or obligation. The constitution of a country being once settled upon some compact, tacit or expressed, there is no power existing of force to alter it, without the breach of the covenant, or the consent of all the parties. Such is the nature of a contract.[55]

If a contract could as well be tacit as explicit, however, the idea of government depending on and being confined by a pre-existing constitution was compromised. Moreover, in Burke's language, 'contract' silently elided via 'compact'

---

[53] Burke, *Letter to a Member*, p. 49.
[54] J. P. Kenyon, *Revolution Principles: the Politics of Party 1689–1720* (Cambridge, 1977).
[55] [Burke], *Appeal*, p. 118.

into 'covenant', which suggested a contract less between man and man than between man and God. It was to this argument on 1688 that Burke's Nonconformist critics replied, for their different understanding of contract gave them the right of resistance that Burke denied.

Yet in this area Dissenters, especially the most vocal of them, and especially Price and Priestley, were too preoccupied with the long-standing and recently revitalised litany of denominational grievances against the Church of England fully to exploit the opportunity created by the French Revolution. It was left to Thomas Paine, standing outside the familiar denominational polemic, to probe most effectively the weaknesses of Burke's argument. These weaknesses were not Burke's foolish lapses. They were the contradictions inherent in the Whig defence of 1688 from the outset,[56] cracks which had been papered over in various ways in successive decades, but which yawned once again as the structure of the state felt the strain of the new doctrines of 1789.

Burke's *Reflections* is therefore an important late defence of the mainstream Whig rationale for 1688. Great works of political theory often arise from the attempt to square the circle or to reconcile the irreconcilable. In Burke's case this involved the attempt to preserve dignified, virtuous government, built on law, precedent and security of property, echoing its hereditary commitments in the institutions of its monarchy, nobility and church, while at the same time attempting to deny that 1688 had constituted a violation of legitimacy fully comparable to that of 1789. Burke's defence of this historical interpretation was heroic; it stemmed the tide for a time; but it went down to final defeat in 1832.

### (iii) Burke's knowledge of France

English Whigs had well-rehearsed positions on what had occurred in England in 1688, but their knowledge of France was seldom what they boasted it to be; none of them predicted in 1788 the internal collapse of French monarchical government, still less what was to follow. As its full title made clear, Burke's *Reflections* was only in part about France; he recorded that he was 'Solicitous chiefly for the peace of my own country' (p. [11]). Burke's knowledge of France and his foresight nevertheless compared well with those of most of his Foxite colleagues. His early biographer Sir James Prior quoted Burke speaking of 'three or four journeys he had made in France ... previous to the year 1773'; one visit may have occurred in 1757.[57] His vi-

---

[56]For which, see especially Kenyon, *Revolution Principles*.

[57]Prior, *Memoir of Burke*, I, p. 46. The year was not mentioned in the first edition of Prior's *Memoir* (1824); by the fifth edition (1854), '1773' had become '1775'. Burke

sion was that of a Whig critic of absolute monarchy. In 1769, after a careful discussion of French finances, he had written: 'no man, I believe, who has considered their affairs with any degree of attention or information, but must hourly look for some extraordinary convulsion in that whole system; the effect of which on France, and even on all Europe, it is difficult to conjecture.'[58] From an early date, he scrutinised French society for clues to the general causes of an impending catastrophe.

Despite his apprehensions of French finances, which were to prove prescient, his early insight was to work towards an understanding of the intellectual origins of France's problems in the realm of morals, manners and opinions. With the benefit of hindsight, Burke's executors depicted him as uttering early and far-seeing warnings against *philosophes* and heterodox Dissenters alike. Burke's belief in the 'pernicious effects of the new philosophy', they claimed, were 'confirmed' during his visit to Paris in 1773. He had there been 'courted and caressed, as a man of eminence, by the literary cabal which was then preparing the way for the overthrow of Altars and Thrones'.[59] In a speech in the House of Commons on 17 March 1773, soon after his return, he had warned against 'a confederacy of the powers of darkness' represented by a part of the Nonconformists, 'the wicked Dissenters' who challenged revealed religion, the 'infidels': 'Under the systematick attacks of these people, I see some of the props of good government already begin to fail; I see propagated principles, which will not leave to Religion even a toleration.'[60] Although this was probably more important in retrospect, Laurence and King may not have been wholly wrong. Burke may have sensed the wider implications of the *philosophes*' crusade, a theme which recent scholarship has illuminated. Nor was he alone in predicting such consequences. Horace Walpole, who was hardly a paranoid friend of the established order, reached similar conclusions on a visit to Paris in 1765:

> do you know who *the philosophers* are, or what the term means here? In the first place, it comprehends almost everybody; and in the next, means men, who avow-

---

to Richard Shackleton, 10 August 1757: Burke, *Correspondence*, I, p. 123 and n. Evidence for these earlier visits is lacking, but since information on Burke's career before the 1760s is patchy, the absence of other evidence is less telling than Burke's statement that they occurred.

[58] Edmund Burke, *Observations on a Late State of the Nation* (London, 1769), p. 59.

[59] [Laurence and King, eds.], Burke, *Two Letters*, pp. xxxvi–xxxviii.

[60] 'Speech on the Second Reading of a Bill for the Relief of Protestant Dissenters (1773)' in Burke, *Works*, X, pp. 22–40, at 37–9; *Parl Hist*, XVII, cols. 770–83. Burke spoke in favour of the Bill, supporting Dissenters but warning against men who opposed revealed religion.

ing war against popery, aim, many of them, at a subversion of all religion, and still many more, at the destruction of regal power. How do you know this? you will say; you, who have been but six weeks in France, three of which you have been confined to your chamber. True: but in the first period I went everywhere, and heard nothing else; in the latter, I have been extremely visited, and have had long and explicit conversations with many, who think as I tell you, and with a few of the other side, who are no less persuaded that there are such intentions.[61]

In this perspective, what was remarkable about the French Revolution was that it was so long delayed.

Burke was never xenophobic: his wish was to move freely among the enlightened elite of Ireland, England and France, and the small number of his journeys across the Channel does not prove his insularity. His main opponents in England were not necessarily better informed about French affairs, and often argued from vaguely-conceived abstract principles rather than from knowledge or practical experience of that country.[62] Richard Price confessed in 1788:

> What is now passing in France is an object of my anxious attention. I am by no means properly informed about the nature and circumstances of the struggle; but as far as it is a struggle for a free constitution of government and the recovery of their rights by the people I heartily wish it success whatever may be the consequence to this country, for I have learnt to consider myself more as a citizen of the world than of any particular country, and to such a person every advance that the cause of public liberty makes must be agreeable.[63]

Thomas Jefferson replied to Price in a series of euphoric letters from Paris which confirmed Price's generalised faith in revolutionary ideals.[64] Price's nephew, the Dissenting minister George Cadogan Morgan, also wrote from Paris rejoicing at 'a king DRAGGED *in submissive triumph*'.[65] Price, in remote

---

[61]Walpole to Henry Seymour Conway, 28 October 1765, in W. S. Lewis et al. (eds.), *The Yale Edition of Horace Walpole's Correspondence* 39 (New Haven, 1974), pp. 22–3.

[62]There were exceptions. Thomas Christie was in France for six months from late 1789, and in 1792. Mary Wollstonecraft lived in France from December 1792 to early 1795. Not all of their experience was embodied in the replies to Burke's *Reflections*. That work was published on 1 November 1790; Mary Wollstonecraft's *A Vindication of the Rights of Men* followed on 29 November. Thomas Christie's *Letters on the Revolution of France* appeared in May 1791, before his longer period of residence in that country.

[63]Price to Thomas Jefferson, 26 October 1788, in Price, *Correspondence*, III, p. 182.

[64]Jefferson to Price, 8 January, 19 May, 12 and 17 July, 13 September 1789: ibid., pp. 195–9, 223–5, 231–7, 257–8.

[65]Ibid., p. 250; Burke, *Reflections*, p. [250].

Wales in the late summer of 1789, noted: 'I know little of what passes in the Political world except what I learn from the Gazeeter [sic] which I receive every morning from London, and supplies me with an intelligence from France which is often very delightful to me.'⁶⁶ On this slender evidential base, Price preached his sensational sermon on 4 November which provoked Burke's far better-informed reply.

Both Fox and Burke had connections in France, but they were very different. Fox saw that country through the eyes of kindred reforming spirits among the French nobility, men like Lafayette, the vicomte de Noailles and the duc d'Orléans. Burke already recognised their English counterparts as blind to the wider implications of their reforming schemes. His contacts were more miscellaneous, and evidently included a French bishop, middle-ranking French clergy, French noblemen, one of the leading political players, Jacques Necker, and his chief critic, Charles-Alexandre de Calonne, as well as a cross-section of popular provincial opinion which was, presumably, uncongenial to the Whig patricians.⁶⁷ Neither Fox nor Sheridan replied to Burke's *Reflections* either verbally or in print with a reasoned case based on any superior knowledge of events in France, for they had no such expertise; instead, Fox distanced himself from his still-loyal colleague, and tried to evade the detailed attention that the situation demanded. For the Foxite Whigs the early stage of the French Revolution was, at most, a tourist attraction that confirmed their prejudices.

'I do not pretend to know France as correctly as some others', Burke admitted candidly (p. [202]), but he knew much. He displayed detailed knowledge of that country's government as early as his pamphlet *Observations on a Late State of the Nation* (1769). His spoken French was not fluent, and he often confessed 'my misfortune of not speaking French well'.⁶⁸ Yet despite the reproaches of his enemies this was a shortcoming which he shared with Thomas Jefferson and Thomas Paine,⁶⁹ whose optimistic view of the Revolution British Jacobins wished to think rested on more authentic knowledge. Jefferson and Paine both lived in Paris for considerable periods while holding emi-

⁶⁶Price to Lansdowne, 9 September 1789: Price, *Correspondence*, III, pp. 255–7.

⁶⁷'Noms de ceux qui ont écrit à M. Bourke', Sheffield MSS Bk. 10, 18–19 (microfilm). The occasion on which this list was compiled is unknown, but it suggests a much wider range of contacts than with the circle of *bienpensants* favoured by the Foxites.

⁶⁸Burke to the Chevalier de la Bintinaye, 2 October 1791: Burke, *Correspondence*, VI, pp. 423–4.

⁶⁹Conor Cruise O'Brien, *The Long Affair: Thomas Jefferson and the French Revolution* (London, 1996), p. 36; John Keane, *Tom Paine: A Political Life* (London, 1995), pp. 313, 350–1, 368, 375, 402, 423, 437.

nent positions in public life (Jefferson from August 1784 to October 1789): it is their ignorance of spoken French and their consequently superficial understanding of events in France which is the larger issue. The same may have been true of Charles James Fox. Napoleon, who met Fox in Paris during the Peace of Amiens in 1802, later recalled their brief encounter in unflattering terms: '*Il me combattait avec chaleur en son mauvais français.*'[70] Nor was Burke's command of the language as slight as his enemies wished to suggest. William Smith visited Burke shortly after the publication of the *Appeal from the New to the Old Whigs*. Present at dinner were many French *émigrés*, whose English was poor. Smith recalled:

> Mr. Burke, consequently, addressed much of his conversation to them in French; he did not seem to pronounce it or speak it well, but was perfectly able to express himself intelligibly, and with reasonable fluency; and this was manifestly all that he aimed at. He appeared not merely above the vanity of attempting to make a display of proficiency; but also above the more excusable feeling of reluctance to betray a want of it.[71]

Moreover, Burke read French perfectly well and in the *Reflections* quoted long passages in that language without bothering to translate. The little-known manuscript version of Burke's library catalogue, dated 1813 and now in the Bodleian Library, contains a substantial number of French works, more than the better-known printed sale catalogue of 1833, and suggests that Burke's attention to French culture had long been considerable, both for pleasure and business. In 1789–90 and later, Burke took pains to consult French sources. His views on French finances had been derived from study of the seemingly-authoritative volumes of Necker (1784), but Burke was not solely dependent on him: the *Reflections* gave full discussions of reports to the National Assembly on the state of national finances by Necker in May 1789 (pp. [175, 327]) and Vernier in August 1790 (p. [331]). Despite his friendship with Necker, Burke continued urgently to revise his views on this subject in directions critical of the Genevan banker in response to later reading of the writings on finance of Necker's rival and critic Calonne: these changes were included in the third edition of the *Reflections*, published on 16 November 1790 (pp. [190–3, 197–8]; Appendix I).

William Windham, MP, was in Paris in August and September 1789, and on his return brought Burke books 'recommended to me by a Deputy' and which 'contain, I apprehend, a pretty general view of the state of opinions

---

[70]Stanley Ayling, *The Life of Charles James Fox* (London, 1991), p. 213.

[71]William Smith, 'Recollections of the Right Hon. Edmund Burke', in Prior, *Memoir of Burke*, II, pp. 527–32, at 528.

prevailing at the commencement of this business in France'.[72] Burke corresponded with a Deputy in the National Assembly, Adrien-Jean-François Duport, about the latter's plans for judicial reform, and assured the Frenchman that his, Burke's, opinions as expressed in the debate on the army estimates were drawn from a reading of French sources and were not 'infused into my mind' by *émigrés* in London:

> I had then scarcely read any thing upon the subject, except the general Instructions given to the Representatives; and the proceedings of the National Assembly, extremely at variance with those instructions; and some pieces supposed to be written by the Comte de Mirabeau; together with the facts which appear'd uncontradicted in some foreign and domestick papers. From them I had formed my opinions. Since that time I have read more largely

as well as talking to *émigrés* '(but not so often as I wished)'.[73] Burke applied himself mainly to written evidence.

In 1789–90, according to his executors, Burke assiduously collected information on the French Revolution: 'he sought information from every quarter, as if the subject had been wholly new to him. He desired all persons of his acquaintance who were going to Paris (and curiosity attracted many) to bring him whatever they could collect of the greatest circulation, both on the one side and the other. He had also many correspondents, not only among the English and Americans residing there, but also among the natives', correspondents who included men as enthusiastic about the Revolution as Thomas Paine, Thomas Christie and Anacharsis Cloots.[74] Burke's belief that France would be divided into electoral districts each geometrically square, derived from an early plan which was modified when enacted in February 1790, was for example confirmed by Paine's long and detailed letter to him from Paris of 17 January 1790.[75] Burke's son Richard also had his French sources, which would presumably have been shared with his father, and between (at least) June 1789 and September 1790 Richard Burke received reports from Jean-Baptiste Decrétot, a Deputy in the Third Estate, about events in that body and

---

[72]Windham to Burke, 15 September 1789: Burke, *Correspondence*, VI, pp. 20–2. Windham reported: 'it does not appear to me, that there is any near prospect of civil commotion'.

[73]Burke to Duport, [post 29 March 1790]: Burke, *Correspondence*, VI, pp. 104–9.

[74][Laurence and King, eds.], Burke, *Two Letters*, pp. xxxviii–xxxix.

[75]Paine to Burke, 17 January 1790: Burke, *Correspondence*, VI, pp. 67–76, at 74. Burke let his account of the electoral system stand, evidently for rhetorical effect: his point was that such a model could have been seriously proposed, and what this established about the attitudes of the revolutionaries. The object of the new system, even as modified, was to erase ancient identities and loyalties.

its successor the National Assembly.[76] Richard Burke evidently made contributions to his father's text at one point (p. [165]), and may have done so at others. As with similar crusades into which the elder Burke threw himself, he was formidably industrious in mastering his subject. When James Mackintosh, author of the very different *Vindiciae Gallicae* (1791), met his former opponent in December 1796, even he confessed that Burke was 'minutely and accurately informed, to a wonderful exactness, with respect to every fact relative to the French Revolution'.[77]

The text of the *Reflections* alone demonstrates that Burke read a range of French pamphlets, including those summarising the *cahiers de doléances*, listing the deputies of the Estates-General and analysing their social composition (pp. [59, 61, 188]). He read a pamphlet containing the speeches and reports at the opening of the Estates-General. He knew the writings of the *monarchiens* and early *émigrés* Lally-Tollendal and Mounier (pp. [109–10]). He read pamphlets by Gaston Camus on the Civil Constitution of the Clergy, and by Rabaut Saint-Etienne (pp. [225, 247]). Burke followed daily events in *Le Moniteur*[78] and the *Courier Français*[79] as well as in the *Procès-verbal*,[80] the full account of debates in the National Assembly, and in English newspapers (pp. [253, 305, 320]). Burke gave extended and detailed analysis to many aspects of the Revolution: to the early scheme for an electoral system (pp. [253–66]); to the war minister, du Pin's, report to the National Assembly on 4 June 1790 on the collapse of military discipline (p. [304]); to the mayor of Paris, Bailly's, report to the Assembly on 13 August 1790 on the state of the capital (p. [349]). The *Reflections* contain evidence of substantial knowledge of France, though naturally some points could be corrected or improved upon by later observers.[81]

[76]Burke, *Correspondence*, VI, p. 10n.

[77]Thomas Green's report of Mackintosh's remark in 1799, in Robert James Mackintosh, *Memoirs of the Life of the Right Honourable Sir James Mackintosh* (2 vols., London, 1835), I, p. 92.

[78]*Gazette Nationale, on Le Moniteur Universel* (5 May 1789–).

[79]The journal begun as *Assemblée Nationale, ou Courier François*, launched on 26 June 1789, and changed its spelling to *Assemblée nationale, ou Courier Français* from 1 August 1789; from 31 August 1789 it appeared as *Courier Français, du [date]. Assemblée Nationale*. Burke's citing of it as the *Courier François* may be evidence that his acquaintance with it began early.

[80]*Proces-Verbal de l'Assemblée Nationale, imprimée par son ordre* (Paris, 1789–).

[81]Burke's use of his French sources, and the degree of accuracy of his discussions of the events of 1789–90, are considered in detail in the notes to the text of the *Reflections*. He presented a copy of his book to William Windham with an explanation: 'It is possible enough, that in the infinite variety of matter contained in my general Subject I

On some matters, therefore, Burke was right and his critics wrong. Priestley ridiculed the idea that 'the present members of the National Assembly are not eligible into the next';[82] but it was so, and the meeting of the newly-elected Legislative Assembly in October 1791 ushered in a new phrase of the Revolution which led quickly to war, massacre and regicide. Burke argued that France possessed an 'ancient constitution' which might serve as the basis for a reformed, law-bound government on the English model. This was, in part, to see the French situation in English terms, yet Burke was not alone among his countrymen in this respect: the best-informed English commentator on France, Arthur Young, in Paris in June 1789, similarly considered that the French court's great mistake was not to provide regulations for the Estates-General before their reassembly which would have 'taken the constitution of England for their model', combining the clergy and nobility in an upper house to counterbalance the commons in a lower.[83] It was the collapse of the three Estates into a single body that removed any checks and balances from French politics, argued Young. Although he took a much lower view of the *parlements* than Burke, and was a strong advocate of reform in France, even Young thought a limited, constitutional monarchy a possible outcome before May 1789. Burke took sides in a French debate, but it was not an ignorant or a prejudiced choice.

On the basis of this first-hand knowledge and careful reading, Burke drew few fundamental distinctions between English and French society. He acknowledged differences of degree: the distance between the moneyed and the landed interests was greater in France, and their interaction less; but the face of France presented a society modern, sophisticated, prosperous, second only to England and in many respects not second (pp. [194–5]). Between their governments, indeed, he claimed wide differences of kind, for Burke subscribed to the familiar Whig reproof of French monarchy by comparison with the libertarian regime established in England in 1688. But in every other aspect of society, including nobility, church, commerce and technology, Burke was not drawn to assert essential differences. His disdainful comments on the unsuit-

---

may have made some Mistakes, and I wrote sometimes in circumstances not favourable to accuracy. I wrote from the Memory of what I had read; and was not able always to get the documents from whence I had been supplied when I wished to verifye my facts with precision. But I hope my errours will be found to be rather mistakes than misrepresentations': Burke to Windham, 27 October 1790: Burke, *Correspondence*, VI, pp. 142–3.

[82]Priestley, *Letters to Burke*, p. 16. This decision of the National Constituent Assembly had been reported in *The Times* of 25 September 1789.

[83]Young, *Travels in France*, p. 128.

ability of the French professions, especially lawyers and doctors, for political power were matched by no Burkeian boasts that the professions played a dominant role in England. True, the way was open in England for merit to rise; but, according to Burke, 'The temple of honour ought to be seated on an eminence' (p. [74]), an unacknowledged borrowing from the Francophile Bolingbroke, and, in England, it was: 'the road to eminence and power, from obscure condition, ought not to be made too easy, nor a thing too much of course' (p. [74]). He did not observe that, in England, landless talent already had a secure place. Historians later dismissed Burke's analysis for his failure to distinguish the French case from the English and especially for failing to perceive the widespread hatred of the aristocracy in France which had undermined their position even before 1789; others, more recently, have seen greater points of similarity between the two cultures.

Burke's Foxite contemporaries saw in France what they wished to see. They fatally underestimated the extent of personal violence, lawlessness, destruction of property and military insubordination in those supposedly peaceful and idealistic years, 1789–90. Burke gave full weight to the dark side of the Revolution, but in this he did not project personal nightmares onto a peaceful constitutional experiment; he echoed French sources, including the fearful complaints of deputies in the National Assembly itself, printed in *Le Moniteur*. As an early *émigré* also noted in a pamphlet which Burke evidently read, 'Le 7 Août [1789], les Ministres du Roi vinrent à l'Assemblée, le Garde-des-Sceaux nous présenta un tableau effrayant de l'anarchie & des crimes impunis qui désolaient le Royaume.'[84] Burke considered that Louis XVI had been effectively deposed by the events of 5–6 October 1789, but this judgement was far from being prophetic: *The Times*, which carried regular and detailed reports from its correspondent in Paris, had been drawing analogies with Charles I and observing that Louis's power had been reduced to a shadow from July 1789.[85]

Burke rightly saw that discipline in the French army had disintegrated at an early date. Open mutiny was unusual in 1789, but related phenomena were widespread: the discrediting of the authority of officers, inability to carry out orders, increasing desertion and fraternisation with revolutionaries, and an obvious, and widely-reported, unwillingness by troops to fire on civilians. The army consequently proved a broken reed in the hands of the monar-

[84] *Mémoire de M. le Comte de Lally-Tollendal, ou Seconde lettre A ses Commettans* (Paris, 1790), p. 115; Burke, *Reflections*, pp. [102, 109].
[85] *The Times*, 2, 3, 4, 25, 28, 31 July; 4, 20 August; 8, 22 September 1789 (Louis XVI 'a state prisoner').

chy in 1789, and it was this collapse of hierarchical authority that made the military repression of the Revolution in that year impossible. It led inexorably to widespread and open mutinies in 1790.[86] The minister of war, du Pin, correctly briefed the National Assembly on 4 July 1790: the degree of insubordination in the army was so great that it would create 'a military democracy' and force the officers to emigrate. After Louis XVI's failed flight to Varennes in June 1791, they did so in large numbers.[87] If Burke's views on the Revolution took shape by his speech of 9 February 1790, this does not prove ignorance or prejudice on Burke's part; it shows Burke reaching a conclusion based on a justifiable analogy with events in England, and on a knowledge of French primary sources which he continued to expand. It was a conclusion derived, Burke claimed, from the observation that 'As much injustice and tyranny has been practised in a few months by a French democracy, as in all the arbitrary monarchies in Europe in the forty years of my observation.'[88]

Foxite Whigs pictured the years 1789 and 1790 as peaceful, the period when the Revolution made great strides towards its constitutional ideals, uncompromised by the violence which later blew it off course. Burke's reaction in the *Reflections* could, by contrast, be made to seem extreme. Yet in the same years 1789–90 the London press focused on the opposite features: it detailed mob violence, murder and theft; its images were of heads carried on pikes, chateaux in flames, regiments in disarray. By 20 July 1789, *The Times* was writing bluntly of 'the bloodshed of a civil war ... the mob has risen to a degree of ferocity, unexampled in the annals of the country'.[89] Although eclipsed by the scale of the suffering in 1791–4, and although neglected in

[86]*The Times*, 3, 20 July; 7, 11, 27 August; 3 October 1789; 11 June; 16, 17, 23 August 1790.

[87]Samuel F. Scott, *The Response of the Royal Army to the French Revolution: The Role and Development of the Line Army 1787–93* (Oxford, 1978), pp. 78–97.

[88]Burke to Thomas Mercer, 26 February 1790: Burke, *Correspondence*, VI, pp. 92–8, at 96.

[89]The reports of *The Times*'s correspondent in Paris were dramatic. On 28 July 1789: 'The Provinces are in a state of rebellion from one end of France to the other ... The proscriptions against particular persons extend every day, and strike terror among all ranks of people'; on 31 July: 'There is neither law nor police at this moment in Paris. Our Sovereign Lord the Mob govern the city at their pleasure; they seize whom they please, and, in defiance of every subsisting law of the nation, and every dictate of reason, they put whom they chuse to death, without judgment, and without mercy.' Such stories were sometimes contradicted by editorial comment in London which congratulated the French on achieving a revolution 'with so little bloodshed': *The Times*, 6 August 1789. Reports of the destruction of property, murder and outrage continued throughout 1790.

subsequent historiography, the early violence and passion of the Revolution undoubtedly existed. They were not spun out of Burke's imagination. Burke's libertarian and crusading career had inspired a young revolutionary, Charles Depont, to look up to him as a guardian of liberty, but by the time Depont's letter of 4 November 1789 asking for a blessing on the Revolution had arrived, Burke had come to very different conclusions. The speed with which he did so, and the depth of his insight into the Revolution, demand further explanation.

## (iv) The genesis of the 'Reflections'

Burke's *Reflections* was soon caught up in a controversy in which it was later assumed that the opposing position was most cogently expressed by Paine's *Rights of Man*. Burke's political thought has usually been interpreted in the light of that assumption, and compared especially with Paine's version of natural rights theory. It might better be argued that it was *Rights of Man* that was more influential on the evolving terms of the debate from the 1790s to the 1820s, while the *Reflections* stood in an older controversial framework; Burke's intervention was appropriately provoked by Price, not by Paine. In the 1770s and 1780s, Burke's thought had been shaped by other controversies and addressed different issues: theological heterodoxy within the Church of England; the American Revolution; parliamentary reform; the Regency Crisis; India; the attempted repeal of the Test and Corporation Acts. Burke wrote a reply to a sermon by a Dissenting minister; he did not address a secular intellectual.[90] His denunciations of metaphysics and unaided reason were aimed at Price, not Robespierre.

It was this older context that nevertheless allowed Burke his insight into the French Revolution, for this was not in every respect as novel an episode as it later seemed. Even in 1772, speaking in the Commons against the Feathers Tavern petition to release Anglican clergy from the obligation to subscribe the Thirty-nine Articles, Burke warned: 'If you make this a season for religious alterations, depend upon it you will soon find it a season of religious tumults and religious wars'.[91] By 1790, reforming doctrine in England had already gone significantly further than it was to do even in revolutionary France, and English observers had had a decade in which to observe its practical implications. Burke well knew that these principles did not originate in America or France, although 1789 gave them an immense boost. His perception of a link

[90]Locating Burke in a controversy (at the outset) with Price rather than Paine is thus analogous to replacing Locke in a controversy with Filmer rather than Hobbes.

[91]Burke, *Works*, X, p. 10.

between newly-emergent heterodoxy and threats to the political order can be traced at least as far back as 1780. In the debate of 8 May that year, the veteran campaigner and ex-Wilkesite John Sawbridge moved another of his regular (and regularly unsuccessful) motions in the Commons calling for annual parliaments. Burke made an impassioned speech against: 'It is always to be lamented when men are driven to search into the foundations of the Commonwealth ... popular Election is a mighty evil.'[92] Burke's friend the duke of Richmond, a Unitarian, wrote to ask for a copy of his speech; despite Burke's obsequious efforts to prevent a breach,[93] on 3 June 1780 Richmond moved in the Lords for leave to introduce a reform bill on the sensational basis of universal manhood suffrage, equal electoral areas, electoral registers and annual general elections: not even the French electoral proposals of 1789 went as far.[94] Ineptly, Richmond's motion coincided with the Gordon riots. The Lords refused their assent, but the issue would not thereafter disappear. Nor did the possibility of major civil disorder.

In March 1782, Burke's patron Rockingham became First Lord of the Treasury. Three members of his cabinet (Fox, Richmond and Shelburne) were in some way publicly committed to parliamentary reform. Richmond extorted a promise from Rockingham that the question would be dealt with, and a meeting at Richmond's house persuaded the new MP, William Pitt, to take up the cause. On 7 May 1782 Pitt moved in the Commons for a committee of enquiry into the state of the representation, seconded by John Sawbridge.[95] Against this combined threat of pressure from without and betrayal from within, Burke drafted a major speech which anticipated many of the themes of the *Reflections*. He analysed the reformers into two schools, one demanding change on the basis of 'the supposed rights of man as man', the other arguing that 'the Representation is not so politically framed as to answer the theory of its institution'.

> As to the first sort of Reformer, it is ridiculous to talk to them of the British Constitution upon any or upon all of its bases; for they lay it down, that every man ought to govern himself, and that where he cannot go himself he must send his Representative; that all other government is usurpation, and is so far from having

[92]Burke, *Works*, X, 72–91, at 72–3 (there undated); *Parl Hist*, XXI, cols. 594–615; Cone, *Burke*, I, p. 376.

[93]Burke to Richmond, [post 8 May 1780], Burke, *Correspondence*, IV, pp. 235–8.

[94]Alison Gilbert Olson, *The Radical Duke: Career and Correspondence of Charles Lennox third Duke of Richmond* (Oxford, 1961), pp. 48–63. Richmond had given notice of his plan to Burke's friend Walker King, who passed on the information: King to Burke, 5 November 1779, in Burke, *Correspondence*, IV, pp 165–8.

[95]Cone, *Burke*, II, pp. 49–50; *Parl Hist*, XXII, cols. 1416–38.

a claim to our obedience, it is not only our right, but our duty, to resist it. Nine tenths of the Reformers argue thus, that is on the natural right.

Such a theory would demolish the House of Lords and the Crown, not merely the Commons. Given this principle, why should the people have only a one third share in the legislature? 'How came they neither to have the choice of King, or Lords, or Judges, or Generals, or Admirals, or Bishops, or Priests, or Ministers, or Justices of Peace? Why, what have you to answer in favour of the prior rights of the Crown and Peerage but this—our Constitution is a prescriptive Constitution; it is a Constitution, whose sole authority is, that it has existed time out of mind.'[96] 'Prescription is the most solid of all titles, not only to property, but, which is to secure that property, to Government.' Prescription as a 'ground of authority' meant it was a presumption in favour of

> any settled scheme of government against any untried project, that a nation has long existed and flourished under it. It is a better presumption even of the *choice* of a nation, far better than any sudden and temporary arrangement by actual election. Because a nation is not an idea only of local extent, and individual momentary aggregation, but it is an idea of continuity, which extends in time as well as in numbers, and in space. And this is a choice not of one day, or one set of people, not a tumultuary and giddy choice; it is a deliberate election of ages and of generations; it is a Constitution made by what is ten thousand times better than choice, it is made by the peculiar circumstances, occasions, tempers, dispositions, and moral, civil, and social habitudes of the people, which disclose themselves only in a long space of time.

The House of Commons was 'not made upon any given theory, but existing prescriptively', like the Crown and the Lords. 'To ask whether a thing, which has always been the same, stands to its usual principle, seems to me to be perfectly absurd; for how do you know the principles but from the construction?' Burke saw the logical flaw at the heart of the 'Commonwealth' position:

> On what grounds do we go, to restore our Constitution to what it has been at some given period, or to reform and re-construct it upon principles more conformable to a sound theory of government? A prescriptive Government, such as ours, never was the work of any Legislator, never was made upon any foregone theory. It seems to me a preposterous way of reasoning, and a perfect confusion of ideas, to take the theories, which learned and speculative men have made from that Government, and then supposing it made on those theories, which were made from it, to accuse the Government as not corresponding with them.[97]

[96]Such an argument, of course, made problematic the assumption that government (let alone civil society) had originated via a contract; but Burke did not yet explore this contradiction.

[97]'Speech On a Motion made in the House of Commons, the 7th of May 1782, for a Committee to inquire into the state of the Representation of the Commons in Parliament', in Burke, *Works*, X, pp. 92–108, at 93–9.

But Burke did not deliver the speech, evidently in order not to antagonise those of his colleagues, including Fox, Sheridan and Lord John Cavendish, who spoke in favour of reform.[98] Nor did Burke publish the speech. When he finally made public these views in 1790, the scale of the hostile reaction explains something of his reticence in 1782. Meanwhile, for the rest of the 1780s, Burke's target was not Fox but the reformer William Pitt.[99] Burke continued to be apprehensive about the reform movement, and in the *Reflections* recorded his suspicion (correctly, as we now know) that the Revolution Society, hitherto a non-political club of Dissenters, had been taken over by political extremists for use as a 'front organisation' (pp. [4–5]).

In the *Reflections*, his riposte to Price, Burke addressed a long-standing loyalty and spectacularly renounced it. Burke had been a lifelong friend of Dissenters and reformers, even of the Unitarian Joseph Priestley. Most of the 'friends of America' in London during the war of 1776–83 were Dissenters. The electoral support of the Dissenting interest was a valuable one, and the Rockinghamite Whigs were able credibly to appeal to it in opposition to the government of the loyal churchman Lord North, Chancellor of the University of Oxford and principled defender of the established status of the Church of England. Dissenters might easily join in a denunciation of North's government for its waste, intolerance, and tyrannical oppression of their American co-religionists. In 1783 this suddenly changed when Fox and North forged an alliance and, backed by a Commons majority, forced the king to give them ministerial office: this use of power, later commonplace, was still often condemned. Fox's India Bill, reforming the vast and anomalous East India Company, similarly opened him and his party to charges of subverting the constitution in order to create a fiefdom of private patronage for their own faction. The effect on Dissenting opinion was cataclysmic. When George III threw out Fox and North in 1784, many Dissenters sided electorally with the new Prime Minister, William Pitt, and the Foxites suffered a major reverse in the general election which followed.

Worse was to come: in November 1788 the king was diagnosed as mentally ill. The constitution made no automatic provision for a Regency: political conflict now turned on the powers of the obvious candidate (the Foxites' patron George, Prince of Wales) and on whether conditions might constitu-

[98]Cone, *Burke*, II, p. 49. The motion was defeated by 161 votes to 141: Burke's intervention would have been unnecessary.

[99]In a debate on 18 April 1785 over Pitt's proposal for parliamentary reform, Burke let slip that his opposition was lest Pitt's scheme let in a more extensive one from the duke of Richmond: *Parl Hist* XXV, cols. 432–78, at 469–70; Cone, *Burke*, II, p. 50. But Burke did not follow it up.

tionally be laid upon him as Regent. On this abstruse legal issue depended the survival of William Pitt's ministry or its replacement by its Foxite rivals: suddenly, the crushing electoral verdict of 1784 seemed about to be reversed. Seduced by this prospect, Burke found himself arguing to advance the Prince's position on extreme hereditarian grounds: that the Revolution of 1688 had not made the crown elective; that the Regent's powers should be unlimited by parliament; that he should succeed at once to full monarchical authority by hereditary right as if George III were naturally dead.[100] It was not a position to endear the Foxites either to the Dissenters or to the king, who, inconveniently for them, recovered in February 1789. Even Fox had distanced himself from Burke's extreme position as the crisis unfolded, searching for a compromise which finally proved unavailable. Paine did not forget Burke's new monarchical zeal during the Regency Crisis, and later argued ironically that Burke had not carried his principles far enough: 'Hard as Mr. Burke laboured the Regency Bill and hereditary succession two years ago, and much as he dived for precedents, he still had not boldness enough to bring up William of Normandy, and say, *There is the head of the list, there is the fountain of honour*, the son of a prostitute, and the plunderer of the English nation.'[101] Paine was right to argue that Burke had not engaged in such a regress: his renewed hereditarian emphasis was still within the framework of traditional Whig doctrine on the significance of that foundational event, the Revolution of 1688. Yet in ideological as well as parliamentary terms, the Regency crisis had a profound effect on Burke's position.

To condemn the French Revolution meant breaking with the Foxite Whigs, but Burke's position within that party was already difficult, even tenuous. In the late 1780s his career seemed over. On 4 May 1789 he was censured by the House of Commons for calling Warren Hastings a murderer, and Burke's crusade over India seemed conclusively to have lost credibility. Fox now inclined to Sheridan rather than to Burke, and by November 1789 Burke wrote privately of a 'defeat' over the Hastings trial produced by the 'desertion' of 'our pretended friends' among the Foxites. By January 1790 he knew that Fox himself had deserted the cause, and his indignation reached its

---

[100]Burke later explained: 'You cannot forget, that I supported the Prince's Title to the *Regency* upon the Principle of his Hereditary Right to the Crown: and I endeavourd to explode the false Notions, drawn from what has been Stated as the Revolution Maxims, by much the same arguments which I afterwards used in my printed reflexions.' Burke therefore complained of the Prince's ingratitude: 'I am in disgrace at Carleton House': Burke to William Weddell, 31 January 1792, in Burke, *Correspondence*, VII, p. 58.

[101]Paine, *Rights of Man*, p. 120.

height.[102] *The Times* of 1 June 1789 reported Burke 'in reality almost exhausted in strength of mind, as well as strength of body'. On 25 December it
wrote of him as a failed place-hunter. On 2 January 1790 it satirised his ob-
sessive pursuit of Warren Hastings, and on 15 January printed an imaginary
account of a loquacious and self-righteous Burke once more losing the attention of the House of Commons. Burke's was 'a name which should never be
mentioned without a mingled sentiment of admiration and disregard', added
the same paper on 18 January. On 2 February it predicted that Burke 'it is said
goes to Ireland, gets a seat in the senate there, and quits England for ever. This
is said to be owing to the very indecent inattentive manner, in which the British House treats his speeches'. All this was now to change with Burke's denunciation of the French Revolution in his speech of 9 February 1790, an act
which, by putting principle before party, won the respect of *The Times* and of
a large section of public opinion.

The reformers' ideological position was, meanwhile, evolving in a direction opposite to Burke's. Dissenters had long subscribed to an ecclesiology
which implied a contractarian, voluntarist view of civil authority also. Activated especially by advancing theological heterodoxy within their ranks, and
given a new field of action by the American revolution, some Dissenting intellectuals began to express their burgeoning millenarian vision in secular
terms. Thus activated, they began to be enlisted by the hotter spirits on the
fringes of the Foxite Whigs.[103] Against this background, the attention of Dissenters now turned again to those emblems of their inferior status within an
Anglican confessional state, the Corporation Act of 1661 and Test Act of
1673. In the spring of 1789, a Bristol Nonconformist, Richard Bright, had
written asking for Burke's support in an attempt to repeal these Acts. Burke
replied, indignant that the Dissenters were not backing him in his attempts 'to
relieve twenty Millions of Dissenters from the Church of England, in Asia
from real grievances' through his prosecution of Warren Hastings.

> There are no Men on Earth to whom I have been more attached, and with a more
> sincere Esteem and Affection, than to some amongst the Dissenters. From my ear-
> liest years my Connexions have been very much with them. I flatter myself that I
> have still friends of that denomination. They were once indulgent enough to Me,
> to think, that, (according to my scanty Power of obliging) they had some sort of
> obligation to me.
>     In the Year 1784, a great Change took place; and all of them who seem'd to act
> in Corps, have held me out to publick Odium, as one of a gang of Rebels and

[102]Frank O'Gorman, *The Whig Party and the French Revolution* (London, 1967),
pp. 42–6.
[103]See Burke, *Reflections*, p. [4] n.

Regicides, which had conspired at one blow to subvert the Monarchy, to annihilate, without Cause, all the Corporate privileges in the Kingdom, and totally to destroy this Constitution.

In 1784, the Dissenters had made a 'Slaughter' of 'the most honourable and Virtuous Men in the Kingdom'.[104] The motion for the repeal of the Acts was lost on 8 May 1789. Burke absented himself.

While Burke was beginning the *Reflections*, the Dissenting campaign continued undeterred. On 13 February 1790 Bright wrote again asking that Burke support a further application. Burke replied, excusing his absence on 8 May 1789 on grounds of ill health, and professing 'I never have for a moment departed from my Esteem and affection for you, and for other Gentlemen of your description', but admitting 'many considerations ... which make me less desirous, than formerly I had been, of becoming active in the Service of the Dissenters'. Many related to the French Revolution:

> Since the last years applications many things have either happened, or come to my knowlege, which add not a little to my disposition to persevere in my former State of inactivity. Extraordinary things have happend in France; extraordinary things have been said and done here, and publishd with great ostentation, in order to draw us into a connexion and concurrence with that nation upon the principles of its proceedings, and to lead us to an imitation of them. I think such designs, as far as they go, highly dangerous to the constitution and the prosperity of this Country. I have had lately put into my hands, and but very lately, two extraordinary works,[105] so sanctiond, as to leave no Doubt upon my Mind, that a considerable party is formed, and is proceeding systematically, to the destruction of this Constitution in some of its essential parts. I was much surprised to find religious assemblies turned into sort of places of exercise and discipline for politicks; and for the nourishment of a party which seems to have contention and power much more than Piety for its Object.[106]

The two 'extraordinary works' were those condemned by Burke in his speech on 2 March 1790.[107]

[104]Burke to Richard Bright, 8–9 May 1789: Burke, *Correspondence*, V, pp. 470–2.
[105]Evidently [Samuel Palmer], *The Protestant-Dissenter's Catechism. Containing, I. A Brief History of the Nonconformists: II. The Reasons of the Dissent from the National Church* (London, 1772) and Robert Robinson, *A Plan of Lectures on the Principles of Nonconformity. For the Instruction of Catechumens* (Cambridge, 1778), each a systematic attack on the established Church, and each often reprinted. If these were the two works Burke was given, his ignorance of them since their first publication is significant. It is not known who drew these works to Burke's attention; Horsley is a possibility.
[106]Burke to Bright, 18 February 1790: Burke, *Correspondence*, VI, pp. 82–5.
[107]For which, see below, n. 138.

February 1790 saw the culmination of a nation-wide series of meetings,
part of a campaign against the repeal of the Acts. The texts of the resolutions
passed at these meetings are evidence of the wide diffusion of ideas of the essential connection of Church and State and the subordination of natural
rights to statutory privileges: Burke was not alone in these claims, but in the
mainstream.[108] By 1791, Burke believed that 'nine tenths' of the Dissenters
were 'entirely devoted, some with greater some with less zeal, to the principles
of the French Revolution'.[109] He probably exaggerated, but was not wholly
wrong, and it was not an emotional or sudden over-reaction which led him to
that assessment. While writing the *Reflections*, Burke had been briefed by a
friend on the extreme claims of the Dissenting intelligentsia associated with
Price, Priestley and the movement for parliamentary reform. On this basis,
Burke wrote: 'Some of them are so heated with their particular theories, that
they give more than hints that the fall of the civil powers, with all the dreadful
consequences of that fall, provided they might be of service to their theories,
would not be unacceptable to them, or very remote from their wishes' (p.
[85]). He then quoted Priestley's *History of the Corruptions of Christianity*
(1782), demanding 'the fall of the civil powers' and predicting a millenarian
revolution independently of any consideration of events in France.[110]

On these English issues, then, Burke's mind had been formed long before
the French Revolution. English Dissent, in the versions patronised by the reforming nobility like the Unitarians Richmond, Grafton and Shelburne, had
created a social constituency in England whose doctrines demanded a fundamental reconstruction of the state. Burke now thought he saw something similar in France, where the intellectual leaven was provided by the *philosophes*.
Together, he inferred, the mixture was explosive. It pointed to the sweeping
away of the authority of society's basic institutions.[111] Hereditary right, pre-

---

[108]Anthony Lincoln, *Some Political & Social Ideas of English Dissent 1763–1800*
(Cambridge, 1938), pp. 261–7; *A Collection of the resolutions passed at the meetings
of the clergy of the Church of England, of the counties, corporations, cities, and towns,
and of the Society for Promoting Christian Knowledge; assembled to take into consideration the late application of the Dissenters to Parliament, for the repeal of the Corporation and Test Acts* (London, 1790).

[109]Burke to Dundas, 30 September 1791: Burke, *Correspondence*, VI, pp. 418–22,
at 419.

[110]It is not known who drew this work to his attention. Again, it may have been
Horsley.

[111]For the essential accuracy of Burke's insight into English Dissent, see A. M. C.
Waterman, 'The nexus between theology and political doctrine in Church and Dissent', in Knud Haakonssen (ed.), *Enlightenment and Religion: Rational Dissent in
eighteenth-century Britain* (Cambridge, 1996), pp. 193–218.

scription, and contract were interdependent with hierarchy, order, and property. Orthodox religion provided the providential rationale of such an order, and the Church hierarchy was intimately involved with the social hierarchy: no bishop, no king, no gentleman. Prescription, liberty as an inheritance, the links between generations, everything venerable were now to be interpreted as being in one scale; in the other scale now sat the omnicompetent individual owing no allegiance to family, nation or rank; religious Dissent; natural rights doctrine; landless talent; militant atheism; revolutionary violence. So Burke arranged the alternatives. To conceive of them in this stark and antithetical way was, however, novel. Many in England, both in government and opposition, thought otherwise. That Whig reformer William Pitt regarded the Revolution as a problem that might be managed: co-existence, if possible, was his goal. Foxite Whigs often thought the ideals of the Revolution attainable, both in France and England, without the dire consequences that Burke predicted as inevitable.

Yet Burke's outright condemnation of the French Revolution was not a foregone conclusion. Although his position on English Dissent was long-rehearsed and well-informed, his early reaction to news from France was ambiguous, tentative and not precipitate. In a letter of 9 August 1789, he was undecided about French events. He recorded 'England gazing with astonishment at a French struggle for Liberty and not knowing whether to blame or to applaud! The thing indeed, though I thought I saw something like it in progress for several years, has still something in it paradoxical and Mysterious. The spirit it is impossible not to admire; but the old Parisian ferocity has broken out in a shocking manner.'[112] He clearly had in mind the Massacre of St Bartholomew and the wars of the Fronde. Burke the libertarian Whig was moved to admire; Burke the friend of order was repelled. He read the two letters published in *The Gazetteer* in August 1789 on events in Paris, and later quoted them in the *Reflections* (pp. [97, 128]). By September, he wrote with apprehension of 'the Democracy that is the Spirit, and in a good measure too, the form, of the constitution they have in hand: It is except the Idea of the Crowns being hereditary much more truly democratical than that of North America'.[113] The crucial episode for him seems to have been the events of 5–6 October 1789, the subject of the most lurid and heightened passage in the *Reflections*. Burke wrote to his son Richard on 10 October: 'This day I heard from Laurence who has sent me papers confirming the portentous state of

[112]Burke to Lord Charlemont, 9 August 1789: Burke, *Correspondence*, VI, p. 10.
[113]Burke to William Windham, 27 September 1789: Burke, *Correspondence*, VI, pp. 24–6.

France—where the Elements which compose Human Society seem all to be dissolved, and a world of Monsters to be produced in the place of it—where Mirabeau presides as the Grand Anarch; and the late Grand Monarch makes a figure as ridiculous as pitiable.'[114]

On 4 November 1789 a French admirer wrote to Burke with a plea that he endorse the Revolution.[115] Burke's reply, written in November but not then sent, warned: 'If I should seem any where to express myself in the language of disapprobation, be so good as to consider it as no more than the expression of doubt.' He advocated a limited, law-bound liberty, but feared that 'You may have subverted Monarchy, but not recover'd freedom.' He recommended prudence and virtue, but without the indignant denunciation of the *Reflections*.[116] His apprehensions were nevertheless growing. The same month, Burke was describing France as 'a country undone' and, although welcoming her inability 'despotically to give the Law to Europe', apprehended 'many inconveniencies not only to Europe at large, but to this Country in particular from the total political extinction of a great civilized Nation situated in the heart of this our Western System'.[117]

Parliament re-convened after the extended summer and autumn recess on 21 January 1790. Burke's letter to Charles-Jean-François Depont the previous November showed no evident fear that the French example would be immediately exported to England. Burke's increasingly concerned but still balanced appreciation of the situation changed profoundly after he returned to London, however, for he now read Price's sermon of 4 November 1789 in its printed form, *A Discourse on the Love of our Country*, and the appendix of documents which Price added.[118] It was now that he received a letter from Paine assuring him that 'The Revolution in France is certainly a Forerunner to other Revolutions in Europe', and explaining that no foreign court, not even Prussia, would intervene in France: 'they are afraid of their Armies and their

[114]Burke to Richard Burke, 10 October 1789: Burke, *Correspondence*, VI, pp. 29–30.

[115]Charles-Jean-François Depont to Burke, 4 November 1789: Burke, *Correspondence*, VI, pp. 31–2.

[116]Burke to Depont, [November 1789]: Burke, *Correspondence*, VI, pp. 39–50, at 41.

[117]Burke to Fitzwilliam, 12 November 1789: Burke, *Correspondence*, VI, pp. 34–7.

[118]Burke later recalled: 'When I came to Town, though I had heard of Dr. Price's Sermon, I had not read it'; he was led to do so by a conversation with a leading Dissenter at a dinner party who assured him 'that the dissenters never could be reconciled to us … as long as we were led by Fox', whom Burke was still then defending. Burke to William Weddell, 31 January 1792, in Burke, *Correspondence*, VII, p. 56.

Subjects catching the Contagion'.[119] Price's sermon and Paine's letter turned a future, hypothetical, foreign problem into an immediate, actual and domestic danger.

Price's sermon was a sensational document, which provoked some twenty-one critical replies before Burke's *Reflections* appeared, and others later: Burke's response to Price was fully in line with the hostile tone and systematic defence of the Church mounted by these other tracts.[120] Price had echoed the usual Whig eulogies of 'our deliverance at the Revolution from the dangers of popery and arbitrary power', and of 'LIBERTY' as 'the object of patriotic zeal ... inseparable from knowledge and virtue'.[121] Any Whig would have agreed. But the sermon also contained a novel political programme. First, Price sought to redefine national identity,[122] in order to make universally applicable his Dissenting political theology. A 'love of our country' was commendable, but had to be freed from 'mistakes and prejudices'. By 'our country', he argued, was meant 'not the soil or the spot of earth on which we happen to have been born', but 'that body of companions and friends and kindred who are associated with us under the same constitution of government, protected by the same laws, and bound together by the same civil polity'. Even in this sense, love of country 'does not imply any conviction of the superior value of it to other countries, or any particular preference of its laws and constitution of government'. Finally, love of country, as redefined by Price, disavowed 'that spirit of rivalship and ambition which has been common among nations.—What has the love of their country hitherto been among mankind? What has it been but a love of domination, a desire of conquest, and a thirst for grandeur and glory, by extending territory and enslaving surrounding countries?' This was nothing less than a systematic attempt to undermine English identity, grounded as it was on the providential destiny of an estab-

---

[119]Paine to Burke, 17 January 1790: Burke, *Correspondence*, VI, pp. 67–75, at 71. *The Times* of 4 November 1789 had similarly reported: 'The spirit of Revolution and revolt is not confined to France and Flanders only, but seems to be extending to the inner territories of Germany.'

[120]Gayle Trusdel Pendleton, 'Towards a Bibliography of the *Reflections* and *Rights of Man* Controversy', *Bulletin of Research in the Humanities* 85 (1982), pp. 65–103, at 68–9. Pendleton recorded a total of twenty-seven replies to Price (excluding Burke's), three of them deploying the divine-right arguments that Burke so clearly disavowed in the *Reflections*.

[121]Price, *Discourse*, pp. 2, 19.

[122]'Nationalism' was a term coined in the nineteenth century for a new conception of identity, ascribed to a homogeneity of race, vernacular language and culture. Such assumptions about the necessary foundations of group identity were not common at the time Burke wrote.

lished church, on reverence for legal and political institutions, and a shared history. In its place, Price urged 'the Religion of Benevolence', practiced by 'citizens of the world'.[123]

Second, Price lightly dismissed 'most' of the currently-existing governments of the world as 'usurpations on the rights of men' and sought a political model which, once appreciated, would make it 'impossible' for men to 'submit' to those governments. That political model involved the abolition of 'that gloomy and cruel superstition ... which has hitherto gone under the name of religion', including, by implication, the established Church. The 'overthrow of priestcraft and tyranny', in familiar heterodox Dissenting fashion, were linked goals for Price. Civil government was only 'an institution of human prudence' for delivering to its citizens 'that liberty to which all have an equal right'. Given that function, 'a King is no more than the first servant of the public'.[124] The political model was, therefore, the Revolution of 1688, in the interpretation given to it within the tradition even of orthodox Dissent. According to Price, 1688 had indeed established those principles as the accepted ones of the English constitution in a moment when 'the fetters which despotism had been long preparing for us were broken': a 'tyrant' had been 'expelled' and 'a Sovereign of our own choice appointed in his room'. As a result, 'our consciences were emancipated'. Price then summed up his and the Dissenters' interpretation of the Revolution in the formula which Burke found so provoking.[125] Even so, although the Revolution was a 'great work, it was by no means a perfect work ... In particular ... the toleration then obtained was imperfect.' Price's chief target was the Corporation and Test Acts, and these laws, the emblems or bulwarks of Anglican ascendancy, provided the engine of his and his co-religionists' passionate denunciations of the social order of their day. Eventual success was not open to doubt: Dissenters were on the side of history.[126]

Third, a legislature which had blocked the repeal of these Acts was now to be swept away. The 'INEQUALITY OF OUR REPRESENTATION' was 'so gross and so palpable, as to make it excellent chiefly in form and theory'. Without representation in the legislature, government was 'nothing but an usurpation'. Price was not specific about how far Britain's government yet was from such a state, but his implications were clear. They were rhetorically heightened in Price's inflammatory peroration:

[123]Price, *Discourse*, pp. 2–5, 8, 10.
[124]Price, *Discourse*, pp. 12–14, 20–1, 23.
[125]Price, *Discourse*, pp. 31–2, 34; Burke, *Reflections*, p. [20].
[126]Price, *Discourse*, pp. 34–7.

After sharing in the benefits of one Revolution [1688], I have been spared to be a witness to two other Revolutions [1776, 1789], both glorious.—And now me-thinks, I see the ardour for liberty catching and spreading; a general amendment beginning in human affairs; the dominion of kings changed for the dominion of laws, and the dominion of priests giving way to the dominion of reason and con-science.

Be encouraged all ye friends of freedom, and writers in its defence! The times are auspicious. Your labours have not been in vain. Behold kingdoms, admon-ished by you, starting from sleep, breaking their fetters, and claiming justice from their oppressors! Behold, the light you have struck out, after setting AMERICA free, reflected to FRANCE, and there kindled into a blaze that lays despotism in ashes, and warms and illuminates EUROPE![127]

Price wrote of 'the friends of freedom' everywhere, not just of the American colonists and the example set by their achievement of independence.

In language redolent of the Book of Revelation, Burke closed his *Reflec-tions* with the warning that the French commonwealth would be 'purified by fire and blood' (p. [356]). This imagery can easily be presented as dispropor-tionate to what are claimed to be the moderate, idealistic and consensual stages of the Revolution in 1789–90, however apt for the apocalyptic events of 1791–4. It should however be remembered that Burke was responding only secondarily to events in Paris, and primarily to an English Dissenting cam-paign which was rhetorically heightened, extensive, and in some cases, even from the 1760s, literally millenarian. In these areas, Burke's diagnosis was es-sentially accurate. The consequences of heterodox theology had been mani-fest in the parliamentary arena in the programmes of Unitarians like Rich-mond. Price's Arianism was already publicly avowed, defended by him as a 'middle scheme' between Trinitarianism and Socinianism.[128] He had also gone on record as advocating universal suffrage in principle, and in practice when 'prudent'.[129] Burke had fought against these principles in England throughout the 1780s; now a new setting made them dramatically and immediately threatening.

The international ambitions of the French Revolution were no secret. On 15 July 1790, *The Times* reported the meeting of reformers at the Crown and Anchor Tavern and noted Price, 'with a French national cockade in the but-

[127]Price, *Discourse*, pp. 39, 49–50.

[128]Richard Price, *Sermons on the Christian Doctrine as received by the Different Denominations of Christians* (London, 1787), p. 71 and passim.

[129]*A Collection of the Letters Which have been addressed to the Volunteers of Ire-land, on the Subject of a Parliamentary Reform, by the Earl of Effingham, Doctor Price, Major Cartwright, Doctor Jebb, and the Rev. Mr. Wyvill* (London, 1783), pp. 80–8, at 83–4.

ton-hole of his coat ... saying, that in France there was a plan in agitation for proposing a perpetual union with this country'. What Burke mentioned first as objectionable in Price's *Discourse* and its attached documents was its 'manifest design of connecting the affairs of France with those of England, by drawing us into an imitation of the conduct of the National Assembly' (p. [10]). He wrote to an unknown correspondent, presumably at this time, lamenting the influence of 'Voltaire and Rousseau as legislators ... I see some people here are willing that we should become their scholars too, and reform our state on the French model. They have begun; and it is high time for those who wish to preserve *morem majorum*, to look about them.'[130] On 5 February a tract was published entitled *A Review of the Case of the Protestant Dissenters with Reference to the Corporation and Test Acts*. Although anonymous, it was quickly ascribed to Bishop Samuel Horsley, who had been Priestley's chief theological opponent in controversies dating from 1783; the tract was soon acknowledged as a classic statement of the case against Dissent, built around the argument that 'the principles of a Nonconformist in religion, and a Republican in politics, are inseparably united'.[131]

It was in this setting that Burke made his first public pronouncement on the revolution in the debate on the Army Estimates on 9 February 1790, provoked by the euphemistic praise heaped on France by Pitt and Fox. His choice of words was sensational. France had 'lost every thing'; he 'trembled at the uncertainty of all human greatness'.

> Since the House had been prorogued in the summer much work was done in France. The French had shewn themselves the ablest architects of ruin that had hitherto existed in the world. In that very short space of time they had completely pulled down to the ground, their monarchy; their church; their nobility; their law; their revenue; their army; their navy; their commerce; their arts; and their manufactures.[132]

England's danger was 'an imitation of the excesses of an irrational, unprincipled, proscribing, confiscating, plundering, ferocious, bloody and tyrannical democracy'; in religion, 'the danger of their example is no longer from intolerance, but from Atheism; a foul, unnatural vice, foe to all the dignity and consolation of mankind; which seems in France, for a long time, to have been

----

[130]Burke to unknown [?Paine], [?January 1790], in Burke, *Correspondence*, VI, pp. 78–82, at 81.

[131]*A Review of the Case*, p. 29; F. C. Mather, *High Church Prophet: Bishop Samuel Horsley (1733–1806) and the Caroline Tradition in the Later Georgian Church* (Oxford, 1992), pp. 55–63, 73–4.

[132]Burke, *Speech ... 9 Feb 1790*, pp. 6–8, 11.

embodied into a faction, accredited, and almost avowed'. Burke warned England against 'an imitation of the French spirit of Reform'. The French had gloried in the revolution 'as if revolutions were good things in themselves. All the horrors, and all the crimes of the anarchy which led to their revolution, which attend its progress, and which may virtually attend it in its establishment, pass for nothing with the lovers of revolutions.'[133]

Reactions to Burke's speech anticipated reactions to his *Reflections*. Earl Stanhope responded with bitter indignation, stigmatising 'the curious tenets of your Political Creed', reminding him that the Revolution of 1688 had 'given a wholesome lesson to *Tories*', and implying that Burke's doctrines were 'WHIG Principles from *St. Omers*'.[134] A systematic work by Burke on events in France was long awaited. A pamphlet was advertised on 13 February 1790 as 'in the Press, and speedily will be published',[135] but Burke worked on, revising, extending, rewriting,[136] and changing its balance from an examination of the English Dissenters towards an analysis of the French Revolution itself. It is an open question whether Burke saw a copy of Bishop Samuel Horsley's paper entitled 'Thoughts upon Civil government, and its Relation to Religion' of February 1790, which emphasised in phrases that anticipated the *Reflections* how 'all Kingdoms and States in this World', despite their different governments, 'are to be regarded as the Provinces of this great and universal Kingdom' of God; it defended 'the intimate and inseparable Union of Religion and Civil Government' on the basis of religious truth, not political expediency.[137] On 2 March 1790 the third and decisive motion for the repeal of the Test and Corporation Acts was moved in the Commons by Fox himself,

[133]Burke, *Speech ... 9 Feb 1790*, pp. 12, 15, 17.

[134]*A Letter from Earl Stanhope, to the Right Honourable Edmund Burke: containing a short Answer to his late Speech on the French Revolution* (London, 1790), pp. 6, 25, 34.

[135]*The World*, 13 February 1790. Burke's title was then *Reflections on certain proceedings of the Revolution Society, of the 4th of November, 1789, concerning the affairs of France.*

[136]A fragment of Burke's drafts survive, printed by J. T. Boulton, 'The *Reflections*: Burke's Preliminary Draft and Methods of Composition', *Durham University Journal* 14 (1953), pp. 114–19. It establishes 'the scrupulous care with which Burke ordered his thoughts before writing'.

[137]Lambeth Palace Library, Horsley Papers, MS 1767, fos. 198–203, ed. Andrew Robinson, in Stephen Taylor (ed.), *From Cranmer to Davidson* (Church of England Record Society, vol. 7, Woodbridge, 1999), pp. 203–12. Horsley may also have been the author of *An Apology for the Liturgy and Clergy of the Church of England* (London, 1790), a classic reply to the Unitarian duke of Grafton. It is sometimes ascribed to Bishop Samuel Hallifax.

cynically bidding for the votes of Dissenters in the forthcoming general election. Burke now attended and opposed repeal in a major speech.[138] The motion went down to defeat by the crushing majority of 294 to 105: the link between Dissent and Republicanism had been clearly made in the parliamentary arena. On 4 March Henry Flood, chairman of the Society for Constitutional Information, introduced proposals for parliamentary reform, again with Fox's blessing. Again Burke spoke against, and the motion was frustrated by the adjournment.[139] To Burke, it can only have seemed that Fox had given a decisive answer to the question of Whig identity.

Events across the Channel now presented themselves as the larger analogues of English conflicts; the crucial contest for the soul of the Whig party would be fought over the interpretation of the French Revolution. Burke followed French affairs more and more closely, distracted from the general election at home. The latest events recorded in the *Reflections* were in August 1790: the speech of Bailly, mayor of Paris, to the National Assembly on 13th, a speech which was reported in England in the *Public Advertiser* of 19th; the festival of the Patriotic Society at Nantes on 23rd (p. [227]); the proposal in the National Assembly on 28th and 29th to melt church bells for coin (p. [348]).[140] Burke probably finished writing at the beginning of September.[141] When the book finally appeared on 1 November 1790, it was an immediate best-seller. One hostile pamphleteer complained how 'the moment that Mr. Burke's pamphlet was announced, Dodsley's shop was crowded with purchasers; the industry of the printers could scarce satisfy the impatience of the public, and the runners of the booksellers groaned beneath the *weight* of the Right Honourable Gentleman's composition'.[142] Why was Burke's book so successful, then and later?

[138]For the debate on 2 March 1790, see *Parl Hist* XXVIII, cols. 387–452; for Burke's speech, ibid., 432–43. For the circulation of Priestley's threats, see *Reflections*, p. [85]n.

[139]For the debate on 4 March 1790, see *Parl Hist* XXVIII, cols. 452–79; for Burke's two speeches, ibid., 477–9.

[140](This last had been anticipated on 16 January 1790.) Burke did, however, write of the report of a committee on reviewing treaties as in the future (p. [162]): it reported on 25 August.

[141]Burke did not write of Necker's departure from office on 4 September: *Reflections*, p. [297].

[142]*Short Observations on the Right Hon. Edmund Burke's Reflections* (London, 1790), p. 4.

## (v) Burke's theory of the French Revolution

Burke confronted in the French Revolution a vast and bewildering catastrophe, and was drawn to explain it in different ways, not wholly consistent. Broadly, Burke had two interpretations of the Revolution; they are still echoed, and unresolved, in the work of modern historians who enjoy far greater access to the evidence than any of Burke's contemporaries could command. One might say that two Burkes observed events on the other side of the Channel. The Whig Burke deplored France's absolute monarchy and applauded the reforms of 1787–8. This Burke argued that France had the remains of an ancient constitution, like England's; that France (after its recent reforms) had a good and viable constitution on the day the Estates-General met in separate orders; and that peaceful, constitutional progress from that point had been possible. This Burke stood in an older humanist tradition in thinking that this auspicious moment in human affairs had then been overwhelmed by an unheralded catastrophe, a sudden turn in Fortune's wheel which destroyed virtuous plans and dragged down noble individuals without obvious just cause: a revolution.

The other Burke began to develop insights into the Revolution that led him to be pilloried as a Tory by his allies the Foxite Whigs, and to be seen in retrospect as the catalyst of nineteenth-century conservatism. This other Burke saw the Revolution as doomed from the outset to end in apocalyptic catastrophe. It had been long heralded by *philosophes* who had eroded the moral ties that bind civilised society and subordinate it to the divine will. This other Burke claimed in retrospect to have inferred disaster from the list of names of those elected to the Estates-General, even before that body had met and recast itself as a unicameral National Assembly claiming to exercise sovereignty. This other Burke saw in the Revolution an egalitarian principle destructive of all authority and all order; he saw violence and lawlessness at the heart of the Revolution from its outset. This Burke moved away from picturing the Revolution as a sudden, incomprehensible event and began to find ways of understanding it as a thing in itself, a dynamic, uncontrollable spectre; revolution not as an event, but as an episode, a process, a principle.

These two Burkes were the same man, and although his comments on the Revolution moved away from the first interpretation and towards the second even as he was writing the *Reflections*, both were present in the work, held in an unresolved tension. Since these were the major questions that haunted him, his book did not address many other aspects of French society, politics, law or political theory that modern scholars seek to explore. In some ways, and on first reading, Burke's *Reflections* is a disappointment: it contains no extended

account of the forms or essence of French monarchical society;[143] no apologia
for the *ancien régime* other than to say that it could have been peacefully reformed; no authoritative narrative of the quotidian course of French politics;
no structural analysis of revolution as such; not even a worked-out conspiracy
theory. In these areas the book did not teach the French things about their
Revolution of which they were unaware. But in its insights into the ideological
origin of revolution, the nature of revolutionary violence, the religious underpinnings of social order, the political logic of a government's sudden collapse
and the tragic unfolding of fateful consequences, Burke said something about
France which was unique.

Burke's condemnation of the Revolution was all the more remarkable because his defence of France's old order was strictly limited and qualified. He
did not argue that France had an admirable constitution before 1789 which
was then overthrown by an unjustifiable act of resistance; on the contrary, he
condemned France's absolute monarchy in familiar Whig fashion, and only
asserted that the foundations of an ancient constitution still survived, on
which a limited monarchy after the English model could have been built. To
call the old order 'full of abuses' but 'a despotism rather in appearance than
reality' (pp. [188–9]) was cool praise indeed. Examined closely, it can be seen
that the *Reflections* offered no systematic theoretical defences of monarchy,
of nobility, of the Church, of landownership or of seigneurial rights; at most,
Burke argued pragmatically that these institutions were underwritten by prescription, that they were not as evil as they had been depicted, that they included many good men, that some good results flowed from them, and that
they were a proper basis for Whig reform.

Burke offered no narrative of how the Revolution had come about, and offered only selective criticisms of France's proposed new constitution. His
English enemies seized on such omissions in Burke's account and claimed that
they were weaknesses. Paine later complained: 'As Mr. Burke has not written
on constitutions, so neither has he written on the French revolution. He gives
no account of its commencement or its progress.'[144] Yet despite this claim,
Price and Priestley actually gave less attention than Burke to the specific nature of events in France. Paine provided a brief narrative of the background to
the Revolution, tracing what he argued were its causes from the American
war and following politics up to the fall of the Bastille, but apart from a short

---

[143]His picture of French monarchical society indeed echoed in some respects the
idealised picture of India that he had built up in order to condemn the administration
of Warren Hastings: Lock, *Burke*, pp. 531–2.

[144]Paine, *Rights of Man*, pp. 84–5.

narrative covering 5–6 October 1789 he did not continue his account to explain the acceleration of events after 14 July that year, although this was the emerging point at issue between himself and Burke.[145] Paine did not record that he was in England during the fall of the Bastille and the October Days, although he sought to imply that his account throughout had the authority of an eye-witness. As the Revolution progressed, Price, Priestley and Paine shied away from detailed analysis of it. Paine's *Rights of Man. Part the Second* (1792) remarkably said almost nothing about France. Burke's engagement with the Revolution from 1789 to his death in 1797 was the most consistent and profound of these four figures, but even he did not provide a synoptic narrative of events, or a structural analysis of their significance. Burke's conception of what had happened in France is, paradoxically, not easy to explain. The paradox was created by Burke's belief that the French Revolution, unlike the English, had been unnecessary and regressive; an unnecessary revolution was dominated by contingency, and difficult to account for in terms of major antecedent causes.

Burke was not alone in this perception. Most of his contemporaries struggled to accept the fact that they had not anticipated what happened in France: revolution seemed to overwhelm the most populous, most magnificent, most politically stable nation in Europe like some natural catastrophe. In structural terms, this collapse seemed capricious; Burke was not alone in seeking an alternative explanation in terms of public morality. His account was strikingly similar to that which the journalist Louis Sébastien Mercier later gave of the destruction of the French church:

> Nothing announced so sudden a destruction. The people in general seemed attached to the ceremonies of catholicism; but there are bodies struck with lightning, who seem still to preserve their life and organization, but touch them, and they crumble into dust ... It is not their [the altars'] overthrow which ought to astonish, but it is having seen them fall in one day, with all the circumstances of the most profound contempt or hatred. The progress of irreligion was extremely rapid among the vulgar, who armed themselves at once with hammers and levers to break the sacred images before which six months back they bent the knee.[146]

Such events seemed from the outside to be fanaticism or frenzy rather than a stage in the beneficient unfolding logic of history.

Burke did briefly explore some structural explanations of the Revolution.

---

[145]Paine, *Rights of Man*, pp. 24–31, 85–108. Before the publication of the *Reflections*, Paine was in France from May to September 1787, December 1787 to June 1788, November 1789 to March 1790, and July to October 1790.

[146]Mercier, *New Picture of Paris*, II, pp. 75–6.

He appreciated the existence of a conflict between the landed and the monied interest in France, conflicts over status in which wealthy men, not newly ennobled, 'struck at the nobility through the crown and the church'. He saw a 'state of real, though not always perceived warfare' between these interests, as the wealthy commons 'were not fully admitted to the rank and estimation which wealth, in reason and good policy, ought to bestow in every country'. He saw an alliance between the monied interest and 'the political Men of Letters', themselves pursuing 'something like a regular plan for the destruction of the Christian religion' (pp. [163–5, 204]). But it was the last that Burke really stressed, rather than any conflict within French society over careers, status, seigneurial dues or tax burdens. He denied that 'the oppression of the people' was significant, although instances of it existed, and denied that nobility or clergy had any 'considerable share' in oppression (pp. [203–4, 206]). The real causes of the Revolution were not, in Burke's view, systemic ones,[147] and in this he was in agreement with most of his English contemporaries. It is open to argument whether any French observers, on the basis of the daily frictions present in all societies, predicted what was about to happen in their own.[148] Only later did historians develop the broad explanatory models which helped men to come to terms with catastrophe, and later still that other historians dismantled them.[149] Contemporaries of the French Revolution, lacking such comforting interpretative schemes, were brought face to face with the bewildering diversity of a cataclysm. Burke's insight into the nature of revolution was a profoundly pessimistic one: chaos has no history. This had a corollary, prominent in Burke's pages: political violence has no moral justification.

His attempt to devise systemic explanations had failed in the face of a paradox: the awesome scale of the catastrophe was grotesquely disproportionate to the ostensible causes. Things had not happened on their merits: 'The financial difficulties were only pretexts and instruments of those who ac-

---

[147]Nevertheless, Burke continued to seek information on the extent of peasant grievances over land tenure, rents, evictions, *métayage*, bad harvests, 'personal feudal Duties', tithes and the Church's behaviour as a landowner, e.g. Burke to vicomte de Cicé, 24 January 1791: Burke, *Correspondence*, VI, pp. 206–8.

[148]Some have seen an anticipation of the Revolution in the writings of the Abbé Mably, especially *Des droits et devoirs du citoyen* (1750), but these general prefigurings did not prepare contemporaries for what actually happened in 1788–9.

[149]'By uncoupling 1789 from the bourgeoisie, one rediscovers something of the mysterious indeterminacy of those celebrated events': François Furet, 'Transformations in the Historiography of the Revolution', in Ferenc Fehér (ed.), *The French Revolution and the Birth of Modernity* (Berkeley, 1990), pp. 264–77, at 272.

complished the ruin of that Monarchy. They were not the causes of it.'[150] Burke recorded his bewilderment; the spectacle produced 'alternate laughter and tears' (pp. [11–12]). As he had elsewhere argued, 'In most of the capital changes that are recorded in the principles and system of any government, a public benefit of some kind or other has been pretended. The revolution commenced in something plausible; in something which earned the appearance at least of punishment of delinquency, or correction of abuse.'[151] That was not true of France, which had already been embarked on a substantial programme of reform before 1789. Burke's account of the Revolution confronted the inexplicable cataclysm of events, and he struggled to find answers adequate to their scale.

Burke's analysis therefore had little in common with the over-determined models of many later historians. He did not, like Tocqueville, see an absolute republic as a natural offspring of an absolute monarchy, although he had a typically Whiggish low regard for the latter. He did not see the Revolution as essentially a class war, the bourgeoisie seizing power from a decaying feudal order, although he appreciated the growth of 'the middle classes', who became 'the seat of all the active politicks'.[152] He defended the rational Whig order of 1688 not against the 'rise' of any new 'class' but chiefly against what he saw as betrayal from within by reforming members of the existing elite.[153] Burke did not fear communist levelling, although he feared the insecurity of all property. He did not (as Jefferson did) regard 1789 as the logical extension of 1776. Despite his role in the American Revolution, Burke did not see himself living in an age of Atlantic revolutions, and did not diagnose the essential source of the revolutionary ideology as democratic. Although he clearly understood the ideological emblem of the Revolution as 'the rights of man', Burke said little about natural rights theories as such. These absences from Burke's thought share a common cause: he did not regard 1789 as a step forward into a new world, a new world which needed new definition. He regarded the French Revolution as a step back into a world violent, irrational,

[150]Burke, *Two Letters ... on the Proposals for Peace*, p. 6. Ironically, Burke thereby echoed the objection of colonial loyalists that the American Revolution was unintelligible in the light of 'such trivial Causes, as those alledged by these unhappy People': Daniel Leonard, quoted in Gordon S. Wood, *The Creation of the American Republic 1776–1787* (Chapel Hill, 1969), p. 4.

[151]Burke, *Speech ... Feb. 28, 1785*, p. 10.

[152]Burke, *Two Letters ... on the Proposals for Peace*, p. 184.

[153]'Class' did not carry its later meaning until the 1820s at the earliest, and available evidence makes problematic any idea that the eighteenth century saw the 'rise' of any 'middle class' in England: Clark, *English Society 1660–1832*, ch. 2.

and fanatical in a way that recalled sixteenth-century wars of religion. Yet this insight was not a hasty response to the events in France in 1789–90 alone; it drew on Burke's experience of the dynamics of English and Irish society also. His critics were right to say that his claims about France often rested on English analogies, express or implicit. That did not mean that those claims were necessarily wrong.

Burke was not, however, a consistent systematiser. He condemned France's reforming nobility for having rashly initiated processes subversive of social order which they then proved unable to control. Yet this argument in some ways contradicted Burke's Whig faith that a limited, restrained, constitutional revolution was possible, as had been demonstrated in England in 1688, so that France in 1789 might have built a limited monarchy on the still-surviving foundations of its version of an ancient constitution. Two historical episodes might return to haunt a Whig framing such an argument: 1642 and 1776. As a Whig, Burke presumably approved the constitutional revolution effected during the early years of the Long Parliament; as a Whig, he shied away from asking whether such a constitutional revolution might lead inexorably to the catastrophe of civil war. The same Whig Burke had been a prominent friend of the American colonies during their constitutional disputes with Britain of the 1760s and early 1770s; he was not eager to ask whether armed conflict and social revolution from 1776 was a result of what he and his parliamentary allies had encouraged.

The strangest omission in the *Reflections* was any comparison of the French Revolution with the American,[154] but serious thought on the inner nature of that earlier episode itself had been markedly absent from Burke's writings, speeches and correspondence after 1776. His critique of Lord North's government for the unwisdom of its colonial policies did not compensate for the absence of enquiry by Burke into the powerful impetus towards revolution within America, irrespective of British policies. The terms of his opposition to North had committed Burke to the argument that America's revolution was merely a defence of English liberties against tyrannical innovations, but this argument, however politically useful, made unnecessary or inconvenient any investigation of the internal forces which transformed American society. Yet all the themes which most agitated Burke about the French

[154]*The Times* of 6, 17 and 21 July 1789, by contrast, quickly explained France's revolution as a direct consequence of her involvement in the American War. See also Friedrich von Gentz's *The Origin and Principles of the American Revolution, Compared with the Origins and Principles of the French Revolution* [trans. John Quincy Adams] (Philadelphia, 1800).

Revolution in 1789–90 had been present in the American also: the principled rejection of monarchy; the disavowal of nobility and the hereditary principle; representatives exceeding their instructions to make a revolution not foreseen by the people; militant, politicized religion or irreligion; the destruction of religious establishments; the election of clergy; the expropriation of property; the destruction of livelihoods; paper money; inflation; the intimidation of individuals by the mob; widespread violence (though as yet stopping short of massacre); the sudden rise to power of low and base individuals; the flood of expropriated émigrés.[155] It may be that such features were not self-evidently integral to the French Revolution when Burke condemned it in his speech on the army estimates in February 1790: if so, his unacknowledged recollection of the American Revolution (in which they were inescapable) becomes all the more important.

In the *Reflections*, Burke asserted that pure democracy was not desirable in France or 'any other great country' and argued from Aristotle about the similarities between 'a democracy' and 'a tyranny', especially 'the most cruel oppressions' of the majority upon the minority, without citing, or attempting to exonerate, the American example. Ironically, his censure of France's reforming patricians for failing to anticipate the consequences of their actions applied equally to his own party before 1776. Burke's charge that the French had rebelled against a 'mild and lawful monarch, with more fury, outrage, and insult, than ever any people has been known to rise against the most illegal usurper, or the most sanguinary tyrant' similarly echoed colonial loyalists' denunciations of the American rebellion (pp. [56, 185–6]). Englishmen after 1783 preferred to close their eyes to the consequences of defeat; Burke did not comment on them; but it is not clear whether his agonizings of 1790 constituted a delayed response to what he had unknowingly encouraged in America a decade and a half earlier, or whether he had learned nothing from that episode.[156]

[155]For the scale of the upheaval in America, see Gordon S. Wood, *The Radicalism of the American Revolution* (New York, 1992) and J. C. D. Clark, *The Language of Liberty 1660–1832* (Cambridge, 1994). The American Revolution contained both 'conservative' and 'radical' elements; in recent scholarship the second of these has assumed much more prominence than it once did, and the old contrast between American and French Revolutions has consequently weakened.

[156]See [Burke], *Appeal*, pp. 36–41, for his defence against the charge of inconsistent conduct over the American and French Revolutions. Burke argued against the thesis that 'the Americans had from the beginning aimed at independence'; Franklin had always maintained to Burke that America only sought 'a security to its *ancient* condition'; Americans were 'purely on the defensive in that rebellion. He considered the

Yet the second Burke could develop exactly because the first Burke had not denounced republics as such. Burke had not condemned the United States for its constitution of 1787, and in the *Reflections* professed not to offer a view of the relative merits of monarchical and republican government: he only denied that 'the present scheme of things in France, did at all deserve the respectable name of a republic ... what was done in France was a wild attempt to methodize anarchy; to perpetuate and fix disorder ... it was a foul, impious, monstrous thing, wholly out of the course of moral nature.'[157] Although the *Reflections* criticised France's proposed electoral machinery for its inconsistencies, Burke was right to insist that he had not entered into a full appraisal of what was reported to be France's forthcoming constitution. What he had focused on was the principle of anarchy which would undermine all constitutions, and the problem in assessing Burke's thought is to understand his conception of that principle. His insights were into the nature and causes of antinomianism, and its devastating consequences: gratuitous violence, revolutionary violence as an end in itself.[158]

In this insight, Burke is not supported by some recent scholarship. It has been shown that the actions of the crowd in *ancien-régime* as well as in revolutionary France were not necessarily violent and could exercise the function of representing the community:[159] to this extent, Irish rural vendettas or the Gordon riots of 1780 would not have been a reliable guide to what took place in France in 1789–90. It is even possible to some degree to correlate outbreaks of French rural violence with the pattern of peasant grievances expressed in the *cahiers de doléances*, and to interpret the actions of these crowds as, in large part, restrained and purposive.[160] This is a familiar preliminary to eulogies of the Revolution as emancipatory, as essential to the modernisation of French society, and as integral to the achievement of democracy, eulogies which in England began with the Foxite Whigs. Burke evidently knew little of peasant grievances; but, however expressed, these were only a part of the problem. Burke seems instead to have had in mind all those other acts of vio-

---

Americans as standing at that time, and in that controversy, in the same relation to England, as England did to king James the Second, in 1688.' Burke's Foxite contemporaries were right to think this insufficient.

[157][Burke], *Appeal*, p. 10.

[158]This theme is prominent in Simon Schama, *Citizens: a chronicle of the French Revolution* (New York, 1989).

[159]Colin Lucas, 'The Crowd and Politics between *Ancien Régime* and Revolution in France', *Journal of Modern History* 60 (1988), pp. 421–57.

[160]E.g. John Markoff, 'Violence, Emancipation, and Democracy: The Countryside and the French Revolution', *American Historial Review* 100 (1995), pp. 360–86.

lence, murder and mutilation which pointed towards better-known episodes like the September Massacres, the Terror and the Vendée, and for which merely functional explanations seem less adequate: even the September Massacres were premeditated, calmly organised and specific in their targets, not the result of blind panic.

Taking seriously such phenomena, Burke did not see the Revolution as an agency of (what we now term) modernisation. On the contrary, the violence which he saw at its heart was one reason why he depicted it as a regressive, atavistic force, blasting the promise of France's reforms in the preceding years. Violence, dynamic, uncontrolled and contagious, was essential to bring about the sort of transformations seen in France in 1789–90. Burke did not attempt to quantify that violence, but he possessed an insight into its essence.[161] In 1791, he wrote:

> Having found the advantage of assassination in the formation of their tyranny, it is the grand resource in which they trust for the support of it. Whoever opposes any of their proceedings, or is suspected of a design to oppose them, is to answer with his life, or the lives of his wife and children.[162]

Burke's language seemed extreme; it was soon to seem prophetic.

The dramatic imagery of the *Reflections* when discussing violence conceals the fact that the Whig Burke's account of what had happened in France in 1788, and up to the meeting of the Estates-General on 5 May 1789, echoed both conventional Whig formulae and one reading of constitutional debates in France itself before that date. Some historians have argued that Burke's main misreading of eighteenth-century France was to picture it as a society with an ancient constitution, like England's, which might be reinvigorated by a return to first principles: they observe that even the *monarchiens* of August–September 1789 believed in the sovereignty of the people, and that their proposals were far from the English constitution.[163] Burke did not stress, and probably failed to appreciate, his differences from the men he regarded as al-

---

[161]This perception of the savagery at the heart of the Revolution was not peculiar to Burke, but quickly became widespread in England in the 1790s: see David Bindman, *The Shadow of the Guillotine: Britain and the French Revolution* (London, 1989). This reaction can only partly be explained in terms of long-standing anti-French sentiment or of a reading of the *Reflections*. Paine in *Rights of Man* claimed that the French people had been brutalised by their government under the monarchy; this, too, was insufficient to explain the novel element in revolutionary violence.

[162]Burke, *Letter to a Member*, p. 44.

[163]Burke continued to be assured by a French source, even after the publication of the *Reflections*, that Lally Tollendal and Mounier 'aimed at a British Constitution': Menonville to Burke, 17 November 1790: Burke, *Correspondence*, VII, p. 168.

lies. Yet neither did Burke advocate the imposition on France of any single model of government, even England's. Other historians have pointed to confident expectations in France itself during 1788–9 of the possibility of reform within a limited monarchy. Whatever the feasibility of that speculation, Burke thought he endorsed the commonplaces of eighteenth-century French argument in balancing his condemnation of absolute monarchy with the claim that France too had its ancient constitution, eroded by 'waste and dilapidation' but capable of being repaired (p. [50]), capable of being the basis for an ideal constitution in which institutions, corporations or privileged groups checked and balanced each other to the common good. Tocqueville later denied this, claiming that monarchical absolutism had wiped clean the slate of French society and thereby provided the basis for the new absolutism of the Revolution. Since the National Assembly deliberately renounced what English observers thought was the model of the English constitution in the euphoria of August–September 1789, no definitive answer to this question was provided by events. It is possible, however, that Burke was not as wrong as Tocqueville led later generations to believe. Tocqueville's book *L'Ancien régime et la Révolution* (Paris, 1856) was partly written to refute Burke's *Reflections*, yet despite Tocqueville's brilliance the effect of some recent scholarship has been partly to redress the balance towards Burke's analysis.

Burke was sometimes charged with having failed to appreciate the widespread support for the Revolution in France, even within the Church and nobility; but his belief was that that enthusiasm had extended only to the early objectives of a limited, constitutional reform. Burke pointed out how the *cahiers de doléances* showed that, even up to early 1789, the instructions to the deputies in the Estates-General 'were filled with projects for the reformation of that government, without the remotest suggestion of a design to destroy it' (p. [188]). Necker's standard study of French finances, published in 1784, 'gives an idea of the state of France, very remote from the portrait of a country whose government was a perfect grievance, an absolute evil, admitting no cure but through the violent and uncertain remedy of a total revolution' (p. [192]). By 5 May 1789, the outcome in France had been such as any English Whig might approve. By that date, 'Upon a free constitution there was but one opinion in France. The absolute monarchy was at an end. It breathed its last, without a groan, without struggle, without convulsion. All the struggle, all the dissension arose afterwards upon the preference of a despotic democracy to a government of reciprocal controul. The triumph of the victorious party was over the principles of a British constitution' (p. [200]). Burke divided from his Foxite colleagues in his view that events in France had then gone disastrously wrong.

His developing explanation for this catastrophe was novel, and possibly contradicted his earlier defence of France's old order.[164] This other Burke did not argue that random mob violence had unpredictably intruded and undeservedly overturned a Whig constitutional experiment, although he did discuss the effect of mob intimidation on the National Assembly. He argued that the catastrophic outcome was implicit in the very composition of the Estates-General: 'I may speak it upon an assurance almost approaching to absolute knowledge, that nothing has been done that has not been contrived from the beginning, even before the states had assembled. *Nulla nova mihi res inopinave surgit*. They are the same men and the same designs that they were from the first, though varied in their appearance.'[165] If the deputies to the Estates-General were the first character in Burke's scenario of predestined disaster, the reforming nobility were the second, degrading themselves and thereby their whole order by their involvement in low designs: this claim was the setting for Burke's remark about attachment to the 'little platoon', that platoon being, for him, the 'men of quality' with whom Burke aligned himself (pp. [68–70]). It was this outrage at the debasement of the noble, not a nineteenth-century objection to class mobility, that informed Burke's claim that 'those who attempt to level, never equalize'; they merely invert 'the natural order of things' (p. [72]).

The third actor in Burke's unfolding drama was the mob, representing 'epidemical fanaticism' and moved by a 'black and savage atrocity of mind' (pp. [225–6]). Burke candidly recorded what the English friends of the Revolution chose not to see: even its early stages, in 1789–90, were marked by lawlessness, expropriation, violence, bloodshed and murder. Who but a tyrant, demanded Burke, 'could think of seizing on the property of men, unaccused, unheard, untried, by whole descriptions, by hundreds and thousands together?' (p. [157]) Some have seen in this an anticipation of twentieth-century genocide against whole categories of humanity identified by class or race, but these categories were not anticipated in Burke's analysis. Other historians have recently returned to the related idea that the Terror was inherent in the Revolution from the beginning,[166] a position which would explain

---

[164]'The French have made their way through the destruction of their country, to a bad constitution, when they were absolutely in possession of a good one. They were in possession of it the day the States [i.e. Estates-General] met in separate orders': Burke, *Speech ... 9 Feb. 1790*, p. 17.

[165]Burke, *Letter to a Member*, p. 6. 'Nothing confronts me which is new or unexpected': Virgil, *Aeneid*, VI, 103–4.

[166]See T. C. W. Blanning (ed.), *The Rise and Fall of the French Revolution* (Chicago, 1996), Introduction.

Burke's seeming prophecies about the future course of revolutionary violence. Yet Burke's understanding of fanaticism was not new in 1789 or specific to France. In 1757, his and William Burke's account of the savagery to which human nature could be degraded in America anticipated much of the language he used to describe the passion and violence witnessed on 5–6 October 1789 when the royal family were forcibly brought from Versailles to Paris (p. [99] n). Burke's reference to the Theban and Thracian orgies (p. [107]) reminds us that such features of group mentality were linked to religion long before they were blamed on an alleged structural process termed 'revolution'. As the greatest journalist of the Revolution also wrote of the wave of iconoclasm which later accompanied the campaign of de-Christianization, the people 'did not proceed to this destruction with the fury of fanaticism, but with derision, with an irony, a saturnalian kind of gaiety, well fitted to astonish the observer'.[167]

Burke was less of a prophet than he later appeared, but a better analyst of the phenomena of his own day. He condemned France's new paper currency, the *assignats*, but not because he foresaw the massive and crippling inflation which was to follow (p. [182n]); rather, Burke regarded a paper currency as a device of the 'monied interest' to make possible the expropriation of the French Church, to conceal the financial collapse which the Revolution had caused, and to give large numbers of men an interest in the Revolution's continuance.

Burke published the *Reflections* before most of the more memorable and sanguinary episodes of the Revolution had occurred, but he had already seen enough to realise that a dynamic had been unleashed which would not stop at the constitutional reforms of mid and late 1789. Any analysis of the causes of the Revolution depended on what events to include within that term. In the *Reflections*, Burke insisted that the Revolution extended forward in time to include the horrors of 5–6 October 1789; Depont replied[168] that it was over, by implication, that summer. This was not special pleading on Depont's part: the usual European understanding was that a revolution was a sudden event.[169] Burke was feeling his way towards a new understanding of revolution

---

[167]Mercier, *New Picture of Paris*, II, p. 77.

[168]Charles-Jean-François Depont to Burke, 29 December 1789: Burke, *Correspondence* VI, pp. 59–61.

[169]From an extensive literature, see especially Jean Marie Goulemot, *Discours, révolutions, et histoire: Représentations de l'histoire et discours sur les révolutions de l'âge classique aux Lumières* (Paris, 1975); Alain Rey, *'Révolution': histoire d'un mot* (Paris, 1989) and Keith Michael Baker, 'Revolution', in Colin Lucas (ed.), *The French Revolution and the Creation of Modern Political Culture* II (Oxford, 1989), pp. 41–

as a process extending over time,[170] an understanding that within a few years
was taken up and systematised within French discourse. In Burke's mind, too,
the events in France were on the way to being pictured as an entity, whether
called 'the Revolution' or identified by a term descriptive of an ideology, Jacobinism. Burke sensed the presence of something dynamic, expansive, protean, inhuman and profoundly evil: it was this that led him towards defining
the Revolution as a thing in itself.

> Before this of France, the annals of all time have not furnished an instance of a
> *compleat* revolution. That revolution seems to have extended even to the constitu-
> tion of the mind of man. It has this of wonderful in it, that it resembles what Lord
> Verulam says of the operations of nature: It was perfect, not only in all its ele-
> ments and principles, but in all it's members and it's organs from the very begin-
> ning.[171]

By 1796, Burke pictured it still more vividly:

> out of the tomb of the murdered Monarchy in France, has arisen a vast, tremen-
> dous, unformed spectre, in a far more terrific guise than any which ever yet have
> overpowered the imagination, and subdued the fortitude of man. Going straight
> forward to it's end, unappalled by peril, unchecked by remorse, despising all
> common maxims and all common means, that hideous phantom overpowered
> those who could not believe it was possible she should at all exist, except on the
> principles, which habit rather than nature had persuaded them were necessary to
> their own particular welfare and to their own ordinary modes of action.[172]

However shapeless this spectre, specific explanations of an unfolding phenomenon still seemed to be demanded. Burke condemned the role of France's
reforming nobility but he did not give priority to a conspiracy theory, which
would have negated explanation, although such theories had been common-

---

62. Baker cites the journal *Révolutions de Paris*, which began on 18 July 1789 with the
old meanings of the term, to show the emergence of a new one: 'Projected indefinitely
into the future, Revolution ceases to be a moment of crisis and becomes an extended
present at once immediate and universal, a "mythic present" in which eternity and
contingency meet.'

[170]*The Times* of 13 July 1789 reported: 'The revolution in the change of government appears to be complete.' On 14 October 1789 it wrote of the events of 5–6 October as a second revolution, and predicted a third; on 17 June 1790 it wrote of the
'strange revolutions' in the states of Sweden, France, Holland and Poland. Burke's library also included two well-known works by an author who used the same sense of
'revolution' as event to structure his histories: the Abbé René Vertot, *Histoire des
révolutions arrivées dans le gouvernement de la République romaine* (6th edn., 1767)
and *Histoire des révolutions de Portugal*.

[171]Burke, *Letter to a Noble Lord*, pp. 3–4.

[172]Burke, *Two Letters ... on the Proposals for Peace*, pp. 6–7.

place among American revolutionaries of the 1770s and were to be so among European counter-revolutionaries in the 1790s, and despite Burke's own willingness to acknowledge human agency. Burke, like Paine, in the final analysis argued for 'a revolution in sentiments, manners, and moral opinions' which had preceded the Revolution (p. [119]), and began the task of seeking general causes of a long-term process.[173] One cause was, centrally, the role of that French 'literary cabal' which 'had some years ago formed something like a regular plan for the destruction of the Christian religion. This object they pursued with a degree of zeal which hitherto had been discovered only in the propagators of some new system of piety' (p. [165]).

The Revolution consequently took the form of a war of religion in which, for the first time, atheism usurped the place of theology: in this insight, Burke heralded the age of ideology which succeeded. What the National Assembly

> had held out as a large and liberal toleration, is in reality a cruel and insidious religious persecution; infinitely more bitter than any which had been heard of within this century ... it had a feature in it worse than the old persecutions ... the old persecutors acted, or pretended to act, from zeal towards some system of piety and virtue: they gave strong preferences to their own; and if they drove people from one religion, they provided for them another, in which men might take refuge, and expect consolation ... their new persecution is not against a variety in conscience, but against all conscience ... it professes contempt towards its object; and whilst it treats all religion with scorn, is not so much as neutral about the modes: It unites the opposite evils of intolerance and indifference.[174]

This 'literary cabal' then had its impact in association with the reforming French nobility, the equivalents of Stanhope and Grafton. Despite this similarity, Burke drew a contrast between an English public culture in which a heterodox, satirical, levelling and freethinking initiative had been largely frustrated and a French public culture in which philosophical atheism had been far more influential.[175]

These were arguments which some recent scholarship on the two countries has now endorsed, though the sense in which the *philosophes* might be given a degree of causal responsibility for the Revolution was even then controversial. An alternative scenario was soon available from men who wished to shift the blame to the actions of rival politicans. Mounier wrote:

[173]Paine (*Rights of Man*, p. 85) similarly attributed the Revolution to 'a mental revolution priorily existing in France'.

[174][Burke], *Appeal*, p. 11.

[175]For the 'aggressive anticlericalism' of many of the deputies of the National Assembly, see Burke, *Reflections*, p. [168] n.

There is a material difference in saying that it [philosophy] has occasioned the Revolution of France, and all the misfortunes which have followed it, or in acknowledging that some philosophers, misled by their passions and fallacious systems, have placed themselves among the number of the factious; and that the chiefs of these factions have employed, after the fall of the ancient government, the errors of some philosophers, in order to destroy the religious sentiments and the morality of the people.[176]

Lally-Tollendal confirmed: 'Je savois que les écrits du célèbre Jean-Jacques [Rousseau], étoient un des évangiles du jour; beaucoup plus cité peut-être qu'entendu.'[177] But Mounier and Lally-Tollendal, like the *monarchiens* in general, were reformers. They were not as far removed from the *philosophes* as the Whig Burke wished to think. The other Burke was therefore able to develop ideological explanations of the Revolution after he found that systemic, structural explanations were inadequate.

It was not democracy in the sense of the new ideology of universal suffrage which preoccupied Burke when considering France, but rather the freethinking or Deist critique of the hierarchical and hereditary principle of which Paine later became the most famous spokesman. The early expressions of the Revolution, especially the collapse of the armed forces, therefore showed what was really at work just as much as the Revolution's later phases. Desertions from the army were

a desertion to a cause, the real object of which was to level all those institutions, and to break all those connections, natural and civil, that regulate and hold together the community by a chain of subordination; to raise soldiers against their officers; servants against their masters; tradesmen against their customers; artificers against their employers; tenants against their landlords; curates against their bishops; and children against their parents ... this cause of theirs was not an enemy to servitude, but to society.[178]

The subversion of hierarchy was not the same as the establishment of equality. Burke predicted that the Revolution would not end in a pure democracy but in a 'base oligarchy': 'France will be wholly governed by the agitators in corporations, by societies in the towns formed of directors of assignats, and trustees for the sale of church lands, attornies, agents, money-jobbers, speculators, and adventurers' (p. [283]; cf. p. [185]), a reasonable if uncomplimen-

---

[176]J. J. Mounier, *On the Influence attributed to Philosophers, Free-Masons, and to the Illuminati, on the Revolution of France* (Tübingen, 1801; trans. J. Walker, London, 1801), p. 114.

[177]*Mémoire de m. le comte de Lally-Tollendal, ou seconde lettre A ses Commettants* (Paris, Janvier 1790), p. 7.

[178]Burke, *Speech ... 9 Feb. 1790*, p. 22.

tary account of the Directory. It was such an oligarchy which Burke expected
to give way to a military dictatorship (p. [318]), a prediction fulfilled by the
*coup* of Napoleon Bonaparte on 9 November 1799.

Although Burke's *Reflections* was read in France in the 1790s, it would be
hard to argue that his prophecies were self-fulfilling; nor was Pitt's ministry
eager to join the crusade to extirpate Jacobin doctrine, as Burke demanded.
Consequently, the force of Burke's analysis for his contemporaries derived
not just from his rhetorical skill, but from the way in which his strangely
haunting intuitions were apparently realised in the years to come. Yet, as we
have seen, many of what now appear to be Burke's premonitions were in reality solidly grounded on evidence already widely available when he wrote. In
particular, Paine soon claimed that Burke's *Reflections* was a gratuitous attack on the Revolution: 'Neither the people of France, nor the National Assembly, were troubling themselves about the affairs of England, or the English
Parliament.'[179] The evidence of the contacts between the London Revolution
Society and its French allies presented in this edition suggests, on the contrary,
that the dynamic urge to export the Revolution, and to create a united Europe
re-forged in the heat of revolutionary doctrine, was present even in 1789–90.

Burke later offered a retrospect on the leading themes of the Revolution,
and the motives which led him to write his call to arms against it, in terms
which echoed Gibbon:

> In the long series of ages which have furnished the matter of history, never was so
> beautiful and so august a spectacle presented to the moral eye, as Europe afforded
> the day before the revolution in France. I knew indeed that this prosperity con-
> tained in itself the seeds of its own danger. In one part of the society it caused lax-
> ity and debility. In the other it produced bold spirits and dark designs. A false
> philosophy passed from academies into courts, and the great themselves were in-
> fected with the theories which conducted to their ruin. Knowledge which in the
> two last centuries either did not exist at all, or existed solidly on right principles
> and in chosen hands, was now diffused, weakened and perverted. General wealth
> loosened morals, relaxed vigilance, and increased presumption. Men of talent be-
> gan to compare, in the partition of the common stock of public prosperity, the
> proportions of the dividends, with the merits of the claimants. As usual, they
> found their portion not equal to their estimate (or perhaps to the public estimate)
> of their own worth. When it was once discovered by the revolution in France that
> a struggle between establishment and rapacity could be maintained, though but
> for one year, and in one place, I was sure that a practicable breach was made in the
> whole order of things and in every country. Religion, that held the materials of the
> fabrick together, was first systematically loosened. All other opinions, under the
> name of prejudices, must fall along with it; and Property, left undefended by prin-

[179]Paine, *Rights of Man*, p. 5.

ciples, became a repository of spoils to tempt cupidity, and not a magazine to furnish arms for defence. I knew, that attacked on all sides by the infernal energies of talents set in action by vice and disorder, authority could not stand upon authority alone. It wanted some other support than the poise of its own gravity. Situations formerly supported persons. It now became necessary that personal qualities should support situations. Formerly, where authority was found, wisdom and virtue were presumed. But now the veil was torn, and to keep off sacrilegious intrusion, it was necessary that in the sanctuary of government something should be disclosed not only venerable, but dreadful. Government was at once to shew itself full of virtue and full of force. It was to invite partizans by making it appear to the world that a generous cause was to be asserted; one fit for a generous people to engage in.[180]

So Burke's analysis of the nature of the Revolution shaped the rhetorical strategies he chose to combat it: neither democracy nor representative government nor republics were intrinsically wrong. What had caused the Revolution was that sea change in morals, manners and religious opinions which was to be resisted in England by the reassertion of the necessary unity of Church and State, and by the depiction of England's social and political hierarchies as ancient, venerable, and warmly attractive. This was not the Burke of 1765.

### (vi) The political theory of the 'Reflections'

Burke's *Reflections* was a work of practical political rhetoric, not of abstract, systematic analysis. Most of Burke's arguments in favour of England's social and political order were eighteenth-century commonplaces. Burke presented no elaborate theory (as had Locke) to justify inequalities of property, and was equally assured about the secure foundations of inequalities of rank: these questions were not central to his political thought. He made rhetorical use of the ideas of natural law and of the general good (i.e. utility), but as with most Whigs of the 1790s these were truisms rather than sharply conceived premises from which distinct conclusions flowed. It was a truism that government was for the good of the governed and a truism that it should be conducted in accord with higher morality or natural law. Practically, however, the Whig device of man's ancient surrender of natural rights on entering into civil society meant that imprescriptible limits had long ago been set to the extent to which the individual could appeal either to natural law or to utility against the requirements of the state. Burke frequently framed arguments like 'The will of the many, and their interest, must very often differ' (p. [76]), a position which flattered neither utility nor natural law. The subservience of the idea of a law of nature to Burke's practical purposes is shown by his argu-

[180]Burke, *Two Letters*, pp. 116–18.

ment, on the authority of the French lawyer Domat, that prescription itself was part of the law of nature (p. [223]): natural law was a more flexible doctrine than orthodox Whiggery.[181] The truisms of Whiggery nevertheless achieved tremendous emotional and political force in the *Reflections* by being defined as antithetical to the implications of the events of 1789, and from Burke's claim that the enemy within (English Dissent, in alliance with its noble patrons) was about to throw England into the French maelstrom.

Burke's book, then, re-emphasised practice, experience and wisdom against revolutionary theory. This was not unique. *The Times* of 25 August 1789 reported:

> The National Assembly forms at present a very curious subject of political speculation. In the members which compose it, we are supposed to see the REPRESENTATIVE WISDOM of FRANCE. And how is this wisdom employed? In forming UTOPIAN plans of reformation which cannot succeed,—in laying down Theories of Government which cannot be reduced to practice, in short, in building castles in the air, and neglecting the means not only to preserve good order, but even to quench the spirit of licentiousness, rapine and freebooting which prevails in and threatens to desolate every part of the kingdom.[182]

To be against theory is not to be without a theory, however, and Burke's *Reflections* can be shown to embody distinct principles of government.

As a mainstream Whig, Burke argued against (without citing) Locke's extremist doctrine in *Two Treatises of Government* (1690) that the people had a right to dissolve civil society at any time and for any reason they considered adequate. Burke also implicitly rejected (if he knew of it) Locke's argument in his *Essay Concerning Humane Understanding* (1690) that the antiquity of an idea did not confer prescriptive authority.[183] Nevertheless, Burke's account of the formation of government, the specific local arrangements between rulers and ruled, was contractual. He differed from Dissenters like Price and Priestley, and from freethinkers like Paine, in coming to see the earlier contract which created civil society itself within a providential setting as an expression

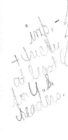

[181]Paul Lucas, 'On Edmund Burke's Doctrine of Prescription; or, an Appeal from the New to the Old Lawyers', *Historical Journal* 11 (1968), pp. 35–63, at 42–3; F. P. Lock, *Burke's Reflections on the Revolution in France* (London, 1985), pp. 94–6.

[182]It repeated its condemnation of the Assembly for debating '*abstract* propositions and *elementary* principles of Government' on 3 September 1789.

[183]John Locke, *An Essay Concerning Humane Understanding* (London, 1690), Book IV, ch. xvi, s. 10 (p. 338): 'any Testimony, the farther off it is from the original Truth, the less force and proof it has ... So that *in traditional Truths, each remove weakens the force of the proof* ... I find among some Men, the quite contrary commonly practised, who look on Opinions to gain force by growing older ...'

of the necessary and eternal nature of things, and ultimately of divine dispensations. As the *Reflections* developed, Burke came to envelop that initial contract within providentialist language. This was the significance of the magnificent but obscure rhetoric of the famous passage of the *Reflections* which asserted that, although 'Society is indeed a contract', nevertheless 'Each contract of each particular state is but a clause in the great primaeval contract of eternal society' written by God and which made society a partnership between the living, the dead and the yet unborn (p. [143–4]). After the nineteenth century, it was natural to read this rhetoric in Hegelian terms. Burke, however, had no such organic conception of society, and the terms which should be emphasized in such famous passages are the legal ones: *contract, partnership, inheritance, entail, trust, incorporation*. Burke, trained as a lawyer, saw society as an awesomely complex piece of machinery, produced like the universe itself by the watchmaker God described by Anglican latitudinarianism.[184] Burke therefore appealed to assumptions widely held in his day; it was Paine who broke from them with the two-dimensional individualism of his argument that each generation was sovereign, owing nothing to and owed nothing by later or earlier generations.

It was Burke the lawyer who was closely in touch with seventeenth-century English common lawyers' theories of the ancient constitution as something antecedent to royal grant and therefore libertarian by virtue of its antiquity.[185] The ancient constitution as a legal construct also embodied for such men, as for Burke, an accumulation of just decisions and adaptations to circumstance beyond the capacity of the individual's ahistorical reason: the antiquity of the ancient constitution was therefore presumptive evidence of its wisdom also. In an age of increasing legislation Burke adhered to the idea of law as custom rather than as command, for in its very historical and customary nature resided its justice.

Whatever the rhetoric, Burke's view of the continuing authority of government had two components. One was the legalistic claim that 'The constitution of a country being once settled upon some compact, tacit or expressed,

[184]It should also be compared with Aristotle, *Politics*, I, i, 8: 'Hence every city-state exists by nature, inasmuch as the first partnerships so exist; for the city-state is the end of the other partnerships, and nature is an end, since that which each thing is when its growth is completed we speak of as being the nature of each thing, for instance of a man, a horse, a household.'

[185]This theme was revealed by J. G. A. Pocock, *The Ancient Constitution and the Feudal Law* (1957; 2nd edn., Cambridge, 1987), and expanded in idem, 'Burke and the Ancient Constitution: A Problem in the History of Ideas', *Historical Journal* 3 (1960).

there is no power existing of force to alter it, without the breach of the covenant, or the consent of all the parties.' The second component was the claim
that the people, by a majority vote, 'cannot alter the moral any more than they
can alter the physical nature of things'. This meant that 'Duties are not voluntary. Duty and will are even contradictory terms. Now though society might
be at first a voluntary act (which in many cases it undoubtedly was) its continuance is a covenant.'[186] The Dissenters' model citizen was a member of a
'voluntary society', free at all times to choose his social activities in every respect; Burke's was one who abided by 'a fixed compact sanctioned by the inviolable oath which holds all physical and moral natures, each in their appointed place' (p. [144]). This 'inviolable oath', it now appeared, was not one
that any man had actually taken. It was a locution that had developed beyond
the normal language of eighteenth-century Whiggism, though without renouncing it. In Burke's positive vision, duty and contract joined hands.

   Part of Burke's theory was generated negatively, by reaction against events
in France as he pictured them. The French Revolution was directed against
monarchy, against the hereditary principle, against the social hierarchy which
the hereditary principle underpinned, and against the orthodox, established
religion which was staffed by gentlemen and which validated the patrician
ideal. These attacks had little to do with democracy in the sense of the new
doctrine of universal suffrage recently worked out in England. Even Paine's
*Rights of Man* advocated representative government, not participatory democracy built on universal suffrage. Burke's *Reflections* contained an elaborate critique of the cumbersome representative machinery initially proposed
for the French constitution; Burke said little about the new ideology of individual political entitlement, which was not the central point at issue in France.
Burke belonged to one world, pictured by his contemporaries as modern and
by later generations as an *ancien régime*, and despite his insights into totalitarian violence, his understanding of the world that was being born was as
limited as Paine's: the world pictured by most of his contemporaries as primitive, atavistic and chaotic, and pictured later as a new dawn for mankind.

   Burke did not therefore conceptualise an *'ancien régime'*,[187] and the *Reflections* did not defend any such reification. He did not idealise or romanticise an
'old order', though he defended the social forms of his age with the arts of

---

[186][Burke], *Appeal*, pp. 118, 121. Burke was not a consistent thinker: this late remark about *society* being at first a voluntary act echoed his earlier, more strongly
Whig, position. It might also have been a locution designed to disarm Foxite critics.
   [187]For his first reaction to such a concept, evidently as used by an *émigré*, see below,
n. 228.

classical rhetoric. As we have seen, his account of the merits of French society were qualified with Whig criticisms which, though discreetly expressed, were profound. He did not defend an old world against a new world; he defended his modern world (Whig, commercial, rational, patrician, Anglican) against assault by atavistic moral, intellectual and political vices. For these reasons, Burke was not a 'traditionalist' in our sense of preferring 'the old' to 'the new'; although continuity between the present and the past was, for Burke, an essential component of moral and political rationality, it was only as important as continuity between the present and the future. Burke described the descent of English liberties legalistically rather than sentimentally as 'an *entailed inheritance*', and observed: 'By adhering in this manner and on those principles to our forefathers, we are guided not by the superstition of antiquarians, but by the spirit of philosophic analogy' (pp. [47, 49]). Burke analysed his enemies as the regressive party. When he warned that 'it would well become us to ascertain, as well as we can, what form it is that our incantations are about to call up from darkness and the sleep of ages',[188] it was the English friends of the Revolution who were pictured as reawakening an atavistic menace.

As a modern Whig, Burke was not defending feudalism, any more than, as a landowner, he was anticipating capitalism. It is true that the most rhetorically charged passage in the *Reflections* deals with Marie Antoinette, and culminates in the lament that 'the age of chivalry is gone' (p. [113]). Yet nowhere did Burke defend feudalism as a social order, and this passage is open to two better explanations. First, its role in Burke's analysis of revolution. The normal European meaning of the word 'revolution' had been less a circular return to origins than a sudden and unexpected turn of Fortune's wheel. In this sense, 'revolution' was a commonplace idea in European discourse in the eighteenth century, meaning a sudden, astonishing and incomprehensible transformation in some aspect of human affairs. What astonished and awed the observer was, prominently, the spectacle of great men dragged down by malign Fortune, the noble and good laid low, and the elevation to power of the base. This had been a familiar image of Western literature since Giovanni Boccaccio's *De Casibus Virorum Illustrium*, and became a central component in sixteenth-century English drama's conception of tragedy. The expropriation of affluent and dignified clergy, the systematic denigration of nobility, and the dragging down of the weakest and therefore most symbolic element of the hierarchy, the queen, were integral components of Burke's definition of what had happened in France as a revolution. That, too, was why it was tragic, and why Burke responded to the events of 5–6 October 1789 in such

---

[188][Burke], *Appeal*, p. 124.

dramatic language.[189] Second, Burke's conception of chivalry did not anticipate the Victorian Gothic revival. His interpretation of it within a progressive
Whig historical scenario accurately reflected the new role given to the chival-
ric ethic by historians and sociologists from the 1760s, like Richard Hurd and
Adam Ferguson (p. [113] n). In this model, chivalry had been an early stage on
the road to the rational modernity of the *ancien régime*; it was the revolutionaries who were putting the clock back to an age of barbarism by rejecting politeness, by dishonouring women, by subverting trade.[190]

In the *Reflections*, Burke did not lament the fall of the Bastille on 14 July
or the abolition of feudal dues by the National Assembly on 4 August 1789.
He was exercised instead by illegality, expropriation, personal violence, mob
threats. He was indignant at the inversion of hierarchy. He regarded the
events of 5–6 October as tantamount to the fall of the monarchy. Above all,
Burke was emotionally engaged by two things: the fall of great men, and the
fall of the Church. Contemplating the revolution, he wrote, especially the
'atrocious spectacle' of 5–6 October 1789, one reflects (not, as we might now
do, on republics, democracy or majoritarian tyranny, but) on 'the tremendous
uncertainty of human greatness', and 'our minds (as it has long since been observed) are purified by terror and pity' (pp. [119–20]). Tragedy and revolution were the same 'when kings are hurl'd from their thrones by the Supreme
Director of the great drama, and become the objects of insult to the base' (p.
[119]). The same tragedy overwhelmed the French Church, 'casting down
men of exalted ranks and sacred function ... from the highest situation in the
commonwealth ... to a state of indigence, depression and contempt' (p.
[157]). It was this 'unmerited fall' of the French clergy, argued Burke, which
evoked English feelings (p. [216]).[191]

The early stages of the French Revolution embodied a programme for the
reform of the Church, not its disestablishment, as the Civil Constitution of the

---

[189]For an argument that Burke's response to the queen's sufferings embodied the
principles of Adam Smith's *The Theory of Moral Sentiments*, see Dreyer, 'Genesis of
Burke's *Reflections*', p. 475. Burke was often charged with over-dramatising these
events, especially the violent intrusion of the mob into the queen's bedroom and her
flight; his account in fact followed quite closely that given in *The Times* of 12 and 13
October 1789.

[190]For which see Smith, *The Gothic Bequest*.

[191]This theme can be traced in Burke as early as his sympathy for the gentry families
ruined by their part in the rebellion of 1745: Conor Cruise O'Brien, *The Great Melody:
A Thematic Biography and Commented Anthology of Edmund Burke* (London, 1992),
pp. 27–8. It is present also in his sympathy for the Indian grandees ruined by Warren
Hastings: Lock, *Burke's Reflections*, p. 29.

Clergy made clear.[192] Burke did not denounce this in principle. Controversies in England since the Feathers Tavern petition of 1772, and Burke's systematic reply to Price,[193] meant however that the *Reflections* offered an extended defence of that which had been first attacked in England, 'our church establishment', far beyond the rebuttal of specific reforming proposals. It 'consecrated the commonwealth' (p. [136]). This honourable and dignified 'system' created in its clergy 'high and worthy notions' and so made the state, in its religious aspects, mirror the hierarchical aspects of the state in its civil aspects. Christianity was a creed that taught 'humility'; it countered 'the lust of selfish will' (p. [140]) which Burke analysed as the essence of Rousseau's doctrine. Although the state was a human creation, God willed its connection with 'the source and archetype of all perfection', by implication the Church (p. [146]). Burke's opinions on the role of religion in society were 'so worked into my mind, that I am unable to distinguish what I have learned from others from the results of my own meditation' (p. [147]). For 'the majority of the people of England ... Church and State are ideas inseparable in their minds, and scarcely is the one ever mentioned without mentioning the other' (pp. [147–8]). Burke did not only speak of religion and society; Church and State, too, were his images. Although many defences of the established Church had been published in eighteenth-century England, none had drawn such general connections with the shape of the social order. Only in this context of theologically orthodox Anglicanism does Burke seem other than the anti-rationalist thinker perceived by a later, and secular, age. Burke defended church establishments as 'the first of our prejudices, not a prejudice destitute of reason, but involved in a profound and extensive wisdom' (p. [136]). Prejudice reflected a prior access to divine rationality and 'the nature of things' which human reason might clarify but not supplant.

Burke was not alone in tracing social stability to the cohesive effects of religion: this was a commonplace in eighteenth-century England. Successive Dissenting attempts to secure the repeal of the Test and Corporation Acts had been the occasions for many Anglican commentators on all points on the spectrum of churchmanship to defend the union of Church and State by deploying the resources of denominational discourse on which Burke drew. Nor was that characteristically English preoccupation the sole source of reflection on this issue. Even in the society most individualised by the *philosophes*,

[192]Its text, as voted on 12 July 1790, is printed in Roberts (ed.), *Documents*, pp. 225–31.

[193]For Burke's priorities in replying to Price throughout his career, see Dreyer, 'Genesis of Burke's *Reflections*', passim.

Burke's admired minister of finance had recently passed some time out of office in composing a work which maintained:

> One could not have taken an active part in the administration of public affairs; or made it the object of stedfast attention; one could not have compared the several relations of this great whole, with the natural dispositions of minds and characters; nor indeed observed men in a perpetual state of rivalry and competition, without perceiving, how much the wisest governments need support from the influence of that invisible spring which acts in secret on the consciences of individuals ... What then would be the consequence, if once the salutary chain of religious sentiments were broken? What would be the event, if the action of that powerful spring were ever entirely destroyed? You would soon see every part of the social structure tremble from its foundation, and the hand of government unable to sustain the vast and tottering edifice.[194]

Burke explored those consequences. He was, however, drawn in two directions on the proper role of religion in politics. He condemned Price's circle for propagating a 'political gospel' (p. [18]), asserted that 'politics and the pulpit are terms that have little agreement' and proposed himself as championing only 'civil liberty and civil government' (p. [14]). Yet, warming to his task, Burke soon turned to praise the church establishment in England in more extensive terms.

After 1789, his novel insight into the Revolution was that 'a theory concerning government may become as much a cause of fanaticism as a *dogma* in religion'.[195] But it was a theory concerning government which acted like a religious creed and in England had denominational links. What Burke saw as the threat in England was not just the moneyed interest as such,[196] nor talent divorced from property, but an intelligentsia; and not a secular intelligentsia but 'literary caballers, and intriguing philosophers ... political theologians, and theological politicians' (p. [13]), in association with reformist members of the nobility whom Burke termed 'lay-divines' (p. [14]), men whose 'titled pulpits' would give forth 'democratic and levelling principles' (p. [16]). These zealots had 'made a philosophy and a religion of their hostility' to religious establishments (p. [135]). It was not Parisian revolutionaries but English Dissenters to whom Burke's most keen insights applied: 'They despise experience as the wisdom of unlettered men ... they have wrought under-ground a mine

---

[194]Jacques Necker, *Of the Importance of Religious Opinions. Translated from the French* (London, 1788), p. iii.

[195][Burke], *Appeal*, p. 99.

[196]For this subject, see J. G. A. Pocock, 'The political economy of Burke's analysis of the French Revolution' (1982), in Pocock, *Virtue, Commerce and History*, pp. 193–212.

that will blow up at one grand explosion all examples of antiquity, all precedents, charters, and acts of parliament. They have "the rights of men"' (p. [86]). The rights of man and theological heterodoxy were, in Burke's mind, integrally related. This was the lesson he drew from recent English experience.

The role of religion in Burke's thought was partly disguised, since the proof-texts in the *Reflections* were rarely drawn from Scripture (which was often cited by Paine) and never from works of political theology, but overwhelmingly from the classics. Burke quoted these with facility and often without translation, from Latin and Greek, for an audience among whom he assumed an equal knowledge. He was not a Romantic, and died in 1797, the year before the publication of Wordsworth's and Coleridge's *Lyrical Ballads*. Burke's frame of cultural reference, like that of most of the English elite, was the humanist literature and philosophy of the ancient world. The two posthumous catalogues of Burke's library, dated 1813 and 1833, demonstrate a marked preponderance of the Greek and Latin classics, in the best editions and only a few in translation, over the great texts of Anglican divinity or political thought. Burke did not dispute with Price on the meaning of the Anglican tradition. Horne, Horsley and Hallifax, that Trinity of scholar-bishops of the 1780s, did not openly feature in the *Reflections*. Burke's culture was a classical one, the slight inaccuracies in his chosen texts suggesting quotation from his well-stocked memory: Cicero (10), Horace (7), Virgil (5), Juvenal (3), Livy, Lucan, Martial, Tacitus, Terence (1 each). Some of these were merely apt Latin phrases, the common coin of educated debate; most expressed a more serious purpose.

Burke's account of the logic of history and the evolution of societies was not proto-Darwinian but retro-Virgilian; his understanding of social cohesion and the continuity of generations was not an anticipation of Hegel, but an open affirmation of a debt to Horace. Juvenal and Horace were called on to reprove the folly of Richard Price and condemn as rhetorical and false, but threatening and serious, the genre of sermons on the anniversary of 1688 (pp. [16, 18, 93]). Virgil and Horace mocked the presumption of literary men and the affront their metaphysics offered to the gods (pp. [86, 92]).[197] The same lesson from Horace was transposed to recent French politicians: republican virtue was not won by dishevelled clothes or 'grim and savage look' (p. [251]). Raw orators had ruined a state before, as Cicero recalled (p. [331]), condemning an unrighteous rebellion in which the confiscation and sale of the property of the vanquished only sowed the seeds of future civil war (p. [171]).

---

[197]In 1791, Burke quoted Persius to confirm his argument that 'human will has no place' in 'moral investigation': [Burke], *Appeal*, p. 123.

In Burke's pages, by implication, Lucan mocked the unashamed lawlessness of the French legislature and warned of the unaccountable anonymity of the multitude; Martial condemned the inhumanity of the new French constitution and Tacitus spoke against the collapse of ancient loyalties in the French army (pp. [102, 265, 267]). All this mattered more since France was complimented in Virgil's phrase as 'the cradle of our race' (p. [118]).

⁜ Burke's vision of a dignified, duty-bound, ancestral social order was similarly illustrated. Cicero explained how the gods presided over all, making the laws their own and taking notice of human conduct, and how the gods took delight in those human associations, states, which were instituted to secure justice (pp. [134, 145]). Horace had observed that poems must win the hearts of their readers; so too, argued Burke, must states win the hearts of their members. Utilitarian calculations of self-interest were not enough. Men did not choose the state into which they were born, but Cicero showed men's duty to the state where providence had placed them (pp. [115, 231]). Cicero too explained why wise men 'always favour noble birth', why nobility was useful to the state, why the long and stable possession of property was just and its confiscation outrageous (pp. [205, 228]). Horace spoke for the ideal of the uncorrupt rural freeholder tilling his 'ancestral acres'; Cicero's aged farmer who, despite approaching death, carried on planting 'for the immortal gods' joined the rural vision with a politico-theology in which, beneath divine providence, the present generation linked their ancestors with their posterity (pp. [278–9]). Virgil in the *Georgics* had used the bee-hive as a symbol of political society, where 'the race abides immortal' despite the transience of its members' individual lives, and Virgil's *Aeneid*, appropriated by eighteenth-century England as its national epic, sang the praises of another island, a 'holy land, most dear to the mother of the Nereids and Aegean Neptune', anchored safely in 'mid-sea' by the loving gods (pp. [31, 278]).

Classical reference was bound up with Burke's sense of his public role. He claimed to 'take my full share, along with the rest of the world, in my individual and private capacity, in speculating on what has been done or is doing in any place ancient or modern; in the republic of Rome or the republic of Paris' (p. [5]). For Burke, antiquity ranked with precedents, charters and acts of parliament as a source of venerable but immediately present authority. It was in this setting that Burke developed his stress on prescription, by which he sought to secure property and the reliability of law, usage and custom which went with security of property (p. [223]). For Burke, the argument from antiquity did not therefore mean an appeal to the irrational, a tracing back of human institutions to a deep and mysterious darkness; it meant an appeal to long-successful reason, practical reason that had vindicated its rationality in the clear light of countless days. Burke's doctrine of prescription was not a proto-Hegelian claim to identify the world-spirit of his age. It derived from the reverence for divine purposes which he drew from Virgil and Christianity; from the idea of an 'ancient constitution'; and from an eighteenth-century latitudinarian reading of nature as 'wisdom without reflection, and above it' (p. [47]). This combination produced Burke's aphorism: 'People will not look forward to posterity, who never look backward to their ancestors' (pp. [47–8]). As a modern Whig, it was forward that Burke wished to look.

Men in 'traditional' societies do not praise 'tradition'. Burke's doctrine of prescription was evoked not by nostalgia or reaction but by dissent from what he saw as a systematic doctrine, shared by English Dissenters and French revolutionaries, that men were under no inherited obligations and were entirely free to remake their societies at will. Burke had evidently not seen this element in the American revolution, though it had been present from the moment when some colonists went beyond arguments from the 'rights of Englishmen' and the ancient constitution to appeal to a revitalised and literally-intended understanding of natural law: as James Otis had asserted, 'There can be no prescription old enough to supersede the law of nature, and the grant of God Almighty; who has given to all men a natural right to be *free*, and they have it ordinarily in their power to make themselves so, if they please.'[198] The same rejection had been present in England in Dissenting or freethinking initiatives aimed against the established Church. The requirement that Oxford undergraduates subscribe the Thirty-nine Articles at their matriculation 'has been required and submitted to for near Two Hundred Years', announced one defender of the Anglican ascendancy in 1772; 'The Wisdom of Ages ought not in Justice to give Way suddenly to every seeming Difficulty.' It followed that 'The University has a *prescriptive Right* to the present Mode of Subscription, having exercised it near two Hundred Years.'[199] It was a familiar usage.

Burke was not unique, but his sense of the polarization of options in 1789 produced in him a uniquely heightened sense of the alternative to the ancient constitution: 'I cannot conceive how any man can have brought himself to that pitch of presumption, to consider his country as nothing but carte blanche, upon which he may scribble whatever he pleases' (p. [231]). The enemy now focused not only on the substance of the social fabric, but its title to authority:

[198]James Otis, *The Rights of the British Colonies Asserted and proved* (Boston, 1764), p. 12.

[199]*A Collection of Papers, Designed to Explain and Vindicate the Present Mode of Subscription required by The University of Oxford, from all Young Persons at their Matriculation* (Oxford, 1772), pp. 5, 15, 21.

'The learned professors of the Rights of Man regard prescription, not as a title to bar all claim, set up against old possession—but they look on prescription as itself a bar against the possessor and the proprietor. They hold an immemorial possession to be no more than a long continued, and therefore an aggravated injustice.'[200] Not even here did Burke prefigure the organic metaphors which were to mark some areas of nineteenth-century political thought. Such metaphors still derived from claims about the role of divine providence in human society; they were encouraged by the publication of the *Reflections*, but not created by them. Burke's arguments were eighteenth-century ones. Burke's latitudinarian God was still a watch-maker, who had created a Whig constitution of checks and balances: 'An ignorant man, who is not fool enough to meddle with his clock, is however sufficiently confident to think he can safely take to pieces, and put together at his pleasure, a moral machine of another guise importance and complexity, composed of far other wheels, and springs, and balances, and counteracting and co-operating powers.'[201] Burke's originality was not in coining a new political discourse built around dark instinct, organic metaphor or collectivism; his images, traced to their sources, prove to be echoes of Scripture or the classics, not anti-rationalist provocations (pp. [117, 127]). Burke's theoretical assumptions were those of his age.

Divine providence played a more complex part in this scheme. The 'order of the world' was established by 'the disposition of a stupendous wisdom' (p. [48]), but the catastrophes of human existence had to be ascribed to the same cause: 'It is often impossible, in these political enquiries, to find any proportion between the apparent force of any moral causes we may assign and their known operation. We are therefore obliged to deliver up that operation to mere chance, or more piously (perhaps more rationally) to the occasional interposition and irresistible hand of the Great Disposer.' Burke was a true son of the Enlightenment in his insistence that great events might have small causes; 'a thousand accidents might have prevented the operation of what the most clear-sighted were not able to discern, nor the most provident to divine'.[202] In his belief that this was consistent with the intervention in human affairs of divine providence, Burke was also an Anglican. But why should God have permitted the catastrophe of the French Revolution to overwhelm Christendom? Burke had no answer, and by his death in 1797 he verged on despair that the Revolution would finally triumph.

[200] Burke, *Letter to a Noble Lord*, p. 53.
[201] [Burke], *Appeal*, p. 113.
[202] Burke, *Two Letters ... on the Proposals for Peace*, pp. 3–5.

## (vii) Burke's crusade against the Revolution

Some classics of political theory, like *The Federalist*, owe their lasting importance to an attempt to square the circle, to reconcile equally desirable opposites. Others, like Locke's *Two Treatises*, owe their long currency to their resolutely ignoring the destructive consequences of the simple but ruthless courses of action which they recommend. Burke's *Reflections* was closer to the first of these. Its importance lay in its agonised attempt to hold together a middle ground, or (from another perspective) to reconcile the principles of 1688 with the necessary preconditions of stable government. Yet, paradoxically, the first result of the *Reflections* was to call down on Burke's head an unprecedented stream of vilification and abuse as if he himself had been the extremist. No other writer against the French Revolution was so reviled, though others were more unambiguously hostile to it than Burke, and intervened from positions on the opposite, anti-reformist wing of the political spectrum. The odium was so extreme not least because Burke was execrated by his own party: he was an insider, a colleague of Fox and Sheridan, a correspondent of Paine and Priestley, who had deserted their cause and revealed their hypocrisies and self-deceptions.

Burke's enemies were often unable to argue on the basis of better detailed knowledge of French affairs, and instead produced a variety of *ad hominem* arguments to explain this desertion. Some denounced him as a crypto-Papist. Some claimed that Burke had been bribed with a secret pension. Some asserted that he acted out of malice towards the Dissenters for their having abandoned the Foxite Whigs in the 1784 general election. Some proposed that Burke had merely found a new target for the crusading zeal he had poured into the pursuit of Warren Hastings: 'Mr. Burke had long been occupied in painting the crimes of India; and it was easy for a heated imagination to substitute Europe.'[203] Some called Burke unbalanced or even insane, and when rejection and ostracism provoked Burke to more heightened rhetoric, this argument could be insidiously exploited by those who had been his friends. This was, however, as recent scholarship has demonstrated, a minority position in the reaction to the *Reflections*.

Despite this abuse, the war of ideas began to swing Burke's way even before the execution of Louis XVI, and finally did so decisively: of a total of 340 publications identified by one scholar as falling within the Price-Burke-Paine

[203]*Short Observations on the Right Hon. Edmund Burke's Reflections* (London, 1790), p. 10.

controversy, 104 works have been identified as 'reformist' in sympathy, 213 as 'conservative'.[204] In the light of this evidence, it could scarcely be argued that Burke's book was not taken seriously. The argument followed this course, however, not because Burke created a school of thought but because he acted as a catalyst of pre-existing traditions of discourse.[205] Burke was not a lone, embattled defender of the political order against the revolutionary tide; rather, he gave powerful but partial expression to a number of pro-establishment discourses with which, as an ex-reformer himself, he did not exactly coincide.

Burke's moral analysis of the causes of political revolution found a particular echo in an English culture whose formal High Church rationales were already heavily reinforced by Evangelical moral exhortation: the English counter-revolution of the 1790s was to a considerable degree a religious crusade,[206] a phenomenon for which Burke's latitudinarian and Foxite origins had hardly prepared him. Burke had not been noted for any devotion to the memory of that un-Whiggish figure, King Charles I; yet the execution of Louis XVI on 21 January 1793 produced a sudden revitalisation of the flagging genre of political sermons on the anniversary of Charles's execution, 30 January.[207] Burke's stand against the Revolution meant that he was caught up in a pre-

[204]Pendleton, 'Bibliography', pp. 74–5. Of the 340, 20 accounts of trials should be excluded as falling in neither camp. The breakdown by years is revealing: in 1789, 1 'reformist' tract to 2 'conservative'; in 1790, 17 to 11; in 1791, 35 to 44; in 1792, 28 to 72; in 1793, 15 to 69; in 1794–7, 8 reformist publications to 15 conservative. The large number of 'conservative' writings was often unknown to historians before Pendleton's bibliographic survey of 1982, and Burke was consequently treated as almost the only spokesman for the anti-revolutionary cause. What was wrongly assumed to be Burke's lonely position seemed to call for *ad hominem* explanations, often of his extremism, frustrated ambition or psychological imbalance. Such speculations are now shown to be inappropriate. Nevertheless, other published items failed to meet Pendleton's criteria for inclusion in her sample, and the balance of opinion between loyalists and revolutionaries cannot be established by statistics alone.

[205]Mark Philp, 'Vulgar Conservatism, 1792–3', *English Historical Review* 110 (1995), pp. 42–69 at 56, notes the absence of Burke's name from the papers and publications of John Reeves's Association for the Preservation of Liberty and Property against Republicans and Levellers, the leading loyalist organisation.

[206]R. A. Soloway, 'Reform or Ruin: English Moral Thought during the First French Republic', *Review of Politics* 25 (1963), pp. 110–28.

[207]The most notable, and politically articulate, was Samuel Horsley, *A Sermon Preached before the Lords Spiritual and Temporal ... January 30, 1793, Being the Anniversary of the Martyrdom of King Charles the First. With an Appendix Concerning the Political Principles of Calvin* (London, 1793).

dominantly Anglican backlash;[208] without that social constituency, it is not clear that his warnings could have been the catalyst that they became. Nor was he the only catalyst: his crusade was also parallelled by, among others', Horsley's and Horne's.[209] Burke's rhetoric in the 1790s was heightened, but not out of line with that of many senior and learned churchmen, some of whom even agreed with Priestley in seeing a literally apocalyptic pattern in the disasters that overwhelmed many European states. Even so, Burke's initial arguments were not identical with the developing debate of the 1790s. The theme of economic 'levelling' was not central to Burke's *Reflections*, or perhaps even to Paine's *Rights of Man*; it has been argued that it came to dominate discussions of English 'Jacobinism'.[210] Equally, the American example had considerable prominence in the debate of the 1790s,[211] yet (as we have seen) Burke offered no thoughts on the nature and significance of the American Revolution.

The war of ideas was partly about political mobilisation, partly about the refutation or vindication of what the *Reflections* had said. Burke's arguments were therefore sometimes polemically misrepresented by his opponents. Burke was a lifelong reformer, and had written that 'A state without the means of some change is without the means of its conservation'; Priestley claimed that 'On [Burke's] principles, the *church*, or the *state*, once established, must for ever remain the same.' Burke consistently disparaged early eighteenth-century Tories and their doctrines of hereditary right; Priestley argued that the principles of the *Reflections* were 'in fact, no other than those of *passive obedience and non-resistance*, peculiar to the Tories and the friends of arbitrary power, such as were echoed from the pulpits of all the high church party, in the reigns of the Stuarts, and of Queen Anne'. Priestley quoted out of context Burke's assertion that the absolute power of the French monarchy

[208]See, for example, Richard Allen Soloway, *Prelates and People: Ecclesiastical Social Thought in England 1783–1852* (London, 1969), pp. 19–45.

[209]Mather, *Horsley*, pp. 250–68; Nigel Aston, 'Horne and Heterodoxy: The Defence of Anglican Beliefs in the Late Enlightenment', *English Historical Review* 108 (1993), pp. 895–919.

[210]Gregory Claeys, 'The French Revolution Debate and British Political Thought', *History of Political Thought* 11 (1990), pp. 59–80, at 60. By the end of his life, however, Burke could write: 'The present war is, above all others (of which we have heard or read) a war against landed property': *A Third Letter to a Member of the Present Parliament, on the Proposals for Peace with the Regicide Directory of France. By the Late Right Hon. Edmund Burke* (London, 1797), p. 144.

[211]Mark Philp, 'The Role of America in the 'Debate on France' 1791–5: Thomas Paine's Insertion', *Utilitas* 5 (1993), pp. 221–37.

was 'inconsistent with law and liberty' without completing Burke's argument, that Louis XVI's government had shown 'an earnest endeavour towards the prosperity and improvement of the country' in a major programme of reform.[212]

Yet, elsewhere, Burke's enemies were correct in pointing out his lifelong Whiggery. Priestley acutely observed that although the *Reflections* defended the sacredness of 'an hereditary principle of succession', the work also conceded 'a power of change in its application in cases of extreme emergency', and acknowledged that 'the great end and object of all government' was 'the good of the people': civil society was 'made for the advantage of man'. Priestley seized on Burke's Whig dicta that 'all the kingdoms of Europe were, at a remote period, elective' and that George III 'holds his rank no longer than while the legal conditions of the compact of sovereignty are performed by him'; Priestley exulted: 'This, Sir, is granting all that we, seditious as our doctrine is, contend for.'[213]

That was not the case, however. The aspirations of the English friends of the French Revolution went far beyond the Whig principles of 1688, as Burke correctly appreciated and as recent scholarship has confirmed. In the debate which developed on French events, Burke therefore addressed a widening critique of English society. If the *Reflections* was substantially about English controversies, the same was often much more the case of Burke's critics. Price never produced any extended discussion of the French Revolution to vindicate his euphoric predictions.[214] Although Price's death in April 1791 spared him the sight of the Revolution's later stages, Priestley, too, produced a reply to Burke which said little specific about France and much in reiteration of the familiar Dissenting preoccupations with undermining the established status of the Church of England.[215] Although Priestley lived until 1804, he produced no systematic account of French politics. Nor, most surprisingly, did Thomas Paine, whose *Rights of Man. Part the Second* (1792) moved further away from specific engagement with the detailed reality of what had happened in the state in which he spent so much time, and whose political testament, *The Age of Reason*, written while Paine was awaiting arrest and execution during the Terror, abandoned analysis of the Revolution altogether and returned to its author's central preoccupation, the attack on orthodox Christian theology.

[212]Burke, *Reflections*, pp. [29, 39, 195]; Priestley, *Letters to Burke*, pp. viii, 4, 23.

[213]Burke, *Reflections*, pp. [19, 29, 87]; Priestley, *Letters to Burke*, pp. 2–3, 23, 31.

[214]His only reply to Burke, often overlooked, was some additional material in the fourth edition of his *Discourse on the Love of Our Country*, printed as Appendix II below.

[215]Priestley, *Letters to Burke*, passim.

Although Burke (as his admirers later thought) won the war of ideas, he lost many of its battles: his position was often uneasy. From the outset, Burke was both idolised and vilified. In December 1790 Trinity College Dublin awarded Burke an honorary doctorate. The same month, fifty resident senior members of Oxford petitioned their university to grant him an honorary DCL 'in Consideration of his very able Representation of the true Principles of our Constitution Ecclesiastical and Civil, in his late Publication'. With Oxford's usual ineptness, the motion was then defeated in the Caput (the executive body composed of heads of houses) on the grounds that the members of that body, as the *St. James's Chronicle* reported, were 'less forcibly impressed by the obligations of the Church of England to this eloquent defender of Roman Catholic institutions'. In 1793 the nominal leader of the Whig opposition, the duke of Portland, became Chancellor of Oxford, and renewed the offer on his own authority: this time, it was Burke who rejected it with contempt.[216]

In one way, Burke's gamble worked. The *Reflections* was rhetorically brilliant, and posed a henceforth unavoidable challenge both to the Revolution and to its English friends. The book quickly sold in large numbers, was repeatedly reprinted in London, published in translation in Paris on 29 November 1790, and reprinted elsewhere on the continent also. It provoked a pamphlet controversy in which successive reformers revealingly exposed the extent of their intentions and were often polarised into extreme positions.[217] Most famously, this was the experience of Burke's former friend Thomas Paine; and it may be that if Burke departed from what had been shared ground between them, Paine departed from that common ground much further, in the opposite direction.[218] Although *Rights of Man* was a publishing triumph, selling far more copies than the *Reflections*, Paine was provoked into defining his version of the reformist cause in ways that for decades largely denied it practical success.[219]

[216]Burke, *Correspondence*, VI, pp. 192–5.

[217]Pendleton, 'Bibliography' remains the best guide to this debate.

[218]Paine returned from America to France in May 1787 and travelled to England in September that year to promote his scheme for the construction of an iron bridge evidently with no expectation that events were to commit him to a second revolution. Paine's *Rights of Man*, as he claimed, was indeed provoked by Burke's *Reflections*.

[219]For qualifications to the familiar picture of Paine as the 'theoretical mastermind' of reform in the 1790s, see especially Günther Lottes, *Politische Aufklärung und plebejisches Publikum. Zur Theorie und Praxis des englischen Radikalismus im späten 18. Jahrhundert* (Munich, 1979) and 'Radicalism, revolution and political culture: an Anglo-French comparison' in Mark Philp (ed.), *The French Revolution and British Popular Politics* (Cambridge, 1991).

In parliament, the Foxite Whigs could no longer ignore or marginalise Burke, as they had increasingly done since Rockingham's death in 1782. Burke had set the agenda: they were challenged to be for him or against him. If Fox temporised, avoiding a definitive pronouncement on the Revolution in reply to the *Reflections,* this did not provide a lasting solution to his party's problems: a definitive breach with Burke came in the Commons' debate of 6 May 1791. Loyalist opinion now had a rallying point, and the popular politics of the 1790s was to be characterised by the mushrooming of Loyalist Associations that meted out rough justice to suspected local Jacobins. Reformers had been diverse in their origins, principles and programmes, but they were now faced with the inconvenient and often inappropriate choice either to side with and apologise for the revolutionary cause as Burke had defined it, or to renounce their party and join the cause of Church and King. Burke nevertheless was only one among many voices calling for a re-emphasis on the image of Church and State, a familiar one in eighteenth-century England but not a cherished ideal of the Foxite Whigs. Around the uniquely resilient state form created by this English union of the civil and the sacred, opinion rallied. Within this stout practical and theoretical formulation, England rode out the storm of the French Revolution. It would be too simple to say that England avoided revolution because of the force of anti-revolutionary ideology;[220] nevertheless, the contrast is marked between England's case and that of France, where monarchical ideology had been largely driven from public debate by 1789.

Yet, in another way, Burke failed. His Manichaean analysis of the limitless evil and the boundless dynamism of the Revolution entailed a crusade of extirpation against a force with which, he predicted, no negotiation or compromise would ever be possible. In this perception, Burke still went beyond the views of many Englishmen in the 1790s.[221] In that decade, Burke converted, or partly converted, to support the English state form that he had spent so long trying to challenge and to reconstruct. Yet that state form had always embraced a variety of discourses which explained and defended it, like its French counterpart: Burke now became more loyalist than the loyalists, a sure recipe for disappointment. William Pitt, frigid in temperament, a reformer from

[220]For the complexities of the role of ideology in political mobilisation see Mark Philp, 'Vulgar Conservatism' and idem (ed.), *French Revolution and British Popular Politics.*

[221]For the mixed reaction of the newspapers, see Lucyle Werkmeister, *A Newspaper History of England, c. 1792–1793* (Lincoln, Nebraska, 1967); Jeremy Black, 'The challenge of the Revolution and the British press', *Studies on Voltaire and the Eighteenth Century* 287 (1991), pp. 131–41.

principle, reacted coldly to the *Reflections* and continued to resist Burke's subsequent calls for intervention in France.[222]

Only from a late twentieth-century perspective does the nature of political totalitarianism seem more self-evident. It was France which declared war on Britain in 1793, not vice versa. Even then, practical British statesmen, aware of France's immense strength and Britain's military limitations, often saw a negotiated, compromised peace as an option worth pursuing. Burke's campaign against the Revolution therefore became increasingly frenzied, and in his last comment on it, the *Letters on a Regicide Peace* of 1796–7, he warned in his most highly-wrought language against the danger of a betrayal from within. The question was unresolved at his death, and in 1802 just such a compromise peace was made. If Britain found itself renewing a cataclysmic struggle with Napoleonic France in 1803, and pursuing this conflict to the final Armageddon of 1814–15, it was more from necessity than prior Burkeian conviction. Perhaps, indeed, on Burke's earlier reformist Whig principles, a war of extermination against Jacobinism was impossible to sustain.[223]

Philip Francis had instantly recognised on the basis of an early draft of the *Reflections* that, as he advised the author, 'your appeal in effect is to all Europe'.[224] By contrast with that challenge, the reaction of Fox's friends was merely parochial. Rejected and denigrated by the Whig intelligentsia at home, Burke achieved more recognition abroad. Even here, however, he did not sweep all before him. French *émigrés* displayed diverse preferences across the spectrum of alternatives from aristocratic constitutionalism, through monarchical absolutism to theocratic monarchy, the first in decline after 1792 for tactical reasons, the third rising to prominence from the middle of the decade. Burke normally avoided endorsing the specific views of the *émigrés*, and they normally identified with his in equally general terms. His relations with that divided and quarrelsome group, and with the princes of the blood who provided their leadership in exile, were complex and unsatisfactory to him.[225]

In the long retrospect of the nineteenth century, these complexities were

[222]John Ehrman, *The Younger Pitt: The Reluctant Transition* (London, 1983), pp. 80–1; Jeremy Black, *British foreign policy in an age of revolutions, 1783–1793* (Cambridge, 1994), pp. 352–3, 355–67, 'Burke and the Revolution'.

[223]Nor did he renounce those principles: 'The opinions maintained in that book [*Reflections*] never can lead to an extreme, because their foundation is laid in an opposition to extremes': [Burke], *Appeal*, p. 112.

[224]Francis to Burke, 19 February 1790: Burke, *Correspondence*, VI, pp. 85–7.

[225]Colin Lucas, 'Edmund Burke and the Émigrés' in François Furet and Mona Ozouf (eds.), *The Transformation of Political Culture 1789–1848* (Oxford, 1989), pp. 101–14, at 102–4.

forgotten: Burke was remembered throughout Europe as the inspiration for counter-revolutionaries everywhere, and after 1815 it was difficult not to think that the counter-revolution had succeeded. This crusade, seemingly inescapable by the late 1790s, was also presciently there in Burke's writings from the early stages. It was in May 1791, before the September Massacres, the execution of Louis XVI and the Terror, that Burke wrote: 'Never shall I think any country in Europe to be secure, whilst there is established, in the very centre of it, a state (if so it may be called) founded on principles of anarchy, and which is, in reality, a college of armed fanatics, for the propagation of the principles of assassination, robbery, rebellion, fraud, faction, oppression, and impiety.'[226] The closer the observer to actual revolution, the more compelling this characterisation of it seemed.

James Mackintosh was the first to identify Burke's *Reflections* as 'the manifesto of a counter revolution'. Mackintosh mocked Burke's claimed moderation:

> Confident in the protection of all the Monarchs of Europe, whom he alarms for the security of their thrones, and having insured the moderation of a fanatical rabble, by giving out among them the savage *war-whoop* of atheism, he already fancies himself in full march to Paris, not there to re-instate the deposed despotism (He disclaims the purpose, and who would not trust such virtuous disavowals) but at the head of this army of priests, nobles, mercenaries, and fanatics, to dictate as the tutelar genius of France, the establishment, without commotion or carnage, of a just and temperate freedom, equally hostile to the views of kingly or popular tyrants.[227]

Yet, whatever the political dynamics of a restoration would have been in 1791–2, Burke's Whig libertarianism was real and he did not stand for any simple reimposition of an *ancien régime*. The extirpation of Jacobinism did not entail the restoration of an unreformed absolute monarchy. In 1791, Burke looked forward with caution to a restoration, evidently advising an *émigré*:

> When such a complete convulsion has shaken the State, and hardly left any thing whatsoever, either in civil arrangements, or in the Characters and disposition of mens minds, exactly where it was, whatever shall be settled although in the former persons and upon old forms, will be in some measure a new thing and will labour under something of the weakness as well as other inconveniences of a Change. My poor opinion is that you mean to establish what you call 'L'ancien Regime', If any

---

[226]Burke, *Letter to a Member*, p. 20.

[227]James Mackintosh, *Vindiciae Gallicae. Defence of the French Revolution and its English Admirers against the Accusations of the Right Hon. Edmund Burke* (London, 1791), pp. xi–xiii.

one means that system of Court Intrigue miscalled a Government as it stood, at Versailles before the present confusions as the thing to be establishd, that I beleive will be found absolutely impossible; and if you consider the Nature, as well of persons, as of affairs, I flatter myself you must be of my opinion. That was tho' not so violent a State of Anarchy as well as the present. If it were even possible to lay things down exactly as they stood, before the series of experimental politicks began, I am quite sure that they could not long continue in that situation. In one Sense of L'Ancien Regime I am clear that nothing else can reasonably be done.[228]

In October 1791 he recommended offering the French people a security 'that after having changed a sort of despotism for a sort of Anarchy, they should not change back from anarchy to despotism'.[229] In 1793, he criticised a group among the *émigrés* whom he called 'soldiers of fortune': 'They are, if not enemies, at least not friends to the orders of their own state; not to the Princes, the Clergy, or the Nobility; they possess only an attachment to the Monarchy, or rather to the persons of the late King and Queen. In all other respects their conversation is Jacobin.'[230]

Burke was a Whig constitutionalist; but his continental admirers were normally ignorant of the finer points of English debate, and saw in Burke merely the most eloquent enemy of Jacobinism.[231] They read only the *Reflections*, in translation; they were unaware of the extent of Burke's Whig views, expressed more candidly in his other published speeches and tracts. Consequently, they interpreted Burke's doctrines in the light of their own. In that second role, Burke was widely influential among the anti-revolutionaries in continental Europe. It would, however, be wrong simply to equate him with the ideologists of the Catholic counter-revolution. Although Burke was honoured in such circles, he acted there too as a catalyst rather than as the framer

*[handwritten marginal note: — I agree, esp b/c he wasn't RC.]*

---

[228]Burke to unknown, [1791]: Burke, *Correspondence*, VI, pp. 479–80.

[229]Burke to the Chevalier de la Bintinaye, 2 October 1791: Burke, *Correspondence*, VI, pp. 423–4.

[230]Edmund Burke, 'Remarks on the Policy of the Allies with Respect to France. Begun in October, 1793' in Burke, *Three Memorials on French Affairs. Written in the Years 1791, 1792 and 1793* (London, 1797), pp. 149–50, cited in Lucas, 'Burke and the Émigrés', p. 109.

[231]For an argument that this misreading of Burke was the German norm, see Rod Preece, 'Edmund Burke and his European Reception', *The Eighteenth Century* 21 (1980), pp. 255–73. Significantly, Burke plays no prominent part in the ideology discussed by Klaus Epstein, *The Genesis of German Conservatism* (Princeton, 1966), which covers in detail the period c. 1770–1806. His influence is equally faint on the French theorists discussed by Paul H. Beik, 'The French Revolution Seen From the Right: Social Theories in Motion, 1789–1799', *Transactions of the American Philosophical Society* 46 (1956), pp. 1–122, and by James L. Osen, *Royalist Political Thought During the French Revolution* (Westport, Conn., 1995).

of a Europe-wide consensus. Burke and the legitimists shared much in their negative critique of the Revolution, a critique which Burke pioneered, but shared much less in their positive prescriptions for the society to be restored: the counter-revolution spanned a spectrum of opinion. He was most at home with the *monarchiens*, the exponents of limited monarchy like Mounier and Lally-Tollendal, but could also blame them for initiating a revolution which then became uncontrollable.

Burke was least in tune with the ultras, the followers of the princes of the blood who organised the first military action against the Revolution in 1792: the comte de Provence, brother of Louis XVI, and to reign himself as Louis XVIII in 1814–24; the king's next brother the comte d'Artois, king as Charles X in 1824–30; the king's cousin, the prince de Condé. The *monarchiens* or *Anglophiles* were the first casualties of the Revolution, however. It was the legitimism of the princes which came to dominate the *émigré* movement, together with the Catholic doctrines of men like Joseph, comte de Maistre (1753–1821),[232] Louis, vicomte de Bonald (1754–1840)[233] or the abbé Barruel (1741–1820). Burke proved more influential on German-speaking anti-revolutionaries like Friedrich von Gentz (1764–1832), Ernst Brandes (1758–1810) and August Wilhelm Rehberg (1752–1836); but in Germany, constitutionalism became a liberal rather than a conservative ideology, standing for revolution rather than for the anti-libertarian, holistic views of order and authority with which German admirers wrongly associated Burke. The Germanic counterpart to the Whig constitutionalism for which Burke really stood proved an insufficient basis for German national unification, as was clear in the failed revolutions of 1848, and German politics was to owe more to Bismarck than to Burke.

Although Burke, the Protestant Whig, was essentially different from the French Catholic theorists of princely legitimism, Burke's position did partly overlap with theirs. Both stressed legitimacy, though in identifying it Burke gave greater emphasis to law than to divine institution. Both argued for a reverential attitude towards the state, customs and morals. Both opposed the abstract, timeless analysis of social relations that they saw at the heart of Jacobinism. Both therefore opposed democracy as a system which they described as

---

[232]Richard A. Lebrun, *Throne and Altar: The Religious and Political Thought of Joseph de Maistre* (Ottawa, 1965), and idem, *Joseph de Maistre: An Intellectual Militant* (Kingston, Canada, 1988).

[233]W. Jay Reedy, 'Burke and Bonald: Paradigms of Late Eighteenth-Century Conservatism', *Historical Reflections/Réflexions Historiques* 8 (1981), pp. 69–93, and David Klinck, *The French Counterrevolutionary Theorist, Louis de Bonald (1754–1840)* (New York, 1996) show his differences from Burke.

falsely voluntarist and egalitarian, issuing in a geometrical dismembering of a real, complex and living body. Both emphasised diversities between peoples rather than any common humanity. Both defended established religion against Dissent or atheism. Both ascribed a greater dignity to the state than to the individual, though Burke because the state was the awesome creation of generations of individuals, Bonald and Maistre because the state was created by God before man could really be termed man. Both saw a superior logic in the social order which forbad individuals from wilful meddling, though Burke identified that logic more with a political contract which bound the individual to his ancestors and descendants where the Catholic theorists identified it more openly with transcendent divine purposes. Both therefore had reasons for arguing that a democratically-expressed majority was not free to do just as it wished, and both had reasons (if not exactly the same reasons) for expecting that the unrestrained exercise of that asserted right would end in tyranny and slaughter.

Not all of the characteristics of the restored monarchy in France are to be blamed on the theorists who defended it. Maistre is wrongly taken to be an apologist for arbitrary monarchical power; like Burke, Maistre as a jurist defended France's ancient constitution, especially the role played in it by the *parlements*, the superiority of fundamental laws even to kings, and the need for the nation to consent to taxation. Like Burke, Maistre honoured the nobility but recognised the claims of merit.[234] Maistre's view of the Papacy, expressed in *Du Pape* (1819), was less a rationale for a Catholic theocracy than for a means of confining civil princes to a middle position between tyranny and anarchy. More than Burke, Maistre argued that 'the priesthood in France needed to be regenerated'. Like Burke, he diagnosed in France the assault of 'the Goddess of Reason against Christianity'. Like Burke, Maistre analysed the Revolution as intrinsically evil from the beginning, having a 'satanic quality'.[235] Maistre, too, claimed: 'Either every imaginable institution is founded on a religious concept or it is only a passing phenomenon.' In France, 'Philosophy having corroded the cement that united men, there are no longer any moral bonds.' For England, that meant that 'If England ever banished the words *Church and State* from its political vocabulary, its government would perish just like that of its rival.' Maistre was equally sceptical of abstract constitution-making.[236]

[234]Joseph de Maistre, *Considerations on France*, ed. Richard A. Lebrun (Cambridge, 1994), pp. 64–6, 89–90.
[235]Ibid., pp. 18, 21, 38–40.
[236]Ibid., pp. 41, 47, 49–53, 63.

Yet continental Catholic political thought was a thing in itself, not the off-spring of an English Protestant Whig. Burke condemned English divine-right doctrine as he recalled it from the early eighteenth century as anachronistic, long 'exploded'; Catholic thinkers preached just such doctrines. At his coronation in 1824, Charles X of France even resumed the practice of touching for the 'King's Evil', the thaumaturgic gauge of a title by divine right. Burke approved the French Revolution up to the meeting of the Estates-General; the collapse of the absolute monarchy in 1788 was perfectly acceptable to him, and he merely wished to proceed from there by Whig means. Continental legitimists wished to put the clock back. Burke had nothing in common with Maistre's alleged grounding of political conduct in the irrational or his exultation in the terror of authority. Suffering, war and the executioner were not Burke's symbols, as they were allegedly Maistre's.[237] There was an overlap in their list of society's enemies (lawyers, intellectuals, financiers); but for Maistre, Protestantism was at the root of the problem, and Burke defended Protestantism against the Papacy that Maistre exalted.

Both diagnosed a religious origin to the Revolution, but where Burke traced this to the French *philosophes'* and English Dissenters' assaults on shared religious orthodoxy and was sceptical of papal claims, the Catholic theocrats traced it to the principles of individualism and the right of private judgement which they found in the Protestant Reformation, and began to talk up Papal infallibility in ways that anticipated the first Vatican Council of 1870. Rulers in Maistre's vision were guardians, regulators, controllers; in Burke's vision they were the virtuous defenders of popular liberties against the threats of royal tyranny and corruption. Maistre was a lifelong student of what is now termed the Enlightenment who renounced it; he saw its logical culmination in the French Revolution and sought thenceforth to extirpate Enlightened doctrine. Burke was a lifelong student of the Enlightenment who saw in the French Revolution the ultimate threat to those modern, rational, libertarian, enlightened Whig values that he sought to defend.[238]

[237]It is open to doubt whether these themes were as important to Maistre as they have sometimes been claimed to be.

[238]'Burke's claims for the English aristocracy were rooted in the prescriptive quality of property and the empirical experience of history. In Bonald's society, the aristocracy were distinguished by function: the function of defending the society externally and internally. For Bonald, individualism simply did not exist: it was not the man who was honoured but the family, and aristocrats in particular were not free since they could not escape from the obligations of their hereditary profession. Furthermore, for Bonald, conservation was not a counsel of empirical wisdom as it was for Burke, but a principle inseparable from the divine institution of society, the ultimate human deriva-

## (viii) Burke's later influence

Faced with the agonising option which Burke had largely created, the Foxite parliamentary party first ostracised him, then split in 1794, the majority, led by the duke of Portland, joining the equally Whig William Pitt in a coalition ministry, leaving the minority, led by Fox himself, in isolated opposition. With only a brief interlude in 1806–7, this Whig group was to be out of office until 1830. The intellectual shallowness of the Foxite Whigs, and of their heirs the Holland House circle, was primarily the consequence of their refusal of that serious engagement with the problems with which the French Revolution and Edmund Burke had confronted them. With no credible answers to these new questions, their patrician high-mindedness made them unelectable. By contrast, the Foxite Burke was inappropriately recruited as the champion of what became that pragmatic and meritocratic institution, Lord Eldon's Church-State. Burke's account of 1688, his rationale for the union of Church and State, and his analysis of the danger of parliamentary reform (though not his sympathy for Catholic claims) provided or confirmed some of the theoretical underpinning for the Whig ministries of Pitt, Addington, Portland, Perceval, Liverpool, Canning, Goderich and Wellington. Although the term 'Tory' was sometimes, and increasingly, used to describe these ministerialists from about the 1820s, their ideology remained largely Burke's.

Yet this social and political order was smashed in 1828–32: Burke's positive prescriptions were made increasingly irrelevant by sweeping ecclesiastical, parliamentary and local government reform, and Burke's views were thereafter open to reinterpretation and appropriation for use in different contexts. That new creation of the 1830s, 'conservatism', adopted Burke as its patron saint. In that role, anomalously, he was used to sanctify Peelite utilitarianism, a creed hostile to the symbiosis of Church and State of which the young Gladstone was the last defender, hostile to the interests of the great landowners who had been Burke's patrons, neglectful of the status of a gentleman that had so preoccupied the historical Burke. Thanks to this misreading, the monarchical constitutionalist Maistre was denigrated in England as an extremist, and the Whig constitutionalist Burke (whose prescriptions had arguably failed in America in 1765–76, in France in 1788–89 and in England in 1828–32) was revered.

Attention now shifted from Burke's texts on the role of the Church in con-

---

tion from God's self-conservation born of God's self-love': Lucas, 'Burke and the Émigrés', p. 107.

secrating the state and the inviolability of the social order to his dicta about evolution, especially that a state without some means of change is without the means of its own conservation, and to those of his writings, especially *Thoughts on the Cause of the Present Discontents* (1770), in which he had seemed to anticipate a justification for the Victorian party system. Burke offered a rationale for the role of religion in society, a means of appreciating the practical wisdom embedded in ancient institutions, and a critique of schemes of reform derived from abstract principles which could be used in the new world after 1832: Burke was not a Conservative, but he made Victorian Conservatism possible.[239] Yet his legacy did not descend to one party only. Victorian Liberals too could sympathise with Burke the prophet of cabinet government, with Burke's stance on the American Revolution, and with his case for the conciliation of Irish Catholics. If it was difficult after 1832 to build any systematic political theory around the historical Burke's principles, the social and political order having changed out of recognition, a Burkeian style nevertheless passed into English discourse; his emphasis on social continuities and on the role of the particular circumstances and dispositions of peoples meant that 'It is in historiography rather than in theoretical statement that we find the fullest expression of Burkean political ideas in nineteenth-century England.'[240]

In these new roles, Burke's writings enjoyed lasting currency. Where Locke's *Two Treatises of Government* were relatively neglected, not often reprinted until the 1930s, Burke was reprinted, collected, abstracted and anthologised until the First World War. This was, however, a new, 'usable' Burke. The historical Burke had been significantly different. His writings lacked terms like 'conservatism', 'liberalism' and 'radicalism' that were to be the building blocks of a new conceptualisation of politics from the 1820s and 30s: none of these ideologies existed in his lifetime. He was neither a 'traditionalist' nor a 'reactionary' in the nineteenth-century sense, and would not have understood that later term, 'nostalgia'. Retrospectively imposing this vocabulary obscures the reasons for which some men in his lifetime defended and others opposed the established order. Burke's mythical role as the father of English Conservatism derived not least from later commentators' ignorance of the languages of anti-revolutionary, pro-establishment discourse

---

[239]It is another question whether he also made it impossible for it to succeed, if he placed at its heart a Whig theory of beneficent and inevitable reform; if he lacked a systematic defence of the old order; and if his central religious beliefs were latitudinarian ones.

[240]J. W. Burrow, *A Liberal Descent: Victorian historians and the English past* (Cambridge, 1981), p. 131 and passim.

upon which Burke drew. Nationalism, traditionalism and capitalism, in their mid-Victorian senses, are terms that equally misdescribe what the historical Burke had tried to do.[241] Burke's aim until the 1780s was to win power within the old order of society by condemning its vices and championing its virtues. Burke's aim in the 1790s was to defend the old order as such, virtues and vices together, against a new system of ideas which (he maintained) called for its total overthrow.

After immense suffering and the devastation of a continent, the crowned heads closed the lid on Pandora's box in 1815. The world they restored could not be the world they had lost, but the triumph of the princes in 1814–15 meant that Metternich's Europe was not to be one that squared easily with Burke's values. An England more intellectually indebted than were continental European states to Burke's Whig analysis of the French Revolution was an England which, after 1815, found itself coldly disposed to a European order whose restored monarchs had allegedly learned nothing and forgotten nothing. Into the nineteenth century, British foreign policy, whether shaped by Canning, Wellington, Peel, Palmerston or Gladstone, was generally favourable to what came to be called, in the new language of politics, liberalism and nationalism, and looked with disfavour on princely absolutism. Nineteenth-century Britain tended to promote movements of national or colonial liberation or unification against these restored monarchies, and so to widen a schism that Burke had contributed to cause. Between European reformers and Roman Catholics there was, in 1788–9, potentially much common ground. Nevertheless, things turned out very differently. Many of the more disastrous episodes of European history in the next two centuries were permitted by the conflict, not the co-operation, of these two schools. In the long and genocidal shadow cast by 1789, only Burke's Anglican England survived largely unscathed.

[241] It was once commonplace to think that Burke 'Has a feeling for biology and biological analogy' that anticipated the nineteenth century; that the *Reflections* were 'a great apology for romanticism'; that 'Burke was prior to Hegel, but he had an Hegel within him'; that he expounded 'conservatism': Ernest Barker, 'Burke on the French Revolution', in *Essays on Government* (Oxford, 1945), pp. 216, 220, 225, 235. It will now be clear that these and other similar characterisations of Burke as an anti-rationalist are equally misconceptions.

# A note on the text

## Choice of copy text

The textual history of the *Reflections* has been established by Professor William B. Todd. His edition (New York: Holt, Reinhart & Winston, 1959) made available the final version to receive Burke's own revisions, reprinting the 'seventh edition' (i.e. tenth impression) of 1791. This text (with a single correction in the 'ninth edition') was used in the Pelican (1968) and Oxford (1989) editions. The present version is the first modern edition to be taken from the first edition (1 November 1790). This has been chosen as the copy text since scholarly practice now favours the recovery of an author's first thoughts and since it can be shown that it was the first or the unchanged 'second edition' which Paine used for his reply in *Rights of Man*.[1] To do otherwise would be to compromise the integrity of Burke's text. Readers who wish to trace Burke's alterations in subsequent editions may now do so without access to the originals: this presentation allows us to appreciate that Burke continued to pursue French sources on the Revolution, and even in the last months of 1790 moved closer to Calonne's interpretation and away from Necker's.

Inconsistencies in spelling and accents were present in all editions (as well as in Burke's French sources) and have been reproduced here without correction. Following W. B. Todd, this edition includes five footnotes apparently representing Burke's marginal notes to his copy of the 1792 edition of his *Works*, printed in the 1803 edition, together with one footnote in the 1803

[1]Burke, *Reflections*, p. [241]; William B. Todd, *A Bibliography of Edmund Burke* (2nd edn., Godalming, 1982), pp. 142–8. The 'second edition' in its four impressions contained some reset pages, but the contents were identical with the first edition.

edition by another hand (*Reflections*, pp. [117, 165, 167, 169, 171, 211]). In classical translations, I have often adopted the version of the Loeb Classics.

All editors of the *Reflections* owe a debt to the work of their predecessors. The edition of E. J. Payne (Oxford, 1875) contained a wealth of detailed notes. Conor Cruise O'Brien's Penguin edition (Harmondsworth, 1968) emphasized Burke as an Irishman. L. G. Mitchell's edition (Oxford, 1989) focused on the Foxite Whigs' rejection of Burke and his interpretation of the Revolution. J. G. A. Pocock's edition (Indianapolis, 1987) contained a masterly introduction surveying Burke's political theory in many of its aspects, and an Appendix by W. R. E. Velema on Burke's influence abroad. Finally, a French edition, introduced by Philippe Raynaud and with annotations by Alfred Fierro and Georges Liébert (Paris, 1989) took seriously Burke's knowledge of, and insight into, events in France, and has been an invaluable guide to that dimension of Burke's book.

*Textual citation*

Burke's own footnotes are here indicated by '[B]': text preceding that sign is Burke's; text following it is the present editor's. Since the *Reflections* was begun as a letter, it lacks divisions into chapters and sections which make references within a systematic work like Locke's *Two Treatises* easy. The present edition for the first time makes cross-referencing possible by inserting in the text the page numbers of the first edition in square brackets: [2] signifies the beginning of Burke's p. 2. *All cross-references in the introduction, footnotes, and index within square brackets are to the page numbers of the first edition (1790).*

*Terminology*

It should be remembered throughout that the nouns 'liberalism', 'conservatism' and 'radicalism' were coined after Burke's lifetime; the adjectives 'conservative', 'liberal' and 'radical' did not carry political meanings for Burke or any of his contemporaries. Their use by modern readers can only obscure the real meaning of eighteenth-century discourse.[2]

[2]For a fuller account of the significance of concepts, see J. C. D. Clark, *English Society 1660–1832* (Cambridge, 2000), 'Keywords'.

# Biographical guide

Emmanuel-Armand de Vignerot du Plessis-Richelieu, duc d'AIGUILLON (1720–88). Governor of Brittany (1753–69) and Upper Alsace (1761–70), he succeeded Choiseul as Minister of Foreign Affairs. At the instigation of the *parlement* of Brittany, he had been prosecuted for maladministration in the *parlement* of Paris, which convicted him on 4 July 1770. Louis XV halted the prosecution in a *lit de justice*. His son, Armand-Désiré de Vignerot du Plessis-Richelieu, duc d'AIGUILLON (1761–1800), enormously wealthy, was a reforming ally of the duc d'Orléans. He seconded the motion of Noailles in the National Assembly on 4 August 1789 for the abolition of feudal dues, was a member of the Breton Club, precursor of the Jacobins, opposed an English-style constitution, and was suspected of complicity in the events of 5–6 October 1789. After the flight to Varennes, he changed his mind. In 1792 he fled to London, moved to Hamburg in 1795, and died before he could return to France.

Jean de Dieu Raymond de Boisgelin de Cucé (1732–1804), archbishop of AIX. A reforming churchman, he was briefly President of the National Assembly in November 1789; in that role, he drafted the Assembly's reply to the Revolution Society's address, but failed to prevent the Revolution proceeding to the nationalisation of Church property and imposing the Civil Constitution of the Clergy. He fled to England in 1792, where he lived as an *émigré*; returning to France after the Concordat, he became archbishop of Tours and a cardinal, and preached at the coronation of Napoleon in 1804.

Jean-Sylvain BAILLY (1736–93). An astronomer and member of the Academy of Sciences, he was mayor of Paris from July 1789 to November 1791. He was later accused of complicity in the flight to Varennes and responsibility for the massacre in the Champ de Mars on 17 July 1791, arrested in September 1793, and executed.

Antoine-Pierre-Joseph-Marie BARNAVE (1761–93). A lawyer from Dauphiné and a powerful orator, he broke with Mounier and was by late 1789 an influential member of the Jacobin Club. The rise of the more extreme Brissotins and the flight to Varennes converted him to the defence of constitutional monarchy. The discovery of his negotiations with Louis XVI led to his arrest in August 1792; while imprisoned, he wrote *Introduction à la Révolution française*. He was guillotined in November 1793.

Charles-Alexandre de CALONNE (1734–1802). As Controller-General of Finances from 1783 to April 1787, he attempted to implement a range of economic reforms and to balance the budget after Necker's financial expedients during the American war. Failing in this because of the resistance of the nobility and *parlements* to his tax reforms, he lived in London from 1787 to November 1790 and published a series of works justifying his conduct: *Requête au roi* (London, 1787); *Réponse de M. Calonne à l'écrit de M. Necker* (London, 1787); *Lettre adressée au roi, le 9 février 1787* (London, 1789); *Notes sur la mémoire remis par M. Necker au Comite des subsistances établi par l'Assemblée nationale* (London, 1789); *De l'état de la France tel qu'il peut et tel qu'il doit être* (London, 1790). These writings drew him to Burke.

Étienne-François, duc de CHOISEUL (1719–85). Minister of Foreign Affairs under Louis XV 1758–61 and 1766–70, also minister of war (1761–70) and of the navy (1761–6). He was regarded as the chief instigator of the Seven Years' War with Britain (1756–63), disastrous in its outcome for France; his lavish habits were equally disastrous for his own finances, and he died in debt. He was a friend of the *Encylopédistes* and helped to secure the expulsion of the Jesuits from France in 1763.

Thomas CHUBB (1679–1747), Deist. A tallow chandler and glove maker of Salisbury, his theological writings were subsidised by the Whig Sir Joseph Jekyll. These were published together in *A Collection of Tracts* (1730), and supplemented by *A Discourse concerning Reason* (1731), *The True Gospel of Jesus Christ Asserted* (1738), *A Discourse on Miracles* (1741) and other works.

Sir Edward COKE (1552–1634), jurist. He was chief justice of common pleas, 1606, and chief justice of the king's bench, 1613. In these offices he became a champion of the common law against the royal prerogative; his *Institutes of the Laws of England* and *Reports* achieved the status of classic expositions of the common law.

Anthony COLLINS (1676–1729), Deist. A landowner, educated at Eton and King's College, Cambridge, he was a friend of Locke and a theological controversalist. Author of *Priestcraft in Perfection* (1709), *A Discourse of Freethinking* (1713), *A Discourse on the Grounds and Reasons of the Christian Religion* (1724) and other works.

Marie-Jean-Antoine-Nicholas Caritat, marquis de CONDORCET (1743–94). A mathematician, member of the Academy of Sciences and a liberal reformer, he was the leading *philosophe* to live to see the Revolution. He played a leading role in the Legislative Assembly and the Convention until denounced by the Jacobins for supporting the Girondins. Imprisoned, he poisoned himself in his cell.

Charles-Jean-François DEPONT (1767–96). His father Jean-Samuel was Intendant of Metz from 1778 to 1790, and had been introduced to Burke in 1785 by Madame de Genlis. Jean-Samuel had secured a flying start for his son's career in the *ancien régime*: Charles became Advocate-general of the Parlement of Metz in 1784, aged 16, and a *conseiller* of the Parlement of Paris in 1789, aged 22. Both had visited London in 1785, and Charles had stayed with Edmund Burke at Beaconsfield. By 1789, Charles was an ardent revolutionary and an active member of the National Assembly. He was elected to the Patriot Committee of Metz in September 1789 and addressed the National Assembly in that capacity on 26 November.

Lord George GORDON (1751–93), MP 1774–80, the erratic President of the Protestant Association, presented to the House of Commons in June 1780 a massive petition against the Catholic Relief Act of 1778. When the House refused to receive it, as a violation of the Act against Tumultuous Petitioning of 1661, Gordon was suspected of fomenting the destructive anti-popery riots in London of 5–6 June 1780 which bear his name. The heavy loss of life and destruction of property in these mob actions, and their successful suppression by a resolute sovereign, provided a model for English observers of the French Revolution. Acquitted of treason in 1781, Gordon adopted Judaism, was imprisoned for libel in 1788, and died in the rebuilt Newgate gaol in 1793, a fervent admirer of the French Revolution, allegedly after singing the *Ça ira*.

Augustus Henry FitzRoy (1735–1811), 3rd duke of GRAFTON from 1757. In 1768 he was elected Chancellor of Cambridge University but refused the customary degree of LL.D. at his installation to avoid subscribing the Thirty-nine Articles. His extra-marital affairs were widely discussed (e.g. *Memoirs of the Amours, Intrigues and Adventures of Charles Augustus [sc. Augustus Henry] Fitz-Roy, Duke of Grafton, with Miss Parsons* (London, 1769)); his wife left him in 1769. He was soon associated with the Unitarian meeting house illegally established by Theophilus Lindsey in Essex Street, London, in 1774, a centre for reformers. His theological opinions were set out in two tracts, both published anonymously: *Hints, &c. submitted to the Serious Attention of the Clergy, Nobility and Gentry, newly associated, by a Layman* (London, 1789) and *The Serious Reflections of a Rational Christian, written down at different times, from 1788 to 1797* ([London], 1797).

The ducs de GUISE played a leading role at the head of the Catholic party in the French wars of religion: François (1520–63), his son Henri (1550–88), and Louis II de Guise, cardinal de Lorraine (1555–88): the last two ordered the massacre of St. Bartholomew. Gaspard de COLIGNY (1519–72), admiral of France, and his brother François, seigneur d'ANDELOT (1521–69), were equally prominent in the Protestant party. Louis II de Bourbon, prince de CONDÉ (1621–86), was a military leader of the Fronde and an enemy of Mazarin.

HENRI IV (1553–1610), head of the Protestant party, succeeded to the French throne in 1589, re-established peace, and embraced Catholicism in 1593.

Earl of HOLLAND: Sir Henry Rich (1590–1649), dubious favourite and courtier of James I, created first earl of Holland (1624). He made a fortune out of a variety of court appointments but turned against Charles I in 1642. In 1643 he rejoined the court, and again abandoned it. Failing to persuade Parliament of his loyalty, he backed the King in the second civil war in 1647, was defeated, captured and executed.

Jean Joseph, marquis de LABORDE (1724–94), was a leading banker and financier to the French government, whose son, François-Louis-Joseph Laborde de Méréville, acquired the office of keeper of the Royal Treasury in 1785 and who associated his father in that office. The Laborde family was connected to the world of high finance by a series of marriage alliances. Jean Joseph was tried during the Terror for exporting gold, and guillotined on 18 April 1794.

Marie-Joseph Gilbert Motier, marquis de LA FAYETTE (1757–1834). A general in the French army supporting the American revolutionaries, he became a flamboyant advocate of their cause. As an ardent aristocratic reformer he served in the Assembly of Notables in 1787 and became the first commander of the National Guard in Paris in 1789–91. He then accepted an army command, but tried to restrain the revolution and retain a limited monarchy; failing, and denounced by the National Assembly, he became an *émigré* in Austria in 1792.

Trophime Gérard, marquis de LALLY-TOLLENDAL (1751–1830). His father had been executed in 1766 for surrendering Pondicherry to the English; he persuaded Voltaire to campaign to overturn that verdict, and succeeded in 1778. Lally-Tollendal became a celebrity and a reformer, and in 1789 was elected a deputy in the Second Estate of the Estates-General where he worked with the *monarchiens* for a limited monarchy. After the events of 5–6 October 1789 he fled to Switzerland, defended his role as a reformer, and returned to Paris briefly in 1792 in an attempt to save Louis XVI. Arrested, he was released in time to escape the September Massacres, fled to England and lived there as an *émigré*.

John LAW (1671–1729). A Scot, the son of a banker, he sought to make his career in England. After killing a man in a duel in 1694 he was imprisoned but escaped and fled to Holland, where he studied finance. Unable to obtain backing for his schemes in Scotland, in 1715 he was finally able to persuade the Regent of France to adopt his plans for reducing France's war debt. These included the establishment in 1717 of the *Compagnie de la Louisiane ou d'Occident*, known as the Mississippi Company. This was part of an interlocking series of financial projects which fuelled a speculative mania and led to a spectacular crash in 1720. It provided Burke's model for the system of finance built around the issue of *assignats* during the French Revolution.

Armand-Marc, comte de MONTMORIN-Saint-Herem (1745–92); diplomat, Minister of Foreign Affairs from February 1787, he played a prominent part in the ministry after the fall of Necker on 4 September 1790. He resigned in November 1791, was imprisoned in August 1792 and murdered there by the mob in the September Massacres.

Thomas MORGAN (d. 1743), Deist. A farmer's son, educated at the expense of a Dissenting minister, he served in that capacity himself in Somerset and Wiltshire until dismissed in 1720 for heterodoxy. He was active in anti-Trinitarian controversy from 1719, his publications assembled in A *Collection of Tracts* (1720), and continued in writings including *The Moral Philosopher* (1737) and other works.

Jean-Joseph MOUNIER (1758–1806). A judge at Grenoble, in 1789 he was elected a deputy to the Third Estate of the Estates-General, where he campaigned unsuccessfully for a constitution on the English model. He failed to persuade the king to defend Versailles by force on 5 October 1789 and on 8 October returned to his native Dauphiné. Fearing for his safety, in May 1790 he fled abroad, and lived as an *émigré* until 1801.

Anne-Louis-Henri de la Fare (1752–1829), bishop of NANCY (1787). A defender of the rights of the clergy in the Estates-General, he attacked the suppression of monastic orders in the National Assembly. Refusing to take the oath required by the Civil Constitution of the Clergy, he became an *émigré* in 1791.

Jacques NECKER (1732–1804), Genevan banker, Treasurer from 1765 and then Director-General of Finances in 1776–81 and 1788–90. He acquired widespread popularity by resisting tax increases, financing the American war by massive loans, and by producing the first (albeit misleading) published version of national accounts, the *Compte rendu au roi* of 1781. The problems he bequeathed to his successors after 1781 proved insoluble, and he was himself unable to prevent the financial collapse of the old order when he was recalled to office after the national bankruptcy of August 1788. His popularity and reputation for financial genius finally evaporated, and amid mounting hostility he was dismissed on 8 September 1790 and returned to Switzerland.

Louis-Marie d'Ayen, vicomte de NOAILLES (1756–1804). He fought with his friend La Fayette during the American War of Independence, and sat as a deputy for the nobility in the Estates-General. Joining the Third Estate, he pursued a career as a reformer in the National Assembly, and proposed there the motion for the abolition of feudal dues on the night of 4 August 1789. He was a member of the Breton Club and contributed to the abolition of titles of nobility on 29 June 1790. After service in the revolutionary army in 1791–2, he became an *émigré* in 1792, first in England, then the United States.

Hugh PETERS (1598–1660). Ordained in the Church of England, his religious opinions led him to emigrate first to Holland, then to New England; in 1641 he returned and became an army chaplain to the Parliamentarian forces, siding with the Independents against the Presbyterians. Peters reached the apogee of his influence during Cromwell's rule; in 1660 he was exempted from the Act of Indemnity, tried for treason, and executed.

Richard PRICE (1723–91), from 1758 minister of a Dissenting congregation at Newington Green, and from 1771 also at Hackney, near London. He acquired a wide reputation as a writer on ethics and finance, but also notoriously intervened in political questions with his tract *Observations on Civil Liberty and the Justice and Policy of the War with America* (London, 1776). Price had aligned himself against Burke by his association with Rockingham's rival Shelburne, who had offered Price the post of private secretary on forming his administration in 1782.

Dr. Joseph PRIESTLEY (1733–1804), Dissenting minister, Socinian and scientist. His attacks on Trinitarianism and the Anglican establishment dated from the 1760s and in 1772 secured him the position of librarian and political aide to the Earl of Shelburne (q.v.), on the recommendation of Richard Price; Shelburne terminated the arrangement in 1780. Priestley was minister to a Dissenting congregation in Birmingham from 1780, increasingly drawn into a theological controversy on the Trinity with the Rev. Samuel Horsley. Priestley had aligned himself with the cause of revolution in America in tracts of 1769 and 1774; his sermon on 5 November 1789 tendentiously commemorating the Glorious Revolution was only overshadowed by Price's. On 26 August 1792 the National Assembly in Paris rewarded Priestley with French citizenship, and the department of l'Orne elected him to membership of that body. He declined, and in 1794 left for America.

Louis-Alexandre, duc de la Roche-Guygon et de La ROCHEFOUCAULD d'Enville (1743–92). A friend of Earl Stanhope and a kindred spirit, he was a member of the Assembly of Notables in 1787 and one of the first of his order in the Estates-General to join the Third Estate; he conveyed the address of the Revolution Society to the National Assembly and secured the Assembly's acknowledgement of it. He was stoned to death in front of his wife and mother during a revolutionary riot in 1792.

François Alexandre Frédéric, duc de La ROCHEFOUCAULD-LIANCOURT (1747–1827), economist and reformer, master of the robes to Louis XVI and an army officer. In August 1792, anticipating the fall of the monarchy, he became an *émigré* in England. His estates were returned to him by Napoleon, and he was again a focus of aristocratic opposition to the Bourbon monarchy after its restoration.

Dominique de la Rochefoucauld (1712–1800), cardinal and archbishop of ROUEN. From an impoverished branch of the ducal family, he chaired the First Estate in the Estates-General and opposed its union with the Third. He fought against all the anticlerical measures of the National Assembly and became an *émigré* only after the fall of the monarchy in August 1792.

Jean-Paul Rabaut SAINT-ÉTIENNE (1743–93). Son of a Protestant minister, his campaign on behalf of his co-religionists led to the decree of toleration of November 1787. His heightened rhetoric of destruction and renewal was held to be symptomatic by Burke (*Reflections*, p. [247]): this accurately reflected his role in the Constitutional Committee of the National Assembly in 1789 and 1790. After the royal family's flight to Varennes, Saint-Étienne adopted more extreme positions and was guillotined with his friends the Girondins.

John SELDEN (1584–1654), jurist, antiquarian and MP, championed common law rights against Charles I's use of the prerogative, and was one of the authors of the Petition of Right.

William Petty (1737–1805), from 1761 second earl of SHELBURNE in the Irish peerage and Baron Wycombe, created 1st marquis Lansdowne (1784). An ally of the elder Pitt in the 1760s, he became an outspoken critic of Lord North's ministry, backing the attempts of Dissenters to abolish the requirement of subscription to most of the Thirty-nine Articles to obtain the protection of the Toleration Act, and attacking the government's policy towards America. He succeeded to the leadership of Chatham's followers after his death in 1778 and became the most prominent noble patron of the reformist intelligentsia, including Price and Priestley. Shelburne joined Rockingham's administration as Secretary of State in 1782. His principled objection to party cohesion (the opposite position to Burke's) went with growing distrust and jealousy between himself and Charles James Fox, and when Shelburne became First Lord of the Treasury on Rockingham's death, Fox and the Rockingham party resigned; in February 1783 Fox allied with North to force Shelburne's resignation. The younger Pitt rewarded him with a marquisate. In the Lords, he defended Warren Hastings and supported Pitt's ministry during the Regency Crisis. He hailed the French Revolution; by 1793 he was an outspoken opponent of the war with France, and attacked the ministry's measures against domestic subversion. Shelburne was widely and intensely disliked in Foxite circles. Burke declared in 1782: 'If lord Shelburne was not a Cataline, or a Borgia in morals, it must not be ascribed to any thing but his understanding': *Parl Hist* XXIII, col. 183.

Richard Brinsley SHERIDAN (1751–1816). An MP from 1780, he had been associated with schemes for parliamentary reform from the outset of his career: this, and the immorality of his private life, alienated him from Burke. His close friendships with Fox and the Prince of Wales, and the success of his parliamentary oratory, also made him Burke's greatest rival in the Whig opposition. It was Sheridan who led the party's attack on Burke after Burke's denunciation of the French Revolution in the Commons debate of 9 February 1790. Sheridan wrote 'fragmentary drafts' of a reply to Burke's *Reflections*, but did not succeed in completing a text. By 1793 he was often pictured as an English *sansculotte*: R. G. Thorne (ed.), *The History of Parliament: The House of Commons 1790–1820* (5 vols., London, 1986), V, pp. 143–69.

Emmanuel Joseph SIEYÈS (1748–1836), priest, Freemason and revolutionary. He wrote, for the Constituent Assembly, the *Reconaissance et exposition raisonnée des Droits de l'Homme et du Citoyen* (July 1789) and *Qu'est-ce que le Tiers-Etat?* (1789). He sat in the Estates-General in the Third Estate, to which he was elected for Paris, and played a part in the drafting of the Declaration of the Rights of Man and of the Citizen; as a deputy in the Convention, he voted for the death of the king. Robespierre referred to him as 'the mole of the Revolution'. Burke wrote: 'Abbé Sieyès has whole nests of pigeon-holes full of constitutions ready made, ticketed, sorted and numbered; suited to every season and every fancy; some with the top of the pattern at the bottom, and some with the bottom at the top; some plain, some flowered ...': *Letter to a Noble Lord*, pp. 63–4. He became a rich man after 1799 by endorsing Napoleon's *coup* and aiding his drafting of yet another constitution.

John 1st baron SOMERS (1651–1716). Junior counsel for the seven bishops, 1688; he sat in the Convention Parliament, which he urged to resolve that James II had abdicated; he took the lead in the Commons' committee that drafted the Declaration of Rights; was confidant of William III; solicitor general, 1689; attorney general 1692; lord keeper, 1693 and lord chancellor, 1697–1700. A leader of the Junto Whigs in Anne's reign, he played a large part in framing the Regency Act (1706) and Act of Union (1707). He was lord president 1708–10; a friend of Gilbert Burnet, Matthew Tindal and John Toland.

Charles, 3rd earl STANHOPE (1753–1816). He had long been associated with intellectual reformers: as Lord Mahon he sat as MP for Shelburne's pocket borough of Chipping Wycombe from 1780 until he succeeded to his democrat father's earldom on 7 March 1786. In the Commons he spoke against the American war and introduced a series of Bills for parliamentary reform. In the Lords he sponsored in 1789 Bills to relieve Anglicans from the requirement of subscription to the Thirty-nine Articles and to obstruct clergy in the recovery of their tithes: the Bills failed on 18 May and 3 July. He had become the chairman of the Revolution Society on its re-foundation in 1788. In that role he forwarded the Society's congratulatory address on the fall of the Bastille, moved on 4 November 1789, and also forwarded to Rochefoucauld the congratulatory address on the establishment of liberty in France, proposed by Sheridan at the Crown and Anchor tavern on 14 July 1790. He was among Burke's earliest opponents, replying to Burke's speech on the army estimates of 9 February 1790 with *A Letter from Earl Stanhope to the Right Honourable Edmund Burke: containing a Short Answer to his late Speech on the French Revolution*, denouncing the French government before the Revolution as a 'Feudal Tyranny' whose people were '*literally starving*', boasting of the role of the Revolution Society, and reproaching Burke with the superior wisdom of Fox and Sheridan. Stanhope went on to oppose British involvement in the war against France, and earned the nickname 'Citizen' Stanhope. An assiduous inventor, he ill-treated and disinherited his children. His patrician indignation when his third daughter eloped to marry an apothecary exposed him to much satire.

Maximilien de Béthune, duc de SULLY (1559–1641) was the chief counsellor, and successful finance minister, of Henri IV of France (q.v.).

Matthew TINDAL (1657–1733), Deist. Son of a minister intruded into a Devonshire living during the Commonwealth. Educated at Oxford, he lived as a law fellow of All Souls College from 1678, notorious for his private life and heterodoxy. He converted to Catholicism under James II and, having failed to obtain the Wardenship of his college, re-converted in 1688. Thereafter he engaged in theological polemic in *The Rights of the Christian Church Asserted* (1706), *Christianity as Old as the Creation* (1730) and other works.

John TOLAND (1670–1722), Deist. Born in Ireland, possibly the illegitimate son of a Catholic priest, he was educated at Glasgow University and Leyden. His *Christianity Not Mysterious* (1696) caused an outcry and made him a notorious figure, argued against by orthodox divines, and making a tenuous living in the underworld of London journalism, publishing and politics, subsidised by Shaftesbury. His other works included *Amyntor* (1699), *Nazarenus* (1718) and many pamphlets on contemporary politics.

Jean-Frédéric, comte de La TOUR DU PIN (1727–94); Minister of War from 7 August 1789 to 16 November 1790 (see *Reflections*, p. [305]). He was guillotined in 1794.

Anne-Robert-Jacques TURGOT (1727–81). A leading Physiocrat, he was Controller General of Finances 1774–6 and a famous reformer, abolishing internal tolls and promoting domestic free trade in grain. He wrote *Réflexions sur la formation et la distribution des richesses* (1776).

# Bibliography

## (A) Bibliographies

Burke scholarship is well served by bibliographical guides. William B. Todd, *A Bibliography of Edmund Burke* (London, 1964; 2nd edn., Godalming, Surrey, 1982) provides an exhaustive list of works by Burke himself published between 1748 and 1827. Burke's own library can be reconstructed from his sale catalogue, *Catalogue of the Library of the Late Right Hon. Edmund Burke, the Library of the Late Sir M. B. Clare, MD some Articles from Gibbon's Library, &c. &c.* ([London], 1833), the owners of which are separately listed, and from the manuscript catalogue of his library dated 1813, Bodleian MS Eng Misc D722.

For recent work Clara I. Gandy and Peter J. Stanlis, *Edmund Burke: A Bibliography of Secondary Studies to 1982* (New York, 1983) is detailed up to that date, and is followed by Leonard W. Cowie, *Edmund Burke 1729–1797: A Bibliography* (Westport, Connecticut, 1994). Both focus on modern secondary writings, although Cowie covers manuscript and archival resources also. Gayle Trusdel Pendleton, 'Towards a Bibliography of the *Reflections* and *Rights of Man* Controvery', *Bulletin of Research in the Humanities* 85 (1982), pp. 65–103, provides a detailed list of the pamphlet controversy generated by Burke's *Reflections*. For recent work on the French Revolution, the exhaustive study is Alfred Fierro (ed.), *Bibliographie de la Révolution française 1940–1988* (2 vols., Paris, 1989). A useful shorter guide is William Doyle, *The French Revolution: a bibliography of works in English* (London, 1988).

## (B) Edmund Burke

*(i) Biography and political career.* T. W. Copeland et al. (eds.), *The Correspondence of Edmund Burke* (10 vols., Cambridge, 1958–78) is standard,

supplemented by the microfilm edition of Burke's papers, *Politics in the Age of Revolution, 1715–1848. Part I. The Papers of Edmund Burke, 1729–1797* (Adam Matthew Publications, 1994) and F. P. Lock (ed.), 'Unpublished Burke Letters, 1783–96', *English Historical Review* 112 (1997), pp. 119–41. Carl B. Cone, *Edmund Burke and the Nature of Politics* (2 vols., Lexington, Kentucky) is now being superseded by a major two-volume biography, F. P. Lock, *Edmund Burke*; vol. I, covering 1730–84 (Oxford, 1998) had appeared when this edition was completed. T. H. D. Mahoney, *Edmund Burke and Ireland* (Cambridge, Mass., 1960) began the process of relocating Burke in his native culture, re-emphasised by Conor Cruise O'Brien's vividly personal *The Great Melody: A Thematic Biography and Commented Anthology of Edmund Burke* (London, 1992). Stanley Ayling, *Edmund Burke* (London, 1968) is convenient. Nicholas K. Robinson, *Edmund Burke: A Life in Caricature* (New Haven, Conn., 1996) provides a visual survey. For Burke's main allies, see Ross Hoffman, *The Marquis: A Study of Lord Rockingham 1730–1782* (New York, 1973) and John W. Derry, *Charles James Fox* (London, 1972). Frank O'Gorman, *The Whig Party and the French Revolution* (London, 1967), Leslie Mitchell, *Charles James Fox and the Disintegration of the Whig Party 1782–1794* (Oxford, 1971) and B. W. Hill, 'Fox and Burke: the Whig party and the question of principles, 1784–1789', *English Historical Review* 89 (1974), pp. 1–24 provide a political background. P. J. Marshall, *The Impeachment of Warren Hastings* (London, 1965) illuminates Burke's great crusade.

*(ii) Editions and anthologies.* R. B. McDowell (ed.), *The Writings and Speeches of Edmund Burke, IX, I. The Revolutionary War 1794–1797 II. Ireland* (Oxford, 1991) is the indispensable sequel to the *Reflections*. Anthologies of Burke's writings, with bibliographic guides, include B. W. Hill (ed.), *Edmund Burke on Government, Politics and Religion* (Brighton, 1975), Iain Hampsher-Monk (ed.), *The Political Philosophy of Edmund Burke* (London, 1987), Ian Harris (ed.), *Edmund Burke: Pre-Revolutionary Writings* (Cambridge, 1993) and David Womersley (ed.), *Edmund Burke: A Philosophical Enquiry into the Origin of our Ideas of the Sublime and Beautiful and Other Pre-Revolutionary Writings* (Harmondsworth, 1998). Marilyn Butler (ed.), *Burke, Paine, Godwin and the Revolution Controversy* (Cambridge, 1984) provides extracts from pamphlets of the 1790s, including Burke's. Gregory Claeys (ed.), *The Political Writings of the 1790s* (8 vols., London, 1995) is an admirably extensive collection of reprinted texts.

*(iii) Political theory.* Burke has been subject to many interpretive influences in the twentieth century. Alfred Cobban's *Edmund Burke and the Revolt against the Eighteenth Century* (London, 1929) examined his thought against that of the Romantics, Wordsworth, Coleridge and Southey. For the

largely American neo-conservative depiction of Burke as indebted chiefly to a classical and medieval tradition of natural law, especially in Aristotle and Aquinas, see Russell Kirk, *The Conservative Mind from Burke to Santayana* (New York, 1953); P. J. Stanlis, *Edmund Burke and the Natural Law* (Ann Arbor, 1958); Francis J. Canavan, SJ, *The Political Reason of Edmund Burke* (Durham, N.C., 1960); Burleigh Taylor Wilkins, *The Problem of Burke's Political Philosophy* (Oxford, 1967) and Joseph L. Pappin III, *The Metaphysics of Edmund Burke* (New York, 1993). J. R. Dinwiddy, 'Utility and natural law in Burke's thought: a reconsideration', *Studies in Burke and His Time* 16 (1974–5), pp. 105–28 reacted against this American natural-law school by emphasising Burke as an utilitarian. C. B. Macpherson, *Burke* (Oxford, 1981) provided a late Marxist interpretation, and Isaac Kramnick, *The Rage of Edmund Burke* (New York, 1979) a late psychoanalytical one. Tom Furniss, *Edmund Burke's Aesthetic Ideology: Language, gender and political economy in revolution* (Cambridge, 1993) offers a literary critic's reading of texts, as does Steven Blakemore, *Burke and the Fall of Language: the French Revolution as Linguistic Event* (Hanover, New Hampshire, 1988) and idem, *Intertextual War: Edmund Burke and the French Revolution in the Writings of Mary Wollstonecraft, Thomas Paine, and James Mackintosh* (Cranbury, NJ, 1997). None of these interpretations is followed in this edition.

A more historical approach can be traced from Charles Parkin, *The Moral Basis of Burke's Political Thought* (Cambridge, 1956), which pointed to links with religion at a time when the Church of England attracted little attention from students of political theory, and James T. Boulton, *The Language of Politics in the Age of Wilkes and Burke* (London, 1963). A contextualising in practical politics was continued by Frank O'Gorman, *Edmund Burke: His Political Philosophy* (London, 1973), and F. P. Lock, *Burke's Reflections* (below). Derek Roper, *Reviewing before the Edinburgh, 1788–1802* (London, 1978) discussed the reception of Price and Burke. Frederick A. Dreyer, *Burke's Politics: A Study in Whig Orthodoxy* (Waterloo, Canada, 1979) depicted him as a Whig in a tradition indebted primarily to Locke. On Burke's relation to the Enlightenment, Seamus F. Deane, 'Burke and the French Philosophes', *Studies in Burke and his Time* 10 (1968–9), pp. 1111–37 and idem, *The French Revolution and Enlightenment in England 1789–1832* (Cambridge, Mass., 1988). On prescription, see especially J. G. A. Pocock, 'Burke and the Ancient Constitution: A Problem in the History of Ideas', *Historical Journal* 3 (1960), pp. 125–43, reprinted in idem, *Politics, Language and Time* (London, 1971) and Paul Lucas, 'On Edmund Burke's Doctrine of Prescription; or, an Appeal from the New to the Old Lawyers', *Historical Journal* 11

(1968), pp. 35–63. For the 1790s, R. R. Fennessy, *Burke, Paine and the Rights of Man: a difference of political opinion* (The Hague, 1963) is the leading monograph on the controversy. See also Ian Hampsher-Monk, 'Rhetoric and Opinion in the Politics of Edmund Burke', *History of Political Thought* 9 (1988), pp. 455–84, Gregory Claeys, 'The French Revolution Debate and British Political Thought', *History of Political Thought* 11 (1990), pp. 59–8; J. G. A. Pocock, 'Edmund Burke and the Redefinition of Enthusiasm: the Context as Counter-Revolution' in *The French Revolution and the Creation of Modern Political Culture*, III (1989), Mark Philp, 'Vulgar Conservatism, 1792–3', *English Historical Review* 110 (1995), pp. 42–69 and 'English Republicanism in the 1790s', *Journal of Political Philosophy* 6 (1998), pp. 235–62.

Frederick Dreyer, 'Burke's Religion', *Studies in Burke and His Time* 17 (1976), pp. 199–212 argues for his latitudinarianism; Nigel Aston, 'A 'lay divine': Burke, Christianity, and the Preservation of the British State, 1790–1797', in Aston (ed.), *Religious Change in Europe 1650–1914* (Oxford, 1997), cautions against the term but presents a similar picture. Ian Hampsher-Monk, 'Burke and the Religious Sources of Skeptical Conservatism', in J. van der Zande and R. H. Popkin (eds.), *The Skeptical Tradition around 1800* (The Hague, 1998) traces Burke's politics to a school of Anglican argument against Deists. See also Francis Canavan, *Edmund Burke: Prescription and Providence* (Durham, N.C., 1987) and Norman Ravitch, 'Far Short of Bigotry: Edmund Burke on Church Establishments and Confessional States', *Journal of Church and State* 37 (1995), pp. 365–83. Elizabeth Lambert, 'Edmund Burke's Religion', *English Language Notes* 32 (1994), pp. 19–28, refuted the idea of his deathbed return to the Roman church. On Anglican orthodoxy, see R. A. Soloway, *Prelates and People: Ecclesiastical Social Thought in England 1783–1852* (London, 1969); Robert Hole, *Pulpits, politics and public order in England 1760–1832* (Cambridge, 1989), F. C. Mather, *High Church Prophet: Bishop Samuel Horsley (1733–1806) and the Caroline Tradition in the Later Georgian Church* (Oxford, 1992), Nigel Aston, 'Horne and Heterodoxy: The Defence of Anglican Beliefs in the Late Enlightenment', *English Historical Review* 108 (1993), pp. 895–919, and Samuel Horsley, 'Thoughts upon Civil government, and its Relation to Religion', ed. Andrew Robinson, in Stephen Taylor (ed.), *From Cranmer to Davidson* (Church of England Record Society, vol. 7, Woodbridge, 1999), pp. 203–12. Burke's view of the essentially marginal nature of heterodoxy in an England dominated intellectually and politically by its established Church is confirmed by a number of recent studies, including John Gascoigne, *Cambridge in the Age of the Enlightenment* (Cambridge, 1991); John Walsh, Colin Haydon and Stephen Taylor (eds.), *The*

*Church of England c. 1689-c. 1833: From Toleration to Tractarianism* (Cambridge, 1993), and Roger D. Lund (ed.), *The Margins of Orthodoxy: Heterodox Writings and Cultural Response, 1660–1750* (Cambridge, 1995).

Studies of the wider intellectual setting have influenced Burke scholarship, including J. W. Burrow, *A Liberal Descent: Victorian Historians and the English Past* (Cambridge, 1981); Reed Browning, *Political and Constitutional Ideas of the Court Whigs* (Baton Rouge, 1982); J. G. A. Pocock, *Virtue, Commerce and History: Essays on Political Thought and History, Chiefly in the Eighteenth Century* (Cambridge, 1985), including especially 'The varieties of Whiggism from Exclusion to Reform: A history of ideology and discourse', pp. 215–310; R. J. Smith, *The Gothic Bequest: Medieval institutions in British thought, 1688–1863* (Cambridge, 1987); Robert Hole, *Pulpits, politics and public order in England 1760–1832* (Cambridge, 1989); James J. Sack, *From Jacobite to Conservative: Reaction and orthodoxy in Britain, c. 1760–1832* (Cambridge, 1993); and Robert Eccleshall, 'Anglican Political Thought in the century after the Revolution of 1688' in D. George Boyce, Robert Eccleshall and Vincent Geoghegan (eds.), *Political Thought in Ireland Since the Seventeenth Century* (London, 1993). For continental comparisons, see C. P. Courtney, *Montesquieu and Burke* (Oxford, 1963); Michel Ganzin, *La Pensée politique d'Edmund Burke* (Paris, 1972); David R. Cameron, *The Social Thought of Rousseau and Burke: a comparative study* (London, 1973); and P. J. Stanlis, *Edmund Burke: the Enlightenment and Revolution* (New Brunswick, NJ, 1991). For the present editor's contribution, see J. C. D. Clark, *English Society 1688–1832* (1985), 2nd edn. as *English Society 1660–1832: religion, ideology and politics during the ancien regime* (Cambridge, 2000).

*(iv) Burke's Reflections.* The correspondent who provoked Burke to begin the *Reflections* was identified by H. V. F. Somerset, 'A Burke Discovery', *English: The Magazine of the English Association* 8 (1951), pp. 171–83; cf. Robert Forster, *Merchants, Landlords, Magistrates: the Depont Family in Eighteenth-Century France* (Baltimore, 1980). On the composition of Burke's reply, see J. T. Boulton, 'The *Reflections*: Burke's preliminary draft and methods of composition', *Durham University Journal* 14 (1958), pp. 114–9; A. Goodwin, 'The Political Genesis of Edmund Burke's *Reflections on the Revolution in France*', *Bulletin of the John Rylands Library* 50 (1967–8), pp. 336–64; Frederick A. Dreyer, 'The Genesis of Burke's *Reflections*', *Journal of Modern History* 50 (1978), pp. 462–79 and F. P. Lock, *Burke's Reflections on the Revolution in France* (London, 1985). Ian Crowe (ed.), *Edmund Burke: His Life and Legacy* (Dublin, 1997) illustrates his continued salience in present political debate, as does Roger Scruton, 'Man's Second Disobedience: a Vindication of Burke', in Ceri Crossley and Ian Small (eds.), *The French Revolution and*

*British Culture* (Oxford, 1989) and David Musselwhite, 'Reflections on Burke's *Reflections, 1790–1990*' in Peter Hulme and Ludmilla Jordanova (eds.), *The Enlightenment and its Shadows* (London, 1990).

*(C) England*

   *(i) The Revolution of 1688.* The central recent studies are: J. R. Jones, *The Revolution of 1688 in England* (London, 1972); H. T. Dickinson, 'The Eighteenth-Century Debate on the Glorious Revolution', *History* 61 (1976), pp. 28–45; J. P. Kenyon, *Revolution Principles: The Politics of Party 1689–1720* (Cambridge, 1977); W. A. Speck, *Reluctant Revolutionaries: Englishmen and the Revolution of 1688* (Oxford, 1988) and Howard Nenner, *The Right to be King: The Succession to the Crown of England, 1603–1714* (London, 1995).

   *(ii) Dissent.* General studies include Anthony Lincoln, *Some Political & Social Ideas of English Dissent 1763–1800* (Cambridge, 1938); Ursula Henriques, *Religious Toleration in England 1787–1833* (London, 1961); Richard Burgess Barlow, *Citizenship and Conscience: a study in the theory and practice of religious toleration in England during the eighteenth century* (Philadelphia, 1962); and Gordon Rupp, *Religion in England 1688–1791* (Oxford, 1986). The starting point in a debate on political mobilisation is now James Bradley, *Religion, Revolution and English Radicalism: Nonconformity in Eighteenth-Century Politics and Society* (Cambridge, 1990). On Burke's first opponent, see D. O. Thomas, *The Honest Mind: the Thought and Work of Richard Price* (Oxford, 1977), and W. Bernard Peach and D. O. Thomas (eds.), *The Correspondence of Richard Price* (3 vols., Cardiff, 1983–94). W. Bernard Peach (ed.), *Richard Price and the Ethical Foundations of the American Revolution* (Durham, NC, 1979) is an edition of his writings on the American question. Priestley is not yet so well served, but see Clarke Garrett, *Respectable Folly: Millenarians and the French Revolution in France and England* (Baltimore, 1975); Jack Fruchtman, Jr., 'The Apocalyptic Politics of Richard Price and Joseph Priestley: A Study in Late Eighteenth-Century English Republican Millennialism', *Transactions of the American Philosophical Society* 73 (1983), pp. 1–125 and Robert E. Schofield, *The Enlightenment of Joseph Priestley: A Study of His Life and Work from 1733 to 1773* (University Park, Pennsylvania, 1997).

   *(iii) The crisis of the 1790s.* George Stead Veitch, *The Genesis of Parliamentary Reform* (1914; ed. Ian R. Christie, London, 1965) was an early classic, not wholly superseded by later work: Eugene Charlton Black, *The Association: British Extraparliamentary Political Organization 1769–1793* (Cambridge, Mass., 1963); John Cannon, *Parliamentary Reform 1640–1832* (Cambridge, 1973); Albert Goodwin, *The Friends of Liberty: The English Demo-*

*cratic Movement in the age of the French Revolution* (London, 1979); Günther Lottes, *Politische Aufklärung und plebejisches Publikum. Zur Theorie und Praxis des englischen Radikalismus im späten 18. Jahrhundert* (Munich, 1979); Robert R. Dozier, *For King, Constitution and Country: The English Loyalists and the French Revolution* (Lexington, Kentucky, 1983); Ian R. Christie, *Stress and Stability in Late Eighteenth-Century Britain: Reflections on the British Avoidance of Revolution* (Oxford, 1984) and Mark Philp (ed.), *The French Revolution and British Popular Politics* (Cambridge, 1991). On the reformist Whigs, see Ghita Stanhope and G. P. Gooch, *The Life of Charles, Third Earl Stanhope* (London, 1914), which needs to be replaced; Peter Brown, *The Chathamites* (London, 1967); Derek Jarrett, *The Begetters of Revolution: England's involvement with France, 1759–1789* (London, 1973); and E. Pariset, 'La Société de la Révolution de Londres dans ses rapports avec Burke et l'Assemblée Constituante', *La Révolution Française* 29 (1895), pp. 297–325. Studies of Paine now begin from Jack Fruchtman, Jr., *Thomas Paine: Apostle of Freedom* (New York, 1994) and John Keene, *Tom Paine: A Political Life* (London, 1995). Thomas Paine, *Rights of Man, Common Sense, and Other Political Writings*, ed. Mark Philp (Oxford, 1995) is the most helpful and accurate anthology. David Bindman, *The Shadow of the Guillotine: Britain and the French Revolution* (London, 1989) assembles iconographic evidence.

*(D) France*

*(i) The Old Order.* William Doyle, *The Old European Order, 1660–1800* (2nd edn., Oxford, 1992) and Jeremy Black, *Eighteenth Century Europe* (2nd edn., London, 1999) are able overviews. For France, Roland Mousnier, *The Institutions of France under the Absolute Monarchy 1598–1789* (1974–80; trans. Brian Pearce, 2 vols., Chicago, 1979–84) is definitive. See also Pierre Goubert, *L'Ancien Régime* (2 vols., 2nd edn., Paris, 1969); Pierre Goubert and Daniel Roche, *Les Français et l'Ancien Régime* (2 vols., Paris, 1984); Gail Bossenga, *The politics of privilege: old regime and revolution in Lille* (Cambridge, 1991); and James B. Collins, *The State in Early Modern France* (Cambridge, 1995). B. F. Stone, *The Parlement of Paris, 1774–1789* (Durham, N.C., 1981) and idem, *The French Parlements and the Crisis of the Old Regime* (Chapel Hill, 1986) explore aspects of what Burke regarded as France's 'ancient constitution'. David Parker, *Class and State in Ancien Régime France: the road to modernity?* (London, 1996) explores some Anglo-French comparisons; John Lough, *France on the Eve of Revolution: British Travellers' Observations 1763–1788* (London, 1987) helps Burke's reactions to be set in context.

*(ii) The Attack on the Old Order.* Daniel Mornet's *Les Origines intellectuelles de la Révolution française: 1715–1787* (Paris, 1933) adopted an approach which relegated ideas to a subordinate role; this was echoed in (for example) Joan McDonald, *Rousseau and the French Revolution 1762–1791* (London, 1965) and Peter Gay, *The Party of Humanity* (New York, 1964). More recent historians have been retrieving the nature of the Revolution as an ideological conflict, e.g. Keith Baker, *Inventing the French Revolution: Essays on French Political Culture in the Eighteenth Century* (Cambridge, 1990) and T. C. W. Blanning (ed.), *The Rise and Fall of the French Revolution* (Chicago, 1996). Carol Blum, *Rousseau and the Republic of Virtue: The Language of Politics in the French Revolution* (Ithaca, NY, 1986) did much to re-identify its subject as the founder of a new public morality, as Burke had claimed. Norman Hampson, *Will & Circumstance: Montesquieu, Rousseau and the French Revolution* (London, 1983) emphasised the explicit indebtedness of the revolutionaries to these thinkers.

A fundamental reinterpretation of the social dimension of the Enlightenment and its published works began with Ira O. Wade, *The Clandestine Organization and Diffusion of Philosophic Ideas in France from 1700 to 1750* (Princeton, 1938; New York, 1967); it has now won acceptance. See, passim, the work of Robert Darnton: *The Business of Enlightenment: A Publishing History of the Encyclopédie, 1775–1800* (Cambridge, Mass., 1979); idem, *The Literary Underground of the Old Regime* (Cambridge, Mass., 1982); idem, *The Corpus of Clandestine Literature in France, 1769–1789* (New York, 1995); idem, *The Forbidden Best-Sellers of Pre-Revolutionary France* (London, 1996). See also Olivier René Bloch (ed.), *Le Matérialisme du XVIIIe siècle et la littérature clandestine* (Paris, 1982); Roger Chartier, *The Cultural Origins of the French Revolution* (1990; trans. Lydia Cochrane, Durham, NC, 1991), which addresses questions of linkages between culture and political action; Daniel Roche, *Les républicains des lettres: Gens de culture et Lumières au XVIIIᵉ siècle* (Paris, 1988) and idem, *La France des lumières* (Paris, 1993). For the denigration of the monarchy, see Henri d'Alméras, *Marie-Antoinette et les pamphlets royalistes et révolutionnaires* (Paris, [1907]) and Chantal Thomas, *The Wicked Queen: the origins of the myth of Marie-Antoinette* (1989; trans., New York, 1997).

Other distinguished studies of the *philosophes* include J. Q. C. Mackrell, *The Attack on 'Feudalism' in Eighteenth-Century France* (London, 1973); Alan Charles Kors, *D'Holbach's Coterie: An Enlightenment in Paris* (Princeton, 1976); and Harry C. Payne, *The Philosophes and the People* (New Haven, Conn., 1976). John Lough, *The Philosophes and Post-Revolutionary France* (Oxford, 1982) explores their programmes and assesses their impact.

Dale Van Kley, *The Religious Origins of the French Revolution: From Calvin to the Civil Constitution* (New Haven, Conn., 1996) points to the importance of a Jansenist mentality operating via Rousseau.

*(iii) The nobility before the Revolution.* Surveys include John McManners, 'France' in A. Goodwin (ed.), *The European Nobility in the Eighteenth Century* (London, 1953); Guy Chaussinand-Nogaret, *The French nobility in the eighteenth century* (1976; trans. William Doyle, Cambridge, 1985); and François Bluche, *La Vie quotidienne de la noblesse française au XVIII° siècle* (Paris, 1973). For specific studies, see for example Jean Meyer, *La Noblesse bretonne au XVIII° siècle* (2 vols., Paris, 1966) and Robert Forster, *The House of Saulx-Tavanes: Versailles and Burgundy 1700–1830* (Baltimore, 1971).

*(iv) The Church before the Revolution.* John McManners, *French Ecclesiastical Society under the Ancien Régime: a study of Angers in the Eighteenth Century* (Manchester, 1961), more wide-ranging than its title, takes the story to the Civil Constitution of the Clergy in 1791. For a magisterial overview, see McManners, *Church and Society in Eighteenth Century France* (2 vols., Oxford, 1998). For the theological dimension, see Bernard Plongeron, *Théologie et politique au siècle des lumières (1770–1820)* (Geneva, 1973). Social surveys include Bernard Plongeron, *La Vie quotidienne du clergé français au XVIII° siècle* (1974; 2nd edn., Paris, 1988) and Jean Quéniart, *Les Hommes, l'Eglise et Dieu dans la France du XVIII° siècle* (Paris, 1978). Burke's generally favourable view of the higher clergy is confirmed, with qualifications, in Nigel Aston, *The End of an Élite: The French Bishops and the Coming of the Revolution 1786–1790* (Oxford, 1992); for English comparisons, Norman Ravitch, *Sword and Mitre: Government and Episcopate in France and England in the Age of Aristocracy* (The Hague, 1966). The almost complete domination of the episcopate by noble families is shown by John McManners, 'Aristocratic Vocations: The Bishops of France in the 18th Century', *Studies in Church History* 15 (1978), pp. 305–25.

*(v) Taxation and finance.* Important studies include S. E. Harris, *The Assignats* (Cambridge, Mass., 1930); Betty Behrens, 'Nobles, Privileges and Taxes in France at the End of the Ancien Régime', *Economic History Review* 15 (1963), pp. 451–75; Norman Ravitch, 'The Taxing of the Clergy in Eighteenth-Century France', *Church History* 33 (1964), pp. 157–74; J. F. Bosher, *French Finances 1707–1795: From Business to Bureacracy* (Cambridge, 1970); François Hincker, *Les Français devant l'impôt sous l'Ancien Regime* (Paris, 1971); the exchange between G. J. Cavanaugh and Betty Behrens, in *French Historical Studies* 8 (1974), pp. 681–92 and 9 (1976), 521–31; J. G. A. Pocock, 'The Political Economy of Burke's Analysis of the French Revolution', *Historical Journal* 25 (1982), pp. 331–49, reprinted in idem, *Virtue, Com-*

*merce and History* (Cambridge, 1985); and Florin Aftalion, *The French Revolution: an economic interpretation* (1987; trans. Martin Thom, Cambridge, 1990).

*(vi) The Revolution: surveys.* Important modern overviews include: François Furet and Denis Richet, *French Revolution* (1965; trans. Stephen Hardman, London, 1970); D. M. G. Sutherland, *France 1789–1815: Revolution and Counterrevolution* (Oxford, 1986); William Doyle, *The Oxford History of the French Revolution* (Oxford, 1989); and J. F. Bosher, *The French Revolution* (London, 1989). François Furet, *Interpreting the French Revolution* (1978; trans. Elborg Forster, Cambridge, 1981) played a large part in the modern revolution in revolutionary studies. His *Revolutionary France 1770–1880* (1988; trans. Antonia Nevill, Oxford, 1992) is an Olympian summing-up. Recent collections of essays include Colin Lucas (ed.), *Rewriting the French Revolution* (Oxford, 1991) and, most notably, K. M. Baker, C. Lucas, F. Furet and M. Ozouf (eds.), *The French Revolution and the Creation of Modern Political Culture* (4 vols., Oxford, 1987–94).

*(vii) The Revolution: documents and reference.* J. M. Roberts (ed.), *French Revolution Documents*, I (Oxford, 1966) extends to August 1792. François Furet and Mona Ozouf (eds.), *A Critical Dictionary of the French Revolution* (1988; trans. Arthur Goldhammer, Cambridge, Mass., 1989); Samuel F. Scott and Barry Rothaus (eds.), *Historical Dictionary of the French Revolution* (2 vols., Westport, Conn., 1985); Albert Soboul, *Dictionnaire historique de la Révolution française* (ed. Jean-René Suratteau and François Gendron, Paris, 1989) and Lynn Hunt (ed.), *The French Revolution and Human Rights: A Brief Documentary History* (Boston, 1996) are important aids to study.

*(viii) The Revolution: opening stages.* Georges Lefebvre, *The Coming of the French Revolution* (1939; trans. R. R. Palmer, Princeton, 1987) is a Marxist classic, now treated with caution. Modern surveys include: Jean Egret, *The French Prerevolution 1787–1788* (1962; trans. Wesley B. Camp, Chicago, 1977); Michel Vovelle, *The fall of the French monarchy 1787–1792* (1972; trans. Susan Burke, Cambridge, 1984); William Doyle, *Origins of the French Revolution* (1980; 3rd edn., Oxford, 1999); Norman Hampson, *Prelude to Terror: The Constituent Assembly and the Failure of Consensus, 1789–91* (Oxford, 1988); P. M. Jones, *Reform and Revolution in France: The Politics of Transition, 1774–1791* (Cambridge, 1995); and François Furet and Ran Halévi, *La monarchie républicaine: la constitution de 1791* (Paris, 1996).

J. M. Thompson, *English Witnesses of the French Revolution* (Oxford, 1938) and Peter Vansittart (ed.), *Voices of the Revolution* (London, 1989) provide anthologies of reactions. David V. Erdman, *Commerce des Lumières:*

*John Oswald and the British in Paris, 1790–1793* (Columbia, Missouri, 1986) illuminates Anglo-French contacts. For French opinion, Pierre Goubert and Michel Denis, *1789: les Français ont la parole: cahiers de doléances des Etats Généraux* (Paris, 1964); Beatrice Fry Hyslop, *Répertoire critique des cahiers de doléances pour les Etats Généraux de 1789* (Paris, 1933); idem, *A Guide to the General Cahiers of 1789* (New York, 1936). Malcolm Crook, *Elections in the French Revolution: an apprenticeship in democracy, 1789–1799* (Cambridge, 1996) is a statistical study.

French adulation of the example of 1688 has been little studied since Gabriel Bonno, *La Constitution britannique devant l'opinion française de Montesquieu à Bonaparte* (Paris, 1932), but see Edna Hindie LeMay, 'Les modèles anglais et américain à l'Assemblée constituante', *Transactions of the Fifth International Congress on the Enlightenment* II (Oxford, 1980), pp. 872–84. Mitchell B. Garrett, *The Estates General of 1789: The Problems of Composition and Organization* (New York, 1935) is an account of the controversy which followed the summoning of that body over its structure and ordering. On the Estates General see also M. G. Hutt, 'The rôle of the Curés in the Estates General of 1789', *Journal of Ecclesiastical History* 6 (1955), pp. 190–220; James Michael Murphy, Bernard Higonnet and Patrice Higonnet, 'Notes sur la composition de l'Assemblée Constituante', *Annales Historiques de la Révolution Française* 46 (1974), pp. 321–6; Ruth F. Necheles, 'The Curés in the Estates General of 1789', *Journal of Modern History* 46 (1974), pp. 425–44 and Edna Hindie LeMay, 'La Composition de l'Assemblée Nationale Constituante: les hommes de la continuité?', *Revue d'histoire moderne et contemporaine* 24 (1977), pp. 341–63. Harriet B. Applewhite, *Political Alignment in the French National Assembly, 1789–1791* (Baton Rouge, 1993) provided a statistical analysis. Michael P. Fitzsimmons, *The Remaking of France: The National Assembly and the Constitution of 1791* (Cambridge, 1994) and Timothy Tackett, *Becoming a Revolutionary: the deputies of the French National Assembly and the emergence of a revolutionary culture (1789–1790)* (Princeton, 1996) provide overviews.

On the revolution's acceleration, see Jacques Godechot, *The Taking of the Bastille, 14 July 1789* (1965; trans. Jean Stewart, London, 1970); Joseph Durieux, *Les Vainqueurs de la Bastille* (Paris, 1911); Patrick Kessel, *La Nuit du 4 Août 1789* (Paris, 1969); George Armstrong Kelly, 'From Lèse-Majesté to Lèse-Nation' in Kelly, *Mortal Politics in Eighteenth-Century France*, special issue of *Historical Reflections/Réflexions Historiques* 13 (1986), pp. 208–34, and Simon Schama, *Citizens: a chronicle of the French Revolution* (London, 1989).

*(ix) Leading actors featured in Burke's Reflections.* Gene A. Brucker,

*Jean-Sylvain Bailly: Revolutionary Mayor of Paris* (Westport, Conn., 1984); Robert Lacour-Gayet, *Calonne: Financier, Réformateur, Contre-Révolution-naire, 1734–1802* (Paris, 1963); Barbara Luttrell, *Mirabeau* (New York, 1990); Henri Grange, *Les idées de Necker* (Paris, 1974); Robert D. Harris, *Necker: Reform Statesman of the Ancien Regime* (Berkeley, 1979) and *Necker and the Revolution of 1789* (Lanham, 1986); Robert Howell Griffiths, *Le Centre perdu: Malouet et les 'monarchiens' dans la Révolution française* (Grenoble, 1988); Jean Egret, *La Révolution des notables. Mounier et les monarchiens* (Paris, 1950); George Armstrong Kelly, 'The Machine of the Duc d'Orléans and the New Politics', *Journal of Modern History* 51 (1979–80), pp. 667–84; Murray Forsyth, *Reason and Revolution: The Political Thought of the Abbé Sieyès* (Leicester, 1987); William Sewell, Jr., *The Abbé Sieyès and What is the Third Estate?* (Durham, 1994); and L. S. Greenbaum, *Talleyrand, Statesman-Priest* (Washington, 1970).

*(x) The events of 5–6 October 1789.* Albert Mathiez, 'Etude critique sur les journées des 5 et 6 octobre 1789', *Revue historique* 67 (1898), pp. 241–81; 68 (1898), pp. 258–94; 69 (1899), pp. 41–66; George Rudé, 'Deux documents relatifs aux journées d'octobre', *Annales Historique de la Révolution Française* 22 (1950), pp. 76–77; Jacques Godechot, 'Quatre lettres sur les journées de 11–23 juillet et 5–6 octobre 1789', ibid. 42 (1970), pp. 646–56; Pierre Dominique, *Paris enlève le Roi octobre 1789* (Paris, 1973).

*(xi) The role of Paris.* In the series *Nouvelle Histoire de Paris*, see Jean Chagniot, *Paris au XVIII<sup>e</sup> siècle* (Paris, 1988) and Marcel Reinhard, *La Révolution 1789–1799* (Paris, 1971). Other studies which focus on events in Paris include George Rudé, *The Crowd in the French Revolution* (Oxford, 1959); J. T. Gilchrist and W. J. Murray, *The Press in the French Revolution: A Selection of Documents taken from the Press of the Revolution for the years 1789–1794* (London, 1971); Jack Richard Censer, *Prelude to Power: the Parisian Radical Press 1789–1791* (Baltimore, 1976); Michael L. Kennedy, *The Jacobin Clubs in the French Revolution: The First Years* (Princeton, 1982); R. B. Rose, *The Making of the Sans Culottes: democratic ideas and institutions in Paris, 1789–92* (Manchester, 1983) and Barry M. Shapiro, *Revolutionary Justice in Paris, 1789–1790* (Cambridge, 1993).

*(xii) De-Christianisation: the Church in the Revolution.* Older surveys include A. Aulard, *Christianity and the French Revolution* (London, 1927); André Latreille, *L'Eglise catholique et la Révolution française* (2 vols., Paris, 1946–50), which covered 1775–1815; and Jean Leflon, *La crise révolutionnaire, 1789–1846* (Paris, 1949). Jean de Viguerie, *Christianisme et Révolution* (Paris, 1986) and Paul Christophe, *1789, les prêtres dans la Révolution* (Paris, 1986) are modern surveys from the Estates-General to 1801. English readers

may begin with John McManners, *The French Revolution and the Church* (London, 1969) and Michel Vovelle, *The Revolution against the Church: From Reason to the Supreme Being* (1988; trans. Alan José, Cambridge, 1991). Timothy Tackett, *Religion, Revolution and Regional Culture in Eighteenth-Century France: The Ecclesiastical Oath of 1791* (Princeton, 1986) uses the oath as a point of access for a study of the clergy. Charles A. Gliozzo, 'The Philosophes and Religion: Intellectual Origins of the Dechristianisation Movement in the French Revolution', *Church History* 40 (1971), pp. 273–83 and Mona Ozouf, 'De-Christianisation', in François Furet and Mona Ozouf (eds.), *A Critical Dictionary of the French Revolution* (Cambridge, Mass., 1989), pp. 20–32 focus on this theme. Timothy Tackett, 'The West in France in 1789: the religious factor in the origins of counterrevolution', *Journal of Modern History* 54 (1982), pp. 715–45 reveals the religious origins of counter-revolution.

*(xiii) Revolutionary symbolism.* The major studies are Jean Starobinski, *1789: The Emblems of Reason* (1973; trans. Barbara Bray, Charlottesville, 1982); Mona Ozouf, *Festivals and the French Revolution* (1976; trans. Alan Sheridan, Cambridge, Mass., 1988); Maurice Agulhon, *Marianne into battle: Republican imagery and symbolism in France, 1789–1880* (1979; trans. Janet Lloyd, Cambridge, 1981); Ronald Paulson, *Representations of Revolution (1789–1820)* (New Haven, 1983) and Lynn Hunt, *Politics, Culture, and Class in the French Revolution* (Berkeley, 1984).

*(xiv) The impact of revolution on France.* J. L. Talmon, *The Origins of Totalitarian Democracy* (London, 1952) was a key text which presented a cerebral interpretation of its subject without much attention to the practical significance of violence. For a growing appreciation of this theme for 1789–90, see Samuel F. Scott, 'Problems of Law and Order during 1790, the "Peaceful" year of the French Revolution', *American Historical Review* 80 (1975), pp. 859–88; Colin Lucas, 'The Crowd and Politics between *Ancien Régime* and Revolution in France', *Journal of Modern History* 60 (1988), pp. 421–57; Simon Schama, *Citizens: A Chronicle of the French Revolution* (London, 1989); Brian Singer, 'Violence in the French Revolution: Forms of Ingestion/Forms of Expulsion', in Ferenc Fehér (ed.), *The French Revolution and the Birth of Modernity* (Berkeley, 1990); W. D. Edmonds, *Jacobinism and the Revolt of Lyon 1789–1793* (Oxford, 1990) and Simone Bernard-Griffiths, Marie-Claude Chemin and Jean Ehrard (eds.), *Révolution française et 'vandalisme révolutionnaire'* (Oxford, 1992); John Markoff, 'Violence, Emancipation, and Democracy: The Countryside and the French Revolution', *American Historical Review* 100 (1995), pp. 360–86. For a later period, studies include Pierre Carron, *Les Massacres du septembre* (Paris, 1935); Frédéric Blu-

che, *Septembre 1792. Logiques d'un massacre* (Paris, 1986); G. Lefebvre, *La Première Terreur* (Paris, 1952); Stanley Loomis, *Paris in the Terror June 1793–July 1794* (London, 1964); Colin Lucas, *The Structure of the Terror: The Example of Javogues and the Loire* (Oxford, 1973); Donald Greer, *The Incidence of the Terror during the French Revolution: a statistical interpretation* (Cambridge, Mass., 1935); Charles Tilly, *The Vendée* (Cambridge, Mass., 1964); Reynaud Secher, *Le génocide franco-française: La Vendée-Vengée* (Paris, 1986); Jean-Clement Martin, *La Vendée et la France* (Paris, 1987); Maurice Hutt, *Chouannerie and Counter-Revolution* (2 vols., Cambridge, 1983); and Donald Sutherland, *The Chouans* (Oxford, 1982). René Sedillot, *Le coût de la Révolution française* (Paris, 1987) and Jacques Dupâquier and Joseph Goy, 'Révolution et population', chapter 2 of Dupâquier (ed.), *Histoire de la population française* III (Paris, 1988) assess the impact of the Revolution in demographic terms.

For the subversion of the armed forces, see Samuel F. Scott, *The Response of the Royal Army to the French Revolution: The Role and Development of the Line Army 1787–93* (Oxford, 1978); Jean-Paul Bertaud, *The Army of the French Revolution* (1979; trans. R. R. Palmer, Princeton, 1988); Joseph Martray, *La destruction de la marine française par la Révolution* (Paris, 1988); and William S. Cormack, *Revolution and Political Conflict in the French Navy 1789–1794* (Cambridge, 1995). Patrice Higonnet, *Class, Ideology and the Rights of Nobles during the French Revolution* (Oxford, 1981) covers anti-noble persecution during 1789–99. On the *émigrés*, see Donald Greer, *The Incidence of the Emigration during the French Revolution* (Cambridge, Mass., 1951) and Jean Vidalenc, *Les émigrés français, 1789–1825* (Caen, 1963). On revolutionary expropriations, Marcel Marion, *La Vente des biens nationaux pendant la Révolution* (Paris, 1908) was a thorough study that emphasised their vast extent; see also Georges Lefebvre, 'La vente des biens nationaux', in Lefebvre, *Études sur la Révolution française* (Paris, 1954), and P. M. Jones, *The Peasantry in the French Revolution* (Cambridge, 1988). On the distortion of law, see Philippe Sagnac, *La Législation civile de la Révolution française (1789–1804)* (Paris, 1898) and Edmond Seligman, *La Justice en France pendant la Révolution (1789–1792)* (Paris, 1901).

For the ambiguities of natural rights doctrines in practice, see Mitchell B. Garrett, *The French Colonial Question, 1789–1791: Dealings of the Constituent Assembly with Problems Arising from the Revolution in the West Indies* (1916; New York, 1970). Scholarship on the role of women has differed over the impact of the Revolution, e.g. Harriet B. Applewhite and Darline G. Levy (eds.), *Women and Politics in the Age of the Democratic Revolution* (Ann Arbor, Michigan, 1993) and Joan Landes, *Women and the Public Sphere in the Age of the French Revolution* (Ithaca, NY, 1988). Darline Gay Levy, Harriet Branson Applewhite and Mary Durham Johnson (eds.), *Women in Revolutionary Paris 1789–1795* (Urbana, 1979) print documents.

*(E) Burke's European influence*

For Burke's impact overseas, see Rod Preece, 'Edmund Burke and his European Reputation', *The Eighteenth Century* 21 (1980), pp. 255–73; Colin Lucas, 'Edmund Burke and the Émigrés', in *The French Revolution and the Creation of Modern Political Culture*, III (1989), 101–14, which shows Burke's ambiguous relation with them; Yves Chiron, *Edmund Burke et la Révolution française* (Paris, 1987); idem, 'The Influence of Burke's Writings in Post-Revolutionary France', in Crowe (eds.), *Edmund Burke: His Life and Legacy* (1997). For the propaganda war, William James Murray, *The Right Wing Press in the French Revolution 1789–92* (London, 1986). Philip Mansel, *The Court of France 1789–1830* (Cambridge, 1988) showed how it survived. Emmanuel Vingtrinier, *La contre-révolution, première periode, 1789–1791* (2 vols., Paris, 1924–5), Philippe Jules Fernand Baldensperger, *Le movement des idées dans l'émigration française, 1789–1815* (Paris, 1925) and Alphonse Victor Roche, *Les Idées traditionalistes en France de Rivarol à Maurras* (Univ. of Illinois Press, 1937), are now partly superseded by Paul H. Beik, 'The French Revolution seen from the Right: Social Theories in Motion, 1789–1799', *Transactions of the American Philosophical Society* 46 (1956), pp. 1–122, Jacques Godechot, *The Counter Revolution: Doctrine and Action 1789–1804* (1961, trans. Salvator Attanasio, London, 1972), James Roberts, *The Counter-Revolution in France 1787–1830* (New York, 1990), and James L. Osen, *Royalist Political Thought During the French Revolution* (Westport, Conn., 1995).

Frederic Holdsworth, *Joseph de Maistre et l'Angleterre* (Paris, 1935), Béla Menczer (ed.), *Catholic Political Thought 1789–1848* (London, 1952), Dominique Bagge, *Les Idées politiques en France sous la Restauration* (Paris, 1952), W. Jay Reedy, 'Burke and Bonald: Paradigms of Late Eighteenth-Century Conservatism', *Historical Reflections/Réflexions Historiques* 8 (1981), pp. 69–93, David Klinck, *The French Counterrevolutionary Theorist, Louis de Bonald (1754–1840)* (New York, 1996), Richard A. Lebrun, *Throne and Altar: The Religious and Political Thought of Joseph de Maistre* (Ottawa, 1965), idem, *Joseph de Maistre: An Intellectual Militant* (Kingston, Canada, 1988) and Joseph de Maistre, *Considerations on France* (1797; trans. Richard A. Lebrun, Montreal, 1974) show how Burke functioned as a catalyst rather than a framer. Modern surveys include T. C. W. Blanning, 'The role of religion in European counter-revolution 1789–1815', in Derek Beales and Geoffrey

Best (eds.), *History, Society and the Churches: Essays in Honour of Owen Chadwick* (Cambridge, 1985) and Marcel Reinhard, *Religion, Révolution et Contre-Révolution* (Paris, 1960). Linking British and European thinkers is not easy. Bruce Mazlish, *Burke, Bonald and de Maistre: a study in conservatism* (Ann Arbor, 1958), attempted to do so by employing an ideal construct, 'conservatism', which none of them ever addressed.

For the German dimension, see especially T. C. W. Blanning, *Reform and Revolution in Mainz, 1743–1803* (Cambridge, 1974); idem, *The French Revolution in Germany: Occupation and Resistance in the Rhineland 1792–1802* (Oxford, 1983); idem, *The Origins of the French Revolutionary Wars* (London, 1986). Frieda Braune, *Edmund Burke in Deutschland: Ein Beitrag zur Geschichte des historisch-politischen Denkens* (Heidelberg, 1917) began modern attention. See also G. P. Gooch, *Germany and the French Revolution* (London, 1920); Harro de Wet Jensen, *Das Konservative Welt- und staatsbild Edmund Burkes* (Halle, 1934); Reinhold Aris, *History of Political Thought in Germany from 1789 to 1815* (London, 1936); Jacques Droz, *L'Allemagne et la Révolution française* (Paris, 1949), especially part 4, ch. 2, 'L'influence de Burke en Allemagne: Brandes et Rehberg'; Stephan Skalweit, *Burke und Frankreich* (Cologne, 1956); Hans Barth, *The Idea of Order* (trans. E. W. Hankamer and W. M. Newell, Dordrecht, 1960); Klaus Epstein, *The Genesis of German Conservatism* (Princeton, 1966); Bernhard Groethuysen, *Philosophie der Französichen Revolution* (Berlin, 1971); Hans-Gerd Schumann (ed.), *Konservatismus* (Cologne, 1974); Regina Wecker, *Geschichte und Geschichtsverständnis bei Edmund Burke* (Bern and Frankfurt am Main, 1981). Important recent work in German includes Günther Lottes, 'Die Französische Revolution und der moderne politische Konservatismus', in Reinhard Koselleck and Rolf Reichardt (eds.), *Die Französische Revolution als Bruch des gesellschaftlichen Bewusstseins* (Munich, 1988) and Lottes, 'Hegels Schrift über die Reformbill in Kontext des Deutschen Diskurses über Englands Verfassung im 19. Jahrundert', in Christoph Jamme and Elisabeth Weisser-Lohmann (eds.), *Politik und Geschichte: Zu den Intentionen von G. W. F. Hegels Reformbill-Schrift* (Bonn, 1995). H. T. Mason and William Doyle (eds.), *The Impact of the French Revolution on European Consciousness* (Gloucester, 1989) includes Blanning, 'France during the Revolution through German eyes'; Geoffrey Best (ed.), *The Permanent Revolution: the French Revolution and its Legacy 1789–1989* (London, 1988) collects essays on the Revolution's lasting influence.

# REFLECTIONS

## ON THE

# REVOLUTION IN FRANCE,

### AND ON THE

## PROCEEDINGS IN CERTAIN SOCIETIES

## IN LONDON

#### RELATIVE TO THAT EVENT.

### IN A

# LETTER

#### INTENDED TO HAVE BEEN SENT TO A GENTLEMAN

#### IN PARIS.

#### BY THE RIGHT HONOURABLE

# EDMUND BURKE.

———————

## LONDON:

### PRINTED FOR J. DODSLEY, IN PALL-MALL.

#### M.DCC.XC.

[Overleaf: Facsimile of the title page of the first edition of Burke's *Reflections on the Revolution in France*. Courtesy of the Bodleian Library, Oxford.]

[iii] *IT may not be unnecessary to inform the Reader, that the following Reflections had their origin in a correspondence between the Author and a very young gentleman at Paris,*[1] *who did him the honour of desiring his opinion upon the important transactions, which then, and ever since, have so much occupied the attention of all men.*[2] *An answer was written some time in the month of October 1789;*[3] *but it was kept back upon prudential considerations. That letter is alluded to in the beginning of the following sheets. It has been since forwarded to the person to whom it was addressed. The reasons for the delay in sending it were assigned in a short letter*[4] *to the same gentleman. This produced on his part a new and pressing application for the Author's sentiments.*[5]

[1]Charles-Jean-François Depont: see Biographical Guide.

[2]Depont to Burke, 4 November 1789: H. V. F. Somerset, 'A Burke Discovery', *English* 8 (1951), p. 173; Burke, *Correspondence*, VI, p. 31. Depont hailed Burke as 'le Grand homme qui fait trembler les ministres et qui encourage les jeunes Gens amants de la Liberté', and asked Burke a leading question: 'If you will deign to assure him that the French are worthy of being free, that they know how to distinguish liberty from licence, and a legitimate government from a despotic power—if you will deign also to assure him that the Revolution now begun will succeed—proud in your support he will never be beaten down by the discouragement which often follows hope.'

[3]Burke to Depont, [November 1789]: Burke, *Correspondence*, VI, p. 39. Burke evidently misremembered the month of his reply. The letter was Burke's first considered response to the events of the Revolution.

[4]Missing. Burke probably thought that the post was still subject to censorship in France.

[5]Depont to Burke, 29 December 1789: Somerset, 'Burke Discovery', p. 174; Burke, *Correspondence*, VI, p. 59: 'Ah! tell me, you whom I look to as a guide and master, tell me that the events which have taken place have been the necessary consequences of a change which circumstances rendered indispensable! Ah, tell me that I may hope to see my country worthy to enjoy liberty, English liberty!' When Burke finally sent his young admirer a copy of the *Reflections*, the Frenchman was appalled: 'When I took the liberty, last year, of asking your opinion on the political events in France, I had certainly no idea that my letter would lead to the publication of the work you have so kindly sent me. I will even confess that I should never have made the request, had I been able to foresee its effect; and that if I had at that time known your opinions, far from begging you to express them, I should have besought you not to make them public': Depont to Burke, 6 December 1790: Somerset, 'Burke Discovery', p. 175. This letter, translated, was published as a pamphlet with Depont's permission: *Answer to the Reflections of the Right Hon. Edmund Burke. By M. Depont* (London, 1791).

*The Author began a second and more full discussion on the subject. This he had some thoughts of publishing early in the last spring;[6] but the matter gaining upon him, he found that what he had undertaken not only far exceeded the measure of a letter, but that its importance required rather a more detailed consideration than at that time he had any leisure to bestow upon it. However, having thrown down his first thoughts in the form of a letter, and indeed when he sat down to write, having intended [iv] it for a private letter, he found it difficult to change the form of address, when his sentiments had grown into a greater extent, and had received another direction. A different plan, he is sensible, might be more favourable to a commodious division and distribution of his matter.*

'Burke's first public disavowal of the French Revolution came in the House of Commons on 9 February 1790; it was published as as a pamphlet (see Abbreviations). Stanhope replied: 'In your speech, you allude to certain *"wicked persons"* (to use your own elegant expression) "who have shewn," you say, "a strong disposition to imitate the French Spirit of reform;" but, who the persons are, who are glanced at by this *dark* insinuation, it is difficult to determine. But, from the title of another Pamphlet, which an Advertisement in the Papers has announced is speedily to be expected *from you*, it is conjectured, that the Revolution Society in London was in your contemplation when you made that Speech': *A Letter from Earl Stanhope, to the Right Honourable Edmund Burke: Containing a short Answer to his late Speech on the French Revolution* (London, 1790), pp. 20–1. One such advertisement appeared in the *London Chronicle* for 13–16 February 1790: '*In the Press, and speedily will be published,* Reflections on certain Proceedings of the Revolution Society of the 4th of November 1789, concerning the Affairs of France. In a Letter from Mr. Edmund Burke to a Gentleman in Paris. Printed for J. Dodsley, in Pall-mall.'

[1] DEAR SIR,

YOU are pleased to call again, and with some earnestness, for my thoughts on the late proceedings in France. I will not give you reason to imagine, that I think my sentiments of such value as to wish myself to be solicited about them. They are of too little consequence to be very anxiously either communicated or withheld. It was from attention to you, and to you only, that I hesitated at the time, when you first desired to receive them. In the first letter I had the honour to write to you, and which at length I send, I wrote neither for nor from any description of men; nor shall I in this. My errors, if any, are my own. My reputation alone is to answer for them.

You see, Sir, by the long letter I have transmitted to you, that, though I do most heartily wish that France may be animated by a spirit of [2] rational liberty, and that I think you bound, in all honest policy, to provide a permanent body, in which that spirit may reside, and an effectual organ, by which it may act, it is my misfortune to entertain great doubts concerning several material points in your late transactions.

You imagined, when you wrote last, that I might possibly be reckoned among the approvers of certain proceedings in France, from the solemn public seal of sanction they have received from two clubs of gentlemen in London, called the Constitutional Society, and the Revolution Society.

I certainly have the honour to belong to more clubs than one, in which the constitution of this kingdom, and the principles of the glorious Revolution, are held in high reverence;[7] and I reckon myself among the most forward in my zeal for maintaining that constitution and those principles in their utmost purity and vigour. It is because I do so, that I think it necessary for me, that there should be no mistake. Those who cultivate the memory of our revolution, and those who are attached to the constitution of this kingdom, will take good care how they are involved with persons who, under the pretext of zeal

[7]Burke was pleased to be elected to Brooks's in 1783: Burke, *Correspondence*, V, p. 76. By June 1791, with overt distaste, he was to describe a supper there as 'a sort of Academy' for the 'Doctrines' of 'Paine, Priestley, Price, Rouse, Mackintosh, Christie, &ca &ca &ca': ibid., VI, p. 273. Burke was also a member of the Whig Club, founded in 1784 for the Foxite opposition in Parliament; he and forty-two of his supporters resigned from it in February 1793 in a protest against the Club's stance on the French Revolution: ibid., VII, pp. 353–5.

towards the Revolution and constitution, too frequently wander from their true principles; and are ready on every occasion to depart from the firm but cautious and deliberate spirit which produced the one, and which presides in the other. Before I proceed to answer the more material [3] particulars in your letter, I shall beg leave to give you such information as I have been able to obtain of the two clubs which have thought proper, as bodies, to interfere in the concerns of France; first assuring you, that I am not, and that I have never been, a member of either of those societies.

The first, calling itself Constitutional Society, or Society for Constitutional Information, or by some such title, is, I believe, of seven or eight years standing.[8] The institution of this society appears to be of a charitable, and so far of a laudable, nature: it was intended for the circulation, at the expence of the members, of many books, which few others would be at the expence of buying; and which might lie on the hands of the booksellers, to the great loss of an useful body of men. Whether the books so charitably circulated, were ever as charitably read, is more than I know. Possibly several of them have been exported to France; and, like goods not in request here, may with you have found a market. I have heard much talk of the lights to be drawn from books that are sent from hence. What improvements they have had in their passage (as it is said some liquors are meliorated by crossing the sea) I cannot tell: But I never heard a man of common judgment, or the least degree of information, speak a word in praise of the greater part of the publications circulated by that society;[9] nor have their proceedings [4] been accounted, except by some of themselves, as of any serious consequence.

[8]It was founded by Major John Cartwright, John Jebb and Thomas Brand Hollis in April 1780, but in the face of failure had become lethargic by c. 1785: see Eugene Charlton Black, *The Association: British Extraparliamentary Political Organization 1769–1793* (Cambridge, Mass., 1963), ch. 5. The Society was apparently not mentioned in Burke's correspondence before the publication of the *Reflections*; although historians have since given the SCI a leading role in what hindsight identifies as a coherent movement towards parliamentary reform, Burke may hitherto have been hardly aware of its existence. He may not have known of Cartwright's programmatic remark that 'Moderation in practice may be commendable, but moderation in principle is detestable': quoted Black, *The Association*, p. 174. Despite its ostensibly innocent purposes, the SCI, when it met on 27 November 1789 after a summer's break, took its lead from the reinvented Revolution Society, with the membership of which it suspiciously overlapped. This co-operation continued in 1790, and, via Sheridan, drew in the Whig Club. In 1791, the SCI was responsible for the 'energetic promotion' of Paine's *Rights of Man*: Albert Goodwin, *The Friends of Liberty: The English Democratic Movement in the age of the French revolution* (London, 1979), pp. 114–5, 120–4, 177.

[9]The ostensible purpose of the Society was the reprinting and circulation of the

Your National Assembly seems to entertain much the same opinion that I do of this poor charitable club. As a nation, you reserved the whole stock of your eloquent acknowledgments for the Revolution Society;[10] when their fellows in the Constitutional were, in equity, entitled to some share. Since you have selected the Revolution Society as the great object of your national thanks and praises, you will think me excuseable in making its late conduct the subject of my observations. The National Assembly of France[11] has given importance to these gentlemen by adopting them; and they return the favour,

---

Whig classics (Coke, Sidney, Milton, Somers). Burke here distinguished between such unread tomes and the works of more recent authors who made up the greater part of the Society's output (John Cartwright, John Jebb, Capel Lofft, Thomas Northcote, the duke of Richmond, Granville Sharp). By 1783, the Society had linked Richmond's extreme demands for universal suffrage with Northcote's extreme demands for disestablishment.

[10]A Society for Commemorating the Glorious Revolution, usually abbreviated to the Revolution Society, had existed 'for many years' according to Price, 'consisting chiefly of Dissenters' (Price to Lansdowne, 30 October 1788, in Price, *Correspondence*, III, pp. 184–7). The printed 'Rules of the Revolution Society', n.d. (MS 24.90 (1), Dr. Williams's Library, London) reveal a social club, confined to Protestant Dissenters, having as its main aim the relief of impoverished Dissenting ministers. The 'Rules' admit that meetings had been suspended for some time, but its refoundation was not political: 'It is not our wish by this name to be considered as a political Club.' The Club changed profoundly, argued Eugene Black, when it was taken over in 1788 by 'reform veterans' to avoid using 'the old, partially discredited organizations'. 'As the centenary of 1688 approached, veterans of metropolitan extraparliamentary activity saw in the event a fortuitous device to secure the repeal of the Test and Corporation Acts and to revive the movement for radical parliamentary reform': Black, *The Association*, p. 214. For its resuscitation, and the creation of a formal membership list, subscription, committee, minutes and secretary see *An Abstract of the History and Proceedings of the Revolution Society, in London. To which is annexed a copy of the Bill of Rights* ([London], 1789), the Preface dated 1 May 1789. At the first meeting of the Society on 4 November 1788 were present most of the members of the Society for Constitutional Information, and many politically-active Dissenting ministers including Dr. Rees, minister of the Old Jewry (ibid., pp. 8–17). The minute book of the Revolution Society (British Library Add MSS 64814), dating from 1788, claimed (without evidence) a genealogy extending back to the Revolution: the 'Character of King William' allegedly read at each annual meeting appears to be a piece of late eighteenth-century prose (f. 52).

[11]The Estates-General had met at Versailles on 5 May 1789, sitting in its three ancient orders of clergy, nobility and commons. On 17 June the Third Estate, some clergy and a few nobles combined into a single body, which claimed the hitherto-unknown title of the National Assembly. It carried through the legislative reforms of the first stage of the Revolution, approved the draft constitution, and dissolved itself on 30 September 1791 to make way for a new body, the Legislative Assembly.

by acting as a sort of sub-committee in England for extending the principles of the National Assembly.[12] Henceforward we must consider them as a kind of privileged persons; as no inconsiderable members in the diplomatic body. This is one among the revolutions which have given splendour to obscurity, and distinction to undiscerned merit. Until very lately I do not recollect to have heard of this club. I am quite sure that it never occupied a moment of my thoughts; nor, I believe, those of any person out of their own set. I find, upon enquiry, that on the anniversary of the Revolution in 1688, a club of dissenters,[13] but of what denomination I know not, have long had the custom of

[12]Burke was correct. The Appendix to Price's *Discourse*, extended in the third and again in the fourth editions, printed documents which showed these links. At the meeting of the newly politicised Revolution Society in the London Tavern on 4 November 1789, after his sermon, Price proposed an Address to the National Assembly: 'The Society for commemorating the Revolution in Great Britain, disdaining national partialities, and rejoicing in every triumph of liberty and justice over arbitrary power, offer to the National Assembly of France their congratulations on the Revolution in that country, and on the prospect it gives to the two first kingdoms in the world, of a common participation in the blessings of civil and religious liberty. They cannot help adding their ardent wishes of a happy settlement of so important a Revolution, and at the same time expressing the particular satisfaction, with which they reflect on the tendency of the glorious example given in France to encourage other nations to assert the unalienable rights of mankind, and thereby to introduce a general reformation in the governments of Europe, and to make the world free and happy.' The Society passed it unanimously and sent it to the duc de La Rochefoucauld in Paris, asking him to present it to the National Assembly, and 'intimating' that the Revolution Society considered the Assembly 'as acting for the world as well as for the great kingdom it represented' (Price, *Discourse*, Appendix, pp. 13–14). For the Assembly's enthusiastic response, see below. The Revolution Society's address was printed in *Le Moniteur* no. 88 of 10 November 1789, with that paper's comment: 'Jamais hommage ne flatta plus vivement l'Assemblée nationale que ce témoignage éclatant d'estime de la part d'une société aussi illustre par ses lumieres que pas son civisme, d'une société qui comptait parmi ses membres les Price, les Stanhope et une infinité d'autres célebres défenseurs des droits de l'humanité.'

[13]Dissenters had long supported informal commemorations of the Revolution, possibly in reply to the Church's services on 30 January (the execution of Charles I) and 29 May (the restoration of Charles II). This tradition was now exploited by the extreme reformers to take over this yearly gathering and create a 'front organisation'. It was not an effective disguise, however: by 1791 even Fox would 'have nothing to do' with the Revolution Society, which was 'effectively dead': Black, *The Association*, p. 216. The coherence of this older, informal, Dissenting practice has sometimes been overstated. Even its exploiters conceded that 'For a long course of years this institution was chiefly confined to the City of London': *An Abstract of the History and Proceedings of the Revolution Society*, p. 6.

hearing a sermon in one of their [5] churches; and that afterwards they spent the day cheerfully, as other clubs do, at the tavern. But I never heard that any public measure, or political system, much less that the merits of the constitution of any foreign nation, had been the subject of a formal proceeding at their festivals; until, to my inexpressible surprize, I found them in a sort of public capacity, by a congratulatory address, giving an authoritative sanction to the proceedings of the National Assembly in France.

In the antient principles and conduct of the club, so far at least as they were declared, I see nothing to which I, or any sober man, could possibly take exception. I think it very probable, that for some purpose, new members may have entered among them; and that some truly christian politicians, who love to dispense benefits, but are careful to conceal the hand which distributes the dole, may have made them the instruments of their pious designs.[14] Whatever I may have reason to suspect concerning private management, I shall speak of nothing as of a certainty, but what is public.

For one, I should be sorry to be thought, directly or indirectly, concerned in their proceedings. I certainly take my full share, along with the rest of the world, in my individual and private capacity, in speculating on what has been done, or is doing, on the public stage; in any place antient or modern; in the republic of Rome, or the republic of Paris; but having no [6] general apostolical mission, being a citizen of a particular state, and being bound up, in a considerable degree, by its public will, I should think it, at least improper and irregular, for me to open a formal public correspondence with the actual government of a foreign nation, without the express authority of the government under which I live.[15]

I should be still more unwilling to enter into that correspondence, under any thing like an equivocal description, which to many, unacquainted with our usages, might make the address, in which I joined, appear as the act of persons in some sort of corporate capacity, acknowledged by the laws of this kingdom, and authorized to speak the sense of some part of it. On account of the ambiguity and uncertainty of unauthorized general descriptions, and of the deceit which may be practised under them, and not from mere formality, the House of Commons would reject the most sneaking petition for the most

[14]Burke, as a practicing politician, was well aware that such bodies could be revitalised by 'private management', the covert aid of the Whig nobility's immense wealth. The phrase 'truly christian' was an ironic allusion to their theological heterodoxy or infidelity.

[15]Burke presumably believed that his own actions during the American Revolution did not come within this definition: Cone, *Burke*, I, pp. 299, 331–5.

trifling object, under that mode of signature to which you have thrown open the folding-doors of your presence chamber,[16] and have ushered into your National Assembly, with as much ceremony and parade, and with as great a bustle of applause, as if you had been visited by the whole representative majesty of the whole English nation. If what this society has thought proper to send forth had been a piece of argument, it would have signified little whose argument it was. It would be neither the more nor [7] the less convincing on account of the party it came from. But this is only a vote and resolution. It stands solely on authority; and in this case it is the mere authority of individuals, few of whom appear. Their signatures ought, in my opinion, to have been annexed to their instrument.[17] The world would then have the means of knowing how many they are; who they are; and of what value their opinions may be, from their personal abilities, from their knowledge, their experience, or their lead and authority in this state. To me, who am but a plain man, the proceeding looks a little too refined, and too ingenious; it has too much the air of a political stratagem, adopted for the sake of giving, under an high-sounding name, an importance to the public declarations of this club, which, when the matter came to be closely inspected, they did not altogether so well deserve. It is a policy that has very much the complexion of a fraud.[18]

[16]Burke's objection was that the Revolution Society pretended to be an official, national body, but had no such standing. Nor would the House of Commons accept an anonymous petition, not signed by individuals. Burke's implication that petitions carried more weight if presented by corporate bodies was an overstatement that still contained an element of truth in 1790, but ceased to be the case as petitioning became part of a developing popular politics. The numbers of petitions presented to Parliament grew exponentially: in 1785–9, 880; 1801–5, 1,026; 1811–15, 4,498; 1827–31, 24,492: *Report from Select Committee on Public Petitions* (London, 1832), p. 10. The corporation of the City of London had the special privilege of presenting petitions at the bar of the House of Commons by its sheriffs rather than by a Member, but every individual also had a right to petition, subject only to the Act of 1661 ('An Act against Tumults and Disorders, upon Pretence of preparing or presenting publick Petitions, or other Addresses to his Majesty or the Parliament', 13 Car. II, s. 1, c. 5). This made criminal the soliciting of more than twenty signatures to a petition calling 'for Alteration of Matters established by Law in Church or State', unless the petition received the sanction of three magistrates, or the majority of a Grand Jury, or, in London, of the Lord Mayor, Aldermen and Common Council.

[17]The Society's Address to the National Assembly was signed only by its chairman, Earl Stanhope.

[18]The Society was not deterred from continuing its exchanges with revolutionary groups in France; these mutual congratulations even grew in numbers and euphoria. By 1792, the Society had exchanged encouraging addresses with at least fifty-six local French societies. In response to Burke's *Appeal from the New to the Old Whigs*, the

I flatter myself that I love a manly, moral, regulated liberty[19] as well as any gentleman of that society, be he who he will; and perhaps I have given as good proofs of my attachment to that cause, in the whole course of my public con-. duct. I think I envy liberty as little as they do, to any other nation. But I cannot stand forward, and give praise or blame to any thing which relates to human actions, and human concerns, on a simple view of the object, as it stands stripped of every relation, in all the nakedness and solitude of metaphysical abstraction.[20] Circumstances [8] (which with some gentlemen pass for nothing) give in reality to every political principle its distinguishing colour, and discriminating effect. The circumstances are what render every civil and political scheme beneficial or noxious to mankind. Abstractedly speaking, government,[21] as well as liberty, is good; yet could I, in common sense, ten years ago, have felicitated France on her enjoyment of a government (for she then had a government) without enquiry what the nature of that government was, or how it was administered? Can I now congratulate the same nation upon its freedom? Is it because liberty in the abstract may be classed amongst the blessings of mankind, that I am seriously to felicitate a madman, who has escaped from the protecting restraint and wholesome darkness of his cell, on his restoration to the enjoyment of light and liberty? Am I to congratulate an highwayman and murderer, who has broke prison, upon the recovery of his natural rights? This would be to act over again the scene of the criminals condemned to the gallies, and their heroic deliverer, the metaphysic Knight of the Sorrowful Countenance.[22]

---

Society published the main texts of these exchanges, to February 1792, in *The Correspondence of the Revolution Society in London, with the National Assembly, and with Various Societies of the Friends of Liberty in France and England* (London, 1792). For the French dimension see Veitch, *Genesis of Parliamentary Reform*, pp. 126–59, 357–9; E. Pariset, 'La Société de la Révolution de Londres dans ses rapports avec Burke et l'Assemblée Constituante', *La Révolution Française* 29 (1895), pp. 297–325. Veitch suggested that the 'real importance' of the Revolution Society 'seems to end with the cessation of its French correspondence' in February 1792: *Genesis*, p. 159.

[19]Cf. Burke's closing discussion of liberty, *Reflections*, p. [352].

[20]For one academic claim that Burke was not anti-metaphysical, but that his implicit metaphysics is to be understood in the context of an Aristotelian and Thomist tradition of natural law, see Bibliography, B iii. Whatever the truth of this argument, Burke certainly came to use the term 'metaphysics' in a derogatory sense for the doctrines associated with the French Revolution, e.g. *Reflections*, pp. [86, 90, 134, 272–4, 313, 321, 325, 344, 348].

[21]I.e. the condition of living under government.

[22]Miguel de Cervantes Saavedra (1547–1616), *The History of the Valorous and Witty Knight-Errant, Don Quixote Of the Mancha*, trans. Thomas Shelton (4 vols., London, 1740), Book III, chapter 8. Don Quixote here frees a chain-gang of prisoners

When I see the spirit of liberty in action, I see a strong principle at work; and this, for a while, is all I can possibly know of it. The wild *gas*, the fixed air[23] is plainly broke loose: but we ought to suspend our judgment until the first effervescence is a little subsided, till the liquor is cleared, and until we see something deeper [9] than the agitation of a troubled and frothy surface. I must be tolerably sure, before I venture publicly to congratulate men upon a blessing, that they have really received one. Flattery corrupts both the receiver and the giver; and adulation is not of more service to the people than to kings. I should therefore suspend my congratulations on the new liberty of France, until I was informed how it had been combined with government; with public force; with the discipline and obedience of armies; with the collection of an effective and well-distributed revenue; with morality and religion; with the solidity of property; with peace and order; with civil and social manners. All these (in their way) are good things too; and, without them, liberty is not a benefit whilst it lasts, and is not likely to continue long. The effect of liberty to individuals is, that they may do what they please. We ought to see what it will please them to do, before we risque congratulations, which may be soon turned into complaints. Prudence would dictate this in the case of separate insulated private men; but liberty, when men act in bodies, is *power*. Considerate people before they declare themselves will observe the use which is made of *power*; and particularly of so trying a thing as *new* power in *new* persons, of whose principles, tempers, and dispositions, they have little or no experi-

---

being led under guard to serve their sentences in the gallies, invoking high ideals of liberty and ignoring their crimes which, in turn, they narrate. The criminals then refuse Quixote's request to present themselves before Lady Dulcinea of Toboso, to prove the knight's generosity; instead they turn on Quixote, beat him, and rob him, leaving him 'most discontent to see himself so much misused by those very same to whom he had done so much Good' (ibid., I, p. 194). Burke owned a copy of this edition: *LC*, p. 4.

[23]'Fixed air' was carbon dioxide, as observed in the bubbles of mineral water. 'The pressure of the atmosphere assists very considerably in keeping fixed air confined in water; for in an exhausted receiver [i.e. a vacuum], Pyrmont water will absolutely boil, by the copious discharge of its air': Joseph Priestley, *Experiments and Observations on Different Kinds of Air* (3 vols., London, 1775–7), I, pp. 25–43, at 34. Burke knew Priestley before 1770, saw him occasionally through the 1780s, and visited his laboratory in Birmingham in 1782. Priestley used the term 'fixed air' in a letter to Burke of 11 December 1782: Burke, *Correspondence*, VI, pp. 53–4. Burke owned a work listed as *Priestley's Discoveries* (LC MS fo. 33) and intervened in September 1789 to obtain permission for Priestley to dedicate a new edition of the *Experiments and Observations* to the Prince of Wales: Burke, *Correspondence*, VI, pp. 14–15. Burke openly confessed to Fox the need to curry the favour of the Dissenters in the approaching General Election.

ence, and in situations where those who appear the most stirring in the scene may possibly not be the real movers.[24][10]

All these considerations however were below the transcendental dignity of the Revolution Society. Whilst I continued in the country, from whence I had the honour of writing to you, I had but an imperfect idea of their transactions. On my coming to town,[25] I sent for an account of their proceedings, which had been published by their authority, containing a sermon of Dr. Price,[26] with the Duke de Rochefaucault's[27] and the Archbishop of Aix's[28] letter, and several

[24]The duc d'Orléans was widely believed to be playing a covert role in inciting disorder as a prelude to seizing the throne himself (see *Reflections*, p. [69]). Burke had an accurate sense that all was not as it seemed in the conduct of the Revolution.

[25]Burke remained at Beaconsfield during the autumn of 1789, when Parliament did not sit. He was still there on 12 January 1790, and came to London some time before 23 January (*Correspondence*, VI, pp. 67, 76). Price's sermon on 4 November 1789 had been published on 5 December (Price, *Correspondence*, III, p. 260) and produced a controversy in the press. Parliament reassembled for the King's speech on 21 January 1790.

[26]As Burke's footnotes made clear, he bought the third edition (see Abbreviations): the successive editions marked its success. As printed, it was a longer version of Price's actual sermon. At its meeting on 4 November 1789, the Society had resolved 'That the Thanks of the Meeting be given to the Rev. Dr. Price, for his excellent Sermon preached this day, and that he be requested to publish the same, together with *that part* which, for want of time and strength, he did not deliver': *The Correspondence of the Revolution Society*, pp. 3–4.

[27]See Biographical Guide. The duc de La Rochefoucauld (to Price, 2 December 1789, in Price, *Discourse*, Appendix, p. 14) claimed that the National Assembly had received the Address with 'lively applause'; they had 'seen in that address the dawn of a glorious day, in which two nations who have always esteemed one another notwithstanding their political divisions and the diversity of their governments, shall contract an ultimate union, founded on the similarity of their opinions and their common enthusiasm for liberty'. From an early date, cosmopolitan Frenchmen announced their goal of an ever-closer union of their reluctant neighbours.

[28]See Biographical Guide. The Archbishop of Aix, President of the National Assembly, to Earl Stanhope, as Chairman of the Revolution Society, 5 December 1789, in Price, *Discourse*, Appendix, p. 19, claimed: 'The National Assembly discovers in the Address of the Revolution Society of England, those principles of universal benevolence which ought to bind together, in all countries of the world, the true friends to the happiness and liberty of mankind.' Other replies followed, equally euphoric, from the patriotic societies of Dijon and Lille. In the Society's answer to the Dijon society, Stanhope told its president that the English society 'concur heartily in the wishes expressed by him, and the other members of the Patriotic Club, of a FRATERNAL UNION between this country and theirs. Among the benefits of the revolution in FRANCE they reckon its tendency to produce such an union ...' (p. 32).

other documents annexed. The whole of that publication, with the manifest design of connecting the affairs of France with those of England, by drawing us into an imitation of the conduct of the National Assembly, gave me a considerable degree of uneasiness. The effect of that conduct upon the power, credit, prosperity, and tranquillity of France, became every day more evident. The form of constitution to be settled, for its future polity, became more clear. We are now in a condition to discern, with tolerable exactness, the true nature of the object held up to our imitation. If the prudence of reserve and decorum dictates silence in some circumstances, in others prudence of an higher order may justify us in speaking our thoughts. The beginnings of confusion with us in England are at present feeble enough; but with you, we have seen an infancy still more feeble, growing by moments into a strength to heap mountains upon mountains,[29] and to wage war with Heaven itself. Whenever our neighbour's house is on fire, it [11] cannot be amiss for the engines to play a little on our own. Better to be despised for too anxious apprehensions, than ruined by too confident a security.

Solicitous chiefly for the peace of my own country, but by no means unconcerned for your's, I wish to communicate more largely, what was at first intended only for your private satisfaction. I shall still keep your affairs in my eye, and continue to address myself to you. Indulging myself in the freedom of epistolary intercourse, I beg leave to throw out my thoughts, and express my feelings, just as they arise in my mind, with very little attention to formal method. I set out with the proceedings of the Revolution Society; but I shall not confine myself to them. Is it possible I should? It looks to me as if I were in a great crisis, not of the affairs of France alone, but of all Europe, perhaps of more than Europe. All circumstances taken together, the French revolution is the most astonishing that has hitherto happened in the world.[30] The most wonderful things are brought about in many instances by means the most absurd and ridiculous; in the most ridiculous modes; and, apparently, by the most contemptible instruments.[31] Every thing seems out of nature in this

[29]See Edmund Waller, *On the Head of a Stag*: 'Heav'n with these engines had been scal'd, / When mountains heap'd on mountains fail'd.' Elijah Fenton (ed.), *The Works of Edmund Waller, Esq; In Verse and Prose* (London, 1744), p. 85; cf. Virgil, *Georgics*, I, 281. Burke owned a copy of the 1729 edition of Waller's *Works: LC*, p. 25; LC MS, fo. 33.

[30]In European usage until the 1790s, a 'revolution' was a reversal of fortune or a sudden change; it was judged not by any structural or stadial characteristics but by the degree to which it astonished the observer.

[31]'The Politicians have long observed that the greatest Events may be often traced back to very trivial Causes, and that a petty Competition or casual Friendship, the Pru-

*mixing*        *mixing of social classes*

strange chaos of levity and ferocity, and of all sorts of crimes jumbled together with all sorts of follies. In viewing this monstrous tragi-comic scene, the most opposite passions necessarily succeed, and sometimes mix [12] with each other in the mind; alternate contempt and indignation; alternate laughter and tears; alternate scorn and horror. ]        *how are these alternate?*

It cannot however be denied, that to some this strange scene appeared in quite another point of view. Into them it inspired no other sentiments than those of exultation and rapture. They saw nothing in what has been done in France, but a firm and temperate exertion of freedom; so consistent, on the whole, with morals and with piety, as to make it deserving not only of the secular applause of dashing Machiavelian politicians, but to render it a fit theme for all the devout effusions of sacred eloquence.

On the forenoon of the 4th of November last, Doctor Richard Price, a non-conforming minister of eminence, preached at the dissenting meeting-house of the Old Jewry,[32] to his club or society, a very extraordinary miscella-neous sermon, in which there are some good moral and religious sentiments, and not ill expressed, mixed up in a sort of porridge of various political opinions and reflections: but the revolution in France is the grand ingredient in the cauldron. I consider the address transmitted by the Revolution Society to the National Assembly, through Earl Stanhope,[33] as originating in the principles of the sermon, and as a corollary from them. It was moved by the preacher of that discourse. It was passed by those who came reeking from the effect of the

---

dence of a Slave, or the Garrulity of a Woman have hindered or promoted the most important Schemes, and hastened or retarded the Revolutions of Empire': Samuel Johnson, *The Rambler* 141 (23 July 1751), p. 839. Johnson correctly reported linguistic usage: this was the prevalent English and French sense of 'revolution' until the 1790s. Despite his anticipations of the way in which events in France were to reify 'revolution', Burke still grappled with the power of contingency: 'It is often impossible, in these political enquiries, to find any proportion between the apparent force of any moral causes we may assign and their known operation. We are therefore obliged to deliver up that operation to mere chance, or more piously (perhaps more rationally) to the occasional interposition and irresistible hand of the Great Disposer.' What seemed on the outside an 'intricate plot' was 'the awful drama of Providence, now acting on the moral theatre of the world': Burke, *Two Letters ... on the Proposals for Peace*, pp. 1–4.

[32]The Presbyterian meeting house in the Old Jewry, a street between Gresham Street and the Poultry, was built in 1701. From 1759 to the incumbent in 1789, Abraham Rees, the ministers had been 'acknowledged Arians', a trend perhaps begun by Richard Price, who had been an assistant there in 1744: Walter Wilson, *The History and Antiquities of Dissenting Churches and Meeting Houses, in London, Westminster and Southwark* (4 vols., London, 1808–14), II, pp. 305–6.

[33]See Biographical Guide.

sermon, without any censure or qualification, expressed or implied. [13] If, however, any of the gentlemen concerned shall wish to separate the sermon from the resolution, they know how to acknowledge the one, and to disavow the other. They may do it: I cannot.

For my part, I looked on that sermon as the public declaration of a man much connected with literary caballers, and intriguing philosophers; with political theologians, and theological politicians, both at home and abroad.[34] I know they set him up as a sort of oracle; because, with the best intentions in the world, he naturally *philippizes*,[35] and chaunts his prophetic song in exact unison with their designs.

That sermon is in a strain which I believe has not been heard in this kingdom, in any of the pulpits which are tolerated or encouraged in it, since the year 1648, when a predecessor of Dr. Price, the Reverend Hugh Peters,[36] made the vault of the king's own chapel at St. James's ring with the honour and privilege of the Saints, who, with the "high praises of God in their mouths, and a *two*-edged sword in their hands, were to execute judgment on the heathen, and punishments upon the *people*; to bind their *kings* with chains, and

---

[34]For Price's membership of 'Shelburne's retinue of radical philosophers' from the 1770s, see Peter Brown, *The Chathamites* (London, 1967), pp. 111–86 and Derek Jarrett, *The Begetters of Revolution: England's involvement with France, 1759–1789* (London, 1973), pp. 130–1, 283. Price had been briefed on events in Paris since January 1789 by Thomas Jefferson, the American Ambassador to France; Price sent a copy of his *Discourse* to another American correspondent, John Adams: Thomas, *Price*, pp. 294–5, 303–4.

[35]"To favour, or take the side of, Philip of Macedon … to speak or write as one is corruptly 'inspired' or influenced': *OED*.

[36]See Biographical Guide. At his trial in 1660 several witnesses testified to his sermon at St James's chapel on 28 January 1648, e.g. Walker: 'One Sunday after the King was first brought to his tryal, out of curiosity, I went to hear Mr. *Peters* at *Whitehall*, after he hath made a long prayer, saith he, I have prayed and preached these twenty years, and now I may say, with old *Symeon, Lord now lettest thou thy servant depart in peace, for mine eyes have seen thy salvation,* Afterward he speaks of the Text, of *binding their Kings in chains,* &c. then much reviled the King'; Thomas Tongue testified: 'Upon the 28. of *Jan.* 1648. next day after sentence of the King, I heard *Peters* preach upon this Text in S. *James's* Chappel, 149 *Psal.* 6, 7, 8, 9 verses. *Let the high praises* of God be in their mouth, and a two edged sword *in their hands*, to execute vengeance upon the heathen, and punishments *upon the people,* To bind their Kings with chains, and their Nobles with *fetters of iron*': *An Exact and most Impartial Accompt Of the Indictment, Arraignment, Trial, and Judgement (according to Law) of nine and twenty Regicides, the Murtherers Of His Late Sacred Majesty* (London, 1660), pp. 153–84, at 168, 170, 179–80. Peters's only reply to these allegations was 'These are but single witnesses.'

their *nobles* with fetters of iron."[37] Few harangues from the pulpit, except in the days of your league in France,[38] or in the days of our solemn league and covenant[39] in England, have ever breathed less of the spirit of moderation than [14] this lecture in the Old Jewry. Supposing, however, that something like moderation were visible in this political sermon; yet politics and the pulpit are terms that have little agreement. No sound ought to be heard in the church but the healing voice of Christian charity. The cause of civil liberty and civil government gains as little as that of religion by this confusion of duties. Those who quit their proper character, to assume what does not belong to them, are, for the greater part, ignorant both of the character they leave, and of the character they assume. Wholly unacquainted with the world in which they are so fond of meddling, and inexperienced in all its affairs, on which they pronounce with so much confidence, they have nothing of politics but the passions they excite. Surely the church is a place where one day's truce ought to be allowed to the dissensions and animosities of mankind.

This pulpit style, revived after so long a discontinuance, had to me the air of novelty, and of a novelty not wholly without danger.[40] I do not charge this danger equally to every part of the discourse. The hint given to a noble and reverend lay-divine,[41] who is supposed high in office in one of our universi-

---

[37]Psalm cxlix. [B] 'Let the saints be joyful in glory: let them sing aloud upon their beds. Let the high praises of God be in their mouth, and a two-edged sword in their hand; To execute vengeance upon the heathen, and punishments upon the people: To bind their kings with chains, and their nobles with fetters of iron; To execute upon them the judgement written: this honour have all his saints.'

[38]The League was an alliance of French Catholics in 1585, led by the Guises, to preserve their religion and prevent the accession to the throne of France of Henry of Navarre. The political preaching of the Leaguers incited the assassination of Henri III in 1589.

[39]A number of Scots documents in the sixteenth century, especially the National Covenant of 1581, affirmed a zealous commitment to Presbyterian doctrine and hostility to Rome. Imposed on all Scots, it was again subscribed in 1590 and 1596, revived in 1638 to resist the imposition of an English liturgy, and redrafted in 1643 as the Solemn League and Covenant as the price of Scots' support for the Westminster Parliament in the civil war. It promised 'to reform religion in the Church of England according to God's Holy Word'. The Covenants were declared to be unlawful oaths in 1662.

[40]Anglican clergy regularly preached on political questions, but in an increasingly emollient tone as the century progressed.

[41]The 3rd duke of Grafton, Chancellor of Cambridge University: see Biographical Guide. Grafton's pamphlet entitled *Hints, &c.*, published just before George III's illness, withdrawn and reissued in a revised second edition after the king's recovery, was a recall to religious observance, especially by the social elite, but argued implausibly that the liturgy and articles were the chief obstacles to this: 'the church loses the credit,

ties,[42] and to other lay-divines "of *rank* and literature,"[43] may be proper and seasonable, though somewhat new. If the noble *Seekers*[44] should find nothing to satisfy their pious fancies [15] in the old staple[45] of the national church, or in all the rich variety to be found in the well-assorted warehouses of the dissenting congregations, Dr. Price advises them to improve upon nonconformity; and to set up, each of them, a separate meeting-house upon his own particular principles.[46] It is somewhat remarkable that this reverend divine should be so earnest for setting up new churches, and so perfectly indifferent concerning the doctrine which may be taught in them. His zeal is of a curious character. It is not for the propagation of his own opinions, but of any opinions. It is not for the diffusion of truth, but for the spreading of contradiction. Let the noble teachers but dissent, it is no matter from whom or from

---

and the nation the advantage, that would arise from the example of a very large number of persons of the best character and purest principles of religion, who are restrained by their consciences from joining in our public worship' because of the 'ill-founded and unscriptural' elements which it still contained (p. 3). Despite his tone of patrician urbanity, Grafton like other Unitarians made use of the concepts of 'bigotry', 'ignorance' and 'priestcraft' (e.g. pp. 44–5).

[42]Discourse on the Love of our Country, Nov. 4, 1789, by Dr. Richard Price, 3d edition, p. 17 and 18. [B] Price had written (pp. 16–17): 'I hope you will not mistake what I am now saying, or consider it as the effect of my prejudices as a Dissenter from the established church. The complaint I am making, is the complaint of many of the wisest and best men in the established church itself, who have been long urging the necessity of a revisal of its Liturgy and Articles. [footnote:] See a pamphlet ascribed to a great name, and which would dignify any name, entitled, *Hints, &c submitted to the serious Attention of the Clergy, Nobility, and Gentry, newly assembled. By a Layman, a Friend to the true Principles of the Constituion in Church and State, and to Civil and Religious Liberty.*' ['assembled' *sc.* 'associated']

[43]Burke may be alluding to Shelburne, for whom see Biographical Guide.

[44]Seekers: an early seventeenth-century sect which flourished in the 1640s and 50s. They held that no true Church existed, the then Church having been captured by the spirit of Antichrist; they looked for the foundation of a new Church by new Apostles or Prophets. The term 'Seekers' was generally used of those who suspended formal observances, awaiting a new light.

[45]Staple: 'A town or place, appointed by royal authority, in which was a body of merchants having the exclusive right of purchase of certain classes of goods destined for export; also, the body of merchants so privileged': OED.

[46]"Those who dislike that mode of worship which is prescribed by public authority ought, if they can find *no* worship *out* of the church which they approve, *to set up a separate worship for themselves*; and by doing this, and giving an example of a rational and manly worship, men of *weight* from their *rank* and literature may do the greatest service to society and the world." P. 18. Dr. Price's Sermon. [B] 'and literature' *sc.* 'or literature'.

what. This great point once secured, it is taken for granted their religion will be rational and manly. I doubt whether religion would reap all the benefits which the calculating divine computes from this "great company of great preachers." It would certainly be a valuable addition of non-descripts to the ample collection of known classes, genera and species, which at present beautify the *hortus siccus* of dissent.[47] A sermon from a noble [16] duke, or a noble marquis, or a noble earl, or baron bold, would certainly increase and diversify the amusements of this town, which begins to grow satiated with the uniform round of its vapid dissipations.[48] I should only stipulate that these new *Mess-Johns*[49] in robes and coronets should keep some sort of bounds in the democratic and levelling principles which are expected from their titled pulpits. The new evangelists will, I dare say, disappoint the hopes that are conceived of them. They will not become, literally as well as figuratively, polemic divines, nor be disposed so to drill their congregations that they may, as in former blessed times,[50] preach their doctrines to regiments of dragoons, and corps of infantry and artillery.[51] Such arrangements, however favourable to the cause of compulsory freedom, civil and religious, may not be equally conducive to the national tranquillity. These few restrictions I hope are no great stretches of intolerance, no very violent exertions of despotism.

But I may say of our preacher, "*utinam nugis tota illa dedisset tempora sævitiae.*"[52]—All things in this his fulminating bull are not of so innoxious a tendency. His doctrines affect our constitution in its vital parts. He tells the Revolution Society, in this political sermon, that his majesty "is almost the *only* lawful king in the world, because the *only* one who owes his crown to the *choice of his people.*"[53] As to the kings of *the world*, all of whom (except one) this archpontiff of the *rights of men*, with all the [17] plenitude, and with more than the boldness of the papal deposing power in its meridian fervour of

[47]Hortus siccus: 'An arranged collection of dried plants': OED. Burke's remark refers to the spiritual aridity by the 1790s of much of 'Old Dissent', the congregations of Presbyterians, Congregationalists and Baptists who traced their origins to the seventeenth century.

[48]The London 'season'. Its repetitiousness was often remarked on.

[49]A derogatory nickname for a Scots Presbyterian minister: 'Mess' was a corruption of 'Magister'.

[50]The Great Rebellion of the 1640s.

[51]Cromwell's New Model Army had employed such zealots as chaplains.

[52]'And yet would that he [the tyrannical emperor Domitian] had rather given to follies such as these all those days of cruelty when he robbed the city of its noblest and choicest souls, with none to punish or avenge!': Juvenal, Satires, IV, 150–1.

[53]Price, Discourse, p. 25.

the twelfth century,[54] puts into one sweeping clause of ban and anathema, and proclaims usurpers by circles of longitude and latitude, over the whole globe, it behoves them to consider how they admit into their territories these apostolic missionaries, who are to tell their subjects they are not lawful kings. That is their concern. It is ours, as a domestic interest of some moment, seriously to consider the solidity of the *only* principle upon which these gentlemen acknowledge a king of Great Britain to be entitled to their allegiance.

This doctrine, as applied to the prince now on the British throne, either is nonsense, and therefore neither true nor false, or it affirms a most unfounded, dangerous, illegal, and unconstitutional position. According to this spiritual doctor of politics, if his majesty does not owe his crown to the choice of his people, he is no *lawful* king. Now nothing can be more untrue than that the crown of this kingdom is so held by his majesty. Therefore if you follow their rule, the king of Great Britain, who most certainly does not owe his high office to any form of popular election, is in no respect better than the rest of the gang of usurpers, who reign, or rather rob, all over the face of this our miserable world, without any sort of right or title to the allegiance of their people. The policy of this general doctrine, so qualified, is evident enough.[55] [18] The propagators of this political gospel are in hopes their abstract principle (their principle that a popular choice is necessary to the legal existence of the sovereign magistracy) would be overlooked whilst the king of Great Britain was not affected by it. In the mean time the ears of their congregations would be gradually habituated to it, as if it were a first principle admitted without dispute. For the present it would only operate as a theory, pickled in the preserving juices of pulpit eloquence, and laid by for future use. *Condo et compono quæ mox depromere possim.*[56] By this policy, whilst our government is soothed with a reservation in its favour, to which it has no claim, the security, which it has in common with all governments, so far as opinion is security, is taken away.

Thus these politicians proceed, whilst little notice is taken of their doc-

[54]Pope Innocent III (1198–1216) excommunicated King John, declared him deposed, and invited the king of France to take the throne of England. Opposition to papal claims of a deposing power became a steadily more important element of England's self-definition from the early sixteenth century.

[55]Burke and his critics agreed that authority had often begun in conquest or usurpation. Burke's point was that unless long possession identified a prescriptive right, no title to property or power could be secure. His opponents were driven to the impractical extreme of denying all authority without the consent of the governed.

[56]'I am putting by and setting in order the stores on which I may some day draw': Horace, *Epistles*, Book I, i, 12.

trines; but when they come to be examined upon the plain meaning of their words and the direct tendency of their doctrines, then equivocations and slippery constructions come into play. When they say the king owes his crown to the choice of his people and is therefore the only lawful sovereign in the world, they will perhaps tell us they mean to say no more than that some of the king's predecessors have been called to the throne by some sort of choice; and therefore he owes his crown to the choice of his people. Thus, by a miserable subterfuge, they hope to render their proposition safe, by rendering it [19] nugatory. They are welcome to the asylum they seek for their offence; since they take refuge in their folly. For, if you admit this interpretation, how does their idea of election differ from our idea of inheritance?[57] And how does the settlement of the crown in the Brunswick line derived from James the first,[58] come to legalize our monarchy, rather than that of any of the neighbouring countries? At some time or other, to be sure, all the beginners of dynasties were chosen by those who called them to govern.[59] There is ground enough for the opinion that all the kingdoms of Europe were, at a remote period, elective, with more or fewer limitations in the objects of choice; but whatever kings might have been here or elsewhere, a thousand years ago, or in whatever manner the ruling dynasties of England or France may have begun, the King of Great Britain is at this day king by a fixed rule of succession, according to the laws of his country; and whilst the legal conditions of the compact of sovereignty are performed by him (as they are performed) he holds his crown in contempt of the choice of the Revolution Society,[60] who have not a single vote for a king amongst them, either individually or collectively; though I make no doubt they would soon erect themselves into an electoral college,[61] if things were ripe to give effect to their claim. His majesty's heirs and successors, each in his time and order, will come to the crown with [20] the same contempt of their choice with which his majesty has succeeded to that he wears.

[57]Burke's critics seized on such Whig remarks and used them in a sense opposite to Burke's.

[58]See *Reflections*, pp. [32–3].

[59]By this throwaway line, potentially of immense significance, Burke disclosed his indelibly Whig position.

[60]Burke correctly observed that no genuine element of popular choice entered into the legal rule of succession to the English throne. Paine glossed this passage: 'It is not the Revolution Society that Mr. Burke means; it is the Nation, as well in its *original*, as in its *representative* character': *Rights of Man*, p. 122.

[61]The assembly of the nine Electors to the Holy Roman Empire was known as the electoral college.

Whatever may be the success of evasion in explaining away the gross error of *fact*, which supposes that his majesty (though he holds it in concurrence with the wishes) owes his crown to the choice of his people, yet nothing can evade their full explicit declaration, concerning the principle of a right in the people to choose, which right is directly maintained, and tenaciously adhered to. All the oblique insinuations concerning election bottom in this proposition, and are referable to it. Lest the foundation of the king's exclusive legal title should pass for a mere rant of adulatory freedom, the political Divine proceeds dogmatically to assert,[62] that by the principles of the Revolution the people of England have acquired three fundamental rights, all which, with him, compose one system, and lie together in one short sentence; namely, that we have acquired a right

    1. "To choose our own governors."
    2. "To cashier them for misconduct."
    3. "To frame a government for ourselves."

This new, and hitherto unheard-of bill of rights, though made in the name of the whole people, belongs to those gentlemen and their faction only. The body of the people of England have no share in it. They utterly disclaim it. They [21] will resist the practical assertion of it with their lives and fortunes.[63] They are bound to do so by the laws of their country, made at the time of that very Revolution, which is appealed to in favour of the fictitious rights claimed by the society which abuses its name.

[62]P. 34, Discourse on the Love of our Country, by Dr. Price. [B] Price, *Discourse*, 3rd edn., p. 34, wrote: 'Let us, in particular, take care not to forget the principles of the Revolution. This Society has, very properly, in its Reports, held out these principles, as an instruction to the public. I will only take notice of the three following: First; The right to liberty of conscience in religious matters. Secondly; The right to resist power when abused. And, Thirdly; The right to chuse our own governors; to cashier them for misconduct; and to frame a government for ourselves. On these three principles, and more especially the last, was the Revolution founded.' It might be argued that Price listed five rights; but it is important that Burke challenged only the last three. As a Whig, he did not dispute a right to religious liberty. On Price's next point, Burke like all Whigs was caught between wishing to assert both that Englishmen possessed an ultimate right of resisting tyranny and that 1688 had seen not an exercise of that right, but rather James II's 'virtual abdication'.

[63]Paine (*Rights of Man*, p. 7) mocked the idea that men should risk their lives and fortunes 'to maintain they have *not* rights', but did not reply to Burke's historical and legal evidence relating to 1688. Paine's argument (p. 8–9) was the novel one that Parliament in 1688 had no right 'of binding and controuling posterity to the end of time'. Paine supported this claim rhetorically, arguing that Burke's doctrine was a version of 'the divine right to govern' which 'shortened his journey to Rome' (p. 11). Burke's argument was, in reality, very far from Roman Catholic political teaching.

These gentlemen of the Old Jewry, in all their reasonings on the Revolution of 1688, have a revolution which happened in England about forty years before, and the late French revolution, so much before their eyes, and in their hearts, that they are constantly confounding all the three together. It is necessary that we should separate what they confound.[64] We must recall their erring fancies to the *acts* of the Revolution which we revere, for the discovery of its true *principles*. If the *principles* of the Revolution of 1688 are any where to be found, it is in the statute called the *Declaration of Right*.[65] In that most wise, sober, and considerate declaration, drawn up by great lawyers and great statesmen, and not by warm and inexperienced enthusiasts, not one word is said, nor one suggestion made, of a general right "to choose our own *governors*; to cashier them for misconduct; and to *form* a government for *ourselves*."

This Declaration of Right (the act of the 1st of William and Mary, sess. 2. ch. 2.) is the corner-stone of our constitution, as reinforced, explained, improved, and in its fundamental principles for ever settled.[66] It is called "An act for declaring the rights and liberties of the subject, and for [22] *settling* the *succession* of the crown." You will observe, that these rights and this succession are declared in one body, and bound indissolubly together.

A few years after this period, a second opportunity offered for asserting a right of election to the crown.[67] On the prospect of a total failure of issue from

[64]Burke did not, in the *Reflections*, distinguish between the events of the 1640s and those of 1688–9. It is not clear that English revolutionaries of the 1790s were greatly influenced by the example of the 1640s.

[65]The term 'Declaration of Rights' is now generally confined to the resolution, passed by the Houses of Lords and Commons of the Convention Parliament in February 1689, which reasserted a series of rights as being already part of the constitution and declared William and Mary joint sovereigns: see Lois Schwoerer, *The Declaration of Rights, 1689* (Baltimore, 1981). Its provisions were then enacted as a statute (I W and M, s. 2, c. 2), colloquially termed the 'Bill of Rights'.

[66]It had been a commonplace of state-building or the drafting of constitutions, as of Anglican theology, that obligations, once entered into by oath, were of eternal force. Even Locke had devised a constitution 'to be perpetually established amongst us, unto which we do oblige our selves, our Heirs and Successors, in the most binding ways that can be devised': [John Locke], *The Fundamental Constitutions of Carolina* [n.p., ?1680], p. 1. This hereditary element, integral to the orthodox Anglican understanding of a religious oath and to dynastic succession as a Providential guarantee of legitimacy, was now undermined by the insistence of the heterodox Dissenting intelligentsia that each individual was endowed by God at birth with the full and undiminished range of 'human' rights, so that (perhaps a non-sequitur) each 'generation' was free of any inherited obligations.

[67]Priestley's argument (*Letters to Burke*, pp. 34–42) was both that such a right had

King William, and from the Princess, afterwards Queen Anne, the consideration of the settlement of the crown, and of a further security for the liberties of the people again came before the legislature. Did they this second time make any provision for legalizing the crown on the spurious Revolution principles of the Old Jewry? No. They followed the principles which prevailed in the Declaration of Right; indicating with more precision the persons who were to inherit in the Protestant line. This act also incorporated, by the same policy, our liberties, and an hereditary succession in the same act.[68] Instead of a right to choose our own governors, they declared that the *succession* in that line (the protestant line drawn from James the First) was absolutely necessary "for the peace, quiet, and security of the realm," and that it was equally urgent on them "to maintain a *certainty in the succession* thereof, to which the subjects may safely have recourse for their protection."[69] Both these acts, in which are heard the unerring, unambiguous oracles of Revolution policy, instead of countenancing the delusive, gypsey predictions of a "right to choose our governors," prove to [23] a demonstration how totally adverse the wisdom of the nation was from turning a case of necessity into a rule of law.

Unquestionably there was at the Revolution, in the person of King William, a small and a temporary deviation from the strict order of a regular hereditary succession;[70] but it is against all genuine principles of jurisprudence to draw a principle from a law made in a special case, and regarding an individual person. *Privilegium non transit in exemplum.*[71] If ever there was a time fa-

---

been asserted in 1688 (by Lord Somers) and that what had then been done was in fact 'a *choice* made, both of a particular king *pro tempore*, and also of *a new line of succession* for future kings'.

[68]'An act for the further limitation of the crown, and better securing the rights and liberties of the subject', 1701 (12 and 13 W III, c. 2), known as the Act of Settlement. As a Whig, Burke was obliged to argue that this Act also did not constitute a choice of governors. Early eighteenth-century Jacobites had taken the opposite view.

[69]Act of Settlement, clause I (free quotation). The Act used the familiar phraseology in committing the kingdom to the Hanoverian succession in default of issue from William or Anne: 'and thereunto the said lords spiritual and temporal, and commons, shall and will, in the name of all the people of this realm, most humbly and faithfully submit themselves, their heirs and posterities': *Statutes at Large*, X, pp. 357–60.

[70]Burke's Whiggery here impaled him on the traditional Whig dilemma over the interpretation of the events of 1688–9. He was correct to observe that none of its defining documents had affirmed Price's principles of elective and accountable monarchy; but Burke offered no defence of his claims that the break in the succession was either 'small' or 'temporary'. His quite different point that it was 'an act of necessity' is further explored, with classical authorities, in *Reflections*, p. [43].

[71]'An individual privilege does not create a general rule.' Burke probably took this Roman Law maxim from Domat.

vourable for establishing the principle, that a king of popular choice was the only legal king, without all doubt it was at the Revolution. Its not being done at that time is a proof that the nation was of opinion it ought not to be done at any time. There is no person so completely ignorant of our history, as not to know, that the majority in parliament of both parties were so little disposed to any thing resembling that principle, that at first they were determined to place the vacant crown, not on the head of the prince of Orange, but on that of his wife Mary, daughter of King James, the eldest born of the issue of that king, which they acknowledged as undoubtedly his.[72] It would be to repeat a very trite story, to recall to your memory all those circumstances which demonstrated that their accepting King William was not properly a *choice*; but, to all those who did not wish, in effect to recall King James, or to deluge their country in blood, and again to bring their religion, laws, [24] and liberties into the peril they had just escaped, it was an act of *necessity*, in the strictest moral sense in which necessity can be taken.[73]

In the very act, in which for a time, and in a single case, parliament departed from the strict order of inheritance, in favour of a prince, who, though not next, was however very near in the line of succession, it is curious to observe how Lord Somers,[74] who drew the bill called the Declaration of Right, has comported himself on that delicate occasion. It is curious to observe with what address this temporary solution of continuity is kept from the eye; whilst all that could be found in this act of necessity to countenance the idea of an

[72]James II's son and heir, James Francis Edward Stuart, was born on 10 June 1688 (OS). The wide currency of hereditarian arguments meant that Whigs who sought to bar his right were driven back on the curious (and false) argument that the real child had been born dead, and replaced with another infant surreptitiously brought into the Queen's bedchamber in a warming pan. If so, James II's eldest daughter Mary (b. 1662) was still heir presumptive; if the throne were vacant in 1689, an argument for her title by hereditary descent could be made. This was less strong as a justification for the joint monarchy of William and Mary, and less strong again as a rationale for William's sole rule after Mary's death in 1694.

[73]Burke here placed the best available interpretation on the old Whig dilemma. James II's constructive abdication, and the allegedly vacant throne, could have opened the door to a popular choice of successor; Burke had to argue that the hereditary principle was still paramount. The implausibility of this argument was the fault not of Burke but of the Whigs of 1688–9.

[74]See Biographical Guide. In the eighteenth century, Somers enjoyed a reputation, later forgotten, as the chief constitutional architect of the Protestant succession. Somers was one of the few Whig statesmen of his generation who probably did not seek to insure his position by retaining links with the Stuart court at St Germain in Anne's reign, although William L. Sachse, *Lord Somers: A political portrait* (Manchester, 1975), pp. 223, 313, suggests that this may have occurred.

hereditary succession is brought forward, and fostered, and made the most of, by this great man and by the legislature who followed him. Quitting the dry, imperative style of an act of parliament, he makes the lords and commons fall to a pious, legislative ejaculation, and declare, that they consider it "as a marvellous providence, and merciful goodness of God to this nation, to preserve their said majesties *royal* persons, most happily to reign over us *on the throne of their ancestors,* for which, from the bottom of their hearts, they return their humblest thanks and praises."[75]—The legislature plainly had in view the act of recognition of the first of Queen Elizabeth, Chap. 3d,[76] and of that of James the First, Chap. 1st,[77] both acts strongly declaratory of the inheritable nature of the crown; and in many [25] parts they follow, with a nearly literal precision, the words and even the form of thanksgiving, which is found in these old declaratory statutes.

The two houses, in the act of king William, did not thank God that they had found a fair opportunity to assert a right to choose their own governors, much less to make an election the *only lawful* title to the crown. Their having been in a condition to avoid the very appearance of it, as much as possible, was by them considered as a providential escape. They threw a politic, well-wrought veil over every circumstance tending to weaken the rights, which in the meliorated order of succession they meant to perpetuate; or which might

[75]The Bill of Rights, clause VII (free quotation). Belief in the power of Divine Providence was common to Jacobites and Williamites in 1688, and was still strong among Christians; it was prominently mocked by the 'friends of liberty' in the 1790s.

[76]I Eliz. I, c. 3 (1588), 'An act for recognition of the Queen's highness to the imperial crown of this realm', assured her (clauses I, II, IV) 'that your Highness is rightly, lineally and lawfully descended and come of the blood royal of this realm of England, in and to whose princely person ... the imperial and royal estate, place, crown and dignity of this realm ... are and shall be most fully, rightfully, really and entirely invested and incorporated, united and annexed ... and thereunto most humbly and faithfully we do submit ourselves, our heirs and posterities for ever ... And that it may be enacted by the authority aforesaid, That as well this our declaration, confession and recognition, as also the limitation and declaration of the succession of the imperial crown of this realm, mentioned and contained in the said act made in the said five and thirtieth year of the reign of your said most noble father, shall stand, remain and be the law of this realm for ever': *Statutes at Large,* VI, pp. 123–4.

[77]I Jac. I, c. 1 (1604) 'A most joyful and just recognition of the immediate, lawful and undoubted succession, descent and right of the crown', declared (clause IV) that the crown of England 'did by inherent birthright, and lawful and undoubted succession, descend and come to your most excellent Majesty, as being lineally, justly and lawfully, next and sole heir of the blood royal of this realm ... And thereunto we most humbly and faithfully do submit and oblige ourselves, our heirs and posterities for ever, until the last drop of our bloods be spent': *Statutes at Large,* VII, pp. 73–5.

furnish a precedent for any future departure from what they had then settled for ever. Accordingly, that they might not relax the nerves of their monarchy, and that they might preserve a close conformity to the practice of their ancestors, as it appeared in the declaratory statutes of queen Mary[78] and queen Elizabeth, in the next clause[79] they vest, by recognition, in their majesties, *all* the legal prerogatives of the crown, declaring, "that in them they are most *fully*, rightfully, and *intirely* invested, incorporated, united, and annexed." In the clause which follows,[80] for preventing questions, by reason of any pretended titles to the crown, they declare (observing also in this the traditionary [26] language, along with the traditionary policy of the nation, and repeating as from a rubric the language of the preceding acts of Elizabeth and James) that on the preserving "a *certainty* in the SUCCESSION thereof, the unity, peace, and tranquillity of this nation doth, under God, wholly depend."

They knew that a doubtful title of succession would but too much resemble an election; and that an election would be utterly destructive of the "unity, peace, and tranquillity of this nation," which they thought to be considerations of some moment. To provide for these objects, and therefore to exclude for ever the Old Jewry doctrine of "a right to choose our own governors," they follow with a clause, containing a most solemn pledge, taken from the preceding act of Queen Elizabeth, as solemn a pledge as ever was or can be given in favour of an hereditary succession, and as solemn a renunciation as could be made of the principles by this society imputed to them. "The lords spiritual and temporal, and commons, do, in the name of all the people aforesaid, most humbly and faithfully submit *themselves, their heirs and posterities for ever*; and do faithfully promise, that they will stand to, maintain, and defend their said majesties, and also the *limitation of the crown*, herein specified and contained, to the utmost of their powers," &c. &c.[81] [27]

So far is it from being true, that we acquired a right by the Revolution to elect our kings, that if we had possessed it before,[82] the English nation did at

[78] 1st Mary, Sess. 3. ch. 1. [B] 'An act that the regal power of this realm is as full in the Queen's majesty as ever it was in any of her noble ancestors', recorded that 'the imperial crown of this realm ... is most lawfully, justly and rightfully descended and come unto the Queen's highness that now is, being the very, true and undoubted heir and inheritrix thereof': *Statutes at Large*, VI, pp. 18–19.

[79] These provisions actually occur in the same clause VII.

[80] I.e. clause VIII.

[81] Bill of Rights, clause VIII (free quotation).

[82] Paine (*Rights of Man*, p. 8) pointed to this clause as an admission that the people had had such a right: Burke 'acknowledges [this] to have been the case, not only in England, but throughout Europe, at an early period'.

that time most solemnly renounce and abdicate it, for themselves and for all their posterity for ever. These gentlemen may value themselves as much as they please on their whig principles; but I never desire to be thought a better whig than Lord Somers:[83] or to understand the principles of the Revolution better than those by whom it was brought about: or to read in the declaration of right any mysteries unknown to those whose penetrating style has engraved in our ordinances, and in our hearts, the words and spirit of that immortal law.

It is true that, aided with the powers derived from force and opportunity, the nation was at that time, in some sense, free to take what course it pleased for filling the throne; but only free to do so upon the same grounds on which they might have wholly abolished their monarchy, and every other part of their constitution. However they did not think such bold changes within their commission. It is indeed difficult, perhaps impossible, to give limits to the mere *abstract* competence of the supreme power, such as was exercised by parliament at that time; but the limits of a *moral* competence, subjecting, even in powers more indisputably sovereign, occasional will to permanent reason, and to the steady maxims of faith, justice, and fixed fundamental policy, are perfectly intelligible, and [28] perfectly binding upon those who exercise any authority, under any name, or under any title, in the state. The house of lords, for instance, is not morally competent to dissolve the house of commons; no, nor even to dissolve itself, nor to abdicate, if it would, its portion in the legislature of the kingdom. Though a king may abdicate for his own person, he can-

---

[83]Burke may have consulted the reputation of this author rather than his writings. [John Somers], *A Brief History of the Succession to the Crown of England, &c.* (London, 1688/9) argued that the English Crown had normally been elective before 1066 and had often been so even after that date; that (as with Edward II) Parliament might judge the 'Irregular and Arbitrary Government' of a monarch and depose him, and had 'Elected his Son to reign after him ... in his Fathers Life-time' (pp. 1–3, 6). Henry VII 'was wise enough to think his Title' to the Crown 'was not very good, till it was made so by an Act of Parliament'; even Henry VIII 'never doubted of their Power in setling the Succession and resorted to it very frequently' (p. 10). Somers concluded (p. 13): 'it hath been the constant opinion of all Ages that the Parliament of *England* had an unquestionable power to limit, restrain and qualify the Succession as they pleased, and that in all Ages they have put their power in practice; and that the Historian had reason for saying that seldom or never the third Heir in a right descent enjoyed the Crown of *England*'. Somers's doctrines were much more extreme than Burke perhaps appreciated. Priestley (*Letters to Burke*, p. 35) cited another tract generally ascribed to Somers, *The Judgement of Whole Kingdoms and Nations concerning the Rights, Power and Prerogative of Kings, and the Rights, Privileges and Properties of the People* (London, 1710) to illustrate a position close to elective kingship.

not abdicate for the monarchy. By as strong, or by a stronger reason, the house of commons cannot renounce its share of authority. The engagement and pact of society, which generally goes by the name of the constitution, forbids such invasion and such surrender. The constituent parts of a state are obliged to hold their public faith with each other, and with all those who derive any serious interest under their engagements, as much as the whole state is bound to keep its faith with separate communities. Otherwise competence and power would soon be confounded, and no law be left but the will of a prevailing force. On this principle the succession of the crown has always been what it now is, an hereditary succession by law:[84] in the old line it was a succession by the common law; in the new by the statute law operating on the principles of the common law, not changing the substance, but regulating the mode, and describing the persons.[85] Both these descriptions of law are of the same force, and are derived from an equal authority, emanating from the common agreement and original compact of the state, *communi sponsione reipublicæ*,[86] and as such are equally [29] binding on king, and people too, as long as the terms are observed, and they continue the same body politic.[87]

It is far from impossible to reconcile, if we do not suffer ourselves to be entangled in the mazes of metaphysic sophistry, the use both of a fixed rule and an occasional deviation; the sacredness of an hereditary principle of succession in our government, with a power of change in its application in cases of extreme emergency.[88] Even in that extremity (if we take the measure of our

[84]English history since at least the reign of Henry III had displayed a series of attempts to avoid anarchy and bring order to the succession by emphasising the principle of hereditary right by primogeniture, a theory which had won wide acceptance by the reign of Richard II. Subsequent violations of that principle, like the accessions of Henry Bolingbroke in 1399, Henry Tudor in 1485 and Willem of Orange Nassau in 1689, had to be explained away. If common law had validated the title of Richard II, it might be argued that statute law established the titles of Henry IV, Henry VII and William III; but few monarchs who asserted an hereditary title neglected a parliamentary one also. Burke, as a Whig, was obliged to minimise the difference. For this question see especially Howard Nenner, *The Right to be King: The Succession to the Crown of England, 1603–1714* (London, 1995).

[85]Burke echoed the Athanasian Creed in the *Book of Common Prayer*.

[86]'From the common engagement of the state'. Burke's source was probably Domat.

[87]Burke here assimilated statute law (law as command) to common law (law as custom) and derived the authority of both sorts of law from their antiquity. The contractual origins of the state, which Burke admitted as a truism, thereby became lost in the antiquity of the ancient constitution.

[88]Paine (*Rights of Man*, p. 63) replied: 'Although Mr. Burke has asserted the right of the parliament at the Revolution to bind and controul the nation and posterity for *ever*, he denies, at the same time, that the parliament or the nation had any right to al-

rights by our exercise of them at the Revolution) the change is to be confined to the peccant part only; to the part which produced the necessary deviation; and even then it is to be effected without a decomposition of the whole civil and political mass, for the purpose of originating a new civil order out of the first elements of society.

A state without the means of some change is without the means of its conservation. Without such means it might even risque the loss of that part of the constitution which it wished the most religiously to preserve. The two principles of conservation and correction operated strongly at the two critical periods of the Restoration and Revolution, when England found itself without a king. At both those periods the nation had lost the bond of union in their ancient edifice; they did not, however, dissolve the whole fabric. On the contrary, in both cases they regenerated the deficient part of the old constitution through [30] the parts which were not impaired. They kept these old parts exactly as they were, that the part recovered might be suited to them. They acted by the ancient organized states[89] in the shape of their old organization, and not by the organic *moleculæ*[90] of a disbanded people. At no time, perhaps, did the sovereign legislature manifest a more tender regard to that fundamental principle of British constitutional policy, than at the time of the Revolution, when it deviated from the direct line of hereditary succession. The crown was carried somewhat out of the line in which it had before moved; but the new line was derived from the same stock. It was still a line of hereditary descent; still an hereditary descent in the same blood, though an hereditary descent qualified with protestantism. When the legislature altered the direction, but kept the principle, they shewed that they held it inviolable.[91]

---

ter what he calls the succession of the crown, in any thing but in part, or by a sort of modification.'

[89]I.e. estates, the Lords and Commons, as in the French Estates-General.

[90]Burke's metaphor recalled seventeenth-century physics rather than anticipating nineteenth-century biology. The standard Anglican treatise on materialism had discussed the theories of matter of the ancients, including 'Asclepiades, who supposed all the Corporeal World to be made ... not of Similar Parts (as Anaxagoras) but of Dissimilar and inconcinn *Moleculae*, i.e. Atoms of different Magnitude and Figures': Ralph Cudworth, *The True Intellectual System of the Universe: First wherein, All the Reason and Philosophy Of Atheism is Confuted; and Its Impossibility Demonstrated* (London, 1678), p. 16. Burke owned a copy of Thomas Birch's edition of this work (2 vols., London, 1743): *LC*, p. 7; LC MS, fo. 34.

[91]Before the birth of James Francis Edward Stuart, Mary was heir presumptive; William of Orange hoped to share the throne in his wife's right. Similarly, Sophia, electress and duchess dowager of Hanover, was the daughter of Elizabeth, Queen of Bohemia, herself the daughter of James I.

On this principle, the law of inheritance had admitted some amendment in the old time, and long before the æra of the Revolution. Some time after the conquest[92] great questions arose upon the legal principles of hereditary descent. It became a matter of doubt, whether the heir *per capita* or the heir *per stirpes* was to succeed;[93] but whether the heir *per capita* gave way when the heirdom *per stirpes* took place, or the Catholic heir when the Protestant was preferred, the inheritable principle[94] survived with a sort of immortality through all transmigrations—*multosque* [31] *per annos stat fortuna domus et avi numerantur avorum.*[95] This is the spirit of our constitution, not only in its

[92]I.e. the Norman Conquest. Burke here implied that the use of the two principles of inheritance had not always been a problem. As he had earlier written of successions to the Crown before 1066, 'Very frequent examples occur in the Saxon times, where the son of the deceased king, if under age, was entirely passed over, and his uncle, or some remoter relation, raised to the crown; but there is not a single instance where the election has carried it out of the blood. So that in truth the controversy, which has been managed with such heat, whether in the Saxon times the crown was hereditary or elective, must be determined, in some degree, favourably for the litigants on either side; for it was certainly both hereditary and elective within the bounds, which we have mentioned': Edmund Burke, *An Essay towards an Abridgement of the English History* in Burke, *Works*, X, pp. 333–4. Burke's *Essay towards an Abridgement* was written in 1758, but left unfinished and only partly published in 1812: Cone, *Burke*, I, pp. 30–3. Like others in the 1750s, Burke had sought a formula to reconcile early eighteenth-century ideological conflicts, but noticeably failed to endorse the Tory doctrine of *indefeasible* hereditary right.

[93]Heirs 'per capita' who were in the same relation to a common ancestor shared equally in an inheritance. In Roman law, inheritance was 'per stirpes': each branch of descendants took only the share to which its parent would have been entitled if living. Burke used these terms to distinguish between the Stuart principle of indefeasible primogeniture and the Revolution principle of the choice of the next Protestant heir of the same blood. The point had arisen earlier: descent *per stirpes* had allowed the crown to 'skip a generation' in 1377, so that Edward III 'had been succeeded by his grandson Richard II, the child of Edward's deceased elder son, rather than by any of the Black Prince's surviving brothers': Nenner, *Right to be King*, p. 30.

[94]It might be argued that Burke's desire to depict continuities in English history led him to gloss over the fundamental differences between two forms of inheritance in order to save the hereditary principle itself.

[95]Virgil had used the hive as a metaphor of human society: 'Therefore, though the limit of a narrow span awaits the bees themselves—for never stretches it beyond the seventh summer—yet the race abides immortal, for many a year stands firm the fortune of the house, and grandsires' grandsires are numbered on the roll': *Georgics*, Book IV, 206–9. This was not an example of proto-Hegelian organic theory but an eighteenth-century trope: the passage was quoted as a motto in *The Spectator*, no. 72 (23 May 1711), and in the Dedication to [Lord Bolingbroke], *A Dissertation upon Parties; In Several Letters to Caleb D'Anvers, Esq.* (1735): 'Let the illustrious and royal

settled course but in all its revolutions. Whoever came in, or however he came in, whether he obtained the crown by law, or by force, the hereditary succession was either continued or adopted.

The gentlemen of the Society for Revolutions see nothing in that of 1688 but the deviation from the constitution; and they take the deviation from the principle for the principle. They have little regard to the obvious consequences of their doctrine, though they must see, that it leaves positive authority in very few of the positive institutions of this country. When such an unwarrantable maxim is once established, that no throne is lawful but the elective,[96] no one act of the princes who preceded their æra of fictitious election can be valid. Do these theorists mean to imitate some of their predecessors, who dragged the bodies of our ancient sovereigns out of the quiet of their tombs?[97] Do they mean to attaint and disable backwards all the kings that have reigned before the Revolution, and consequently to stain the throne of England with the blot of a continual usurpation? Do they mean to invalidate, annul, or to call in question, together with the titles of the whole line of our kings, that great body of our statute law which passed under those whom they treat as usurpers? to annul laws of inestimable value to our liberties—of as great [32] value

---

house, that hath been called to the government of these kingdoms, govern them till time shall be no more. But ... whatever happens in the various course of human contingencies, whatever be the fate of particular persons, of houses, or families, let the liberties of Great Britain be immortal': David Mallet (ed.), *The Works Of the late Right Honorable Henry St. John, Lord Viscount Bolingbroke* (5 vols., London, 1754), II, p. 5. Burke owned a copy of this edition: *LC*, p. 6; LC MS, fo. 33. Cf. *Reflections*, p. [187].

[96]Burke had censured both the elective monarchy of Poland and the election of a king of the Romans (the heir to the Emperor): 'These two elective sovereignties not only occasion many mischiefs to those who live under them, but have frequently involved a great part of Europe in blood and confusion': *The Annual Register* (London, 1763), p. 44.

[97]At the Reformation, the body of King Stephen was disinterred from its grave in Faversham Abbey by thieves who stole its lead coffin. During the Great Rebellion, parliamentary troops committed similar acts of sacrilege against the remains of pre-Conquest kings in Winchester Cathedral. Burke's forebodings were realised: in August 1793, the tombs of French kings at the abbey of Saint-Denis and elsewhere were opened and destroyed by order of the Convention, and their contents subjected to insults from the populace. By 1796, Burke had developed and confirmed this image of the revolutionaries: 'Neither sex, nor age—nor the sanctuary of the tomb is sacred to them. They have so determined a hatred to all privileged orders, that they deny even to the departed, the sad immunities of the grave ... they unplumb the dead for bullets to assassinate the living': *Letter to a Noble Lord*, pp. 4–5. During a fever before his own death the following year, Burke asked to be buried in an unmarked grave, although this did not represent his settled wishes. He was buried in Beaconsfield churchyard.

at least as any which have passed at or since the period of the Revolution? If kings, who did not owe their crown to the choice of their people, had no title to make laws, what will become of the statute *de tallagio non concedendo?*—of the *petition of right?*—of the act of *habeas corpus?*[98] Do these new doctors of the rights of men presume to assert, that King James the Second, who came to the crown as next o[f] blood, according to the rules of a then unqualified succession, was not to all intents and purposes a lawful king of England, before he had done any of those acts which were justly construed[99] into an abdication of his crown? If he was not, much trouble in parliament might have been saved at the period these gentlemen commemorate. But King James was a bad king with a good title, and not an usurper. The princes who succeeded[100] according to the act of parliament which settled the crown on the electress Sophia[101] and on her descendents, being Protestants, came in as much by a title of inheritance as King James did. He came in according to the law, as it stood at his accession to the crown; and the princes of the House of Brunswick came to the inheritance of the crown, not by election, but by the law, as it stood at their several accessions of Protestant descent and inheritance, as I hope I have shewn sufficiently.

The law by which this royal family is specifically destined to the succession, is the act of [33] the 12th and 13th of King William. The terms of this act bind "us and our *heirs*, and our *posterity*, to them, their *heirs*, and their *posterity*,"[102] being Protestants, to the end of time, in the same words as the declaration of right had bound us to the heirs of King William and Queen Mary. It

---

[98]The statute *De tallagio non concedendo* (25 Edw. I, 1297) enunciated the principle that taxation could only be raised by the consent of Parliament, though the survival of 'fiscal feudalism' delayed the principle's realisation. The Petition of Right (1628) was a petition to the King from both Houses of Parliament 'concerning divers rights and liberties of the subject'; although it was not a statute, Charles I, by accepting it, gave some authority to its provisions, including the need for parliamentary assent to taxation and the wrongfulness of imprisonment 'without any cause shown'. Habeas corpus was a common-law writ to produce a prisoner in court for some purpose, most notably to restore his liberty. After controversies over the right of the royal prerogative to limit its use, the Habeas Corpus Act of 1679 defined the law on the subject.

[99]In the Commons' motion of 28 January 1689. This was, however, a syntactically ambiguous paragraph: it is not clear what those acts were, whether flight alone or prior misrule.

[100]I.e. George I, George II and George III.

[101]Sophia, Electress of Hanover (1630–1714), granddaughter of James I of England.

[102]Act of Settlement, clause I (free quotation). Burke omitted the qualification: 'according to the limitation and succession of the crown in this act specified and contained'.

therefore secures both an hereditary crown and an hereditary allegiance. On what ground, except the constitutional policy of forming an establishment to secure that kind of succession which is to preclude a choice of the people for ever, could the legislature have fastidiously rejected the fair and abundant choice which our own country presented to them, and searched in strange lands for a foreign princess, from whose womb the line of our future rulers were to derive their title to govern millions of men through a series of ages?

The Princess Sophia was named in the act of settlement of the 12th and 13th of King William, for a *stock* and root of *inheritance* to our kings, and not for her merits as a temporary administratrix of a power, which she might not, and in fact did not, herself ever exercise. She was adopted for one reason, and for one only, because, says the act, "the most excellent Princess Sophia, Electress and Dutchess Dowager of Hanover, is *daughter* of the most excellent Princess Elizabeth,[103] late Queen of Bohemia, *daughter* of our late *sovereign lord* King James the First, of happy memory, and is hereby declared to be the next in *succession* [34] in the Protestant line," &c. &c; "and the crown shall continue to the *heirs* of her body, being Protestants." This limitation was made by parliament, that through the Princess Sophia an inheritable line, not only was to be continued in future but (what they thought very material) that through her it was to be connected with the old stock of inheritance in King James the First; in order that the monarchy might preserve an unbroken unity through all ages, and might be preserved (with safety to our religion) in the old approved mode by descent,[104] in which, if our liberties had been once endangered, they had often, through all storms and struggles of prerogative and privilege, been preserved. They did well. No experience has taught us, that in any other course or method than that of an *hereditary crown*, our liberties can be regularly perpetuated and preserved sacred as our *hereditary right*. An irregular, convulsive movement may be necessary to throw off an irregular, convulsive disease. But the course of succession is the healthy habit of the British constitution. Was it that the legislature wanted, at the act for the limitation of the crown in the Hanoverian line, drawn through the female descendants of James the First, a due sense of the inconveniencies of having two or three, or possibly more, foreigners in succession to the British throne?[105]

[103]Princess Elizabeth (1595–1662), daughter of James I, married Frederick, Elector Palatine, in 1614.

[104]Burke, like the Whigs of 1688, thereby countered the argument that any variation in the principle of primogeniture at once made the crown wholly elective. To the revolutionists of the 1790s this appeared less plausible because of the rise of a cult of *choice*, the exercise of unfettered will by the omnicompetent, timeless individual.

[105]In the Bill of Rights and the Act of Settlement, the Westminster Parliament acted

No!—they had a due sense of the evils which might happen from such foreign rule, and more than a due sense of [35] them. But a more decisive proof cannot be given of the full conviction of the British nation, that the principles of the Revolution did not authorize them to elect kings at their pleasure, and without any attention to the ancient fundamental principles of our government, than their continuing to adopt a plan of hereditary Protestant succession in the old line, with all the dangers and all the inconveniencies of its being a foreign line full before their eyes, and operating with the utmost force upon their minds.

A few years ago I should be ashamed to overload a matter, so capable of supporting itself, by the then unnecessary support of any argument; but this seditious, unconstitutional doctrine is now publicly taught, avowed, and printed. The dislike I feel to revolutions, the signals for which have so often been given from pulpits;[106] the spirit of change that is gone abroad; the total  contempt which prevails with you, and may come to prevail with us, of all ancient institutions, when set in opposition to a present sense of convenience, or to the bent of a present inclination: all these considerations make it not unadviseable, in my opinion, to call back our attention to the true principles of our own domestic laws; that you, my French friend, should begin to know, and that we should continue to cherish them. We ought not, on either side of the water, to suffer ourselves to be imposed upon by the counterfeit wares which some persons, by a [36] double fraud, export to you in illicit bottoms,[107] as raw commodities of British growth though wholly alien to our soil, in order afterwards to smuggle them back again into this country, manufactured after the newest Paris fashion of an improved liberty.

The people of England will not ape the fashions they have never tried; nor go back to those which they have found mischievous on trial. They look upon the legal hereditary succession of their crown as among their rights, not as among their wrongs; as a benefit, not as a grievance; as a security for their liberty, not as a badge of servitude. They look on the frame of their commonwealth, *such as it stands*, to be of inestimable value; and they conceive the un-

---

in the name of the kingdoms of 'England, France and Ireland' (the second being a formulaic survival); until the union of 1707, Scots affairs were transacted through the Edinburgh Parliament.

[106]Burke's critics seized on his recent activity in support of the American colonists. His recognition here of the role of preaching in political mobilisation contrasted with his earlier insistence (*Reflections*, pp. [13–14]) that Price's intervention had revived this idiom 'after so long a discontinuance', i.e. since the 1640s.

[107]The Navigation Acts progressively restricted English maritime trade to English shipping. The most important Acts were those of 1651 and 1660.

disturbed succession of the crown to be a pledge of the stability and perpetuity of all the other members of our constitution.

I shall beg leave, before I go any further, to take notice of some paltry artifices, which the abettors of election as the only lawful title to the crown, are ready to employ, in order to render the support of the just principles of our constitution a task somewhat invidious. These sophisters substitute a fictious cause, and feigned personages, in whose favour they suppose you engaged, whenever you defend the inheritable nature of the crown. It is common with them to dispute as if they were in a conflict with some of those exploded fanatics of slavery, who formerly maintained, what I believe no creature [37] now maintains, "that the crown is held by divine, hereditary, and indefeasible right."[108]—These old fanatics of single arbitrary power dogmatized as if hereditary royalty was the only lawful government in the world, just as our new fanatics of popular arbitrary power, maintain that a popular election is the sole lawful source of authority. The old prerogative enthusiasts, it is true, did speculate foolishly, and perhaps impiously too, as if monarchy had more of a divine sanction than any other mode of government; and as if a right to govern by inheritance were in strictness *indefeasible* in every person, and under every circumstance, which no civil or political right can be. But an absurd opinion concerning the king's hereditary right to the crown does not prejudice one that is rational, and bottomed upon solid principles of law and policy. If all the absurd theories of lawyers and divines were to vitiate the objects in which they are conversant, we should have no law, and no religion, left in the world. But an absurd theory on one side of a question forms no justification for alledging a false fact, or promulgating mischievous maxims on the other.

The second claim of the Revolution Society is "a right of cashiering their governors on *misconduct*." Perhaps the apprehensions our ancestors entertained of forming such a precedent as that "of cashiering for misconduct," was the cause that the declaration of the act which implied the abdication of king James, [38] was, if it had any fault, rather too guarded, and too circumstantial.[109] But all this guard, and all this accumulation of circumstances,

[108]This paragraph placed Burke unambiguously and passionately on the Whig side of the polarity which had divided Britain during the early part of his life.

[109]"That King James the second, having endeavoured to *subvert the constitution* of the kingdom, by breaking the *original contract* between king and people, and by the advice of jesuits, and other wicked persons, having violated the *fundamental* laws, and *having withdrawn himself out of the kingdom*, hath *abdicated* the government, and the throne is thereby *vacant*. [B] *Journals of the House of Commons*, X, p. 14. Burke did

serves to shew the spirit of caution which predominated in the national councils, in a situation in which men irritated by oppression, and elevated by a triumph over it, are apt to abandon themselves to violent and extreme courses: it shews the anxiety of the great men who influenced the conduct of affairs at that great event, to make the Revolution a parent of settlement, and not a nursery of future revolutions.[110]

No government could stand a moment, if it could be blown down with any thing so loose and indefinite as an opinion of *"misconduct."*[111] They who led at the Revolution, grounded the virtual abdication of King James upon no such light and uncertain a principle. They charged him with nothing less than a design, confirmed by a multitude of illegal overt acts, to *subvert the Protestant church and state*, and their *fundamental*, unquestionable laws and liberties: they charged him with having broken the *original contract* between king and people.[112] This was [39] more than *misconduct*. A grave and over-ruling necessity obliged them to take the step they took, and took with infinite reluctance, as under that most rigorous of all laws. Their trust for the future preservation of the constitution was not in future revolutions. The grand policy of all their regulations was to render it almost impracticable for any future sovereign to compel the states of the kingdom to have again recourse to those violent remedies. They left the crown what, in the eye and estimation of law, it had ever been, perfectly irresponsible. In order to lighten the crown still further, they aggravated responsibility on ministers of state. By the statute of the 1st of King William, sess. 2d, called *"the act for declaring the rights and liberties of the subject, and for settling the succession of the crown,"*[113] they enacted, that the ministers should serve the crown on the terms of that declara-

---

not reproduce accurately the punctuation of this crucially ambiguous paragraph. The italics were Burke's.

[110]Burke here responded to the new sense of 'revolution' as a process, to be repeated, rather than an event.

[111]Even Locke had to argue at length, and implausibly, to avoid the charge that his principles would make for constant dissolutions of government: *Two Treatises of Government*, II, ss. 223–40. Burke naturally owned Locke, both the three-volume folio edition of the *Works* (1751) and the 1764 edition of the *Two Treatises*: LS MS, fos. 6, 31; *LC*, p. 13.

[112]It is not clear that Burke was aware that all mention of an original contract was dropped between the Commons' resolution of 28 January 1689 and the Declaration of Rights, presented to William and Mary on 13 February. For the problems of contract theory in 1688, see especially J. P. Kenyon, *Revolution Principles: The Politics of Party 1689–1720* (Cambridge, 1977).

[113]The Act of 1 W and M, s. 2, c. 2, commonly known as the Bill of Rights.

tion. They secured soon after the *frequent meetings of parliament*, by which the whole government would be under the constant inspection and active controul of the popular representative and of the magnates of the kingdom.[114] In the next great constitutional act, that of the 12th and 13th of King William, for the further limitation of the crown, and *better* securing the rights and liberties of the subject, they provided, "that no pardon under the great seal of England should be pleadable to an impeachment by the commons in parliament."[115] The rule laid down for government in the Declaration of Right, [40] the constant inspection of parliament, the practical claim of impeachment,[116] they thought infinitely a better security not only for their constitutional liberty, but against the vices of administration, than the reservation of a right so difficult in the practice, so uncertain in the issue, and often so mischievous in the consequences, as that of "cashiering their governors."

Dr. Price, in this sermon,[117] condemns very properly the practice of gross, adulatory addresses to kings. Instead of this fulsome style, he proposes that his majesty should be told, on occasions of congratulation, that "he is to con-

---

[114]The Triennial Act of 1694 (6 & 7 W and M, c. 2) provided for parliamentary elections at least every three years; it remained in force until the Whigs' Septennial Act of 1716.

[115]The Act of Settlement, clause III. The earl of Danby had escaped impeachment in 1679 by pleading a royal pardon. The legality of such a proceeding remained in dispute until the Act of Settlement.

[116]Burke insisted on the importance and feasibility of the weapon of impeachment. Since that notorious Whig show trial, the impeachment of the Tory Dr. Sacheverell in 1710, Whigs had normally shied away from its use, but Burke was still doggedly pursuing the impeachment of Warren Hastings despite the Foxites' loss of enthusiasm for that cause. Burke evidently owned two copies of that classic anthology of early eighteenth-century political argument, *The Tryal of Dr Henry Sacheverell* (London, 1710): LC, p. 28.

[117]P. 22, 23, 24. [B] Burke's membership of the Foxite opposition found echoes in his otherwise-surprising approval of some of Price's more extreme passages (p. 22): 'Adulation is always odious, and when offered to men in power it corrupts *them*, by giving them improper ideas of their situation; and it debases those who offer it, by manifesting an abjectness founded on improper ideas of *themselves*. I have lately observed in this kingdom too near approaches to this abjectness. In our late addresses to the King, on his recovery from the severe illness with which God hath been pleased to afflict him, we have appeared more like a herd crawling at the feet of a master, than like enlightened and manly citizens rejoicing with a beloved sovereign, but at the same time conscious that he derives all his consequence from themselves.' Perhaps political vicissitudes explain Burke's sympathy for Price: George III's recovery in February 1789 had destroyed the Foxite Whigs' hopes of office when it had at last seemed to be within their grasp.

sider himself as more properly the servant than the sovereign of his people."[118] For a compliment, this new form of address does not seem to be very soothing. Those who are servants, in name, as well as in effect, do not like to be told of their situation, their duty, and their obligations. The slave, in the old play, tells his master, "*Hæc commemoratio est quasi exprobratio.*"[119] It is not pleasant as compliment; it is not wholesome as instruction. After all, if the king were to bring himself to echo this new kind of address, to adopt it in terms, and even to take the appellation of Servant of the People as his royal style, how either he or we should be much mended by it, I cannot imagine. I have seen very assuming letters, signed, Your most obedient, humble servant. The proudest domination that ever was endured on earth took a title of [41] still greater humility than that which is now proposed for sovereigns by the Apostle of Liberty. Kings and nations were trampled upon by the foot of one calling himself "the Servant of Servants;" and mandates for deposing sovereigns were sealed with the signet of "the Fisherman."[120]

I should have considered all this as no more than a sort of flippant vain discourse, in which, as in an unsavoury fume, several persons suffer the spirit of liberty to evaporate, if it were not plainly in support of the idea, and a part of the scheme of "cashiering kings for misconduct." In that light it is worth some observation.

Kings, in one sense, are undoubtedly the servants of the people, because their power has no other rational end than that of the general advantage; but it is not true that they are, in the ordinary sense (by our constitution, at least) any thing like servants; the essence of whose situation is to obey the commands of some other, and to be removeable at pleasure. But the king of Great Britain obeys no other person; all other persons are individually, and collectively too, under him, and owe to him a legal obedience. The law, which knows neither to flatter nor to insult, calls this high magistrate, not our servant, as this humble Divine calls him, but "*our sovereign Lord the King;*" and we, on our parts, have learned to speak only the primitive language of the law, and not the confused jargon of their Babylonian pulpits, [.]

As he is not to obey us, but as we are to [42] obey the law in him, our con-

---

[118]Price, *Discourse*, p. 26.

[119]'Your recounting the circumstances looks like a reproach for ingratitude: with these words the steward Sosia replied when his master reminded him that he had formerly been a slave.' Terence, *Andria*, Act I, 45–6.

[120]The title 'Servus servorum Dei' was first used by Pope Gregory I (590–604) and has been in general use since Gregory VII (1073–85). The term 'The Fisherman' referred to the claim of Bishops of Rome to trace their authority to St. Peter. Burke's passage is hardly flattering of the Roman Church.

stitution has made no sort of provision towards rendering him, as a servant, in any degree responsible. Our constitution knows nothing of a magistrate like the *Justicia* of Arragon;[121] nor of any court legally appointed, nor of any process legally settled for submitting the king to the responsibility belonging to all servants. In this he is not distinguished from the commons and the lords; who, in their several public capacities, can never be called to an account for their conduct; although the Revolution Society chooses to assert, in direct opposition to one of the wisest and most beautiful parts of our constitution, that "a king is no more than the first servant of the public, created by it, *and responsible to it*".[122]

Ill would our ancestors at the Revolution have deserved their fame for wisdom, if they had found no security for their freedom, but in rendering their government feeble in its operations, and precarious in its tenure; if they had been able to contrive no better remedy against arbitrary power than civil confusion. Let these gentlemen state who that *representative* public is to whom they will affirm the king, as a servant, to be responsible. It will be then time enough for me to produce to them the positive statute law which affirms that he is not.

The ceremony of cashiering kings, of which these gentlemen talk so much at their ease, can rarely, if ever, be performed without force. It then becomes a case of war, and not of constitution. [43] Laws are commanded to hold their tongues amongst arms;[123] and tribunals fall to the ground with the peace they are no longer able to uphold. The Revolution of 1688 was obtained by a just war, in the only case in which any war, and much more a civil war, can be just. "Justa bella quibus *necessaria*."[124] The question of dethroning, or, if these gentlemen like the phrase better, "cashiering["] kings, will always be, as it has always been, an extraordinary question of state, and wholly out of the law; a question (like all other questions of state) of dispositions, and of means, and of probable consequences, rather than of positive rights. As it was not made

[121][Somers], *A Brief History of the Succession*, had pointed out how many exceptions there were to divine right monarchy, including 'Aragon, where they do not only elect their King, but tell him plainly at his Coronation, that they will depose him if he observes not the Conditions which they require from him, and have a settled Officer, call *El Justitia*, for that purpose' (p. 15).

[122]Price, *Discourse*, p. 23.

[123]'When arms speak, the laws are silent; they bid none to await their word, since he who chooses to await it must pay an undeserved penalty ere he can exact a deserved one': Cicero, *Pro Milone*, IV, 11–12.

[124]'Samnites, that war is just which is necessary, and righteous are their arms to whom, save only in arms, no hope is left': Livy, Book IX, i, 10–11.

for common abuses, so it is not to be agitated by common minds. The speculative line of demarcation, where obedience ought to end, and resistance must begin, is faint, obscure, and not easily definable.[125] It is not a single act, or a single event, which determines it. Governments must be abused and deranged indeed, before it can be thought of; and the prospect of the future must be as bad as the experience of the past. When things are in that lamentable condition, the nature of the disease is to indicate the remedy to those whom nature has qualified to administer in extremities this critical, ambiguous, bitter portion to a distempered state. Times and occasions, and provocations, will teach their own lessons. The wise will determine from the gravity of the case; the irritable from sensibility to oppression; the high-minded from disdain [44] and indignation at abusive power in unworthy hands; the brave and bold from the love of honourable danger in a generous cause: but, with or without right, a revolution will be the very last resource of the thinking and the good.

The third head of right, asserted by the pulpit of the Old Jewry, namely, the "right to form a government for ourselves," has, at least, as little countenance from any thing done at the Revolution, either in precedent or principle, as the two first of their claims. The Revolution was made to preserve our *antient* indisputable laws and liberties, and that *antient* constitution of government which is our only security for law and liberty. If you are desirous of knowing the spirit of our constitution, and the policy which predominated in that great period which has secured it to this hour, pray look for both in our histories, in our records, in our acts of parliament, and journals of parliament, and not in the sermons of the Old Jewry, and the after-dinner toasts of the Revolution Society.—In the former you will find other ideas and another language. Such a claim is as ill-suited to our temper and wishes as it is unsupported by any appearance of authority. The very idea of the fabrication of a new government, is enough to fill us with disgust and horror. We wished at the period of the Revolution, and do now wish, to derive all we possess as *an inheritance from our* [45] *forefathers.* Upon that body and stock of inheritance we have taken care not to inoculate any cyon alien to the nature of the original plant. All the reformations we have hitherto made, have proceeded upon the principle of reference to antiquity; and I hope, nay I am persuaded, that all those which possibly may be made hereafter, will be carefully formed upon analogical precedent, authority, and example.[126]

*Rings of frankenstein*

[125]Price and his allies offered no clear account of the point at which resistance should be triggered. They relied instead on heightened rhetorical eulogies of liberty and denunciations of tyranny, which begged the question.

[126]This trope had faded in England after the Revolution as ministerial Whigs in-

*critique of inventing new all over again.*

Our oldest reformation is that of Magna Charta. You will see that Sir Edward Coke,[127] that great oracle of our law, and indeed all the great men who follow him, to Blackstone,[128] are industrious to prove the pedigree of our liberties. They endeavour to prove, that the antient charter, the Magna Charta of King John, was connected with another positive charter from Henry I. and that both the one and the other were nothing more than a re-affirmance of the still more antient standing law of the kingdom.[129] In the matter of fact, for the greater part, these authors appear to be in the right; perhaps not always: but if the lawyers mistake in some particulars, it proves my position still the more strongly; because it demonstrates the powerful prepossession towards antiquity, with which the minds of all our lawyers and legislators, and of all the people whom they wish to influence, have been always filled; and the stationary policy of this kingdom in considering their most sacred rights and franchises as an *inheritance*.[130] [46]

In the famous law of the 3d of Charles I. called the *Petition of Right*,[131] the parliament says to the king, "Your subjects have *inherited* this freedom,"

------

creasingly traced English liberties to modern statutes like the Bill of Rights, the Toleration Act and the Act of Settlement. Burke was unusual in reverting to an older body of ideas which was currently employed only by the reformist intelligentsia. For this theme see Bibliography, B iii.

[127]See Biographical Guide.

[128]See Blackstone's Magna Charta, printed at Oxford, 1759. [B] William Blackstone (ed.), *The Great Charter and Charter of the Forest, with other Authentic Instruments* (Oxford, 1759) contained a lengthy historical introduction tracing the drafting of these charters from John to Edward I: documents which 'had been often endangered, and undergone many mutations, for the space of near a century; but were now [in 1300] fixed upon an eternal basis, having in all, before and since this time (as Sir Edward Coke observes) been established, confirmed, and commanded to be put in execution, by two and thirty several acts of parliament' (p. lxxiv).

[129]King John's Magna Carta of 1215 was part of a tradition of political strategems, including Henry I's coronation charter in 1100, in which medieval monarchs made detailed constitutional promises of good lordship. Such documents restated ancient custom and disavowed recent abuses. They owed nothing to the natural rights theories that reformers of the 1790s now attempted to read into them.

[130]For the English tradition of concrete and specific liberties contrasted with metaphysical conceptions of liberty, see especially G. R. Elton, 'Human Rights and the Liberties of Englishmen', *University of Illinois Law Review* (1990), pp. 329–46.

[131]The Petition of Right referred back to earlier statutes, like Edward I's *De Tallagio non Concedendo* 'by which the statutes before mentioned and other the good laws and statutes of this realm your subjects have inherited this freedom, that they should not be compelled to contribute to any tax, tallage, aid or other like charge not set by common consent in parliament': J. P. Kenyon (ed.), *The Stuart Constitution 1603–1688* (2nd edn., Cambridge, 1986), pp. 68–71.

claiming their franchises not on abstract principles "as the rights of men," but
as the rights of Englishmen, and as a patrimony derived from their forefathers. Selden,[132] and the other profoundly learned men, who drew this petition
of right, were as well acquainted, at least, with all the general theories concerning the "rights of men,"[133] as any of the discoursers in our pulpits, or on
your tribune; full as well as Dr. Price, or as the Abbé Seyes.[134] But, for reasons
worthy of that practical wisdom which superseded their theoretic science,
they preferred this positive, recorded, *hereditary* title to all which can be dear
to the man and the citizen, to that vague speculative right, which exposed
their sure inheritance to be scrambled for and torn to pieces by every wild litigious spirit.

The same policy pervades all the laws which have since been made for the
preservation of our liberties. In the 1st of William and Mary, in the famous
statute, called the Declaration of Right, the two houses utter not a syllable of
"a right to frame a government for themselves." You will see, that their whole
care was to secure the religion, laws, and liberties, that had been long possessed, and had been lately endangered. "Taking[135] into their most serious
consideration the *best* means for making such an establishment, [47] that
their religion laws, and liberties, might not be in danger of being again subverted," they auspicate all their proceedings, by stating as some of those *best*
means, "in the *first place*" to do "as their *ancestors in like cases have usually*
done for vindicating their *antient* rights and liberties, to *declare*;"—and then
they pray the king and queen, "that it may be *declared* and enacted, that *all
and singular* the rights and liberties *asserted and declared* are the true *antient*
and indubitable rights and liberties of the people of this kingdom."[136]

You will observe, that from Magna Charta to the Declaration of Right, it
has been the uniform policy of our constitution to claim and assert our liberties, as an *entailed inheritance* derived to us from our forefathers, and to be
transmitted to our posterity;[137] as an estate specially belonging to the people of

[132]See Biographical Guide.

[133]Natural rights theories were, of course, far older than the new language of the
rights of man, traced to 1776 and 1789. See especially Richard Tuck, *Natural Rights
Theories: Their Origin and Development* (Cambridge, 1979).

[134]See Biographical Guide.

[135]I W. and M. [B]

[136]The Bill of Rights (1 W.& M., s. 2, c. 2), clauses I, VI (free quotation).

[137]Cf. Joseph Addison, *Cato. A Tragedy* (London, 1713), p. 42: 'Cato. Remember,
O my Friends, the Laws, the Rights, / The gen'rous Plan of Power deliver'd down / From
Age to Age, by your renown'd Forefathers / (So dearly bought, the Price of so much
Blood) / O let it never perish in your Hands! / But piously transmit it to your Children.'

this kingdom without any reference whatever to any other more general or prior right. By this means our constitution preserves an unity in so great a diversity of its parts. We have an inheritable crown; an inheritable peerage; and an house of commons and a people inheriting privileges, franchises, and liberties, from a long line of ancestors.[138]

This policy appears to me to be the result of profound reflection; or rather the happy effect of following nature, which is wisdom without reflection, and above it.[139] A spirit of innovation is generally the result of a selfish temper and confined views. People will not look forward to posterity, [48] who never look backward to their ancestors. Besides, the people of England well know, that the idea of inheritance furnishes a sure principle of conservation, and a sure principle of transmission; without at all excluding a principle of improvement. It leaves acquisition free; but it secures what it acquires. Whatever advantages are obtained by a state proceeding on these maxims, are locked fast as in a sort of family settlement; grasped as in a kind of mortmain for ever.[140] By a constitutional policy, working after the pattern of nature, we receive, we hold, we transmit our government and our privileges, in the same manner in which we enjoy and transmit our property and our lives. The institutions of policy, the goods of fortune, the gifts of Providence, are handed down, to us and from us, in the same course and order. Our political system is placed in a just correspondence and symmetry with the order of the world, and with the mode of existence decreed to a permanent body composed of transitory parts; wherein, by the disposition of a stupendous wisdom, moulding together the great mysterious incorporation of the human race, the whole, at one time, is never old, or middle-aged, or young, but in a condition of unchangeable constancy, moves on through the varied tenour of perpetual decay, fall, renovation, and progression. Thus, by preserving the method of nature in the conduct of the state, in what we improve we are never wholly new;

[138]Burke thus defended a social order in which each of its component parts had its separate rights.

[139]'Never does Nature say one thing and Wisdom another': Juvenal, *Satires* XIV, line 321.

[140]Mortmain: 'The condition of lands or tenements held inalienably by an ecclesiastical or other corporation', *OED*. By alienating land in perpetuity from the crown and other landlords, mortmain had been looked on with disfavour and regulated by statutes since the reign of Edward I; the last had been the Mortmain Act, 9 Geo. II, c. 36 (1736). This Act had been part of a freethinking Whig campaign against the Church. In 1770, Burke had used the term pejoratively, condemning royal influence as something possessed by the crown 'as in a sort of mortmain', partly returned to the people at the Revolution of 1688: [Burke], *Thoughts*, p. 8. Now, Burke began to give 'mortmain' a favourable meaning.

in what we retain we are [49] never wholly obsolete. By adhering in this manner and on those principles to our forefathers, we are guided not by the superstition of antiquarians,[141] but by the spirit of philosophic analogy. In this choice of inheritance we have given to our frame of polity the image of a relation in blood; binding up the constitution of our country with our dearest domestic ties; adopting our fundamental laws into the bosom of our family affections; keeping inseparable, and cherishing with the warmth of all their combined and mutually reflected charities, our state, our hearths, our sepulchres, and our altars.[142]

Through the same plan of a conformity to nature in our artificial institutions, and by calling in the aid of her unerring and powerful instincts, to fortify the fallible and feeble contrivances of our reason, we have derived several other, and those no small benefits, from considering our liberties in the light of an inheritance. Always acting as if in the presence of canonized forefathers, the spirit of freedom, leading in itself to misrule and excess, is tempered with an awful gravity. This idea of a liberal descent inspires us with a sense of habitual native dignity, which prevents that upstart insolence almost inevitably adhering to and disgracing those who are the first acquirers of any distinction. By this means our liberty becomes a noble freedom. It carries an imposing and majestic aspect. It has a pedigree, and illustrating ancestors. It has its bearings, and its ensigns armorial. It has its gallery [50] of portraits; its monumental inscriptions; its records, evidences, and titles.[143] We procure reverence to our civil institutions on the principle upon which nature teaches us to revere individual men; on account of their age; and on account of those from whom they are descended. All your sophisters cannot produce any thing better adapted to preserve a rational and manly freedom than the course that we have pursued, who have chosen our nature rather than our speculations, our breasts rather than our inventions, for the great conservatories and magazines of our rights and privileges.

You might, if you pleased, have profited of our example, and have given to

[141]Burke distanced himself from an antiquarian tradition in English historical scholarship in figures like William Cole (1714–82), Thomas Hearne (1678–1735), George Hickes (1642–1715) and Humfrey Wanley (1672–1726), a tradition which had often had Tory-Jacobite associations.

[142]Burke's eulogy is more remarkable after a lifetime in politics spent denouncing the corruption of his age and the incompetence of governments; his critics now seized on the apparent contradiction.

[143]Such passages echo the strong sense of family which characterised the Whig nobility, a world into which Burke had been initiated by the 2nd marquis of Rockingham.

your recovered freedom a correspondent dignity. Your privileges,[144] though discontinued, were not lost to memory. Your constitution,[145] it is true, whilst you were out of possession, suffered waste and dilapidation; but you possessed in some parts the walls, and in all the foundations of a noble and venerable castle. You might have repaired those walls; you might have built on those old foundations.[146] Your constitution was suspended before it was perfected; but you had the elements of a constitution very nearly as good as could be wished.[147] In your old states[148] you possessed that variety of parts corre-

[144]I.e. liberties.

[145]Revolutionaries now sought to confine the term 'constitution' to a codified statement of fundamental law, antecedent to government. Burke used the term in its wider sense of all the institutions and practices of government. Paine argued: 'A constitution is a thing *antecedent* to a government, and a government is only the creature of a constitution. The constitution of a country is not the act of its government, but of the people constituting a government.' It was in this sense of the word that Paine challenged: 'Can then Mr Burke produce the English Constitution?': *Rights of Man*, pp. 53–4. An affirmative answer was precluded in advance. The real question was whether Paine's analysis applied to the American and French revolutions.

[146]Many French moderates still acted on the same principle, looking to 1688 as an example. They came to be known as *monarchiens* or *Anglophiles*, led from 1789 by the marquis de Lally-Tollendal, Pierre-Victor Malouet and Jean-Joseph Mounier, and campaigned for a bicameral legislature and a monarchy retaining a power of veto. The *monarchiens* lost the crucial divisions on these points in the National Assembly during September 1789 by wide margins. It was to force Louis XVI to reverse his refusal to promulgate the constitutional measures passed in these divisions, together with the Declaration of the Rights of Man and the abolition of feudalism, that the Paris mob intervened and brought the king by force to the capital on 6 October. Recent historians have sometimes argued that Burke misread eighteenth-century France, since France's 'ancient constitution' had been largely erased by monarchical absolutism. This was not the perspective of many at the time. As Loménie de Brienne, the king's chief minister until 25 August 1788, noted in September 1790 on a memorandum discussing the new provincial assemblies envisaged by the reforms of May 1788: 'Si les bases que je donnois alors conciliées avec l'ancienne constitution eussent été établies, cette ancienne constitution n'eût pas été ébranlée. Il y eût eu moins de trouble, enfin la génération future y auroit peut-être moins gagné, mais la génération présente y auroit trouvé plus de tranquillité, moins de secousses et de dommages; peut-être mesme que petit à petit ce qu'on a établi brusquement se seroit introduit lentement et sans convulsions. Au surplus, il n'étoit pas permis dans le tems de penser à ce qui est venu depuis, et qu'on eût regardé comme impossible. C'étoit beaucoup d'adopter des principes qui étoient déjà favorables à la révolution actuelle et qui sans la completter la proposoient sans la rendre aussi désastreuse pour une multitude d'individus.' Pierre Chevallier (ed.), *Journal de l' Assemblée des Notables de 1787 par le comte de Brienne et Etienne Charles de Loménie de Brienne, archevêque de Toulouse* (Paris, 1960), p. 13n.

[147]Reformers often focused on this controversial component of Burke's argument,

sponding with the various descriptions of which your community was happily composed[;] you had all that combination, and all that opposition of interests, you had that action and counteraction which, in the natural and in the political [51] world, from the reciprocal struggle of discordant powers, draws out the harmony of the universe. These opposed and conflicting interests, which you considered as so great a blemish in your old and in our present constitution, interpose a salutary check to all precipitate resolutions; They render deliberation a matter not of choice, but of necessity; they make all change a subject of *compromise*; which naturally begets moderation; they produce *temperaments*, preventing the sore evil of harsh, crude, unqualified reformations; and rendering all the headlong exertions of arbitrary power, in the few or in the many, for ever impracticable. Through that diversity of members and interests, general liberty had as many securities as there were separate views in the several orders; whilst by pressing down the whole by the weight of a real monarchy, the separate parts would have been prevented from warping and starting from their allotted places.[149]

You had all these advantages in your ancient states; but you chose to act as if you had never been moulded into civil society, and had every thing to begin anew. You began ill, because you began by despising every thing that belonged to you. You set up your trade without a capital. If the last generations of your country appeared without much lustre in your eyes, you might have passed them by, and derived your claims from a more early race of ancestors. Under a pious predilection to those ancestors, your imaginations [52] would have realized in them a standard of virtue and wisdom, beyond the vulgar practice of the hour: and you would have risen with the example to whose imitation you aspired. Respecting your forefathers, you would have been taught to respect yourselves. You would not have chosen to consider the French as a people of yesterday, as a nation of low-born servile wretches until

---

e.g. Philip Francis to Burke, 3 November 1790: Burke, *Correspondence*, VI, pp. 150–5.

[148]The Estates-General. They had last been summoned in 1614.

[149]Burke's analysis here echoed Montesquieu's defence of intermediate institutions (e.g. *The Spirit of the Laws*, Book, II, chapter 4, 'Of the Relation of Laws to the Nature of monarchical Governement'). Revolutionaries of 1776 and 1789 increasingly urged the unchecked, unmediated, absolute authority of 'the people' or 'the nation'. Burke owned the *Oeuvres de Montesquieu* (7 vols., 1757), as well as another copy of the *Esprit des Loix*: LC MS, fos. 3, 10; *LC*, p. 14. It is not clear which edition of the *Oeuvres* is meant: see C. P. Courtney, *Montesquieu and Burke* (Oxford, 1963), p. 31. Courtney documents the continuing parallels between Burke's thought and Montesquieu's.

the emancipating year of 1789.[150] In order to furnish, at the expence of your honour, an excuse to your apologists here for several enormities of yours, you would not have been content to be represented as a gang of Maroon slaves,[151] suddenly broke loose from the house of bondage,[152] and therefore to be pardoned for your abuse of the liberty to which you were not accustomed and ill fitted. Would it not, my worthy friend, have been wiser to have you thought, what I, for one, always thought you, a generous and gallant nation, long misled to your disadvantage by your high and romantic sentiments of fidelity, honour, and loyalty; that events had been unfavourable to you, but that you were not enslaved through any illiberal or servile disposition; that in your most devoted submission, you were actuated by a principle of public spirit, and that it was your country you worshipped, in the person of your king? Had you made it to be understood, that in the delusion of this amiable error you had gone further than your wise ancestors; that you were resolved to resume your ancient privileges, whilst you preserved the spirit of your ancient and your [53] recent loyalty and honour; or, if diffident of yourselves, and not clearly discerning the almost obliterated constitution of your ancestors, you had looked to your neighbours in this land, who had kept alive the ancient principles and models of the old common law of Europe meliorated and adapted to its present state—by following wise examples you would have given new examples of wisdom to the world. You would have rendered the cause of liberty venerable in the eyes of every worthy mind in every nation. You would have shamed despotism from the earth, by shewing that freedom was not only reconcileable, but as, when well disciplined it is, auxiliary to law. You would have had an unoppressive but a productive revenue. You would have had a flourishing commerce to feed it.[153] You would have had a free con-

---

[150]The Legislative Assembly did not adopt the new revolutionary calendar until 2 January 1792, retrospectively designating 1789 as 'L'an I', but a proposal for simultaneously reckoning 'l'Ere de la liberté' from 1 April 1789 had been made in Le Moniteur of 17 May 1790, and from 1 July 1790 that journal's title had boasted: 'Seconde Année de la Liberté', commemorating the fall of the Bastille. The full republican calendar, with its renamed months and decimalised weeks, was promulgated in November 1793 and imposed under threat of a death penalty.

[151]Runaway slaves in the West Indies sometimes established tribes in the hinterland and carried on a guerilla war with the planters.

[152]Cf. Exodus 20.2: 'I am the Lord thy God, which have brought thee out of the land of Egypt, out of the house of bondage.'

[153]Burke overlooked the failure of the reform movement in France in 1787–8, coinciding with a disastrous economic crisis, and culminating in a suspension of payments from the royal treasury on 16 August 1788 which was generally interpreted as national bankruptcy: Doyle, Origins, pp. 96–114, 158–67; this lacuna reflected Burke's ideali-

stitution; a potent monarchy; a disciplined army; a reformed and venerated clergy; a mitigated but spirited nobility, to lead your virtue, not to overlay it; you would have had a liberal order of commons, to emulate and to recruit that nobility; you would have had a protected, satisfied, laborious, and obedient people, taught to seek and to recognize the happiness that is to be found by virtue in all conditions; in which consists the true moral equality of mankind, and not in that monstrous fiction, which, by inspiring false ideas and vain expectations into men destined to travel in the obscure walk of laborious life, serves only to aggravate and imbitter that real inequality, [54] which it never can remove; and which the order of civil life establishes as much for the benefit of those whom it must leave in an humble state, as those whom it is able to exalt to a condition more splendid, but not more happy. You had a smooth and easy career of felicity and glory laid open to you, beyond any thing recorded in the history of the world; but you have shewn that difficulty is good for man.

Compute your gains:[154] see what is got by those extravagant and presumptuous speculations which have taught your leaders to despise all their predecessors, and all their contemporaries, and even to despise themselves, until the moment in which they became truly despicable. By following those false lights, France has bought undisguised calamities at a higher price than any nation has purchased the most unequivocal blessings! France has bought poverty by crime! France has not sacrificed her virtue to her interest; but she has abandoned her interest, that she might prostitute her virtue. All other nations have begun the fabric of a new government, or the reformation of an old, by establishing originally, or by enforcing with greater exactness some rites or other of religion.[155] All other people have laid the foundations of civil freedom in severer manners, and a system of a more austere and masculine morality. France, when she let loose the reins of regal authority, doubled the licence, of

---

sation of English Whiggery as a formula for national prosperity rather than of France's *ancien régime*. Other historians (e.g. Egret, *French Prerevolution*, passim) have treated this reform movement as feasible, and explained its frustration by the resistance to it of the nobility.

[154]English reformers quickly accepted Burke's challenge to draw up a balance-sheet of gains and losses. Their response was unwise: even in 1790, the cold comparison of constitutional innovations with mob violence and expropriation made reformers look inhumane. Accumulating atrocities, culminating in the September Massacres of 1792, the Terror and the savage repression of the rising in the Vendée, were then incorporated in the same balance-sheet. For a modern summing-up, see René Sédillot, *Le coût de la Révolution française* (Paris, 1987).

[155]It is questionable whether Burke included the American republic in this analysis. He almost certainly had in mind the English republic of the 1650s.

a ferocious dissoluteness in manners, and of an insolent irreligion[156] in opinions and practices; [55] and has extended through all ranks of life, as if she were communicating some privilege, or laying open some secluded benefit, all the unhappy corruptions that usually were the disease of wealth and power. This is one of the new principles of equality in France.

France, by the perfidy of her leaders, has utterly disgraced the tone of lenient council in the cabinets of princes, and disarmed it of its most potent topics. She has sanctified the dark suspicious maxims of tyrannous distrust; and taught kings to tremble at (what will hereafter be called) the delusive plausibilities, of moral politicians. Sovereigns will consider those who advise them to place an unlimited confidence in their people, as subverters of their thrones; as traitors who aim at their destruction, by leading their easy good-nature, under specious pretences, to admit combinations of bold and faithless men into a participation of their power. This alone (if there were nothing else) is an irreparable calamity to you and to mankind. Remember that your parliament of Paris told your king, that in calling the states together, he had nothing to fear but the prodigal excess of their zeal in providing for the support of the throne.[157] It is right that these men should hide their heads. It is right that they should bear their part in the ruin which their counsel has brought on their sovereign and their country. Such sanguine declarations tend to lull authority asleep; to encourage it rashly to engage in perilous adventures of untried policy; [56] to neglect those provisions, preparations, and precautions, which distinguish benevolence from imbecillity; and without which no man can answer for the salutary effect of any abstract plan of government or of freedom. For want of these, they have seen the medicine of the state corrupted into its poison. They have seen the French rebel against a mild and lawful monarch,[158]

[156]It has been argued by some historians that in 1789 a conflict between the Revolution and the Church was not inevitable, and that de-Christianisation was a violent but brief movement confined to 1793–4. Other scholars see the Revolution as essentially anti-Christian from the outset: see Bibliography, D xii.

[157]After the failed royal *coup* of 8 May 1788, the Paris *Parlement* reconvened on 25 September and the following day enthusiastically registered a royal edict for the summoning of the Estates-General. See Armand Brette, *Receuil de documents relatifs à la convocation des États généraux de 1789* (4 vols., Paris, 1894–1915), I, pp. 28–9. For the *Parlement*'s deliberations on the same subject on 21 December 1788, see Jules Flammermont (ed.), *Remontrances du Parlement de Paris au XVIII<sup>e</sup> Siècle* (3 vols., Paris, 1888–99), III, pp. 777–99.

[158]Paine commented (*Rights of Man*, p. 17): 'It was not against Louis the XVIth, but against the despotic principles of the government, that the nation revolted.' Burke's discussion of the Revolution continually reverts to the personal, human consequences of principled action.

with more fury, outrage, and insult, than ever any people has been known to rise against the most illegal usurper, or the most sanguinary tyrant. Their resistance was made to concession; their revolt was from protection; their blow was aimed at an hand holding out graces, favours, and immunities.[159] —This was unnatural. The rest is in order.[160] They have found their punishment in their success. Laws overturned; tribunals subverted; industry without vigour; commerce expiring; the revenue unpaid, yet the people impoverished; a church pillaged, and a state not relieved; civil and military anarchy made the constitution of the kingdom; every thing human and divine sacrificed to the idol of public credit, and national bankruptcy the consequence; and to crown all, the paper securities of new, precarious, tottering power, the discredited paper securities of impoverished fraud, and beggared rapine, held out as a currency for the support of an empire, in lieu of the two great recognized species[161] that represent the lasting conventional credit of mankind, which disappeared [57] and hid themselves in the earth from whence they came, when the principle of property, whose creatures and representatives they are, was systematically subverted.[162]

[159]Louis XVI's governments had a strong record of domestic reform: see especially Egret, *French Prerevolution*, passim and Burke, *Reflections*, p. [195]. Yet the attempts of French ministers like Calonne and Brienne in 1786–88 to reform the state and its finances were often resisted and denounced by the clergy and nobility as despotic violations of ancient privileges and liberties. This rhetoric had been given a forum in the Assembly of Notables, which (having last met in 1626) was recalled at Versailles on 22 February 1787; its resistance was followed by that of the *parlements*, which often refused to register Brienne's reforms from July that year, and were overridden by royal prerogative. When the Paris *Parlement* issued a major claim of constitutional right on 3 May 1788, the ministry responded on 8 May by establishing a Plenary Court which would largely supersede the *parlements* in their familiar role: this royal *coup d'etat* was often termed a '*révolution*'. Denunciation of the arbitrary actions of the monarchy now reached a peak, and induced Brienne in July 1788 to promise an eventual summoning of the Estates-General. On 8 August he agreed to suspend the introduction of the Plenary Courts and summon the Estates-General in 1789, not 1792. The collapse of the *ancien régime* is arguably to be dated to 16 August 1788, when the royal treasury suspended payments in specie: Doyle, *Origins*, pp. 96–114; Hampson, *Prelude*, pp. 21–41.

[160]I.e. followed logically.

[161]Gold and silver.

[162]It has been argued that the National Assembly was chiefly composed of Catholics who sought to reform the Church and make it 'a buttress of regenerated France', with only grudging religious toleration (John McManners, *The French Revolution and the Church* (London, 1969), pp. 24–5), but the attack on privilege soon became uncontrollable. On 4 August 1789 the Assembly voted the abolition of tithes; on 2 November it voted that church property was '*à la disposition de la Nation*', which would hence-

Were all these dreadful things necessary? were they the inevitable results of the desperate struggle of determined patriots, compelled to wade through blood and tumult, to the quiet shore of a tranquil and prosperous liberty? No! nothing like it. The fresh ruins of France, which shock our feelings wherever we can turn our eyes, are not the devastation of civil war; they are the sad but instructive monuments of rash and ignorant counsel in time of profound peace. They are the display of inconsiderate and presumptuous, because unresisted and irresistible authority. The persons who have thus squandered away the precious treasure of their crimes, the persons who have made this prodigal and wild waste of public evils (the last stake reserved for the ultimate ransom of the state) have met in their progress with little, or rather with no opposition at all. Their whole march was more like a triumphal procession than the progress of a war. Their pioneers have gone before them, and demolished and laid every thing level at their feet. Not one drop of *their* blood have they shed in the cause of the country they have ruined. They have made no sacrifices to their projects of greater consequence than their shoe-buckles,[163] whilst they were imprisoning their king, [58] murdering their fellow citizens,[164] and bathing in tears, and plunging in poverty and distress, thousands of worthy men and worthy families. Their cruelty has not even been the base result of fear. It has been the effect of their sense of perfect safety, in authorizing treasons, robberies, rapes, assassinations, slaughters, and burnings throughout their harrassed land.[165] But the cause of all was plain from the beginning.

---

forth pay salaries to the clergy; on 19 December the Assembly voted to begin the auction of the ecclesiastical property so confiscated. On 13 February 1790 it withdrew official recognition of monastic vows, forbade taking them in future, and ordered the suppression of contemplative and mendicant orders. In March 1790, this expropriated wealth became the insecure backing for the new paper currency, the *assignats*: see *Reflections*, p. [182].

[163]*Le Moniteur* prominently paraded the *dons patriotiques* made by ordinary citizens of their gold shoe buckles. Burke suggested that the revolutionaries' donations to the public cause were only token. See *Reflections*, p. [80].

[164]Paine (*Rights of Man*, p. 20) claimed that 'in the instance of France, we see a revolution generated in the rational contemplation of the rights of man, and distinguishing from the beginning between persons and principles.' Paine never adequately addressed the problem of revolutionary violence.

[165]Food riots in the countryside early in 1789 grew in July, and the drive to abolish seigneurial dues began to find expression in the looting of chateaux and abbeys. The hysteria was heightened by the 'Grande Peur', set off by spontaneous rumours of counter-revolutionary bands. In this fevered context, the nobility was swayed into surrendering its feudal or seigneurial rights at the astonishing and uncontrolled session of the National Assembly on the night of 4 August. At that moment, the task of the Assembly expanded from the drafting of a new constitution to the reconstruction of

This unforced choice, this fond election of evil, would appear perfectly unaccountable, if we did not consider the composition of the National Assembly; I do not mean its formal constitution, which, as it now stands, is exceptionable enough, but the materials of which in a great measure it is composed, which is of ten thousand times greater consequence than all the formalities in the world. If we were to know nothing of this Assembly but by its title and function, no colours could paint to the imagination any thing more venerable. In that light the mind of an enquirer, subdued by such an awful image as that of the virtue and wisdom of a whole people collected into a focus, would pause and hesitate in condemning things even of the very worst aspect. Instead of blameable, they would appear only mysterious. But no name, no power, no function, no artificial institution whatsoever, can make the men of whom any system of authority is composed, any other than God, and nature, and education, and their habits of life have made them.[166] Capacities [59] beyond these the people have not to give. Virtue and wisdom may be the objects of their choice; but their choice confers neither the one nor the other on those upon whom they lay their ordaining hands. They have not the engagement of nature, they have not the promise of revelation for any such powers.

After I had read over the list of the persons and descriptions elected into the *Tiers Etat*,[167] nothing which they afterwards did could appear astonishing. Among them, indeed, I saw some of known rank; some of shining talents; but

---

French society. For this aspect of disorder see Georges Lefebvre, *The Great Fear of 1789*, trans. Joan White (London, 1973). Samuel Scott, 'Problems of Law and Order during 1790, the "Peaceful" Year of the French Revolution', *American Historical Review* 80 (1975), pp. 859–88, showed how the wide extent of violence and lawlessness had been omitted from subsequent historical writing, and provided evidence that violence was not confined to 'traditional' forms like the food riot: it included military insubordination and peasant '*jacqueries* against feudal obligations'. These produced a 'widespread, if not general, breakdown of law and order during 1790 ... Although Paris was spared, many of the greatest cities in France—Lille, Nancy, Montauban, Nîmes, Marseilles, Lyon, and others—were the scenes of bitter struggles', pp. 880, 887.

[166]In the eighteenth-century debate between 'nature' and 'nurture', Burke thus adopted an intermediate position.

[167]This could have been *Liste complette de Messieurs les Députés aux États Généraux* ([Paris], 1789); or *Liste de Messieurs les Députés aux États-Généraux & de leur Suppléants, divisée par Gouvernements* ([Paris], 1789); or *Liste, par ordre alphabétique, de bailliages et sénéchaussées, de MM. les députés aux États-Généraux, Convoqués à Versailles le 27 Avril 1789* (Paris, 1789). Lists of deputies to the three Estates, with their occupations or ranks, were also printed in [Louis Marie Prudhomme and F. S. Laurent de Mezières], *Résumé général, ou Extrait des Cahiers de Pouvoirs, Instructions, Demandes et Doléances* (3 vols., [Paris], 1789). Burke may have seen this work: see *Reflections*, p. [188].

of any practical experience in the state, not one man was to be found. The best were only men of theory.[168] But whatever the distinguished few may have been, it is the substance and mass of the body which constitutes its character, and must finally determine its direction. In all bodies, those who will lead, must also, in a considerable degree, follow. They must conform their propositions to the taste, talent, and disposition of those whom they wish to conduct: therefore, if an Assembly is viciously or feebly composed in a very great part of it, nothing but such a supreme degree of virtue as very rarely appears in the world, and for that reason cannot enter into calculation, will prevent the men of talents disseminated through it from becoming only the expert instruments of absurd projects! If what is the more likely event, instead of that unusual degree of virtue, they should be actuated by sinister ambition and a lust of meretricious glory, then the feeble part of the [60] Assembly, to whom at first they conform, becomes in its turn the dupe and instrument of their designs. In this political traffick the leaders will be obliged to bow to the ignorance of their followers, and the followers to become subservient to the worst designs of their leaders.

To secure any degree of sobriety in the propositions made by the leaders in any public assembly, they ought to respect, in some degree perhaps to fear, those whom they conduct. To be led any otherwise than blindly, the followers must be qualified, if not for actors, at least for judges; they must also be judges of natural weight and authority. Nothing can secure a steady and moderate conduct in such assemblies, but that the body of them should be respectably composed, in point of condition in life, of permanent property, of education, and of such habits as enlarge and liberalize the understanding.

In the calling of the states general of France, the first thing which struck me, was a great departure from the antient course. I found the representation for the Third Estate composed of six hundred persons. They were equal in number to the representatives of both the other orders. If the orders were to act separately, the number would not, beyond the consideration of the expence, be of much moment.[169] But when it became apparent that the three or-

[168]Tocqueville later made the same point central to his argument. 'Men of letters were not daily involved in public affairs as in England; on the contrary, they had never been further removed from them ... However, they ... constantly concerned themselves with topics relating to government; in fact, that was their real occupation ... The very situation of these writers prepared them to like general and abstract theories of government and to trust in them blindly ... they didn't have any idea of the dangers which always accompany even the most necessary revolutions': Tocqueville, *Old Regime*, pp. 195, 197.

[169]On 5 July 1788 Brienne, the king's chief minister, promised to summon the Es-

ders were to be melted down into one, the policy and necessary effect of this numerous representation became obvious. A [61] very small desertion from either of the other two orders must throw the power of both into the hands of the third. In fact, the whole power of the state was soon resolved into that body.[170] Its due composition became therefore of infinitely the greater importance.

Judge, sir, of my surprize, when I found that a very great proportion of the Assembly (a majority, I believe, of the members who attended)[171] was com-

---

tates-General and to consider suggestions about the form they should now take in the light of modern conditions. A controversy followed. The *Parlement* of Paris favoured an Estates-General composed of three equal and separate orders, each voting separately, the assent of all three being necessary for the passage of legislation. Others, like Pétion and Sieyès, stood for a Third Estate increased to numerical equality with the other two, a formula implying voting by simple majority in a body amalgamating the three orders. Brienne's successor Necker persuaded Louis XVI that the representatives of the Third Estate should be doubled to 600 (a measure decreed by an act of the council dated 27 December 1788) but left the question of how the three Orders should vote to be decided by the Estates-General. The *Parlement* of Paris, argued Burke, ought to have protested against the 'doubling of the Third': 'Under pretence of resuscitating the ancient constitution, the Parliament saw one of the strongest acts of innovation, and the most leading in its consequences, carried into effect before their eyes; and an innovation through the medium of despotism; that is, they suffered the King's ministers to new model the whole representation of the *Tiers Etat*, and, in a great measure, that of the clergy too, and to destroy the antient proportions of the orders. These changes, unquestionably the King had no right to make; and here the Parliaments failed in their duty, and along with their country, have perished by the failure': *Letter to a Member*, pp. 60–1. Arthur Young commented: 'If there is any one circumstance to which all the horrors that have passed in France may be more properly attributed than to any other, it is the double representation given to the *tiers etat* by Mr. Neckar, directly contrary to every respectable authority': Arthur Young, *The Example of France, a Warning to Britain* (London, 1793), p. 40.

[170]The Estates-General met on 5 May 1789 and were quickly deadlocked by disagreement on the question of voting by majority, or by orders. On 10 June the Third Estate broke the stalemate by passing Sieyès's motion to begin the verification of members' credentials in a joint session, whether or not the other Estates agreed: the Third Estate now began to act on behalf of the nation. On 17 June, with the participation of a few clergy who had broken ranks with their First Estate, the Third Estate adopted the novel title of National Assembly. Implicitly claiming sovereignty, this body then passed resolutions provisionally confirming existing taxes and guaranteeing the national debt. By 22 June, the Assembly had been joined by 149 clerical deputies and 3 nobles. Louis XVI failed to undo this on 23 June; the rest of the clergy and many of the nobles now joined the Third Estate, and the king ordered the rest to do so on 27 June: Doyle, *Origins*, pp. 168–77; Hampson, *Prelude*, pp. 33–49.

[171]A contemporary list analysed the Third Estate as consisting of 353 *Hommes de*

posed of practitioners in the law.[172] It was composed not of distinguished magistrates,[173] who had given pledges to their country of their science, prudence, and integrity; not of leading advocates, the glory of the bar; not of renowned professors in universities;—but for the far greater part, as it must in such a number, of the inferior, unlearned, mechanical, merely instrumental members of the profession. There were distinguished exceptions; but the general composition was of obscure provincial advocates, of stewards of petty local jurisdictions, country attornies, notaries, and the whole train of the ministers of municipal litigation, the fomentors and conductors of the petty war of village vexation.[174] From the moment I read the list I saw distinctly, and very nearly as it has happened, all that was to follow.[175]

The degree of estimation in which any profession is held becomes the standard of the estimation in which the professors hold themselves. Whatever the personal merits of many individual [62] lawyers might have been, and in many it was undoubtedly very considerable, in that military kingdom, no part of the profession had been much regarded, except the highest of all, who often united to their professional offices great family splendour, and were invested with great power and authority. These certainly were highly respected, and

---

*Robe* as against 242 in the various categories of *Arts & Métiers: Liste complette de Messieurs les Députes*. A modern analysis of the Third Estate by occupational category gives: *avocats* 27.9 per cent, royal judiciary 25.0 per cent, merchants 11.1 per cent, royal administrators (ie judges and lawyers in royal administrative courts) 5.9 per cent, mayors 5.5 per cent, farmers 5.2 per cent, bourgeois 3.2 per cent, doctors 3.0 per cent. Other lawyers included *notaires* 1.8 per cent, seigneurial judges 1.2 per cent, *procureurs* 0.4 per cent: Harriet B. Applewhite, *Political Alignment in the French National Assembly, 1789–1791* (Baton Rouge, 1993), p. 42.

[172]Perhaps unwisely, Priestley conceded the point with an analogy: 'The first American Congress, I very well remember, was said to consist chiefly of lawyers': *Letters to Burke*, p. 14, quoting David Ramsay, *The History of the American Revolution* (2 vols., Philadelphia, 1789), I, p. 134: 'Of the whole number of deputies, which formed the Continental Congress, of 1774, one half were lawyers.'

[173]Magistrates of the supreme courts ranked with the nobility; in 1789, 27 senior lawyers were listed among 289 members of the Second Estate: *Liste complette de Messieurs les Députés*.

[174]Elections to the Third Estate were in two stages. First, delegates were elected who met in each *bailliage* (bailiwick). It was they who chose deputies to the Estates-General. This indirect system favoured men of some substance with experience of public speaking, often lawyers.

[175]Paine, referring to his correspondence with Burke from Paris, wrote: 'Mr. Burke certainly did not see all that was to follow. I have endeavored to impress him, as well before as after the States-General met, that there would be a *revolution*; but was not able to make him see it, neither would he believe it': *Rights of Man*, p. 101.

even with no small degree of awe. The next rank was not much esteemed; the mechanical part was in a very low degree of repute.

Whenever the supreme authority is invested in a body so composed, it must evidently produce the consequences of supreme authority placed in the hands of men not taught habitually to respect themselves; who had no previous fortune in character at stake; who could not be expected to bear with moderation, or to conduct with discretion, a power which they themselves, more than any others, must be surprized to find in their hands. Who could flatter himself that these men, suddenly, and, as it were, by enchantment, snatched from the humblest rank of subordination, would not be intoxicated with their unprepared greatness? Who could conceive, that men who are habitually meddling, daring, subtle, active, of litigious dispositions and unquiet minds, would easily fall back into their old condition of obscure contention, and laborious, low, unprofitable chicane? Who could doubt but that, at any [63] expence to the state, of which they understood nothing, they must pursue their private interests, which they understood but too well? It was not an event depending on chance or contingency. It was inevitable; it was necessary; it was planted in the nature of things. They must *join* (if their capacity did not permit them to *lead*) in any project which could procure to them a *litigious constitution*; which could lay open to them those innumerable lucrative jobs which follow in the train of all great convulsions and revolutions[176] in the state, and particularly in all great and violent permutations of property. Was it to be expected that they would attend to the stability of property, whose existence had always depended upon whatever rendered property questionable, ambiguous, and insecure? Their objects would be enlarged with their elevation, but their disposition and habits, and mode of accomplishing their designs, must remain the same.

Well! but these men were to be tempered and restrained by other descriptions, of more sober minds, and more enlarged understandings. Were they then to be awed by the super-eminent authority and awful dignity of an handful of country clowns who have seats in that Assembly, some of whom are said not to be able to read and write? and by not a greater number of traders, who, though somewhat more instructed, and more conspicuous in the order of society, had never known any thing beyond their counting-house? [64] No! both these descriptions were more formed to be overborne and swayed by the intrigues and artifices of lawyers, than to become their counterpoise. With such a dangerous disproportion, the whole must needs be governed by them. To the faculty of law was joined a pretty considerable proportion of the fac-

---

[176]Burke used the two terms as synonyms.

ulty of medicine.[177] This faculty had not, any more than that of the law, possessed in France its just estimation. Its professors therefore must have the qualities of men not habituated to sentiments of dignity. But supposing they had ranked as they ought to do, and as with us they do actually, the sides of sick beds are not the academies for forming statesmen and legislators. Then came the dealers in stocks and funds, who must be eager, at any expence, to change their ideal paper wealth for the more solid substance of land. To these were joined men of other descriptions, from whom as little knowledge of or attention to the interests of a great state was to be expected, and as little regard to the stability of any institution; men formed to be instruments, not controls. Such in general was the composition of the *Tiers Etat* in the National Assembly; in which was scarcely to be perceived the slightest traces of what we call the natural landed interest of the country.[178]

We know that the British house of commons, without shutting its doors to any merit in any class,[179] is, by the sure operation of adequate causes, [65] filled with every thing illustrious in rank, in descent, in hereditary and in acquired opulence, in cultivated talents, in military, civil, naval, and politic distinction, that the country can afford.[180] But supposing, what hardly can be

[177]In fact only 15 members of the National Assembly were listed as doctors, compared with 353 *Hommes de Robe* plus other lawyers: *Liste complette de Messieurs les Députes.*

[178]Of the Third Estate, 'between 10 and 11 percent of deputies described themselves as some sort of landowner, and the true proportion of landowners must have been far higher': Doyle, *Origins*, p. 155. Yet they scarcely corresponded to the ideal type of the country gentleman, a JP with broad acres, with which Burke was familiar at Westminster. An Act of 1710 ('An Act for securing the Freedom of Parliaments, by the farther qualifying the Members to sit in the House of Commons', 9 Anne, c. 5) required of English and Welsh MPs an income from land as a qualification for taking their seats (£600 p.a. for a county MP, £300 p.a. for a borough MP). Although this was a party strategem during the Tory high tide of 1710–14, most Whigs too either were or sought to be landowners, and the Act was not repealed until 1838. About half of British MPs were country gentlemen without other employment. Of a total of 2041 MPs in the Parliaments of 1714–54, 708 have been identified as army and naval officers, barristers, professional men, merchants and industrialists. Of the 2143 MPs in the Parliaments of 1790–1820, similar categories, with diplomats included, account for 1270 Members: Romney Sedgwick (ed.), *The History of Parliament: The House of Commons 1715–1754* (2 vols., London, 1970), I, pp. 136–51; R. G. Thorne (ed.), *The History of Parliament: The House of Commons 1790–1820* (5 vols., London, 1986), I, pp. 278–326.

[179]Burke's argument is confirmed by Ian R. Christie, *British 'non-elite' MPs, 1715–1820* (Oxford, 1995).

[180]In the absence of political parties and of a tradition of representative politics, the new deputies were a miscellaneous collection; as one historian observes, 'many were

supposed as a case, that the house of commons should be composed in the same manner with the Tiers Etat in France, would this dominion of chicane be borne with patience, or even conceived without horror? God forbid I should insinuate any thing derogatory to that profession, which is another priesthood, administering the rites of sacred justice. But whilst I revere men in the functions which belong to them, and would do, as much as one man can do, to prevent their exclusion from any, I cannot, to flatter them, give the lye to nature. They are good and useful in the composition; they must be mischievous if they preponderate so as virtually to become the whole.[181] Their very excellence in their peculiar functions may be far from a qualification for others. It cannot escape observation, that when men are too much confined to professional and faculty habits, and, as it were, inveterate in the recurrent employment of that narrow circle, they are rather disabled than qualified for whatever depends on the knowledge of mankind, on experience in mixed affairs, on a comprehensive connected view of the various complicated external and internal interests which go to the formation of that multifarious thing called a state? [66]

After all, if the house of commons were to have an wholly profesional and faculty composition, what is the power of the house of commons, circumscribed and shut in by the immoveable barriers of laws, usages, positive rules of doctrine and practice, counterpoized by the house of lords, and every moment of its existence at the discretion of the crown to continue, prorogue, or dissolve us?[182] The power of the house of commons, direct or indirect, is indeed great; and long may it be able to preserve its greatness, and the spirit belonging to true greatness, at the full; and it will do so, as long as it can keep the breakers of law in India from becoming the makers of law for England.[183] The

---

parish priests or local lawyers who would never have got into the British House of Commons': Hampson, *Prelude to Terror*, p. 41.

[181]Of 558 MPs at Westminster, in the years 1754–90 about 30 at each general election were practising barristers, but only a handful were attornies. The number of the latter doubled in the years 1790–1820, but barristers still outnumbered them by 300 to 23: Sir Lewis Namier and John Brooke (eds.), *The History of Parliament: The House of Commons 1754–1790* (3 vols., London, 1964), I, pp. 126, 128; Thorne (ed.), *The House of Commons, 1790–1820*, I, pp. 300, 304.

[182]In March 1784, George III had used his power to dissolve Parliament before the maximum term provided by the Septennial Act. The general election resulted in a majority for William Pitt's administration, formed in December 1783, and a disastrous reverse for the Foxite opposition, Burke among them.

[183]The delinquents allegedly included Warren Hastings, whose impeachment Burke pursued from 1786 to 1795, but India was an earlier preoccupation. For Burke's ironical denunciation of the nabob Paul Benfield (1741–1810), who obtained the seat of

power, however, of the house of commons, when least diminished, is as a drop of water in the ocean, compared to that residing in a settled majority of your National Assembly. That Assembly, since the destruction of the orders, has no fundamental law, no strict convention, no respected usage to restrain it. Instead of finding themselves obliged to conform to a fixed constitution, they have a power to make a constitution which shall conform to their designs. Nothing in heaven or upon earth can serve as a control on them. What ought to be the heads, the hearts, the dispositions, that are qualified, or that dare, not only to make laws under a fixed constitution, but at one heat to strike out a totally new constitution for a great kingdom, and in every part of it, from the monarch on the throne to the vestry of a [67] parish? But—"*fools rush in where angels fear to tread.*"[184] In such a state of unbounded power, for undefined and undefinable purposes, the evil of a moral and almost physical inaptitude of the man to the function must be the greatest we can conceive to happen in the management of human affairs.

Having considered the composition of the third estate as it stood in its original frame, I took a view of the representatives of the clergy. There too it appeared, that full as little regard was had to the general security of property, or to the aptitude of the deputies for their public purposes, in the principles of their election. That election was so contrived as to send a very large proportion of mere country curates[185] to the great and arduous work of new-modelling a state; men who never had seen the state so much as in a picture; men who knew nothing of the world beyond the bounds of an obscure village;

---

Cricklade by outright bribery in 1780 as a means of restoring his corruptly-acquired fortune in India, see *Speech ... Feb. 28, 1785*. Benfield had almost been unseated on petition, but, according to Burke, 'Paul Benfield made (reckoning himself) no fewer than eight members in the last parliament'. Burke identified Benfield's attorney, Richard Atkinson, as the real author of Pitt's India Bill: 'Paul Benfield's associate and agent was held up to the world as legislator of Indostan'. Atkinson set up an office 'where the whole business of the last general election [of 1784] was managed'. 'I believe, after this exposure of facts, no man can entertain a doubt of the collusion of ministers with the corrupt interest of the delinquents in India' (ibid., pp. 83–5, 90–1).

[184]"Nay, run to *Altars*; *there* they'll talk you dead; / For *Fools* rush in where *Angels* fear to tread': [Alexander Pope], *An Essay on Criticism* (London, 1711), p. 36, lines 7–8. Burke sided with Pope's satire of religious reformers.

[185]Necker's regulations governing elections to the Estates-General, published in January 1789, gave preponderance to the *curés* over cathedral chapters and monasteries: McManners, *French Revolution and the Church*, pp. 17–18. The outcome reflected this, for the First Estate of the clergy was analysed as consisting of 79 *Haut Clergé*, including 10 archbishops and 35 bishops, against 214 *Clergé pastoral: Liste complette de Messieurs les Députes*. The English term 'curate' came to mean the untenured assistant to a clergyman holding a benefice, a more junior station.

who, immersed in hopeless poverty, could regard all property, whether secular or ecclesiastical, with no other eye than that of envy; among whom must be many, who, for the smallest hope of the meanest dividend in plunder, would readily join in any attempts upon a body of wealth, in which they could hardly look to have any share, except in a general scramble. Instead of balancing the power of the active chicaners in the other assembly, these curates must necessarily become the active coadjutors, or at best the passive instruments of those[186] with whom they had been habitually guided in their petty village concerns.[68] They too could hardly be the most conscientious of their kind, who, presuming upon their incompetent understanding, could intrigue for a trust which led them from their natural relation to their flocks, and their natural spheres of action, to undertake the regeneration of kingdoms. This preponderating weight being added to the force of the body chicane in the Tiers Etat, compleated that momentum of ignorance, rashness, presumption, and lust of plunder, which nothing has been able to resist.[187]

To observing men it must have appeared from the beginning, that the majority of the Third Estate, in conjunction with such a deputation from the clergy as I have described, whilst it pursued the destruction of the nobility, would inevitably become subservient to the worst designs of individuals in that class. In the spoil and humiliation of their own order these individuals would possess a sure fund for the pay of their new followers. To squander away the objects which made the happiness of their fellows, would be to them no sacrifice at all. Turbulent, discontented men of quality, in proportion as they are puffed up with personal pride and arrogance, generally despise their own order.[188] One of the first symptoms they discover of a selfish and mischievous ambition, is a profligate disregard of a dignity which they partake with

[186]I.e. the lawyers.

[187]Demands for reform had been heard within the French church since the middle of the century in favour of some redistribution of its great wealth from prelates and monasteries to the parish curés. Many of them initially proved to be better off as salaried employees of the state than they had been under the old order, and the Revolution in its early stages attracted the idealistic as well as self-interested support of large numbers of the clergy: McManners, *French Revolution and the Church*, pp. 15–17. For the Revolution as 'The Revolt of the Curés' see McManners, *Church and Society in Eighteenth-Century France* (2 vols., Oxford, 1998), II, pp. 705–44. Burke did not appreciate the idealistic desire for national regeneration which was widespread in France before episodes like the September massacres and the Terror, and was obliged to explain away the lesser clergy's involvement in the Revolution.

[188]Burke implied the Whig nobility, like Bedford, Grafton, Lansdowne, Lauderdale, and Stanhope.

others. To be attached to the subdivision,[189] to love the little platoon we belong to in society, is the first principle (the germ as it were) of public affections. It is the first link in the series [69] by which we proceed towards a love
to our country and to mankind.[190] The interests of that portion of social arrangement is a trust in the hands of all those who compose it; and as none but
bad men would justify it in abuse, none but traitors would barter it away for
their own personal advantage.[191]

[189]The interdependence of Creation was a familiar trope, and echoed the idea of the
'Great Chain of Being'. As Pope expressed it: 'God loves from Whole to Parts: but human Soul / Must rise from Individual to the Whole. / Self-love but serves the virtuous
mind to wake, / As the small pebble stirs the peaceful Lake, / The Centre mov'd, a Circle strait succeeds, / Another still, and still another spreads; / Friend, Parent, Neighbour, first it will embrace, / His Country next, and next all Human-race': [Alexander
Pope], An Essay on Man. In Epistles to a Friend (London, [1733]), Epistle 4, lines 356–
363.
    [190]This was not a unique insight on Burke's part. As Hume had observed: '... as Na-
ture has implanted in every one a superior Affection to his own Country, we never expect any Regard to distant Nations, where the smallest Competition arises. Not to
mention, that while every Man consults the Good of his own Community, we are sensible, that the general Interest of Mankind is better promoted, than by any loose inde-
terminate Views to the Good of a Species, whence no beneficial Action could ever result, for want of a duly limited Object, on which they could exert themselves ... 'Tis
wisely ordain'd by Nature, that private Connexions should commonly prevail over
universal Views and Considerations; otherwise our Affections and Actions would be
dissipated and lost, for Want of a proper limited Object': David Hume, An Enquiry
Concerning the Principles of Morals (London, 1751), s. V, pp. 93n, 100n.
    [191]Cf. Edmund Burke to Philip Francis, 19 November 1790, in Burke, Correspon-
dence, VI, pp. 170–3: 'You put the case, as if in the predominant faction in France
there were at the head of it a set of wise and excellent patriots, proceeding with vigour
indeed; but with all the attention to order and justice, which that vigour admitted: but
that they are disgraced by the disorders of an ungovernable Mob. This, if you please,
you may suppose, but I suppose no such thing. I charge all these disorders not on the
Mob, but on the Duke of Orleans, and Mirabeau, and Barnave, and Bailly, and La-
meth, and La Fayette, and the rest of that faction, who, I conceive, spent immense sums
of money, and used innumerable arts to instigate the populace throughout France to
the enormities they committed'. This was not an unusual opinion. Writing from Paris,
Thomas Paine had briefed Burke on the forcible transfer of the king from Versailles to
Paris on 6 October: 'The March to Versailles has yet some Mystery in it. I beleive the
Duke of Orleans knows as much of this business as anybody knows': Paine to Burke,
17 January 1790, Burke, Correspondence, VI, pp. 67–75. Thomas Jefferson, also in
Paris, wrote to Richard Price, John Jay and James Madison with even more explicit
warnings against the ambitions of d'Orléans and Mirabeau: Price, Correspondence,
III, p. 258. This was Louis-Philippe-Joseph de Bourbon, duc d'Orléans (1747–93),
who was evidently exploiting the Revolution in an attempt to supplant Louis XVI. To
remove him from the scene, the French court had sent him on a diplomatic mission to

There were, in the time of our civil troubles in England (I do not know whether you have any such in your Assembly in France) several persons, like the then Earl of Holland,[192] who by themselves or their families had brought an odium on the throne, by the prodigal dispensation of its bounties towards them, who afterwards joined in the rebellions arising from the discontents of which they were themselves the cause; men who helped to subvert that throne to which they owed, some of them, their existence, others all that power which they employed to ruin their benefactor. If any bounds are set to the rapacious demands of that sort of people, or that others are permitted to partake in the objects they would engross, revenge and envy soon fill up the craving void that is left in their avarice. Confounded by the complication of distempered passions, their reason is disturbed; their views become vast and perplexed; to others inexplicable; to themselves uncertain. They find, on all sides, bounds to their unprincipled ambition in any fixed order of things. But in the fog and haze of confusion all is enlarged, and appears without any limit. [70]

When men of rank[193] sacrifice all ideas of dignity to an ambition without a distinct object, and work with low instruments and for low ends, the whole composition becomes low and base. Does not something like this now appear in France? Does it not produce something ignoble and inglorious? a kind of meanness in all the prevalent policy? a tendency in all that is done to lower along with individuals all the dignity and importance of the state?[194] Other revolutions have been conducted by persons, who whilst they attempted or effected changes in the commonwealth, sanctified their ambition by advancing

---

London from October 1789 to July 1790: there he moved in the circle of the Prince of Wales and Charles James Fox; he already knew Lansdowne from a visit in 1789. For evidence of d'Orléans's complicity in the disorders of the 14 July and 6 October 1789, see George Armstrong Kelly, 'The Machine of the Duc d'Orléans and the New Politics', *Journal of Modern History* 51 (1979–80), pp. 667–84.

[192]See Biographical Guide.

[193]I.e. the English noblemen who supported the Revolution Society. Burke's resentment at the political conduct of sections of the Whig nobility long preceded the 1790s and his *Letter to a Noble Lord* (1796): see *Reflections*, p. [93]. Paine (*Rights of Man*, pp. 123–4) provided confirmation: 'I remember taking notice of a speech in what is called the English House of Peers, by the then Earl of Shelburne, and I think it was at the time he was Minister, which is applicable to this case. I do not directly charge my memory with every particular; but the words and the purport, as nearly as I remember, were these: *That the form of a Government was a matter wholly at the will of a Nation at all times: that if it chose a monarchical form, it had a right to have it so; and if it afterwards chose to be a Republic, it had a right to be a Republic, and to say to a King, we have no longer any occasion for you.*'

[194]For France 'destroyed by men of mean or secondary capacities', see [Burke], *Appeal*, p. 7.

the dignity of the people whose peace they troubled. They had long views. They aimed at the rule, not at the destruction of their country. They were men of great civil, and great military talents, and if the terror, the ornament of their age. They were not like Jew brokers[195] contending with each other who could best remedy with fraudulent circulation and depreciated paper the wretchedness and ruin brought on their country by their degenerate councils. The compliment made to one of the great bad men of the old stamp (Cromwell) by his kinsman, a favourite poet of that time, shews what it was he proposed, and what indeed to a great degree he accomplished in the success of his ambition:

"Still as *you* rise, the *state*, exalted too,
Finds no distemper whilst 'tis chang'd by *you*;
Chang'd like the world's great scene, when without noise
The rising sun night's *vulgar* lights destroys."[196][71]

These disturbers were not so much like men usurping power, as asserting their natural place in society. Their rising was to illuminate and beautify the world. Their conquest over their competitors was by outshining them. The hand that, like a destroying angel, smote the country, communicated to it the force and energy under which it suffered. I do not say (God forbid) I do not say, that the virtues of such men were to be taken as a balance to their crimes; but they were some corrective to their effects. Such was, as I said, our Cromwell.[197] Such were your whole race of Guises, Condés, and Colignis.[198] Such the Richlieus, who in more quiet times acted in the spirit of a civil war.[199] Such, as better men, and in a less dubious cause, were your Henry the 4th and your

---

[195]On the basis of such remarks, Burke is sometimes accused of antisemitism; yet his objections are evidently to financiers rather than to their race. Paine, however, went far further, citing as evidence that 'aristocracy has a tendency to degenerate the human species' the assertion: 'By the universal oeconomy of nature it is known, and by the instance of the Jews it is proved, that the human species has a tendency to degenerate, in any small number of persons, when separated from the general stock of society, and intermarrying constantly with each other': *Rights of Man*, p. 71.

[196][Edmund Waller], *A Panegyrick to My Lord Protector, by a Gentleman that Loves the Peace, Union and Prosperity of the English Nation* (London, 1655), p. 7, lines 7–10. Burke here shared Samuel Johnson's partial admiration for the talents of Oliver Cromwell, whose politics he naturally condemned. Edmund Waller (1606–87) was John Hampden's cousin, and Cromwell's kinsman by marriage. See *Reflections*, p. [10].

[197]For Burke's balanced appreciation of Cromwell, acknowledging his usurpation but crediting him with respect for the rule of law and with the achievement of stable government, see Burke, *Letter to a Member*, pp. 14–16, 48.

[198]See Biographical Guide, under 'Guise'.

[199]See Biographical Guide.

Sully,[200] though nursed in civil confusions, and not wholly without some of their taint. It is a thing to be wondered at, to see how very soon France, when she had a moment to respire, recovered and emerged from the longest and most dreadful civil war that ever was known in any nation. Why? Because, among all their massacres, they had not slain the *mind* in their country. A conscious dignity, a noble pride, a generous sense of glory and emulation, was not extinguished. On the contrary, it was kindled and inflamed. The organs also of the state, however shattered, existed. All the prizes of honour and virtue, all the rewards, all the distinctions, remained. But your present confusion, like a palsy, has attacked the fountain [72] of life itself. Every person in your country, in a situation to be actuated by a principle of honour, is disgraced and degraded, and can entertain no sensation of life, except in a mortified and humiliated indignation. But this generation will quickly pass away. The next generation of the nobility will resemble the artificers and clowns, and money-jobbers, usurers, and Jews,[201] who will be always their fellows, sometimes their masters. Believe me, Sir, those who atempt to level, never equalize.[202] In all societies, consisting of various descriptions of citizens, some description must be uppermost. The levellers therefore only change and pervert the natural order of things; they load the edifice of society, by setting up in the air what the solidity of the structure requires to be on the ground. The associations of taylors and carpenters, of which the republic (of Paris, for instance) is composed, cannot be equal to the situation, into which, by the worst of usurpations, an usurpation on the prerogatives of nature, you attempt to force them.

The chancellor of France at the opening of the states, said, in a tone of oratorial flourish, that all occupations were honourable.[203] If he meant only, that no honest employment was disgraceful, he would not have gone beyond the truth. But in asserting, that any thing is honourable, we imply some distinction in its favour. The occupation of an hair-dresser, or of a working tallow-chandler, cannot be a matter of honour to any [73] person—to say nothing of

[200]See Biographical Guide.

[201]Burke explained his position more clearly in *Letter to a Member*, pp. 17–18.

[202]Paine claimed that, in abolishing titles of nobility, 'France has not levelled; it has exalted': *Rights of Man*, p. 67.

[203]Charles-Louis-François de Paule de Barentin (1738–1819), garde des Sceaux. His speech was printed in *Ouverture des États-Généraux, faite à Versailles le 5 mai 1789. Discours du Roi; Discours de M. le Garde des Sceaux; Rapport de M. le Directeur Général des Finances, fait par ordre du roi* (Paris, 1789), p. 16: 'Le vice & l'inutilité méritent seuls le mépris des hommes, & toutes les professions utiles sont honorables ... Tous les citoyens du royaume, quelle que soit leur condition, ne sont-ils pas les membres d'une même famille!' See *Reflections*, p. [175].

a number of other more servile employments. Such descriptions of men ought not to suffer oppression from the state; but the state suffers oppression, if such as they, either individually or collectively, are permitted to rule. In this you think you are combating prejudice, but you are at war with nature.[204]

I do not, my dear Sir, conceive you to be of that sophistical captious spirit, or of that uncandid dulness, as to require, for every general observation or sentiment, an explicit detail of all the correctives and exceptions, which reason will presume to be included in all the general propositions which come from reasonable men. You do not imagine, that I wish to confine power, authority, and distinction to blood, and names, and titles. No, Sir. There is no qualification for government, [74] but virtue and wisdom, actual or presumptive. Wherever they are actually found, they have, in whatever state, condition, profession or trade, the passport of Heaven to human place and honour. Woe to the country which would madly and impiously reject the service of the talents and virtues, civil, military, or religious, that are given to grace and to serve it; and would condemn to obscurity every thing formed to diffuse lustre and glory around a state.[205] Woe to that country too, that passing into the opposite extreme, considers a low education, a mean contracted view of things, a sordid mercenary occupation, as a preferable title to command. Every thing ought to be open; but not indifferently to every man. No rotation; no appointment by lot; no mode of election operating in the spirit of sortition or rotation, can be generally good in a government conversant in extensive objects.[206] Because they have no tendency, direct or indirect, to fit the man to the

---

[204]Ecclesiasticus, chap. xxxviii. verse 24, 25. "The wisdom of a learned man cometh by opportunity of leisure: and he that hath little business shall become wise."— "How can he get wisdom that holdeth the plough, and that glorieth in the goad; that driveth oxen; and is occupied in their labours; and whose talk is of bullocks."

Ver. 27. "So every carpenter and work-master that laboureth night and day." &c.

Ver. 33. "They shall not be sought for in public counsel, nor sit high in the congregation: They shall not sit on the judges seat, nor understand the sentence of judgment: they cannot declare justice and judgment, and they shall not be found where parables are spoken."

Ver. 34. "But they will maintain the state of the world."

I do not determine whether this book be canonical, as the Gallican church (till lately) has considered it, or apocryphal, as here it is taken. I am sure it contains a great deal of sense, and truth. [B] The Apocrypha are books of the Old Testament surviving in Greek, but not in Hebrew. St Jerome accepted them into the Latin Vulgate Bible; Protestant reformers ascribed them a lesser authority.

[205]Priestley challenged: 'Let Mr Burke's conduct with respect to the Test Act, be compared with' this passage: Letters to Burke, p. 129. Evidently Burke did not assume that virtue and wisdom were to be found in the ranks of Dissenters.

[206]Soame Jenyns, in 1772, had bluntly contradicted Burke's fanciful theory of the

duty. I do not hesitate to say, that the road to eminence and power, from obscure condition, ought not to be made too easy, nor a thing too much of
course.[207] If rare merit be the rarest of all rare things, it ought to pass through
some sort of probation. The temple of honour ought to be seated on an eminence.[208] If it be open through virtue, let it be remembered too, that virtue is
never tried but by some difficulty, and some struggle.[209]

Nothing is a due and adequate representation of a state, that does not represent its ability, as [75] well as its property. But as ability is a vigorous and active principle, and as property is sluggish, inert, and timid, it never can be safe
from the invasions of ability, unless it be, out of all proportion, predominant

---

high-minded integrity of the Rockingham Whigs. Parties, argued Jenyns, no longer, as
in the past, arose 'from any differences of opinions, or any contradictory articles in our
political creeds ... from whence it appears to me plainly demonstrable, that all our present dissentions are nothing more than an outrageous contest for power and profit' by
men pursuing 'the wild career of their headlong ambition'. Jenyns's solution, possibly
ironic but in retrospect proto-Jacobin, was that ministers should be chosen annually by
lot. Such a step would release the opposition (by implication, Burke's) from its sordid
pursuit of power: [Soame Jenyns], *A Scheme for the Coalition of Parties, humbly submitted to the Publick* (London, 1772), pp. 7, 12–13. In 1796, Burke recalled his anxieties of the early 1780s: 'Many of the changes, by a great misnomer called parliamentary reforms, went, not in the intention of all the professors and supporters of them,
undoubtedly, but went in their certain, and, in my opinion, not very remote effect,
home to the utter destruction of the Constitution of this kingdom. Had they taken
place, not France, but England, would have had the honour of leading up the death-
dance of Democratick Revolution': *Letter to a Noble Lord*, p. 13. Jenyns's 'Thoughts
on a Parliamentary Reform' [1784] and 'A Scheme for the Coalition of Parties. 1782'
were reprinted in Charles Nalson Cole (ed.), *The Works of Soame Jenyns, Esq.* (4 vols.,
London, 1790), II, pp. 235, 249. Burke owned Jenyns's *Miscellanies, Free Thoughts*
and *Free Reflections*: LC MS, fos. 21, 25, 27.

[207]Men like Burke in the circles of the marquis of Rockingham and Charles James
Fox increasingly found their faction dominated by noblemen and great landowners, or
by careerists who wasted their talents in dissipation: the meritocratic ethic was increasingly associated with the governing coalition assembled by the crown and now led
by the younger Pitt. Burke was obliged to praise talent without conceding to it any
overriding claim.

[208]Burke borrowed, without acknowledgement, from Bolingbroke's *The Idea of a
Patriot King*: 'Virtue is not placed on a rugged mountain of difficult and dangerous access, as they who would excuse the indolence of their temper, or the perverseness of
their will, desire to have it believed; but she is seated, however, on an eminence': Bolingbroke, *Works*, III, p. 38.

[209]'At every step of my progress in life (for in every step I was traversed and opposed), and at every turnpike I met, I was obliged to shew my passport, and again and
again to prove my sole title to the honour of being useful to my Country': Burke, *Letter
to a Noble Lord*, p. 29.

in the representation. It must be represented too in great masses of accumulation, or it is not rightly protected. The characteristic essence of property, formed out of the combined principles of its acquisition and conservation, is to be *unequal*.[210] The great masses therefore which excite envy, and tempt rapacity, must be put out of the possibility of danger. Then they form a natural rampart about the lesser properties in all their gradations. The same quantity of property, which is by the natural course of things, divided among many, has not the same operation. Its defensive power is weakened as it is diffused. In this diffusion each man's portion is less than what, in the eagerness of his desires, he may flatter himself to obtain by dissipating the accumulations of others. The plunder of the few would indeed give but a share inconceivably small in the distribution to the many. But the many are not capable of making this calculation; and those who lead them to rapine, never intend this distribution.

The perpetuation of property in our families is the most valuable and most interesting circumstance attending it, that which demonstrates most of a benevolent disposition in its owners, and that which tends most to the perpetuation of society itself. The possessors of family wealth, and of the distinction which attends [76] hereditary possession (as most concerned in it) are the natural securities for this transmission. With us, the house of peers is formed upon this principle. It is wholly composed of hereditary property and hereditary distinction; and made therefore the third of the legislature;[211] and in the last event, the sole judge of all property in all its subdivisions. The house of commons too, though not necessarily, yet in fact, is always so composed in the far greater part. Let those large proprietors be what they will, and they have their chance of being amongst the best, they are at the very worst, the ballast in the vessel of the commonwealth. For though hereditary wealth, and the rank which goes with it, are too much idolized by creeping sycophants, and the blind abject admirers of power, they are too rashly slighted in shallow speculations of the petulant, assuming, short-sighted coxcombs of philosophy.[212] Some decent regulated pre-eminence, some preference (not exclusive appropriation) given to birth, is neither unnatural, nor unjust, nor impolitic.

[210]Locke, *Two Treatises*, II, ss. 26–50, 54, had provided an elaborate if implausible Whig justification for the vast inequalities of landed property which the Whigs sanctioned. See *Reflections*, p. [38].

[211]'The Crown in Parliament', i.e. King, Lords and Commons.

[212]Burke had spent most of his life as a friend of the authors and intellectuals of his age, and did not now reject the life of the mind. He did, however, champion a middle course against what he regarded as extremism, as in writing to an agent of the *émigré* princes at Brussels to urge the new Emperor Leopold II not to pursue a widely unpopular anti-clerical policy like that of his predecessor Joseph II: 'it is not very easy to

It is said, that twenty-four millions ought to prevail over two hundred thousand.[213] True; if the constitution of a kingdom be a problem of arithmetic. This sort of discourse does well enough with the lamp-post[214] for its second: to men who *may* reason calmly, it is ridiculous. The will of the many, and their interest, must very often differ; and great will be the difference when they make an evil choice. A government of five hundred country attornies [77] and obscure curates is not good for twenty-four millions of men, though it were chosen by eight and forty millions; nor is it the better for being guided by a dozen of persons of quality, who have betrayed their trust in order to obtain that power. At present, you seem in every thing to have strayed out of the high road of nature. The property of France does not govern it. Of course property is destroyed, and rational liberty has no existence. All you have got for the present is a paper circulation, and a stock-jobbing constitution: and as to the future, do you seriously think that the territory of France, upon the republican system of eighty-three independent municipalities,[215] (to say nothing of the parts that compose them) can ever be governed as one body, or can ever be set in motion by the impulse of one mind? When the National Assembly has completed its work,[216] it will have accomplished its ruin. These commonwealths will not long bear a state of subjection to the republic of Paris. They will not bear that this one body should monopolize the captivity of the king, and the dominion over the assembly calling itself National. Each will keep its own portion of the spoil of the church to itself; and it will not suffer either that spoil, or the more just fruits of their industry, or the natural produce of their

---

suppress (by the methods lately used) what you call 'the *monkish fury*' without exciting fury of another Kind ... It were better to forget once for all, the *Encyclopedie* and the whole body of Economists and to revert to those old rules and principles which have hitherto made princes great and nations happy. Let not a Prince circumstanced like him weakly fall in love either with Monks or nobles': Burke to Claude-François de Rivarol, 1 June 1791: Burke, *Correspondence*, VI, pp. 265–70.

[213]This was a familiar argument, originating in [Emmanuel Joseph, comte de Sieyès], *Qu'est-ce que le tiers-état?* ([Paris, 1789]): see 3rd edn., pp. 52–3. Sieyès had written of twenty-five or twenty-six million people aligned against two hundred thousand '*Privilégiés*'.

[214]The French practice of the mob lynching its suspects by hanging them at lamp-posts began in the summer of 1789. An early victim was the Intendant of Paris, Berthier de Sauvigny (1737–89).

[215]On 16 February 1790 the National Assembly voted to replace France's ancient and complex administrative units with 83 new *départements* (*Le Moniteur*, 17 February 1790). Burke did not appreciate how limited their powers would be against that of the nation.

[216]I.e. that of drafting a new constitution for France.

soil, to be sent to swell the insolence, or pamper the luxury of the mechanics of Paris. In this they will see none of the equality, under the pretence of which they have been tempted to throw off their allegiance [78] to their sovereign, as well as the antient constitution of their country. There can be no capital city in such a constitution as they have lately made.[217] They have forgot, that when they framed democratic governments, they had virtually dismembered their country. The person whom they persevere in calling king, has not power left to him by the hundredth part sufficient to hold together this collection of republics. The republic of Paris will endeavour indeed to compleat the debauchery of the army, and illegally to perpetuate the assembly, without resort to its constituents, as the means of continuing its despotism.[218] It will make efforts, by becoming the heart of a boundless paper circulation, to draw every thing to itself; but in vain. All this policy in the end will appear as feeble as it is now violent.

If this be your actual situation, compared to the situation to which you were called, as it were by the voice of God and man, I cannot find it in my heart to congratulate you on the choice you have made, or the success which has attended your endeavours. I can as little recommend to any other nation a conduct grounded on such principles, and productive of such effects. That I must leave to those who can see further into your affairs than I am able to do, and who best know how far your actions are favourable to their designs. The gentlemen of the Revolution Society, who were so early in their congratula-

---

[217]Burke evidently did not anticipate the way in which the provincial anarchy of the Revolution would be suppressed to create a new republic far more dominated by Paris than its predecessor had been by Versailles. By contrast, Arthur Young, in 1789, found opinion in the provinces undecided, awaiting the outcome of events in Paris: *Travels in France*, p. 137. See Bibliography, D xi.

[218]Burke did have some insight into the centralising pressure of totalitarian democracy. Arthur Young wrote from Paris on 10 January 1790: 'The violent democrats, who have the reputation of being so much republican in principle, that they do not admit any political necessity for having even the name of a king, are called the *enragés*. They have a meeting at the Jacobins, called the revolution club, which assembles every night ... and they are so numerous, that all material business is there decided, before it is discussed by the National Assembly. I called this morning on several persons, all of whom are great democrats; and mentioning this circumstance to them, as one which savoured too much of a Paris junto governing the kingdom, an idea, which must, in the long run, be unpopular and hazardous; I was answered, that the predominancy which Paris assumed, at present, was absolutely necessary, for the safety of the whole nation; for if nothing were done, but by procuring a previous common consent, all great opportunities would be lost, and the National Assembly left constantly exposed to the danger of a counter-revolution': *Travels in France*, pp. 267–8. See also Burke, *Reflections*, pp. [284–5].

tions, appear to be strongly of opinion that there is some scheme of politics relative to this [79] country, in which your proceedings may, in some way, be useful.[219] For your Dr. Price, who seems to have speculated himself into no small degree of fervour upon this subject, addresses his auditory in the following very remarkable words: "I cannot conclude without recalling *particularly* to your recollection a consideration which I have *more than once alluded to*, and which probably your thoughts have *been all along anticipating*; a consideration with which my *mind is impressed more than I can express*. I mean the consideration of the *favourableness of the present times to all exertions in the cause of liberty*."[220]

It is plain that the mind of this *political* Preacher was at the time big with some extraordinary design; and it is very probable, that the thoughts of his audience, who understood him better than I do, did all along run before him in his reflection, and in the whole train of consequences to which it led.

Before I read that sermon, I really thought I had lived in a free country; and it was an error I cherished, because it gave me a greater liking to the country I lived in. I was indeed aware, that a jealous, ever-waking vigilance, to guard the treasure of our liberty, not only from invasion, but from decay and corruption, was our best wisdom and our first duty. However, I considered that treasure rather as a possession to be secured than as a prize to be contended for. I did not discern how the present time came to be so very favourable to all *exertions* in the cause of freedom. The present [80] time differs from any other only by the circumstance of what is doing in France. If the example of that nation is to have an influence on this, I can easily conceive why some of their proceedings which have an unpleasant aspect, and are not quite reconcileable to humanity, generosity, good faith, and justice, are palliated with so much milky good-nature towards the actors, and borne with so much heroic fortitude towards the sufferers. It is certainly not prudent to discredit the authority of an example we mean to follow. But allowing this, we are led to a very natural question;—What is that cause of liberty, and what are those exertions in its favour, to which the example of France is so singularly auspicious? Is our monarchy to be annihilated, with all the laws, all the tribunals, and all the antient corporations of the kingdom? Is every land-mark of the country to be done away in favour of a geometrical and arithmetical constitution? Is the

[219]This is clear from the Society's addresses reprinted in *The Correspondence of the Revolution Society*. French interest in Price's sermon also continued. When he replied to Burke's critique in the *Reflections* with a new introduction to the fourth edition of the *Discourse*, Price's new material was published, in translation, in *Le Moniteur* (6 December 1790).

[220]Price, *Discourse*, 3rd edn., pp. 48–9 (free quotation): 'liberty' sc. 'public liberty'.

house of lords to be voted useless?[221] Is episcopacy to be abolished?[222] Are the church lands to be sold to Jews and jobbers; or given to bribe new-invented municipal republics into a participation in sacrilege? Are all the taxes to be voted grievances, and the revenue reduced to a patriotic contribution, or patriotic presents? Are silver shoe-buckles to be substituted in the place of the land tax and the malt tax, for the support of the naval strength of this kingdom?[223] Are all orders, ranks, and distinctions to be confounded, that out of universal anarchy, joined to national bankruptcy, [81] three or four thousand democracies should be formed into eighty-three, and that they may all, by some sort of unknown attractive power, be organized into one? For this great end, is the army to be seduced from its discipline and its fidelity, first, by every kind of debauchery, and then by the terrible precedent of a donative in the encrease of pay? Are the curates to be seduced from their bishops, by holding out to them the delusive hope of a dole out of the spoils of their own order? Are the citizens of London to be drawn from their allegiance, by feeding them at the expence of their fellow-subjects? Are all the public revenues levied in their city to be put under their administration? Is what remains of the plundered stock of public revenue to be employed in the wild project of maintaining two armies to watch over and to fight with each other?[224]—If these are the ends and means of the Revolution Society, I admit they are well adapted to each other; and France may furnish them for both with precedents in point.

[221]On 6 February 1648/9 the House of Commons resolved 'That the House of Peers in Parliament is useless and dangerous, and ought to be abolished: And that an Act be brought in, to that Purpose': *Journals of the House of Commons*, VI, p. 132.

[222]The exclusion of bishops from the House of Lords was one of the early measures of the Long Parliament, which passed 'An Act for Disenabling all Persons in Holy Orders to exercise any Temporal Jurisdiction or Authority' (17 Car. I, c. 27) on 5 February 1641/2 (it received the royal assent and was reversed after the Restoration). A Bill for the abolition of church government by archbishops, bishops, deans, archdeacons and others was passed on 26 January 1642/3 but not accepted by the king. After ordinances for the erection of Presbyterian government, Parliament acted without royal authority to abolish episcopacy on 9 October 1646: William A. Shaw, *A History of the English Church during the Civil Wars and under the Commonwealth* (2 vols., London, 1900), I, pp. 118, 121, 196; II, p. 210.

[223]In England the land tax and the excise duty on malt were both appropriated in the estimates for raising 'supplies' to the navy, ordnance, army and miscellaneous services. In the euphoria or fear of the French Revolution, some groups were inspired, or terrified, into making 'patriotic presents' to the state. Some sacrificed their shoe-buckles in a symbolic rejection of an item of patrician dress. See Burke, *Reflections*, pp. [57, 333].

[224]The French National Guard now constituted a second army. Its purpose could only be to oppose the army of the crown.

I see that your example is held out to shame us. I know that we are supposed a dull sluggish race,[225] rendered passive by finding our situation tolerable; and prevented by a mediocrity of freedom from ever attaining to its full
perfection. Your leaders in France began by affecting to admire, almost to
adore, the British constitution; but as they advanced they came to look upon it
with a sovereign contempt.[226] The friends of your National Assembly amongst
us have full as mean an [82] opinion of what was formerly thought the glory
of their country. The Revolution Society has discovered that the English nation is not free. They are convinced that the inequality in our representation is
a "defect in our constitution so *gross and palpable*, as to make it excellent
chiefly in *form* and *theory*."[227] That a representation in the legislature of a
kingdom is not only the basis of all constitutional liberty in it, but of "*all le-*

---

[225]Cf: 'I admit, indeed, that my praises of the British Government loaded with all its
encumbrances; clogged with its peers and its beef; its parsons and its pudding; its
Commons and its beer; and its dull slavish liberty of going about just as one pleases,
had something to provoke a Jockey of Norfolk' [Charles Howard, 11th duke of Norfolk (1746–1815)]: *A Letter to ******* ********, in Edmund Burke, *Two Letters on
the Conduct of our Domestick Parties, with regard to French Politicks* (London,
1797), pp. 101–2.

[226]French admiration of the British constitution, widespread in the eighteenth century, quickly died in the face of the demand of Sieyès in *Qu'est-ce que le tiers état* (January 1789) that the French abandon '*l'espirit d'imitation*' and become themselves an
example for other nations. By June 1789, Arthur Young, in France, had come to understand French demands for 'the regeneration of the kingdom' as meaning 'a theoretic
perfection of government, questionable in its origin, hazardous in its progress, and vi-
sionary in its end': its advocates, from the National Assembly to the provinces, 'all affect to hold the constitution of England cheap in respect of liberty: and as that is unquestionably, and by their own admission the best the world ever saw, they profess to
appeal from practice to theory, which, in the arrangement of a question of science,
might be admitted (though with caution); but, in establishing the complex interests of a
great kingdom, in *securing* freedom to 25 millions of people, seems to me the very ac-
iné of imprudence, the very quintessence of insanity': *Travels in France*, p. 127. In
August 1789, Mounier, in *Considérations sur les gouvernments, et principalement sur
celui qui convient à la France*, agreed: 'Il y a peu de temps ... on professait l'admiration
la plus outrée pour la constitution d'Angleterre. Aujourd'hui on affecte de la mépriser':
Fierro and Liébert, pp. 639–40. Condorcet was soon arguing that, comparing the
events of 1688 and 10 August 1792, 'the cause of the French is exactly similar to that
of the English', but that, in the conduct of the two revolutions, 'every circumstance
gives the advantage to the French nation' since the Convention Parliament of 1689
could be swayed by 'the will of about two hundred heads of powerful families' and was
therefore 'an attack on the rights of natural equality': Jean-Antoine-Nicolas de Caritat,
marquis de Condorcet, *Reflections on the English Revolution of 1688, and that of the
French, August 10, 1792 ... translated from the French* (London, 1792), pp. 1, 7, 9.

[227]Discourse on the Love of our Country, 3d edit. p. 39. [B]

*gitimate government*; that without it a *government* is nothing but an *usurpa-tion*;"—that "when the representation is *partial*, the kingdom possesses lib-erty only *partially*; and if extremely partial it gives only a *semblance*; and if not only extremely partial, but corruptly chosen, it becomes a *nuisance*." Dr. Price considers this inadequacy of representation as our *fundamental griev-ance*; and though, as to the corruption of this semblance of representation, he hopes it is not yet arrived to its full perfection of depravity; he fears that "nothing will be done towards gaining for us this *essential blessing*, until some *great abuse of power* again provokes our resentment, or some *great ca-lamity* again alarms our fears, or perhaps till the acquisition of a *pure and equal representation by other countries*, whilst we are *mocked* with the *shadow*, kindles our shame." To this be subjoins a note in these words. "A representation, chosen chiefly by the Treasury, and a *few* thousands [83] of the *dregs* of the people, who are generally paid for their votes."[228]

You will smile here at the consistency of those democratists, who, when they are not on their guard, treat the humbler part of the community with the greatest contempt, whilst, at the same time, they pretend to make them the depositories of all power. It would require a long discourse to point out to you the many fallacies that lurk in the generality and equivocal nature of the terms "inadequate representation." I shall only say here, in justice to that old-fashioned constitution, under which we have long prospered, that our repre-sentation has been found perfectly adequate to all the purposes for which a representation of the people can be desired or devised. I defy the enemies of our constitution to shew the contrary. To detail the particulars in which it is found so well to promote its ends, would demand a treatise on our practical constitution. I state here the doctrine of the Revolutionists, only that you and others may see, what an opinion these gentlemen entertain of the constitution of their country, and why they seem to think that some great abuse of power,

---

[228]Burke paraphrased Price, *Discourse*, 3rd edn., pp. 39–42. He omitted Price's passage on p. 41: 'At the time of the American war, associations were formed for this purpose [parliamentary reform] in LONDON, and other parts of the kingdom; and our present Minister [Pitt] himself has, since that war, directed to it an effort which made him a favourite of many of us.' Burke, like the Rockingham Whigs in general, had sup-ported 'Economical Reform' (the elimination of waste and corruption, the limitation of future pensions) and opposed parliamentary reform. From the 1770s, if not earlier, the latter had been advocated on the basis of abstract principles which entailed annual parliaments, universal manhood suffrage, equal electoral districts and the secret ballot. Burke's antipathy to elaborate schemes of social reconstruction was widely shared, and long preceded the French Revolution. It also brought him into collision from the early 1780s with aristocratic reformers in England like the duke of Richmond: see In-troduction, above.

or some great calamity, as giving a chance for the blessing of a constitution according to their ideas, would be much palliated to their feelings; you see *why they* are so much enamoured of your fair and equal representation, which being once obtained, the same effects might follow. You see they consider our house of commons as only "a semblance," "a form," [84] "a theory," "a shadow," "a mockery," perhaps "a nuisance."

These gentlemen value themselves on being systematic; and not without reason. They must therefore look on this gross and palpable defect of representation, this fundamental grievance (so they call it) as a thing not only vicious in itself, but as rendering our whole government absolutely *illegitimate*, and not at all better than a downright *usurpation*. Another revolution, to get rid of this illegitimate and usurped government, would of course be perfectly justifiable, if not absolutely necessary. Indeed their principle, if you observe it with any attention, goes much further than to an alteration in the election of the house of commons; for, if popular representation, or choice, is necessary to the *legitimacy* of all government, the house of lords is, at one stroke, bastardized and corrupted in blood. That house is no representative of the people at all, even in "semblance or in form." [229] The case of the crown is altogether as bad. In vain the crown may endeavour to screen itself against these gentlemen by the authority of the establishment made on the Revolution. The Revolution which is resorted to for a title, on their system, wants a title itself. The Revolution is built, according to their theory, upon a basis not more solid than our present formalities, as it was made by an house of lords not representing any one but themselves; and by an house of commons exactly such [85] as the present, that is, as they term it, by a mere "shadow and mockery" of representation.

Some of them are so heated with their particular religious theories, that

---

[229]In 1770, Burke had argued for the representative character of the House of Commons (and, by implication, of the other branches of government) despite the lack of uniformity in the franchise: 'it is not the derivation of the power of that House from the people, which makes it in a distinct sense their representative. The King is the representative of the people; so are the Lords; so are the Judges. They all are trustees for the people ...' ([Burke], *Thoughts*, p. 35). On 8 April 1778 Burke's enemy Shelburne, in the upper House, argued: 'I shall never submit to the doctrines I have heard this day from the woolsack, that the other House [of Commons] are the only representatives and guardians of the people's rights. I boldly maintain the contrary. I say this House are equally the representatives of the people': *Parl Hist* XIX, col. 1048. In 1784, Burke reversed his position, arguing, against Shelburne, that 'The collective sense of his people his Majesty is to receive from his Commons in Parliament assembled' (Burke, *Representation ... 1784*, p. 3). Burke now returned to his former position. See *Reflections*, p. [269].

they give more than hints that the fall of the civil powers, with all the dreadful consequences of that fall, provided they might be of service to their theories, would not be unacceptable to them, or very remote from their wishes. A man amongst them of great authority,[230] and certainly of great talents, speaking of a supposed alliance between church and state, says, "perhaps *we must wait for the fall of the civil powers* before this most unnatural alliance be broken. Calamitous no doubt will that time be. But what convulsion in the political world ought to be a subject of lamentation, if it be attended with so desirable an effect?"[231] You see with what a steady eye these gentlemen are prepared to view the greatest calamities which can befall their country![232]

[230]Dr. Joseph Priestley: see Biographical Guide. His tract *Letters to the Rev. Edward Burn, of St Mary's Chapel, Birmingham, in Answer to His, on the Infallibility of the Apostolic Testimony, concerning the Person of Christ* (Birmingham, 1790) portrayed its author as a moderate reformer but contained the sensational passage: 'I rejoice to see the warmth with which the cause of *orthodoxy* (that is of long established opinions, however erroneous) and that of the *hierarchy* is now taken up by its friends. Because if their system be not well founded, they are only accelerating its destruction. In fact, they are assisting me in the proper disposal of those grains of *gunpowder*, which have been some time accumulating, and at which they have taken so great an alarm, and which will certainly blow it up at length; and perhaps as suddenly, as unexpectedly, and as completely, as the overthrow of the late arbitrary government of France ... They [the clergy] are labouring for its destruction much more than I am. If I be laying *gunpowder*, they are providing the *match*, and *their* part of the business seems to be in greater forwardness than *mine*' (pp. ix–x). Quickly circulated, this tract helped to defeat Fox's motion in the Commons on 2 March 1790 for the repeal of the Test and Corporation Acts.

[231]Joseph Priestley, *An History of the Corruptions of Christianity* (2 vols., Birmingham, 1782), II, p. 484 ('effect' *sc.* 'event'). Burke correctly saw the millenarian streak in Priestley's writing. This, the final paragraph of his work, began: 'It is nothing but the *alliance* of the kingdom of Christ with the kingdoms of this world (an alliance which our Lord himself expressly disclaimed) that supports the grossest corruptions of Christianity' [i.e. Trinitarianism]. It continued with the words Burke quoted, and concluded: 'May the *Kingdom of God*, and of Christ (that which I conceive to be intended in the Lord's prayer) truly and fully *come*, though all the kingdoms of the world be removed, in order to make way for it!' Priestley repeated this prediction with added emphasis in *The present State of Europe compared with Antient Prophecies; A Sermon, preached at the Gravel Pit Meeting in Hackney, February 28, 1794, Being the Day appointed for a General Fast* (London, 1794): 'great calamities, such as the world has never yet experienced, will precede that happy state of things, in which 'the kingdoms of this world will become the kingdom of our Lord Jesus Christ'... it appears to me highly probable ... that the present disturbances in Europe are the beginning of those very calamitous times' (p. 2). For this theme, see Bibliograpy, C ii.

[232]Priestley, unabashed, confirmed Burke's argument: 'the dissolution of this fatal alliance is still the object of our most ardent wishes'. He remembered that Burke had

It is no wonder therefore, that with these ideas of every thing in their constitution and government at home, either in church or state, as illegitimate and usurped, or, at best as a vain mockery, they look abroad with an eager and passionate enthusiasm. Whilst they are possessed by these notions, it is vain to talk to them of the practice of their ancestors, the fundamental laws of their country, the fixed form of a constitution, whose merits are confirmed by the solid test of long experience, and an increasing public strength and national prosperity. [86] They despise experience as the wisdom of unlettered men; and as for the rest, they have wrought under-ground a mine that will blow up at one grand explosion all examples of antiquity, all precedents, charters, and acts of parliament. They have "the rights of men." Against these there can be no prescription; against these no agreement is binding: these admit no temperament, and no compromise: any thing withheld from their full demand is so much of fraud and injustice. Against these their rights of men let no government look for security in the length of its continuance, or in the justice and lenity of its administration. The objections of these speculatists, if its forms do not quadrate with their theories, are as valid against such an old and beneficent government as against the most violent tyranny, or the greenest usurpation. They are always at issue with governments, not on a question of abuse, but a question of competency, and a question of title. I have nothing to say to the clumsy subtilty of their political metaphysics. Let them be their amusement in the schools.—"Illa *se jactet in aula—Æolus, et clauso ventorum carcere regnet.*"[233]—But let them not break prison to burst like a *Levanter*,[234] to sweep the earth with their hurricane, and to break up the fountains of the great deep to overwhelm us.

Far am I from denying in theory; full as far is my heart from withholding in practice (if I were of power to give or to withhold) the *real* rights of men. In denying their false claims [87] of right, I do not mean to injure those which are real, and are such as their pretended rights would totally destroy. If civil society be made for the advantage of man, all the advantages for which it is made become his right. It is an institution of beneficence; and law itself is only beneficence acting by a rule. Men have a right to live by that rule; they have a right to justice; as between their fellows, whether their fellows are in politic function or in ordinary occupation. They have a right to the fruits of their in-

---

made no opposition to the two earlier attempts to repeal the Test and Corporation Acts, and was indignant that Burke should intervene to oppose the third: *Letters to Burke*, pp. 128–9.

[233]'In that hall let Aeolus lord it and rule within the barred prison of the winds': Virgil, *Aeneid*, Book I, 140–1.

[234]Levanter: in the Mediterranean, a storm blowing from the east.

*Marx?*

#2

#3-6

*ought to soc. benefits.*

*and here's where D. can use him.*

dustry; and to the means of making their industry fruitful. They have a right to the acquisitions of their parents; to the nourishment and improvement of their offspring; to instruction in life, and to consolation in death. Whatever each man can separately do, without trespassing upon others, he has a right to do for himself; and he has a right to a fair portion of all which society, with all its combinations of skill and force, can do in his favour. But as to the share of power, authority, and direction which each individual ought to have in the management of the state, that I must deny to be amongst the direct original rights of man in civil society; for I have in my contemplation the civil social man, and no other. It is a thing to be settled by convention.

*ought to undef.*

*but no natural right to gov.*

If civil society be the offspring of convention, that convention must be its law. That convention must limit and modify all the descriptions of constitution which are formed under it. Every sort of legislative, judicial, or executory power are its creatures. [88] They can have no being in any other state of things; and how can any man claim, under the conventions of civil society, rights which do not so much as suppose its existence? Rights which are absolutely repugnant to it? One of the first motives to civil society, and which becomes one of its fundamental rules, is, *that no man should be judge in his own cause.* By this each person has at once divested himself of the first fundamental right of uncovenanted man, that is, to judge for himself, and to assert his own cause. He abdicates all right to be his own governor. He inclusively, in a great measure, abandons the right of self-defence, the first law of nature. Men cannot enjoy the rights of an uncivil and of a civil state together. That he may obtain justice he gives up his right of determining what it is in points the most essential to him. That he may secure some liberty, he makes a surrender in trust of the whole of it.[235]

*nothing new here - sounds like soc. compact theory.*

Government is not made in virtue of natural rights, which may and do exist in total independence of it; and exist in much greater clearness, and in a much greater degree of abstract perfection: but their abstract perfection is their practical defect.[236] By having a right to every thing they want every thing. Government is a contrivance of human wisdom to provide for human *wants.* Men have a right that these wants should be provided for by this wisdom. Among these wants is to be reckoned the want, out of civil society, of a suffi-

[235]This account of the origin of political society was nevertheless a commonplace, not necessarily owed to the Whig classics; see, for example, Lucretius, *De Rerum Natura,* V, 1136–60.

[236]Whigs in office conventionally argued that man had surrendered his natural rights on entering civil society. It is open to argument how far Burke went in allowing a continuing appeal to natural rights or to 'nature'.

cient restraint upon their passions.[237] Society requires not [89] only that the passions of individuals should be subjected, but that even in the mass and body as well as in the individuals, the inclinations of men should frequently be thwarted, their will controlled, and their passions brought into subjection. This can only be done *by a power out of themselves*; and not, in the exercise of its function, subject to that will and to those passions which it is its office to bridle and subdue. In this sense the restraints on men, as well as their liberties, are to be reckoned among their rights. But as the liberties and the restrictions vary with times and circumstances, and admit of infinite modifications, they cannot be settled upon any abstract rule; and nothing is so foolish as to discuss them upon that principle.[238]

The moment you abate any thing from the full rights of men, each to govern himself, and suffer any artificial positive limitation upon those rights, from that moment the whole organization of government becomes a consideration of convenience. This it is which makes the constitution of a state, and the due distribution of its powers, a matter of the most delicate and complicated skill. It requires a deep knowledge of human nature and human necessities, and of the things which facilitate or obstruct the various ends which are to be pursued by the mechanism of civil institutions. The state is to have recruits to its strength, and remedies to its distempers. What is the use of discussing a man's abstract right to food or to medicine?[239] The question is upon the method of procuring [90] and administering them. In that deliberation I shall always advise to call in the aid of the farmer and the physician, rather

[237]In Whig fashion, Burke apparently analysed the state as created through contract by pre-existing individuals. This distinguished him both from early eighteenth-century Tories, and from the obvious classical source: 'It is clear therefore that the state is also prior by nature to the individual; for if each individual when separate is not self-sufficient, he must be related to the whole state as other parts are to their whole': Aristotle, *Politics*, I, i, 12. If so, Burke was close to the position advanced by Paine. Paine argued against the view 'that government is a compact between those who govern and those who are governed … for as man must have existed before governments existed, there necessarily was a time when governments did not exist, and consequently there could originally exist no governors to form a contract with. The fact therefore must be, that the *individuals themselves*, each in his own personal and sovereign right, *entered into a compact with each other* to produce a government': *Rights of Man*, p. 52. Paine did not claim to be correcting Burke at this point.

[238]Whig theorists had commonly declared that men surrendered their natural rights on entering into civil society. Burke now extended that point to make civil society wholly dependent on practical wisdom.

[239]Natural rights theories had already begun to proliferate by designating more and more goods as 'rights'.

than the professor of metaphysics. The science of constructing a common-wealth, or renovating it, or reforming it, is, like every other experimental science, not to be taught *à priori*. Nor is it a short experience that can instruct us in that practical science; because the real effects of moral causes are not always immediate; but that which in the first instance is prejudicial may be excellent in its remoter operation; and its excellence may arise even from the ill effects it produces in the beginning. The reverse also happens; and very plausible schemes, with very pleasing commencements, have often shameful and lamentable conclusions. In states there are often some obscure and almost latent causes, things which appear at first view of little moment, on which a very great part of its prosperity or adversity may most essentially depend. The science of government being therefore so practical in itself, and intended for such practical purposes, a matter which requires experience, and even more experience than any person can gain in his whole life, however sagacious and observing he may be, it is with infinite caution that any man ought to venture upon pulling down an edifice which has answered in any tolerable degree for ages the common purposes of society, or of building it up again, without having models and patterns of approved utility before his eyes.

These metaphysic rights entering into common [91] life, like rays of light which pierce into a dense medium, are, by the laws of nature, refracted from their straight line. Indeed in the gross and complicated mass of human passions and concerns, the primitive rights of men undergo such a variety of refractions and reflections, that it becomes absurd to talk of them as if they continued in the simplicity of their original direction. The nature of man is intricate; the objects of society are of the greatest possible complexity; and therefore no simple disposition or direction of power can be suitable either to man's nature, or to the quality of his affairs.[240] When I hear the simplicity of contrivance aimed at and boasted of in any new political constitutions, I am at no loss to decide that the artificers are grossly ignorant of their trade, or totally negligent of their duty. The simple governments are fundamentally defective, to say no worse of them. If you were to contemplate society in but one point of view, all these simple modes of polity are infinitely captivating. In effect each would answer its single end much more perfectly than the more complex is able to attain all its complex purposes. But it is better that the whole should be imperfectly and anomalously answered, than that, while some parts are provided for with great exactness, others might be totally neglected, or perhaps materially injured, by the over-care of a favourite member.

---

[240]For Burke's long-standing insistence on the difficulty of changing the constitution see, for example, [Burke], *Thoughts*, p. 51.

The pretended rights of these theorists are all extremes; and in proportion as they are metaphysically true, they are morally and politically [92] false.[241] The rights of men are in a sort of *middle*, incapable of definition, but not impossible to be discerned. The rights of men in governments are their advantages; and these are often in balances between differences of good; in compromises sometimes between good and evil, and sometimes, between evil and evil. Political reason is a computing principle; adding, subtracting, multiplying, and dividing, morally and not metaphysically or mathematically, true moral denominations.[242]

By these theorists the right of the people is almost always sophistically confounded with their power.[243] The body of the community, whenever it can come to act, can meet with no effectual resistance; but till power and right are the same, the whole body of them has no right inconsistent with virtue, and the first of all virtues, prudence. Men have no right to what is not reasonable, and to what is not for their benefit; for though a pleasant writer said, *Liceat perire poetis*, when one of them, in cold blood, is said to have leaped into the flames of a volcanic revolution, *Ardentem frigidus Ætnam insiluit*,[244] I consider such a frolic rather as an unjustifiable poetic licence, than as one of the franchises of Parnassus; and whether he were poet or divine, or politician that chose to exercise this kind of right, I think that more wise, because more charitable thoughts would urge me rather to save the man, than to preserve his brazen slippers as the monuments of his folly. [93]

[241]'It is a certain though a strange truth, that in politics almost all principles that are speculatively right are practically wrong: the reason of which is, that they proceed on a supposition that men act rationally; which being by no means true, all that is built on so false a foundation, on experiment falls to the ground': Soame Jenyns, 'Reflections on Several Subjects' in Cole (ed.), *Works of Soame Jenyns*, II, p. 225. Burke's attention, if he read this work, may have been caught by an unwelcome passage on the preceding page: 'opposition is the most unpromising school in which a minister can receive his education; it being as unlikely that a man should learn the science of government by the practice of disturbing it, as that he should acquire the skill of an architect by pulling down houses, or the trade of a glazier by breaking of windows'.

[242]Paine (*Rights of Man*, p. 119) claimed this passage meant: '*That government is governed by no principle whatever; that it can make evil good, or good evil, just as it pleases. In short, that government is arbitrary power.*'

[243]'In fine as in democracies the people seem to do very near whatever they please, liberty has been placed in this form of government, and the power of the people has been confounded with their liberty': Montesquieu, *The Spirit of the Laws*, Book XI, ch. 2 (I, p. 213).

[244]'Empedocles, eager to be thought a god immortal, calmly leapt into burning Aetna. Let poets have the right and power to destroy themselves': Horace, *De Arte Poetica*, 465–6.

The kind of anniversary sermons, to which a great part of what I write refers, if men are not shamed out of their present course, in commemorating the fact, will cheat many out of the principles, and deprive them of the benefits of the Revolution they commemorate. I confess to you, Sir, I never liked this continual talk of resistance and revolution, or the practice of making the extreme medicine of the constitution its daily bread. It renders the habit of society dangerously valetudinary: it is taking periodical doses of mercury sublimate, and swallowing down repeated provocatives of cantharides[245] to our love of liberty.

✳ This distemper of remedy, grown habitual, relaxes and wears out, by a vulgar and prostituted use, the spring of that spirit which is to be exerted on great occasions. It was in the most patient period of Roman servitude that themes of tyrannicide made the ordinary exercise of boys at school—*cum perimit sævos classis numerosa tyrannos*.[246] In the ordinary state of things, it produces in a country like ours the worst effects, even on the cause of that liberty which it abuses with the dissoluteness of an extravagant speculation. Almost all the high-bred republicans of my time have, after a short space, become the most decided, thorough-paced courtiers;[247] they soon left the business of a tedious, moderate, but practical resistance to those of us[248] whom, in the pride and intoxication of their theories, they have slighted, as not much better than tories.[249] Hypocrisy, of course, delights in the [94] most sublime speculations; for, never intending to go beyond speculation, it costs nothing to have it magnificent. But even in cases where rather levity than fraud was to be suspected in these ranting speculations, the issue has been much the same.

---

[245]Mercury sublimate was a familiar drug, used to treat venereal disease. In overdose, mercury poisoning produced symptoms of irritability and nervousness resembling mania. Used to cure felt, mercury sometimes produced these symptoms in hatters. Cantharides was a drug made of dried beetle, 'Spanish Fly', once considered an aphrodisiac. Burke may have implied that revolutionaries were forced to take a harmful remedy for a disease which their own actions had produced.

[246]'Or do you teach rhetoric? O Vettius! What iron bowels must you have when your troop of scholars slays the cruel tyrant' [in a rhetorical exercise]: Juvenal, *Satires*, VII, 150–1.

[247]Burke referred to the earlier part of his career, in which the Bedford, Grenville and Chatham factions had all joined the court party. The phrase 'high-bred republicans' was more appropriate, however, for the reforming nobility of the 1790s.

[248]The Rockingham Whigs.

[249]Burke again signalled his aversion from early-Hanoverian Toryism. After c. 1760, the term 'Tory' survived, after the parliamentary party had disintegrated, as a term of reproach, intended to signify an excessive attachment to monarchy and a contempt for liberty.

These professors, finding their extreme principles not applicable to cases which call only for a qualified, or, as I may say, civil and legal resistance, in such cases employ no resistance at all. It is with them a war or a revolution, or it is nothing. Finding their schemes of politics not adapted to the state of the world in which they live, they often come to think lightly of all public principle; and are ready, on their part, to abandon for a very trivial interest what they find of very trivial value. Some indeed are of more steady and persevering natures; but these are eager politicians out of parliament, who have little to tempt them to abandon their favourite projects. They have some change in the church or state, or both, constantly in their view.[250] When that is the case, they are always bad citizens, and perfectly unsure connexions. For, considering their speculative designs as of infinite value, and the actual arrangement of the state as of no estimation, they are at best indifferent about it. They see no merit in the good, and no fault in the vicious management of public affairs; they rather rejoice in the latter, as more propitious to revolution. They see no merit or demerit in any man, or any action, or any political principle, any further than as they may forward or retard their design [95] of change: they therefore take up, one day, the most violent and stretched prerogative, and another time the wildest democratic ideas of freedom, and pass from the one to the other without any sort of regard to cause, to person, or to party.

In France you are now in the crisis of a revolution,[251] and in the transit from one form of government to another—you cannot see that character of men exactly in the same situation in which we see it in this country. With us it is militant; with you it is triumphant; and you know how it can act when its power is commensurate to its will. I would not be supposed to confine those observations to any description of men, or to comprehend all men of any description within them—No! far from it. I am as incapable of that injustice, as I am of keeping terms with those who profess principles of extremes; and who under the name of religion teach little else than wild and dangerous politics. The worst of these politics of revolution is this; they temper and harden the breast, in order to prepare it for the desperate strokes which are sometimes used in extreme occasions. But as these occasions may never arrive, the mind receives a gratuitous taint; and the moral sentiments suffer not a little, when no political purpose is served by the depravation. This sort of people are so

---

[250]For Tocqueville's endorsement, for France, of Burke's analysis of the lack of experience of men of letters, see *Old Regime*, bk. 3, ch. 1, 'How Around the Middle of the Eighteenth Century Intellectuals Became the Country's Leading Politicians, and the Effects Which Resulted from This.'

[251]In passages like this, Burke began to extend the meaning of 'revolution' from an event to a process.

taken up with their theories about the rights of man, that they have totally forgot his nature. Without opening one new avenue to the understanding, they have succeeded in stopping up those that lead to the heart. They have perverted [96] in themselves, and in those that attend to them, all the well-placed sympathies of the human breast.

This famous sermon of the Old Jewry breathes nothing but this spirit through all the political part. Plots, massacres, assassinations, seem to some people a trivial price for obtaining a revolution. A cheap, bloodless reformation, a guiltless liberty,[252] appear flat and vapid to their taste. There must be a great change of scene; there must be a magnificent stage effect; there must be a grand spectacle to rouze the imagination, grown torpid with the lazy enjoyment of sixty years security, and the still unanimating repose of public prosperity. The Preacher found them all in the French revolution. This inspires a juvenile warmth through his whole frame. His enthusiasm kindles as he advances; and when he arrives at his peroration, it is in a full blaze. Then viewing, from the Pisgah of his pulpit,[253] the free, moral, happy, flourishing, and glorious state of France, as in a bird-eye landscape of a promised land, he breaks out into the following rapture:[254]

"What an eventful period is this! I am *thankful* that I have lived to it; I could almost say, *Lord, now lettest thou thy servant depart in peace, for mine eyes have seen thy salvation.*—I have lived to see a *diffusion* of knowledge, which has undermined superstition and error.—I have lived to see *the rights of men* better understood than ever; and nations panting for liberty which seemed to have lost the idea of it.—I have lived to see *Thirty Millions* [97] *of People*, indignant and resolute, spurning at slavery, and demanding liberty with an irresistible voice. *Their King led in triumph, and an arbitrary monarch surrendering himself to his subjects.*"[255]

[252]Cf. 'Blamelesse Liberty': Thomas Hobbes, *De Corpore Politico. Or the Elements of Law, Moral & Politick* (London, 1650), p. 4.

[253]Cf. Deuteronomy 34.1: 'And Moses went up from the plains of Moab, unto the mountain of Nebo, to the top of Pisgah, that is over against Jericho; and the Lord showed him all the land of Gilead unto Dan.' This was Moses' first sight of the promised land.

[254]Price, *Discourse*, 3rd edn., p. 49.

[255]Another of these reverend gentlemen, who was witness to some of the spectacles which Paris has lately exhibited—expresses himself thus, "*A king dragged in submissive triumph by his conquering subjects* is one of those appearances of grandeur which seldom rise in the prospect of human affairs, and which, during the remainder of my life, I shall think of with wonder and gratification." These gentlemen agree marvellously in their feelings. [B] The author of this letter, probably published in the *Gazetteer* of 14 September 1789, was Price's nephew George Cadogan Morgan, who had in

Before I proceed further, I have to remark, that Dr. Price seems rather to over-value the great acquisitions of light which he has obtained and diffused in this age. The last century appears to me to have been quite as much enlightened. It had, though in a different place, a triumph as memorable as that of Dr. Price; and some of the great preachers of that period partook of it as eagerly as he has done in the triumph of France. On the trial of the Rev. Hugh Peters for high treason, it was deposed, that when King Charles was brought to London for his trial, the Apostle of Liberty in that day conducted the *triumph*. "I saw," says the witness, "his majesty in the coach with six horses, and Peters riding before the king *triumphing*."[256] Dr. Price, when he talks as if he had made a discovery, only follows a precedent; for, after the commencement of the king's trial, this precursor, the same Dr. Peters, concluding a long prayer at the royal chapel at Whitehall, [98] (he had very triumphantly chosen his place) said, "I have prayed and preached these twenty years; and now I may say with old Simeon, *Lord, now lettest thou thy servant depart in peace, for mine eyes have seen thy salvation.*"[257] Peters had not the fruits of his prayer; for he neither departed so soon as he wished, nor in peace. He became (what I heartily hope none of his followers may be in this country) himself a sacrifice to the triumph which he led as Pontiff. They dealt at the Restoration, perhaps, too hardly with this poor good man. But we owe it to his memory and his sufferings, that he had as much illumination, and as much zeal, and had as effectually undermined all *the superstition and error* which might impede the great business he was engaged in, as any who follow and repeat after him, in this age, which would assume to itself an exclusive title to the knowl-

---

1786 been appointed Price's assistant minister in the meeting house at Newington Green. See D. O. Thomas, 'George Cadogan Morgan (1754–98)', *The Price-Priestley Newsletter* 3 (1979), pp. 53–70, and 'Edmund Burke and the Reverend Dissenting Gentlemen', *Notes and Queries* 29 (June 1982), pp. 202–4. Although Morgan had not written of 6 October 1789, the extremism of his language is even more remarkable. See also *Reflections*, p. [128].

[256]Priestley (*Letters to Burke*, p. 48) announced: 'in my opinion, there was sufficient cause for triumph'; January 30, the anniversary of Charles I's execution, was 'a *proud day* for England'.

[257]State Trials, vol. ii. p. 360, p. 363. [B] Burke used *A Complete Collection of State-Trials, and Proceedings upon High-Treason, and other Crimes and Misdemeanours; from The Reign of King Richard II to The End of the Reign of King George I* (10 vols., London, 1730–66). For the trial of Hugh Peters, see II, pp. 353–65: witnesses deposed that Peters in a sermon on 20 December 1648 had compared Charles I to Barabbas, arguing against the king's release. In sermons on 21 and 28 January 1649, Peters's text was Psalm cxlix: 8, 'To bind their kings in Chains, and their Nobles in Links of Iron'.

edge of the rights of men, and all the glorious consequences of that knowledge.

After this sally of the preacher of the Old Jewry, which differs only in place and time, but agrees perfectly with the spirit and letter of the rapture of 1648, the Revolution Society, the fabricators of governments, the heroic band of *cashierers* of *monarchs,* electors of sovereigns, and leaders of kings in triumph, strutting with a proud consciousness of the diffusion of knowledge, of which every member had obtained so large a share in the donative, were in haste to make a generous diffusion of the knowledge [99] they had thus gratuitously received. To make this bountiful communication, they adjourned from the church in the Old Jewry, to the London Tavern; where the same Dr. Price, in whom the fumes of his oracular tripod were not entirely evaporated, moved and carried the resolution, or address of congratulation, transmitted by Lord Stanhope to the National Assembly of France.[258]

I find a preacher of the gospel prophaning the beautiful and prophetic ejaculation, commonly called "*nunc dimittis,*" made on the first presentation of our Saviour in the Temple, and applying it, with an inhuman and unnatural rapture, to the most horrid, atrocious, and afflicting spectacle, that perhaps ever was exhibited to the pity and indignation of mankind. This "*leading in triumph,*" a thing in its best form unmanly and irreligious, which fills our Preacher with such unhallowed transports, must shock, I believe, the moral taste of every well-born mind. Several English were the stupified and indignant spectators of that triumph.[259] It was (unless we have been strangely deceived) a spectacle more resembling a procession of American savages, entering into Onondaga,[260] after some of their murders called victories, and leading into hovels hung round with scalps, their captives, overpowered with the scoffs and buffets of women as ferocious as themselves, much more than it resembled the triumphal pomp of a civilized martial nation;—if a civilized na-

[258]Price's reply to Burke was an eight page Preface and an addition to the Appendix of the fourth edition of A Discourse on the Love of our Country, published on 25 November 1790 (see below, Appendix II). Price dealt with few of Burke's points. He claimed that he had referred to Louis XVI's entry into Paris in July 1789, not to the events of 5–6 October. His evidence was merely that 'The letters quoted by him [Burke] in p. 99 [sc. 97] and 128, were dated in *July* 1789', and so referred to the earlier event. This was irrelevant (nor did the letter on p. 128 refer to a royal visit), and did not dispel a widespread belief that Price, in his sermon of November, had indeed exulted at the atrocities committed a month before.

[259]Burke referred to the action of the women of the Paris mob in forcibly moving the royal family from Versailles to the capital on 5–6 October 1789.

[260]Onondaga, near Lake Ontario, was the site of the main Jesuit mission to the American Indians.

tion, or any men who had a sense of generosity, were capable of a personal triumph over the fallen and afflicted.[261] [100]

This, my dear Sir, was not the triumph of France. I must believe that, as a nation, it overwhelmed you with shame and horror. I must believe that the National Assembly find themselves in a state of the greatest humiliation, in not being able to punish the authors of this triumph, or the actors in it; and that they are in a situation in which any enquiry they may make upon the subject, must be destitute even of the appearance of liberty or impartiality. The apology of that Assembly is found in their situation; but when we approve what they *must* bear, it is in us the degenerate choice of a vitiated mind.

With a compelled appearance of deliberation, they vote under the dominion of a stern necessity. They sit in the heart, as it were, of a foreign republic: they have their residence in a city whose constitution has emanated neither from the charter of their king, nor from their legislative power.[262] There they

[261]Not all Europeans depicted Native Americans as 'noble savages'. William Burke had emphasised the similarity of the 'Aborigines of America' across the northern and southern continents, their capacity to execute 'an horrible revenge' on enemies, their 'shocking barbarities' including cannibalism, their adornment of their houses with the scalps of their victims. This cruelty reached its peak in war, the Indians' martial spirit roused by 'the most hideous howlings' in which 'the women add their cries to those of the men'. In the conflict itself, 'the conquerors satiate their savage fury with the most shocking insults and barbarities to the dead, biting their flesh, tearing the scalp from their heads, and wallowing in their blood like wild beasts', the victory celebrated on the return of the warriors with 'an extravagance and phrenzy of joy' in which prisoners were tortured to death. In this civic festival 'The women, forgetting the human as well as the female nature, and transformed into something worse than furies, act their parts, and even outdo the men in this scene of horror'. William Burke did not present this as evidence of the inherent racial inferiority of the Indians, but as proof of 'to what an inconceivable degree of barbarity the passions of men let loose will carry them. It will point out to us the advantages of a religion that teaches a compassion to our enemies, which is neither known nor practised in other religions; and it will make us more sensible than some appear to be, of the value of commerce, the arts of a civilized life, and the lights of literature; which, if they have abated the force of some of the natural virtues by the luxury which attends them, have taken out likewise the sting of our natural vices, and softened the ferocity of the human race without enervating their courage': [William Burke, revised by Edmund Burke], *An Account of the European Settlements in America* (2 vols., London, 1757), I, pp. 161, 165, 182, 187, 190–4. For early English perceptions of Americans, see H. C. Porter, *The Inconstant Savage: England and the North American Indian 1500–1660* (London, 1979).

[262]After the forcible removal of the royal family from Versailles to Paris on 6 October 1789, the National Assembly decided to follow on 12 October. Once in Paris, they were overawed by the mob. It was while the Assembly was in Paris that it passed most of its decrees against the Church. *The Times* reported on 26 October 1789: 'The

are surrounded by an army[263] not raised either by the authority of their crown, or by their command; and which, if they should order to dissolve itself, would instantly dissolve them. There they sit, after a gang of assassins had driven away all the men of moderate minds and moderating authority amongst them, and left them as a sort of dregs and refuse, under the apparent lead of those in whom they do not so much as pretend to have any confidence.[264] There they sit, in mockery of legislation, repeating in resolutions the words of those whom they detest and despise. Captives themselves, they compel a captive king to issue as royal edicts, at third hand, the polluted nonsense [101] of their most licentious and giddy coffee-houses. It is notorious, that all their measures are decided before they are debated. It is beyond doubt, that under the terror of the bayonet, and the lamp-post, and the torch to their houses, they are obliged to adopt all the crude and desperate measures suggested by clubs composed of a monstrous medley of all conditions, tongues, and nations. Among these are found persons, in comparison of whom Catiline would be thought scrupulous, and Cethegus[265] a man of sobriety and moderation. Nor is it in these clubs alone that the publick measures are deformed into

---

translation of the National Assembly to Paris, might be a matter of indifference at any other moment than the present, but it is now accompanied by circumstances so extraordinary, as to be extremely alarming. The Assembly is now placed in the centre of public opinion, which will be at instant call to direct or arrest their proceedings. It is here the danger exists …'

[263]The National Guard or *milice bourgeoise*, nominally 48,000 men, ordered to be assembled by the revolutionary government of Paris on 13 July 1789. Napoleon suppressed it after his *coup* of 1799.

[264]A moderate Deputy, François-Louis-Thibault de Menonville, who resolutely continued to attend, protested at this passage (Menonville to Burke, 17 November 1790: Burke, *Correspondence*, VI, pp. 162–9). Burke explained himself in *Letter to a Member of the National Assembly*, and corrected the passage in later editions of the *Reflections* to read: 'There they sit, after a gang of assassins had driven away some hundreds of the members; whilst those who held the same moderate principles, with more patience or better hope, continued every day exposed to outrageous insults and murderous threats. There a majority, sometimes real, sometimes pretended, captive itself, compels a captive king …' Burke was correct in arguing that many Deputies fled the National Assembly after 6 October 1789. The first great wave of emigration from France, including Lally-Tollendal and Mounier, also began at this time. At its first meeting in Paris on 19 October, the National Assembly was some three hundred members smaller than at its last meeting at Versailles on 15 October.

[265]Lucius Sergius Catilina. Repeatedly disappointed in elections for the consulate, he organised a conspiracy to seize power which was frustrated by Cicero: Catiline was caught and killed in 62 BC. Publius Claudius Cethegus was an ally of Sulla and played a leading part in the proscriptions at Rome after 87 BC.

monsters. They undergo a previous distortion in academies,[266] intended as so many seminaries for these clubs, which are set up in all the places of publick resort. In these meetings of all sorts, every counsel, in proportion as it is daring, and violent, and perfidious, is taken for the mark of superior genius. Humanity and compassion are ridiculed as the fruits of superstition and ignorance. Tenderness to individuals is considered as treason to the public. Liberty is always to be estimated perfect as property is rendered insecure. Amidst assassination, massacre, and confiscation, perpetrated or meditated, they are forming plans for the good order of future society. Embracing in their arms the carcases of base criminals, and promoting their relations on the title of their offences,[267] they drive hundreds of virtuous persons to the same end, by forcing them to subsist by beggary or by crime. [102]

The Assembly, their organ, acts before them the farce of deliberation with as little decency as liberty. They act like the comedians of a fair before a riotous audience; they act amidst the tumultuous cries of a mixed mob of ferocious men, and of women lost to shame, who, according to their insolent fancies, direct, control, applaud, explode[268] them; and sometimes mix and take their seats amongst them; domineering over them with a strange mixture of servile petulance and proud presumptuous authority.[269] As they have inverted order in all things, the gallery is in the place of the house. This Assembly, which overthrows kings and kingdoms, has not even the physiognomy and aspect of a grave legislative body—*nec color imperii, nec frons erat ulla senatus.*[270] They have a power given to them, like that of the evil principle, to sub-

[266]See Michael L. Kennedy, *The Jacobin Clubs in the French Revolution: The First Years* (Princeton, 1982).

[267]The National Assembly provided for 'les vainqueurs de la Bastille', including the widows of men killed in the assault, and enlisted them in civic processions: *Le Moniteur*, 21 June 1790.

[268]'Explode': shout down, reject.

[269]Lally-Tollendal recorded of the session of 5 October 1789: 'J'avois été à l'assemblée, dans la soirée. J'y avois vu ces femmes équivoques et ces hommes déguisés, siégeant pêle-mêle avec les députés, interrompant les uns, appellant les autres par leurs noms, nous prescrivant le sujet de nos délibérations. J'y avois vu ces scènes de crapule et de fureur qui avoient forcé de lever la séance, et j'étois retourné dans la chambre du roi': *Mémoire de M. le Comte de Lally-Tollendal, ou seconde lettre A ses Commettans* (Paris, 'Janvier 1790'), pp. 163–4 (dated from Lausanne, 30 December 1789). The public was excluded from the floor of the House of Commons at Westminster and the galleries were cleared in the event of disorder there. The principles of the French Revolution evidently implied a legislature open to the populace.

[270]'No tyrant need blush in future: there will be no pretence of military command, and the Senate will never again be used as a screen': Lucan, *Pharsalia*, Book IX, 206–7. Lucan attributed these remarks to Cato, on the death of Pompey. 'erat' *sc.* 'erit'.

vert and destroy; but none to construct, except such machines as may be fitted for further subversion and further destruction.

Who is it that admires, and from the heart is attached to national representative assemblies, but must turn with horror and disgust from such a profane burlesque, and abominable perversion of that sacred institute? Lovers of monarchy, lovers of republicks, must alike abhor it. The members of your Assembly must themselves groan under the tyranny of which they have all the shame, none of the direction, and little of the profit. I am sure many of the members who compose even the majority of that body, must feel as I do, notwithstanding the applauses of the Revolution Society. [103]—Miserable king! miserable Assembly! How must that assembly be silently scandalized with those of their members, who would call a day which seemed to blot the sun out of Heaven, "un beau jour!"[271] How must they be inwardly indignant at hearing others, who thought fit to declare to them, "that the vessel of the state would fly forward in her course towards regeneration with more speed than ever,"[272] from the stiff gale of treason and murder, which preceded our Preacher's triumph! What must they have felt, whilst with outward patience and inward indignation they heard of the slaughter of innocent gentlemen in their houses, that "the blood spilled was not the most pure?"[273] What must they have felt, when they were besieged by complaints of disorders which shook their country to its foundations, at being compelled coolly to tell the complainants, that they were under the protection of the law, and that they would address the king (the captive king) to cause the laws to be enforced for their protection; when the enslaved ministers of that captive king had formally notified to them, that there were neither law, nor authority, nor power left to protect? What must they have felt at being obliged, as a felicitation on the present new year, to request their captive king to forget the stormy period of the last, on account of the great good which *he* was likely to produce to his

[271]6th of October, 1789. [B] According to Lally-Tollendal's letter (printed in *Reflections*, pp. [109–10]) these were the words used by Jean-Sylvain Bailly, mayor of Paris, to describe that day. Since it rained heavily, he was probably not referring to the weather.

[272]The expression 'vessel of state' was used by Mirabeau in a debate in the National Assembly on 6 October, and reported in the *Procès-verbal*.

[273]On 23 July 1789 Lally-Tollendal condemned in the National Assembly the murders of Joseph-François Foullon and Berthier de Sauvigny the day before. Barnave replied: 'On veut nous attendrir, messieurs, en faveur du sang qui a été versé hier à Paris: ce *sang était-il donc si pur?*': Fierro and Liébert, pp. 648–9. *Le Moniteur*, 23–24 July 1789, attributed to Barnave the less immediately offensive words: 'Il ne faut pas se laisser trop alarmer par les orages, inseparables des mouvemens d'une révolution.'

people; to the complete attainment of which good they adjourned the practical demonstrations [104] of their loyalty, assuring him of their obedience, when he should no longer possess any authority to command?[274]

This address was made with much good-nature and affection, to be sure. But among the revolutions in France, must be reckoned a considerable revolution in their ideas of politeness.[275] In England we are said to learn manners at second-hand from your side of the water, and that we dress our behaviour in the frippery of France.[276] If so, we are still in the old cut; and have not so far conformed to the new Parisian mode of good-breeding, as to think it quite in the most refined strain of delicate compliment (whether in condolence or congratulation) to say, to the most humiliated creature that crawls upon the earth, that great public benefits are derived from the murder of his servants, the attempted assassination of himself and of his wife, and the mortification, disgrace, and degradation, that he has personally suffered. It is a topic of consolation which our ordinary[277] of Newgate would be too humane to use to a criminal at the foot of the gallows. I should have thought that the hangman of Paris, now that he is liberalized by the vote of the National Assembly, and is

[274]On 1 January 1790 the National Assembly presented the King with an address: 'Sire, l'Assemblée nationale vient offrir à votre majeste le tribut d'amour et de respect qu'elle lui offrira dans tous les tems. Le restaurateur de la liberté publique, le roi qui, dans des circonstances difficiles, n'a écouté que son amour pour la fidelle Nation dont il est le chef, mérite tous nos hommages, et nous les présentons avec un dévoûment parfait.

Les sollicitudes paternelles de votre majesté auront un terme prochain; les représentans de la Nation osent l'en assurer. Cette considération ajoute au zele qu'ils mettent dans leurs travaux: pour se consoler des peines de leur longue carriere, ils songent à cet heureux jour, où paraissant en corps devant un prince ami du Peuple, ils lui présenteront un receuil de lois calculées pour son bonheur et pour celui de tous les Français; où leur tendresse respecteuse suppliera un roi chéri d'oublier les désordres d'une époque orageuse, de ne plus se souvenir que de la prosperité et du contentement qu'il aura repandus sur le plus beau royaume de l'Europe; où votre majesté reconnaîtra, pour l'expérience, que sur le trône, ainsi que dans les rangs les plus obscurs, les mouvemens d'un cœur génereux sont la source des véritables plaisirs.

Alors on connaîtra toute la loyauté de Français; alors on sera bien convaincu qu'ils abhorrent et savent réprimer la license; qu'au moment où leur énergie a causé des alarmes, ils ne voulaient qu'affermir l'autorité légitime; et que si la liberté est devenue pour eux un bien nécessaire, ils la méritent par leur respect pour les lois et pour le vertueux monarque qui doit les maintenir': Le Moniteur, 4 January 1790.

[275]Contemporaries still had no clear idea of 'revolution' as a unitary process which displayed itself in various aspects.

[276]'Frippery': '1. Old clothes; cast-off garments ... 2. Finery in dress, esp. tawdry finery': OED.

[277]'Ordinary': chaplain.

allowed his rank and arms in the Herald's College of the rights of men, would be too generous, too gallant a man, too full of the sense of his new dignity, to employ that cutting consolation to any of the persons whom the *leze nation* might bring under the administration of his *executive powers.*[278]

A man is fallen indeed, when he is thus flattered. [105] The anodyne draught of oblivion, thus drugged, is well calculated to preserve a galling wakefulness, and to feed the living ulcer of a corroding memory. Thus to administer the opiate potion of amnesty, powdered with all the ingredients of scorn and contempt, is to hold to his lips, instead of "the balm of hurt minds,"[279] the cup of human misery full to the brim, and to force him to drink it to the dregs.

Yielding to reasons, at least as forcible as those which were so delicately urged in the compliment on the new year, the king of France will probably endeavour to forget these events, and that compliment. But history, who keeps a durable record of all our acts, and exercises her awful censure over the proceedings of all sorts of sovereigns, will not forget, either those events, or the æra of this liberal refinement in the intercourse of mankind. History will record, that on the morning of the 6th of October 1789, the king and queen of France, after a day of confusion, alarm, dismay, and slaughter, lay down, under the pledged security of public faith, to indulge nature in a few hours of respite, and troubled melancholy repose. From this sleep the queen was first startled by the voice of the centinel at her door, who cried out to her, to save herself by flight—that this was the last proof of fidelity he could give—that they were upon him, and he was dead.[280] Instantly he was cut down. A band of cruel ruffians and assassins, reeking with his blood, rushed into the chamber of the queen, and pierced [106] with an hundred strokes of bayonets and poniards the bed, from whence this persecuted woman had but just time to fly almost naked, and through ways unknown to the murderers had escaped to seek refuge at the feet of a king and husband, not secure of his own life for a moment.

This king, to say no more of him, and this queen, and their infant children (who once would have been the pride and hope of a great and generous people) were then forced to abandon the sanctuary of the most splendid palace in the world, which they left swimming in blood, polluted by massacre, and

---

[278]In September 1789 the National Assembly had redefined treason from *lèse majesté* to *lèse nation*. See George Armstrong Kelly, 'From *Lèse-Majesté* to *Lèse-Nation*' in Kelly, *Mortal Politics in Eighteenth-Century France*, special issue of *Historical Reflections/Réflexions Historiques* 13 (1986), pp. 208–34.

[279]William Shakespeare, *Macbeth*, Act II, scene 2.

[280]M. de Miomandre.

strewed with scattered limbs and mutilated carcases. Thence they were conducted into the capital of their kingdom. Two had been selected[281] from the
u[n]provoked, unresisted, promiscuous slaughter, which was made of the
gentlemen of birth and family who composed the king's body guard. These
two gentlemen, with all the parade of an execution of justice, were cruelly and
publickly dragged to the block, and beheaded in the great court of the palace.
Their heads were stuck upon spears, and led the procession; whilst the royal
captives who followed in the train were slowly moved along, amidst the horrid yells, and shrilling screams, and frantic dances, and infamous contumelies,
and all the unutterable abominations of the furies of hell, in the abused shape
of the vilest of women. After they had been made to taste, drop by drop, more
than the bitterness of death, in the slow torture of a journey of twelve [107]
miles, protracted to six hours, they were, under a guard, composed of those
very soldiers who had thus conducted them through this famous triumph,
lodged in one of the old palaces[282] of Paris, now converted into a Bastile for
kings.[283]

Is this a triumph to be consecrated at altars? to be commemorated with
grateful thanksgiving? to be offered to the divine humanity with fervent prayer
and enthusiastick ejaculation?—These Theban and Thracian Orgies,[284] acted

[281]M. de Huttes and M. Varicourt. The atrocities were much worse than Burke recorded. Priestley, who disparaged Burke's knowledge of events in France, flatly denied
his account of these events, and revealingly added that Marie Antoinette 'may think
herself fortunate, in such a revolution as this has been, to have escaped with life': *Let
ters to Burke*, pp. 17–18. Paine estimated only 'the loss of two or three lives': *Rights of
Man*, p. 41. Even the *Courier Français* (8 October 1789) recorded the burial of seventeen victims. *The Times* of 17 October 1789 reported: 'On an accurate return, since
made of the people killed on both sides in this affray, we find the number to be about
106.'

[282]The Tuileries.

[283]The friends of the Revolution in England tried to disparage Burke's account of
the events of 5–6 October as rhetorical exaggeration, but despite Burke's heightened
language the essential accuracy of his account is established by eye-witnesses: see Bibliography, D x. Paine (*Rights of Man*, p. 42) claimed that 'not an act of molestation
was committed during the whole march'. *Le Moniteur*, over five issues from 8–9 October to 12–13 October, carried lengthy and graphic accounts which paralleled
Burke's images of frenzy and violence.

[284]The orgies celebrated in Thebes (Boetia) and the hills of Thrace to honour the
god Dionysus involved his frenzied worshippers in tearing to pieces a bull, representing
the god, and eating its raw flesh. These devotees, drunken, dressed in animal skins and
often female, were emblematic of ecstatic license before this state of mind was associated with political revolutions. France's most able journalist recorded: 'A people suddenly released from a political and religious yoke are no longer a people; they are an

in France, and applauded only in the Old Jewry,[285] I assure you, kindle prophetic enthusiasm in the minds but of very few people in this kingdom; although a saint and apostle, who may have revelations of his own, and who has so completely vanquished all the mean superstitions of the heart, may incline to think it pious and decorous to compare it with the entrance into the world of the Prince of Peace, proclaimed in an holy temple by a venerable sage, and not long before not worse announced by the voice of angels to the quiet innocence of shepherds.

At first I was at a loss to account for this fit of unguarded transport. I knew, indeed, that the sufferings of monarchs make a delicious repast to some sort of palates. There were reflexions which might serve to keep this appetite within some bounds of temperance. But when I took one circumstance into my consideration, I was obliged to confess, that much allowance ought to be made for the Society, and that the temptation was too strong for common discretion; I mean, the circumstance of the Io [108] Pæan[286] of the triumph, the animating cry which called "for *all* the BISHOPS to be hanged on the lampposts"[287], might well have brought forth a burst of enthusiasm on the foreseen consequences of this happy day. I allow to so much enthusiasm some little deviation from prudence. I allow this prophet to break forth into hymns of joy and thanksgiving on an event which appears like the precursor of the Millenium, and the projected fifth monarchy,[288] in the destruction of all church establishments. There was, however (as in all human affairs there is) in the midst of this joy something to exercise the patience of these worthy gentle-

---

enfuriated populace, dancing before the sanctuary, yelling the Carmagnole, and the dancers (I exaggerate nothing) almost without breeches, their neck and breast bare, their stockings about their heels, they imitated by their rapid turnings those whirlwinds, the forerunners of tempests, which ravage and destroy wherever they take place': Mercier, *New Picture of Paris*, II, p. 83.

[285]Burke reasonably inferred that Price's references to a 'king led in triumph' were to the events of 6 October. In the Preface to the fourth edition of his *Discourse*, Price protested that he had referred to an earlier royal entry into Paris in July 1789: see Appendix II below.

[286]'Io Paean', from the chorus of the Greek hymn to Apollo; in English a song of triumph.

[287]Tous les Evêques à la lanterne. [B]

[288]Millennium: the thousand-year reign of the saints on earth, foretold in Revelations, which would precede (or, according to another interpretation, succeed) the Second Coming of Christ. The Fifth Monarchy is prophesied in Daniel 2.44: the great monarchies of Assyria, Persia, Greece and Rome would be succeeded by a fifth, subsequently identified with the Millennium. The Fifth Monarchy Men were an extremist sect of the 1640s and 1650s who proclaimed the imminence of this event.

men, and to try the long-suffering of their faith. The actual murder of the king and queen, and their child, was wanting to the other auspicious circumstances of this *"beautiful day."* The actual murder of the bishops, though called for by so many holy ejaculations, was also wanting. A groupe of regicide and sacrilegious slaughter, was indeed boldly sketched, but it was only sketched. It unhappily was left unfinished, in this great history-piece of the massacre of innocents. What hardy pencil of a great master, from the school of the rights of men, will finish it, is to be seen hereafter. The age has not yet the compleat benefit of that diffusion of knowledge that has undermined superstition and error; and the king of France wants another object or two, to consign to oblivion, [109] in consideration of all the good which is to arise from his own sufferings, and the patriotic crimes of an enlightened age.[289] [110]

[289]It is proper here to refer to a letter written upon this subject by an eye-witness. That eye-witness was one of the most honest, intelligent, and eloquent members of the National Assembly, one of the most active and zealous reformers of the state. He was obliged to secede from the assembly; and he afterwards became a voluntary exile, on account of the horrors of this pious triumph, and the dispositions of men, who, profiting of crimes, if not causing them, have taken the lead in public affairs.

EXTRACT of M. de Lally Tollendal's Second Letter to a Friend.

Parlons du parti que j'ai pris; il est bien justifié dans ma conscience.—Ni cette ville coupable, ni cette assemblée plus coupable encore, ne meritoient que je me justifie; mais j'ai à cœur que vous, et les personnes qui pensent comme vous, ne me condamnent pas.—Ma santé, je vous jure, me rendoit mes fonctions impossibles; mais meme en les mettant de coté il a eté au-dessus de mes forces de supporter plus long-tems l'horreur que me causoit ce sang,—ces têtes,—cette reine *presque egorgée,*—ce roi,—amené *esclave,*—entrant à Paris, au milieu de ses assassins, et precedé des tetes de ses malheureux gardes.—Ces perfides jannissaires, ces assassins, ces femmes cannibales, ce cri de, TOUS LES EVEQUES A LA LANTERNE, dans le moment ou le roi entre sa capitale avec deux eveques de son conseil dans sa voiture. Un *coup de fusil,* que j'ai vu tirer dans un *des carosses de la reine.* M. Bailley appellant cela *un beau jour.* L'assemblée ayant declaré froidement le matin, qu'il n'étoit pas de sa dignité d'aller toute entiere environner le roi. M. Mirabeau disant impunement dans cette assemblée, que le vaisseau de l'état, loin d'etre arrêté dans sa course, s'élanceroit avec plus de rapidité que jamais vers sa régénération. M. Barnave, riant avec lui, quand des flots de sang couloient autour de nous. [110] Le vertueux Mounier* echappant par miracle à vingt assassins, qui avoient voulu faire de sa tete un trophée de plus.

Voila ce qui me fit jurer de ne plus mettre le pied *dans cette caverne d'Antropophages* [the National Assembly] où je n'avois plus de force d'élever la voix, ou depuis six semaines je l'avois elevée en vain. Moi, Mounier, et tous les honnêtes gens, ont le dernier effort à faire pour le bien étoit d'en sortir. Aucune idée de crainte ne s'est approchée de moi. Je rougirois de m'en defendre. J'avois encore reçû sur la route de la part de ce peuple, moins coupable que ceux qui l'ont enivré de fureur, des acclamations, et des applaudissemens, dont d'autres auroient été flattés, et qui m'ont fait fre-

Although this work of our new light and knowledge, did not go to the length, that in all probability it was intended it should be carried; yet I must think, that such treatment of any human creatures must be shocking to any but those [111] who are made for accomplishing Revolutions. But I cannot stop here. Influenced by the inborn feelings of my nature, and not being illuminated by a single ray of this new-sprung modern light, I confess to you, Sir, that the exalted rank of the persons suffering, and particularly the sex, the beauty, and the amiable qualities of the descendant of so many kings and emperors, with the tender age of royal infants, insensible only through infancy and innocence of the cruel outrages to which their parents were exposed, instead of being a subject of exultation, adds not a little to my sensibility on that most melancholy occasion.

----

mir. C'est à l'indignation, c'est à l'horreur. C'est aux convulsions physiques, que le seul aspect du sang me fait eprouver que j'ai cedé. On brave une seule mort; on la brave plusieurs fois, quand elle peut être utile. Mais aucune puissance sous le Ciel, mais aucune opinion publique ou privée n'ont le droit de me condamner à souffrir inutilement mille supplices par minute, et à perir de désespoir, de rage, au milieu des *triomphes*, du crime que je n'ai pu arrêter. Ils me proscriront, ils confisqueront mes biens. Je labourerai la terre, et je ne les verrai plus.—Voila ma justification. Vous pourez la lire, la montrer, la laisser copier; tant pis pour ceux qui ne la comprendront pas; ce ne sera alors moi qui auroit eut tort de la leur donner.

This military man had not so good nerves as the peaceable gentleman of the Old Jewry.—See Mons. Mounier's narrative of these transactions; a man also of honour and virtue, and talents, and therefore a fugitive.

*N.B. Mr. Mounier was then speaker of the National Assembly. He has since been obliged to live in exile, though one of the firmest assertors of liberty. [B] See Biographical Guide. Burke quoted most of *Extrait d'une lettre de M. de Lally Tollendal a Mme la comtesse de ***, Pour servir à sa justification* ([Paris], 1789), pp. 3–7. Burke's transcription was not wholly accurate, and the capitals, and some of the italics, were his. Burke exaggerated: Lally-Tollendal recorded Mounier escaping from nineteen, not twenty, assassins. 'Moi, Mounier' *sc.* 'Moi, Madame'; 'ont le dernier' *sc.* 'ont vu le dernier'. Priestley (*Letters to Burke*, pp. ix–xi) implied that Burke had misquoted and misrepresented Lally-Tollendal, and tried to argue that the Frenchman approved of the work of the National Assembly. Priestley was in fact quoting misleadingly from another work (*Mémoire de M. le Comte de Lally-Tollendal, ou seconde lettre A ses Commettans* (Paris, 'Janvier 1790')), and ignored Burke's point about the impact on these good intentions of revolutionary violence. Priestley further ignored Lally-Tollendal's argument (ibid., pp. 108–11) that the National Assembly did not have the legislative authority of a national convention. Burke also referred to *Exposé de la conduite de M. Mounier, dans l'Assemblée nationale, Et des Motifs de son retour en Dauphiné* (Paris, '17 Novembre 1789'), which narrated the history of the National Assembly and described the events of 5–6 October, not to Mounier's *Nouvelles Observations sur les États-Généraux de France* (Paris, 1789): this was an historical and theoretical work, published before the Estates-General met.

I hear that the august person, who was the principal object of our preacher's triumph, though he supported himself, felt much on that shameful occasion. As a man, it became him to feel for his wife and his children, and the faithful guards of his person, that were massacred in cold blood about him; as a prince, it became him to feel for the strange and frightful transformation of his civilized subjects, and to be more grieved for them, than solicitous for himself. It derogates little from his fortitude, while it adds infinitely to the honour of his humanity. I am very sorry to say it, very sorry indeed, that such personages are in a situation in which it is not unbecoming to praise the virtues of the great.

I hear, and I rejoice to hear, that the great lady,[290] the other object of the triumph, has borne that day (one is interested that beings made for suffering should suffer well) and that she bears [112] all the succeeding days, that she bears the imprisonment of her husband, and her own captivity, and the exile of her friends, and the insulting adulation of addresses, and the whole weight of her accumulated wrongs, with a serene patience, in a matter suited to her rank and race, and becoming the offspring of a sovereign[291] distinguished for her piety and her courage; that like her she has lofty sentiments; that she feels with the dignity of a Roman matron; that in the last extremity she will save herself from the last disgrace, and that if she must fall, she will fall by no ignoble hand.

It is now sixteen or seventeen years since I saw the queen of France, then the dauphiness, at Versailles;[292] and surely never lighted on this orb, which she

[290]Revolutionaries who wished to pose as restorers of the ancient constitution and so credited Louis XVI with good intentions were drawn to disparage monarchical government by painting Marie Antoinette in the opposite colours as 'of a quite different disposition, being ambitious, subtle, penetrating and obstinate; and, holding an improper ascendancy over her royal consort, would by all means have him to be absolute. The queen, and her tyrannical party, exercised every effort to crush the proceedings of the National Assembly; but they were as strongly opposed by those who were real friends to their king, to freeedom, and their country': *Tyranny Annihilated: or, the Triumph of Freedom over Despotism* (London, [1789]), p. 9. Burke's rhetorical praise of the queen may in part have been intended to redress this imbalance.

[291]Maria Theresia (1717–80), Empress of Austria from 1740.

[292]For Burke's visit in January-March 1773 see Burke, *Correspondence*, II, pp. 411–25: he did not at that time remark on Marie Antoinette, though for reports of the Queen's striking good looks even in 1787–90 see J. M. Thompson, *English Witnesses of the French Revolution* (Oxford, 1938), pp. 10, 18, 48, 90–1. It should be noted that Burke wrote in the genre of *de casibus* tragedy and offered no analysis of the political conduct of Marie Antoinette or Louis XVI. There is no reason to think that he was uncritical of the actions of either.

hardly seemed to touch, a more delightful vision. I saw her just above the horizon, decorating and cheering the elevated sphere she just began to move in,—glittering like the morning-star, full of life, and splendor, and joy. Oh! what a revolution! and what an heart must I have, to contemplate without emotion that elevation and that fall![293] Little did I dream that, when she added titles of veneration to those of enthusiastic, distant, respectful love, that she should ever be obliged to carry the sharp antidote against disgrace concealed in that bosom; little did I dream that I should have lived to see such disasters fallen upon her in a nation of gallant men, in a nation of men of honour and of cavaliers. I thought ten thousand swords must have leaped from their scabbards to avenge [113] even a look that threatened her with insult.—But the age of chivalry is gone.—That of sophisters, œconomists, and calculators, has succeeded; and the glory of Europe is extinguished for ever. Never, never more, shall we behold that generous loyalty to rank and sex, that proud submission, that dignified obedience, that subordination of the heart, which kept alive, even in servitude itself, the spirit of an exalted freedom. The unbought grace of life, the cheap defence of nations, the nurse of manly sentiment and heroic enterprize is gone! It is gone, that sensibility of principle, that chastity of honour, which felt a stain like a wound, which inspired courage whilst it mitigated ferocity, which ennobled whatever it touched, and under which vice itself lost half its evil, by losing all its grossness.[294]

This mixed system of opinion and sentiment had its origin in the antient chivalry; and the principle, though varied in its appearance by the varying state of human affairs, subsisted and influenced through a long succession of generations, even to the time we live in. If it should ever be totally extin-

[293]Burke showed his friend Philip Francis a manuscript and later the proofs of the first 32 pages of the *Reflections*, the contents of which were subsequently much revised. Francis urged more 'deliberation' and 'circumspection'. Insinuating that he, and 'the world', thought Marie Antoinette 'a Messalina', Francis cautioned: 'In my opinion all that you say of the Queen is pure foppery': Francis to Burke, 19 February 1790: Burke, *Correspondence*, VI, pp. 85–7. Burke already knew, from their long friendship, that 'we differ only in every thing'. He protested against Francis's claim 'that I found no other Cause than the Beauty of the Queen of France (which I now suppose pretty much faded) for disapproving the Conduct which has been held towards her ... It is for those who applaud or palliate assassination, regicide, and base insults to Women of illustrious place, to prove the Crimes in the sufferers which they allege to justifye their own': Burke to Francis, 20 February [1790], ibid., VI, pp. 88–92.

[294]This was not the Burkes' only explanation of social progress. In *An Account of the European Settlements in America*, I, p. 192 (see Burke, *Reflections*, p. [99]), William and Edmund Burke drew attention in the same context to the effects of religion, commerce and literature.

guished, the loss I fear will be great. It is this which has given its character to modern Europe.[295] It is this which has distinguished it under all its forms of government, and distinguished it to its advantage, from the states of Asia, and possibly from those states which flourished in the most brilliant periods of the antique world. It was this, which, without confounding ranks, had produced a noble equality, and handed it down through all the gradations [114] of social life. It was this opinion which mitigated kings into companions, and raised private men to be fellows with kings. Without force, or opposition, it subdued the fierceness of pride and power; it obliged sovereigns to submit to the soft collar of social esteem, compelled stern authority to submit to elegance, and gave a domination vanquisher of laws, to be subdued by manners.[296]

[ But now all is to be changed. All the pleasing illusions, which made power gentle, and obedience liberal, which harmonized the different shades of life, and which, by a bland assimilation, incorporated into politics the sentiments which beautify and soften private society, are to be dissolved by this new conquering empire of light and reason. All the decent drapery of life is to be rudely torn off. All the superadded ideas, furnished from the wardrobe of a moral imagination, which the heart owns, and the understanding ratifies, as necessary to cover the defects of our naked shivering nature, and to raise it to

[295]In defending chivalry, Burke was neither anticipating the Victorian Gothic revival nor reverting to feudalism in a spirit of blind reaction. The most modern authors were already analysing chivalry as an important stage in the evolution of manners. Adam Ferguson, in *An Essay on the History of Civil Society* (Edinburgh, 1767), Part IV, sections 3–4, 'Of the Manners of Polished and Commercial Nations', had emphasized the difference between the public policy of modern states and the vindictiveness and cruelty of Greece and Rome, and ascribed this in large part to chivalry, 'the maxims of a refined courtesy' and a 'scrupulous honour'. It had an equal significance for gender relations: 'The system of chivalry, when completely formed, proceeded on a marvellous respect and veneration to the fair sex.' In all, 'chivalry, uniting with the genius of our policy, has probably suggested those peculiarities in the law of nations, by which modern states are distinguished from the ancient' (ibid., pp. 297–8, 307–9, 311). Burke owned a copy of this work: LC MS, fo. 33. Richard Hurd, later a bishop, had called for chivalry to be understood as an 'institution' in terms of its purposes, not dismissed as 'the usual caprice and absurdity of barbarians'. It produced an 'eagerness to run to the succour of the distressed', especially a 'refined gallantry' towards women prisoners: Richard Hurd, *Moral and Political Dialogues; with Letters on Chivalry and Romance* (3 vols., London, 1765), III, pp. 193–4, 204, 209. Burke owned a copy of this work: LC MS, fo. 23; LC, p. 12.

[296]Burke referred to 'politeness' or civility, held to be the distinguishing characteristic of modern European societies before the Revolution, and now destroyed by the recrudescence of primitive forces. Burke's attitude was unrelated to nostalgia.

*enduring principle* (handwritten margin note)

dignity in our own estimation, are to be exploded as a ridiculous, absurd, and antiquated fashion.

On this scheme of things, a king is but a man; a queen is but a woman; a woman is but an animal; and an animal not of the highest order. All homage paid to the sex in general as such, and without distinct views, is to be regarded as romance and folly.[297] Regicide, and parricide, and sacrilege, are but fictions of superstition, corrupting jurisprudence by destroying [115] its simplicity. The murder of a king, or a queen, or a bishop, or a father, are only common homicide; and if the people are by any chance, or in any way gainers by it, a sort of homicide much the most pardonable, and into which we ought not to make too severe a scrutiny.[298]

On the scheme of this barbarous philosophy, which is the offspring of cold hearts and muddy understandings, and which is as void of solid wisdom, as it is destitute of all taste and elegance, laws are to be supported only by their own terrors, and by the concern, which each individual may find in them, from his own private speculations, or can spare to them from his own private interests. In the groves of *their* academy, at the end of every visto, you see nothing but the gallows. Nothing is left which engages the affections on the part of the commonwealth. On the principles of this mechanic philosophy, our institutions can never be embodied, if I may use the expression, in persons; so as to create in us love, veneration, admiration, or attachment. But that sort of reason which banishes the affections is incapable of filling their

[297]Women were not necessarily gainers by the new freedoms of the Revolution. At Paris on 10 January 1790, Arthur Young noted: 'Dine[d] with a large party, at the duke de La Rochefaucauld's; ladies and gentlemen, and all equally politicians; but I may remark another effect of this revolution, by no means unnatural, which is, that of lessening, or rather reducing to nothing, the enormous influence of the [female] sex: they mixed themselves before in every thing, in order to govern every thing: I think I see an end to it very clearly': Young, *Travels in France*, p. 268. He sensed the dissolution of the salon society of the *ancien régime*. For similar analyses by writers as diverse as Mme. de Staël and Nietzsche, see Fierro and Liébert, pp. 652–3.

[298]'In spite of their solemn declarations, their soothing addresses, and the multiplied oaths which they have taken, and forced others to take, they will assassinate the king when his name will no longer be necessary to their designs; but not a moment sooner. They will probably first assassinate the queen, whenever the renewed menace of such an assassination loses its effect upon the anxious mind of an affectionate husband': Burke, *Letter to a Member*, p. 26. In fact, Louis XVI was executed on 21 January 1793, Marie Antoinette on 16 October. A translation by John Wilkes's daughter of Burke's passage eulogising Marie Antoinette eventually reached the Queen 'who before she had read half the Lines, she Burst into a flood of Tears, and was a long Time before she was sufficiently composed to peruse the remainder': Edward Jerningham to Burke, [before 11 January 1791]: Burke, *Correspondence*, VI, pp. 203–4.

place. These public affections, combined with manners, are required sometimes as supplements, sometimes as correctives, always as aids to law. The
precept given by a wise man, as well as a great critic, for the construction of
poems, is equally true as to states. *Non satis est pulchra esse poemata, dulcia
sunto.*[299] There ought to be a system of manners in every nation which a well-
[116] formed mind would be disposed to relish. To make us love our country,
our country ought to be lovely.

But power, of some kind or other, will survive the shock in which manners
and opinions perish; and it will find other and worse means for its support.
The usurpation which, in order to subvert antient institutions, has destroyed
antient principles, will hold power by arts similar to those by which it has acquired it. When the old feudal and chivalrous spirit of *Fealty*, which, by freeing kings from fear, freed both kings and subjects from the precautions of tyranny, shall be extinct in the minds of men, plots and assassinations will be anticipated by preventive murder and preventive confiscation, and that long roll
of grim and bloody maxims, which form the political code of all power, not
standing on its own honour, and the honour of those who are to obey it. Kings
will be tyrants from policy when subjects are rebels from principle.

When antient opinions and rules of life are taken away, the loss cannot
possibly be estimated. From that moment we have no compass to govern us;
nor can we know distinctly to what port we steer. Europe undoubtedly, taken
in a mass, was in a flourishing condition the day on which your Revolution
was compleated.[300] How much of that prosperous state was owing to the spirit
of our old manners and opinions is not easy to say; but as such causes cannot
be indifferent in their operation, we must presume, that, on the whole, their
operation was beneficial. [117]

We are but too apt to consider things in the state in which we find them,
without sufficiently adverting to the causes by which they have been produced, and possibly may be upheld. Nothing is more certain, than that our
manners, our civilization, and all the good things which are connected with
manners, and with civilization, have, in this European world of ours, depended for ages upon two principles; and were indeed the result of both combined; I mean the spirit of a gentleman, and the spirit of religion. The nobility
and the clergy, the one by profession, the other by patronage, kept learning in
existence, even in the midst of arms and confusions, and whilst governments

[299]'Not enough is it for poems to have beauty: they must have charm, and lead the
hearer's soul where they will': Horace, *De Arte Poetica*, 99–100; 'sunto' *sc.* 'sunt'.

[300]Burke here treated the French Revolution as an event, completed presumably in
the summer of 1789.

were rather in their causes than formed. Learning paid back what it received to nobility and to priesthood; and paid it with usury, by enlarging their ideas, and by furnishing their minds. Happy if they had all continued to know their indissoluble union, and their proper place! Happy if learning, not debauched by ambition, had been satisfied to continue the instructor, and not aspired to be the master! Along with its natural protectors and guardians, learning will be cast into the mire, and trodden down under the hoofs of a swinish multitude.[301]

If, as I suspect, modern letters owe more than they are always willing to own to antient manners, so do other interests which we value full as much as they are worth. Even commerce, and trade, and manufacture, the gods of our œconomical politicians, are themselves perhaps but [118] creatures; are themselves but effects, which, as first causes, we choose to worship. They certainly grew under the same shade in which learning flourished. They too may decay with their natural protecting principles. With you, for the present at least, they all threaten to disappear together. Where trade and manufactures are wanting to a people, and the spirit of nobility and religion remains, sentiment supplies, and not always ill supplies their place; but if commerce and the arts should be lost in an experiment to try how well a state may stand without these old fundamental principles, what sort of a thing must be a nation of gross, stupid, ferocious, and at the same time, poor and sordid barbarians, destitute of religion, honour, or manly pride, possessing nothing at present, and hoping for nothing hereafter?

I wish you may not be going fast, and by the shortest cut, to that horrible and disgustful situation. Already there appears a poverty of conception, a coarseness and vulgarity in all the proceedings of the assembly and of all their instructors. Their liberty is not liberal.[302] Their science is presumptuous ignorance. Their humanity is savage and brutal.

---

[301]This image was seized on by Burke's detractors in the 1790s. It was, in fact, a familiar Biblical allusion, not evidence of any contempt on Burke's part for plebeians: 'Give not that which is holy unto the dogs, neither cast ye your pearls before swine, lest they trample them under their feet, and turn again and rend you': Matthew 7.6. Burke's enemies also misquoted his phrase as '*the* swinish multitude', implying that he had attributed that characteristic to the people as such. He had, in fact, written of particular mobs in Paris. In the 1803 edition, a footnote was added here: 'See the fate of Bailly and Condorcet, supposed to be here particularly alluded to. Compare the circumstances of the trial, and execution of the former with this prediction.'

[302]Samuel Johnson offered the following definitions of 'liberal': '1. Not mean; not low in birth; not low in mind. 2. Becoming a gentleman. 3. Munificent; generous; bountiful; not parcimonious': *A Dictionary of the English Language* (London, 1755). The word lacked a specifically political meaning in Burke's lifetime.

It is not clear, whether in England we learned those grand and decorous principles, and manners, of which considerable traces yet remain, from you, or whether you took them from us. But to you, I think, we trace them best. You seem to me to be—*gentis incunabula nostræ.*[303] France has always more or less influenced manners in England; and when your fountain is choaked up and polluted, [119] the stream will not run long, or not run clear with us, or perhaps with any nation. This gives all Europe, in my opinion, but too close and connected a concern in what is done in France. Excuse me, therefore, if I have dwelt too long on the atrocious spectacle of the sixth of October 1789, or have given too much scope to the reflexions which have arisen in my mind on occasion of the most important of all revolutions, which may be dated from that day, I mean a revolution in sentiments, manners, and moral opinions. As thing now stand, with every thing respectable destroyed without us, and an attempt to destroy within us every principle of respect, one is almost forced to apologize for harbouring the common feelings of men.

Why do I feel so differently from the Reverend Dr. Price, and those of his lay flock, who will choose to adopt the sentiments of his discourse?—For this plain reason—because it is *natural* I should; because we are so made as to be affected at such spectacles with melancholy sentiments upon the unstable condition of mortal prosperity, and the tremendous uncertainty of human greatness; because in those natural feelings we learn great lessons; because in events like these our passions instruct our reason; because when kings are hurl'd from their thrones by the Supreme Director of this great drama, and become the objects of insult to the base, and of pity to the good, we behold such disasters in the moral, as we should behold a miracle in the physical order of things. We are alarmed into [120] reflexion; our minds (as it has long since been observed)[304] are purified by terror and pity; our weak unthinking pride is humbled, under the dispensations of a mysterious wisdom.—Some tears might be drawn from me, if such a spectacle were exhibited on the stage. I should be truly ashamed of finding in myself that superficial, theatric sense of painted distress, whilst I could exult over it in real life. With such a perverted mind, I could never venture to shew my face at a tragedy. People would think the tears that Garrick formerly, or that Siddons not long since, have extorted from me,[305] were the tears of hypocrisy; I should know them to be the tears of folly.

---

[303]'The cradle of our race': Virgil, *Aeneid*, Book III, 105. Perhaps Burke echoed Cicero, *Letters to Atticus* II, 15: 'I shall certainly be off to "My native hills, the cradle of my youth".'

[304]Aristotle, *Poetics*, VI.

[305]David Garrick (1717–79), actor; Sara Siddons (1755–1831), actress. Burke was a close friend of Garrick.

Indeed the theatre is a better school of moral sentiments than churches, where the feelings of humanity are thus outraged. Poets, who have to deal with an audience not yet graduated in the school of the rights of men, and who must apply themselves to the moral constitution of the heart, would not dare to produce such a triumph as a matter of exultation. There, where men follow their natural impulses, they would not bear the odious maxims of a Machiavelian policy, whether applied to the attainment of monarchical or democratic tyranny. They would reject them on the modern, as they once did on the antient stage,[306] where they could not bear even the hypothetical proposition of such wickedness in the mouth of a personated tyrant, though suitable to the character he sustained. No theatric audience in Athens would bear what has been [121] borne, in the midst of the real tragedy of this triumphal day; a principal actor weighing, as it were in scales hung in a shop of horrors,—so much actual crime against so much contingent advantage,—and after putting in and out weights, declaring that the balance was on the side of the advantages. They would not bear to see the crimes of new democracy posted as in a ledger against the crimes of old despotism, and the bookkeepers of politics finding democracy still in debt, but by no means unable or unwilling to pay the balance. In the theatre, the first intuitive glance, without any elaborate process of reasoning, would shew, that this method of political computation, would justify every extent of crime. They would see, that on these principles, even where the very worst acts were not perpetrated, it was owing rather to the fortune of the conspirators than to their parsimony in the expenditure of treachery and blood. They would soon see, that criminal means once tolerated are soon preferred. They present a shorter cut to the object than through the highway of the moral virtues. Justifying perfidy and murder for public benefit, public benefit would soon become the pretext, and perfidy and murder the end; until rapacity, malice, revenge, and fear more dreadful than revenge, could satiate their insatiable appetites. Such must be consequences of losing in the splendour of these triumphs of the rights of men, all natural sense of wrong and right.[307]

[305]Seneca recounted the reaction of an audience to a speech beginning 'Call me a scoundrel, only call me rich!': 'When these last-quoted lines were spoken at a performance of one of the tragedies of Euripides, the whole audience rose with one accord to hiss the actor and the play off the stage': *Ad Lucilium Epistolae Morales*, CXV.

[307]'Till the justice of the world is awakened, such as these will go on, without admonition, and without provocation, to every extremity. Those who have made the exhibition of the 14th of July [1790], are capable of every evil. They do not commit crimes for their designs; but they form designs that they may commit crimes': Burke, *Letter to a Member*, p. 29.

But the Reverend Pastor exults in this "leading [122] in triumph," because truly Louis XVIth was "an arbitrary monarch;" that is, in other words, neither more nor less, than because he was Louis the XVIth, and because he had the misfortune to be born king of France, with the prerogatives of which, a long line of ancestors, and a long acquiescence of the people, without any act of his, had put him in possession. A misfortune it has indeed turned out to him, that he was born king of France. But misfortune is not crime, nor is indiscretion always the greatest guilt. I shall never think that a prince, the acts of whose whole reign were a series of concessions to his subjects, who was willing to relax his authority, to remit his prerogatives, to call his people to a share of freedom, not known, perhaps not desired by their ancestors; such a prince, though he should be subject to the common frailties attached to men and to princes, though he should have once thought it necessary to provide force against the desperate designs manifestly carrying on against his person, and the remnants of his authority; though all this should be taken into consideration, I shall be led with great difficulty to think he deserves the cruel and insulting triumph of Paris, and of Dr. Price. I tremble for the cause of liberty, from such an example to kings. I tremble for the cause of humanity, in the unpunished outrages of the most wicked of mankind. But there are some people of that low and degenerate fashion of mind, that they look up with a sort of complacent awe and admiration to kings, who know [123] to keep firm in their seat, to hold a strict hand over their subjects, to assert their prerogative, and by the awakened vigilance of a severe despotism, to guard against the very first approaches of freedom. Against such as these they never elevate their voice. Deserters from principle, listed with fortune, they never see any good in suffering virtue, nor any crime in prosperous usurpation.

If it could have been made clear to me, that the king and queen of France (those I mean who were such before the triumph) were inexorable and cruel tyrants, that they had formed a deliberate scheme for massacring the National Assembly (I think I have seen something like the latter insinuated in certain publications)[308] I should think their captivity just. If this be true, much more ought to have been done, but done, in my opinion, in another manner. The punishment of real tyrants is a noble and awful act of justice;[309] and it has with truth been said to be consolatory to the human mind.[310] But if I were to punish

[308]This may be a reference to Jean Paul Marat's paper *L'Ami du Peuple* (1789–92).

[309]Burke thereby affirmed his belief in the Whig doctrine of a right of resistance.

[310]'... do you not understand that it is enough for brave men to have learned how beautiful in act, how grateful in benefit, how glorious in report, it is to slay a tyrant?': Cicero, *Philippics*, II, xlvi.

a wicked king, I should regard the dignity in avenging the crime. Justice is grave and decorous, and in its punishments rather seems to submit to a necessity, than to make a choice. Had Nero,[311] or Agrippina,[312] or Louis the eleventh,[313] or Charles the ninth,[314] been the subject; if Charles the twelfth of Sweden, after the murder of Patkul,[315] or his predecessor Christina, after the murder of Monaldeschi,[316] had fallen into your hands, Sir, or into mine, I am sure our conduct would have been different.[317] [124]

If the French King, or King of the French, (or by whatever name he is known in the new vocabulary of your constitution)[318] has in his own person, and that of his queen, really deserved these unavowed but unavenged murderous attempts, and those subsequent indignities more cruel than murder, such a person would ill deserve even that subordinate executory trust, which I understand is to be placed in him; nor is he fit to be called chief in a nation which he has outraged and oppressed. A worse choice for such an office in a new commonwealth, than that of a deposed tyrant, could not possibly be made. But to degrade and insult a man as the worst of criminals, and afterwards to trust him in your highest concerns, as a faithful, honest, and zealous servant, is not consistent in reasoning, nor prudent in policy, nor safe in practice. Those who could make such an appointment must be guilty of a more flagrant breach of trust than any they have yet committed against the people. As this is the only crime in which your leading politicians could have acted in-

---

[311]Nero (37–68), Roman emperor 54–68 AD.

[312]Agrippina (16–59), daughter of Germanicus and mother of Nero. She secured the imperial throne for her son by her first marriage by murdering her third husband, the emperor Claudius. Thereafter she attempted to rule through her son; Nero had her murdered in turn.

[313]Louis XI (1423–83, King of France from 1461) was seen in retrospect as the initiator of the absolute monarchy completed by Louis XIV.

[314]Charles IX (1550–74, King of France from 1560) took part in the Massacre of St Bartholomew, 1572.

[315]Patkul was a Livonian patriot, handed over to Charles XII by Augustus of Poland under the terms of a treaty, and judicially murdered in 1707.

[316]Giovanni Rinaldo, marquis Monaldeschi, an Italian, formerly a favourite of Queen Christina of Sweden (1626–89), had published an account of her intrigues. On 10 October 1657 she had him brought into her presence at Fontainebleau and assassinated.

[317]As a Whig, Burke did not add George I of Great Britain (1660–1727). While heir-apparent to the Electorate of Hanover, he had divorced and imprisoned his wife, and arranged for her lover, Count Königsmarck, to be secretly murdered.

[318]The title of Louis XVI was changed from 'King of France' to 'King of the French' from 10 October 1789 (Le Moniteur, 9–10 October 1789). The title was intended to express a contractual rather than a proprietorial basis for his authority.

consistently, I conclude that there is no sort of ground for these horrid insinuations. I think no better of all the other calumnies.

In England, we give no credit to them. We are generous enemies: We are faithful allies. We spurn from us with disgust and indignation the slanders of those who bring us their anecdotes with the attestation of the flower-de-luce on their shoulder.[319] We have Lord George Gordon fast in Newgate; and neither his being a public proselyte [125] to Judaism, nor his having, in his zeal against Catholick priests and all sort of ecclesiastics, raised a mob (excuse the term, it is still in use here) which pulled down all our prisons, have preserved to him a liberty, of which he did not render himself worthy by a virtuous use of it.[320] We have rebuilt Newgate,[321] and tenanted the mansion. We have prisons almost as strong as the Bastile, for those who dare to libel the queens of France. In this spiritual retreat, let the noble libeller remain. Let him there meditate on his Thalmud, until he learns a conduct more becoming his birth and parts, and not so disgraceful to the antient religion to which he has become a proselyte; or until some persons from your side of the water, to please your new Hebrew brethren,[322] shall ransom him. He may then be enabled to purchase, with the old hoards of the synagogue, and a very small poundage, on the long compound interest of the thirty pieces of silver (Dr. Price has shewn us what miracles compound interest will perform in 1790 years)[323] the lands which are lately discovered to have been usurped by the Gallican church. Send us your popish Archbishop of Paris,[324] and we will send you our protestant Rabbin. We shall treat the person you send us in exchange like a

[319]Jeanne de Saint-Rémy de Valois, comtesse de la Motte, had been convicted in France in July 1786 for her role in the 'Diamond Necklace' affair, branded on both shoulders and imprisoned. She escaped to England where she was responsible for a flood of pamphlets denouncing the Queen of France. The chief of these was *Mémoires justificatifs de la Comtesse de Valois de la Motte, écrits par elle-même* (London, 1788). Lord George Gordon had criticised Marie Antoinette in the *Public Advertiser* over the same affair and this led to one of his two convictions for libel in June 1787. For this tide of obscene libel, see Bibliography, D ii.

[320]See Biographical Guide.

[321]Newgate prison had been burnt during the Gordon riots of June 1780.

[322]The National Assembly had voted on 28 January 1790 to guarantee the Jews their existing rights, and to accord them the status of '*citoyens actifs*'. After successive decrees in their favour, a general measure of emancipation was passed on 27 September 1791: Fierro and Liébert, p. 656.

[323]Burke satirised Price, who had not calculated the effect of compound interest since the birth of Christ: Richard Price, *Observations on Reversionary Payments* (London, 1771), especially Appendix, pp. 277–9. Burke owned a copy of the third edition of this work (London, 1773): LC, p. 19; LC MS, fo. 29.

[324]Antoine-Éléonore-Léon Leclerc de Juigné (1728–1811).

gentleman and an honest man, as he is; but pray let him bring with him the fund of his hospitality, bounty, and charity; and, depend upon it, we shall never confiscate a shilling of that honourable and pious fund, nor think of enriching the treasury with the spoils of the poor-box.

To tell you the truth, my dear Sir, I think the [126] honour of our nation to be somewhat concerned in the disclaimer of the proceedings of this society of the Old Jewry and the London Tavern. I have no man's proxy. I speak only from myself; when I disclaim, as I do with all possible earnestness, all communion with the actors in that triumph, or with the admirers of it. When I assert any thing else, as concerning the people of England, I speak from observation not from authority; but I speak from the experience I have had in a pretty extensive and mixed communication with the inhabitants of this kingdom, of all descriptions and ranks, and after a course of attentive observation, began early in life, and continued for near forty years.[325] I have often been astonished, considering that we are divided from you but by a slender dyke of about twenty-four miles, and that the mutual intercourse between the two countries has lately been very great, to find how little you seem to know of us. I suspect that this is owing to your forming a judgment of this nation from certain publications, which do, very erroneously, if they do at all, represent the opinions and dispositions generally prevalent in England. The vanity, restlessness, petulance, and sp[i]rit of intrigue of several petty cabals,[326] who attempt to hide their total want of consequence in bustle and noise, and puffing, and mutual quotation of each other, makes you imagine that our contemptuous neglect of their abilities is a mark of general acquiescence in their opinions. No such thing, I assure you. Because half a dozen grashoppers under a fern make the field ring [127] with their importunate chink, whilst thousands of great cattle, reposed beneath the shadow of the British oak, chew the cud and are silent, pray do not imagine, that those who make the noise are the only inhabitants of the field; that, of course, they are many in number; or that, after all, they are other than the little shrivelled, meagre, hopping, though loud and troublesome insects of the hour.[327]

[325]Burke, born and educated in Ireland, settled in England in 1750.

[326]The image of England which had become current in eighteenth-century France was chiefly indebted to France's reformist intelligentsia, who wished to use a neighbouring nation as an example. The *philosophes* naturally found their social contacts, and soulmates, among England's reformist or disaffected nobility, from Bolingbroke to Shelburne and Holland House. See especially Derek Jarrett, *The begetters of Revolution: England's involvement with France, 1759–1789* (London, 1973).

[327]Burke echoed Virgil: '... let us haste to the cool fields, as the morning-star begins to rise, while the day is young, while the grass is hoar, and the dew on the tender blade

I almost venture to affirm, that not one in a hundred amongst us participates in the "triumph" of the Revolution Society. If the king and queen of France, and their children, were to fall into our hands by the chance of war,[328] in the most acrimonious of all hostilities (I deprecate such an event, I deprecate such hostility) they would be treated with another sort of triumphal entry into London. We formerly have had a king of France[329] in that situation; you have read[330] how he was treated by the victor in the field; and in what manner he was afterwards received in England. Four hundred years have gone over us; but I believe we are not materially changed since that period. Thanks to our sullen resistance to innovation, thanks to the cold sluggishness of our national character, we still bear the stamp of our forefathers. We have not (as I conceive) lost the generosity and dignity of thinking of the fourteenth century; nor as yet have we subtilized ourselves into savages. We are not the converts of Rousseau;[331] we are not the disciples of Voltaire; Helvetius has made no

most sweet to the cattle. Then, when heaven's fourth hour has brought thirst to all, and the plaintive cicadas rend the thickets with song, I will bid the flocks at the side of wells or deep pools drink of the water that runs in oaken channels. But in midday heat let them seek out a shady dell, where haply Jove's mighty oak with its ancient trunk stretches out giant branches, or where the grove, black with many holms, lies brooding with hallowed shade': Virgil, *Georgics*, III. Like Burke's remark about 'a swinish multitude' (*Reflections*, p. [117]) this, too, was an easily-recognised allusion, not a provocative new metaphor.

[328]It may be that Burke had already begun to contemplate war with revolutionary France.

[329]John (1319–64), captured by Edward the 'Black Prince' at the battle of Poitiers, 1356 and held captive in London, 1356–60.

[330]The episode features prominently in Froissart's *Chronicle*.

[331]In a letter of January 1790 to an unknown recipient (*Correspondence*, VI, pp. 78–81), Burke argued against the influence of Montesquieu on the revolutionaries, but argued for the influence of Voltaire and Rousseau, the second being 'not a little deranged in his intellects, to my almost certain knowledge'. Burke's *Letter to a Member of the National Assembly* contained an extended and insightful critique of Rousseau (pp. 31–43) on the basis of Burke's knowledge of him during Rousseau's visit to England in 1766. Rousseau was, claimed Burke, the model of the deputies of the National Assembly: 'Him they study; him they meditate; him they turn over in all the time they can spare from the laborious mischief of the day, or the debauches of the night.' Burke explained Rousseau as the framer of a new public morality: rejecting 'True humility, the basis of the Christian system ... [the revolutionaries'] object is to merge all natural and social sentiment in inordinate vanity', and it was Rousseau who was 'the great professor and founder of *the philosophy of vanity* ... It is that new-invented virtue which your masters canonize, that led their moral hero constantly to exhaust the stores of his powerful rhetoric in the expression of universal benevolence; whilst his heart was incapable of harbouring one spark of common parental affection. Benevolence to the

progress amongst us.[332] Atheists are not our preachers; madmen are not our lawgivers. We [128] know that *we* have made no discoveries; and we think that no discoveries are to be made, in morality;[333] nor many in the great principles of government, nor in the ideas of liberty, which were understood long before we were born, altogether as well as they will be after the grave has heaped its mould upon our presumption, and the silent tomb shall have imposed its law on our pert loquacity. In England we have not yet been completely embowelled of our natural entrails; we still feel within us, and we cherish and cultivate, those inbred sentiments which are the faithful guardians, the active monitors of our duty, the true supporters of all liberal and manly morals. We have not been drawn and trussed, in order that we may be filled, like stuffed birds in a museum, with chaff and rags, and paltry, blurred shreds of paper about the rights of man.[334] We preserve the whole of our feelings still native and entire, unsophisticated by pedantry and infidelity. We have real hearts of flesh and blood beating in our bosoms.[335] We fear God;[336] we look up with awe to kings; with affection to parliaments; with duty to magistrates; with reverence to priests; and with respect to nobility.[337] Why?

---

whole species, and want of feeling for every individual with whom the professors come in contact, form the character of the new philosophy.' Burke's analysis became basic to the developing critique of the *bienpensants*.

[332]It was until recently conventional to minimise the impact of Rousseau and others of the more prominent *philosophes*. For their partial scholarly rehabilitation, see Bibliography, D ii. Robert Darnton, *The Forbidden Best-Sellers of Revolutionary France* (London, 1996), pp. xviii, 65–7, 169–80, and work there cited, makes clear the lasting circulation of Helvétius's *De l'Esprit*, 'first published in 1758, held up until the 1780s, eclipsing by far the demand for *Emile*' (p. 67).

[333]Burke may have implied that such is the thesis of Richard Price, *A Review of the Principal Difficulties in Morals* (London, 1758).

[334]Paine (*Rights of Man*, pp. 44–5) replied: 'Does Mr. Burke mean to deny that *man* has any rights?' Paine argued that human rights could accurately be traced from 'the divine origin of the rights of man at the creation'.

[335]Cf. Ezekiel, 11.19–20: 'And I will give them one heart, and I will put a new spirit within you; and I will take the stony heart out of their flesh, and will give them an heart of flesh: That they may walk in my statutes, and keep mine ordinances, and do them: and they shall be my people, and I will be their God.'

[336]Paine (*Rights of Man*, pp. 47–8) objected to this passage as 'Mr Burke's catalogue of barriers that he has set up between man and his Maker'.

[337]The English are, I conceive, misrepresented in a Letter published in one of the papers, by a gentleman thought to be a dissenting minister.—When writing to Dr. Price, of the spirit which prevails at Paris, he says, "The spirit of the people in this place has abolished all the proud *distinctions* which the *king* and *nobles* had usurped in their minds; [129] whether they talk of "*the king, the noble, or the priest*, their whole language is that of the most *enlightened and liberal amongst the English*." If this gentle-

Because when such [129] ideas are brought before our minds, it is *natural* to be so affected; because all other feelings are false and spurious, and tend to corrupt our minds, to vitiate our primary morals, to render us unfit for rational liberty; and by teaching us a servile, licentious, and abandoned insolence, to be our low sport for a few holidays, to make us perfectly fit for, and justly deserving of slavery, through the whole course of our lives.

You see, Sir, that in this enlightened age I am bold enough to confess, that we are generally men of untaught feelings; that instead of casting away all our old prejudices, we cherish them to a very considerable degree, and, to take more shame to ourselves, we cherish them because they are prejudices; and the longer they have lasted, and the more generally they have prevailed, the more we cherish them.[338] We are afraid to put men to live and trade each on his own private stock of reason; because we suspect that this stock in each man is small, and that the individuals would do better to avail themselves of the general bank and capital of nations, and of ages. Many of our men of speculation, instead of exploding general prejudices, employ their sagacity to discover the latent wisdom which prevails in them.[339] If they find what they seek, and they seldom fail, they think it more wise to continue the prejudice, [130] with the reason involved, than to cast away the coat of prejudice, and to leave nothing but the naked reason; because prejudice, with its reason, has a motive to give action to that reason, and an affection which will give it permanence. Prejudice is of ready application in the emergency; it previously engages the mind in a steady course of wisdom and virtue, and does not leave the man hesitating in the moment of decision, sceptical, puzzled, and unresolved.

---

man means to confine the terms *enlightened and liberal* to one set of men in England, it may be true. It is not generally so. [B] The letter was by Price's nephew George Cadogan Morgan, also a Dissenting minister: see *Reflections*, p. [97].

[338]Priestley typically commented: 'The spirit of free and rational enquiry is now abroad, and without any aid from the powers of this world, will not fail to overturn all error and false religion, wherever it is found, and neither the church of Rome, nor the church of England, will be able to stand before it': *Letters to Burke*, pp. 111–2.

[339]This may be an allusion to Samuel Johnson; but other authors wrote similarly. *The World* no. 112 (20 February 1755), an issue ascribed to the Earl of Chesterfield by a ms. note in the Bodleian's copy, argued that the present age had gone 'too far' in exploding 'errors and prejudices' in the name of reason: 'The bulk of mankind have neither leisure nor knowledge sufficient to reason right: why then should they be taught to reason at all? Will not honest instinct prompt, and wholsome prejudices guide them much better than half-reasoning?' Burke owned a copy of the collected edition of this periodical (3 vols., London, 1761): *LC*, p. 23; LC MS, fo. 21. This idea was not identical with the presumption in favour of legal precedents discussed in Blackstone, *Commentaries* I, p. 70.

Prejudice renders a man's virtue his habit; and not a series of unconnected acts. Through just prejudice, his duty becomes a part of his nature.[340]

Your literary men, and your politicians, and so do the whole clan of the enlightened among us, essentially differ in these points. They have no respect for the wisdom of others; but they pay it off by a very full measure of confidence in their own. With them it is a sufficient motive to destroy an old scheme of things, because it is an old one. As to the new, they are in no sort of fear with regard to the duration of a building run up in haste; because duration is no object to those who think little or nothing has been done before their time, and who place all their hopes in discovery. They conceive, very systematically, that all things which give perpetuity are mischievous, and therefore they are at inexpiable war with all establishments. They think that government may vary like modes of dress, and with as little ill effect. That there needs no principle of attachment, except a sense [131] of present conveniency, to any constitution of the state. They always speak as if they were of opinion that there is a singular species of compact between them and their magistrates, which binds the magistrate, but which has nothing reciprocal in it, but that the majesty of the people has a right to dissolve it without any reason, but its will. Their attachment to their country itself, is only so far as it agrees with some of their fleeting projects; it begins and ends with that scheme of polity which falls in with their momentary opinion.

These doctrines, or rather sentiments, seem prevalent with your new statesmen. But they are wholly different from those on which we have always acted in this country.

I hear it is sometimes given out in France, that what is doing among you is after the example of England.[341] I beg leave to affirm, that scarcely any thing done with you has originated from the practice or the prevalent opinions of this people, either in the act or in the spirit of the proceeding. Let me add, that

---

[340]'... a man becomes just by doing just actions and temperate by doing temperate actions ... But the mass of mankind, instead of doing virtuous acts, have recourse to discussing virtue, and fancy that they are pursuing philosophy and that this will make them good men': Aristotle, *Nicomachean Ethics*, II, iv, 6. Burke owned a copy of William Wilkinson's Greek and Latin version of Aristotle's *Ethics* (Oxford, 1716): *LC*, p. 2.

[341]Many of the Foxite Whigs and the Dissenting interest continued to make this claim, perhaps ignorant that the *anglomanes* like Mounier, Clermont-Tonnere, Malouet, Lally-Tollendal and Mallet du Pan, had lost the crucial votes over an English-style constitution in the National Assembly in September 1789. Since Mounier and Lally-Tollendal were among the earliest and most public *émigrés*, the Foxites' insistence on the continued relevance of 1688 and the English constitution may have been disingenuous.

we are as unwilling to learn these lessons from France, as we are sure that we never taught them to that nation. The cabals here who take a sort of share in your transactions as yet consist but of an handful of people. If unfortunately by their intrigues, their sermons, their publications, and by a confidence derived from an expected union with the counsels and forces of the French nation, they should draw considerable numbers into their faction, and in consequence [132] should seriously attempt any thing here in imitation of what has been done with you, the event, I dare venture to prophesy, will be, that, with some trouble to their country, they will soon accomplish their own destruction. This people refused to change their law in remote ages, from respect to the infallibility of popes;[342] and they will not now alter it from a pious implicit faith in the dogmatism of philosophers; though the former was armed with the anathema and crusade, and though the latter should act with the libel and the lamp-iron.

Formerly your affairs were your own concern only. We felt for them as men; but we kept aloof from them, because we were not citizens of France. But when we see the model held up to ourselves, we must feel as Englishmen, and feeling, we must provide as Englishmen. Your affairs, in spite of us, are made a part of our interest; so far at least as to keep at a distance your panacea, or your plague. If it be a panacea, we do not want it. We know the consequences of unnecessary physic. If it be a plague; it is such a plague, that the precautions of the most severe quarantine ought to be established against it.

I hear on all hands that a cabal, calling itself philosophic, receives the glory of many of the late proceedings; and that their opinions and systems are the true actuating spirit of the whole of them. I have heard of no party in England, literary or political, at any time, known by such a description. It is not with you composed of those men, is it? whom the vulgar, in their blunt, [133] homely style, commonly call Atheists and Infidels?[343] If it be, I admit that we too have had writers of that description, who made some noise in their day. At present they repose in lasting oblivion. Who, born within the last forty years, has read one word of Collins, and Toland, and Tindal, and Chubb, and Morgan, and that whole race who called themselves Freethinkers?[344] Who now reads Bolingbroke? Who ever read him through? Ask the booksellers of London what is become of all these lights of the world.[345] In as few years their few

[342]Remarks like this, which recur in Burke's writings, are evidence against any emotional proclivity to the Roman Catholic church.

[343]See *Reflections*, p. [165].

[344]For these Deists see Biographical Guide. Their backgrounds were miscellaneous; Burke was right to argue that they had no organizational unity.

[345]Burke's famous dismissal of Bolingbroke was intended only to clinch his dis-

successors will go to the family vault of "all the Capulets."[346] But whatever they were, or are, with us, they were and are wholly unconnected individuals. With us they kept the common nature of their kind, and were not gregarious. They never acted in corps, nor were known as a faction in the state, nor presumed to influence, in that name or character, or for the purposes of such a faction, on any of our public concerns. Whether they ought so to exist, and so be permitted to act, is another question. As such cabals have not existed in England, so neither has the spirit of them had any influence in establishing the original frame of our constitution, or in any one of the several reparations and improvements it has undergone. The whole has been done under the auspices, and is confirmed by the sanctions of religion and piety. The whole has emanated from the simplicity of our national character, and from a sort of native plainness and directness of understanding, which for a long time characterized [134] those men who have successively obtained authority amongst us. This disposition still remains, at least in the great body of the people.

We know,[347] and what is better we feel inwardly, that religion is the basis of civil society, and the source of all good and of all comfort.[348] In England we are so convinced of this, that there is no rust of superstition, with which the

---

missal of a phase of English thought. Burke adopted a particularly unfavourable interpretation in characterising these men as atheists: they were more familiarly known as Deists, but equally identified as a defeated school in the classic account, John Leland, *A View of the Principal Deistical Writers that have Appeared in England in the last and present Century; with Observations upon them, and some Account of the Answers that have been published against them* (2 vols., London, 1754–5). In the House of Commons in 1773, Burke called Leland's 'The best book, that ever, perhaps, has been written against these people': Burke, *Works*, X, p. 36. Burke's enemies were revealingly indignant that he had dismissed the Deists, but his view of them was widely shared by Christians.

[346]William Shakespeare, *Romeo and Juliet*, Act IV, scene i.

[347]Priestley revealingly glossed this sentence: 'You certainly magnify the benefits derived from religion itself too much': *Letters to Burke*, p. 86.

[348]Sit igitur hoc ab initio persuasum civibus, dominos esse omnium rerum ac moderatores, deos; eaque, quae gerantur, eorum geri vi, ditione, ac numine; eosdemque optime de genere hominum mereri; et qualis quisque sit, quid agat, quid in se admittat, qua mente, qua pietate colat religiones intueri: piorum et impiorum habere rationem. His enim rebus imbutae mentes haud sane abhorrebunt ab utili et a vera sententia. Cic. de Legibus, l. 2. [B] 'So in the very beginning we must persuade our citizens that the gods are the lords and rulers of all things, and that what is done, is done by their will and authority; that they are likewise great benefactors of man, observing the character of every individual, what he does, of what wrong he is guilty, and with what intentions and with what piety he fulfils his religious duties; and that they take note of the pious and the impious. For surely minds which are imbued with such ideas will not fail to form true and useful opinions': Cicero, *De Legibus*, Book II, vii.

accumulated absurdity of the human mind might have crusted it over in the course of ages, that ninety-nine in an hundred of the people of England would not prefer to impiety. We shall never be such fools as to call in an enemy to the substance of any system to remove its corruptions, to supply its defects, or to perfect its construction. If our religious tenets should ever want a further elucidation, we shall not call on atheism to explain them. We shall not light up our temple from that unhallowed fire. It will be illuminated with other lights. It will be perfumed with other incense, than the infectious stuff which is imported by the smugglers of adulterated metaphysics. If our ecclesiastical establishment should want a revision, it is not avarice or rapacity, public or private, that we shall employ for the audit, or receipt, or application of its consecrated revenue.—Violently condemning neither [135] the Greek nor the Armenian, nor, since heats are subsided, the Roman system of religion, we prefer the Protestant;[349] not because we think it has less of the Christian religion in it, but because, in our judgment, it has more. We are protestants, not from indifference but from zeal.[350]

We know, and it is our pride to know, that man is by his constitution a religious animal;[351] that atheism is against, not only our reason but our instincts; and that it cannot prevail long. But if, in the moment of riot, and in a drunken delirium from the hot spirit drawn out of the alembick of hell, which in France is now so furiously boiling, we should uncover our nakedness by throwing off that Christian religion which has hitherto been our boast and comfort, and one great source of civilization amongst us, and among many other nations, we are apprehensive (being well aware that the mind will not endure a void) that some uncouth, pernicious, and degrading superstition, might take place of it.

For that reason, before we take from our establishment the natural human means of estimation, and give it up to contempt, as you have done, and in

---

[349]Burke's argument anticipated his later defence of 'the four Grand divisions of Christianity' as 'all *prescriptive* religions', agreed on 'the great points' of theology and 'at inexpiable war' with Jacobinism. Although Burke did not specify whether he meant the Roman, Anglican, Russian Orthodox and Greek Orthodox churches, or Calvinists, Catholics, Lutheran and Orthodox, no Roman Catholic would have given such parity of esteem to the other divisions. He added that 'Had we lived an hundred and fifty years ago, I should have been as earnest and anxious as any one for this sort of Abjuration' of the Pope's political authority as had recently been required by an oath from Irish Catholics: Burke to William Smith, 29 January 1795, in Burke, *Correspondence*, VIII, pp. 127–33.

[350]This may be Burke's answer to the charge that, coming from an Irish Catholic family, his membership of the Church of England was for temporal advantage only.

[351]Cf. Aristotle, *Politics*, I, i, 9: 'man is by nature a political animal'.

doing it have incurred the penalties you well deserve to suffer, we desire that some other may be presented to us in the place of it. We shall then form our judgment.

On these ideas, instead of quarrelling with establishments, as some do, who have made a philosophy and a religion of their hostility to such institutions, we cleave closely to them. We are resolved to keep an established church, an [136] established monarchy, an established aristocracy, and an established democracy, each in the degree it exists, and in no greater. I shall shew you presently how much of each of these we possess.

It has been the misfortune (not as these gentlemen think it, the glory) of this age, that every thing is to be discussed, as if the constitution of our country were to be always a subject rather of altercation than enjoyment. For this reason, as well as for the satisfaction of those among you (if any such you have among you) who may wish to profit of examples, I venture to trouble you with a few thoughts upon each of these establishments. I do not think they were unwise in antient Rome, who, when they wished to new-model their laws, sent commissioners to examine the best constituted republics within their reach.³⁵²

First, I beg leave to speak of our church establishment, which is the first of our prejudices, not a prejudice destitute of reason, but involving in it profound and extensive wisdom.³⁵³ I speak of it first. It is first, and last, and midst in our minds.³⁵⁴ For, taking ground on that religious system, of which we are now in possession, we continue to act on the early received, and uniformly continued sense of mankind. That sense not only, like a wise architect, hath built up the august fabric of states, but like a provident proprietor, to preserve the structure from prophanation and ruin, as a sacred temple, purged from all the impurities of fraud, and violence, and injustice, and tyranny, hath solemnly and for ever consecrated the commonwealth, and all that officiate in it. This consecration is made, that all who administer [137] in the government of men, in which they stand in the person of God himself, should have high and worthy notions of their function and destination; that their hope should be

³⁵²The Decemvirate are supposed to have ordered a mission to Athens for this purpose.

³⁵³Passages like this led the Unitarian Joseph Priestley, an implacable enemy of the Church of England, to charge Burke with 'confounding ... the idea of *religion* itself, with that of the *civil establishment* of it': *Letters to Burke*, p. 52. Priestley ignored the ancient Anglican arguments, dating at least to John Jewel and Richard Hooker in the sixteenth century, for the necessary unity of church and state, and the legitimate division of the universal church into national churches.

³⁵⁴Cf. Milton, *Paradise Lost*, V, 165.

full of immortality; that they should not look to the paltry pelf of the moment, nor to the temporary and transient praise of the vulgar, but to a solid, permanent existence, in the permanent part of their nature, and to a permanent fame and glory, in the example they leave as a rich inheritance to the world.

Such sublime principles ought to be infused into persons of exalted situations; and religious establishments provided, that may continually revive and enforce them. Every sort of moral, every sort of civil, every sort of politic institution, aiding the rational and natural ties that connect the human understanding and affections to the divine, are not more than necessary, in order to build up that wonderful structure, Man; whose prerogative it is, to be in a great degree a creature of his own making; and who when made as he ought to be made, is destined to hold no trivial place in the creation. But whenever man is put over men, as the better nature ought ever to preside, in that case more particularly, he should as nearly as possible be approximated to his perfection.

The consecration of the state, by a state religious establishment, is necessary also to operate with an wholesome awe upon free citizens; because, in order to secure their freedom, they must enjoy some determinate portion of power. To [138] them therefore a religion connected with the state, and with their duty towards it, becomes even more necessary than in such societies, where the people by the terms of their subjection are confined to private sentiments, and the management of their own family concerns. All persons possessing any portion of power ought to be strongly and awefully impressed with an idea that they act in trust; and that they are to account for their conduct in that trust to the one great master, author and founder of society.

This principle ought even to be more strongly impressed upon the minds of those who compose the collective sovereignty than upon those of single princes. Without instruments, these princes can do nothing. Whoever uses instruments, in finding helps, finds also impediments. Their power is therefore by no means compleat; nor are they safe in extreme abuse. Such persons, however elevated by flattery, arrogance, and self-opinion, must be sensible that, whether covered or not by positive law, in some way or other they are accountable even here for the abuse of their trust. If they are not cut off by a rebellion of their people, they may be strangled by the very Janissaries kept for their security against all other rebellion. Thus we have seen the king of France sold by his soldiers for an encrease of pay. But where popular authority is absolute and unrestrained, the people have an infinitely greater, because a far better founded confidence in their own power. They are themselves, in a great measure, [139] their own instruments. They are nearer to their objects. Besides, they are less under responsibility to one of the greatest controlling powers on earth, the sense of fame and estimation. The share of infamy that is likely to fall to the lot of each individual in public acts, is small indeed; the operation of opinion being in the inverse ratio to the number of those who abuse power. Their own approbation of their own acts has to them the appearance of a public judgment in their favour. A perfect democracy is therefore the most shameless thing in the world. As it is the most shameless, it is also the most fearless. No man apprehends in his person he can be made subject to punishment. Certainly the people at large never ought: for as all punishments are for example towards the conservation of the people at large, the people at large can never become the subject of punishment by any human hand.[355] It is therefore of infinite importance that they should not be suffered to imagine that their will, any more than that of kings, is the standard of right and wrong. They ought to be persuaded that they are full as little entitled, and far less qualified, with safety to themselves, to use any arbitrary power whatsoever; that therefore they are not, under a false shew of liberty, but, in truth, to exercise an unnatural inverted domination, tyrannically to exact, from those who officiate in the state, not an entire devotion to their interest, which is their right, [140] but an abject submission to their occasional will; extinguishing thereby, in all those who serve them, all moral principle, all sense of dignity, all use of judgment, and all consistency of character, whilst by the very same process they give themselves up a proper, a suitable, but a most contemptible prey to the servile ambition of popular sycophants or courtly flatterers.

When the people have emptied themselves of all the lust of selfish will,[356] which without religion it is utterly impossible they ever should, when they are conscious that they exercise, and exercise perhaps in an higher link of the order of delegation, the power, which to be legitimate must be according to that eternal immutable law, in which will and reason are the same, they will be more careful how they place power in base and incapable hands. In their nomination to office, they will not appoint to the exercise of authority, as to a pitiful job, but as to an holy function; not according to their sordid selfish in-

---

[355]Quicquid multis peccatur inultum. [B] 'There was an end of timid muttering, an end of anger hidden in the secret heart; for what often binds a wavering allegiance—that each fears those to whom he himself is a terror, and each thinks that he alone resents the injustice of oppression—that motive had lost its hold. For their mere numbers had dispelled their fears and made them bold: the sin of thousands always goes unpunished': Lucan, *Pharsalia*, Book V, 256–60. Burke owned a copy of *Lucan's Pharsalia. Translated into English Verse by Nicholas Rowe, Esq; Servant to His Majesty* (London, 1718): 'For Laws, in great Rebellions, lose their End, / And all go free, when Multitudes offend' (p. 185) *LC*, p. 18. See *Reflections*, p. [352].

[356]Cf. Burke's discussion of Rousseau in these terms, *Reflections*, p. [127].

terest, nor to their wanton caprice, nor to their arbitrary will; but they will confer that power (which any man may well tremble to give or to receive) on those only, in whom they may discern that predominant proportion of active virtue and wisdom, taken together and fitted to the charge, such, as in the great and inevitable mixed mass of human imperfections and infirmities, is to be found.

When they are habitually convinced that no evil can be acceptable, either in the act or the permission, to him whose essence is good, they [141] will be better able to extirpate out of the minds of all magistrates, civil, ecclesiastical, or military, any thing that bears the least resemblance to a proud and lawless domination.

But one of the first and most leading principles on which the commonwealth and the laws are consecrated, is lest the temporary possessors and life-renters[357] in it, unmindful of what they have received from their ancestors, or of what is due to their posterity, should act as if they were the entire masters; that they should not think it amongst their rights to cut off the entail,[358] or commit waste on the inheritance, by destroying at their pleasure the whole original fabric of their society; hazarding to leave to those who come after them, a ruin instead of an habitation—and teaching these successors as little to respect their contrivances, as they had themselves respected the institutions of their forefathers. By this unprincipled facility of changing the state as often, and as much, and in as many ways as there are floating fancies or fashions, the whole chain and continuity of the commonwealth would be broken. No one generation could link with the other. Men would become little better than the flies of a summer.

And first of all the science of jurisprudence, the pride of the human intellect, which, with all its defects, redundancies, and errors, is the collected reason of ages,[359] combining the principles of original justice with the infinite va-

---

[357]Tenants for life.

[358]I.e. depriving heirs of their entitlements under a legal settlement. Cf. [Burke], *Appeal*, p. 19: 'With regard to futurity, we are to treat it like a ward. We are not so to attempt an improvement of his fortune, as to put the capital of his estate to any hazard.'

[359]Blackstone, *Commentaries*, III, ch. 22, provided a classic defence of English law, despite its apparent uncertainty and complexity: 'When therefore a body of laws, of so high antiquity as the English, is in general so clear and perspicuous, it argues deep wisdom and foresight in such as laid the foundations, and great care and circumspection, in such as have built the superstructure' (p. 328). It was in the context of this defence of the wisdom and antiquity of the old order that Blackstone introduced his characterisation of the English as 'a nation of freemen, a polite and commercial people' (p. 326): like Burke, he saw no contradiction between 'ancient' and 'modern'. Burke owned a copy of this work: LC MS, fo. 24; *LC*, p. 6.

riety of human concerns, as a heap of old exploded errors, would be no longer studied. [142] Personal self-sufficiency and arrogance (the certain attendants upon all those who have never experienced a wisdom greater than their own) would usurp the tribunal. Of course, no certain laws, establishing invariable grounds of hope and fear, would keep the actions of men in a certain course, or direct them to a certain end. Nothing stable in the modes of holding property, or exercising function, could form a solid ground on which any parent could speculate in the education of his offspring, or in a choice for their future establishment in the world. No principles would be early worked into the habits. As soon as the most able instructor had completed his laborious course of institution, instead of sending forth his pupil, accomplished in a virtuous discipline, fitted to procure him attention and respect, in his place in society, he would find every thing altered; and that he had turned out a poor creature to the contempt and derision of the world, ignorant of the true grounds of estimation. Who would insure a tender and delicate sense of honour to beat almost with the first pulses of the heart, when no man could know what would be the test of honour in a nation, continually varying the standard of its coin? No part of life would retain its acquisitions. Barbarism with regard to science and literature, unskilfulness with regard to arts and manufactures, would infallibly succeed to the want of a steady education and settled principle; and thus the commonwealth itself would, in a few generations, crumble away, be disconnected into the [143] dust and powder of individuality, and at length dispersed to all the winds of heaven.

To avoid therefore the evils of inconstancy and versatility, ten thousand times worse than those of obstinacy and the blindest prejudice, we have consecrated the state, that no man should approach to look into defects or corruptions but with due caution; that he should never dream of beginning its reformation by its subversion; that he should approach to the faults of the state as to the wounds of a father, with pious awe and trembling sollicitude. By this wise prejudice we are taught to look with horror on those children of their country who are prompt rashly to hack that aged parent in pieces, and put him into the kettle of magicians, in hopes that by their poisonous weeds, and wild incantations, they may regenerate the paternal constitution, and renovate their father's life.[360]

Society is indeed a contract. Subordinate contracts for objects of mere oc-

[360]Burke had used the same image in his speech on parliamentary reform, 1782. For the story of the daughters of Pelias, king of Thessaly, being misled by Medea to attempt to rejuvenate their aged father by cutting him to pieces and boiling him with herbs in a cauldron see Ovid, *Metamorphoses*, Book VII.

casional interest may be dissolved at pleasure—but the state ought not to be considered as nothing better than a partnership agreement in a trade of pepper and coffee, callico or tobacco, or some other such low concern, to be taken up for a little temporary interest, and to be dissolved by the fancy of the parties. It is to be looked on with other reverence; because it is not a partnership in things subservient only to the gross animal existence of a temporary and perishable nature. It is a partnership in all science; a partnership in all art; a partnership in every virtue, and in all perfection.[361] As the [144] ends of such a partnership cannot be obtained in many generations, it becomes a partnership not only between those who are living, but between those who are living, those who are dead, and those who are to be born.[362] Each contract of each particular state is but a clause in the great primæval contract of eternal society, linking the lower with the higher natures, connecting the visible and invisible world, according to a fixed compact sanctioned by the inviolable oath which holds all physical and all moral natures, each in their appointed place. This law is not subject to the will of those, who by an obligation above them, and infinitely superior, are bound to submit their will to that law. The municipal corporations of that universal kingdom[363] are not morally at liberty at their pleasure, and on their speculations of a contingent improvement, wholly to separate and tear asunder the bands of their subordinate community, and to dissolve it into an unsocial, uncivil, unconnected chaos of elementary principles. It is the first and supreme necessity only, a necessity that is not chosen but chooses, a necessity paramount to deliberation, that admits no discussion, and demands no evidence, which alone can justify a resort to anarchy. This necessity is no exception to the rule; because this necessity itself is a part too of that moral and physical disposition of things to which man must be obedient by consent or force; but if that which is only submission to necessity should be made the object of choice, the law is [145] broken, nature is disobeyed, and the rebellious are outlawed, cast forth, and exiled, from this world of reason, and order, and peace, and virtue, and fruitful penitence, into the antagonist world of madness, discord, vice, confusion, and unavailing sorrow.

These, my dear Sir, are, were, and I think long will be the sentiments of not

[361]Burke echoed Aristotle: 'Every state is as we see a sort of partnership, and every partnership is formed with a view to some good (since all the actions of all mankind are done with a view to what they think to be good'): Aristotle, *Politics* I, i, 1. Burke now extended this familiar idea beyond his source's meaning.

[362]Paine was indignant that such an 'obligation' might exist between generations: *Rights of Man*, p. 11.

[363]In such phrases, Burke anticipated his preoccupation of the 1790s, the need for a crusade by Christian Europe against the French Revolution and its principles.

the least learned and reflecting part of this kingdom. They who are included in this description, form their opinions on such grounds as such persons ought to form them. The less enquiring receive them from an authority which those whom Providence dooms to live on trust need not be ashamed to rely on. These two sorts of men move in the same direction, tho' in a different place. They both move with the order of the universe. They all know or feel this great antient truth: "Quod illi principi et præpotenti Deo qui omnem hunc mundum regit, nihil eorum quæ quidem fiant in terris acceptius quam concilia et cætus hominum jure sociati quæ civitates appellantur."[364] They take this tenet of the head and heart, not from the great name[365] which it immediately bears, nor from the greater[366] from whence it is derived; but from that which alone can give true weight and sanction to any learned opinion, the common nature and common relation of men. Persuaded that all things ought to be done with reference, and referring all to the point of reference to which all should be directed, they think themselves bound, not only as individuals in the sanctuary of the heart, or as congregated in that [146] personal capacity, to renew the memory of their high origin and cast; but also in their corporate character to perform their national homage to the institutor, and author and protector of civil society; without which civil society man could not by any possibility arrive at the perfection of which his nature is capable, nor even make a remote and faint approach to it. They conceive that He who gave our nature to be perfected by our virtue, willed also the necessary means of its perfection—He willed therefore the state—He willed its connexion with the source and original archetype of all perfection.[367] They who are convinced of this his will, which is the law of laws and the sovereign of sovereigns, cannot think it reprehensible, that this our corporate fealty and homage, that this our

---

[364]"For nothing of all that is done on earth is more pleasing to that supreme God who rules the whole universe than the assemblies and gatherings of men associated in justice, which are called states': Cicero, *De Re Publica*, Book VI, xiii. A version of this passage from the dream of Scipio was used as a motto on the title page of Emmerich de Vattel's *The Law of Nations; or Principles of the Law of Nature: applied to the Conduct and Affairs of Nations and Sovereigns* (2 vols., London, 1759–60). 'Cicero, as great a master in the conduct of a state as in eloquence and philosophy, did not content himself with rejecting the vulgar maxim, that the republic could not be happily governed without committing injustice; he went so far as to establish the contrary as an invariable truth, and maintained that no-one could administer the public affairs in a salutary manner, if he did not attach himself to the most exact justice': ibid., I, p. xiv. Burke owned a copy of this edition of Vattel: *LC*, p. 24; LC MS, fo. 9.

[365]Scipio.

[366]Cicero.

[367]Priestley guessed that Burke meant the Church: *Letters to Burke*, p. 68.

recognition of a signiory paramount, I had almost said this oblation of the state itself, as a worthy offering on the high altar of universal praise,[368] should be performed as all publick solemn acts are performed, in buildings, in musick, in decoration, in speech, in the dignity of persons, according to the customs of mankind, taught by their nature; that is, with modest splendour, with unassuming state, with mild majesty and sober pomp. For those purposes they think some part of the wealth of the country is as usefully employed as it can be, in fomenting the luxury of individuals. It is the publick ornament. It is the publick consolation. It nourishes the publick hope. The poorest man finds his own importance and dignity [147] in it, whilst the wealth and pride of individuals at every moment makes the man of humble rank and fortune sensible of his inferiority, and degrades and vilifies his condition. It is for the man in humble life, and to raise his nature, and to put him in mind of a state in which the privileges of opulence will cease, when he will be equal by nature, and may be more than equal by virtue, that this portion of the general wealth of his country is employed and sanctified.

I assure you I do not aim at singularity. I give you opinions which have been accepted amongst us, from very early times to this moment, with a continued and general approbation, and which indeed are so worked into my mind, that I am unable to distinguish what I have learned from others from the results of my own meditation.

It is on some such principles that the majority of the people of England, far from thinking a religious, national establishment unlawful, hardly think it lawful to be without one. In France you are wholly mistaken if you do not believe us above all other things attached to it, and beyond all other nations; and when this people has acted unwisely and unjustifiably in its favour (as in some instances they have done most certainly) in their very errors you will at least discover their zeal.

This principle runs through the whole system of their polity. They do not consider their church establishment as convenient, but as essential to their state; not as a thing heterogeneous and separable; something added for accommodation;[369] [148] what they may either keep up or lay aside, according

[368]Burke's phraseology echoes the service of Holy Communion in the *Book of Common Prayer*.

[369]Burke here added an implication of the indissolubility of a contract to the argument of William Warburton, in *The Alliance between Church and State: or, The Necessity and Equity of An Established Religion and A Test Law Demonstrated* (London, 1736) that Church and State were separate bodies, and that the State formed an alliance with the largest Christian denomination within it to advance the cause of public morality. Burke owned a copy of the third edition of this work (London, 1748): *LC*, p. 23.

to their temporary ideas of convenience. They consider it as the foundation of their whole constitution, with which, and with every part of which, it holds an indissoluble union. Church and state are ideas inseparable in their minds, and scarcely is the one ever mentioned without mentioning the other.[370]

✳ Our education is so formed as to confirm and fix this impression. Our education is in a manner wholly in the hands of ecclesiastics, and in all stages from infancy to manhood. Even when our youth, leaving schools and universities, enter that most important period of life which begins to link experience and study together, and when with that view they visit other countries, instead of old domestics whom we have seen as governors to principal men from other parts, three-fourths of those who go abroad with our young nobility and gentlemen are ecclesiastics; not as austere masters, nor as mere followers; but as friends and companions of a graver character, and not seldom persons as well born as themselves. With them, as relations, they most commonly keep up a close connexion through life. By this connexion we conceive that we attach our gentlemen to the church; and we liberalize the church by an intercourse with the leading characters of the country.[371]

So tenacious are we of the old ecclesiastical modes and fashions of institution, that very little alteration has been made in them since the fourteenth or fifteenth century;[372] adhering in this particular, [149] as in all things else, to our old settled maxim, never entirely nor at once to depart from antiquity. We found these old institutions, on the whole, favourable to morality and discipline; and we thought they were susceptible of amendment, without altering the ground. We thought that they were capable of receiving and meliorating, and above all of preserving the accessions of science and literature, as the or-

---

[370]Paine commented: 'One of the continual choruses of Mr. Burke's book is, "Church and State:" he does not mean some one particular church, or some one particular state, but any church and state; and he uses the term as a general figure to hold forth the political doctrine of always uniting the church with the state in every country': *Rights of Man*, p. 76. Burke had not, however, argued cynically for the political expediency of exploiting religion to promote social stability, or for the unimportance of differences in Christian belief. Even a latitudinarian like Burke might believe that the church consecrated the state.

[371]The clerical tutor may have been disparaged in the households of the freethinking nobility, but the prevalence of the custom of employing them as companions in foreign travel argues for different attitudes as the norm. See William Gibson, *A Social History of the Domestic Chaplain, 1530–1840* (London, 1997). Dissenters would naturally not have made the tour.

[372]Burke here implicitly rejected the Dissenting, Low Church and Roman Catholic contention that the English Reformation had been a fundamental discontinuity.

der of Providence should successively produce them. And after all, with this Gothic and monkish education (for such it is in the ground-work) we may put in our claim to as ample and as early a share in all the improvements in science, in arts, and in literature, which have illuminated and adorned the modern world, as any other nation in Europe; we think one main cause of this improvement was our not despising the patrimony of knowledge which was left us by our forefathers.

It is from our attachment to a church establishment that the English nation did not think it wise to entrust that great fundamental interest of the whole to what they trust no part of their civil or military public service, that is to the unsteady and precarious contribution of individuals. They go further. They certainly never have suffered and never will suffer the fixed estate of the church to be converted into a pension, to depend on the treasury, and to be delayed, withheld, or perhaps to be extinguished by fiscal difficulties; which difficulties may sometimes be pretended for political purposes, and are in fact often brought on by the extravagance, [150] negligence, and rapacity of politicians. The people of England think that they have constitutional motives, as well as religious, against any project of turning their independent clergy into ecclesiastical pensioners of state. They tremble for their liberty, from the influence of a clergy dependent on the crown; they tremble for the public tranquillity from the disorders of a factious clergy, if it were made to depend upon any other than the crown. They therefore made their church, like their king and their nobility, independent.[373]

From the united considerations of religion and constitutional policy, from their opinion of a duty to make a sure provision for the consolation of the feeble and the instruction of the ignorant, they have incorporated and identified the estate of the church with the mass of *private property*, of which the state is not the proprietor, either for use or dominion, but the guardian only and the regulator. They have ordained that the provision of this establishment might

[373]In a debate on 6 February 1772, Burke had spoken against the 'Feathers Tavern' petition from a group of Anglican clergy against the requirement, imposed by the Act of Uniformity, to subscribe the Thirty-nine Articles. In that speech, Burke commended Locke's definition of the Church as 'a voluntary society' and treated a church as 'only a certain system of religious doctrines and practices fixed and ascertained by some Law ... and the Establishment is a tax laid by the same sovereign authority for payment of those, who so teach and so practise': *Works*, X, pp. 11, 19. In the face of the expropriation of the goods of the French church, Burke began to move away from his earlier latitudinarian position towards a conception of the Church as a body independent of the state.

be as stable as the earth on which it stands, and should not fluctuate with the Euripus[374] of funds and actions.

The men of England, the men, I mean, of light and leading in England, whose wisdom (if they have any) is open and direct, would be ashamed, as of a silly deceitful trick, to profess any religion in name, which by their proceedings they appeared to contemn. If by their conduct (the only language that rarely lies) they seemed to regard the great ruling principle of the moral and the natural world, as a mere invention to [151] keep the vulgar in obedience, they apprehend that by such a conduct they would defeat the politic purpose they have in view. They would find it difficult to make others to believe in a system to which they manifestly gave no credit themselves. The Christian statesmen of this land would indeed first provide for the *multitude*; because it is the *multitude*; and is therefore, as such, the first object in the ecclesiastical institution, and in all institutions.[375] They have been taught, that the circumstance of the gospel's being preached to the poor, was one of the great tests of its true mission.[376] They think, therefore, that those do not believe it, who do not take care it should be preached to the poor. But as they know that charity is not confined to any one description, but ought to apply itself to all men who have wants, they are not deprived of a due and anxious sensation of pity to the distresses of the miserable great. They are not repelled through a fastidious delicacy, at the stench of their arrogance and presumption, from a medicinal attention to their mental blotches and running sores. They are sensible, that religious instruction is of more consequence to them than to any others; from the greatness of the temptation to which they are exposed; from the important consequences that attend their faults; from the contagion of their ill example; from the necessity of bowing down the stubborn neck of their pride and ambition to the yoke of moderation and virtue; from a consideration of the fat stupidity and gross ignorance concerning [152] what imports men most to know, which prevails at courts, and at the head of armies, and in senates, as much as at the loom and in the field.

[374]Euripus was the treacherous channel between the island of Euboea and the Greek mainland.

[375]Priestley (*Letters to Burke*, p. 58) interpreted this passage as Burke's endorsement of the argument of William Warburton, that the state should provide for the largest religious denomination; Priestley asked how this would apply in Ireland, where the established Church was supported by only a minority of the population.

[376]Cf. Luke 7.22: 'Then Jesus answering, said unto them, Go your way, and tell John what things ye have seen and heard, how that the blind see, the lame walk, the lepers are cleansed, the deaf hear, the dead are raised, to the poor the gospel is preached.'

The English people are satisfied, that to the great the consolations of religion are as necessary as its instructions. They too are among the unhappy. They feel personal pain and domestic sorrow. In these they have no privilege, but are subject to pay their full contingent to the contributions levied on mortality. They want this sovereign balm under their gnawing cares and anxieties, which being less conversant about the limited wants of animal life, range without limit, and are diversified by infinite combinations in the wild and unbounded regions of imagination. Some charitable dole is wanting to these, our often very unhappy brethren, to fill the gloomy void which reigns in minds which have nothing on earth to hope or fear; something to relieve in the killing languor and over-laboured lassitude of those who have nothing to do; something to excite an appetite to existence in the palled satiety which attends on all pleasures which may be bought, where nature is not left to her own process, where even[377] desire is anticipated, and therefore fruition defeated by meditated schemes and contrivances of delight; and no interval, no obstacle, is interposed between the wish and the accomplishment.

The people of England know how little influence the teachers of religion are likely to have [153] with the wealthy and powerful of long standing, and how much less with the newly fortunate, if they appear in a manner no way assorted to those with whom they must associate, and over whom they must even exercise, in some cases, something like an authority. What must they think of that body of teachers, if they see it in no part above the establishment of their domestic servants? If the poverty were voluntary, there might be some difference. Strong instances of self-denial operate powerfully on our minds; and a man who has no wants has obtained great freedom and firmness, and even dignity. But as the mass of any description of men are but men, and their poverty cannot be voluntary, that disrespect which attends upon all Lay poverty, will not depart from the Ecclesiastical.[378] Our provident constitution has therefore taken care that those who are to instruct presumptuous ignorance,

[377]Possibly the printer's misreading of 'every'.

[378]It had been a familiar complaint of Anglicans in the seventeenth century that the poverty of the clergy lowered their standing and diminished their pastoral effectiveness. These complaints, and defences, were generally replaced in the early eighteenth century by a different sort of charge: that the clergy were too close to the civil power, or men of too successfully worldly lives. Cf. Peter Maurice, *The true Causes of the Contempt of Christian Ministers. A Sermon Preach'd before the University of Oxford ... November 30, 1718* (Oxford, 1719); [John Hildrop], *The Contempt of the Clergy Considered. In a Letter to a Friend* (London, 1739). Dissenters seized any opportunity to denounce the Church for its wealth; churchmen usually noticed the limited resources available for its work.

those who are to be censors over insolent vice, should neither incur their contempt, nor live upon their alms; nor will it tempt the rich to a neglect of the
true medicine of their minds. For these reasons, whilst we provide first for the
poor, and with a parental sollicitude, we have not relegated religion (like
something we were ashamed to shew) to obscure municipalities or rustic vil-
lages. No! We will have her to exalt her mitred front in courts and parliaments. We will have her mixed throughout the whole mass of life, and
blended with all the classes of society. The people of England will shew to the
haughty [154] potentates of the world, and to their talking sophisters, that a
free, a generous, an informed nation, honours the high magist[r]ates of its
church; that it will not suffer the insolence of wealth and titles, or any other
species of proud pretension, to look down with scorn upon what they look up
to with reverence; nor presume to trample on that acquired personal nobility,
which they intend always to be, and which often is the fruit, not the reward,
(for what can be the reward?) of learning, piety, and virtue. They can see,
without pain or grudging, an Archbishop precede a Duke. They can see a
Bishop of Durham, or a Bishop of Winchester, in possession of ten thousand
pounds a year;[379] and cannot conceive why it is in worse hands than estates to
the like amount in the hands of this Earl, or that Squire; although it may be
true, that so many dogs and horses are not kept by the former, and fed with
the victuals which ought to nourish the children of the people. It is true, the
whole church revenue is not always employed, and to every shilling, in charity; nor perhaps ought it; but something is generally so employed. It is better
to cherish virtue and humanity, by leaving much to free will, even with some
loss to the object, than to attempt to make men mere machines and instruments of a political benevolence.[380] The world on the whole will gain by a liberty, without which virtue cannot exist.

When once the commonwealth has established [155] the estates of the
church as property, it can, consistently, hear nothing of the more or the less.
Too much and too little are treason against property. What evil can arise from

---

[379]The income of English bishoprics at this time is difficult to discover. It was certainly in excess of the nominal figures recorded in, for example, John Lloyd, *Thesaurus
Ecclesiasticus; an improved edition of the Liber Valorum* (London, 1788). But Burke's
'ten thousand pounds' was a rhetorical flourish.

[380]This was a familiar position. Samuel Horsley had recently argued that 'the most
natural and the best method of relief, is by voluntary contribution ... The law should
be careful not to do too much', lest the moral impact of the threat of poverty and of its
relief should be dissipated: Horsley, *A Sermon Preached at the Anniversary Meeting of
the Sons of the Clergy, in the Cathedral Church of St Paul, On Thursday, May 18,
1786* (London, [1786]), pp. 13–14.

the quantity in any hand, whilst the supreme authority has the full, sovereign superintendance over this, as over all property, to prevent every species of abuse; and, whenever it notably deviates, to give to it a direction agreeable to the purposes of its institution.

In England most of us conceive that it is envy and malignity towards those who are often the beginners of their own fortune, and not a love of the self-denial and mortification of the antient church, that makes some look askance at the distinctions, and honours, and revenues, which, taken from no person, are set apart for virtue. The ears of the people of England are distinguishing. They hear these men speak broad. Their tongue betrays them. Their language is in the *patois* of fraud; in the cant and gibberish of hypocrisy. The people of England must think so, when these praters affect to carry back the clergy to that primative evangelic poverty which, in the spirit, ought always to exist in them, (and in us too, however we may like it) but in the thing must be varied, when the relation of that body to the state is altered; when manners, when modes of life, when indeed the whole order of human affairs has undergone a total revolution. We shall believe those reformers to be then honest enthusiasts, not as now we think them, [156] cheats and deceivers, when we see them throwing their own goods into common, and submitting their own persons to the austere discipline of the early church.

With these ideas rooted in their minds, the commons of Great Britain, in the national emergencies, will never seek their resource from the confiscation of the estates of the church and poor.[381] Sacrilege and proscription are not among the ways and means in our committee of supply. The Jews in Change Alley have not yet dared to hint their hopes of a mortgage on the revenues belonging to the see of Canterbury. I am not afraid that I shall be disavowed, when I assure you that there is not *one* public man in this kingdom, whom you would wish to quote; no not one of any party or description, who does not reprobate the dishonest, perfidious, and cruel confiscation which the national assembly has been compelled to make of that property which it was their first duty to protect.

It is with the exultation of a little natural pride I tell you, that those

---

[381]Priestley was indignant at Burke's argument that the poor, like the church, had a sacred right to support. The poor law, Priestley argued, was an Elizabethan invention; 'To many persons, as well as to myself, our method of providing for the poor, is no proof of the wisdom of our ancestors. It takes from man the necessity of *foresight*, and instead of being the most provident, makes him the most improvident of all creatures. So far are our poor laws from encouraging industry, that they encourage idleness, and of course profligacy. Such is the state of this country, burthened with taxes to support the church, and the poor …': *Letters to Burke*, p. 117.

amongst us who have wished to pledge the societies of Paris in the cup of their abominations,[382] have been disappointed. The robbery of your church has proved a security to the possessions of ours. It has roused the people. They see with horror and alarm that enormous and shameless act of proscription. It has opened, and will more and more open their eyes upon the selfish enlargement of mind, and the narrow liberality of sentiment [157] of insidious men, which commencing in close hypocrisy and fraud have ended in open violence and rapine. At home we behold similar beginnings. We are on our guard against similar conclusions.

I hope we shall never be so totally lost to all sense of the duties imposed upon us by the law of social union, as, upon any pretext of public service, to confiscate the goods of a single unoffending citizen. Who but a tyrant (a name expressive of every thing which can vitiate and degrade human nature) could think of seizing on the property of men, unaccused, unheard, untried, by whole descriptions, by hundreds and thousands together? who that had not lost every trace of humanity could think of casting down men of exalted rank and sacred function, some of them of an age to call at once for reverence and compassion, of casting them down from the highest situation in the commonwealth, wherein they were maintained by their own landed property, to a state of indigence, depression and contempt?

The confiscators truly have made some allowance to their victims from the scraps and fragments of their own tables from which they have been so harshly driven, and which have been so bountifully spread for a feast to the harpies of usury.[383] But to drive men from independence to live on alms is itself great cruelty. That which might be a tolerable condition to men in one state of life, and not habituated to other things, may, when all these circumstances are altered, be a [158] dreadful revolution; and one to which a virtuous mind would feel pain in condemning any guilt except that which would demand the life of the offender. But to many minds this punishment of *degradation* and *infamy* is worse than death. Undoubtedly it is an infinite aggravation of this cruel suffering, that the persons who were taught a double prejudice in favour of religion, by education and by the place they held in the administration of its functions, are to receive the remnants of their property as alms from the profane and impious hands of those who had plundered them of all the rest; to re-

---

[382]Cf. Revelations 17.4: 'And the woman was arrayed in purple, and scarlet colour, and decked with gold and precious stones and pearls, having a golden cup in her hand, full of abominations and filthiness of her fornication.'

[383]For the Harpies' attack on the feast of the Trojans, see Virgil, *Aeneid*, Book III, 209–57.

ceive, not from the charitable contributions of the faithful, but from the insolent tenderness of known and avowed Atheism, the maintenance of religion,
measured out to them on the standard of the contempt in which it is held; and
for the purpose of rendering those who receive the allowance vile and of no estimation in the eyes of mankind.

But this act of seizure of property, it seems, is a judgment in law, and not a
confiscation. They have, it seems, found out in the academies of the *Palais
Royale*, and the *Jacobins*,[384] that certain men had no right to the possessions
which they held under law, usage, the decisions of courts, and the accumulated prescription of a thousand years. They say that ecclesiastics are fictitious
persons, creatures of the state; whom at pleasure they may destroy, and of
course limit and modify in every particular; that the goods they possess are
not properly [159] theirs, but belong to the state which created the fiction;
and we are therefore not to trouble ourselves with what they may suffer in
their natural feelings and natural persons, on account of what is done towards
them in this their constructive character.[385] Of what import is it, under what
names you injure men, and deprive them of the just emoluments of a profession, in which they were not only permitted but encouraged by the state to engage; and upon the supposed certainty of which emoluments they had formed
the plan of their lives, contracted debts, and led multitudes to an entire dependence upon them?

You do not imagine, sir, that I am going to compliment this miserable distinction of persons with any long discussion. The arguments of tyranny are as

---

[384]The courtyard of the Palais Royal, the Paris residence of the duc d'Orléans, was a
notorious meeting place of orators and politicians who enjoyed there the protection of
the duke. The Club of Jacobins originated as the club of Breton deputies while the National Assembly sat at Versailles. After the move to Paris, it adopted the formal title of
the Société des Amis de la Constitution. It took its nickname from its debating forum,
the hall of a Dominican monastery of the order of St James of Compostella in the Rue
St. Honoré. It was now thrown open to all, and became the dynamic guiding force of
the Revolution.

[385]On 10 October 1789, Talleyrand, bishop of Autun, proposed in the National Assembly that the goods of the Church might justly be appropriated by the nation, if the
nation undertook the charitable obligations for which that wealth had been given to
the Church. The jurist Jacques Guillaume Thouret gave a theoretical basis to this appropriation on 23 October: individuals and corporations (*'personnes morales ou fic-
tives'*) had different property rights, since individuals existed antecedent to the law and
possessed imprescriptible natural rights, but corporations were created by the law and
possessed rights which could be modified by the law. On 2 November the Assembly
decreed *'que tous les biens ecclésiastiques sont à la disposition de la Nation'*, and in
December, adopting Thouret's terms, that the clergy no longer existed as an order: *Le
Moniteur*, 10 October, 26 October, 3 November 1789; Fierro and Liébert, pp. 666–7.

contemptible as its force is dreadful. Had not your confiscators by their early crimes obtained a power which secures indemnity to all the crimes of which they have since been guilty, or that they can commit, it is not the syllogism of the logician but the lash of the executioner that would have refuted a sophistry which becomes an accomplice of theft and murder. The sophistick tyrants of Paris are loud in their declamations against the departed regal tyrants who in former ages have vexed the world. They are thus bold, because they are safe from the dungeons and iron cages of their old masters. Shall we be more tender of the tyrants of our own time, when we see them acting worse tragedies [160] under our eyes? shall we not use the same liberty that they do, when we can use it with the same safety? when to speak honest truth only requires a contempt of the opinions of those whose actions we abhor?

This outrage on all the rights of property was at first covered with what, on the system of their conduct, was the most astonishing of all pretexts—a regard to national faith. The enemies to property at first pretended a most tender, delicate, and scrupulous anxiety for keeping the king's engagements with the public creditor.[386] These professors of the rights of men are so busy in teaching others, that they have not leisure to learn any thing themselves; otherwise they would have known that it is to the property of the citizen, and not to the demands of the creditor of the state, that the first and original faith of civil society is pledged. The claim of the citizen is prior in time, paramount in title, superior in equity. The fortunes of individuals, whether possessed by acquisition, or by descent, or in virtue of a participation in the goods of some community, were no part of the creditor's security, expressed or implied. They never so much as entered into his head when he made his bargain. He well knew that the public, whether represented by a monarch, or by a senate, can pledge nothing but the public estate; and it can have no public estate, except in what it derives from a just and proportioned imposition upon the citizens at large. This was engaged, [161] and nothing else could be engaged to the public creditor. No man can mortgage his injustice as a pawn for his fidelity.

It is impossible to avoid some observation on the contradictions caused by the extreme rigour and the extreme laxity of the new public faith, which influenced in this transaction, and which influenced not according to the nature of the obligation, but to the description of the persons to whom it was engaged. No acts of the old government of the kings of France are held valid in the Na-

[386]The goods of the Church were initially pledged as security for France's debts, contracted under the monarchy and assumed by the National Assembly. Since many of its deputies held government bonds, Burke regarded their behaviour as hypocritical.

tional Assembly, except its pecuniary engagements; acts of all others of the most ambiguous legality. The rest of the acts of that royal government are considered in so odious a light, that to have a claim under its authority is looked on as a sort of crime. A pension, given as a reward for service to the state, is surely as good a ground of property as any security for money advanced to the state. It is a better; for money is paid, and well paid, to obtain that service. We have however seen multitudes of people under this description in France, who never had been deprived of their allowances by the most arbitrary ministers, in the most arbitrary times, by this assembly of the rights of men, robbed without mercy. They were told, in answer to their claim to the bread earned with their blood, that their services had not been rendered to the country that now exists.[387]

This laxity of public faith is not confined to those unfortunate persons. The assembly, with [162] perfect consistency it must be owned, is engaged in a respectable deliberation how far it is bound by the treaties made with other nations under the former government, and their Committee is to report which of them they ought to ratify, and which not.[388] By this means they have put the external fidelity of this virgin state on a par with its internal.

It is not easy to conceive upon what rational principle the royal government should not, of the two, rather have possessed the power of rewarding service, and making treaties, in virtue of its prerogative, than that of pledging to creditors the revenue of the state actual and possible. The treasure of the nation, of all things, has been the least allowed to the prerogative of the king of France, or to the prerogative of any king in Europe. To mortgage the public revenue implies the sovereign dominion, in the fullest sense, over the public purse. It goes far beyond the trust even of a temporary and occasional taxation. The acts however of that dangerous power (the distinctive mark of a boundless despotism) have been alone held sacred. Whence arose this preference given by a democratic assembly to a body of property deriving its title from the most critical and obnoxious of all the exertions of monarchical authority? Reason can furnish nothing to reconcile inconsistency; nor can partial favour be accounted for upon equitable principles. But the contradic-

---

[387]The National Assembly considered the problem of the enormous burden of pensions granted by the monarchy in its sessions of 26 and 31 December 1789 and 4 January 1790 (*Le Moniteur*, 26 December 1789, 1, 2, 6 January 1790). It eventually decided to terminate royal pensions, but to recreate them with limitations and reductions: it seems that Burke's worst fears were not realised.

[388]Mirabeau presented the report of the Committee to the National Assembly on 25 August 1790; the Assembly decreed that France's treaties would remain valid only until they were reviewed or modified: *Le Moniteur*, 26 August 1790.

tion and partiality which admit no justification, are not the less [163] without an adequate cause; and that cause I do not think it difficult to discover.

By the vast debt of France a great monied interest had insensibly grown up, and with it a great power.[389] By the ancient usages which prevailed in that kingdom, the general circulation of property, and in particular the mutual convertibility of land into money, and of money into land, had always been a matter of difficulty. Family settlements, rather more general and more strict than they are in England, the *jus retractus*,[390] the great mass of landed property held by the crown, and by a maxim of the French law held unalienably,[391] the vast estates of the ecclesiastic corporations,—all these had kept the landed and monied interests more separated in France, less miscible, and the owners of the two distinct species of property not so well disposed to each other as they are in this country.[392]

The monied property was long looked on with rather an evil eye by the people. They saw it connected with their distresses, and aggravating them. It was no less envied by the old landed interests, partly for the same reasons that rendered it obnoxious to the people, but much more so as it eclipsed, by the splendour of an ostentatious luxury, the unendowed pedigrees and naked titles of several

[389]For this theme, see especially J. G. A. Pocock, 'The Political Economy of Burke's Analysis of the French Revolution', in idem, *Virtue, Commerce and History* (Cambridge, 1985), pp. 193–212.

[390]The *droit de retrait*, or *prélation*. A variety of laws provided means by which lands formerly part of an estate could be compulsorily repurchased by the original owner. These included the *Retrait Seignurial*, which allowed a lord at any time to repurchase lands which had once been part of his fief. The law was seldom invoked by 1789, but its existence was a grievance. For a legal definition of the system, see Claude Pocquet, *Traité des Fiefs* (3rd edn., Paris, 1741), pp. 406–524.

[391]In 1566 the distinction between the monarch's private and public estates was abolished, and all royal lands became inalienable. Although they were sometimes in practice sold, such alienated lands remained subject to the threat of resumption under the *jus retractus*.

[392]Burke argued that there was a clearer distinction between the landed and monied interests in France than in England, not that there was little or no intermingling between the two in France. The involvement of the nobility in industrial investment (though mainly in mining and metallurgy, obviously related to landownership) is stressed in Guy Chaussinand-Nogaret, *The French nobility in the eighteenth century: From feudalism to enlightenment*, trans. William Doyle (Cambridge, 1985), ch. 5, 'The nobility and capitalism'. A comparative study would greatly diminish the scale of these achievements when placed beside those of the English nobility and gentry. Chaussinand-Nogaret notes that 'In quantitative terms the noble contribution remained modest though far from negligible ... in practice [noble entrepreneurs] were drawn from a numerically limited group' (pp. 90–1).

among the nobility. Even when the nobility, which represented the more permanent landed interest, united themselves by marriage (which sometimes was the case) with the other description, the wealth which saved the family from ruin, [164] was supposed to contaminate and degrade it.[393] Thus the enmities and heart-burnings of these parties were encreased even by the usual means by which discord is to made to cease, and quarrels are turned into friendship. In the mean time, the pride of the wealthy men, not noble or newly noble, encreased with its cause. They felt with resentment an inferiority, the grounds of which they did not acknowledge. There was no measure to which they were not willing to lend themselves, in order to be revenged of the outrages of this rival pride, and to exalt their wealth to what they considered as its natural rank and estimation. They struck at the nobility through the crown and the church. They attacked them particularly on the side on which they thought them the most vulnerable, that is, the possessions of the church, which, through the patronage of the crown, generally devolved upon the nobility. The bishoprics, and the great commendatory abbies, were, with few exceptions, held by that order.

In this state of real, though not always perceived warfare between the noble ancient landed interest, and the new monied interest, the greatest because the most applicable strength was in the hands of the latter. The monied interest is in its nature more ready for any adventure; and its possessors more disposed to new enterprizes of any kind. Being of a recent acquisition, it falls in more naturally with any novelties. It is therefore the kind of wealth which will be resorted to by all who wish for change. [165]

Along with the monied interest, a new description of men had grown up, with whom that interest soon formed a close and marked union; I mean the political Men of Letters. Men of Letters, fond of distinguishing themselves, are rarely averse to innovation. Since the decline of the life and greatness of Lewis the XIVth, they were not so much cultivated either by him, or by the regent,[394] or the successors to the crown; nor were they engaged to the court by favours and emoluments so systematically as during the splendid period of that ostentatious and not impolitic reign. What they lost in the old court protection they endeavoured to make up by joining in a sort of incorporation of their own; to which the two academies of France,[395] and afterwards the vast undertaking of

[393]Chaussinand-Nogaret, *French nobility*, ch. 6, 'Rites and strategies: the marriage market', emphasises the importance of ancient ancestry, despite intermarriages between *noblesse de robe* and *noblesse d'épée*.

[394]Philippe d'Orléans (1674–1723), Regent 1715–23.

[395]The Académie des sciences and the Académie française were the best known. There were others: the Académie des inscriptions et belles lettres, the Académie de peinture et de sculpture, the Académie d'architecture and the Académie de musique.

the Encyclopædia,[396] carried on by a society of these gentlemen, did not a little contribute.

The literary cabal had some years ago formed something like a regular plan for the destruction of the Christian religion.[397] This object they pursued with a degree of zeal which hitherto had been discovered only in the propagators of some system of piety. They were possessed with a spirit of proselytism in the most fanatical degree; and from thence, by an easy progress, with the spirit of persecution according to their means.[398] What was not to be done towards their great end by any direct or immediate act, might be wrought by a longer process through the medium of opinion. To command that opinion, the first step is to establish a dominion over those who direct it. They contrived to possess themselves, [166] with great method and perseverance, of all the avenues to literary fame. Many of them indeed stood high in the ranks of literature and science. The world had done them justice; and in favour of general talents forgave the evil tendency of their peculiar principles. This was true liberality; which they returned by endeavouring to confine the reputation of sense, learning, and taste to themselves or their followers. I will venture to say that this narrow, exclusive spirit has not been less prejudicial to literature and to taste, than to morals and true philosophy. These Atheistical fathers have a bigotry of their own; and they have learnt to talk against monks with the spirit of a monk. But in some things they are men of the world. The resources of intrigue are called in to supply the defects of argument and wit. To this system of

---

[396]Begun in 1751 by D'Alembert and Diderot, it was compiled by the leading figures of the French intelligentsia and scarcely concealed its reformist sub-text. See Robert Darnton, *The Business of Enlightenment: A Publishing History of the Encyclopédie, 1775–1800* (Cambridge, Mass., 1979).

[397]Burke's interpretation of the social significance of the French Enlightenment, once dismissed as an emotionally-exaggerated conspiracy theory, has been confirmed by recent scholarship: see Bibliography, D ii. Works critical of or hostile to religion made up the largest category of this clandestine literature: Darnton, *Forbidden Best-Sellers*, p. 69. Darnton pointed to a group of influential publications initiating this genre in 1748–51: 'In the space of just a few years in the middle of the eighteenth century, the intellectual topography of France was transformed' (ibid., p. 90). Burke may have been writing of the *philosophes* generically; Fierro and Liébert, pp. 668–71, suggest also a specific group, gathered by d'Holbach and including Diderot, Grimm, Helvétius, Marmontel, Morellet and Raynal. Alan Charles Kors, *D'Holbach's Coterie: An Enlightenment in Paris* (Princeton, 1976) argues against the simple characterisation of this school as a group of materialistic atheists.

[398]In the 1803 edition, a note by Burke appeared as a footnote: 'This (down to the end of the first sentence in the next paragraph) and some other parts here and there, were inserted, on his reading the manuscript, by my lost son.' This was Richard Burke (died August 1794).

literary monopoly was joined an unremitting industry to blacken and discredit in every way, and by every means, all those who did not hold to their faction. To those who have observed the spirit of their conduct, it has long been clear that nothing was wanted but the power of carrying the intolerance of the tongue and of the pen into a persecution which would strike at property, liberty, and life.[399]

The desultory and faint persecution carried on against them, more from compliance with form and decency than with serious resentment, neither weakened their strength, nor relaxed their efforts.[400] The issue of the whole was, that what with opposition, and what with success, a violent and malignant zeal, of a kind hitherto unknown in [167] the world, had taken an entire possession of their minds, and rendered their whole conversation, which otherwise would have been pleasing and instructive, perfectly disgusting. A spirit of cabal, intrigue, and proselytism, pervaded all their thoughts, words, and actions. And, as controversial zeal soon turns its thoughts on force, they began to insinuate themselves into a correspondence with foreign princes; in hopes, through their authority, which at first they flattered, they might bring about the changes they had in view. To them it was indifferent whether these changes were to be accomplished by the thunderbolt of despotism, or by the earthquake of popular commotion.[401] The correspondence between this cabal, and the late king of Prussia,[402] will throw no small light upon the spirit of all their proceedings.[403]

[399]Burke appreciated better than any of the Foxite Whigs the cultural dynamics of the French Enlightenment. Although most of its leading lights had, for prudential reasons, not professed total disbelief, their sceptical or satirical stance was more useful as a critique of orthodox religion and its political consequences. Some, like Diderot and d'Holbach, were nevertheless open about their atheism.

[400]The publication of the *Encylopédie*, the thirty-five volumes of which emerged between 1751 and 1780, was a story of ineffectual persecution frustrated by highly-placed patrons. For the failure of official censorship, see Kors, *D'Holbach's Coterie*, pp. 230–44. On 9 June 1789 Arthur Young, in Paris, recorded his impression that nineteen twentieths of the outpouring of pamphlet literature was hostile to the clergy and nobility: 'Is it not wonderful, that while the press teems with the most levelling and even seditious principles, that if put in execution would overturn the monarchy, nothing in reply appears, and not the least step is taken by the court to restrain this extreme licentiousness of publication': *Travels in France*, p. 104.

[401]Burke was correct that almost all the *philosophes* preferred an efficient absolute monarchy to limited monarchy and to democracy as the most likely agency of swift and sweeping reform, especially of the Church. See Fierro and Liébert, pp. 672–3.

[402]Frederick II 'the Great' (1712–86) patronised the *philosophes*. Some of his letters had already been published in Thomas Holcroft (trans.), *Posthumous Works of Frederic II* (13 vols., London, 1789).

[403]Burke later added a footnote: 'I do not chuse to shock the feeling of the moral reader with any quotation of their vulgar, base, and profane language.'

For the same purpose for which they intrigued with princes, they cultivated, in a distinguished manner, the monied interest of France; and partly through the means furnished by those whose peculiar offices gave them the most extensive and certain means of communication, they carefully occupied all the avenues to opinion.

Writers, especially when they act in a body, and with one direction, have great influence on the public mind; the alliance therefore of these writers with the monied interest[404] had no small effect in removing the popular odium and envy which attended that species of wealth. These writers, like the propagators of all novelties, pretended to a great zeal for the poor, and the lower orders, whilst in their satires they rendered hateful, by every exaggeration, the faults of courts, [168] of nobility, and of priesthood. They became a sort of demagogues. They served as a link to unite, in favour of one object, obnoxious wealth to restless and desperate poverty.

As these two kinds of men appear principal leaders in all the late transactions, their junction and politics will serve to account, not upon any principles of law or of policy, but as a *cause*, for the general fury with which all the landed property of ecclesiastical corporations has been attacked; and the great care which, contrary to their pretended principles, has been taken, of a monied interest originating from the authority of the crown. All the envy against wealth and power, was artificially directed against other descriptions of riches. On what other principles than that which I have stated can we account for an appearance so extraordinary and unnatural as that of the ecclesiastical possessions, which had stood so many successions of ages and shocks of civil violences, and were guarded at once by justice, and by prejudice, being applied to the payment of debts, comparatively recent, invidious, and contracted by a decried and subverted government?[405]

Was the public estate a sufficient stake for the public debts? Assume that it was not, and that a loss *must* be incurred somewhere—When the only estate lawfully possessed, and which the contracting parties had in contemplation at the time in which their bargain was made, happens to fail, who, according to

[404]'Their connection with Turgot and almost all the people of finance' [footnote of 1803]. For Turgot see Biographical Guide, above: as an intellectual and a financier, he fitted Burke's stereotype. Others did so, too: d'Holbach and Helvétius had both held the post of *fermier général*: Fierro and Liébert, p. 673.

[405]'It is clear from their writings that a profound, resolute and aggressive anticlericalism was integral to the thinking of a substantial number of deputies' of the National Assembly: Timothy Tackett, *Becoming a Revolutionary: The Deputies of the French National Assembly and the Emergence of a Revolutionary Culture (1789–1790)* (Princeton, 1996), p. 68 and passim.

the principles of natural and legal equity, ought to be the sufferer? Certainly it ought to be either the party who trusted; or the party who persuaded him to trust; or both; [169] and not third parties who had no concern with the transaction. Upon any insolvency they ought to suffer who were weak enough to lend upon bad security, or they who fraudulently held out a security that was not valid. Laws are acquainted with no other rules of decision. But by the new institute of the rights of men, the only persons, who in equity ought to suffer, are the only persons who are to be saved harmless: those are to answer the debt who neither were lenders or borrowers, mortgagers or mortgagees.

What had the clergy to do with these transactions? What had they to do with any public engagement further than the extent of their own debt? To that, to be sure, their estates were bound to the last acre. Nothing can lead more to the true spirit of the assembly, which sits for public confiscation, with its new equity and its new morality, than an attention to their proceeding with regard to this debt of the clergy. The body of confiscators, true to that monied interest for which they were false to every other, have found the clergy competent to incur a legal debt. Of course they declared them legally entitled to the property which their power of incurring the debt and mortgaging the estate implied; recognizing the rights of those persecuted citizens, in the very act in which they were thus grossly violated.

If, as I said, any persons are to make good deficiencies to the public creditor, besides the public at large, they must be those who managed the agreement. Why therefore are not the estates of all the comptrollers general confiscated?[406] [170] Why not those of the long succession of ministers, financiers, and bankers who have been enriched whilst the nation was impoverished by their dealings and their counsels? Why is not the estate of Mr. Laborde[407] declared forfeited rather than of the archbishop of Paris,[408] who has had nothing to do in the creation or in the jobbing of the public funds. Or, if you must con-

---

[406]The 1803 edition included a footnote: 'All have been confiscated in their turn.' The office of *Contrôleur-Général des Finances*, the usual title of ministers of finance, was at the centre of state finance. See J. F. Bosher, *French Finances 1707–1795: From business to bureaucracy* (Cambridge, 1970), pp. 47–66.

[407]Jean Joseph, marquis de Laborde: see Biographical Guide. Burke may alternatively have referred to his eldest son, François-Louis-Joseph de Laborde de Méréville (1761–1801), Keeper of the Royal Treasury 1785–9, and a deputy in the Third Estate. On 5 December 1789 he presented the Assembly with a plan for a national bank (*Le Moniteur*, 5 December 1789); in 1790 he was appointed one of the commissioners for receiving *dons patriotiques* extracted from the Church. Later he was denounced by the Revolutionary Tribunal and fled to England: Fierro and Liébert, p. 674.

[408]Antoine-Élénor-Léon Leclerc de Juigné (1728–1811), noted for his charity. He became an *émigré* in 1790.

fiscate old landed estates in favour of the money-jobbers, why is the penalty confined to one description? I do not know whether the expences of the duke de Choiseul[409] have left any thing of the infinite sums which he had derived from the bounty of his master, during the transactions of a reign which contributed largely, by every species of prodigality in war and peace, to the present debt of France. If any such remains, why is not this confiscated? I remember to have been in Paris during the time of the old government. I was there just after the duke d'Aiguillon[410] had been snatched (as it was generally thought) from the block by the hand of a protecting despotism. He was a minister, and had some concern in the affairs of that prodigal period. Why do I not see his estate delivered up to the municipalities in which it is situated? The noble family of Noailles have long been servants, (meritorious servants I admit) to the crown of France,[411] and have had of course some share in its bounties. Why do I hear nothing of the application of their estates to the public debt? Why is the estate of the duke de Rochefoucault[412] more sacred than that of the cardinal de Rochefoucault?[413] The former is, I doubt not, a worthy [171] person; and (if it were not a sort of profaneness to talk of the use, as affecting the title to property) he makes a good use of his revenues; but it is no disrespect to him to say, what authentic information well warrants me in saying, that the use made of a property equally valid, by his brother[414] the cardinal archbishop of Rouen, was far more laudable and far more public-spirited.[415] Can one hear of the proscription of such persons, and the confiscation of their effects, without indignation and horror? He is not a man who does not feel such emotions on such occasions. He does not deserve the name of a free man who will not express them.

Few barbarous conquerors have ever made so terrible a revolution in property. None of the heads of the Roman factions, when they established *"crudelem illam Hastam"*[416] in all their auctions of rapine, have ever set up to

[409]See Biographical Guide.

[410]See Biographical Guide.

[411]See Biographical Guide.

[412]See Biographical Guide. Burke may have referred either to the duc de La Rochefoucald (1743–92) or his kinsman the duc de La Rochefoucauld-Liancourt (1747–1827).

[413]See Biographical Guide.

[414]The 1803 edition carried a footnote: 'Not his brother, nor any near relation; but this mistake does not affect the argument.'

[415]This did not save him from the hostility of the populace: Young, *Travels in France*, p. 122.

[416]'In Sulla's case, therefore, an unrighteous victory disgraced a righteous cause. For when he had planted his spear and was selling under the hammer in the forum the property of men who were patriots and men of wealth and, at least, Roman citizens, he

sale the goods of the conquered citizen to such an enormous amount. It must be allowed in favour of those tyrants of antiquity, that what was done by them could hardly be said to be done in cold blood. Their passions were inflamed, their tempers soured, their understandings confused, with the spirit of revenge, with the innumerable reciprocated and recent inflictions and retaliations of blood and rapine. They were driven beyond all bounds of moderation by the apprehension of the return of power with the return of property to the families of those they had injured beyond all hope of forgiveness.

These Roman confiscators, who were yet only [172] in the elements[417] of tyranny, and were not instructed in the rights of men to exercise all sorts of cruelties on each other without provocation, thought it necessary to spread a sort of colour over their injustice. They considered the vanquished party as composed of traitors who had borne arms, or otherwise had acted with hostility against the commonwealth. They regarded them as persons who had forfeited their property by their crimes. With you, in your improved state of the human mind, there was no such formality. You seized upon five millions sterling of annual rent, and turned forty or fifty thousand human creatures out of their houses, because "such was your pleasure." The tyrant, Harry the Eighth of England, as he was not better enlightened than the Roman Marius's and Sylla's,[418] and had not studied in your new schools, did not know what an effectual instrument of despotism was to be found in that grand magazine of offensive weapons, the rights of men. When he resolved to rob the abbies, as the club of the Jacobins have robbed all the ecclesiastics, he began by setting on foot a commission to examine into the crimes and abuses which prevailed in those communities. As it might be expected, his commission reported truths, exaggerations, and falshoods. But truly or falsely it reported abuses and offences. However, as abuses might be corrected, as every crime of persons does not infer a forfeiture with regard to communities, and as property, in that dark age, was not discovered to be a creature of prejudice, all those abuses (and there were enough [173] of them) were hardly thought sufficient ground for such a confiscation as it was for his purposes to make. He there-

---

had the affrontery to announce that "he was selling his spoils" ... And never will the seed and the occasion of civil war be wanting, so long as villains remember that blood-stained spear and hope to see another': Cicero, *De Officiis*, Book II, viii, 27, 29. Roman auctions were normally conducted around a spear thrust into the ground, a symbol inherited from the sale of booty captured in war.

[417]I.e. rudiments.

[418]Henry VIII (reigned 1509–47); Gaius Marius (155–86 BC); Lucius Cornelius Sulla (138–78 BC). The two last were political rivals. Sulla, especially, was a byword for the ruthless use of force to obtain political power.

fore procured the formal surrender of these estates. All these operose proceedings were adopted by one of the most decided tyrants in the rolls of history, as necessary preliminaries, before he could venture, by bribing the members of his two servile houses with a share of the spoil, and holding out to
them an eternal immunity from taxation, to demand a confirmation of his
iniquitous proceedings by an act of parliament. Had fate reserved him to our
times, four technical terms would have done his business, and saved him all
this trouble; he needed nothing more than one short form of incantation—
"*Philosophy, Light, Liberality, the Rights of Men.*"[419]

I can say nothing in praise of those acts of tyranny, which no voice has
hitherto ever commended under any of their false colours; yet in these false
colours an homage was paid by despotism to justice. The power which was
above all fear and all remorse was not set above all shame. Whilst shame
keeps its watch, Virtue is not wholly extinguished in the heart; nor will Mod-
eraton be utterly exiled from the minds of tyrants.

I believe every honest man sympathizes in his reflections with our political
poet on that occasion, and will pray to avert the omen whenever these acts of
rapacious despotism present themselves to his view or his imagination:

> —"May no such storm
> Fall on our times, where ruin must reform. [174]
> Tell me (my muse) what monstrous, dire offence,
> What crimes could any Christian king incense
> To such a rage? Was't luxury, or lust?
> Was *he* so temperate, so chaste, so just?
> Were these their crimes? they were his own much more;
> But wealth is crime enough to him that's poor."[420]

[419]Burke's indignation at the expropriation of the property of the French church
evoked no sympathy in English Dissenters, who coveted the wealth of the Church of
England. Priestley wrote: 'I am clearly of opinion, that the state has a right to dispose
of *all* property within itself; that of the church, as well as of every thing else of a public
nature': *Letters to Burke*, pp. 53, 113–20.

[420]The rest of the passage is this—

> "Who having spent the treasures of his crown,
> Condemns their luxury to feed his own.
> And yet this act, to varnish o'er the shame
> Of sacrilege, must bear devotion's name.
> No crime so bold, but would be understood
> A real, or at least a seeming good,
> Who fears not to do ill, yet fears the name;
> And, free from conscience, is a slave to fame.

This same wealth, which is at all times treason and *lese nation*[421] to indigent and rapacious despotism, under all modes of polity, was your temptation
to violate property, law, and religion, united in one object. But was the state
of France so wretched and undone, that no other resource but rapine re-

Thus he the church at once protects, and spoils:
But princes' swords are sharper than their styles.
And thus to th'ages past he makes amends,
Their charity destroys, their faith defends.
Then did religion in a lazy cell,
In empty aëry contemplations dwell;
And, like the block, unmoved lay: but ours,
As much too active, like the stork devours.
Is there no temp'rate region can be known,
Betwixt their frigid, and our torrid zone? [175]
Could we not wake from that lethargic dream,
But to be restless in a worse extreme?
And for that lethargy was there no cure,
But to be cast into a calenture?
Can knowledge have no bound, but must advance
So far, to make us wish for ignorance?
And rather in the dark to grope our way,
Than, led by a false guide, to err by day?
Who sees these dismal heaps, but would demand,
What barbarous invader sack'd the land?
But when he hears, no Goth, no Turk did bring
This desolation, but a Christian king;
When nothing, but the name of zeal, appears
'Twixt our best actions, and the worst of theirs,
What does he think our sacrilege would spare,
When such th' effects of our devotion are?"
COOPER'S HILL, by Sir JOHN DENHAM. [B]

[Sir John Denham], *Coopers Hill. A Poeme* (London, 1642), pp. 8–10 (free quotation).
Burke might have quoted Denham's ambiguous praise of the securing of Magna Carta
by resistance (p. 16): 'When in that remedy all hope was plac't / Which was, or should
have been at least the last. / For armed subjects can have no pretence / Against their
Princes, but their just defence, / And whether then, or no, I leave to them / To justifie,
who else themselves condemne.' Denham's conclusion would have been equally con-
genial to Burke (p. 19): 'Therefore their boundlesse power tell Princes draw / Within
the Channell, and the shores of Law, / And may that Law, which teaches Kings to sway /
Their Scepters, teach their Subjects to obey.' Sir John Denham (1615–69), poet, fought
for Charles I in 1642 but was quickly captured and obliged to withdraw from the conflict. He remained in the service of the royal family in exile, and his goods were confiscated by Parliament. His predicament was not irrelevant in 1790.

[421] Although the old law of *lèse-majesté* was rarely invoked, the new one of *lèse-nation*
saw a wave of political accusations in November 1789: Fierro and Liébert, pp. 676–7.

mained to preserve its existence? On this point I wish to receive some information. When the states met, was the condition [175] of the finances of France such, that, after œconomising (on principles of justice and mercy) through all departments, no fair repartition of burthens upon all the orders could possibly restore them? If such an equal imposition would have been sufficient, you well know it might easily have been made. Mr. Neckar,[422] in the budget which he laid before the Orders assembled at Versailles, made a detailed exposition of the state of the French nation.[423]

If we give credit to him, it was not necessary to have recourse to any new impositions whatsoever, to put the receipts of France on a balance with its expences. He stated the permanent charges of all descriptions, including the interest of a new loan of four hundred millions, [176] at 531,444,000 livres; the fixed revenue at 475,294,000, making the deficiency 56,150,000, or short of 2,200,000 sterling. But to balance it, he brought forward savings and improvements of revenue (considered as entirely certain) to rather more than the amount of that deficiency; and he concludes with these emphatical words (p. 39) "Quel pays, Messieurs, que celui, ou, *sans impots* et avec de simples objets *inappercus*, on peut faire disparoitre un deficit qui a fait tant de bruit en Europe."[424] As to the re-imbursement, the sinking of debt, and the other great objects of public credit and political arrangement indicated in Mons. Necker's speech, no doubt could be entertained, but that a very moderate and proportioned assessment on the citizens without distinction would have provided for all of them to the fullest extent of their demand.

If this representation of Mons. Necker was false, then the assembly are in the highest degree culpable for having forced the king to accept as his minister, and since the king's deposition,[425] for having employed as *their* minister, a

[422]That Burke should believe Necker rather than Calonne was not unusual, and many in France were of the same view. Most of the Assembly of Notables, recalled in February 1787, showed 'a kind of superstitious reverence' for Necker's optimistic account of national finances as they stood in 1781, and were offended by Calonne's claim in 1787 that the budget had been in deficit even in 1781: Egret, *French Prerevolution*, pp. 21, 62. Burke shared this long-standing idolisation of Necker (see *Reflections*, p. [190]), but more accurate factual evidence on French finances was not available when Burke wrote. Necker's report to the Estates-General on 5 May 1789 only later proved to be a misleading forecast.

[423]Rapport de Mons. le directeur général des finances, fait par ordre du Roi à Versailles. Mai 5, 1789. [B] This work is: *Ouverture des États-Généraux faite a Versailles le 5 Mai 1789. Discours du Roi; Discours de M. le Garde des Sceaux; Rapport de M. le directeur général des finances, fait par ordre du Roi* (Paris, 1789).

[424]The italics were Burke's. 'p. 39' *sc.* 'p. 35'.

[425]Burke evidently regarded the events of 5–6 October 1789 as the king's effective

man who had been capable of abusing so notoriously the confidence of his master and their own; in a matter too of the highest moment, and directly appertaining to his particular office. But if the representation was exact (as, having always, along with you, conceived a high degree of respect for Mr. Neckar, I make no doubt it was) then what can be said in favour of those, who, instead of moderate, reasonable, and general contribution, have in cold blood, and impelled by [177] no necessity, had recourse to a partial and cruel confiscation?[426]

Was that contribution refused on a pretext of privilege, either on the part of the clergy[427] or on that of the nobility? No certainly. As to the clergy, they even ran before the wishes of the third order. Previous to the meeting of the states, they had in all their instructions expressly directed their deputies to renounce every immunity, which put them upon a footing distinct from the condition of their fellow-subjects. In this renunciation the clergy were even more explicit than the nobility.

But let us suppose that the deficiency had remained at the 56 millions, (or £.2,200,000 sterling) as at first stated by Mr. Necker. Let us allow that all the resources he opposed to that deficiency were impudent and groundless fictions; and that the assembly (or their lords of articles[428] at the Jacobins) were from

---

deposition. Formally, Louis XVI was suspended from his functions by the National Assembly on 25 June 1791, and the republic proclaimed on 22 September 1792. Burke's premonitions were shared by some French observers, including Rivarol and Mallet du Pan; Mirabeau wrote to the comte de La Marck in late September 1789: 'Tout est perdu, le roi et la reine y périront, et vous le verrez, la populace battra leurs cadavres' (quoted Fierro and Liébert, p. 678). The Foxite Whigs, in rejecting Burke, failed to read the writing already on the wall.

[426]On 2 November 1789, the National Assembly voted by 586 to 346 to accept Mirabeau's motion to place the goods of the church at the disposal of the nation. Mirabeau claimed that the clergy already accepted the principle of a major reform.

[427]The clergy were not assessed for direct taxation; instead, the elected Assembly of the Clergy, meeting every five years, voted a *don gratuit* or free gift to the king. But the clergy repeatedly (most recently in 1785) resisted a governmental valuation of their wealth; in 1787 prelates in the Assembly of Notables continued the defence of their privileges against Calonne's reforms; in 1788 the Assembly of the Clergy reiterated these protests and voted a *don gratuit* less than a quarter of the sum requested by the government. This contributed to the financial collapse of August 1788. Burke overlooked the widespread resistance of the French clergy to reform before 1789. It was, however, the case that the clergy's *cahiers*, the proposals drawn up for the Estates-General in early 1789, often called for reform of the Church's tax privileges.

[428]In the constitution of Scotland during the Stuart reigns, a committee sat for preparing bills; and none could pass, but those previously approved by them. This committee was called lords of articles. [B] It was abolished in 1640 and again in 1689. See

thence justified in laying the whole burthen of that deficiency on the clergy,—yet allowing all this, a necessity of £.2,200,000 sterling will not support a confiscation to the amount of five millions. The imposition of £.2,200,000 on the clergy, as partial, would have been oppressive and unjust, but it would not have been altogether ruinous to those on whom it was imposed; and therefore it would not have answered the real purpose of the managers. [178]

Perhaps persons, unacquainted with the state of France, on hearing the clergy and the noblesse were privileged in point of taxation, may be led to imagine, that previous to the revolution these bodies had contributed nothing to the state. This is a great mistake. They certainly did not contribute equally with each other, nor either of them equally with the commons. They both however contributed largely.[429] Neither nobility nor clergy enjoyed any exemption from the excise on consumable commodities, from duties of custom, or from any of the other numerous *indirect* impositions, which in France as well as here, make so very large a proportion of all payments to the public. The noblesse paid the capitation. They paid also a land-tax, called the twentieth penny, to the height sometimes of three, sometimes of four shillings in the pound; both of them *direct* impositions of no light nature, and no trivial produce. The clergy of the provinces annexed by conquest to France (which in extent make about an eighth part of the whole but in wealth a much larger proportion) paid likewise to the capitation and the twentieth penny, at the rate paid by the nobility. The clergy in the old provinces did not pay the capitation; but they had redeemed themselves at the expense of about 24 millions, or a little more than a million sterling. They were exempted from the twentieths; but then they made free gifts; they contracted debts for the state; and they were subject to some other charges, the whole computed at about a thirteenth part of [179] their clear income. They ought to have paid annually about forty thousand pounds more, to put them on a par with the contribution of the nobility.[430]

---

C. S. Terry, *The Scottish Parliament: Its Constitution and Procedure, 1603–1707* (Glasgow, 1905); Robert S. Rait, *The Parliaments of Scotland* (Glasgow, 1924); John R. Young, *The Scottish Parliament 1639–1661: A Political and Constitutional Analysis* (Edinburgh, 1996). Rait (pp. 8, 425–9) believed that 'the whole business of Parliament, apart from judicial cases, tended to be entrusted to them, and ... their reports were normally accepted with little discussion.' The Jacobins began, as the Breton Club, as a means of previously formulating and co-ordinating proposals in an Estates-General, and subsequently a National Assembly, which lacked traditions of party organisation.

[429]The clergy and the nobility paid indirect taxes, the *vingtième* and the *capitation*, although these were assessed more heavily on the third estate.

[430]Burke's authority for this statement was probably Necker's estimate that the

When the terrors of this tremendous proscription hung over the clergy, they made an offer of a contribution, through the archbishop of Aix, which, for its extravagance, ought not to have been accepted.[431] But it was evidently and obviously more advantageous to the public creditor, than any thing which could rationally be promised by the confiscation. Why was it not accepted? The reason is plain—There was no desire that the church should be brought to serve the state. The service of the state was made a pretext to destroy the church. One great end in the project would have been defeated, if the plan of extortion had been adopted in lieu of the scheme of confiscation. The new landed interest connected with the new republic, and connected with it for its very being, could not have been created.[432] This was the reason why that extravagant ransom was not accepted.

The madness of the project of confiscation, on the plan that was first pretended, soon became apparent. To bring this unwieldy mass of landed property, enlarged by the confiscation of all the vast landed domain of the crown, at once into markct, was obviously to defeat the profits proposed by the confiscation, by depreciating the value of those lands, and indeed of all the landed estates throughout France. Such a sudden diversion of all its circulating money from trade to land, must be an additional mischief. What [180] step was taken? Did the assembly, on becoming sensible of the inevitable ill effects of their projected sale, revert to the offers of the clergy? No distress could oblige them to travel in a course which was disgraced by any appearance of justice. Giving over all hopes from a general immediate sale, another project seems to have succeeded. They proposed to take stock in exchange for the church lands. In that project great difficulties arose in equalizing the objects to be exchanged. Other obstacles also presented themselves, which threw them

---

French clergy paid 10,050,000 *livres* out of a total annual income of about 110,000,000 *livres*; and that this was 700,000 or 800,000 *livres* per annum less than if they had paid taxes on the same basis as the nobility: Jacques Necker, *De l'administration des finances de la France* (3 vols., [Paris], 1784), II, ch. 9. Necker emphasised the complexity of the question and the uncertainty of the figures. On the basis of the information then available, Burke had some grounds for arguing that the clergy were not substantially under-taxed.

[431]The archbishop of Aix, for the clergy, offered a loan of 400 million *livres* if the National Assembly revoked its suppression of tithes and appropriation of Church goods. In 1788 the Assembly of the Clergy had refused the government's request for a *don gratuit* of 8 million *livres* over two years: Fierro and Liébert, p. 680.

[432]The ideological effects of the sale of Church goods in creating an interest in favour of the Revolution are a matter of debate. See Georges Lefebvre, 'La vente des biens nationaux' in Lefebvre, *Études sur la Révolution française* (Paris, 1954); Marcel Marion, *La Vente des biens nationaux pendant la Révolution* (Paris, 1908).

back again upon some project of sale. The municipalities had taken an alarm. They would not hear of transferring the whole plunder of the kingdom to the stock-holders in Paris.[433] Many of those municipalities had been (upon system) reduced to the most deplorable indigence. Money was no where to be seen. They were therefore led to the point that was so ardently desired. They panted for a currency of any kind which might revive their perishing industry. The municipalities were then to be admitted to a share in the spoil, which evidently rendered the first scheme (if ever it had been seriously entertained) altogether impracticable. Public exigencies pressed upon all sides. The minister of finance reiterated his call for supply with a most urgent, anxious, and boding voice. Thus pressed on all sides, instead of the first plan of converting their bankers into bishops and abbots, instead of paying the old debt, they contracted a new debt, at 3 per cent. creating a new paper currency, founded on an eventual sale of the church lands.[434] They issued [181] this paper currency to satisfy in the first instance chiefly the demands made upon them by the *Bank of discount*,[435] the great machine, or paper-mill, of their fictitious wealth.

The spoil of the church was now become the only resource of all their operations in finance; the vital principle of all their politics; the sole security for the existence of their power. It was necessary by all, even the most violent means, to put every individual on the same bottom, and to bind the nation in one guilty interest to uphold this act, and the authority of those by whom it was done. In order to force the most reluctant into a participation of their pillage, they rendered their paper circulation compulsory in all payments. Those who consider the general tendency of their schemes to this one object as a centre; and a centre from which afterwards all their measures radiate, will not think that I dwell too long upon this part of the proceedings of the national assembly.

To cut off all appearance of connexion between the crown and public justice, and to bring the whole under implicit obedience to the dictators in Paris,

---

[433]'Burke's contention that the Assignats were issued to keep the ecclesiastical lands out of the hands of Paris can find little support in parliamentary debates, or in the literature of the period': S. E. Harris, *The Assignats* (Cambridge, Mass., 1930), p. 12.

[434]The church goods appropriated by the state have been valued at two thousand million *livres*, almost the total of the national debt. In order to realise this sum at once, the Assembly voted on 19 December 1789 to issue bonds backed by these goods, 'billets assignés sur les biens du clergé', soon known as *assignats*. They were issued from January 1790. See Harris, *Assignats* and Michel Bruguière, 'Assignats', in Furet and Ozouf, *Critical Dictionary*, pp. 426–36.

[435]The *Caisse d'Escompte*, planned by Turgot as *Contrôlleur-général des finances*.

the old independent judicature of the parliaments, with all its merits, and all its faults, was wholly abolished.[436] Whilst the parliaments existed, it was evident that the people might some time or other come to resort to them, and rally under the standard of their antient laws. It became however a matter of consideration that the magistrates and officers, in the courts now abolished, *had purchased their places* at a very high rate, for which, as well as for the [182] duty they performed, they received but a very low return of interest. Simple confiscation is a boon only for the clergy;—to the lawyers some appearances of equity are to be observed; and they are to receive compensation to an immense amount. Their compensation becomes part of the national debt, for the liquidation of which there is the one exhaustless fund. The lawyers are to obtain their compensation in the new church paper, which is to march with the new principles of judicature and legislature. The dismissed magistrates are to take their share of martyrdom with the ecclesiastics, or to receive their own property from such a fund and in such a manner, as all those, who have been seasoned with the antient principles of jurisprudence, and had been the sworn guardians of property, must look upon with horror. Even the clergy are to receive their miserable allowance out of the depreciated paper which is stamped with the indelible character of sacrilege, and with the symbols of their own ruin, or they must starve. So violent an outrage upon credit, property, and liberty, as this compulsory paper currency, has seldom been exhibited by the alliance of bankruptcy and tyranny, at any time, or in any nation.[437]

[436]The thirteen *parlements* were suspended on 3 November 1789 and formally abolished by a decree of 6 September 1790. They were judicial bodies with an hereditary membership whose function of registering royal decrees gave them a power of obstructing legislation; this led them to see themselves as representative institutions and claim to be defenders of French liberties. Burke treated the *parlements* as essential parts of France's ancient constitution, but their continual opposition to royal plans for reform had been a major cause of the collapse of the monarchy. Louis XV's minister René Maupeou had abolished them for such reasons in 1771, but Louis XVI restored them on his accession, and his belated attempt on 8 May 1788 to replace them with a more effective administrative system failed. Burke returned to the *parlements* in *Reflections*, pp. [298–301].

[437]The National Assembly had only authorised two issues of *assignats* when Burke's *Reflections* was published. His understanding of the consequences of paper currency focused on confiscation; he did not use the term 'inflation', and though he wrote of a depreciation of 7 per cent (p. [345]) he did not foresee the massive depreciation which was to follow. The first tranche of *assignats* was voted between 19 and 21 December 1789, of 400 million *livres* of notes in high denominations, at first bearing interest at 5 per cent; they represented only 'a simple rescheduling of the government's debt', and retained their value for some months: Michel Bruguière, 'Assignats' in Furet

✳ In the course of all these operations, at length comes out the grand *arcanum*;[438]—that in reality, and in a fair sense, the lands of the church (so far as any thing certain can be gathered from their proceedings) are not to be sold at all. By the late resolutions of the national assembly, they are indeed to be delivered to the highest bidder. But it is to be observed, that *a certain portion only of the purchase money* [183] *is to be laid down*. A period of twelve years is to be given for the payment of the rest. The philosophic purchasers are therefore, on payment of a sort of fine,[439] to be put instantly into possession of the estate. It becomes in some respects a sort of gift to them; to be held on the feudal tenure of zeal to the new establishment. This project is evidently to let in a body of purchasers without money. The consequence will be, that these purchasers, or rather grantees, will pay, not only from the rents as they accrue, which might as well be received by the state, but from the spoil of the materials of buildings, from waste in woods, and from whatever money, by hands habituated to the gripings of usury, they can wring from the miserable peasant. He is to be delivered over to the mercenary and arbitrary discretion of men, who will be stimulated to every species of extortion by the growing demands on the growing profits of an estate held under the precarious settlement of a new political system.

When all the frauds, impostures, violences, rapines, burnings, murders, confiscations, compulsory paper currencies, and every description of tyranny and cruelty employed to bring about and to uphold this revolution, have their natural effect, that is, to shock the moral sentiments of all virtuous and sober minds, the abettors of this philosophic system immediately strain their throats in a declamation against the old monarchical government of France. When they have rendered that deposed power sufficiently black, [184] they then

---

and Ozouf, *Critical Dictionary*, p. 427. Interest was reduced to 3 per cent in April 1790, and the *assignats* at the same moment became legal tender. From 14 May 1790 the Assembly began the sale of confiscated property. On 29 September 1790 a second tranche of 800 million *livres* of *assignats* were voted without interest, though still notionally backed by Church property, despite the warnings of inflation by deputies including Dupont de Nemours and Talleyrand. It is unlikely that Burke learned of this vote in time for it to influence his comments in the *Reflections*, published on 1 November (he wrote of only the first issue, below, p. [344]). Much larger tranches began to be issued from December 1791; by February 1796, 45.6 thousand million *assignats* were in circulation: Fierro and Liébert, pp. 682–3. Burke returned to this theme in *Reflections*, pp. [336–48].

[438] Arcanum: '1. A hidden thing; a mystery, a profound secret ... 2. One of the supposed great secrets of nature which the alchemists aimed at discovering; *hence*, a marvellous remedy, an elixir': *OED*.

[439] 'Fine': a term in English law for a lump sum payment at the renewal of a lease.

proceed in argument, as if all those who disapprove of their new abuses must of course be partizans of the old; that those who reprobate their crude and violent schemes of liberty ought to be treated as advocates for servitude. I admit that their necessities do compel them to this base and contemptible fraud. Nothing can reconcile men to their proceedings and projects but the supposition that there is no third option between them, and some tyranny as odious as can be furnished by the records of history, or by the invention of poets. This prattling of theirs hardly deserves the name of sophistry. It is nothing but plain impudence. Have these gentlemen never heard, in the whole circle of the worlds of theory and practice, of any thing between the despotism of the monarch and the despotism of the multitude? Have they never heard of a monarchy directed by laws, controlled and balanced by the great hereditary wealth and hereditary dignity of a nation;[440] and both again controlled by a judicious check from the reason and feeling of the people at large acting by a suitable and permanent organ?[441] Is it then impossible that a man may be found who, without criminal ill intention, or pitiable absurdity, shall prefer such a mixed and tempered government to either of the extremes; and who may repute that nation to be destitute of all wisdom and of all virtue, which, having in its choice to obtain such a government with ease, *or rather to confirm it when actually possessed*, thought proper to commit a thousand crimes, and [185] to subject their country to a thousand evils, in order to avoid it? Is it then a truth so universally acknowledged, that a pure democracy is the only tolerable form into which human society can be thrown, that a man is not permitted to hesitate about its merits, without the suspicion of being a friend to tyranny, that is, of being a foe to mankind?

I do not know under what description to class the present ruling authority in France. It affects to be a pure democracy, though I think it in a direct train of becoming shortly a mischievous and ignoble oligarchy.[442] But for the present I admit it to be a contrivance of the nature and effect of what it pretends to. I reprobate no form of government merely upon abstract principles.[443]

---

[440]The House of Lords.

[441]The House of Commons.

[442]The establishment of the Directory in November 1795 fulfilled this prediction.

[443]In the Commons, Burke held that he 'was represented as arguing in a manner which implied that the British constitution could not be defended, but by abusing all republics ancient and modern. He said nothing to give the least ground for such a censure. He never abused all republics. He has never professed himself a friend or an enemy to republics or to monarchies in the abstract. He thought that the circumstances and habits of every country, which it is always perilous and productive of the greatest calamities to force, are to decide upon the form of its government.' However, 'the pres-

There may be situations in which the purely democratic form will become necessary. There may be some (very few, and very particularly circumstanced) where it would be clearly desireable. This I do not take to be the case of France, or of any other great country. Until now, we have seen no examples of considerable democracies. The antients were better acquainted with them. Not being wholly unread in the authors, who had seen the most of those constitutions, and who best understood them, I cannot help concurring with their opinion, that an absolute democracy, no more than absolute monarchy, is to be reckoned among the legitimate forms of government. They think it rather the corruption and degeneracy, than the sound constitution of a republic. If I recollect rightly, Aristotle observes, [186] that a democracy has many striking points of resemblance with a tyranny.[444] Of this I am certain, that in a democracy, the majority of the citizens is capable of exercising the most cruel oppressions upon the minority, whenever strong divisions prevail in that kind of polity, as they often must; and that oppression of the minority will extend to far greater numbers, and will be carried on with much greater fury, than can almost ever be apprehended from the dominion of a single sceptre. In such a

---

ent scheme of things in France' did not 'at all deserve the respectable name of a republic': it was 'a foul, impious, monstrous thing, wholly out of the course of moral nature': [Burke], *Appeal*, pp. 10, 45–6. Among other relevant works, Burke owned a copy of the fourth edition of Edward Montagu, *Reflections on the Rise and Fall of the Antient Republicks* (London, 1778): *LC*, p. 14.

[444]When I wrote this I quoted from memory, after many years had elapsed from my reading the passage. A learned friend has found it, and it is as follows:

Τὸ ἦθος τὸ αὐτὸ, καὶ ἄμφω δεσποτικὰ τῶν βελτιόνων, καὶ τὰ ψηφίσματα, ὥσπερ ἐκεῖ τὰ ἐπιταγμάτα· καὶ ὁ δημαγωγὸς καὶ ὁ κόλαξ, οἱ αὐτοὶ καὶ ἀνάλογον· καὶ μάλιστα ἑκάτεροι παρ' ἑκατέροις ἰσχύουσιν, οἱ μὲν κόλακες παρὰ τυράννοις, οἱ δὲ δημαγωγοὶ παρὰ τοῖς δήμοις τοῖς τοιούτοις.—

'The ethical character is the same; both exercise despotism over the better class of citizens; and decrees are in the one, what ordinances and arrêts are in the other: the demagogue too, and the court favourite, are not unfrequently the same identical men, and always bear a close analogy; and these have the principal power, each in their respective forms of government, favourites with the absolute monarch, and demagogues with a people such as I have described.' Arist. Politic. lib. iv. cap. 4. [B]

This was evidently Burke's own translation from the Greek. It was not taken from the obvious English version, *A Treatise on Government. Translated from the Greek of Aristotle. By William Ellis, A. M.* (London, 1776), pp. 195–6, a copy of which Ellis had presented to him. Burke then replied: 'he is satisfied he shall read [the work] in Mr. Ellis's Translation with much greater advantage than he had done when he made vain attempts to understand him in the original by the aid of an ordinary Latin Translation': Burke to William Ellis, 1 January 1779: Burke, *Correspondence*, IV, p. 36. Perhaps Burke had been too modest about his competence in Greek.

popular persecution, individual sufferers are in a much more deplorable condition than in any other. Under a cruel prince they have the balmy compassion of mankind to assuage the smart of their wounds; they have the plaudits of the people to animate their generous constancy under their sufferings: but those who are subjected to wrong under multitudes, are deprived of all external consolation. [187] They seem deserted by mankind; overpowered by a conspiracy of their whole species.

But admitting democracy not to have that inevitable tendency to party tyranny, which I suppose it to have, and admitting it to possess as much good in it when unmixed, as I am sure it possesses when compounded with other forms; does monarchy, on its part, contain nothing at all to recommend it? I do not often quote Bolingbroke, nor have his works, in general, left any permanent impression on my mind.[445] He is a presumptuous and a superficial writer. But he has one observation, which, in my opinion, is not without depth and solidity. He says, that he prefers a monarchy to other governments; because you can better ingraft any description of republic on a monarchy, than any thing of monarchy upon the republican forms.[446] I think him perfectly in the right. The fact is so historically; and it agrees well with the speculation.

I know how easy a topic it is to dwell on the faults of departed greatness. By a revolution in the state, the fawning sycophant of yesterday, is converted into the austere critic of the present hour. But steady independent minds, when they have an object of so serious a concern to mankind as government, under their contemplation, will disdain to assume the part of satirists and de-

---

[445]Burke owned a copy of Mallet's edition of Bolingbroke's *Works* (see *Reflections*, p. [31]) as well as the Rev. Charles Bulkley's *Notes on the Philosophical Writings of Lord Bolingbroke* (London, 1755): *LC*, pp. 3, 6. Nevertheless, Burke's undoubted Whig credentials meant that he was truthful in disavowing Bolingbroke, the loose cannon of early eighteenth-century Tory-Jacobitism. Burke was careful here to distance himself from a political enemy.

[446]'Among many reasons which determine me to prefer monarchy to every other form of government, this is a principal one. When monarchy is the essential form, it may be more easily and more usefully tempered with aristocracy or democracy, or both, than either of them, when they are the essential forms, can be tempered with monarchy. It seems to me, that the introduction of a real permanent monarchical power, or any thing more than the pageantry of it, into either of these, must destroy them and extinguish them, as a great light extinguishes a less. Whereas it may easily be shewn, and the true form of our government will demonstrate, without seeking any other example, that very considerable aristocratical and democratical powers may be grafted on a monarchical stock, without diminishing the lustre, or restraining the power and authority of the prince, enough to alter in any degree the essential form': Bolingbroke, *The Idea of a Patriot King*, in Mallet (ed.), *Works Of ... Bolingbroke*, III, pp. 51-2.

claimers. They will judge of human institutions as they do of human characters. They will sort out the good from the evil, which is mixed in mortal institutions as it is in mortal men.

Your government in France, though usually, and I think justly, reputed the best of the unqualified [188] or ill-qualified monarchies, was still full of abuses. These abuses accumulated in a length of time, as they must accumulate in every monarchy not under the constant inspection of a popular representative. I am no stranger to the faults and defects of the subverted government of France; and I think I am not inclined by nature or policy to make a panegyric upon any thing which is a just and natural object of censure. But the question is not now of the vices of that monarchy, but of its existence. Is it then true, that the French government was such as to be incapable or undeserving of reform; so that it was of absolute necessity the whole fabric should be at once pulled down, and the area cleared for the erection of a theoretic experimental edifice in its place? All France was of a different opinion in the beginning of the year 1789. The instructions to the representatives to the states-general, from every district in that kingdom, were filled with projects for the reformation of that government, without the remotest suggestion of a design to destroy it.[447] Had such a design been then even insinuated, I believe there would have been but one voice, and that voice for rejecting it with scorn and horror. Men have been sometimes led by degrees, sometimes hurried into things, the whole of which, if they could have seen together, they never would have permitted the most remote approach. When those instructions were given, there was no question but that abuses existed, and that they demanded a reform; nor is there now. In the interval between the instructions and the revolution, things changed their shape; and in consequence of that change, the true question at present is, [189] Whether those who would have reformed, or those who have destroyed, are in the right?[448]

[447]The *cahiers de doléances* were drawn up by the electoral assemblies which chose the deputies of the Estates-General. Burke claimed knowledge of the 'first instructions to the representatives of the several orders', and to have read 'the general instructions given to the Representatives; and the proceedings of the National Assembly': Burke, *Correspondence*, VI, pp. 21, 79, 105. This source may have been [Louis Marie Prudhomme and F. S. Laurent de Mezières], *Résumé général, ou Extrait des Cahiers de Pouvoirs, Instructions, Demandes et Doléances* (3 vols., [Paris], 1789), or [Pierre-Samuel Dupont de Nemours], *Tableau comparatif des demandes contenues dans les Cahiers des Trois Ordres* ([Paris], 1789). For the *cahiers*, see Bibliography, D viii.

[448]Dupont de Nemours, *Tableau comparatif*, p. 9, recorded widespread support (even from Paris) for the opening assertions: 'Article premier. 1. Déclarer que la France est un Gouvernement monarchique tempéré par les loix ... 2. Que le Roi est seul revêtu du pouvoir législatif & exécutif, limité néamoins par les loix constitutionelles & fon-

To hear some men speak of the late monarchy of France, you would imagine that they were talking of Persia bleeding under the ferocious sword of Tæhmas Kouli Khân;[449] or at least describing the barbarous anarchic despotism of Turkey,[450] where the finest countries in the most genial climates in the world are wasted by peace more than any countries have been worried by war; where arts are unknown, where manufactures languish, where science is extinguished, where agriculture decays, where the human race itself melts away and perishes under the eye of the observer. Was this the case of France? I have no way of determining the question but by a reference to facts. Facts do not support this resemblance. Along with much evil, there is some good in monarchy itself; and some corrective to its evil, from religion, from laws, from manners, from opinions, the French monarchy must have received; which rendered it (though by no means a free, and therefore by no means a good constitution) a despotism rather in appearance than in reality.[451]

Among the standards upon which the effects of government on any country are to be estimated, I must consider the state of its population as not the least certain. No country in which population flourishes, and is in progressive improvement, can be under a *very* mischievous government. About sixty

damentales du Royaume. Art. II. Que la personne du Roi est toujours sacrée & inviolable. Art. III. Que la Couronne est héréditaire ...': Burke had some grounds for reading the *cahiers* as plans for Whiggish reform. Although Tocqueville, with the benefit of hindsight, read them as unwitting plans for revolution (*Old Regime*, p. 199) Arthur Young, who also studied the *cahiers*, agreed with Burke in interpreting them as calls for English-style liberties and an English monarchy: 'The assemblies that drew them up, most certainly never demanded, in express terms, the abolition of the monarchy, or the transfer of all the regal authority to the deputies', but, by implication, the assembly 'is plainly meant to be a body *solely* possessing the legislative authority': *Travels in France*, pp. 553–4.

[449]Nadir Shah, Shah of Persia from 1736 to his assassination in 1747, made his way to the throne from humble origins and then embarked on a bloody campaign of conquest and massacre in Afghanistan and India, made possible by internal repression, which attracted horrified attention in Western Europe. See [Samuel Johnson, ed. and trans.], *The History of Tahmas Kuli Khan, Shah, or Sophi of Persia* (London, 1740; reprinted by the Samuel Johnson Society of Southern California, n.p., 1993, ed. O M Brack, Jr.), and Laurence Lockhart, *Nadir Shah* (London, 1938).

[450]For Turkey as the defining example of arbitrary power, see Montesquieu, *The Spirit of the Laws*, book III, ch. 9. Burke owned a copy of the second edition of Demetrius [Cantemir], *The History of the Growth and Decay of the Othman Empire*, trans. Nicholas Tindal (London, 1756): *LC*, p. 9; LC MS, fo. 35.

[451]As such passages show, Burke, as a Foxite Whig, had no enthusiasm for monarchy in principle and considerable reservations in practice.

years ago, the Intendants of the generalities[452] of France made, with other matters, a report of the population of their several districts.[453] I have [190] not the
books, which are very voluminous, by me, nor do I know where to procure
them (I am obliged to speak by memory, and therefore the less positively) but I
think the population of France was by them, even at that period, estimated at
twenty-two millions of souls. At the end of the last century it had been generally calculated at eighteen. On either of these estimations France was not ill-
peopled. Mr. Necker, who is an authority for his own time at least equal to the
Intendants for theirs, reckons, and upon apparently sure principles, the people of France, in the year 1780, at twenty-four millions six hundred and sev-
enty thousand.[454] But was this the probable ultimate term under the old establishment? Dr. Price is of opinion, that the growth of population in France was
by no means at its *acmé* in that year. I certainly defer to Dr. Price's authority a
good deal more in these speculations, than I do in his general politics. This
gentleman, taking ground on Mr. Necker's data, is very confident, that since
the period of that minister's calculation, the French population has encreased
rapidly; so rapidly that in the year 1789 he will not consent to rate the people
of that kingdom at a lower number than thirty millions. After abating much
(and much I think ought to be abated) from the sanguine calculation of Dr.
Price, I have no doubt that the population of France did encrease considerably
during this later period: but supposing that it encreased to nothing more than
will be sufficient to compleat the 24,670,000 to 25 millions, still a population
of 25 millions, and that [191] in an increasing progress, on a space of about
twenty-seven thousand square leagues, is immense. It is, for instance, a good
deal more than the proportionable population of this island, or even than that
of England, the best-peopled part of the united kingdom.[455]

---

[452]For administrative purposes, France under the monarchy had been divided into
units called *généralités*, each governed by a royal official, the *intendant*.

[453]This was evidently the census ordered in 1730 and completed in 1745 by *con-
trôleur général* Orry. It actually estimated a population of 17,017,737: Jacques Dupâquier (ed.), *Histoire de la population française. 2-De la Renaissance à 1789* (Paris,
1988), pp. 38, 56.

[454]See Jacques Necker, *De l'Administration des Finances de la France* (3 vols., [Par-
is], 1784), I, p. 221. Although translated by T. Mortimer (3 vols., London, 1785),
Burke used the French edition, which he owned: LC MS, fo. 2.

[455]Arthur Young estimated France's population as even higher, at 26,363,074; 'If
England were equally well peopled, there should be upon 46,915,933 acres rather
more than 9,000,000 souls. And for our two islands, to equal France in this respect,
there should be in them 19,867,117 souls; instead of which there are not more than
15,000,000.' Price had estimated the French population as over 30,000,000: Young,
*Travels in France*, pp. 464–75.

It is not universally true, that France is a fertile country. Considerable tracts of it are barren, and labour under other natural disadvantages. In the portions of that territory, where things are more favourable, as far as I am able to discover, the numbers of the people correspond to the indulgence of nature.[456] The Generality of Lisle (this I admit is the strongest example) upon an extent of 404½ leagues, about ten years ago, contained 734,600 souls, which is 1772 inhabitants to each square league.[457] The middle term for the rest of France is about 900 inhabitants to the same admeasurement.

I do not attribute this population to the deposed government; because I do not like to compliment the contrivances of men, with what is due in a great degree to the bounty of Providence. But that decried government could not have obstructed, most probably it favoured, the operation of those causes (whatever they were) whether of nature in the soil, or in habits of industry among the people, which has produced so large a number of the species throughout that whole kingdom, and exhibited in some particular places such [192] prodigies of population. I never will suppose that fabrick of a state to be the worst of all political institutions, which, by experience, is found to contain a principle favourable (however latent it may be) to the encrease of mankind.[458]

The wealth of a country is another, and no contemptible standard, by which we may judge whether, on the whole, a government be protecting or destructive. France far exceeds England in the multitude of her people; but I apprehend that her comparative wealth is much inferior to ours; that it is not so equal in the distribution, nor so ready in the circulation. I believe the difference in the form of the two governments to be amongst the causes of this advantage on the side of England. I speak of England, not of the whole British dominions; which, if compared with those of France, will, in some degree, weaken the comparative rate of wealth upon our side. But that wealth, which will not endure a comparison with the riches of England, may constitute a very respectable degree of opulence. Mr. Necker's book published in 1785,[459] contains an accurate and interesting collection of facts relative to publick œconomy and to political arithmetic; and his speculations on the subject are generally wise

[456]De l'Administration des Finances de la France, par Mons. Neckar, vol. i. p. 288. [B]

[457]Burke quoted Necker, De l'administration des finances, I, p. 253.

[458]The argument that an increasing population was a sign of good government was a commonplace, and made the only undisputed criterion in Jean-Jacques Rousseau, The Social Contract, Book III, chapter ix.

[459]De l'Administration des Finances de la France, par M. Neckar. [B] '1785' sc. '1784'.

and liberal. In that work he gives an idea of the state of France, very remote from the portrait of a country whose government was a perfect grievance, an absolute evil, admitting no cure but through the violent and uncertain remedy of a total revolution. [193] He affirms, that from the year 1726 to the year 1784, there was coined at the mint of France, in the species of gold and silver, to the amount of about one hundred millions of pounds sterling.[460]

It is impossible that Mr. Necker should be mistaken in the amount of the bullion which has been coined in the mint. It is a matter of official record. The reasonings of this able financier, concerning the quantity of gold and silver which remained for circulation, when he wrote in 1785, that is about four years before the deposition and imprisonment of the French King, are not of equal certainty; but they are laid on grounds so apparently solid, that it is not easy to refuse a considerable degree of assent to his calculation. He calculates the *numeraire*, or what we call *specie*, then actually existing in France, at about eighty-eight millions of the same English money. A great accumulation of wealth for one country, large as that country is! Mr. Necker was so far from considering this influx of wealth as likely to cease, when he wrote in 1785, that he presumes upon a future annual increase of two per cent. upon the money brought into France during the periods from which he computed.[461]

Some adequate cause must have originally introduced all the money coined at its mint into that kingdom; and some cause as operative must have kept at home, or returned into its bosom, such a vast flood of treasure as Mr. Necker calculates to remain for domestic circulation. Suppose any reasonable deductions from M. Necker's computation; [194] the remainder must still amount to an immense sum. Causes thus powerful to acquire and to retain, cannot be found in discouraged industry, insecure property, and a positively destructive government. Indeed, when I consider the face of the kingdom of France; the multitude and opulence of her cities; the useful magnificence of her spacious high roads and bridges; the opportunity of her artificial canals and navigations opening the conveniences of maritime communication through a solid continent of so immense an extent; when I turn my eyes to the stupendous works of her ports and harbours, and to her whole naval apparatus, whether for war or trade; when I bring before my view the number of her fortifications, constructed with so bold and masterly a skill, and made and maintained at so prodigious a charge, presenting an armed front and impenetrable barrier to her enemies upon every side; when I recollect how very small

[460]Vol. iii. chap. 8. and chap. 9. [B] Necker's estimate from 1726 to 1 January 1784 was 2,500 million *livres*: *De l'administration des finances*, III, p. 59.
[461]Ibid., III, p. 68.

a part of that extensive region is without cultivation, and to what complete perfection the culture of many of the best productions of the earth have been brought in France;[462] when I reflect on the excellence of her manufactures and fabrics, second to none but ours, and in some particulars not second; when I contemplate the grand foundations of charity, public and private; when I survey the state of all the arts that beautify and polish life; when I reckon the men she has bred for extending her fame in war, her able statesmen, the multitude of her profound lawyers and theologians, her philosophers, her critics, her historians and antiquaries, her poets, and her orators [195] sacred and profane, I behold in all this something which awes and commands the imagination, which checks the mind on the brink of precipitate and indiscriminate censure, and which demands, that we should very seriously examine, what and how great are the latent vices that could authorise us at once to level so specious a fabric with the ground. I do not recognize, in this view of things, the despotism of Turkey. Nor do I discern the character of a government that has been, on the whole, so oppressive, or so corrupt, or so negligent, as to be utterly unfit *for all reformation*. I must think such a government well deserved to have its excellencies heightened; its faults corrected; and its capacities improved into a British constitution.[463]

Whoever has examined into the proceedings of that deposed government for several years back, cannot fail to have observed, amidst the inconstancy and fluctuation natural to courts, an earnest endeavour towards the prosperity and improvement of the country; he must admit, that it had long been employed, in some instances, wholly to remove, in many considerably to correct, the abusive practices and usages that had prevailed in the state; and that even the unlimited power of the sovereign over the persons of his subjects, inconsistent, as undoubtedly it was, with law and liberty, had yet been every day growing more mitigated in the exercise. So far from refusing itself to reformation, that government was open, with a censurable degree of facility, to all sorts of projects and projectors on the subject.[464] Rather too much counte-

---

[462]Arthur Young judged that 'The proportion of poor land in England, to the total of the Kingdom, is greater than the similar proportion in France', but estimated English grain productivity as greater than that of France in a proportion of 28 to 18: *Travels in France*, pp. 291, 342–3.

[463]As a Whig, Burke subscribed to the view that commerce and manufacture flourished best under a checked and balanced government. He differed from the English enthusiasts for the French Revolution in believing that the France of the *ancien régime* had possessed at least the foundations of such a constitution.

[464]In the reign of Louis XVI these reforms, often resisted by the *parlements*, included: free trade in grain (1774); the end of the *corvée*, forced labour on major roads

nance was given to the spirit of innovation, [196] which soon was turned against those who fostered it, and ended in their ruin. It is but cold, and no very flattering justice to that fallen monarchy, to say, that, for many years, it trespassed more by levity and want of judgment in several of its schemes, than from any defect in diligence or in public spirit. To compare the government of France for the last fifteen or sixteen years with wise and well-constituted establishments, during that, or during any period, is not to act with fairness. But if in point of prodigality in the expenditure of money, or in point of rigour in the exercise of power, it be compared with any of the former reigns, I believe candid judges will give little credit to the good intentions of those who dwell perpetually on the donations to favourites, or on the expences of the court, or on the horrors of the Bastile in the reign of Louis the XVIth.[465]

Whether the system, if it deserves such a name, now built on the ruins of that antient monarchy, will be able to give a better account of the population and wealth of the country, which it has taken under its care, is a matter very doubtful. Instead of improving by the change, I apprehend that a long series of years must be told before it can recover in any degree the effects of this philosophic revolution, and before the nation can be replaced on its former footing.[466] If Dr. Price should think fit, a few years hence, to favour us with an estimate of the population of France, he will hardly be able to make up his tale of thirty millions of souls,[467] as computed in 1789, or the assembly's computation of twenty-six millions in that year; or even [197] Mr. Necker's twenty-five millions in 1780. I hear that there are considerable emigrations from France;[468]

---

(1776); the reduction of the use of *lettres de cachet* (1784); the abolition of censorship of the post, freedom of worship for Protestants, and the institution of provincial assemblies (1787); the abolition of judicial torture and provision for defence of the accused (1788); the wide franchise decreed for elections to the Estates-General (January 1789): Fierro and Liébert, p. 688.

[465]Burke later added a footnote: 'The world is obliged to Mr. de Calonne for the pains he has taken to refute the scandalous exaggerations relative to some of the royal expenses, and to detect the fallacious account given of pensions, for the wicked purpose of provoking the populace to all sorts of crimes.' For Calonne, see Biographical Guide.

[466]Demographers have argued that Burke was correct: the Revolution, despite its initial emancipations, had a profoundly depressing effect on French economic and demographic development in the nineteenth century by comparison with England, Germany and Russia, with results evident in 1914. See Dupâquier, *Histoire de la population française 3—De 1789 à 1914* (Paris, 1988), pp. 3, 63–115.

[467]In the fourth edition of his *Discourse*, Price added a 'Postscript' to p. 4 of the Appendix in which he repeated his estimate that France's population in 1780 was thirty million.

[468]Of the 145,000 *émigrés* listed in 1800, 20 per cent had left between 1789 and 1792. The real total has been estimated at 200,000: Fierro and Liébert, p. 690. See

and that many quitting that voluptuous climate, and that seductive *Circean* liberty,[469] have taken refuge in the frozen regions, and under the British despotism, of Canada.

In the present disappearance of coin, no person could think it the same country, in which the present minister of the finances has been able to discover fourscore millions sterling in specie. From its general aspect one would conclude that it had been for some time past under the special direction of the learned academicians of Laputa and Balnibarbi.[470] Already the population of Paris has so declined, that Mr. Necker stated to the national assembly the provision to be made for its subsistence at a fifth less than what had formerly been found requisite.[471] It is said (and I have never heard it contradicted) that an hundred thousand people are out of employment in that city, though it is

---

Dupâquier (ed.), *Histoire de la population française*, III, p. 76; Donald Greer, *The Incidence of the Emigration during the French Revolution* (Cambridge, Mass., 1951) and Jean Vidalenc, *Les émigrés français, 1789–1825* (Caen, 1963).

[469]Cf. Homer, *Odyssey*, Book X. Circe was a witch who cast a spell over Odysseus and his companions, compelling them to remain on her island for a year.

[470]See Gulliver's Travels for the idea of countries governed by philosophers. [B] For the islands of Laputa and Balnibarbi see [Jonathan Swift], *Travels into several Remote Nations of the World ... By Lemuel Gulliver* (2 vols., London, 1726), II, part III. Swift stressed the disastrous effects in daily life of a preoccupation with abstract speculation. Laputa's houses were 'very ill built' because of 'the Contempt they bear to practical Geometry; which they despise as Vulgar and Mechanick, those Instructions they give being too refined for the Intellectuals of their Workmen, which occasions perpetual mistakes. And although they are dextrous enough upon a Piece of Paper in the management of the Rule, the Pencil and the Divider, yet in the common Actions and behaviour of Life, I have not seen a more clumsy, awkward, and unhandy People, nor so slow and perplexed in their Conceptions upon all other Subjects, except those of Mathematicks and Musick.' In Lagado, capital of Balnibarbi, the houses were 'very strangely Built, and most of them out of Repair. The People in the Streets walked fast, looked wild, their Eyes fixed, and were generally in Rags ... I never knew a Soil so unhappily cultivated, Houses so ill contrived and so ruinous, or a People whose Countenances and Habit expressed so much Misery and Want.' This was the effect of 'an Academy of PROJECTORS in *Lagado*', copied in every town in the kingdom. 'The only Inconvenience is, that none of these Projects are yet brought to Perfection, and in the mean time the whole Country lies miserably wast, the Houses in Ruins, and the People without Food or Cloths. By all which, instead of being discouraged, they are fifty times more violently bent upon prosecuting their Schemes, driven equally on by Hope and Despair' (ibid., pp. 26–7, 52–3, 58–9). Scepticism about abstract learning long preceded the reaction against Jacobinism.

[471]Burke later added a footnote: 'Mr. de Calonne states the falling off of the population of Paris as far more considerable; and it may be so, since the period of Mr. Necker's calculation.' The destruction of the Paris archives in the Commune of 1871 makes this claim impossible to verify.

become the seat of the imprisoned court and national assembly. Nothing, I am credibly informed, can exceed the shocking and disgusting spectacle of mendicancy displayed in that capital. Indeed, the votes of the national assembly leave no doubt of the fact. They have lately appointed a standing committee of mendicancy.[472] They are contriving at once a vigorous police on this subject, and, for the first time, the imposition of a tax to maintain the poor, for whose present relief great sums appear on the face of the public accounts of the [198] year.[473] In the mean time, the leaders of the legislative clubs and cof-

[472]It reported to the National Assembly for the first time on 12 June 1790: Roberts (ed.), *Documents*, p. 238. The *comité de mendacité* (1790–1) encouraged the view that France's population was too great in relation to its means of support. Jean-Baptiste Carrier inferred that 'pour rendre la république plus heureuse, il fallait supprimer au moins la moitié de ses habitants'; Jean-Marie Collot d'Herbois considered that 'la transpiration politique devait être assez abondante pour ne s'arrêter qu'après la destruction de 12 à 15 millions de Français': Dupâquier (ed.), *Histoire de la population française*, III (Paris, 1988), p. 64. Burke was evidently not aware of this genocidal aspect of revolutionary rationalism.

[473]Travaux de charité pour subvenir au

| | Liv. | | £ | s. | d. |
|---|---|---|---|---|---|
| manque de travail à Paris et dans les provinces | 3,866,920 | St$^g$ | 161,121 | 13 | 4 |
| Destruction de vagabondage et de la mendicité | 1,671,417 | – | 69,642 | 7 | 6 |
| Primes pour l'importation de grains | 5,671,907 | – | 236,329 | 9 | 2 |
| Liv. | 11,210,244 | St$^g$ | 467,093 | 10 | 0 |

As I am not quite satisfied with the nature and extent of the annexed article in the public accounts, I do not insert it in the above reference; but if it be understood of the purchase of provision for the poor, it is immense indeed, and swells the total to a formidable bulk.

| | Liv. | | £ | s. | d. |
|---|---|---|---|---|---|
| Dépenses relatives aux subsistances, deduction fait des récouvrements qui ont eu lieu | 39,871,790 | – | 1,661,324 | 11 | 8 |
| Total    –    Liv. | 51,082,034 | St$^g$ | 2,128,418 | 1 | 8 |

[B] Burke subsequently added: 'When I sent this book to the press I entertained some doubt concerning the nature and extent of the last article in the above accounts, which is only under a general head, without any detail. Since then I have seen M. de Calonne's work. I must think it a great loss to me that I had not that advantage earlier. M. de Calonne thinks this article to be on account of general subsistence: but as he is not able to comprehend how so great a loss as upwards of £.1,661,000 sterling could be sustained on the difference between the price and the sale of grain, he seems to attribute this enormous head of charge to secret expenses of the revolution. I cannot say any

fee-houses are intoxicated with admiration at their own wisdom and ability. They speak with the most sovereign contempt of the rest of the world. They tell the people, to comfort them in the rags with which they have cloathed them, that they are a nation of philosophers; and, sometimes, by all the arts of quackish parade, by shew, tumult, and bustle, sometimes by the alarms of plots and invasions, they attempt to drown the cries of indigence, and to divert the eyes of the observer from the ruin and wretchedness of the state.[474] A brave people will certainly prefer liberty, accompanied with a virtuous poverty, to a depraved and wealthy servitude. But before the price of comfort and opulence is paid, one ought to be pretty sure, it is real liberty which is purchased, and that she is to be purchased at no other price. I shall always, however, consider that liberty as very equivocal in her appearance, which has not wisdom and justice for her companions; and does not lead prosperity and plenty in her train. [199]

---

thing positively on that subject. The reader is capable of judging, by the aggregate of these immense charges, on the state and condition of France; and the system of publick oeconomy adopted in that nation. These articles of account produced no enquiry or discussion in the National Assembly.' This work was Charles-Alexandre de Calonne, *De l'état de la France, présent & à venir* (London and Paris, October 1790); see *Reflections*, p. [268]. Burke owned a copy: LC MS, fo. 4.

[474]On 24 July 1789, Arthur Young reported a rumour at Colmar that 'the Queen had a plot, nearly on the point of execution, to blow up the National Assembly by a mine, and to march the army instantly to massacre all Paris ... Thus it is in revolutions, one rascal writes, and a hundred thousand fools believe.' At Dijon on 31 July, 'The current report at present, to which all possible credit is given, is, that the Queen has been convicted of a plot to poison the King and Monsieur, and give the regency to the count d'Artois; to set fire to Paris, and blow up the *Palais Royale* by a mine!' On 10 January 1790, some 'great democrats' at Paris told him of 'jealousies ... at Versailles, where some plots (they added) are, without doubt, hatching at this moment, which have the King's person for their object ... I remarked, in all these conversations, that the belief of plots, among the disgusted party, for setting the King at liberty, is general; they seem almost persuaded, that the revolution will not be absolutely finished before some such attempts are made'. On 13 January, 'The report of plots, to carry off the King, is in the mouth of every one; and it is said, these movements of the people, as well as those at Versailles, are not what they appear to be, mere mobs, but instigated by the aristocrats; and if permitted to rise to such a height as to entangle the Paris militia, will prove the part only of a conspiracy against the new government ... Dine at the Palais Royal, with a select party; politicians they must be, if they are Frenchmen. The question was discussed, Are the plots and conspiracies of which we hear so much at present, real, or are they invented by the leaders of the revolution, to keep up the spirits of the militia, in order to enable themselves to secure the government on its new foundation irreversibly?': *Travels in France*, pp. 143, 151, 268, 271-2; Fierro and Liébert, pp. 690-2.

The advocates for this revolution, not satisfied with exaggerating the vices of their antient government, strike at the fame of their country itself, by painting almost all that could have attracted the attention of strangers, I mean their nobility and their clergy, as objects of horror. If this were only a libel, there had not been much in it. But it has practical consequences. Had your nobility and gentry, who formed the great body of your landed men, and the whole of your military officers, resembled those of Germany, at the period[475] when the Hanse-towns were necessitated to confederate against the nobles in defence of their property—had they been like the *Orsini* and *Vitelli* in Italy,[476] who used to sally from their fortified dens to rob the trader and traveller— had they been such as the *Mamalukes* in Egypt, or the *Nayres* on the coast of Malabar,[477] I do admit, that too critical an enquiry might not be adviseable into the means of freeing the world from such a nuisance. The statues of Equity and Mercy might be veiled for a moment. The tenderest minds, confounded with the dreadful exigence in which morality submits to the suspension of its own rules in favour of its own principles, might turn aside whilst fraud and violence were accomplishing the destruction of a pretended nobility which disgraced whilst it persecuted human nature. The persons most abhorrent from blood, and treason, and arbitrary confiscation, might remain silent spectators of this civil war between the vices.

But did the privileged nobility who met under the king's precept at Versailles, in 1789, or their [200] constituents, deserve to be looked on as the *Nayres* or *Mamalukes* of this age, or as the *Orsini* and *Vitelli* of ancient times? If I had then asked the question, I should have passed for a madman. What have they since done that they were to be driven into exile, that their persons should be hunted about, mangled, and tortured, their families dispersed, their houses laid in ashes, that their order should be abolished, and the memory of it, if possible, extinguished, by ordaining them to change the very names by which they were usually known?[478] Read their instructions to their representa-

[475]I.e. after the death of Frederick II in 1250.

[476]The Vitelli were important condottieri in the late fifteenth century; the Orsini were a Roman princely family whose conflict with the Colonna broke out again in 1484.

[477]The Nairs were a military caste which once dominated Malabar; they had been subdued in 1763 by Hyder Ali. The Mamalukes were a warrior class who ruled in Egypt and Syria between the thirteenth and sixteenth centuries.

[478]The National Assembly voted on 20 June 1790 'que la noblesse héréditaire est pour toujours abolie'; that titles of nobility were not to be used; that all honorific forms of address, liveries, and armorial bearings, including coats of arms painted on the sides of carriages, were forbidden: *Le Moniteur*, 21 June 1790; Roberts (ed.), *Documents*, p. 240.

tives. They breathe the spirit of liberty as warmly, and they recommend ref-ormation as strongly, as any other order.[479] Their privileges relative to contri-bution were voluntarily surrendered;[480] as the king, from the beginning, sur-rendered all pretence to a right of taxation. Upon a free constitution there was but one opinion in France. The absolute monarchy was at an end. It breathed its last, without a groan, without struggle, without convulsion. All the strug-gle, all the dissension arose afterwards upon the preference of a despotic de-mocracy to a government of reciprocal controul. The triumph of the victori-ous party was over the principles of a British constitution.[481]

I have observed the affectation, which, for many years past, has prevailed in Paris even to a degree perfectly childish, of idolizing the memory of your Henry the Fourth.[482] If any thing could put one out of humour with that orna-ment to the kingly character, it would be this overdone style of insidious panegyric. The persons who have worked this engine the most busily, are those who have [201] ended their panegyrics in dethroning his successor and descendant; a man, as good-natured at the least, as Henry the Fourth; alto-gether as fond of his people; and who has done infinitely more to correct the

[479]Burke's account of the *cahiers de doléances* of the Second Estate is confirmed by the quantifying survey in Chaussinand-Nogaret, *French nobility*, pp. 130–65. They show substantial support for voting by head rather than by order in the Estates-General; were critical of 'Despotism, favouritism, intrigue, irresponsibility, waste'; and focused on 'ministerial and bureaucratic arbitrariness, restrictions on individual liberty, and bad management of public services. And the call for change centered on new values: democratisation of government, individualism, and rationalisation of the state.' There was similarly little support for the preservation of noble privileges like the inequality of taxation or the sole right to bear arms, and substantial support for the ennobling of merit: ibid., pp. 140, 150–6.

[480]In the National Assembly on the night of 4 August 1789.

[481]The British constitution had been proposed as a model by Lally-Tollendal, Maury, Mounier and others. The question came to turn on whether the new consti-tution would provide for a legislature with one or two chambers. The bicameralists were decisively defeated in a vote of the National Assembly on 10 September 1789.

[482]Henri IV (1553–1610). Burke owned a copy of H. C. Davila, *The History of the Civil Wars of France* ([London], 1678) (*LC*, p. 10; LC MS, fo. 29) and took a more balanced view of a monarch who still enjoyed wide symbolic popularity, even during the Revolution. This edition of Davila contained a preface by the licenser, Sir Roger L'Estrange, which explained how Charles I while at Oxford had commanded that that translation be continued and finished, and 'read it there, with such eager-ness, that no Diligence could Write it out faire, so fast as he daily called for it; wish-ing he had had it some years sooner, out of a Beliefe, that being forewarned thereby, He might have prevented many of those Mischiefs we then groaned under; and which the Grand Contrivers of them, had drawn from this Original, as Spiders do Poison from the most wholsome Plants.'

antient vices of the state than that great monarch did, or we are sure he ever meant to do. Well it is for his panegyrists that they have not him to deal with. For Henry of Navarre was a resolute, active, and politic prince. He possessed indeed great humanity and mildness; but an humanity and mildness that never stood in the way of his interests. He never sought to be loved without putting himself first in a condition to be feared. He used soft language with determined conduct. He asserted and maintained his authority in the gross, and distributed his acts of concession only in the detail. He spent the income of his prerogatives nobly; but he took care not to break in upon the capital; never abandoning for a moment any of the claims, which he made under the fundamental laws, nor sparing to shed the blood of those who opposed him, often in the field, sometimes upon the scaffold.[483] Because he knew how to make his virtues respected by the ungrateful, he has merited the praises of those whom, if they had lived in his time, he would have shut up in the Bastile, and brought to punishment along with the regicides whom he hanged after he had famished Paris into a surrender.[484]

If these panegyrists are in earnest in their admiration of Henry the Fourth, they must remember, that they cannot think more highly of him, than he did of the noblesse of France; whose virtue, honour, courage, patriotism, and loyalty were his constant theme. [202]

But the nobility of France are degenerated since the days of Henry the Fourth.—This is possible. But it is more than I can believe to be true in any great degree. I do not pretend to know France as correctly as some others; but I have endeavoured through my whole life to make myself acquainted with human nature; otherwise I should be unfit to take even my humble part in the service of mankind. In that study I could not pass by a vast portion of our nature, as it appeared modified in a country but twenty-four miles from the shore of this island. On my best observation, compared with my best enquiries, I found your nobility for the greater part composed of men of an high spirit, and of a delicate sense of honour, both with regard to themselves individually and with regard to their whole corps, over whom they kept, beyond what is common in other countries, a censorial eye. They were tolerably well-bred; very officious, humane, and hospitable; in their conversation frank and open; with a good military tone; and reasonably tinctured with literature, par-

[483]Charles de Gontaut, duc de Biron (1562–1602) fought for Henri IV against the League, and subsequently served the king as a diplomat. He was executed for treason.

[484]This passage produced an exchange between Burke and the translator of the *Reflections*, Pierre-Gaëton Dupont (1762–1817), who challenged its harshness: Burke, *Correspondence*, VI, pp. 144–9.

ticularly of the authors in their own language. Many had pretensions far above this description. I speak of those who were generally met with.[485]

As to their behaviour to the inferior classes, they appeared to me to comport themselves towards them with good-nature, and with something more nearly approaching to familiarity, than is generally practised with us in the intercourse between the higher and lower ranks of life. To strike any person, even in the most abject condition, was a thing in a manner unknown, and would be highly disgraceful. Instances of other ill-treatment of [203] the humble part of the community were rare; and as to attacks made upon the property or the personal liberty of the commons, I never heard of any whatsoever from *them*; nor, whilst the laws were in vigour under the antient government, would such tyranny in subjects have been permitted. As men of landed estates, I had no fault to find with their conduct, though much to reprehend, and much to wish changed, in many of the old tenures. Where the letting of their land was by rent, I could not discover that their agreements with their farmers were oppressive; nor when they were in partnership with the farmer,[486] as often was the case, have I heard that they had taken the lion's share. The proportions seemed not inequitable. There might be exceptions; but certainly they were exceptions only. I have no reason to believe that in these respects the landed noblesse of France were worse than the landed gentry of this country; certainly in no respect more vexatious than the landholders, not noble, of their own nation. In cities the nobility had no manner of power; in the country very little. You know, Sir, that much of the civil government, and the police in the most essential parts, was not in the hands of that nobility which presents itself first to our consideration. The revenue, the system and collection of which were the most grievous parts of the French government, was not administered by the men of the sword; nor were they answerable for the vices of its principle, or the vexations, where any such existed, in its management.

Denying, as I am well warranted to do, that the nobility had any considerable share in the oppression [204] of the people, in cases in which real oppression existed, I am ready to admit that they were not without considerable faults and errors. A foolish imitation of the worst part of the manners of England, which impaired their natural character without substituting in its place what perhaps they meant, has certainly rendered them worse than formerly

---

[485]Burke's subjective assessment is not contradicted by modern works listed in the Bibliography, D iii.

[486]The system was known as *métayage*; the farmer was the *métayer*. Arthur Young was much more critical of this system than Burke.

they were. Habitual dissoluteness of manners continued beyond the pardonable period of life, was more common amongst them than it is with us; and it
reigned with the less hope of remedy, though possibly with something of less
mischief, by being covered with more exterior decorum. They countenanced
too much that licentious philosophy which has helped to bring on their ruin.
There was another error amongst them more fatal. Those of the commons,
who approached to or exceeded many of the nobility in point of wealth, were
not fully admitted to the rank and estimation which wealth, in reason and
good policy, ought to bestow in every country; though I think not equally
with that of other nobility. The two kinds of aristocracy were too punctili-
ously kept asunder; less so, however, than in Germany and some other nations. This separation, as I have already taken the liberty of suggesting to you,
I conceive to be one principal cause of the destruction of the old nobility. The
military, particularly, was too exclusively reserved for men of family.[487] But
after all, this was an error of opinion, which a conflicting opinion would have
rectified. A permanent assembly, in which the commons had their share of
power, would soon abolish whatever was too invidious and insulting in these
distinctions; and even the faults in the morals of the nobility [205] would have
been probably corrected by the greater varieties of occupation and pursuit to
which a constitution by orders would have given rise.

All this violent cry against the nobility I take to be a mere work of art. To
be honoured and even privileged by the laws, opinions, and inveterate usages
of our country, growing out of the prejudice of ages, has nothing to provoke
horror and indignation in any man. Even to be too tenacious of those privileges, is not absolutely a crime. The strong struggle in every individual to preserve possession of what he has found to belong to him and to distinguish
him, is one of the securities against injustice and despotism implanted in our
nature. It operates as an instinct to secure property, and to preserve communities in a settled state. What is there to shock in this? Nobility is a graceful ornament to the civil order. It is the Corinthian capital of polished society. *Om-*

*interes-*
*ting.*

---

[487]It had become more exclusive after the decree of 1781 which restricted entry to
the ranks of officers to men able to demonstrate four generations of nobility. Nevertheless, the object of this measure was not to use aristocratic exclusiveness as a defence
of caste but to promote professional efficiency by ensuring the recruitment of candidates seriously committed to a military career rather than the newly ennobled, seeking
honorific office: Samuel F. Scott, *The Response of the Royal Army to the French
Revolution: The Role and Development of the Line Army, 1787–1793* (Oxford,
1978), pp. 29–31. Only 6.71% of a sample of noble *cahiers* included a demand that the
noble monopoly of commissioned ranks be maintained: Chaussinand-Nogaret, *French
nobility*, p. 151.

*nes boni nobilitati semper favemus,*[488] was the saying of a wise and good man. It is indeed one sign of a liberal and benevolent mind to incline to it with some sort of partial propensity. He feels no ennobling principle in his own heart who wishes to level all the artificial institutions which have been adopted for giving a body to opinion, and permanence to fugitive esteem. It is a sour, malignant, envious disposition, without taste for the reality or for any image or representation of virtue, that sees with joy the unmerited fall of what had long flourished in splendour and in honour. I do not like to see any thing destroyed; any void produced in society; any ruin on the face of the land. It was therefore with no disappointment or dissatisfaction, that my [206] enquiries and observation did not present to me any incorrigible vices in the noblesse of France, or any abuse which could not be removed by a reform very short of abolition. Your noblesse did not deserve punishment; but to degrade is to punish.

It was with the same satisfaction I found that the result of my enquiry concerning your clergy was not dissimilar.[489] It is no soothing news to my ears, that great bodies of men are incurably corrupt. It is not with much credulity I listen to any, when they speak evil of those whom they are going to plunder. I rather suspect that vices are feigned or exaggerated, when profit is looked for in their punishment. An enemy is a bad witness: a robber is a worse. Vices and abuses there were undoubtedly in that order, and must be. It was an old establishment, and not frequently revised. But I saw no crimes in the individuals that merited confiscation of their substance, nor those cruel insults and degradations, and that unnatural persecution which have been substituted in the place of meliorating regulation.[490]

[488]'All we who are good citizens always favour noble birth, both because it is good for the state that there should be noblemen, worthy of their ancestors, and because the memory of distinguished men and of those who have deserved well of the state lives in our hearts even after they are dead': Cicero, *Pro Sestio*, IX, 21.

[489]The attack on the French clergy in the wave of blasphemous and obscene writing that preceded the revolution consisted largely of *ad hominem* abuse and contained little abstract discussion of their collective role in society. For recent academic appraisals see Bibliography, D iv.

[490]Arthur Young reached a similar conclusion: 'The clergy in France have been supposed, by many persons in England, to merit their fate from their peculiar profligacy. But the idea is not accurate: that so large a body of men, possessed of very great revenues, should be free from vice, would be improbable, or rather impossible; but they preserved, what is not always preserved in England, an exterior decency of behaviour.—One did not find among them poachers or fox-hunters, who, having spent the morning in scampering after hounds, dedicate the evening to the bottle, and reel from inebriety to the pulpit. Such advertisements were never seen in France, as I have heard

If there had been any just cause for this new religious persecution, the atheistic libellers, who act as trumpeters to animate the populace to plunder, do not love any body so much as not to dwell with complacence on the vices of the existing clergy. This they have not done. They find themselves obliged to rake into the histories of former ages (which they have ransacked with a malignant and profligate industry) for every instance of oppression and persecution which has been made by that body or in its favour, in order to justify, upon very iniquitous, because very illogical principles of retaliation, [207] their own persecutions, and their own cruelties. After destroying all other genealogies and family distinctions, they invent a sort of pedigree of crimes. It is not very just to chastise men for the offences of their natural ancestors; but to take the fiction of ancestry in a corporate succession, as a ground for punishing men who have no relation to guilty acts, except in names and general descriptions, is a sort of refinement in injustice belonging to the philosophy of this enlightened age. The assembly punishes men, many, if not most, of whom abhor the violent conduct of ecclesiastics in former times as much as their present persecutors can do, and who would be as loud and as strong in the expression of that sense, if they were not well aware of the purposes for which all this declamation is employed.

Corporate bodies are immortal for the good of the members, but not for their punishment. Nations themselves are such corporations. As well might we in England think of waging inexpiable war upon all Frenchmen for the evils which they have brought upon us in the several periods of our mutual hostilities. You might, on your part, think yourselves justified in falling upon all Englishmen on account of the unparalleled calamities brought upon the people of France by the unjust invasions of our Henries and our Edwards. Indeed we should be mutually justified in this exterminatory war upon each other, full as much as you are in the unprovoked persecution of your present countrymen, on account of the conduct of men of the same name in other times.

We do not draw the moral lessons we might from history. On the contrary, without care it [208] may be used to vitiate our minds and to destroy our happiness. In history a great volume is unrolled for our instruction, drawing the materials of future wisdom from the past errors and infirmities of mankind. It may, in the perversion, serve for a magazine, furnishing offensive and defensive weapons for parties in church and state, and supplying the means of keeping alive, or reviving dissensions and animosities, and adding

---

of in England:—*Wanted a curacy in a good sporting country, where the duty is light, and the neighbourhood convivial*': Young, *Travels in France*, p. 543.

fuel to civil fury. History consists, for the greater part, of the miseries brought upon the world by pride, ambition, avarice, revenge, lust, sedition, hypocrisy, ungoverned zeal, and all the train of disorderly appetites, which shake the public with the same

—"troublous storms that toss
The private state, and render life unsweet."[491]

These vices are the *causes* of those storms. Religion, morals, laws, prerogatives, privileges, liberties, rights of men, are the *pretexts*. The pretexts are always found in some specious appearance of a real good. You would not secure men from tyranny and sedition, by rooting out of the mind the principles to which these fraudulent pretexts apply? If you did, you would root out every thing that is valuable in the human breast. As these are the pretexts, so the ordinary actors and instruments in great public evils are kings, priests, magistrates, senates, parliaments, national assemblies, judges, and captains. You would not cure the evil by resolving, that there should be no more monarchs, nor ministers of state, nor of the gospel; no interpreters of law; no general officers; no public councils. You might change [209] the names. The things in some shape must remain. A certain *quantum* of power must always exist in the community, in some hands, and under some appellation. Wise men will apply their remedies to vices, not to names; to the causes of evil which are permanent, not to the occasional organs by which they act, and the transitory modes in which they appear. Otherwise you will be wise historically, a fool in practice. Seldom have two ages the same fashion in their pretexts and the same modes of mischief. Wickedness is a little more inventive. Whilst you are discussing fashion, the fashion is gone by. The very same vice assumes a new body. The spirit transmigrates; and, far from losing its principle of life by the change of its appearance, it is renovated in its new organs with the fresh vigour of a juvenile activity. It walks abroad; it continues its ravages; whilst you are gibbeting the carcass, or demolishing the tomb. You are terrifying yourself with ghosts and apparitions, whilst your house is the haunt of robbers. It is thus with all those, who, attending only to the shell and husk of history, think they are waging war with intolerance, pride, and cruelty, whilst, under colour

---

[491][Edmund Spenser], *The Faerie Queene* (London, 1590), Book II, canto VII, xiv, p. 275 (free quotation): 'Long were to tell the troublous stormes, that tosse / The priuate state, and make the life vnsweet: / Who swelling sayles in Caspian sea doth crosse, / And in frayle wood on *Adrian* gulf doth fleet, / Doth not, I weene, so many euils meet. / Then *Mammon* wexing wroth, And why then, sayd, / Are mortall men so fond and vndiscreet, / So euill thing to seeke vnto their ayd, / And hauing not complaine, and hauing it vpbrayd?'

of abhorring the ill principles of antiquated parties, they are authorizing and feeding the same odious vices in different factions, and perhaps in worse.

Your citizens of Paris formerly had lent themselves as the ready instruments to slaughter the followers of Calvin, at the infamous massacre of St. Bartholomew.[492] What should we say to those who could think of retaliating on the Parisians of this day the abominations and horrors of that time? They are [210] indeed brought to abhor *that* massacre. Ferocious as they are, it is not difficult to make them dislike it; because the politicians and fashionable teachers have no interest in giving their passions exactly the same direction. Still however they find it their interest to keep the same savage dispositions alive. It was but the other day that they caused this very massacre to be acted on the stage for the diversion of the descendants of those who committed it.[493] In this tragic farce they produced the cardinal of Lorraine in his robes of function, ordering general slaughter.[494] Was this spectacle intended to make the Parisians abhor persecution, and loath the effusion of blood?—No, it was to teach them to persecute their own pastors; it was to excite them, by raising a disgust and horror of their clergy, to an alacrity in hunting down to destruction an order, which, if it ought to exist at all, ought to exist not only in safety, but in reverence. It was to stimulate their cannibal appetites[495] (which one

[492]About two thousand Protestants were massacred in Paris on the night of St. Bartholomew's day, 23–24 August 1572.

[493]*Charles IX ou l'école des rois*, a tragedy by Marie-Joseph Chénier (1764–1811), had been banned by the royal censor in 1788 but performed on 8 November 1789. Danton commented: 'Si *Figaro* a tué la noblesse, *Charles IX* tuera la *royauté*'; Camille Desmoulins added: 'Messieurs, voilà une pièce qui avance plus la chute de la royauté et de la piétaille que les journées de juillet et d'octobre': quoted Fierro and Liébert, p. 706.

[494]Louis II de Guise (1555–88), cardinal of Lorraine. The American ambassador, Gouverneur Morris, saw the play and noted in his diary on 10 November 1789: 'It is a very extraordinary piece to be represented in a Catholic country. A cardinal, who excites the king to violate his oaths and murder his subjects, then in a meeting of assassins consecrates their daggers, absolves them from their crimes, and promises everlasting felicity, all this with the solemnities of the established religion. A murmur of horror runs through the audience. There are several observations calculated for the present times, and, I think, this piece, if it runs through the provinces, as it probably will, must give a fatal blow to the Catholic religion ... Surely there never was a nation which verged faster towards anarchy': Anne Cary Morris (ed.), *The Diary and Letters of Gouverneur Morris* (2 vols., New York, 1888), I, pp. 223–4.

[495]Burke's knowledge of the savagery of American Indians, and of the effects of mob frenzy in the Thracian orgies (*Reflections*, above, pp. [99, 107]) led him to use 'cannibal' as a metaphor. Reports from France of the atrocities of the Revolution sometimes however contained claims that acts of cannibalism had actually taken place,

would think had been gorged sufficiently) by variety and seasoning; and to quicken them to an alertness in new murders and massacres, if it should suit the purpose of the Guises of the day. An assembly, in which sat a multitude of priests and prelates, was obliged to suffer this indignity at its door. The author was not sent to the gallies, nor the players to the house of correction. Not long after this exhibition, those players came forward to the assembly to claim the rites of that very religion which they had dared to expose,[496] and to shew their prostituted faces in the senate, whilst the archbishop of Paris,[497] whose function was known to his people only by [211] his prayers and benedictions, and his wealth only by his alms, is forced to abandon his house, and to fly from his flock (as from ravenous wolves) because, truly, in the sixteenth century, the Cardinal of Lorraine was a rebel and a murderer.[498]

Such is the effect of the perversion of history, by those, who, for the same nefarious purposes, have perverted every other part of learning. But those who will stand upon that elevation of reason, which places centuries under our eye, and brings things to the true point of comparison, which obscures little names, and effaces the colours of little parties, and to which nothing can ascend but the spirit and moral quality of human actions, will say to the teachers of the Palais Royal,—the Cardinal of Lorraine was the murderer of the sixteenth century, you have the glory of being the murderers in the eighteenth; and this is the only difference between you. But history, in the nineteenth century, better understood, and better employed, will, I trust, teach a civilized posterity to abhor the misdeeds of both these barbarous ages. It will teach future priests and magistrates not to retaliate upon the speculative and

---

e.g. John Talbot Dillon, *Historical and Critical Memoirs of the General Revolution in France In the Year 1789* (London, 1790), p. 323, gave credence to 'the report, that the heart of Berthier was carried in triumph into a coffee-house, and that Frenchmen signalized their vengeance, by steeping it in their wine.—Human nature repugns at the recital of such acts! We conceive ourselves transported to the Cape of Good Hope, and amongst Hottentots; or amongst the cannibals in the new discovered islands.' Dillon was otherwise an uncritical eulogist of the Revolution. For later reports, see *Plain Truth: or, an Impartial Account of the Proceedings at Paris During the last Nine Months ... By an Eye Witness* (London, 1792), p. 31; James Fennell, *A Review of the Proceedings of Paris during the last Summer* (London, [1792]), p. 470.

[496]The actor François-Joseph Talma, who played Charles IX, lodged a complaint before the National Assembly on 12 July 1790 against the *curé* of Saint-Sulpice, who had refused to officiate at his wedding: Fierro and Liébert, p. 709. This was M. de Pancemont, later a nonjuring priest: Reinhard, *Paris: La Révolution*, pp. 186, 196.

[497]Antoine-Éléonor Leclerc de Juigné (1728–1811).

[498]The 1803 edition carried a footnote: 'This is on a supposition of the truth of this story; but he was not in France at the time. One name serves as well as another.'

inactive atheists of future times, the enormities committed by the present practical zealots and furious fanatics of that wretched error, which, in its quiescent state, is more than punished whenever it is embraced. It will teach posterity not to make war upon either religion or philosophy, for the abuse which the hypocrites of both have made of the two most valuable blessings conferred upon us by the bounty of the universal Patron, [212] who in all things eminently favours and protects the race of man.

If your clergy, or any clergy, should shew themselves vicious beyond the fair bounds allowed to human infirmity, and to those professional faults which can hardly be separated from professional virtues, though their vices never can countenance the exercise of oppression, I do admit, that they would naturally have the effect of abating very much of our indignation against the tyrants who exceed measure and justice in their punishment. I can allow in clergymen, through all their divisions, some tenaciousness of their own opinion; some overflowings of zeal for its propagation; some predilection to their own state and office; some attachment to the interest of their own corps; some preference to those who listen with docility to their doctrines, beyond those who scorn and deride them. I allow all this, because I am a man who have to deal with men, and who would not, through a violence of toleration, run into the greatest of all intolerance. I must bear with infirmities until they fester into crimes.

Undoubtedly, the natural progress of the passions, from frailty to vice, ought to be prevented by a watchful eye and a firm hand. But is it true that the body of your clergy had past those limits of a just allowance? From the general style of your late publications of all sorts, one would be led to believe that your clergy in France were a sort of monsters; an horrible composition of superstition, ignorance, sloth, fraud, avarice, and tyranny. But [213] is this true? Is it true, that the lapse of time, the cessation of conflicting interests, the woful experience of the evils resulting from party rage, has had no sort of influence gradually to meliorate their minds? Is it true, that they were daily renewing invasions on the civil power, troubling the domestic quiet of their country, and rendering the operations of its government feeble and precarious? Is it true, that the clergy of our times have pressed down the laity with an iron hand, and were, in all places, lighting up the fires of a savage persecution? Did they by every fraud endeavour to encrease their estates? Did they use to exceed the due demands on estates that were their own? Or, rigidly screwing up right into wrong, did they convert a legal claim into a vexatious extortion? When not possessed of power, were they filled with the vices of those who envy it? Were they enflamed with a violent litigious spirit of controversy? Goaded on with the ambition of intellectual sovereignty, were they ready to fly in the face of all magistracy, to fire churches, to massacre the priests of other descriptions, to pull down altars, and to make their way over the ruins of subverted governments to an empire of doctrine, sometimes flattering, sometimes forcing the consciences of men from the jurisdiction of public institutions into a submission to their personal authority, beginning with a claim of liberty and ending with an abuse of power?[499]

These, or some of these, were the vices objected, and not wholly without foundation, to several of the churchmen of former times, who belonged to [214] the two great parties[500] which then divided and distracted Europe.

If there was in France, as in other countries there visibly is, a great abatement, rather than any increase of these vices, instead of loading the present clergy with the crimes of other men, and the odious character of other times, in common equity they ought to be praised, encouraged, and supported, in their departure from a spirit which disgraced their predecessors, and for having assumed a temper of mind and manners more suitable to their sacred function.

When my occasions took me into France, towards the close of the late reign, the clergy, under all their forms, engaged a considerable part of my curiosity.[501] So far from finding (except from one set of men, not then very numerous though very active) the complaints and discontents against that body, which some publications had given me reason to expect, I perceived little or no public or private uneasiness on their account. On further examination, I found the clergy in general, persons of moderate minds and decorous manners; I include the seculars, and the regulars of both sexes. I had not the good fortune to know a great many of the parochial clergy; but in general I received a perfectly good account of their morals, and of their attention to their duties. With some of the higher clergy I had a personal acquaintance;[502] and of the rest in that class, very good means of information. They were, almost all of

[499]French Protestants had been subject to persecution in France in the seventeenth century, extending into the early eighteenth: these episodes had been kept before the English public in widely current anti-Catholic polemic. The execution of the Protestant Jean Calas (1762) was probably the last such case, and anti-Catholic invective in England had faded in the late eighteenth century. By the 1790s it was chiefly found among heterodox Dissenters and freethinkers. Their critique was not consistent: English Dissenters denounced French bishops for being 'infidels'; freethinkers reproached the clergy for their Christian belief.

[500]Catholic and Protestant.

[501]Burke visited France in 1773; Louis XV died on 10 May 1774.

[502]Burke's enemies attacked him for knowing little of the French church. His knowledge and personal acquaintance was, however, considerably wider than that of the other Foxite Whigs.

them, persons of noble birth. They resembled others of their own rank; and where there was [215] any difference, it was in their favour. They were more fully educated than the military noblesse; so as by no means to disgrace their profession by ignorance, or by want of fitness for the exercise of their authority. They seemed to me, beyond the clerical character, liberal and open; with the hearts of gentlemen, and men of honour; neither insolent nor servile in their manners and conduct. They seemed to me rather a superior class;[503] a set of men, amongst whom you would not be surprised to find a *Fenelon*.[504] I saw among the clergy in Paris (many of the description are not to be met with any where) men of great learning and candour;[505] and I had reason to believe, that this description was not confined to Paris. What I found in other places, I know was accidental; and therefore to be presumed a fair sample. I spent a few days in a provincial town,[506] where, in the absence of the bishop, I passed my evenings with three clergymen, his vicars general, persons who would have done honour to any church. They were all well informed; two of them of deep, general, and extensive erudition, antient and modern, oriental and western; particularly in their own profession. They had a more extensive knowledge of our English divines than I expected; and they entered into the genius of those writers with a critical accuracy. One of these gentlemen is since dead, the Abbé *Morangis*.[507] I pay this tribute, without reluctance, to the memory of that noble, reverend, learned, and excellent person; and I should do the same, with equal cheerfulness, to the merits of the others, who I believe are still living, [216] if I did not fear to hurt those whom I am unable to serve.

Some of these ecclesiastics of rank, are, by all titles, persons deserving of general respect. They are deserving of gratitude from me, and from many English. If this letter should ever come into their hands, I hope they will believe there are those of our nation who feel for their unmerited fall, and for the cruel confiscation of their fortunes, with no common sensibility. What I say of

[503]See Bibliography, D iv.

[504]François de Salignac de la Mothe-Fénelon (1651–1715), archbishop of Cambrai 1695.

[505]The clergy of Paris, in particular, were in touch with the desire for reform so prevalent in France in 1788–9, and this was one reason which led them to be divided as the Revolution progressed. Of 966 whose decision is known, 545 subscribed the oath required by the Civil Constitution of the Clergy, though often after threats from the mob and pressure from the city authorities: Marcel Reinhard, *Nouvelle Histoire de Paris: La Revolution 1789–1799* (Paris, 1971), pp. 195–202. This majority was not, therefore, a simple disproof of Burke's argument.

[506]Auxerre, which Burke visited in 1773: *Correspondence*, II, pp. 421–2. Its bishop was Jean-Baptiste-Marie Champion de Cicé (1725–1805), later an *émigré* in England.

[507]Nothing is known of him.

them is a testimony, as far as one feeble voice can go, which I owe to truth. Whenever the question of this unnatural persecution is concerned, I will pay it. No one shall prevent me from being just and grateful. The time is fitted for the duty; and it is particularly becoming to shew our justice and gratitude, when those who have deserved well of us and of mankind are labouring under popular obloquy and the persecutions of oppressive power.[508]

You had before your revolution about an hundred and twenty bishops.[509] A few of them were men of eminent sanctity, and charity without limit. When we talk of the heroic, of course we talk of rare, virtue. I believe the instances of eminent depravity may be as rare amongst them as those of transcendent goodness. Examples of avarice and of licentiousness may be picked out, I do not question it, by those who delight in the investigation which leads to such discoveries. A man, as old as I am, will not be astonished that several, in every description, do not lead that perfect life of self-denial, with regard to wealth or to pleasure, which is wished for by all, by some expected, but by none exacted with more rigour, than by [217] those who are the most attentive to their own interests, or the most indulgent to their own passions. When I was in France, I am certain that the number of vicious prelates was not great. Certain individuals among them not distinguishable for the regularity of their lives, made some amends for their want of the severe virtues, in their possession of the liberal; and were endowed with qualities which made them useful in the church and state. I am told, that with few exceptions, Louis the Sixteenth had been more attentive to character, in his promotions to that rank, than his immediate predecessor; and I believe, (as some spirit of reform has prevailed through the whole reign) that it may be true. But the present ruling power has shewn a disposition only to plunder the church. It has punished *all* prelates; which is to favour the vicious, at least in point of reputation. It has made a degrading pensionary[510] establishment, to which no man of liberal ideas or liberal condition will destine his children. It must settle into the lowest classes of the people. As with you the inferior clergy are not numerous

---

[508]Burke was preoccupied by the expropriations and illegalities of the early stages of the Revolution, and neglected the high ideals which led some clergy to side with it as a means by which the Church could be constructively reformed. His case, not conclusive in 1790 when the *Reflections* appeared, became much more plausible in 1792–3 when the programme of de-Christianisation defined religion as antithetical to the new regime.

[509]There were 18 archbishops and 117 bishops; the National Assembly reduced their number to 83, one for each Department.

[510]I.e. stipendiary. The salaries of clergy were now to be paid by the national government.

enough for their duties; as these duties are, beyond measure, minute and toilsome; as you have left no middle classes of clergy at their ease, in future nothing of science or erudition can exist in the Gallican church.[511] To complete the project, without the least attention to the rights of patrons, the assembly has provided in future an elective clergy;[512] an arrangement which will drive out of the clerical profession all men of sobriety; all who can pretend to independence in their function or their conduct; and which will throw the whole direction of the public mind into the [218] hands of a set of licentious, bold, crafty, factious, flattering wretches, of such condition and such habits of life as will make their contemptible pensions (in comparison of which the stipend of an exciseman is lucrative and honourable) an object of low and illiberal intrigue. Those officers, whom they still call bishops, are to be elected to a provision comparatively mean, through the same arts, (that is, electioneering arts) by men of all religious tenets that are known or can be invented. The new lawgivers have not ascertained any thing whatsoever concerning their qualifications, relative either to doctrine or to morals; no more than they have done with regard to the subordinate clergy; nor does it appear but that both the higher and the lower may, at their discretion, practise or preach any mode of religion or irreligion that they please. I do not yet see what the jurisdiction of bishops over their subordinates is to be; or whether they are to have any jurisdiction at all.

In short, Sir, it seems to me, that this new ecclesiastical establishment is intended only to be temporary, and preparatory to the utter abolition, under any of its forms, of the Christian religion, whenever the minds of men are prepared for this last stroke against it, by the accomplishment of the plan for bringing its ministers into universal contempt. They who will not believe, that the philosophical fanatics who guide in these matters, have long entertained

---

[511]The French church had a deserved reputation for learning, including the writings of the Benedictines of Saint-Maur and the great libraries open to the public, like those of Saint-Victor and Sainte-Geneviève: Fierro and Lièbert, p. 710. Burke's term is not to be confused with 'Gallicanism', the position that the French church should be more independent of Rome.

[512]The Civil Constitution of the Clergy, voted by the National Assembly on 12 July 1790, provided for the election of archbishops, bishops and curés by tax-paying citizens. On 27 November 1790 the National Assembly imposed a loyalty oath on the clergy, so provoking a schism within their ranks. The Dissenting minister Joseph Priestley seized the opportunity to argue that the priesthood had been elective in the early Church: Letters to Burke, pp. 80, 95–103. This was an old ecclesiological debate which the Dissenters had much earlier lost in England, though they could hardly ignore the implications for themselves of Burke's observations on the depressing effect of election on the calibre of the clergy.

such a design, are utterly ignorant of their character and proceedings. These enthusiasts do not scruple to avow their opinion, that a state can subsist without any religion better than with one; and that they are able to supply the place of any [219] good which may be in it, by a project of their own— namely, by a sort of education they have imagined, founded in a knowledge of the physical wants of men; progressively carried to an enlightened self-interest, which, when well understood, they tell us will identify with an interest more enlarged and public. The scheme of this education has been long known.[513] Of late they distinguish it (as they have got an entire new nomenclature of technical terms) by the name of a *Civic Education.*

I hope their partizans in England, (to whom I rather attribute very inconsiderate conduct than the ultimate object in this detestable design) will succeed neither in the pillage of the ecclesiastics, nor in the introduction of a principle of popular election to our bishoprics and parochial cures. This, in the present condition of the world, would be the last corruption of the church; the utter ruin of the clerical character; the most dangerous shock that the state ever received through a misunderstood arrangement of religion.[514] I know well enough that the bishoprics and cures, under kingly and seignoral patronage, as now they are in England, and as they have been lately in France, are sometimes acquired by unworthy methods; but the other mode of ecclesiastical canvas subjects them infinitely more surely and more generally to all the evil arts of low ambition, which, operating on and through greater numbers, will produce mischief in proportion.

Those of you who have robbed the clergy, think that they shall easily reconcile their conduct to all protestant nations; because the clergy, whom they have thus plundered, degraded, and [220] given over to mockery and scorn, are of the Roman Catholic, that is, of *their own* pretended persuasion. I have no doubt that some miserable bigots will be found here as well as elsewhere,

---

[513]Burke may have been thinking, among other things, of Rousseau's *Émile, ou de l'Education* (1762), a copy of which he owned: LC, p. 20; LC MS, fo. 4. The phrase '*éducation civique*' does not appear there, however. It may have originated as a project in patriotic virtue with Turgot's *Memoire au Roi sur les municipalités* of 1775, and with Dupont de Nemours, who edited Turgot's works in 1787. The idea gained much wider currency as the revolution continued.

[514]Burke failed to mention that this had been one of the outcomes of the American Revolution, an episode with which he was still identified in the public mind. For the conversion of the Church of England in America by 1789 into a *de facto* congregational church, its teaching subordinated to the public doctrine of the new regime, see Frederick V. Mills, sr., *Bishops by Ballot: An Eighteenth-Century Ecclesiastical Revolution* (New York, 1978).

who hate sects and parties different from their own, more than they love the substance of religion; and who are more angry with those who differ from them in their particular plans and systems, than displeased with those who attack the foundation of our common hope. These men will write and speak on the subject in the manner that is to be expected from their temper and character. Burnet[515] says, that when he was in France, in the year 1683, "the method which carried over the men of the finest parts to popery was this—they brought themselves to doubt of the whole Christian religion. When that was once done, it seemed a more indifferent thing of what side or form they continued outwardly."[516] If this was then the ecclesiastic policy of France, it is what they have since but too much reason to repent of.[517] They preferred atheism to a form of religion not agreeable to their ideas. They succeeded in destroying that form; and atheism has succeeded in destroying them. I can readily give credit to Burnet's story; because I have observed too much of a similar spirit (for a little of it is "much too much") amongst ourselves. The humour, however, is not general.

The teachers who reformed our religion in England bore no sort of resemblance to your present reforming doctors in Paris. Perhaps they were (like those whom they opposed) rather more than [221] could be wished under the influence of a party spirit; but they were most sincere believers; men of the most fervent and exalted piety; ready to die (as some of them did die) like true heroes in defence of their particular ideas of Christianity; as they would with equal fortitude, and more chearfully, for that stock of general truth, for the branches of which they contended with their blood. These men would have disavowed with horror those wretches who claimed a fellowship with them upon no other titles than those of their having pillaged the persons with whom they maintained controversies, and their having despised the common religion, for the purity of which they exerted themselves with a zeal, which unequivocally bespoke their highest reverence for the substance of that system which they wished to reform. Many of their descendants have retained the same zeal; but, (as less engaged in conflict) with more moderation. They do

[515]Gilbert Burnet (1643–1715). A Scots careerist in the English church, he escaped arrest after the Rye House plot (1683), lived in exile, sided with William of Orange in 1688 and was rewarded with the bishopric of Salisbury. As a fellow Whig, Burke cited him without disapproval.

[516]Gilbert Burnet, *History of His Own Time* (2 vols., London, 1724, 1734), I, p. 567. Burke owned a copy of this work: *LC*, p. 9.

[517]Even Burnet did not claim that this was the policy of the Catholic church in France: he wrote disparagingly of Protestant converts.

not forget that justice and mercy are substantial parts of religion.[518] Impious men do not recommend themselves to their communion by iniquity and cruelty towards any description of their fellow creatures.

We hear these new teachers continually boasting of their spirit of toleration.[519] That those persons should tolerate all opinions, who think none to be of estimation, is a matter of small merit. Equal neglect is not impartial kindness. The species of benevolence, which arises from contempt, is no true charity. There are in England abundance of men who tolerate in the true spirit of toleration. They think the dogmas of religion, [222] though in different degrees, are all of moment; and that amongst them there is, as amongst all things of value, a just ground of preference. They favour, therefore, and they tolerate. They tolerate, not because they despise opinions, but because they respect justice. They would reverently and affectionately protect all religions, because they love and venerate the great principle upon which they all agree, and the great object to which they are all directed.[520] They begin more and more plainly to discern, that we have all a common cause, as against a common enemy.[521] They will not be so misled by the spirit of faction, as not to distinguish what is done in favour of their subdivision, from those acts of hostility, which, through some particular description, are aimed at the whole corps, in which they themselves, under another denomination, are included. It is impossible for me to say what may be the character of every description of men amongst us. But I speak for the greater part; and for them, I must tell you, that sacrilege is no part of their doctrine of good works; that, so far from calling you into their fellowship on such title, if your professors are admitted to their communion, they must carefully conceal their doctrine of the lawfulness of the proscription of innocent men; and that they must make restitution of all stolen goods whatsoever. Till then they are none of ours.

You may suppose that we do not approve your confiscation of the revenues of bishops, and deans, and chapters, and parochial clergy possessing independent [223] estates arising from land, because we have the same sort of establishment in England. That objection, you will say, cannot hold as to the confiscation of the goods of monks and nuns, and the abolition of their order. It is true, that this particular part of your general confiscation does not affect

[518]Cf. Micah 6.8: 'He hath shewed thee, O man, what is good; and what doth the Lord require of thee, but to do justly, and to love mercy, and to walk humbly with thy God.'

[519]For the National Assembly's decree on toleration of non-Catholics of 24 December 1789, see Le Moniteur, 25 December 1789; Roberts (ed.), Documents, p. 222.

[520]Burke here described his own latitudinarian position; cf. Reflections, p. [234].

[521]I.e. religion, against infidelity.

England, as a precedent in point: but the reason applies; and it goes a great way. The long parliament confiscated the lands of deans and chapters in England on the same ideas upon which your assembly set to sale the lands of the monastic orders.[522] But it is in the principle of injustice that the danger lies, and not in the description of persons on whom it is first exercised. I see, in a country very near us, a course of policy pursued, which sets justice, the common concern of mankind, at defiance. With the national assembly of France, possession is nothing; law and usage are nothing. I see the national assembly openly reprobate the doctrine of prescription, which[523] one of the greatest of their own lawyers tells us, with great truth, is a part of the law of nature. He tells us, that the positive ascertainment of its limits, and its security from invasion, were among the causes for which civil society itself has been instituted. If prescription be once shaken, no species of property is secure, when it once becomes an object large enough to tempt the cupidity of indigent power. I see a practice perfectly correspondent to their contempt of this great fundamental part of natural law. I see the confiscators begin with bishops, and chapters, and monasteries; [224] but I do not see them end there. I see the princes of the blood, who, by the oldest usages of that kingdom, held large landed estates, (hardly with the compliment of a debate) deprived of their possessions, and in

[522]Just such a principle had been urged by Sir Symonds D'Ewes in the Commons' debates of 26 March 1640/1 and 15 June 1641. The first parliamentary ordinance of 31 March 1643 for the sequestration of the estates of bishops, deans, chapters and others who had been in arms against Parliament was 'not an ordinance against Church lands in general ... It was simply directed against delinquents in general.' But Parliament was led on to just that step: the ordinance of 9 October 1646 abolishing the government of the Church by bishops and archbishops vested their possessions in trustees for the use of the Commonwealth, specifically with the aim of paying the salaries of 'a preaching ministry'. On 13 October 1646, Parliament applied these lands as security for a loan. On 16 November 1646 a measure was passed for the sale of bishops' lands; on 6 September 1648 a measure for the abolition of deans and chapters was introduced, and a measure for the sale of their lands followed on 13 February 1648/9: W. A. Shaw, *A History of the English Church during the Civil Wars and under the Commonwealth* (2 vols., London, 1900), I, pp. 54–9, 88; II, pp. 204–6, 209–13. Burke was right to draw a parallel with the French case.

[523]Domat. [B] Jean Domat, *The Civil Law in its Natural Order: Together with the Publick Law*, trans. William Strahan (2 vols., London, 1722), I, pp. 483–97. Domat defended prescription as 'wholly natural in the state and condition we are in; and so necessary, that without this remedy every Purchaser and every Possessor being liable to be troubled to all eternity, there would never be any perfect assurance of a sure and peaceable Possession' (ibid., p. 483). Burke owned a copy of this edition of Domat: LC, p. 10; LC MS, fo. 6. Jean Domat (1625–96) had originally published this codification of French law in 1689–94.

lieu of their stable independent property, reduced to the hope of some precarious, charitable pension, at the pleasure of an assembly, which of course
will pay little regard to the rights of pensioners at pleasure, when it despises
those of legal proprietors.[524] Flushed with the insolence of their first inglorious
victories, and pressed by the distresses caused by their lust of unhallowed lucre, disappointed but not discouraged, they have at length ventured completely to subvert all property of all descriptions throughout the extent of a
great kingdom. They have compelled all men, in all transactions of commerce,
in the disposal of lands, in civil dealing, and through the whole communion of
life,[525] to accept as perfect payment and good and lawful tender, the symbols
of their speculations on a projected sale of their plunder. What vestiges of liberty or property have they left? The tenant-right of a cabbage-garden, a year's
interest in a hovel, the good-will of an alehouse, or a baker's shop, the very
shadow of a constructive property, are more ceremoniously treated in our
parliament than with you the oldest and most valuable landed possessions, in
the hands of the most respectable personages, or than the whole body of the
monied and commercial interest of your country. We entertain an high opinion of the legislative authority; but we have never dreamt that parliaments
had any right whatever to violate property, to [225] over-rule prescription or
to force a currency of their own fiction in the place of that which is real, and
recognized by the law of nations. But you, who began with refusing to submit
to the most moderate restraints, have ended by establishing an unheard of
despotism. I find the ground upon which your confiscators go is this; that indeed their proceedings could not be supported in a court of justice; but that
the rules of prescription cannot bind a legislative assembly.[526] So that this leg-

---

[524]The National Assembly debated this issue on 13 August 1790, and so decided on
14 August: *Le Moniteur*, 14 and 15 August 1790.

[525]Burke again used language implying an identity between civil and ecclesiastical
association.

[526]Speech of Mr. Camus, published by order of the National Assembly. [B] Ar-
mand-Gaston Camus (1740–1804), lawyer. A Jansenist and a Gallican, he was one of
the draughtsmen of the Civil Constitution of the Clergy. But in *Résumé de l'opinion de
M. Camus, Dans la Séance du 13 Octobre 1789, an sujet de la motion sur les biens ecclésiastiques* [Paris, 1789], Camus argued against Thouret's distinction between the
property rights of individuals and corporations; Camus contended that the law protected both equally. In *Opinion de M. Camus Dans la Séance du 31 Mai 1790, sur le
plan de constitution du clergé, Proposé par le Comité ecclésiastique. Imprimée par ordre de l'Assemblée Nationale* ([Paris, 1790]), Camus contended for the right of the nation to intervene to regulate the internal arrangements of the Church, including the
abolition of archbishoprics and bishoprics, the redefinition of the boundaries of sees,
the adoption of election to ecclesiastical office, and the disavowal of Roman jurisdic-

islative assembly of a free nation sits, not for the security, but for the destruction of property, and not of property only, but of every rule and maxim which can give it stability, and of those instruments which can alone give it circulation.

When the Anabaptists of Munster,[527] in the sixteenth century, had filled Germany with confusion by their system of levelling and their wild opinions concerning property, to what country in Europe did not the progress of their fury furnish just cause of alarm? Of all things, wisdom is the most terrified with epidemical fanaticism, because of all enemies it is that against which she is the least able to furnish any kind of resource. We cannot be ignorant of the spirit of atheistical fanaticism, that is inspired by a multitude of writings, dispersed with incredible assiduity and expence, and by sermons delivered in all the streets and places of public resort in Paris. These writings and sermons have filled the populace with a [226] black and savage atrocity of mind, which supersedes in them the common feelings of nature, as well as all sentiments of morality and religion; insomuch that these wretches are induced to bear with a sullen patience the intolerable distresses brought upon them by the violent convulsions and permutations that have been made in property?[528] The spirit

---

tion over the church in France. See *Reflections*, p. [323]. Burke's enemies in England found ways of arguing that the possessions of the French church were not 'property', but did not apply this insight to any possessions other than ecclesiastical ones: their animus was clear.

[527]The Anabaptists denied the validity of infant baptism. In Münster they established in 1532 a theocracy in which goods, and women, were held in common. This social experiment was forcibly suppressed in 1535.

[528]Whether the following description is strictly true I know not; but it is what the publishers would have pass for true, in order to animate others. In a letter from Toul, given in one of their papers, is the following passage concerning the people of that district: "Dans la Révolution actuelle, ils ont résisté à toutes les *séductions du bigotisme, aux persécutions et aux tracasseries* des Ennemis de la Révolution. *Oubliant leurs plus grands intérêts* pour rendre hommage aux vues d'ordre général qui ont determiné l'Assemblée Nationale, ils voient, *sans se plaindre*, supprimer cette foule d'établissemens ecclésiastiques par lesquels *ils subsistoient*; et même, en perdant leur siège épiscopal, la seule de toutes ces ressources qui pouvoit, ou plutôt *qui devoit, en toute équité*, leur être conservée; condamnés *à la plus effrayante misère*, sans avoir *été ni pu être entendus, ils ne murmurent point*, ils restent fidèles aux principes du plus pur patriotisme; ils sont encore prêts à *verser leur sang* pour le maintien de la Constitution, qui va reduire leur Ville *à la plus déplorable nullité*." These people are not supposed to have endured those sufferings and injustices in a struggle for liberty, for the same account states truly that they had been always free; their patience in beggary and ruin, and their suffering, without remonstrance, the most flagrant and confessed injustice, if strictly true, can be nothing but the effect of this dire fanaticism. A great multitude all

of proselytism attends this spirit of fanaticism. They have societies to cabal and correspond at home and abroad for the propagation of their tenets. The republic of Berne,[529] one of [227] the happiest, the most prosperous, and the best governed countries upon earth, is one of the great objects, at the destruction of which they aim. I am told they have in some measure succeeded in sowing there the seeds of discontent. They are busy throughout Germany. Spain and Italy have not been untried.[530] England is not left out of the comprehensive scheme of their malignant charity; and in England we find those who stretch out their arms to them, who recommend their examples from more than one pulpit, and who choose, in more than one periodical meeting, publicly to correspond with them, to applaud them, and to hold them up as objects for imitation; who receive from them tokens of confraternity, and standards consecrated amidst their rites and mysteries;[531] who suggest to them leagues of perpetual amity, at the very time when the power, to which our constitution has exclusively delegated the federative capacity of this kingdom, may find it expedient to make war upon them.

It is not my fear of the confiscation of our church property from this example in France that I dread, though I think this would be no trifling evil. The great source of my solicitude is, least it should ever be considered in England as the policy of a state, to seek a resource in confiscations of any kind; or that any

---

over France is in the same condition and the same temper. [B] The 'letter from Toul' has not been identified.

[529]Bern, a canton of Switzerland, had prospered under an oligarchic government. In 1790, the 'club helvétique' was founded in Paris; the activities of its members in their native Switzerland gave rise to charges of attempted subversion. See Ariane Méautis, Le club helvétique de Paris (1790–1791) et la diffusion des idées révolutionnaires en Suisse (Neuchâtel, 1969); Alfred Rufer, La Suisse et la Révolution française (ed. Jean-René Suratteau, Paris, 1974).

[530]The propagation of the Revolution was integral to its nature from the outset: see Albert Sorel, L'Europe et la Révolution française, I, Les Moeurs et les traditions politiques (Paris, 1885); II, La chute de la royauté (Paris, 1887); Jacques Droz, L'Allemagne et la Révolution française (Paris, 1949); Richard Herr, The Eighteenth Century Revolution in Spain (Princeton, 1958); Stuart Woolf, A History of Italy, 1700–1860 (London, 1979); Jacques Godechot, La Grande Nation: l'expansion révolutionnaire de la France dans le monde de 1789 à 1799 (2nd edn., Paris, 1983), which has valuable bibliographies.

[531]See the proceedings of the confederation at Nantz. [B] The Patriotic Society at Nantes celebrated the Revolution at a festival on 23 August 1790; it sent two of its members to the London Revolution Society with a picture of the British and French flags bound together with a ribbon reading 'A l'Union de la France et d'Angleterre'. Their reception was reported to the meeting of the Society on 4 November 1790: Correspondence of the Revolution Society, pp. 64–6, 105–7.

one description of citizens should be brought to regard any of the others as [228] their proper prey.[532] Nations are wading deeper and deeper into an ocean of boundless debt. Public debts, which at first were a security to governments, by interesting many in the public tranquillity, are likely in their excess to become the means of their subversion. If governments provide for these debts by heavy impositions, they perish by becoming odious to the people. If they do not provide for them, they will be undone by the efforts of the most dangerous of all parties; I mean an extensive discontented monied interest, injured and not destroyed. The men who compose this interest look for their security, in the first instance, to the fidelity of government; in the second, to its power. If they find the old governments effete, worn out, and [229] with their springs

---

[532] "Si plures sunt ii quibus improbe datum est, quam illi quibus injuste ademptum est, idcirco plus etiam valent? Non enim numero hæc judicantur sed pondere. Quam autem habet æquitatem, ut agrum multis annis, aut etiam sæculis ante possessum, qui nullum habuit habeat; qui autem habuit amittat. Ac, propter hoc injuriæ genus, Lacedæmonii Lysandrum Ephorum expulerunt: Agin regem (quod nunquam antea apud eos acciderat) necaverunt: exque eo tempore tantæ discordiæ secutæ sunt, ut et tyranni exsisterint, et optimates exterminarentur, et preclarissime constituta respublica dilaberetur. Nec vero solum ipsa cecidit, sed etiam reliquam Græciam evertit contagionibus malorum, quæ a Lacedæmoniis profectæ manarunt latius."—After speaking of the conduct of the model of true patriots, Aratus of Sycion, which was in a very different spirit, he says, "Sic par est agere cum civibus; non ut bis jam vidimus, hastam in foro ponere et bona civium voci subjicere præconis. At ille Græcus (id quod fuit sapientis et præstantis viri) omnibus consulendum esse putavit: eaque est summa ratio et sapientia boni civis, commoda civium non divellere, sed omnes eadem æquitate continere." Cic. Off. l. 2.[B] 'Thus even though they to whom property has been wrongfully awarded be more in number than they from whom it has been unjustly taken, they do not for that reason have more influence; for in such matters influence is measured not by numbers but by weight. And how is it fair that a man who never had any property should take possession of lands that had been occupied for many years or even generations, and that he who had them before should lose possession of them? Now, it was on account of just this sort of wrong-doing that the Spartans banished their ephor Lysander, and put their king Agis to death—an act without precedent in the history of Sparta. From that time on—and for the same reason—dissensions so serious ensued that tyrants arose, the nobles were sent into exile, and the state, though most admirably constituted, crumbled to pieces. Nor did it fall alone, but by the contagion of the ills that, starting in Lacedaemon, spread widely and more widely, it dragged the rest of Greece down to ruin.' 'That is the right way to deal with one's fellow-citizens, and not, as we have already witnessed on two occasions, to plant the spear in the forum and knock down the property of citizens under the auctioneer's hammer. But yon Greek, like a wise and excellent man, thought that he must look out for the welfare of all. And this is the highest statesmanship and the soundest wisdom on the part of a good citizen, not to divide the interests of the citizens but to unite all on the basis of impartial justice': Cicero, De Officiis, Book II, xxii, 79–xiii, 80, and xxiii, 83.

relaxed, so as not to be of sufficient vigour for their purposes, they may seek new ones that shall be possessed of more energy; and this energy will be derived, not from an acquisition of resources, but from a contempt of justice. Revolutions are favourable to confiscation;[533] and it is impossible to know under what obnoxious names the next confiscations will be authorised. I am sure that the principles predominant in France extend to very many persons and descriptions of persons in all countries who think their innoxious indolence their security. This kind of innocence in proprietors may be argued into inutility; and inutility into an unfitness for their estates. Many parts of Europe are in open disorder. In many others there is a hollow murmuring under ground; a confused movement is felt, that threatens a general earthquake in the political world. Already confederacies and correspondences of the most extraordinary nature are forming, in several countries.[534] In such a state of things we ought to hold ourselves upon our guard. In all mutations (if mutations must be) the circumstance which will serve most to blunt the edge of their mischief, and to promote what good may be in them, is, that they should find us with our minds tenacious of justice, and tender of property.

But it will be argued, that this confiscation in France ought not to alarm other nations. They say it is not made from wanton rapacity; that it is a [230] great measure of national policy, adopted to remove an extensive, inveterate, superstitious mischief. It is with the greatest difficulty that I am able to separate policy from justice. Justice is itself the great standing policy of civil society; and any eminent departure from it, under any circumstances, lies under the suspicion of being no policy at all.

[533]Burke was presumably aware of the confiscations of property that were part of the American Revolution.

[534]See two books intitled, Enige Originalschriften des Illuminatenordens.—System und Folgen des Illuminatenordens. Munchen 1787. [B] These were two texts published on the order of the Elector of Bavaria to expose the alleged conspiracy of illuminati after the arrest of their founder, Weishaupt, and the seizure of his papers: *Einige Originalschriften des Illuminatenordens, welche bey dem gewesenem Regierungsrath Zwack durch vorgenommene Hausvisitation zu Landshut den 11 und 12 Octob. 1786, vorgefunden worden* and *System und Folgen des Illuminatenordens aus den gedruckten Originalschriften desselben gezogen. In Briefen* ([München], 1787). See J. M. Roberts, *The Mythology of Secret Societies* (London, 1972). Weishaupt, professor of canon law at Ingolstadt, planned a conspiracy to establish a unified European republic. Since systemic and stadial theories of revolution were still lacking, major upheavals like 1776 and 1789 were generally interpreted in personal terms, and sometimes as grandiose conspiracies. This state of mind was shared by the American revolutionaries and the French counter-revolutionaries, most vividly in the abbé Barruel's *Mémoires pour servir à l'histoire du jacobinisme* (1797). Although Burke was open to the role of personal agency, he markedly downplayed this theme, and the *Reflections* began the search for general causes of catastrophe.

When men are encouraged to go into a certain mode of life by the existing laws, and protected in that mode as in a lawful occupation—when they have accommodated all their ideas, and all their habits to it—when the law had long made their adherence to its rules a ground of reputation, and their departure from them a ground of disgrace and even of penalty—I am sure it is unjust in legislature, by an arbitrary act, to offer a sudden violence to their minds and their feelings; forcibly to degrade them from their state and condition, and to stigmatize with shame and infamy that character and those customs which before had been made the measure of their happiness and honour. If to this be added an expulsion from their habitations, and a confiscation of all their goods, I am not sagacious enough to discover how this despotic sport, made of the feelings, consciences, prejudices, and properties of men, can be discriminated from the rankest tyranny.

If the injustice of the course pursued in France be clear, the policy of the measure, that is, the public benefit to be expected from it, ought to be at least as evident, and at least as important. To a man who acts under the influence of no passion, who [231] has nothing in view in his projects but the public good, a great difference will immediately strike him, between what policy would dictate on the original introduction of such institutions, and on a question of their total abolition, where they have cast their roots wide and deep, and where by long habit things more valuable than themselves are so adapted to them, and in a manner interwoven with them, that the one cannot be destroyed without notably impairing the other. He might be embarrassed, if the case were really such as sophisters represent it in their paltry style of debating. But in this, as in most questions of state, there is a middle. There is something else than the mere alternative of absolute destruction, or unreformed existence. *Spartam nactus es; hanc exorna.*[535] This is, in my opinion, a rule of profound sense, and ought never to depart from the mind of an honest reformer. I cannot conceive how any man can have brought himself to that pitch of presumption, to consider his country as nothing but *carte blanche*, upon which he may scribble whatever he pleases. A man full of warm speculative benevolence may wish his society otherwise constituted than he finds it; but a good patriot, and a true politician, always considers how he shall make the most of the existing materials of his country. A disposition to preserve, and an ability to improve, taken together, would be my standard of a statesman. Every thing else is vulgar in the conception, perilous in the execution.

[535]Cicero, *Letters to Atticus*, IV, 6, quoted a line in Greek, evidently Agamemnon's words to Menelaus, from a surviving fragment of Euripides' *Telephos*, literally translated as 'Sparta has fallen to your lot, do it credit', i.e. make the best of things where you have no choice.

There are moments in the fortune of states when particular men are called to make improvements [232] by great mental exertion. In those moments, even when they seem to enjoy the confidence of their prince and country, and to be invested with full authority they have not always apt instruments. A politician, to do great things, looks for a *power*, what our workmen call a *purchase*;[536] and if he finds that power, in politics as in mechanics he cannot be at a loss to apply it. In the monastic institutions, in my opinion, was found a great *power* for the mechanism of politic benevolence. There were revenues with a public direction; there were men wholly set apart and dedicated to public purposes, without any other than public ties and public principles; men without the possibility of converting the estate of the community into a private fortune; men denied to self-interests, whose avarice is for some community; men to whom personal poverty is honour, and implicit obedience stands in the place of freedom. In vain shall a man look to the possibility of making such things when he wants them. The winds blow as they list.[537] These institutions are the products of enthusiasm; they are the instruments of wisdom.[538] Wisdom cannot create materials; they are the gifts of nature or of chance; her pride is in the use. The perennial existence of bodies corporate and their fortunes, are things particularly suited to a man who has long views; who meditates designs that require time in fashioning; and which propose duration when they are accomplished. He is not deserving to rank high, or even to be mentioned in the order of great statesmen, who, having obtained the command and direction of such a power as [233] existed in the wealth, the discipline, and the habits of such corporations, as those which you have rashly destroyed, cannot find any way of converting it to the great and lasting benefit of his country. On the view of this subject a thousand uses suggest themselves to a contriving mind. To destroy any power, growing wild from the rank productive force of the human mind, is almost tantamount, in the moral world, to the destruction of the apparently active properties of bodies in the material. It would be like the attempt to destroy (if it were in our competence to destroy) the expansive force of fixed air in nitre,[539] or

[536]Purchase: 'A device or appliance by means of which power may be brought to bear with advantage; any contrivance for increasing applied power ... A 'hold', 'fulcrum', or position of advantage for accomplishing something': OED.

[537]Cf. John, 3.8: 'The wind bloweth where it listeth, and thou hearest the sound thereof, but canst not tell whence it cometh, and whither it goeth: so is every one that is born of the Spirit.'

[538]Burke notably omitted any defence of the spiritual significance of monasticism. He even identified its driving forces as 'enthusiasm' (as here) and 'superstition' (p. [235]).

[539]Cf. Burke, *Reflections*, p. [8].

the power of steam, or of electricity, or of magnetism. These energies always existed in nature, and they were always discernible. They seemed, some of them unserviceable, some noxious, some no better than a sport to children; until contemplative ability, combining with practic skill, tamed their wild nature, subdued them to use, and rendered them at once the most powerful and the most tractable agents, in subservience to the great views and designs of men. Did fifty thousand persons, whose mental and whose bodily labour you might direct, and so many hundred thousand a year of a revenue, which was neither lazy nor superstitious, appear too big for your abilities to wield? Had you no way of using the men but by converting monks into pensioners? Had you no way of turning the revenue to account, but through the improvident resource of a [234] spendthrift sale? If you were thus destitute of mental funds, the proceeding is in its natural course. Your politicians do not understand their trade; and therefore they sell their tools.[540]

But the institutions savour of superstition in their very principle; and they nourish it by a permanent and standing influence. This I do not mean to dispute; but this ought not to hinder you from deriving from superstition itself any resources which may thence be furnished for the public advantage. You derive benefits from many dispositions and many passions of the human mind, which are of as doubtful a colour in the moral eye, as superstition itself. It was your business to correct and mitigate every thing which was noxious in this passion, as in all the passions. But is superstition the greatest of all possible vices? In its possible excess I think it becomes a very great evil. It is, however, a moral subject; and of course admits of all degrees and all modifications. Superstition is the religion of feeble minds; and they must be tolerated in an intermixture of it, in some trifling or some enthusiastic shape or other, else you will deprive weak minds of a resource found necessary to the strongest. The body of all true religion consists, to be sure, in obedience to the will of the sovereign of the world; in a confidence in his declarations; and an imitation of his perfections. The rest is our own.[541] It may be prejudicial to the great end; it may be auxiliary. Wise men, who as such, are not *admirers* (not admirers at least of the *Munera Terræ*)[542] are not violently attached to these things, nor do they [235] violently hate them. Wisdom is not the most severe corrector of

[540]For the decree of the National Assembly on 13 February 1790 withdrawing recognition of monastic vows and suppressing monastic orders, see *Le Moniteur*, 15 Febuary 1790; Roberts (ed.), *Documents*, p. 222.
      [541]Such a summary of religion, neglecting the role of the Church and of the sacraments, was a characteristic of latitudinarianism; cf. *Reflections*, pp. [221–2].
      [542]'... all of us who feed upon earth's bounty, be we princes or needy husbandmen': Horace, *Odes*, Book II, xiv, 10.

folly. They are the rival follies, which mutually wage so unrelenting a war; and which make so cruel a use of their advantages, as they can happen to engage the immoderate vulgar on the one side or the other in their quarrels. Prudence would be neuter; but if, in the contention between fond attachment and fierce antipathy concerning things in their nature not made to produce such heats, a prudent man were obliged to make a choice of what errors and excesses of enthusiasm he would condemn or bear, perhaps he would think, that which builds, to be more tolerable than that which demolishes—that which adorns a country, than that which deforms it—that which endows, than that which plunders—that which disposes to mistaken beneficence, than that which stimulates to real injustice—that which leads a man to refuse to himself lawful pleasures, than that which snatches from others the scanty subsistence of their self-denial. Such, I think, is very nearly the state of the question between the ancient founders of monkish superstition, and the superstition of the pretended philosophers of the hour.

For the present I postpone all consideration of the supposed public profit of the sale, which however I conceive to be perfectly delusive. I shall here only consider it as a transfer of property. On the policy of that transfer I shall trouble you with a few thoughts.

In every prosperous community something more is produced than goes to the immediate support of [236] the producer. This surplus forms the income of the landed capitalist. It will be spent by a proprietor who does not labour. But this idleness is itself the spring of labour; this repose the spur to industry. The only concern of the state is, that the capital taken in rent from the land, should be returned again to the industry from whence it came; and that its expenditure should be with the least possible detriment to the morals of those who expend it, and to those of the people to whom it is returned.

In all the views of receipt, expenditure, and personal employment, a sober legislator would carefully compare the possessor whom he was recommended to expel, with the stranger who was proposed to fill his place. Before the inconveniences are incurred which *must* attend all violent revolutions in property through extensive confiscation, we ought to have some rational assurance that the purchasers of the confiscated property will be in a considerable degree more laborious, more virtuous, more sober, less disposed to extort an unreasonable proportion of the gains of the labourer, or to consume on themselves a larger share than is fit for the measure of an individual, or that they should be qualified to dispense the surplus in a more steady and equal mode, so as to answer the purposes of a politic expenditure, than the old possessors, call those possessors, bishops, or canons, or commendatory abbots, or monks, or what you please. The monks are lazy. Be it so. Suppose them no otherwise employed than by singing in the choir. They are as usefully employed as those who neither sing nor say. [237] As usefully even as those who sing upon the stage. They are as usefully employed as if they worked from dawn to dark in the innumerable servile, degrading, unseemly, unmanly, and often most unwholesome and pestiferous occupations, to which by the social œconomy so many wretches are inevitably doomed. If it were not generally pernicious to disturb the natural course of things, and to impede, in any degree, the great wheel of circulation which is turned by the strangely directed labour of these unhappy people, I should be infinitely more inclined forcibly to rescue them from their miserable industry, than violently to disturb the tranquil repose of monastic quietude. Humanity, and perhaps policy, might better justify me in the one than in the other. It is a subject on which I have often reflected, and never reflected without feeling from it. I am sure that no consideration, except the necessity of submitting to the yoke of luxury, and the despotism of fancy, who in their own imperious way will distribute the surplus product of the soil, can justify the toleration of such trades and employments in a well-regulated state. But, for this purpose of distribution, it seems to me, that the idle expences of monks are quite as well directed as the idle expences of us lay-loiterers.[543]

When the advantages of the possession, and of the project, are on a par, there is no motive for a change. But in the present case, perhaps they are not upon a par, and the difference is in favour of the possession. It does not appear to me, that the expences of those whom you are going to expel, do, in fact, take a course so directly and so generally leading to vitiate and [238] degrade and render miserable those through whom they pass, as the expences of those favourites whom you are intruding into their houses. Why should the expenditure of a great landed property, which is a dispersion of the surplus product of the soil, appear intolerable to you or to me, when it takes its course through the accumulation of vast libraries, which are the history of the force and weakness of the human mind; through great collections of antient records, medals, and coins, which attest and explain laws and customs; through paintings and statues, that, by imitating nature, seem to extend the limits of creation; through grand monuments of the dead, which continue the regards and connexions of life beyond the grave; through collections of the specimens of nature, which become a representative assembly of all the classes and fami-

[543]Burke's attitude to French monasticism, though not openly hostile like that of the *philosophes*, was critical. He did not object to the programme of reform, in place since 1768, which had closed smaller monastic houses and transferred their resources to the use of episcopal authorities. Burke protested against theft, not against reform.

lies of the world, that by disposition facilitate, and, by exciting curiosity, open the avenues to science? If, by great permanent establishments, all these objects of expence are better secured from the inconstant sport of personal caprice and personal extravagance, are they worse than if the same tastes prevailed in scattered individuals? Does not the sweat of the mason and carpenter, who toil in order to partake the sweat of the peasant, flow as pleasantly and as salubriously, in the construction and repair of the majestic edifices of religion, as in the painted booths and sordid sties of vice and luxury; as honourably and as profitably in repairing those sacred works, which grow hoary with innumerable years, as on the momentary receptacles of transient voluptuousness; in opera-houses, and brothels, and gaming-houses, [239] and clubhouses, and obelisks in the Champ de Mars?[544] Is the surplus product of the olive and the vine worse employed in the frugal sustenance of persons, whom the fictions of a pious imagination raises to dignity by construing in the service of God, than in pampering the innumerable multitude of those who are degraded by being made useless domestics subservient to the pride of man? Are the decorations of temples an expenditure less worthy a wise man than ribbons, and laces, and national cockades, and petits maisons, and petit soupers,[545] and all the innumerable fopperies and follies in which opulence sports away the burthen of its superfluity?

We tolerate even these; not from love of them, but for fear of worse. We tolerate them, because property and liberty, to a degree, require that toleration. But why proscribe the other, and surely, in every point of view, the more laudable use of estates? Why, through the violation of all property, through an outrage upon every principle of liberty, forcibly carry them from the better to the worse?

This comparison between the new individuals and the old corps is made upon a supposition that no reform could be made in the latter. But in a question of reformation, I always consider corporate bodies, whether sole or consisting of many, to be much more susceptible of a public direction by the power of the state, in the use of their property, and in the regulation of modes and habits of life in their members, than private citizens ever can be, or perhaps ought to be; and this [240] seems to me a very material consideration for those who undertake any thing which merits the name of a politic enterprize.—So far as to the estates of monasteries.

[544]The great *Fête de la féderation* was held in the Champ de Mars on 14 July 1790, as an attempt symbolically to reconstruct national unity, but Burke was not obviously referring to that event; he was presumably referring to the increasingly unrestrained public pleasures of the capital as the revolution subverted public morality.

[545]A *petite maison* was a private place of assignation, at which a man might invite his mistress to a *petit souper*.

With regard to the estates possessed by bishops and canons, and commendatory abbots,[546] I cannot find out for what reason some landed estates may not be held otherwise than by inheritance. Can any philosophic spoiler undertake to demonstrate the positive or the comparative evil, of having a certain, and that too a large portion of landed property,[547] passing in succession thro' persons whose title to it is, always in theory, and often in fact, an eminent degree of piety, morals, and learning; a property which, by its destination, in their turn, and on the score of merit, gives to the noblest families renovation and support, to the lowest the means of dignity and elevation; a property, the tenure of which is the performance of some duty, (whatever value you may choose to set upon that duty) and the character of whose proprietors demands at least an exterior decorum and gravity of manners; who are to exercise a generous but temperate hospitality; part of whose income they are to consider as a trust for charity; and who, even when they fail in their trust, when they slide from their character, and degenerate into a mere common secular nobleman or gentleman, are in no respect worse than those who may succeed them in their forfeited possessions? Is it better that estates should be held by those who have no duty than by those who have one?—by those whose character and destination point to virtues, than by those who have no [241] rule and direction in the expenditure of their estates but their own will and appetite? Nor are these estates held altogether in the character or with the evils supposed inherent in mortmain. They pass from hand to hand with a more rapid circulation than any other. No excess is good; and therefore too great a proportion of landed property may be held officially for life; but it does not seem to me of material injury to any commonwealth, that there should exist some estates that have a chance of being acquired by other means than the previous acquisition of money.

This letter is grown to a great length,[548] though it is indeed short with regard to the infinite extent of the subject. Various avocations have from time to time called my mind from the subject. I was not sorry to give myself leisure to observe whether, in the proceedings of the national assembly,[549] I might not

---

[546]Abbots who also held minor benefices *in commendam*, i.e. in plurality.

[547]Statistics were not available for the share of French land owned by the Church; this also varied widely from region to region. Some revolutionaries were therefore able to estimate the Church's holdings as up to a fifth.

[548]This paragraph marks a natural division in the *Reflections*. Burke appears to have resumed the work at this point in the spring of 1790 after an interval during the parliamentary session.

[549]Burke evidently followed the abbreviated reports of the sessions of the National Assembly published daily in *Le Moniteur*; but it seems that he also read the full version

find reasons to change or to qualify some of my first sentiments. Every thing has confirmed me more strongly in my first opinions. It was my original purpose to take a view of the principles of the national assembly with regard to the great and fundamental establishments; and to compare the whole of what you have substituted in the place of what you have destroyed, with the several members of our British constitution. But this plan is of greater extent than at first I computed, and I find that you have little desire to take the advantage of any examples.[550] At present I must content myself with some remarks upon your establishments; reserving for another time what I [242] proposed to say concerning the spirit of our British monarchy, aristocracy, and democracy, as practically they exist.

I have taken a review of what has been done by the governing power in France. I have certainly spoke of it with freedom. Those whose principle it is to despise the antient permanent sense of mankind, and to set up a scheme of society on new principles, must naturally expect that such of us who think better of the judgment of the human race than of theirs, should consider both them and their devices, as men and schemes upon their trial. They must take it for granted that we attend much to their reason, but not at all to their authority. They have not one of the great influencing prejudices of mankind in their favour. They avow their hostility to opinion. Of course they must expect no support from that influence, which, with every other authority, they have deposed from the seat of its jurisdiction.

I can never consider this assembly as any thing else than a voluntary association of men, who have availed themselves of circumstances, to seize upon the power of the state. They have not the sanction and authority of the character under which they first met. They have assumed another of a very different nature; and have completely altered and inverted all the relations in which

---

in *Procès-verbal de l'Assemblée Nationale*, and the *Courier Français*: see *Reflections*, pp. [253, 305, 320].

[550]Paine replied: 'Mr. Burke had *voluntarily* declined going into a comparison of the English and French constitutions. He apologises (in page 241) for not doing it, by saying that he had not time. Mr. Burke's book was upwards of eight months in hand, and is extended to a volume of three hundred and fifty-six pages. As his omission does injury to his cause, his apology makes it worse; and men on the English side of the water will begin to consider, whether there is not some radical defect in what is called the English constitution, that made it necessary in Mr. Burke to suppress the comparison, to avoid bringing it into view': *Rights of Man*, p. 84. This establishes that Paine used the first or unchanged 'second edition' of the *Reflections*: the third edition, published on 16 November 1790, was extended to 364 pages. It was this third edition which included extensive references to Calonne, and was used as the basis for the French translation. Burke was a more assiduous student of events in France than Paine realised.

they originally stood. They do not hold the authority they exercise under any constitutional law of the state. They have departed from the instructions of the people by whom [243] they were sent;[551] which instructions, as the assembly did not act in virtue of any antient usage or settled law, were the sole source of their authority.[552] The most considerable of their acts have not been done by great majorities; and in this sort of near divisions, which carry only the constructive authority of the whole, strangers will consider reasons as well as resolutions.

If they had set up this new experimental government as a necessary substitute for an expelled tyranny,[553] mankind would anticipate the time of prescription, which, through long usage, mellows into legality governments that were violent in their commencement. All those who have affections which lead them to the conservation of civil order would recognize, even in its cradle, the child as legitimate, which has been produced from those principles of cogent

[551]As a Whig, Burke could not concede that this might have been equally true of England's Convention Parliament in 1689 or America's Continental Congress in 1776.

[552]Burke treated the *cahiers de doléances* addressed to the Estates-General as the original source of the deputies' authority; since those deputies had abolished that body, they lacked a mandate. The question whether the delegates were bound to vote in conformity with the instructions of their constituents had been raised when the Estates-General met, some arguing that this was traditional procedure in order to retain voting by order and resist voting by head in a joint session of the three orders. The conception of the delegate as confined by his instructions was specifically disavowed by Louis XVI on 23 June 1789 in ordering the amalgamation of the three estates; the self-styled National Assembly, in claiming to speak for the French nation, quickly claimed unfettered sovereignty residing in its discussions and expressed by majorities of those deputies voting. Burke himself had famously disavowed the idea that British MPs were bound by the instructions of their constituents in 1774: '*authoritative* instructions; *Mandates* issued, which the Member is bound blindly and implicitly to obey, to vote, and to argue for, though contrary to the clearest conviction of his judgement and conscience; these are things utterly unknown to the laws of this land, and which arise from a fundamental Mistake of the whole order and tenour of our Constitution. Parliament is not a *Congress* of Ambassadors from different and hostile interests; which interests each must maintain, as an Agent and Advocate, against other Agents and Advocates; but Parliament is a *deliberative* Assembly of *one* Nation, with *one* Interest, that of the whole; where, not local Purposes, not local Prejudices ought to guide, but the general Good, resulting from the general Reason of the whole': 'Mr. Edmund Burke's Speech to The Electors of Bristol, On his being declared by the Sheriffs, duly elected one of the Representatives in Parliament for that City, on Thursday the 3d of November, 1774' in *Mr. Edmund Burke's Speeches at His Arrival at Bristol, and at The Conclusion of the Poll* (2nd edn., London, 1775), pp. 28–9. See Burke, *Reflections*, p. [269].

[553]Necessity was Burke's rationale for the Revolution of 1688 in England: see *Reflections*, p. [43].

expediency to which all just governments owe their birth, and on which they justify their continuance. But they will be late and reluctant in giving any sort of countenance to the operations of a power, which has derived its birth from no law and no necessity; but which on the contrary has had its origin in those vices and sinister practices by which the social union is often disturbed and sometimes destroyed. This assembly has hardly a year's prescription. We have their own word for it that they have made a revolution. To make a revolution is a measure which, *prima fronte*, requires an apology. To make a revolution is to subvert the antient state of our country; and no common reasons are called for to justify so violent a proceeding. The sense of mankind [244] authorizes us to examine into the mode of acquiring new power, and to criticise on the use that is made of it with less awe and reverence than that which is usually conceded to a settled and recognized authority.

In obtaining and securing their power, the assembly proceeds upon principles the most opposite from those which appear to direct them in the use of it. An observation on this difference will let us into the true spirit of their conduct. Every thing which they have done, or continue to do, in order to obtain and keep their power, is by the most common arts. They proceed exactly as their ancestors of ambition have done before them. Trace them through all their artifices, frauds, and violences, you can find nothing at all that is new. They follow precedents and examples with the punctilious exactness of a pleader.[554] They never depart an iota from the authentic formulas of tyranny and usurpation. But in all the regulations relative to the public good, the spirit has been the very reverse of this. There they commit the whole to the mercy of untried speculations; they abandon the dearest interests of the public, to those loose theories to which none of them would chuse to trust the slightest of his private concerns. They make this difference, because in their desire of obtaining and securing power they are thoroughly in earnest; there they travel in the beaten road. The public interests, because about them they have no real solicitude, they abandon wholly to chance; I say to chance, because their schemes have nothing in experience to prove their tendency beneficial. [245]

We must always see with a pity not unmixed with respect, the errors of those who are timid and doubtful of themselves with regard to points wherein the happiness of mankind is concerned. But in these gentlemen there is noth-

---

[554]Pleader: a lawyer who drafted the pleas, formal documents following strict precedents, to intiate actions in English law. For this system, see F. W. Maitland, *The Forms of Action at Common Law*, ed. A. H. Chaytor and W. J. Whittaker (Cambridge, 1965); Henry John Stephen, *A Treatise on the Principles of Pleading in Civil Actions* (London, 1824).

ing of the tender parental solicitude which fears to cut up the infant for the sake of an experiment. In the vastness of their promises, and the confidence of their predictions, they far outdo all the boasting of empirics.[555] The arrogance of their pretensions, in a manner provokes, and challenges us to an enquiry into their foundation.

I am convinced that there are men of considerable parts among the popular leaders in the national assembly. Some of them display eloquence in their speeches and their writings. This cannot be without powerful and cultivated talents. But eloquence may exist without a proportionable degree of wisdom.[556] When I speak of ability, I am obliged to distinguish. What they have done towards the support of their system bespeaks no ordinary men. In the system itself, taken as the scheme of a republic constructed for procuring the prosperity and security of the citizen, and for promoting the strength and grandeur of the state, I confess myself unable to find out any thing which displays, in a single instance, the work of a comprehensive and disposing mind, or even the provisions of a vulgar prudence. Their purpose every where seems to have been to evade and slip aside from *difficulty*. This it has been the glory of the great masters in all the arts to confront, and to overcome; and when they had overcome the first difficulty, to turn [246] it into an instrument for new conquests over new difficulties; thus to enable them to extend the empire of their science; and even to push forward beyond the reach of their original thoughts, the land marks of the human understanding itself. Difficulty is a severe instructor, set over us by the supreme ordinance of a parental guardian and legislator, who knows us better than we know ourselves, as he loves us better too. *Pater ipse colendi haud facilem esse viam voluit.*[557] He that wrestles with us strengthens our nerves, and sharpens our skill. Our antagonist is our helper. This amicable conflict with difficulty obliges us to an intimate acquaintance with our object, and compels us to consider it in all its relations. It will not suffer us to be superficial. It is the want of nerves of understanding for such a task; it is the degenerate fondness for tricking short-cuts, and little fallacious facilities, that has in so many parts of the world created governments with arbitrary powers. They have created the late arbitrary monarchy of France. They have created the arbitrary republic of Paris. With them defects in wisdom are to be supplied by the plenitude of force. They get nothing by it.

[555]Empiric: 'An untrained practitioner in physic or surgery; a quack': *OED*.

[556]Cf. Sallust's laconic description of Catiline: 'satis eloquentiae, sapientiae parum'; sufficient eloquence, little wisdom: *The War with Catiline*, V.

[557]'The great Father himself has willed that the path of husbandry should not be smooth': Virgil, *Georgics*, Book I, 121–2.

Commencing their labours on a principle of sloth, they have the common fortune of slothful men. The difficulties which they rather had eluded than escaped, meet them again in their course; they multiply and thicken on them; they are involved, through a labyrinth of confused detail, in an industry without limit, and without direction; and, in conclusion, the whole of their work becomes feeble, vitious, and insecure. [247]

It is this inability to wrestle with difficulty which has obliged the arbitrary assembly of France to commence their schemes of reform with abolition and total destruction.[558] But is it in destroying and pulling down that skill is displayed? Your mob can do this as well at least as your assemblies. The shallowest understanding, the rudest hand, is more than equal to that task. Rage and phrenzy will pull down more in half an hour, than prudence, deliberation, and foresight can build up in an hundred years.[559] The errors and defects of old establishments are visible and palpable. It calls for little ability to point them out; and where absolute power is given, it requires but a word wholly to abolish the vice and the establishment together. The same lazy but restless disposition, which loves sloth and hates quiet, directs these politicians, when they come to work, for supplying the place of what they have destroyed. To

[558]Burke later added a footnote: 'A leading member of the assembly, M. Rabaud de St. Etienne, has expressed the principle of all their proceedings as clearly as possible. Nothing can be more simple:—"*Tous les établissemens en France couronnent le malheur du peuple: pour le rendre heureux il faut le renouveler; changer ses idées; changer ses loix; changer ses moeurs; ... changer les hommes; changer les mots ... tout détruire; oui, tout détuire; puisque tout est à recréer.*" This gentleman was chosen president in an assembly not sitting at the *Quinze vingt,* or the *Petites Maisons;* and composed of persons giving themselves out to be rational beings; but neither his ideas, language, or conduct, differ in the smallest degree from the discourses, opinions, and actions of those within and without the assembly, who direct the operations of the machine now at work in France.' The *Quinze vingts* was Paris's hospital for the blind; the *Petites Maisons* was a lunatic asylum in the rue de Sèvres. For Rabaut Saint-Étienne, see Biographical Guide. Burke cited Saint-Étienne's tract *A la nation française, sur les vices de son gouvernement, sur la nécessité d'établir une Constitution* (Paris, 1788). Similar views were also expressed in his *Considérations sur les intérêts du tiers-état* ([Paris], 1788), an incitement to the regeneration of France.

[559]This was another echo from Burke's past. In 1784 he had denounced the newly-elected House of Commons which had just endorsed George III's ministerial coup in ratifying the king's replacement of the Fox-North coalition by William Pitt in December 1783: 'It required a great length of time, very considerable industry and perseverance, no vulgar policy, the union of many men and many tempers, and the concurrence of events which do not happen every day, to build up an independent House of Commons. Its demolition was accomplished in a moment; and it was the work of ordinary hands. But to construct is a matter of skill; to demolish, force and fury are sufficient.' Burke, *Representation ... 1784,* Preface, p. ii.

make every thing the reverse of what they have seen is quite as easy as to destroy. No difficulties occur in what has never been tried. Criticism is almost
baffled in discovering the defects of what has not existed; and eager enthusiasm, and cheating hope, have all the wide field of imagination in which they
may expatiate with little or no opposition.

— At once to preserve and to reform is quite another thing. When the useful
parts of an old establishment are kept, and what is superadded is to be fitted
to what is retained, a vigorous mind, steady persevering attention, various
powers of comparison and combination, and the resources [248] of an understanding fruitful in expedients are to be exercised; they are to be exercised in a
continued conflict with the combined force of opposite vices; with the obstinacy that rejects all improvement, and the levity that is fatigued and disgusted
with every thing of which it is in possession. But you may object—"A process
of this kind is slow. It is not fit for an assembly, which glories in performing in
a few months the work of ages. Such a mode of reforming, possibly might take
up many years." Without question it might; and it ought. It is one of the excellencies of a method in which time is amongst the assistants, that its operation is slow, and in some cases almost imperceptible. If circumspection and
caution are a part of wisdom, when we work only upon inanimate matter,
surely they become a part of duty too, when the subject of our demolition and
construction is not brick and timber, but sentient beings, by the sudden alteration of whose state, condition, and habits, multitudes may be rendered miserable. But it seems as if it were the prevalent opinion in Paris, that an unfeeling
heart, and an undoubting confidence, are the sole qualifications for a perfect
legislator. Far different are my ideas of that high office. The true lawgiver
ought to have an heart full of sensibility. He ought to love and respect his
kind, and to fear himself. It may be allowed to his temperament to catch his
ultimate object with an intuitive glance; but his movements towards it ought
to be deliberate. Political arrangement, as it is a work for social ends, is to be
only wrought by social means. [249] There mind must conspire with mind.
Time is required to produce that union of minds which alone can produce all
the good we aim at. Our patience will atchieve more than our force. If I might
venture to appeal to what is so much out of fashion in Paris, I mean to experience, I should tell you, that in my course I have known, and, according to my
measure, have co-operated with great men; and I have never yet seen any plan
which has not been mended by the observations of those who were much inferior in understanding to the person who took the lead in the business. By a
slow but well-sustained progress, the effect of each step is watched; the good
or ill success of the first, gives light to us in the second; and so, from light to
light, we are conducted with safety through the whole series. We see, that the

parts of the system do not clash. The evils latent in the most promising contrivances are provided for as they arise. One advantage is as little as possible sacrificed to another. We compensate, we reconcile, we balance. We are enabled to unite into a consistent whole the various anomalies and contending principles that are found in the minds and affairs of men. From hence arises, not an excellence in simplicity, but one far superior, an excellence in composition. Where the great interests of mankind are concerned through a long succession of generations, that succession ought to be admitted into some share in the councils which are so deeply to affect them. If justice requires this, the work itself requires the aid of more minds than one age can furnish. It is from this view of things [250] that the best legislators have been often satisfied with the establishment of some sure, solid, and ruling principle in government; a power like that which some of the philosophers have called a plastic nature;[560] and having fixed the principle, they have left it afterwards to its own operation.

To proceed in this manner, that is, to proceed with a presiding principle, and a prolific energy, is with me the criterion of profound wisdom. What your politicians think the marks of a bold, hardy genius, are only proofs of a deplorable want of ability. By their violent haste, and their defiance of the process of nature, they are delivered over blindly to every projector and adventurer, to every alchymist and empiric. They despair of turning to account any thing that is common. Diet is nothing in their system of remedy. The worst of it is, that this their despair of curing common distempers by regular methods, arises not only from defect of comprehension, but, I fear, from some malignity of disposition. Your legislators seem to have taken their opinions of all professions, ranks, and offices, from the declamations and buffooneries of satirists; who would themselves be astonished if they were held to the letter of their own descriptions. By listening only to these, your leaders regard all things only on the side of their vices and faults, and view those vices and faults under every colour of exaggeration. It is undoubtedly true, though it may seem paradoxical; but in general, those who are habitually employed in finding and displaying faults, are unqualified for the work of reformation: [251] because their minds are not only unfurnished with patterns of the fair and good, but by habit they come to take no delight in the contemplation of those things. By hating vices too much, they come to love men too little. It is therefore not wonderful, that they should be indisposed and unable to serve them. From hence arises the complexional disposition of some of your guides to pull every thing in pieces. At this malicious game they display the whole of their

---

[560]Medieval philosophers coined the term to explain reproduction.

*quadrimanous*[561] activity. As to the rest, the paradoxes of eloquent writers,[562] brought forth purely as a sport of fancy, to try their talents, to rouze attention, and excite surprize, are taken up by these gentlemen, not in the spirit of the original authors, as means of cultivating their taste and improving their style. These paradoxes become with them serious grounds of action, upon which they proceed in regulating the most important concerns of the state. Cicero ludicrously describes Cato as endeavouring to act in the commonwealth upon the school paradoxes which exercised the wits of the junior students in the stoic philosophy.[563] If this was true of Cato, these gentlemen copy after him in the manner of some persons who lived about his time—*pede nudo Catonem.*[564] Mr. Hume told me, that he had from Rousseau himself the secret of his principles of composition.[565] That acute, though eccentric, observer had perceived, that to strike and interest the public, the marvellous must be produced; that the marvellous of the heathen mythology had long since lost its effect; that giants, magicians, fairies, and heroes of romance [252] which succeeded, had exhausted the portion of credulity which belonged to their age; that now nothing was left to a writer but that species of the marvellous, which might still be produced, and with as great an effect as ever, though in another way; that is, the marvellous in life, in manners, in characters, and in extraordinary situations, giving rise to new and unlooked-for strokes in politics and morals. I believe, that were Rousseau alive, and in one of his lucid intervals, he would be shocked at the practical phrenzy of his scholars, who in their para-

[561]Quadrimanous: four handed, i.e. monkey-like, wantonly or thoughtlessly destructive.

[562]Burke had condemned Rousseau's *Letter to d'Alembert* for its 'tendency to paradox' in 1759, and in 1762 reviewed Rousseau's *Émile* equally unfavourably as 'dangerous both to piety and morals', the result of its author's 'paradoxical genius': *Annual Register* (1759), p. 479; (1762), p. 227.

[563]'I have often noticed, Brutus, that your uncle Cato when making a speech in the Senate deals with weighty arguments drawn from philosophy which do not conform with our usual practice in the law-courts and the assembly, but that nevertheless his oratory succeeds in making such things acceptable even to the general public': Cicero, *Paradoxa Stoicorum*, 1.

[564]'What, if a man were to ape Cato with grim and savage look, with bare feet and the cut of a scanty gown, would he thus set before us Cato's virtue and morals?': Horace, *Epistles*, Book I, xix, 12–13.

[565]Jean-Jacques Rousseau took refuge in England in 1766 and enjoyed the protection of David Hume. The paranoid Frenchman later turned against his host, who justified his conduct in a memorandum later published, without Hume's permission, as *A Concise and Genuine Account of the Dispute between Mr. Hume and Mr. Rousseau* (London, 1766). Hume's reported view of Rousseau may have been coloured by this event.

doxes are servile imitators; and even in their incredulity discover an implicit faith.[566]

Men who undertake considerable things, even in a regular way, ought to give us ground to presume ability. But the physician of the state, who, not satisfied with the cure of distempers, undertakes to regenerate constitutions, ought to shew uncommon powers. Some very unusual appearances of wisdom ought to display themselves on the face of the designs of those who appeal to no practice, and who copy after no model. Has any such been manifested? I shall take a view (it shall for the subject be a very short one) of what the assembly has done, with regard, first, to the constitution of the legislature; in the next place, to that of the executive power; then to that of the judicature; afterwards to the model of the army; and conclude with the system of finance, to see whether we can discover in any part of their schemes the portentous ability, which may justify these bold undertakers in the superiority which they assume over mankind. [253]

It is in the model of the sovereign and presiding part of this new republic, that we should expect their grand display. Here they were to prove their title to their proud demands. For the plan itself at large, and for the reasons on which it is grounded, I refer to the journals of the assembly of the 29th of September 1789,[567] and to the subsequent proceedings which have made any alterations in the plan. So far as in a matter somewhat confused I can see light, the system remains substantially as it has been originally framed.[568] My few

[566]Burke's most perceptive analysis of Rousseau is found in his *Letter to a Member of the National Assembly*: see *Reflections*, p. [127].

[567]The text of the resolution of the Committee of the Constitution was presented by Jacques Guillaume Thouret to the National Assembly on 29 September 1789: see *Procès-verbal de l'Assemblée Nationale* 87 (29 September 1789) and *Le Moniteur*, nos. 64–5, of 28–29 and 29 September 1789. It denounced France's old territorial divisons as 'vicieuses sous plusieurs rapports, tant physiques que moraux'. Instead, France would be divided into eighty *départements* of equal area, each eighteen leagues square (plus Paris as a central district); each *département* into nine equal *communes*; each *commune* into nine equal *cantons*. The initial proposal was for the indirect election of deputies through three levels: the *cantons* electing to the *communes*, the *communes* to the *départements*, the *départements* to the National Assembly.

[568]This sentence was probably written in early 1790. The plan of 29 September 1789 did, in fact, continue to evolve, especially by abandoning the idea of a geometric division into squares in the electoral law of 22 December 1789 and the reduction of three stages of indirect election to two. A deputy pointed this out to Burke after the publication of the *Reflections*: 'Not that the Assembly had very much improved the Scheme of their Committee, very much altered it for the better.—But they have altered it, they have taken out some of its degrés of those graduate Elections, you so Justly disapprove, they in some things, in my opinion, have altered it for the worse, but then,

remarks will be such as regard its spirit, its tendency, and its fitness for framing a popular commonwealth, which they profess theirs to be, suited to the
ends for which any commonwealth, and particularly such a commonwealth,
is made. At the same time, I mean to consider its consistency with itself, and its
own principles.

Old establishments are tried by their effects. If the people are happy,
united, wealthy, and powerful, we presume the rest. We conclude that to be
good from whence good is derived. In old establishments various correctives
have been found for their aberrations from theory. Indeed they are the results
of various necessities and expediences. They are not often constructed after
any theory; theories are rather drawn from them. In them we often see the end
best obtained, where the means seem not perfectly reconcileable to what we
may fancy was the original scheme. The means taught by experience may be
better suited to political ends than those contrived in the original project.
They again re-act upon the primitive constitution, and [254] sometimes improve the design itself from which they seem to have departed. I think all this
might be curiously exemplified in the British constitution. At worst, the errors

---

some of your Observations become without Application.' This was unfortunate, since
'the Ennemies of good order, shall cavill on those slig[h]t Faults, to be met with, in
your Work, to keep the Eyes of my countrymen, from the masterly strokes, by whom
you so vividly expose, the Raw and Rash undertaking, of those prentice Bricklayers of
ours, in erecting that noble, that noblest of all Buildings, so very much above their skill
and Ability, the Constitution of a great State': François-Louis-Thibault de Menonville
to Burke, 17 November 1790: Burke, *Correspondence*, VI, p. 163. Burke candidly replied: 'Some of the errors you point out to me in my printed letter are really such. It is
corrected in the edition which I take the liberty of sending to you. As to the cavils
which may be made on some part of my remarks, with regard to the *gradations* in your
new constitution, you observe justly, that they do not affect the substance of my objections. Whether there be a round more or less in the ladder of representation, by which
your workmen ascend from their parochial tyranny to their federal anarchy, when the
whole scale is false, appears to me of little or no importance. I published my thoughts
on that constitution, that my countrymen might be enabled to estimate the wisdom of
the plans which were held out to their imitation. I conceived that the true character of
those plans would be best collected from the committee appointed to prepare them. I
thought that the scheme of their building would be better comprehended in the design
of the architects than in the execution of the masons. It was not worth my reader's
while to occupy himself with the alterations by which bungling practice corrects absurd theory. Such an investigation would be endless: because every day's past experience of impracticability has driven, and every day's future experience will drive, those
men to new devices as exceptionable as the old; and which are no otherwise worthy of
observation than as they give a daily proof of the delusion of their promises, and the
falsehood of their professions': Burke, *Letter to a Member*, pp. 1–2. Burke's enemies in
England chose to overlook this distinction.

and deviations of every kind in reckoning are found and computed, and the ship proceeds in her course. This is the case of old establishments; but in a new and merely theoretic system, it is expected that every contrivance shall appear, on the face of it, to answer its end; especially where the projectors are no way embarrassed with an endeavour to accommodate the new building to an old one, either in the walls or on the foundations.

The French builders, clearing away as mere rubbish whatever they found, and, like their ornamental gardeners,[569] forming every thing into an exact level, propose to rest the whole local and general legislature on three bases of three different kinds; one geometrical, one arithmetical, and the third financial; the first of which they call the *basis of territory*; the second, the *basis of population*; and the third, the *basis of contribution*. For the accomplishment of the first of these purposes they divide the area of their country into eighty-one pieces, regularly square, of eighteen leagues by eighteen. These large divisions are called *Departments*. These they portion, proceeding by square measurement, into seventeen hundred and twenty districts called *Communes*. These again they subdivide, still proceeding by square measurement, into smaller districts called *Cantons*, making in all 6,400.[570]

At first view this geometrical basis of theirs presents not much to admire or to blame. It calls [255] for no great legislative talents. Nothing more than an accurate land surveyor, with his chain, sight, and theodolite, is requisite for such a plan as this. In the old divisions of the country various accidents at various times, and the ebb and flow of various properties and jurisdictions, settled their bounds. These bounds were not made upon any fixed system undoubtedly. They were subject to some inconveniencies; but they were inconveniencies for which use had found remedies, and habit had supplied accommodation and patience.[571] In this new pavement of square within square, and this organisation and semiorganisation made on the system of Empedocles[572]

[569]Burke's library contained a work described as *Theorie des jardins*: LC MS, fo. 12. This was probably [A. I. Dezallier d'Argentville], *La Théorie et la pratique du jardinage* (Paris, 1709).

[570]Burke described the plan presented on 29 September 1789 (sc. 720 *communes*, 6480 *cantons*). The *départements* actually created in January 1790 were divided into districts, *cantons* and *municipalités*. Burke's main point, however, was not the arrangement of these units but the principle of indirect election: Fierro and Liébert, p. 721.

[571]For accounts of how French society of the *ancien régime* actually worked, see Bibliography, D i.

[572]Empedocles (c. 490–420 BC) was responsible for the division of natural phenomena into different combinations of fire, air, water and earth. See also *Reflections*, p. [92].

and Buffon,[573] and not upon any politic principle, it is impossible that innumerable local inconveniencies, to which men are not habituated, must not arise. But these I pass over, because it requires an accurate knowledge of the country, which I do not possess, to specify them.

When these state surveyors came to take a view of their work of measurement, they soon found, that in politics, the most fallacious of all things was geometrical demonstration. They had then recourse to another basis (or rather buttress) to support the building which tottered on that false foundation. It was evident, that the goodness of the soil, the number of the people, their wealth, and the largeness of their contribution, made such infinite variations between square and square as to render mensuration a ridiculous standard of power in the commonwealth, and equality in geometry the most unequal of all measures in the distribution [256] of men. However, they could not give it up. But dividing their political and civil representation into three parts, they allotted one of those parts to the square measurement, without a single fact or calculation to ascertain whether this territorial proportion of representation was fairly assigned, and ought upon any principle really to be a third. Having however given to geometry this portion (of a third for her dower)[574] out of compliment I suppose to that sublime science, they left the other two to be scuffled for between the other parts, of population and contribution.

When they came to provide for population, they were not able to proceed quite so smoothly as they had done in the field of their geometry.[575] Here their arithmetic came to bear upon their juridical metaphysics. Had they stuck to their metaphysic principles, the arithmetical process would be simple indeed. Men, with them, are strictly equal, and are entitled to equal rights in their own government. Each head, on this system, would have its vote, and every man would vote directly for the person who was to represent him in the legislature. "But soft—by regular degrees, not yet."[576] This metaphysic principle,

---

[573]Georges Louis Leclerc, comte de Buffon (1707–88), naturalist, divided the natural world into orders, genera and species. Burke owned Buffon's *Oeuvres complètes*: LC MS, fo. 2.

[574]A widow was legally entitled to a third of her husband's property.

[575]For the section of the Constitutional Committee's report of 29 September 1789 concerning 'Base personelle ou de population', see *Le Moniteur*, 28–9 September 1789. Out of a total French population of 26 million, it envisaged an electorate of 'active citizens' of 4.4 million. It thereby disenfranchised another 2 million adult males (Fierro and Liébert, pp. 722–3).

[576]'Behold! my Lord advances o'er the Green, / Smit with the mighty pleasure, to be seen: / But soft—by regular approach—not yet—/ First thro' the length of yon hot Terras sweat, / And when up ten steep Slopes you've dragged your thighs, / Just at his Study-door he'll bless your Eyes': Alexander Pope, *An Epistle to the Right Honourable*

*& sharp crit.*

to which law, custom, usage, policy, reason, were to yield, is to yield itself to their pleasure. There must be many degrees, and some stages, before the representative can come in contact with his constituent. Indeed, as we shall soon see, these two persons are to have no sort of communion with each other. First, the voters in the *Canton*, who compose what they call *primary assemblies*, are to have a *qualification*. What! a [257] qualification on the indefeasible rights of men? Yes; but it shall be a very small qualification. Our injustice shall be very little oppressive; only the local valuation of three days labour paid to the public. Why, this is not much, I readily admit, for any thing but the utter subversion of your equalising principle. As a qualification it might as well be let alone; for it answers no one purpose for which qualifications are established; and, on your ideas, it excludes from a vote, the man of all others whose natural equality stands the most in need of protection and defence; I mean the man who has nothing else but his natural equality to guard him. You order him to buy the right, which you before told him nature had given to him gratuitously at his birth, and of which no authority on earth could lawfully deprive him. With regard to the person who cannot come up to your market, a tyrannous aristocracy, as against him, is established by you who pretend to be its sworn foe.

*ouch*

The gradation proceeds. These primary assemblies of the *Canton* elect deputies to the *Commune*; one for every two hundred qualified inhabitants. Here is the first medium put between the primary elector and the representative legislator; and here a new turnpike is fixed for taxing the rights of men with a second qualification: for none can be elected into the *Commune* who does not pay the amount of ten days labour. Nor have we yet done. There is still to be another gradation.[577] These *Communes*, chosen by the *Canton*, choose to the *Department*; and the deputies of the *Department* choose their [258] deputies to the *National Assembly*. Here is a third barrier of a senseless qualification. Every deputy to the national assembly must pay, in direct con-

---

*Richard Earl of Burlington. Occasion'd by his Publishing Palladio's Designs of the Baths, Arches, Theatres &c. of Ancient Rome* (London, 1731), p. 11. Pope's poem was a satire on architectural formalism.

[577]Following Menonville's objection, Burke added a footnote to the seventh edition: 'The assembly, in executing the plan of their committee, made some alterations. They have struck out one stage in these gradations; this removes a part of the objection: but the main objection, namely, that in their scheme the first constituent voter has no connection with the representative legislator, remains in all its force. There are other alterations, some possibly for the better, some certainly for the worse; but to the author the merit or demerit of these smaller alterations appear to be of no moment, where the scheme itself is fundamentally vitious and absurd.'

tribution, to the value of a *mark of silver*.[578] Of all these qualifying barriers we must think alike; that they are impotent to secure independence; strong only to destroy the rights of men.[579]

In all this process, which in its fundamental elements affects to consider only *population* upon a principle of natural right, there is a manifest attention to *property*; which, however just and reasonable on other schemes, is on theirs perfectly unsupportable.

When they come to their third basis, that of *Contribution*, we find that they have more completely lost sight of their rights of men. This last basis rests *entirely* on property. A principle totally different from the equality of men, and utterly irreconcileable to it, is thereby admitted; but no sooner is this principle, which is a principle regarding property, admitted, than (as usual) it is subverted; and it is not subverted, (as we shall presently see,) to approximate the inequality of riches to the level of nature. The additional share in the third portion of representation, (a portion reserved exclusively for the higher contribution,) is made to regard the *district* only, and not the individuals in it who pay. It is easy to perceive, by the course of their reasonings, how much they were embarrassed by their contradictory ideas of the rights of men and the privileges of riches. The committee of constitution do as good as admit that they are wholly irreconcileable. [259] "The relation, with regard to the contributions, is without doubt *null* (say they) when the question is on the balance of the political rights as between individual and individual; without which *personal equality would be destroyed*, and *an aristocracy of the rich* would be established. But this inconvenience entirely disappears when the proportional relation of the contribution is only considered in the *great masses*, and is solely between province and province; it serves in that case only to form a just reciprocal proportion between the cities, without affecting the personal rights of the citizens."[580]

[578]This was decreed by the National Assembly in October 1789. A *marc*, 224 grammes of silver, was then worth about 51 *livres*; only about 50,000 Frenchmen qualified. After protests, this provision was abolished by the Assembly on 27 August 1791: Fierro and Liébert, p. 724.

[579]The *Déclaration des droits de l'homme et du citoyen* began: 'Les hommes naissent et demeurent libres et égaux en droits.' Burke's English enemies avoided his main point, that property qualifications for the franchise and indirect election violated the principle of the equality of citizens; they challenged instead his account of the levels through which election passed. French critics of the electoral proposals, however, were candid in pointing out this contradiction.

[580]Burke translated the last paragraph of the Committee's report, under 'Base de contribution', printed in *Le Moniteur*, 28–9 September 1789.

Here the principle of *contribution*, as taken between man and man, is reprobated as *null*, and destructive to equality; and as pernicious too; because it leads to the establishment of an *aristocracy of the rich*. However, it must not be abandoned. And the way of getting rid of the difficulty is to establish the inequality as between department and department, leaving all the individuals in each department upon an exact par. Observe, that this parity between individuals had been before destroyed when the qualifications within the departments were settled; nor does it seem a matter of great importance whether the equality of men be injured by masses or individually. An individual is not of the same importance in a mass represented by a few, as in a mass represented by many. It would be too much to tell a man jealous of his equality, that the elector has the same franchise who votes for three members as he who votes for ten.[581]

Now take it in the other point of view, and suppose [260] their principle of representation according to contribution, that is, according to *riches*, to be well founded, and to be a necessary basis for the republic, how have they provided for the rich by giving to the district, that is to say, to the poor in the district of *Canton* and *Commune*, who are the majority, the power of making an additional number of members on account of the superior contribution of the wealthy? Suppose one man (it is an easy supposition) to contribute ten times more than ten of his neighbours. For this contribution he has one vote out of ten. The poor outvote him by nine voices in virtue of his superior contribution, for (say) *ten* members, instead of out-voting him for only one member. Why are the rich complimented with an aristocratic preference, which they can never feel either as a gratification to pride, or as a security to fortune? The rich indeed require an additional security from the dangers to which they are exposed when a popular power is prevalent; but it is impossible to divine, on this system of unequal masses, how they are protected; because the aristocratic mass is generated from democratic principles; and the prevalence in the general representation has no sort of connection with those on account of whose property this superiority is given. If the contrivers of this scheme meant any sort of favour to the rich in consequence of their contribution, they ought to have conferred the privilege either on the individual rich, or on some class formed of rich persons; because the contest between the rich and the poor is not a struggle between corporation and corporation, but a contest between men [261] and men; a competition not between districts, but between descriptions. It would answer its purpose better if the scheme was inverted; that the votes of the masses were rendered equal; and that the votes within each mass

---

[581]For Burke's textual revisions at this point, see Appendix I.

were proportioned to property. In any other light, I see nothing but danger from the inequality of the masses.

If indeed the masses were to provide for the general treasury by distinct contingents, and that the revenue had not (as it has) many impositions running through the whole, which affect men individually, and not corporately, and which, by their nature, confound all territorial limits, something might be said for the basis of contribution as founded on masses. But of all things, this representation, to be measured by contribution, is the most difficult to settle upon principles of equity, in a country which considers its districts as members of an whole. For a great city, such as Bourdeaux or Paris, appears to pay a vast body of duties, almost out of all assignable proportion to other places, and its mass is considered accordingly. But are these cities the true contributors in that proportion? No. The consumers of the commodities imported into Bourdeaux, who are scattered through all France, pay the import duties of Bourdeaux. The produce of the vintage in Guienne and Languedoc give to that city the means of its contribution growing out of an export commerce. The landholders who spend their estates in Paris, and are thereby the creators of that city, contribute for Paris from the provinces out of which their revenues arise.

If in equity this basis of contribution, as locally [262] ascertained by masses, be inequitable, it is impolitic too. If it be one of the objects to preserve the weak from being crushed by the strong (as in all society undoubtedly it is) how are the smaller and poorer of these masses to be saved from the tyranny of the more wealthy? Is it by adding to their means of oppressing them? When we come to a balance of representation between corporate bodies, provincial interests, emulations, and jealousies are full as likely to arise among them as among individuals; and their divisions are likely to produce much hotter dissention, and something leading much more nearly to a war.[582]

To compare together the three bases, not on their political reason, but on the ideas on which the assembly works, and to try its consistency with itself, we cannot avoid observing, that the principle which the committee call the basis of *population*, does not begin to operate from the same point with the two other principles called the bases of *territory* and of *contribution*, which are both of an aristocratic nature. The consequence is, that where all three begin to operate together, there is the most absurd inequality produced by the operation of the former on the two latter principles. Every canton contains four square leagues, and is estimated to contain, on the average, 4,000 inhabi-

[582]France's declarations of war in 1792 obliterated this potential source of domestic conflict.

tants, or 680 voters in the *primary assemblies*, which vary in numbers with the population of the canton, and send *one deputy* to the *commune* for every 200 voters. *Nine cantons* make a *commune*.

Now let us take *a canton* containing *a sea-port town of trade*, or *a great manufacturing town*. Let us suppose the population of this canton to be [263] 12,700 inhabitants, or 2,193 voters, forming *three primary assemblies*, and sending *ten deputies* to the *commune*.

Oppose to this *one* canton *two* others of the remaining eight in the same commune. These we may suppose to have their fair population of 4,000 inhabitants, and 680 voters each, or 8,000 inhabitants and 1,360 voters, both together. These will form only *two primary assemblies*, and send only *six* deputies to the *commune*.

When the assembly of the *commune* comes to vote on the *basis of territory*, which principle is first admitted to operate in that assembly, the *single canton* which has *half* the territory of the *other two*, will have *ten* voices to *six* in the election of *three deputies* to the assembly of the department, chosen on the express ground of a representation of territory.

This inequality, striking as it is, will be yet highly aggravated, if we suppose, as we fairly may, the *several* other cantons of the *commune* to fall proportionably short of the average population, as much as the *principal canton* exceeds it. Now, as to *the basis of contribution*, which also is a principle admitted first to operate in the assembly of the *commune*. Let us again take *one* canton, such as is stated above. If the whole of the direct contributions paid by a great trading or manufacturing town be divided equally among the inhabitants, each individual will be found to pay much more than an individual living in the country according to the same average.[583] The whole paid by the inhabitants of the former will be more than [264] the whole paid by the inhabitants of the latter—we may fairly assume one-third more. Then the 12,700 inhabitants, or 2,193 voters of the canton will pay as much as 19,050 inhabitants, or 3,289 voters of the *other cantons*, which are nearly the estimated proportion of inhabitants and voters of *five* other cantons. Now the 2,193 voters will, as I before said, send only *ten* deputies to the assembly; the 3,289 voters will send *sixteen*. Thus, for an *equal* share in the contribution of the whole *commune*, there will be a difference of *sixteen* voices to *ten* in voting for deputies to be chosen on the principle of representing the general contribution of the whole *commune*.

By the same mode of computation we shall find 15,875 inhabitants, or

---

[583]Fierro and Liébert point out (p. 725) that Burke, on his evidence, should have argued not that town dwellers paid a third more than country dwellers, but a third less.

2,741 voters of the *other* cantons, who pay *one-sixth* LESS to the contribution of the whole *commune*, will have *three* voices MORE than the 12,700 inhabitants, or 2,193 voters of the *one* canton.

Such is the fantastical and unjust inequality between mass and mass, in this curious repartition of the rights of representation arising out of *territory* and *contribution*. The qualifications which these confer are in truth negative qualifications, that give a right in an inverse proportion to the possession of them.

In this whole contrivance of the three bases, consider it in any light you please, I do not see a variety of objects, reconciled in one consistent whole, but several contradictory principles reluctantly and irreconcileably brought and held together by your philosophers, like wild beasts shut up in a cage, to [265] claw and bite each other to their mutual destruction.[584]

I am afraid I have gone too far into their way of considering the formation of a constitution. They have much, but bad, metaphysics; much, but bad, geometry; much, but false proportionate arithmetic; but if it were all as exact as metaphysics, geometry, and arithmetic ought to be, and if their schemes were perfectly consistent in all their parts, it would make only a more fair and sightly vision. It is remarkable, that in a great arrangement of mankind, not one reference whatsoever is to be found to any thing moral or any thing politic; nothing that relates to the concerns, the actions, the passions, the interests of men. *Hominem non sapiunt.*[585]

You see I only consider this constitution as electoral, and leading by steps to the National Assembly. I do not enter into the internal government of the Departments, and their genealogy through the Communes and Cantons. These local governments are, in the original plan, to be as nearly as possible composed in the same manner and on the same principles with the elective assemblies.[586] They are each of them bodies perfectly compact and rounded in themselves.

You cannot but perceive in this scheme, that it has a direct and immediate tendency to sever France into a variety of republics, and to render them totally independent of each other, without any direct constitutional means of coher-

---

[584]The absence of reliable statistics on population meant that the Legislative Assembly, elected on this system and meeting in October 1791, contained many anomalies. For an argument that Burke's fears were, nevertheless, exaggerated see Fierro and Liébert, pp. 725–8.

[585]'You won't find Centaurs here or Gorgons or Harpies: my page smacks of humanity': Martial, *Epigrams*, Book X, iv, 9–10.

[586]One half of the plan presented on 29 September was concerned with elections to the National Assembly; the other set out a new plan of local government.

ence, connection, or subordination, except what may be derived from their acquiescence in the determinations of the general congress of [266] the ambassadors from each independent republic.[587] Such in reality is the National Assembly, and such governments I admit do exist in the world, though in forms infinitely more suitable to the local and habitual circumstances of their people. But such associations, rather than bodies politic, have generally been the effect of necessity, not choice; and I believe the present French power is the very first body of citizens, who, having obtained full authority to do with their country what they pleased, have chosen to dissever it in this barbarous manner.

It is impossible not to observe, that in the spirit of this geometrical distribution, and arithmetical arrangement, these pretended citizens treat France exactly like a country of conquest. Acting as conquerors, they have imitated the policy of the harshest of that harsh race. The policy of such barbarous victors, who contemn a subdued people, and insult their feelings, has ever been, as much as in them lay, to destroy all vestiges of the antient country, in religion, in polity, in laws, and in manners; to confound all territorial limits; to produce a general poverty; to put up their properties to auction; to crush their princes, nobles, and pontiffs; to lay low every thing which had lifted its head above the level, or which could serve to combine or rally, in their distresses, the disbanded people, under the standard of old opinion. They have made France free in the manner in which those sincere friends to the rights of mankind, the Romans, freed Greece, Macedon, and other nations. They destroyed the bonds of their union, under [267] colour of providing for the independence of each of their cities.[588]

When the members who compose these new bodies of cantons, communes, and departments, arrangements purposely produced through the medium of confusion, begin to act, they will find themselves, in a great measure, strangers to one another. The electors and elected throughout, especially in the rural *cantons*, will be frequently without any civil habitudes or connections, or any of that natural discipline which is the soul of a true republic. Magistrates and collectors of revenue are now no longer acquainted with their districts, bishops with their dioceses, or curates with their parishes. These new colonies of the rights of men

[587]For a discussion of the centralising and decentralising forces at work in the Revolution, see Burke, *Reflections*, pp. [77–8]. Burke was not alone in over-estimating the potential for local autonomy: for Mirabeau's similar predictions, see Fierro and Liébert, p. 729.

[588]Burke wrote of the initial project. The *départements* later created by the constitutional committee of the National Assembly often respected ancient boundaries or changed them only for good reason: Fierro and Liébert, p. 730; Burke, *Reflections*, p. [284].

bear a strong resemblance to that sort of military colonies which Tacitus has observed upon in the declining policy of Rome. In better and wiser days (whatever course they took with foreign nations) they were careful to make the elements of a methodical subordination and settlement to be coeval; and even to lay the foundations of civil discipline in the military.[589] But, when all the good arts had fallen into ruin, they proceeded, as your assembly does, upon the equality of men, and with as little judgment, and as little care for those things which make a republic tolerable [268] or durable. But in this, as well as almost every instance, your new commonwealth is born, and bred, and fed, in those corruptions which mark degenerated and worn out republics. Your child comes into the world with the symptoms of death; the *facies Hippocratica*[590] forms the character of its physiognomy, and the prognostic of its fate.[591]

The confusion, which attends on all such proceedings, they even declare to be one of their objects, and they hope to secure their constitution by a terror of a return of those evils which attended their making it. "By this," say they, "its destruction will become difficult to authority, which cannot break it up without the entire disorganization of the whole state."[592] They presume, that if this authority should ever come to the same degree of power that they have acquired, it would make a more moderate and chastised use of it, and would piously tremble entirely to disorganise the state in the savage manner that they have done. They expect, from the virtues of returning despotism, the security which is to be enjoyed by the offspring of their popular vices.[593]

[589]Non, ut olim, universæ legiones deducebantur cum tribunis, et centurionibus, et sui cujusque ordinis militibus, ut consensu et caritate rempublicam afficerent; sed ignoti inter se, diversis manipulis, sine rectore, sine affectibus mutuis, quasi ex alio genere mortalium, repente in unum collecti, numerus magis quam colonia. Tac. Annal, l. 14. sect. 27. All this will be still more applicable to the unconnected, rotatory, biennial national assemblies, in this absurd and senseless constitution. [B] 'For the days had passed when entire legions — with tribunes, centurions, privates in their proper centuries — were so transplanted as to create, by their unanimity and their comradeship, a little commonwealth. The settlers now were strangers among strangers; men from totally distinct maniples, leaderless; mutually indifferent; suddenly, as if they were anything in the world except soldiers, massed in one place to compose an aggregate rather than a colony.' Tacitus, *Annals*, Book XIV, xxvii.

[590]The appearance of the face just before death, a symptom first described by Hippocrates. Burke owned a copy of Foesio's edition of *Hippocratis Opera* (2 vols., Geneva, 1657): *LC*, p. 17; LC MS, fo. 19.

[591]Burke subsequently moved to this point the two paragraphs on pp. [272–5], 'The legislators ... This is to play a most desperate game.'

[592]Burke quoted the remarks with which Thouret introduced the plan to the National Assembly: *Le Moniteur*, 28–9 September 1789.

[593]For text later inserted here, see Appendix I.

It is this resolution, to break their country into separate republics, which has driven them into the greatest number of their difficulties and contradictions. If it were not for this, all the questions of exact equality, and these balances never to be settled, of individual rights, population, and contribution, would be wholly useless. The representation, though derived from parts, would be a duty which equally regarded the whole. Each deputy to the assembly would be the representative of France, and of all its descriptions, of the many and of the [269] few, of the rich and of the poor, of the great districts and of the small. All these districts would themselves be subordinate to some standing authority, existing independently of them; an authority in which their representation, and every thing that belongs to it, originated, and to which it was pointed. This standing, unalterable, fundamental government would make, and it is the only thing which could make, that territory truly and properly an whole. With us, when we elect popular representatives, we send them to a council, in which each man individually is a subject, and submitted to a government complete in all its ordinary functions. With you the elective assembly is the sovereign, and the sole sovereign: all the members are therefore integral parts of this sole sovereignty. But with us it is totally different. With us the representative, separated from the other parts, can have no action and no existence. The government is the point of reference of the several members and districts of our representation. This is the center of our unity. This government of reference is a trustee for the *whole*,[594] and not for the parts. So is the other branch of our public council, I mean the house of lords.[595] With us the king and the lords are several and joint securities for the equality of each district, each province, each city. When did you hear in Great Britain of any province suffering from the inequality of its representation; what district from having no representation at all? Not only our monarchy and our peerage secure the equality on which our unity depends, but it is the spirit of the house of commons itself. The very inequality of [270] representation, which is so foolishly complained of, is perhaps the very thing which prevents us from thinking or acting as members for districts. Cornwall elects as many members as all Scotland. But is Cornwall better taken care of than Scotland? Few trouble their heads about any of your bases, out of some giddy clubs. Most of those,[596] who wish for any change, upon any plausible grounds, desire it on different ideas.[597]

[594]See *Reflections*, p. [243].
[595]See *Reflections*, p. [84].
[596]Including Burke himself.
[597]A small number of reformers seized on this passage, but Burke correctly noted

Your new constitution is the very reverse of ours in its principle; and I am astonished how any persons could dream of holding out any thing done in it as an example for Great Britain. With you there is little, or rather no, connection between the last representative and the first constituent. The member who goes to the national assembly is not chosen by the people, nor accountable to them. There are three elections before he is chosen: two sets of magistracy intervene between him and the primary assembly, so as to render him, as I have said, an ambassador of a state, and not the representative of the people within a state. By this the whole spirit of the election is changed; nor can any corrective your constitution-mongers have devised render him any thing else than what he is. The very attempt to do it would inevitably introduce a confusion, if possible, more horrid than the present. There is no way to make a connexion between the original constituent and the representative, but by the circuitous means which may lead the candidate to apply in the first instance to the primary electors, in order that by their authoritative instructions (and something more perhaps) these primary electors may force the two succeeding bodies of [271] electors to make a choice agreeable to their wishes. But this would plainly subvert the whole scheme. It would be to plunge them back into that tumult and confusion of popular election, which, by their interposed gradation elections, they mean to avoid, and at length to risque the whole fortune of the state with those who have the least knowledge of it, and the least interest in it. This is a perpetual dilemma, into which they are thrown by the vicious, weak, and contradictory principles they have chosen. Unless the people break up and level this gradation, it is plain that they do not at all substantially elect to the assembly; indeed they elect as little in appearance as reality.

What is it we all seek for in an election? To answer its real purposes, you must first possess the means of knowing the fitness of your man; and then you must retain some hold upon him by personal obligation or dependence. For what end are these primary electors complimented, or rather mocked, with a choice? They can never know any thing of the qualities of him that is to serve them, nor has he any obligation whatsoever to them. Of all the powers unfit to be delegated by those who have any real means of judging, that most peculiarly unfit is what relates to a *personal* choice. In case of abuse, that body of primary electors never can call the representative to an account for his conduct. He is too far removed from them in the chain of representation. If he acts improperly at the end of his two years lease, it does not concern him for two

---

that campaigns demanding a redistribution of parliamentary seats had evoked little popular or parliamentary support during his political career. Burke was also correct that the redistribution of seats was not the leading theme in most schemes of reform.

years more. By the new French constitution, the best and the wisest representative[s] go [272] equally with the worst into this *Limbus Patrum*.[598] Their bottoms are supposed foul, and they must go into dock to be refitted. Every man who has served in an assembly is ineligible for two years after. Just as these magistrates begin to learn their trade, like chimney-sweepers, they are disqualified for exercising it.[599] Superficial, new, petulant acquisition, and interrupted, dronish, broken, ill recollection, is to be the destined character of all your future governors. Your constitution has too much of jealousy to have much of sense in it. You consider the breach of trust in the representative so principally, that you do not at all regard the question of his fitness to execute it.

*interesting argument against term limits.*

This purgatory interval is not unfavourable to a faithless representative, who may be as good a canvasser as he was a bad governor. In this time he may cabal himself into a superiority over the wisest and most virtuous. As, in the end, all the members of this elective constitution are equally fugitive, and exist only for the election, they may be no longer the same persons who had chosen him, to whom he is to be responsible when he solicits for a renewal of his trust. To call all the secondary electors of the *Commune* to account, is ridiculous, impracticable, and unjust; they may themselves have been deceived in their choice, as the third set of electors, those of the *Department*, may be in theirs. In your elections responsibility cannot exist.

The legislators who framed the antient republics knew that their business was too arduous to be accomplished with no better apparatus than the metaphysics of an under-graduate,[600] and the mathematics [273] and arithmetic of an exciseman.[601] They had to do with men, and they were obliged to study human nature. They had to do with citizens, and they were obliged to study the effects of those habits which are communicated by the circumstances of civil life. They were sensible that the operation of this second nature on the first produced a new combination; and thence arose many diversities amongst men, according to their birth, their education, their professions, the periods of their lives, their residence in towns or in the country, their several ways of acquiring and of fixing property, and according to the quality of the property itself, all which rendered them as it were so many different species of animals.

[598]The *limbus patrum* was the term for a temporary state of happiness, distinct from purgatory, in which the just who had lived before Christ would await the Second Coming before entering into Heaven. It was distinguished from the *limbus infantium*, the state of children dying unbaptised.

[599]Child chimney-sweeps were 'disqualified' by growing too large for their trade.

[600]For Burke's undergraduate education, including metaphysics, see Francis J. Canavan, *The Political Reason of Edmund Burke* (Durham, N.C., 1960), pp. 197–211.

[601]Thomas Paine had served as an exciseman, and failed in that career.

From hence they thought themselves obliged to dispose their citizens into such classes, and to place them in such situations in the state as their peculiar habits might qualify them to fill, and to allot to them such appropriated privileges as might secure to them what their specific occasions required, and which might furnish to each description such force as might protect it in the conflict caused by the diversity of interests, that must exist, and must contend in all complex society: for the legislator would have been ashamed, that the coarse husbandman should well know how to assort and to use his sheep, horses, and oxen, and should have enough of common sense not to abstract and equalize them all into animals, without providing for each kind an appropriate food, care, and employment; whilst he, the œconomist, disposer, and shepherd of his own kindred, subliming himself into an airy metaphysician, [274] was resolved to know nothing of his flocks, but as men in general. It is for this reason that Montesquieu observed very justly, that in their classification of the citizens, the great legislators of antiquity made the greatest display of their powers, and even soared above themselves.[602] It is here that your modern legislators have gone deep into the negative series, and sunk even below their own nothing. As the first sort of legislators attended to the different kinds of citizens, and combined them into one commonwealth, the others, the metaphysical and alchemistical legislators, have taken the direct contrary course. They have attempted to confound all sorts of citizens, as well as they could, into one homogeneous mass; and then they divided this their amalgama into a number of incoherent republics. They reduce men to loose counters merely for the sake of simple telling, and not to figures whose power is to arise from their place in the table. The elements of their own metaphysics might have taught them better lessons. The troll of their categorical table might have informed them that there was something else in the intellectual world besides *substance* and *quantity*. They might learn from the catechisms of metaphysics that there were eight heads more,[603] in every complex deliberation, which they have never thought of, though these, of all the ten, are the subject on which the skill of man can operate any thing at all. [275]

So far from this able disposition of some of the old republican legislators, which follows with a solicitous accuracy, the moral conditions and propensities of men, they have levelled and crushed together all the orders which they

---

[602]Cf. Montesquieu, *The Spirit of the Laws*, Book II, ch. 2: 'In a popular state the inhabitants are divided into certain classes. 'Tis in the manner of making this division that great legislators have signalized themselves; and 'tis on this the duration and prosperity of democracy have always depended.'

[603]Qualitas, Relatio, Actio, Passio, Ubi, Quando, Situs, Habitus. [B] Burke here showed his undergraduate training in Aristotelian philosophy.

found, even under the coarse unartificial arrangement of the monarchy, in which mode of government the classing of the citizens is not of so much importance as in a republic. It is true, however, that every such classification, if properly ordered, is good in all forms of government; and composes a strong barrier against the excesses of despotism, as well as it is the necessary means of giving effect and permanence to a republic. For want of something of this kind, if the present project of a republic should fail, all securities to a moderated freedom fail along with it; all the indirect restraints which mitigate despotism are removed; insomuch that if monarchy should ever again obtain an entire ascendency in France, under this or under any other dynasty, it will probably be, if not voluntarily tempered at setting out, by the wise and virtuous counsels of the prince, the most completely arbitrary power that has ever appeared on earth. This is to play a most desperate game[.][604]

Finding no sort of principle of coherence with each other in the nature and constitution of the several new republics of France, I considered what cement the legislators had provided for them from any extraneous materials. Their confederations, their *spectacles*, their civic feasts, and their enthusiasm,[605] I take no notice of; They are nothing but [276] mere tricks; but tracing their policy through their actions, I think I can distinguish the arrangements by which they propose to hold these republics together. The first, is the *confiscation*, with the compulsory paper currency annexed to it; the second, is the supreme power of the city of Paris; the third, is the general army of the state. Of this last I shall reserve what I have to say, until I come to consider the army as an head by itself.[606]

As to the operation of the first (the confiscation and paper currency) merely as a cement, I cannot deny that these, the one depending on the other, may for some time compose some sort of cement, if their madness and folly in the management, and in the tempering of the parts together, does not produce a repulsion in the very outset. But allowing to the scheme some coherence and some duration, it appears to me, that if, after a while, the confiscation should not be found sufficient to support the paper coinage (as I am morally certain it

[604]Cf. Montesquieu, *The Spirit of the Laws*, Book II, ch. 4: 'The intermediate, subordinate and dependent powers, constitute the nature of monarchical government, that is, of that in which a single person governs by fundamental laws ... Abolish the privileges of the lords, of the clergy, and of the cities in a monarchy, and you will soon have a popular state, or else an arbitrary government.'

[605]French revolutionaries deliberately used symbolism and festival in a campaign of cultural reconstruction designed to affirm revolutionary values and forge a new sense of national unity: see Bibliography, D xiii.

[606]*Reflections*, p. [304].

will not) then, instead of cementing, it will add infinitely to the dissociation, distraction, and confusion of these confederate republics, both with relation to each other, and to the several parts within themselves. But if the confiscation should so far succeed as to sink the paper currency, the cement is gone with the circulation. In the mean time its binding force will be very uncertain, and it will straiten or relax with every variation in the credit of the paper.

One thing only is certain in this scheme, which is an effect seemingly collateral, but direct, I have no doubt, in the minds of those who conduct this [277] business; that is, its effect in producing an *Oligarchy* in every one of the republics. A paper circulation, not founded on any real money deposited or engaged for, amounting already to four-and-forty millions of English money, and this currency by force substituted in the place of the coin of the kingdom, becoming thereby the substance of its revenue, as well as the medium of all its commercial and civil intercourse, must put the whole of what power, authority, and influence is left, in any form whatsoever it may assume, into the hands of the managers and conductors of this circulation.

In England we feel the influence of the bank; though it is only the center of a voluntary dealing. He knows little indeed of the influence of money upon mankind, who does not see the force of the management of a monied concern, which is so much more extensive, and in its nature so much more depending on the managers than any of ours. But if we take into consideration the other part essentially connected with it (which consists in continually drawing out for sale portions of the confiscated land, this continual exchanging land for paper, and this mixing it into circulation) we may conceive something of the intensity of its operation. By this means the spirit of money-jobbing and speculation goes into the mass of land itself, and incorporates with it. By this kind of operation, that species of property becomes (as it were) volatized; it assumes an unnatural and monstrous activity, and thereby throws into the hands of the several managers, principal and subordinate, Parisian and provincial, [278] all the representative of money, and perhaps a full tenth part of all the land in France, which has now acquired the worst and most pernicious part of the evil of a paper circulation, the greatest possible uncertainty in its value. They have reversed the Latonian kindness to the landed property of Delos.[607] They have sent theirs to be blown about, like the light fragments of a wreck, *oras et littora circum*.[608] The new dealers being all habitually adventur-

---

[607]In Greek legend, the goddess Leto (in Latin, Latona) anchored the island of Delos to the sea bed to use it as a place to give birth to her two children Artemis and Apollo. Burke accused the French of cutting loose from such secure and divinely appointed moorings.

[608]'In the mid-sea lies a holy land, most dear to the mother of the Nereids and Ae-

ers, and without any fixed habits or local predilections, will purchase to job out again, as the market of paper, or of money, or of land shall present an advantage. For though an holy bishop[609] thinks that agriculture will derive great advantages from the *"enlightened"* usurers who are to purchase the church confiscations, I, who am not a good, but an old farmer, with great humility beg leave to tell his late lordship, that usury is not a tutor of agriculture; and if the word "enlightened" be understood according to the new dictionary, as it always is in your new schools, I cannot conceive how a man's not believing in God can teach him to cultivate the earth with the least of any additional skill or encouragement. "Diis immortalibus sero," said an old Roman, when he held one handle of the plough, whilst Death held the other.[610] Though you were to join in the commission all the directors of the two academies to the directors of the *Caisse d'Escompte*,[611] one old experienced peasant is worth them all. I have got more information, upon one curious and interesting branch of husbandry, in one short conversation with one Carthusian monk, than I have derived from all the Bank directors that I have ever conversed [279] with. However, there is no cause for apprehension from the meddling of money-dealers with rural œconomy. These gentlemen are too wise in their generation. At first, perhaps, their tender and susceptible imaginations may be captivated with the innocent and unprofitable delights of a pastoral life; but in a little time they will find that agriculture is a trade much more laborious, and much less lucrative than that which they had left. After making its panegyric, they will turn their backs on it like their great precursor and prototype.—They may, like him, begin by singing *"Beatus ille"*—but what will be the end?

---

gean Neptune, which, as it wandered round coasts and shores, the grateful archer-god bound fast to lofty Myconos and Gyaros, suffering it to lie unmoved and slight the winds': Virgil, *Aeneid*, Book III, 73–7.

[609]Talleyrand, bishop of Autun, a deputy for the First Estate in the Estates-General, proposed in the National Assembly on 10 October 1789 the appropriation of church goods by the nation. He became an *émigré* in London in 1792 and associated with the marquis of Lansdowne, a circle especially detested by Burke.

[610]"And if you ask a farmer, however old, for whom he is planting, he will unhesitatingly reply, "For the immortal gods, who have willed not only that I should receive these blessings from my ancestors, but also that I should hand them on to posterity"": Cicero, *De Senectute*, VII, 25. Here Burke again returned to the subject known to modern philosophers as 'inter-generational equity'.

[611]The bank established by royal charter in 1776 to discount bills of exchange. It was as close as the *ancien régime* got to a national bank, and it was suppressed by the Convention in 1793. See Bosher, *French Finances*, pp. 257–65.

*Sic cum locutus fœnerator Alphius,*
*Jam jam futurus rusticus*
*Omnem relegit idibus pecuniam,*
*Quærit calendis ponere.*[612]

They will cultivate the *caisse d'Eglise*, under the sacred auspices of this prelate, with much more profit than its vineyards or its corn-fields. They will employ their talents according to their habits and their interests. They will not follow the plough whilst they can direct treasuries, and govern provinces.

Your legislators, in every thing new, are the very first who have founded a commonwealth upon gaming, and infused this spirit into it as its vital breath. The great object in these politics is to metamorphose France, from a great kingdom into one great play-table; to turn its inhabitants into a nation of gamesters; to make speculation as extensive as life; to mix it with all its concerns; and to divert the whole of the hopes and fears of [280] the people from their usual channels, into the impulses, passions, and superstitions of those who live on chances. They loudly proclaim their opinion, that this their present system of a republic cannot possibly exist without this kind of gaming fund; and that the very thread of its life is spun out of the staple of these speculations. The old gaming in funds was mischievous enough undoubtedly; but it was so only to individuals. Even when it had its greatest extent, in the Missisipi and South Sea,[613] it affected but few, comparatively; where it extends further, as in lotteries, the spirit has but a single object. But by bringing the currency of gaming into the minutest matters, and engaging every body in it, and in every thing, a more dreadful epidemic distemper of that kind is spread than yet has appeared in the world. With you a man can neither earn nor buy his dinner, without a speculation. What he receives in the morning will not have the same value at night. What he is compelled to take as pay for an old debt, will not be received as the same when he is to contract a new one; nor will it be the same when by prompt payment he would avoid contracting any debt at all. Industry must wither away. Œconomy must be driven from your country. Careful provision will have no existence. Who will labour without

---

[612]'Happy the man who, far away from business cares, like the pristine race of mortals, works his ancestral acres with his steers, from all money lending free ... When the usurer Alfius had uttered this, on the very point of beginning the life of a farmer, he called in all his funds upon the Ides — and upon the Kalends seeks to put them out again!': Horace, *Epodes*, ii, 1–4, 67–70.

[613]The company founded in France by the financier John Law for developing Louisiana, known as the Mississippi Company, crashed amid scandal in 1720: see Biographical Guide, above, under 'Law'. The South Sea Company crashed in England in similar circumstances in 1721.

_no shit.∅_

knowing the amount of his pay? Who will study to encrease what none can estimate? who will accumulate, when he does not know the value of what he saves? If you abstract it from its uses in gaming, to accumulate your paper wealth, would be not the providence of a man, but the distempered instinct of a jackdaw. [281]

The truly melancholy part of the policy of systematically making a nation of gamesters is this; that tho' all are forced to play, few can understand the game; and fewer still are in a condition to avail themselves of the knowledge. The many must be the dupes of the few who conduct the machine of these speculations. What effect it must have on the country-people is visible. When the peasant first brings his corn to market, the magistrate in the towns obliges him to take the assignat at par; when he goes to the shop with this money, he finds it seven per cent the worse for crossing the way. This market he will not readily resort to again. The townsman can calculate from day to day: not so the inhabitant of the country. The towns-people will be inflamed! they will force the country-people to bring their corn. Resistance will begin, and the murders of Paris and St. Dennis may be renewed through all France.[614]

What signifies the empty compliments paid to the country by giving it perhaps more than its share in the theory of your representation? Where have you placed the real power over monied and landed circulation? Where have you placed the means of raising and falling the value of every man's freehold. The whole of the power obtained by this revolution will settle in the towns among the burghers, and the monied directors who lead them. The landed gentleman, the yeoman, and the peasant have, none of them, habits, or inclinations, or experience, which can lead them to any share in this the sole source of power and influence now left in France. The very nature of a country life, [282] the very nature of landed property, in all the occupations, and all the pleasures they afford, render combination and arrangement (the sole way of procuring and exerting influence) in a manner impossible amongst country-people. Combine them by all the art you can, and all the industry, they are always dissolving into individuality. Any thing in the nature of incorporation is almost impracticable amongst them. Hope, fear, alarm, jealousy, the ephemerous tale that does its business and dies in a day, all these things, which are the reins and spurs by which leaders check or urge the minds of

[614]Burke correctly foretold the food crisis of early 1792. Mob paranoia had already shown itself (among other disorders) in the murder of Berthier de Sauvigny on 22 July 1789, for having allegedly conspired to starve Paris; the murder of the mayor of Saint-Denis on 3 August 1789; and the murder of the baker François in Paris on 21 October 1789 for allegedly hoarding bread, an act that prompted the National Assembly to impose martial law: Fierro and Liébert, p. 735.

followers, are not easily employed, or hardly at all, amongst scattered people. They assemble, they arm, they act with the utmost difficulty, and at the greatest charge. Their efforts, if ever they can be commenced, cannot be sustained. They cannot proceed systematically. If the country gentlemen attempt an influence through the mere income of their property, what is it to that of those who have ten times their income to sell, and who can ruin their property by bringing their plunder to meet it at market. If he wishes to mortgage, he falls the value of his land, and raises the value of assignats. He augments the power of his enemy by the very means he must take to contend with him. The country gentleman therefore, the officer by sea and land, the man of liberal views and habits, attached to no profession, will be as completely excluded from the government of his country as if he were legislatively proscribed. It is obvious, that in the towns, all the things which conspire against the country gentleman, combine in favour [283] of the money manager and director. In towns combination is natural. The habits of burghers, their occupations, their diversion, their business, their idleness, continually bring them into mutual contact. Their virtues and their vices are sociable; they are always in garrison; and they come embodied and half disciplined into the hands of those who mean to form them for civil, or for military action. Those whose operations can take from, or add ten per cent. to, the possessions of every man in France, must be the masters of every man in France.

All these considerations leave no doubt on my mind, that if this monster of a constitution can continue, France will be wholly governed by the agitators in corporations, by societies in the towns formed of directors of assignats, and trustees for the sale of church lands, attornies, agents, money-jobbers, speculators, and adventurers, composing an ignoble oligarchy founded on the destruction of the crown, the church, the nobility, and the people. Here end all the deceitful dreams and visions of the equality and rights of men. In "the Serbonian bog"[615] of this base oligarchy they are all absorbed, sunk, and lost for ever.

Though human eyes cannot trace them, one would be tempted to think some great offences in France must cry to heaven, which has thought fit to punish it with a subjection to a vile and inglorious domination, in which no comfort or compensation is to be found in any, even of those false splendours, which, playing about other tyrannies, prevent mankind from feeling themselves [284] dishonoured even whilst they are oppressed. I must confess I am touched with a sorrow, mixed with some indignation, at the conduct of a few

[615]"A gulf profound as that Serbonian Bog / Betwixt Damiata and Mount Cassius old, / Where Armies whole have sunk': Milton, *Paradise Lost*, II, 592.

men, once of great rank, and still of great character, who, deluded with specious names, have engaged in a business too deep for the line of their understanding to fathom; who have lent their fair reputation, and the authority of
their high-sounding names, to the designs of men with whom they could not
be acquainted; and have thereby made their very virtues operate to the ruin of
their country.

So far as to the first cementing principle.

The second material of cement for their new republic is the superiority of
the city of Paris;[616] and this I admit is strongly connected with the other cementing principle of paper circulation and confiscation. It is in this part of the
project we must look for the cause of the destruction of all the old bounds of
provinces and jurisdictions, ecclesiastical and secular, and the dissolution of
all ancient combinations of things, as well as the formation of so many small
unconnected republics. The power of the city of Paris is evidently one great
spring of all their politics. It is through the power of Paris, now become the
center and focus of jobbing, that the leaders of this faction direct, or rather
command the whole legislative and the whole executive government. Every
thing therefore must be done which can confirm the authority of that city over
the other republics. Paris is compact; she has an enormous strength, wholly
disproportioned to the force of any of the square republics;[617] and this strength
is collected and condensed within a narrow compass. [285] Paris has a natural
and easy connexion of its parts, which will not be affected by any scheme of a
geometrical constitution, nor does it much signify whether its proportion of
representation be more or less, since it has the whole draft of fishes in its drag-
net. The other divisions of the kingdom being hackled and torn to pieces, and
separated from all their habitual means, and even principles of union, cannot,
for some time at least, confederate against her. It was plain that the new incorporation of the city of Paris could not completely and conclusively domi-
neer over France in any other way than by breaking, in every other part of it,
those connections which might balance her power. Nothing was therefore to
be left in all the subordinate members, but weakness, disconnection, and confusion.[618] To confirm this part of the plan, the assembly has lately come to a

[616]Cf. Burke, *Reflections*, pp. [77–8].

[617]Burke was still referring to the scheme proposed on 29 September 1789 for the
division of France into 80 *départements*, plus Paris, each of 18 leagues square. This
geometric plan was abandoned by the assembly on 15 February 1790 in favour of a
pattern of 83 *départements* more respectful of ancient boundaries: *Le Moniteur*, 17
February 1790.

[618]Violent provincial resistance to the republic was experienced in 1791, in the
Midi and Avignon, but the major risings came in 1793, in the Loire, the Vendée and

resolution, that no two of their republics shall have the same commander in chief.

To a person who takes a view of the whole, the strength of Paris thus formed, will appear a system of general weakness. It is boasted, that the geometrical policy has been adopted, that all local ideas should be sunk, and that the people should no longer be Gascons, Picards, Bretons, Normans, but Frenchmen, with one country, one heart, and one assembly.[619] But instead of being all Frenchmen, the greater likelihood is, that the inhabitants of that region will shortly have no country.[620] No man ever was attached by a sense of pride, partiality, or real affection, to a description of square measurement. He never will glory in belonging to the Checquer, [286] N° 71, or to any other badge-ticket. We begin our public affections in our families. No cold relation is a zealous citizen. We pass on to our neighbourhoods, and our habitual provincial connections. These are inns and resting places. Such divisions of our country as have been formed by habit, and not by a sudden jerk of authority, were so many little images of the great country in which the heart found something which it could fill. The love to the whole is not extinguished by this subordinate partiality. Perhaps it is a sort of elemental training to those higher and more large regards, by which alone men come to be affected, as with their own concern, in the prosperity of a kingdom so extensive as that of France. In that general territory itself, as in the old name of provinces, the citizens are interested from old prejudices and unreasoned habits, and not on account of the geometric properties of its figure. The power and preeminence of Paris does certainly press down and hold these republics together, as long as it lasts. But, for the reasons I have already given you, I think it cannot last very long.

Passing from the civil creating, and the civil cementing principles of this constitution, to the national assembly, which is to appear and act as sovereign, we see a body in its constitution with every possible power, and no possible external controul. We see a body without fundamental laws, without es-

---

Lyons. These savage civil wars were disconnected, however, and bore out Burke's prediction that Paris would keep provincial resistance divided.

[619]Lally-Tollendal recorded events in the National Assembly on the night of 4 August 1789: 'Bientôt le Marquis de Blacon élevant la voix au nom du Dauphiné, donna le signal à toutes les Provinces de sacrifier leurs priviléges particuliers. Je me rappelai cette belle expression proferée l'année derniere par ce ce même Dauphiné: *Ne soyons plus Bearnais; Provençaux, Bretons, Dauphinois, soyons Français*': *Mémoire de M. le Comte de Lally-Tollendal, ou seconde lettre A ses Commettans* (Paris, 'Janvier 1790'), p. 112.

[620]Despite the rejection of the geometric plan, this development of a national consciousness was a marked feature of the 1790s.

tablished maxims, without respected rules of proceeding, which nothing can keep firm to any system whatsoever. Their idea of their powers is always taken at the utmost stretch of legislative competency, [287] and their examples for common cases, from the exceptions of the most urgent necessity. The future is to be in most respects like the present assembly; but, by the mode of the new elections and the tendency of the new circulations, it will be purged of the small degree of internal controul existing in a minority chosen originally from various interests, and preserving something of their spirit. If possible, the next assembly must be worse than the present. The present, by destroying and altering every thing, will leave to their successors apparently nothing popular to do. They will be roused by emulation and example to enterprises the boldest and the most absurd. To suppose such an assembly sitting in perfect quietude is ridiculous.[621]

Your all-sufficient legislators, in their hurry to do every thing at once, have forgot one thing that seems essential, and which, I believe, never has been, in the theory or the practice, omitted by any projector of a republic. They have forgot to constitute a *Senate*, or something of that nature and character.[622] Never, before this time, was heard of a body politic composed of one legislative and active assembly, and its executive officers, without such a council; without something to which foreign states might connect themselves; something to which, in the ordinary detail of government, the people could look up; something which might give a bias and steadiness, and preserve something like consistency in the proceedings of state. Such a body kings generally have as a council. A monarchy may exist without it; but it seems to be in the very essence of a republican government. It [288] holds a sort of middle place between the supreme power exercised by the people, or immediately delegated from them, and the mere executive. Of this there are no traces in your consti-

---

[621]The National Constituent Assembly held its last session on 30 September 1791 and was replaced on 1 October by the National Legislative Assembly, a body from which the members of the Constituent Assembly had voted to exclude themselves. Political experience dating from the summoning of the Estates-General was thus immediately lost. It was this new Assembly which led France into war in April 1792, lost control of the Paris mob, suspended Louis XVI from his functions in August, adopted universal suffrage, was upstaged by the Paris Commune, and abolished itself in September, making way for a national Convention to decide the fate of the monarchy.

[622]The National Assembly rejected a plan for a bicameral Assembly on 10 September 1789 by 499 votes to 89, lest it should allow the aristocracy to retrieve power: *Le Moniteur*, 8–12 September 1789. This was a decisive defeat for the *anglomanes*, and it was an English rather than an American model which the National Assembly here rejected.

tution; and in providing nothing of this kind, your Solons and Numas[623] have, as much as in any thing else, discovered a sovereign incapacity.

Let us now turn our eyes to what they have done towards the formation of an executive power.[624] For this they have chosen a degraded king. This their first executive officer is to be a machine, without any sort of deliberative discretion in any one act of his function. At best he is but a channel to convey to the national assembly such matter as may import that body to know. If he had been made the exclusive channel, the power would not have been without its importance; though infinitely perilous to those who would choose to exercise it. But public intelligence and statement of facts may pass to the assembly, with equal authenticity, through any other conveyance. As to the means, therefore, of giving a direction to measures by the statement of an authorized reporter, this office of intelligence is as nothing.

To consider the French scheme of an executive officer in its two natural divisions of civil and political—In the first it must be observed, that, according to the new constitution, the higher parts of judicature, in either of its lines, are not in the king. The king of France is not the fountain of justice. The judges, neither the original nor the appellate, are of his nomination.[625] He neither proposes [289] the candidates, nor has a negative on the choice. He is not even the public prosecutor. He serves only as a notary to authenticate the choice made of the judges in the several districts. By his officers he is to execute their sentence. When we look into the true nature of his authority, he appears to be nothing more than a chief of bumbailiffs, serjeants at mace, catchpoles, jailers, and hangmen. It is impossible to place any thing called royalty in a more degrading point of view. A thousand times better it had been for the dignity of this unhappy prince, that he had nothing at all to do with the administration of justice, deprived as he is of all that is venerable, and all that is consolatory in that function, without power of originating any process; without a power of suspension, mitigation, or pardon. Every thing in justice that is vile and odious is thrown upon him. It was not for nothing that the assembly

[623]Solon (c. 630–c. 560 BC) and Numa Pompilius (715–672 BC) were regarded as the founding fathers of the laws of Athens and Rome respectively.

[624]The draft of the new constitution was submitted to the National Assembly on 5 August 1791, and, after debate, the final text was passed on 3 September. Burke anticipated the outcome from what had been done already by the summer of 1790. This Constitution was to define the law as the highest authority, but it was already clear that the king was only the first officer of the state and that sovereignty resided in the National Assembly.

[625]The constitution was to provide for a directly-elected judiciary, independent of the legislature and the executive.

has been at such pains to remove the stigma from certain offices, when they were resolved to place the person who lately had been their king in a situation but one degree above the executioner, and in an office nearly of the same quality. It is not in nature, that situated as the king of the French now is, he can respect himself, or can be respected by others.

View this new executive officer on the side of his political capacity, as he acts under the orders of the national assembly. To execute laws is a royal office; to execute orders is not to be a king. However, a political executive magistracy, though merely such, is a great trust. It is a trust indeed [290] that has much depending upon its faithful and diligent performance, both in the person presiding in it and in all his subordinates. Means of performing this duty ought to be given by regulation; and dispositions towards it ought to be infused by the circumstances attendant on the trust. It ought to be environed with dignity, authority, and consideration, and it ought to lead to glory. The office of execution is an office of exertion. It is not from impotence we are to expect the tasks of power. What sort of person is a king to command executory service, who has no means whatsoever to reward it? Not in a permanent office; not in a grant of land; no, not in a pension of fifty pounds a year; not in the vainest and most trivial title. In France the king is no more the fountain of honour than he is the fountain of justice. All rewards, all distinctions are in other hands. Those who serve the king can be actuated by no natural motive but fear; by a fear of every thing except their master. His functions of internal coercion are as odious, as those which he exercises in the department of justice. If relief is to be given to any municipality, the assembly gives it. If troops are to be sent to reduce them to obedience to the assembly, the king is to execute the order; and upon every occasion he is to be spattered over with the blood of his people. He has no negative; yet his name and authority is used to enforce every harsh decree. Nay, he must concur in the butchery of those who shall attempt to free him from his imprisonment, or shew the slightest attachment to his person or to his antient authority. [291]

Executive magistracy ought to be constituted in such a manner, that those who compose it should be disposed to love and to venerate those whom they are bound to obey. A purposed neglect, or, what is worse, a literal but perverse and malignant obedience, must be the ruin of the wisest counsels. In vain will the law attempt to anticipate or to follow such studied neglects and fraudulent attentions. To make men act zealously is not in the competence of law. Kings, even such as are truly kings, may and ought to bear the freedom of subjects that are obnoxious to them. They may too, without derogating from themselves, bear even the authority of such persons if it promotes their service. Louis the XIIIth mortally hated the cardinal de Richlieu; but his support of that minister against his rivals was the source of all the glory of his reign, and the solid foundation of his throne itself.[626] Louis the XIVth, when come to the throne, did not love the cardinal Mazarin; but for his interests he preserved him in power.[627] When old, he detested Louvois; but for years, whilst he faithfully served his greatness, he endured his person.[628] When George the IId took Mr. Pitt, who certainly was not agreeable to him, into his councils, he did nothing which could humble a wise sovereign. But these ministers, who were chosen by affairs, not by affections, acted in the name of, and in trust for, kings; and not as their avowed, constitutional, and ostensible masters.[629] I think it impossible that any king, when he has recovered his first terrors, can cordially infuse vivacity and vigour into measures which he knows [292] to be dictated by those who he must be persuaded are in the highest degree ill affected to his person. Will any ministers, who serve such a king (or whatever he may be called) with but a decent appearance of respect, cordially obey the orders of those whom but the other day in his name they had committed to the Bastile? will they obey the orders of those whom, whilst they were exercising despotic justice upon them, they conceived they were treating with lenity; and for whom, in a prison, they thought they had provided an asylum? If you expect such obedience, amongst your other innovations and regenerations, you ought to make a revolution in nature, and provide a new constitution for the human mind. Otherwise, your supreme government cannot harmonize with its executory system. There are cases in which we cannot take up with names and abstractions. You may call half a dozen leading individuals, whom we

[626]Armand Jean du Plessis de Richelieu (1585–1642). Louis XIII initially distrusted him, since Richelieu had begun his political career as adviser to the queen mother, Marie de Medici.

[627]Jules Mazarin (1602–61) succeeded as chief minister on Richelieu's death. When Louis XIII died in 1643, Mazarin retained his position during the Queen's regency and preserved the authority of the monarchy during the Fronde. Louis XIV (1638–1715) retained Mazarin when Louis took over from the regency.

[628]François Michel le Tellier, marquis de Louvois (1641–91), war minister from 1666 to his death.

[629]George II was compelled to accept the elder Pitt into his ministry in 1756. Burke here rehearsed the doctrine on party of the Rockingham Whigs, but George II had taken a less favourable view of this sort of use of a parliamentary majority. In 1744 he protested that the acceptance of the 'Broad Bottom' administration was only in a technical sense by his agreement: 'My work! I was forc'd: I was threatened', and added, famously, 'Ministers are the Kings in this Country'. In 1756–7, he protested to Newcastle against the Pitt-Devonshire ministry: he 'did not look upon himself as King whilst he was in the hands of these scoundrels': P. C. Yorke, The Life and Correspondence of Philip Yorke Earl of Hardwicke (3 vols., Cambridge, 1913), I, pp. 382–3; II, p. 365.

have reason to fear and hate, the nation. It makes no other difference, than to make us fear and hate them the more. If it had been thought justifiable and expedient to make such a revolution by such means, and through such persons, as you have made yours, it would have been more wise to have completed the business of the fifth and sixth of October.[630] The new executive officer would then owe his situation to his real masters; and he might be bound in interest, in the society of crime, and (if in crimes there could be virtues) in gratitude, to serve those who had promoted him to a place of great lucre and great sensual indulgence; and of something more: For more he must have [293] received from those who certainly would not have limited an aggrandized creature, as they have done a submitting antagonist.

A king circumstanced as the present, if he is totally stupified by his misfortunes, so as to think it not the necessity, but the premium and privilege of life, to eat and sleep, without any regard to glory, never can be fit for the office. If he feels as men commonly feel, he must be sensible, that an office so circumstanced is one in which he can obtain no fame or reputation. He has no generous interest that can excite him to action. At best, his conduct will be passive and defensive. To inferior people such an office might be matter of honour. But to be raised to it, and to descend to it, are different things, and suggest different sentiments. Does he *really* name the ministers? They will have a sympathy with him. Are they forced upon him? The whole business between them and the nominal king will be mutual counteraction. In all other countries, the office of ministers of state is of the highest dignity. In France it is full of peril and incapable of glory. Rivals however they will have in their nothingness, whilst shallow ambition exists in the world, or the desire of a miserable salary is an incentive to short-sighted avarice. Those competitors of the ministers are enabled by your constitution to attack them in their vital parts, whilst they have not the means of repelling their charges in any other than the degrading character of culprits. The ministers of state in France are the only persons in that country who are incapable of a share in the national councils.[631] What ministers! What [294] councils! What a nation!—But they are responsible. It is a poor service that is to be had from responsibility. The elevation of mind,

[630]After being brought by force from Versailles to Paris on 6 October 1789, the king was in effect the prisoner of the mob, although not finally suspended from his royal office until August 1792.

[631]On 7 November 1789 the National Assembly rejected Mirabeau's motion to allow ministers to sit and exercise a '*voix consultative*' in the legislature: *Le Moniteur*, 7–9 November 1789. By this adoption of the doctrine of the separation of powers, the Assembly finally made impossible the establishment of a system of parliamentary government resembling that of Britain.

to be derived from fear, will never make a nation glorious. Responsibility prevents crimes. It makes all attempts against the laws dangerous. But for a principle of active and zealous service, none but idiots could think of it. Is the conduct of a war to be trusted to a man who may abhor its principle; who, in every step he may take to render it successful, confirms the power of those by whom he is oppressed? Will foreign states seriously treat with him who has no prerogative of peace or war;[632] no, not so much as in a single vote by himself or his ministers, or by any one whom he can possibly influence. A state of contempt is not a state for a prince: better get rid of him at once.

I know it will be said, that these humours in the court and executive government will continue only through this generation; and that the king has been brought to declare the dauphin shall be educated in a conformity to his situation. If he is made to conform to his situation, he will have no education at all. His training must be worse even than that of an arbitrary monarch. If he reads,—whether he reads or not, some good or evil genius will tell him his ancestors were kings. Thenceforward his object must be to assert himself, and to avenge his parents. This you will say is not his duty. That may be; but it is Nature; and whilst you pique Nature against you, you do unwisely to trust to Duty. In this futile scheme [295] of polity, the state nurses in its bosom, for the present, a source of weakness, perplexity, counter-action, inefficiency, and decay; and it prepares the means of its final ruin. In short, I see nothing in the executive force (I cannot call it authority) that has even an appearance of vigour, or that has the smallest degree of just correspondence or symmetry, or amicable relation, with the supreme power, either as it now exists, or as it is planned for the future government.

You have settled, by an œconomy as perverted as the policy, two establishments of government; one real, one fictitious. Both maintained at a vast expence; but the fictitious at, I think, the greatest. Such a machine as the latter is not worth the grease of its wheels. The expence is exorbitant; and neither the shew nor the use deserve the tenth part of the charge. Oh! but I don't do justice to the talents of the legislators. I don't allow, as I ought to do, for necessity. Their scheme of executive force was not their choice. This pageant must be kept. The people would not consent to part with it. Right; I understand you. You do, in spite of your grand theories, to which you would have

---

[632]After debating the issue between 15 and 22 May 1790, the National Assembly voted that the king might only propose a declaration of war to the Assembly, which alone could pass or reject the motion. At the same time, the Assembly decreed: 'la Nation Française renonce à entreprendre aucune guerre dans la vue de faire des conquêtes, et elle n'emploiera jamais ses forces contre la liberté d'aucun Peuple': *Le Moniteur*, 23–24 May 1790.

heaven and earth to bend, you do know how to conform yourselves to the nature and circumstances of things. But when you were obliged to conform thus far to circumstances, you ought to have carried your submission farther, and to have made what you were obliged to take, a proper instrument, and useful to its end. That was in your power. For instance, among many others, it was in [296] your power to leave to your king the right of peace and war. What! to leave to the executive magistrate the most dangerous of all prerogatives? I know none more dangerous; nor any one more necessary to be so trusted. I do not say that this prerogative ought to be trusted to your king, unless he enjoyed other auxiliary trusts along with it, which he does not now hold. But, if he did possess them, hazardous as they are undoubtedly, advantages would arise from such constitution, more than compensating the risque. There is no other way of keeping other potentates from intriguing distinctly and personally with the members of your assembly, from intermeddling in all your concerns, and fomenting, in the heart of your country, the most pernicious of all factions; factions in the interest and under the direction of foreign powers. From that worst of evils, thank God, we are still free. Your skill, if you had any, would be well employed to find out indirect correctives and controls upon this perilous trust. If you did not like those which in England we have chosen, your leaders might have exerted their abilities in contriving better. If it were necessary to exemplify the consequences of such an executive government as yours, in the management of great affairs, I should refer you to the late reports of M. de Montmorin[633] to the national assembly, and all the other proceedings relative to the differences between Great Britain and Spain.[634] It would be treating your understanding with disrespect to point them out to you.

I hear that the persons who are called ministers have signified an intention of resigning their [297] places.[635] I am rather astonished that they have not re-

[633]See Biographical Guide.

[634]Spain claimed the whole west coast of the American continent, and in 1790 a Spanish settlement at Nootka Sound on Vancouver Island violated Britain's claim to the Pacific coast of Canada. With an Anglo-Spanish conflict threatening, Spain had called on France for support under the Bourbon family pact. The National Assembly responded in May 1790 by expressing sympathy with Spain and mobilising part of its navy, but British diplomacy persuaded the Diplomatic Committee of the National Assembly that Spain, not Britain, was the threat to the French Revolution. Spain, diplomatically isolated, agreed to British demands in the autumn of 1790. See H. V. Evans, 'The Nootka Sound Controversy in Anglo-French Diplomacy—1790', *Journal of Modern History* 46 (1974), pp. 609–40.

[635]Necker had in fact left office on 4 September 1790, while the *Reflections* was in the press.

signed long since. For the universe I would not have stood in the situation in which they have been for this last twelvemonth. They wished well, I take it for granted, to the Revolution. Let this fact be as it may, they could not, placed as they were upon an eminence, though an eminence of humiliation, but be the first to see collectively, and to feel each in his own department, the evils which have been produced by that revolution. In every step which they took, or forbore to take, they must have felt the degraded situation of their country, and their utter incapacity of serving it. They are in a species of subordinate servitude, in which no men before them were ever seen. Without confidence from their sovereign, on whom they were forced, or from the assembly who forced them upon him, all the noble functions of their office are executed by committees of the assembly, without any regard whatsoever to their personal, or their official authority. They are to execute, without power; they are to be responsible, without discretion; they are to deliberate, without choice. In their puzzled situation, under two sovereigns, over neither of whom they have any influence, they must act in such a manner as (in effect, whatever they may intend) sometimes to betray the one, sometimes the other, and always to betray themselves. Such has been their situation; such must be the situation of those who succeed them. I have much respect, and many good wishes, for Mr. Necker. I am obliged to him for attentions.[636] I thought when his enemies [298] had driven him from Versailles, that his exile was a subject of most serious congratulation—*sed multæ urbes et publica vota vicerunt.*[637] He is now sitting on the ruins of the finances, and of the monarchy of France.

A great deal more might be observed on the strange constitution of the executory part of the new government; but fatigue must give bounds to the discussion of subjects, which in themselves have hardly any limits.

As little genius and talent am I able to perceive in the plan of judicature formed by the national assembly. According to their invariable course, the framers of your constitution have begun with the utter abolition of the parliaments.[638] These venerable bodies, like the rest of the old government, stood

---

[636]Burke had first been impressed by Necker's financial skill in October 1779 (Burke, *Correspondence*, IV, p. 154), and praised him in his speech of 11 February 1780, evidently seeing in the Swiss financier an analogue of what came to be called 'Economical Reform'. Burke sent Necker a copy of his speech; this led to a polite exchange of correspondence, and subsequent contacts (ibid., p. 233).

[637]'Kindly Campania gave to Pompey a fever, which he might have prayed for as a boon; but the public prayers [for his recovery] of all those cities gained the day; so his own fortune and that of Rome preserved him to be vanquished and to lose his head': Juvenal, *Satires* X, 284–5.

[638]The *parlements* were suspended by the National Assembly on 3 November 1789,

in need of reform, even though there should be no change made in the monarchy. They required several more alterations to adapt them to the system of a free constitution. But they had particulars in their constitution, and those not a few, which deserved approbation from the wise. They possessed one fundamental excellence; they were independent. The most doubtful circumstance attendant on their office, that of its being vendible, contributed however to this independency of character. They held for life. Indeed they may be said to have held by inheritance. Appointed by the monarch, they were considered as nearly out of his power. The most determined exertions of that authority against them only shewed their radical[639] independence. They composed permanent bodies politic, constituted to resist arbitrary innovation; and from that corporate [299] constitution, and from most of their forms, they were well calculated to afford both certainty and stability to the laws. They had been a safe asylum to secure these laws in all the revolutions of humour and opinion. They had saved that sacred deposit of the country during the reigns of arbitrary princes, and the struggles of arbitrary factions. They kept alive the memory and record of the constitution. They were the great security to private property; which might be said (when personal liberty had no existence) to be, in fact, as well guarded in France as in any other country.[640] Whatever is supreme in a state, ought to have, as much as possible, its judicial authority so constituted as not only not to depend upon it, but in some sort to balance it. It ought to give a security to its justice against its power. It ought to make its judicature, as it were, something exterior to the state.

These parliaments had furnished, not the best certainly, but some considerable corrective to the excesses and vices of the monarchy. Such an independent judicature was ten times more necessary when a democracy became the absolute power of the country. In that constitution, elective, temporary, local judges,[641] such as you have contrived, exercising their dependent func-

---

and abolished by a decree of 6 September 1790: *Le Moniteur*, 3–5 November 1789. Cf. Burke, *Reflections*, p. [181].

[639]Samuel Johnson offered three definitions of 'radical': '1. Primitive; original ... 2. Implanted by nature ... 3. Serving to origination': *A Dictionary of the English Language* (London, 1755). The word did not carry a political meaning in Burke's lifetime.

[640]Burke's eulogy of the *parlements* echoed his vision of the role in the British constitution of the Rockingham Whigs rather than detailed knowledge of the French legislative and judicial machinery: the role of an independent body, in the English case a political party, dedicated to resisting 'arbitrary princes' and 'arbitrary factions'. Behind Burke's Westminster experience stood, in turn, Montesquieu's doctrine of the role of intermediary powers in defending the rule of law against the monarchy.

[641]For elective judges in the new Constitution see Roberts (ed.), *Documents*, pp. 360–2.

tions in a narrow society, must be the worst of all tribunals. In them it will be vain to look for any appearance of justice towards strangers, towards the obnoxious rich, towards the minority of routed parties, towards all those who in the election have supported unsuccessful candidates. It will be impossible to keep the new tribunals clear of the worst spirit of faction. All [300] contrivances by ballot, we know experimentally, to be vain and childish to prevent a discovery of inclinations. Where they may the best answer the purposes of concealment, they answer to produce suspicion, and this is a still more mischievous cause of partiality.

If the parliaments had been preserved, instead of being dissolved at so ruinous a change[642] to the nation, they might have served in this new commonwealth, perhaps not precisely the same (I do not mean an exact parallel) but near the same purposes as the court and senate of Areopagus[643] did in Athens; that is, as one of the balances and correctives to the evils of a light and unjust democracy. Every one knows, that this tribunal was the great stay of that state; every one knows with what care it was upheld, and with what a religious awe it was consecrated. The parliaments were not wholly free from faction, I admit; but this evil was exterior and accidental, and not so much the vice of their constitution itself, as it must be in your new contrivance of sexennial elective judicatories. Several English commend the abolition of the old tribunals, as supposing that they determined every thing by bribery and corruption.[644] But they have stood the test of monarchic and republican scrutiny. The court was well disposed to prove corruption on those bodies when they

[642]Sc. 'charge'?

[643]The 'Hill of Ares' near the Acropolis in Athens; also the Council which met there, first to advise the monarch, later virtually to run the government by the seventh century BC.

[644]In 1792, Arthur Young was to publish a rhetorical denunciation: 'The conduct of the parliaments was profligate and atrocious ... for all that mass of property, which comes in every country to be litigated in courts of justice, there was not even the shadow of security ... They had the power, and were in the constant practice of issuing decrees, without the consent of the crown, and which had the force of laws through the whole of their jurisdiction ... Instances are innumerable, and I may remark, that the bigotry, ignorance, false principles, and tyranny of these bodies were generally conspicuous; and that the court (taxation excepted), never had a dispute with a parliament, but the parliament was sure to be wrong. Their constitution, in respect to the administration of justice, was so truly rotten, that the members sat as judges, even in causes of private property, in which they were themselves the parties, and have, in this capacity, been guilty of oppressions and cruelties, which the crown has rarely dared to attempt': *Travels in France*, pp. 537–8. Tocqueville corrected this overstatement in *The Old Regime*.

were dissolved in 1771.[645]—Those who have again dissolved them would have done the same if they could—but both inquisitions having failed, I conclude, that gross pecuniary corruption must have been rather rare amongst them. [301]

It would have been prudent, along with the parliaments, to preserve their antient power of registering, and of remonstrating at least, upon all the decrees of the national assembly, as they did upon those which passed in the time of the monarchy. It would be a means of squaring the occasional decrees of a democracy to some principles of general jurisprudence. The ruin of the antient democracies was, that they ruled, as you do, by occasional decrees, *psephismata*.[646] This practice soon broke in upon the tenour and consistency of the laws; they abated the respect of the people towards them; and totally destroyed them in the end.

Your vesting the power of remonstrance, which, in the time of the monarchy, existed in the parliament of Paris, in your principal executive officer, whom, in spite of common sense, you persevere in calling king, is the height of absurdity.[647] You ought never to suffer remonstrance from him who is to execute. This is to understand neither council nor execution; neither authority nor obedience. The person whom you call king, ought not to have this power, or he ought to have more.

Your present arrangement is strictly judicial. Instead of imitating your monarchy, and seating your judges on a bench of independence, your object is to reduce them to the most blind obedience. As you have changed all things, you have invented new principles of order. You first appoint judges, who, I suppose, are to determine according to law, and then you let them know, that, at some time or other, you intend to give them some law by which they are to determine. Any studies [302] which they have made (if any they have made) are to be useless to them. But to supply these studies, they are to be sworn to obey all the rules, orders, and instructions, which from time to time they are to receive from the national assembly. These if they submit to, they leave no

[645]On the advice of his minister René Nicolas de Maupeou, Louis XV had abolished the *parlements* in 1771 and decreed that justice should be free. The *parlements* organised a public outcry, presenting themselves as defenders of French liberties; Louis XVI, in an attempt to win popularity on his accession, restored them. See Durand Echeverria, *The Maupeou Revolution: A Study in the history of libertarianism: France, 1770–1774* (Baton Rouge, 1985).

[646]Decrees passed by the vote of the Assembly of Athens.

[647]On 11 September 1789 the National Assembly voted to give the king merely a suspensive veto over legislation for four years. Mirabeau and Lally Tollendal had argued for an absolute veto and ministerial responsibility: *Le Moniteur*, 8–12 September 1789.

ground of law to the subject. They become complete, and most dangerous instruments in the hands of the governing power, which, in the midst of a cause,
or on the prospect of it, may wholly change the rule of decision. If these orders
of the National Assembly come to be contrary to the will of the people who
locally choose those judges, such confusion must happen as is terrible to think
of. For the judges owe their place to the local authority; and the commands
they are sworn to obey come from those who have no share in their appointment. In the mean time they have the example of the court of *Chatelet* to encourage and guide them in the exercise of their functions.[648] That court is to
try criminals sent to it by the National Assembly, or brought before it by other
courses of delaction. They sit under a guard, to save their own lives. They
know not by what law they judge, nor under what authority they act, nor by
what tenure they hold. It is thought that they are sometimes obliged to condemn at peril of their lives. This is not perhaps certain, nor can it be ascertained; but when they acquit, we know, they have seen the persons whom they
discharge, with perfect impunity to the actors, hanged at the door of their
court.[649]

   The assembly indeed promises that they will form a body of law, which
shall be short, simple, clear, [303] and so forth. That is, by their short laws,
they will leave much to the discretion of the judge; whilst they have exploded
the authority of all the learning which could make judicial discretion, (a thing
perilous at best) deserving the appellation of a *sound* discretion.

   It is curious to observe, that the administrative bodies are carefully exempted from the jurisdiction of these new tribunals. That is, those persons are
exempted from the power of the laws, who ought to be the most entirely submitted to them. Those who execute public pecuniary trusts, ought of all men
to be the most strictly held to their duty. One would have thought, that it must
have been among your earliest cares, if you did not mean that those administrative bodies should be real sovereign independent states, to form an awful
tribunal, like your late parliaments, or like our king's-bench,[650] where all cor-

   [648]Le Châtelet was the Paris court, and prison, reserved for serious offences. The
National Assembly used it to try the first cases of *lèse-nation* after 14 July 1789, and
royalists continued to be tried there. It was abolished by a decree of 25 August 1790,
and ceased to act on 24 January 1791.
   [649]*The Times* of 3 June 1790 reported: 'It does not appear at present, whether the
summary executions in Paris originated with a *Patriot mob*, enraged at the Court of
*Chatelet* for dismissing atrocious offenders without punishment, or whether they make
part of the preconcerted system of the Aristocratics.'
   [650]One of the four common-law courts in Westminster Hall (with Common Pleas,
Exchequer and Equity).

porate officers might obtain protection in the legal exercise of their functions, and would find coercion if they trespassed against their legal duty. But the cause of the exemption is plain. These administrative bodies are the great instruments of the present leaders in their progress through democracy to oligarchy. They must therefore be put above the law. It will be said, that the legal tribunals which you have made are unfit to coerce them. They are undoubtedly. They are unfit for any rational purpose. It will be said too, that the administrative bodies will be accountable to the general assembly. This I fear is talking, without much consideration, of the nature of that assembly [304] or of these corporations. However, to be subject to the pleasure of that assembly, is not to be subject to law, either for protection or for constraint.[651]

Has more wisdom been displayed in the constitution of your army than what is discoverable in your plan of judicature? The able arrangement of this part is the more difficult, and requires the greater skill and attention, not only as a great concern in itself, but as it is the third cementing principle in the new body of republicks, which you call the French nation. Truly it is not easy to divine what that army may become at last. You have voted a very large one, and on good appointments, at least fully equal to your apparent means of payment.[652] But what is the principle of its discipline? or whom is it to obey? You have got the wolf by the ears, and I wish you joy of the happy position in which you have chosen to place yourselves, and in which you are well circumstanced for a free deliberation, relatively to that army, or to any thing else.

The minister and secretary of state for the war department, is M. de la Tour du Pin.[653] This gentleman, like his colleagues in administration, is a most zealous assertor of the revolution, and a sanguine admirer of the new constitution, which originated in that event. His statement of facts, relative to the military of France, is important, not only from his official and personal authority, but because it displays very clearly the actual condition of the army in France, and because it throws light on the principles upon which the assembly proceeds in the administration of this critical [305] object. It may enable us to form some judgment how far it may be expedient in this country to imitate the martial policy of France.

M. de la Tour du Pin, on the 4th of last June, comes to give an account of the state of his department, as it exists under the auspices of the national assembly.[654] No man knows it so well; no man can express it better. Addressing

[651]Burke later added a paragraph here: see Appendix I.

[652]A decree of the National Assembly on 28 February 1790 provided for an army of 150,000 men and fixed its rates of pay: *Le Moniteur*, 2 March 1790.

[653]See Biographical Guide.

[654]The speech was summarised in *Le Moniteur* of 5 June 1790 and printed in full in the *Procès-verbal de l'Assemblée Nationale* 309 (4 June 1790). Burke translated, selec-

himself to the National Assembly, he says, "His Majesty has *this day* sent me to apprize you of the multiplied disorders of which *every day* he receives the most distressing intelligence. The army (le corps militaire) threatens to fall into the most turbulent anarchy. Entire regiments have dared to violate at once the respect due to the laws, to the King, to the order established by your decrees, and to the oaths which they have taken with the most awful solemnity. Compelled by my duty to give you information of these excesses, my heart bleeds when I consider who they are that have committed them. Those, against whom it is not in my power to withhold the most grievous complaints, are a part of that very soldiery which to this day have been so full of honour and loyalty, and with whom, for fifty years, I have lived the comrade and the friend.

✳︎ "What incomprehensible spirit of delirium and delusion has all at once led them astray? Whilst you are indefatigable in establishing uniformity in the empire, and moulding the whole into one coherent and consistent body; whilst the French are taught by you, at once the respect which the [306] laws owe to the rights of man, and that which the citizens owe to the laws, the administration of the army presents nothing but disturbance and confusion. I see in more than one corps the bonds of discipline relaxed or broken; the most unheard-of pretensions avowed directly and without any disguise; the ordinances without force; the chiefs without authority; the military chest and the colours carried off; the authority of the King himself [*risum teneatis*][655] proudly defied; the officers despised, degraded, threatened, driven away, and some of them prisoners in the midst of their corps, dragging on a precarious life in the bosom of disgust and humiliation. To fill up the measure of all these horrors, the commandants of places have had their throats cut, under the eyes, and almost in the arms of their own soldiers.

"These evils are great; but they are not the worst consequences which may be produced by such military insurrections. Sooner or later they may menace the nation itself. *The nature of things requires,* that the army should never act but as *an instrument.* The moment that, erecting itself into a deliberative body, it shall act according to its own resolutions, the *government, be it what it may, will immediately degenerate into a military democracy*; a species of political monster, which has always ended by devouring those who have produced it.

---

tively, from the latter; the italics were Burke's. For extensive mutiny and insubordination in the French army during 1790, see especially Scott, *Response of the Royal Army to the French Revolution,* pp. 46–97.

[655]'Try not to laugh.' This was Burke's insertion.

"After all this, who must not be alarmed at the irregular consultations, and turbulent committees, formed in some regiments by the [307] common soldiers and non-commissioned officers, without the knowledge, or even in contempt of the authority of their superiors; although the presence and concurrence of those superiors could give no authority to such monstrous democratic assemblies [comices]."[656]

It is not necessary to add much to this finished picture: finished as far as its canvas admits; but, as I apprehend, not taking in the whole of the nature and complexity of the disorders of this military democracy, which, the minister at war truly and wisely observes, wherever it exists, must be the true constitution of the state, by whatever formal appellation it may pass. For, though he informs the assembly, that the more considerable part of the army have not cast off their obedience, but are still attached to their duty, yet those travellers who have seen the corps whose conduct is the best, rather observe in them the absence of mutiny than the existence of discipline.

I cannot help pausing here for a moment, to reflect upon the expressions of surprise which this Minister has let fall, relative to the excesses he relates. To him the departure of the troops from their antient principles of loyalty and honour seems quite inconceivable. Surely those to whom he addresses himself know the causes of it but too well. They know the doctrines which they have preached, the decrees which they have passed, the practices which they have countenanced. The soldiers remember the 6th of October. They recollect the French guards.[657] They have not forgot the taking of the King's castles in Paris, and [308] at Marseilles.[658] That they murdered, with impunity, the governors

[656]Du Pin's terms was *comices*, which Burke allowed to stand with his translation. This was a new term in French, adopted during the Revolution for an electoral meeting, and borrowed from the Latin *comitia*.

[657]The French Guards were a militarized police unit, based in Paris, and the first to go over to the Revolution. In late June 1789 they increasingly refused to perform their duties; five out of their six battalions mutinied by mid July and played conspicuous parts in the assault on the Bastille, an operation which required more than undisciplined enthusiasm. Its capture thus had the symbolic status of the result of mutiny in the French military as well as of successful popular revolt.

[658]The Bastille, the only defensible place in Paris, was stormed on 14 July 1789 and its governor, the marquis de Launay, who had engaged in lengthy negotiations with the assailants, was taken away and later murdered. On 30 April 1790 the National Guard at Marseilles seized the three forts defending the city; Major de Beausset, who had tried to resist, was lynched. When the king demanded the forts' return, the Marseillais demolished two of them and disarmed the third. This represented a symbolic victory for the Jacobin Club in Marseilles (although these forts, like the Bastille, were of little value as means of coercing the populace); as such, 'this division between rich and poor

in both places, has not passed out of their minds. They do not abandon the principles laid down so ostentatiously and laboriously of the equality of men. They cannot shut their eyes to the degradation of the whole noblesse of France; and the suppression of the very idea of a gentleman. The total abolition of titles and distinctions is not lost upon them.[659] But Mr. du Pin is astonished at their disloyalty, when the doctors of the assembly have taught them at the same time the respect due to laws. It is easy to judge which of the two sorts of lessons men with arms in their hands are likely to learn. As to the authority of the King, we may collect from the minister himself (if any argument on that head were not quite superfluous) that it is not of more consideration with these troops, than it is with every body else. "The King," says he, "has over and over again repeated his orders to put a stop to these excesses: but, in so terrible a crisis *your* [the assembly's] concurrence is become indispensably necessary to prevent the evils which menace the state. *You* unite to the force of the legislative power, *that of opinion* still more important." To be sure the army can have no opinion of the power or authority of the king. Perhaps the soldier has by this time learned, that the assembly itself does not enjoy a much greater degree of liberty than that royal figure.

It is now to be seen what has been proposed in this exigency, one of the greatest that can happen in a state. The Minister requests the assembly [309] to array itself in all its terrors, and to call forth all its majesty. He desires that the grave and severe principles announced by them may give vigour to the King's proclamation. After this we should have looked for courts civil and martial; breaking of some corps, decimating others, and all the terrible means which necessity has employed in such cases to arrest the progress of the most terrible of all evils; particularly, one might expect, that a serious inquiry would be made into the murder of commandants in the view of their soldiers. Not one word of all this, or of any thing like it. After they had been told that the soldiery trampled upon the decrees of the assembly promulgated by the King, the assembly pass new decrees; and they authorise the King to make new proclamations. After the Secretary at War had stated[660] that the regiments

---

in Marseilles would reappear later in the Revolution and lead to greater violence than in 1790': Scott, 'Problems of Law and Order during 1790', pp. 881–2. The bloodshed was unnecessary, for, as Burke was aware, the Bastille had only a symbolic importance: 'a thing in itself of no consequence whatever ... As a prison, it was of as little importance' (Burke to unknown, [January 1790], *Correspondence*, VI, p. 80). Burke's point was that the *ancien régime* was not, in fact, a military despotism.

[659]Titles of nobility were abolished by a decree of the National Assembly on 20 June 1790, a logical consequence of the abolition of feudal dues on 4 August 1789.

[660]In his speech on 4 June 1790.

had paid no regard to oaths *prêtés avec la plus imposante solemnité*—they propose—what? More oaths. They renew decrees and proclamations as they experience their insufficiency, and they multiply oaths in proportion as they weaken, in the minds of men, the sanctions of religion. I hope that handy abridgments of the excellent sermons of Voltaire, d'Alembert, Diderot, and Helvetius, on the Immortality of the Soul, on a particular superintending Providence, and on a Future State of Rewards and Punishments, are sent down to the soldiers along with their civic oaths.[661] Of this I have no doubt; as I understand, that a certain description of reading makes no inconsiderable part of their military exercises, and that they are full as well supplied with the ammunition of pamphlets as of cartridges. [310]

To prevent the mischiefs arising from conspiracies, irregular consultations, seditious committees, and monstrous democratic assemblies ['comitia, comices'] of the soldiers, and all the disorders arising from idleness, luxury, dissipation, and insubordination, I believe the most astonishing means have been used, that ever occurred to men, even in all the inventions of this prolific age. It is no less than this:—The King has promulgated in circular letters to all the regiments his direct authority and encouragement, that the several corps should join themselves with the clubs and confederations in the several municipalities, and mix with them in their feasts and civic entertainments! This jolly discipline, it seems, is to soften the ferocity of their minds; to reconcile them to their bottle companions of other descriptions; and to merge particular conspiracies in more general associations.[662] That this remedy would be pleasing to the soldiers, as they are described by Mr. de la Tour du Pin, I can readily believe; and that, however mutinous otherwise, they will dutifully submit themselves to *these* royal proclamations. But I should question whether all this civic swearing, clubbing, and feasting, would dispose them more than at present they are disposed, to an obedience to their officers; [311] or teach them better to submit to the austere rules of military discipline. It will make

---

[661]François Marie Arouet de Voltaire (1694–1778); Jean le Rond d'Alembert (1717–83); Denis Diderot (1713–84); Claude Adrien Helvétius (1715–71). These authors were the pioneers of scepticism in France, and had sought systematically to undermine such beliefs.

[662]Comme sa Majesté y a reconnu, non une système d'associations particulières, mais une réunion de volontés de tous les François pour la liberté et la prosperité communes, ainsi pour le maintien de l'ordre publique; il a pensé qu'il convenoit que chaque regiment prit part a ces fêtes civiques pour multiplier les rapports, et referrer les liens d'union entre les citoyens et les troupes.—Lest I should not be credited, I insert the words, authorising the troops to feast with the popular confederacies. [B] Burke quoted the closing words of du Pin's address to the National Assembly.

them admirable citizens after the French mode, but not quite so good soldiers after any mode. A doubt might well arise, whether the conversations at these good tables, would fit them a great deal the better for the character of *mere instruments*, which this veteran officer and statesman justly observes, the nature of things always requires an army to be.

Concerning the likelihood of this improvement in discipline, by the free conversation of the soldiers with the municipal festive societies, which is thus officially encouraged by royal authority and sanction, we may judge by the state of the municipalities themselves, furnished to us by the war minister in this very speech. He conceives good hopes of the success of his endeavours towards restoring order *for the present* from the good disposition of certain regiments; but he finds something cloudy with regard to the future. As to preventing the return of confusion "for this, the administration (says he) cannot be answerable to you, as long as they see the municipalities arrogate to themselves an authority over the troops, which your institutions have reserved wholly to the monarch. You have fixed the limits of the military authority and the municipal authority. You have bounded the action, which you have permitted to the latter over the former, to the right of requisition; but never did the letter or the spirit of your decrees authorise the commons in these municipalities to break the officers, to try [312] them, to give orders to the soldiers, to drive them from the posts committed to their guard, to stop them in their marches ordered by the King, or, in a word, to enslave the troops to the caprice of each of the cities or even market towns through which they are to pass."

Such is the character and disposition of the municipal society which is to reclaim the soldiery, to bring them back to the true principles of military subordination, and to render them machines in the hands of the supreme power of the country! Such are the distempers of the French troops![663] Such is their cure! As the army is, so is the navy.[664] The municipalities supersede the orders of the assembly, and the seamen in their turn supersede the orders of the municipalities. From my heart I pity the condition of a respectable servant of the public, like this war minister, obliged in his old age to pledge the assembly in their civic cups, and to enter with an hoary head into all the fantastick vagaries of these juvenile politicians. Such schemes are not like propositions com-

---

[663]At least a third of the units of the French army experienced insubordination during 1790, extending to 'large-scale mutiny': Scott, 'Problems of Law and Order during 1790', pp. 863–4.

[664]Burke's views are confirmed by Joseph Martray, *La destruction de la marine française par la Révolution* (Paris, 1988) and William S. Cormack, *Revolution and Political Conflict in the French Navy 1789–1794* (Cambridge, 1995).

ing from a man of fifty years wear and tear amongst mankind. They seem rather such as ought to be expected from those grand compounders[665] in politics, who shorten the road to their degrees in the state; and have a certain inward fanatical assurance and illumination upon all subjects; upon the credit of which one of their doctors has thought fit, with great applause, and greater success, to caution the assembly not to attend to old men, or to any persons who valued themselves upon their experience. I suppose all the ministers of state must qualify, [313] and take this test; wholly abjuring the errors and heresies of experience and observation. Every man has his own relish. But I think, if I could not attain to the wisdom, I would at least preserve something of the stiff and peremptory dignity of age. These gentlemen deal in regeneration; but at any price I should hardly yield my rigid fibres to be regenerated by them; nor begin, in my grand climacteric,[666] to squall in their new accents, or to stammer, in my second cradle, the elemental sounds of their barbarous metaphysics.[667] *Si isti mihi largiantur ut repueriscam, et in eorum cunis vagiam, valde recusem!*[668]

The imbecility of any part of the puerile and pedantic system, which they call a constitution, cannot be laid open without discovering the utter insufficiency and mischief of every other part with which it comes in contact, or that bears any the remotest relation to it. You cannot propose a remedy for the incompetence of the crown, without displaying the debility of the assembly. You cannot deliberate on the confusion of the army of the state, without disclosing the worse disorders of the armed municipalities. The military lays open the civil, and the civil betrays the military anarchy. I wish every body carefully to peruse the eloquent speech (such it is) of Mons. de la Tour du Pin. He attributes the salvation of the municipalities to the good behaviour of some of the troops. These troops are to preserve the well-disposed part of those municipalities, which is confessed to be the weakest, from the pillage of the worst disposed, which is the strongest. But the municipalities affect a sovereignty, and [314] will command those troops which are necessary for their

[665]A grand compounder at Oxford was an undergraduate who paid higher fees in return for certain privileges and honours.

[666]The ancients held that a man's sixty-third year, a multiple of seven and nine, was of particular significance. Burke, born in 1730, would soon attain that age.

[667]Burke later added a footnote: 'This war-minister has since quitted the school and resigned his office.' He resigned in November 1790.

[668]'Nay, if some god should give me leave to return to infancy from my old age, to weep once more in my cradle, I should vehemently protest; for, truly, after I have run my race I have no wish to be recalled, as it were, from the goal to the starting-place': Cicero, *De Senectute*, XXIII, 83.

protection. Indeed they must command them or court them. The municipalities, by the necessity of their situation, and by the republican powers they have obtained, must, with relation to the military, be the masters, or the servants, or the confederates, or each successively; or they must make a jumble of all together, according to circumstances. What government is there to coerce the army but the municipality, or the municipality but the army? To preserve concord where authority is extinguished, at the hazard of all consequences, the assembly attempts to cure the distempers by the distempers themselves; and they hope to preserve themselves from a purely military democracy, by giving it a debauched interest in the municipal.

If the soldiers once come to mix for any time in the municipal clubs, cabals, and confederacies, an elective attraction will draw them to the lowest and most desperate part. With them will be their habits, affections, and sympathies. The military conspiracies, which are to be remedied by civic confederacies; the rebellious municipalities, which are to be rendered obedient by furnishing them with the means of seducing the very armies of the state that are to keep them in order; all these chimeras of a monstrous and portentous policy, must aggravate the confusions from which they have arisen. There must be blood. The want of common judgment manifested in the construction of all their descriptions of forces, and in all their kinds of civil and judicial authorities, will make it flow. Disorders may be quieted in one time and in one part. [315] They will break out in others; because the evil is radical[669] and intrinsic. All these schemes of mixing mutinous soldiers with seditious citizens, must weaken still more and more the military connection of soldiers with their officers, as well as add military and mutinous audacity to turbulent artificers and peasants. To secure a real army, the officer should be first and last in the eye of the soldier; first and last in his attention, observance, and esteem. Officers it seems there are to be, whose chief qualification must be temper and patience. They are to manage their troops by electioneering arts. They must bear themselves as candidates not as commanders. But as by such means power may be occasionally in their hands, the authority by which they are to be nominated becomes of high importance.

What you may do finally, does not appear; nor is it of much moment, whilst the strange and contradictory relation between your army and all the parts of your republic, as well as the puzzled relation of those parts to each other and to the whole, remain as they are. You seem to have given the provisional nomination of the officers, in the first instance, to the king, with a reserve of approbation by the National Assembly. Men who have an interest to

---

[669]For the term 'radical', see *Reflections*, p. [299].

pursue are extremely sagacious in discovering the true seat of power. They must soon perceive that those who can negative indefinitely, in reality appoint. The officers must therefore look to their intrigues in that assembly, as the sole certain road to promotion. Still, however, by your new constitution they must begin their solicitation [316] at court. This double negotiation for military rank seems to me a contrivance as well adapted, as if it were studied for no other end, to promote faction in the assembly itself, relative to this vast military patronage; and then to poison the corps of officers with factions of a nature still more dangerous to the safety of government, upon any bottom on which it can be placed, and destructive in the end to the efficiency of the army itself. Those officers, who lose the promotions intended for them by the crown, must become of a faction opposite to that of the assembly which has rejected their claims, and must nourish discontents in the heart of the army against the ruling powers. Those officers, on the other hand, who, by carrying their point through an interest in the assembly, feel themselves to be at best only second in the good-will of the crown, though first in that of the assembly, must slight an authority which would not advance, and could not retard their promotion. If to avoid these evils you will have no other rule for command or promotion than seniority, you will have an army of formality; at the same time it will become more independent, and more of a military republic. Not they but the king is the machine. A king is not to be deposed by halves. If he is not every thing in the command of an army, he is nothing. What is the effect of a power placed nominally at the head of the army, who to that army is no object of gratitude, or of fear? Such a cypher is not fit for the administration of an object, of all things the most delicate, the supreme command of [317] military men. They must be constrained (and their inclinations lead them to what their necessities require) by a real, vigorous, effective, decided, personal authority. The authority of the assembly itself suffers by passing through such a debilitating channel as they have chosen. The army will not long look to an assembly acting through the organ of false shew, and palpable imposition. They will not seriously yield obedience to a prisoner. They will either despise a pageant, or they will pity a captive king. This relation of your army to the crown will, if I am not greatly mistaken, become a serious dilemma in your politics.

It is besides to be considered, whether an assembly like yours, even supposing that it was in possession of another sort of organ through which its orders were to pass, is fit for promoting the obedience and discipline of an army. It is known, that armies have hitherto yielded a very precarious and uncertain obedience to any senate, or popular authority; and they will least of all yield it to an assembly which is to have only a continuance of two years. The officers must totally lose the characteristic disposition of military men, if they see with perfect submission and due admiration, the dominion of pleaders; especially when they find, that they have a new court to pay to an endless succession of those pleaders, whose military policy, and the genius of whose command (if they should have any) must be as uncertain as their duration is transient. In the weakness of one kind of authority, and in the fluctuation of all, the officers of an army will [318] remain for some time mutinous and full of faction, until some popular general, who understands the art of conciliating the soldiery, and who possesses the true spirit of command, shall draw the eyes of all men upon himself. Armies will obey him on his personal account. There is no other way of securing military obedience in this state of things. But the moment in which that event shall happen, the person who really commands the army is your master; the master (that is little) of your king, the master of your assembly, the master of your whole republic.[670]

How came the assembly by their present power over the army? Chiefly, to be sure, by debauching the soldiers from their officers. They have begun by a most terrible operation. They have touched the central point, about which the particles that compose armies are at repose. They have destroyed the principle of obedience in the great essential critical link between the officer and the soldier, just where the chain of military subordination commences, and on which the whole of that system depends. The soldier is told, he is a citizen, and has the rights of man and citizen. The right of a man, he is told, is to be his own governor, and to be ruled only by those to whom he delegates that self-government. It is very natural he should think, that he ought most of all to have his choice where he is to yield the greatest degree of obedience. He will therefore, in all probability, systematically do, what he does at present occasionally; that is, he will exercise at least a negative in the choice of his officers. At present the [319] officers are known at best to be only permissive, and on their good behaviour. In fact, there have been many instances in which they have been cashiered by their corps. Here is a second negative on the choice of the king; a negative as effectual at least as the other of the assembly. The soldiers know already that it has been a question, not ill received in the national assembly, whether they ought not to have the direct choice of their officers, or some pro-

---

[670]Burke's intuition was confirmed by Bonaparte's *coup d'état* of 18 Brumaire (9 November 1799). He was not alone in this prediction: for similar remarks by Antoine de Rivarol, see Fierro and Liébert, p. 754. It was, however, a rare prediction in the England of 1790, despite seventeenth-century English precedents. English observers often closed their eyes to the more disturbing features of the French Revolution at its outset, and were indignant when Burke drew attention to them.

portion of them?[671] When such matters are in deliberation, it is no extravagant supposition that they will incline to the opinion most favourable to their pretensions. They will not bear to be deemed the army of an imprisoned king, whilst another army in the same country, with whom too they are to feast and confederate, is to be considered as the free army of a free constitution. They will cast their eyes on the other and more permanent army; I mean the municipal. That corps, they well know, does actually elect its own officers.[672] They may not be able to discern the grounds of distinction on which they are not to elect a Marquis de la Fayette[673] (or what is his new name)[674] of their own? If this election of a commander in chief be a part of the rights of men, why not of theirs? They see elective justices of peace, elective judges, elective curates, elective bishops, elective municipalities and elective commanders of the Parisian army.—Why should they alone be excluded? Are the brave troops of France the only men in that nation who are not the fit judges of military merit, and of the qualifications necessary for a commander in chief? Are they paid by the state, [320] and do they therefore lose the rights of men? They are a part of that nation themselves, and contribute to that pay. And is not the king, is not the national assembly, and are not all who elect the national assembly, likewise paid? Instead of seeing all these forfeit their rights by their receiving a salary, they perceive that in all these cases a salary is given for the exercise of those rights. All your resolutions, all your proceedings, all your debates, all the works of your doctors in religion and politics, have industriously been put into their hands; and you expect that they will apply to their own case just as much of your doctrines and examples as suits your pleasure.

[671]After Burke had finished the *Reflections*, the National Assembly's decree of 21 September 1790 on the army established an elaborate mechanism of promotion which attempted to combine popular election, choice by senior officers, and seniority: *Le Moniteur*, 22 September 1790; Fierro and Liébert, p. 753. The introduction of the principle of a 'career open to talents' into the army had been discussed on 31 August 1790: *Le Moniteur*, 2 September 1790. It was, in part, a response to '*ce torrent d'insurrection militaire*' of which the war minister, Du Pin, had complained to the Assembly on 6 August: *Le Moniteur*, 7 August 1790.

[672]Burke was correct: the National Guard already elected its officers. Later, the mass conscripts to the army in 1792 were given this right from the outset, and the election of officers was made general in 1793 by the reform of Edmond Dubois de Crancé. Fierro and Liébert, p. 754.

[673]See Biographical Guide.

[674]After the abolition of titles of nobility on 20 June 1790, the marquis de La Fayette should have become plain M. Motier. The prohibition of their use was backed by draconian penalties; it could not yet be known that the decree's absurdity would eventually lead to its being ignored.

Every thing depends upon the army in such a government as yours; for you have industriously destroyed all the opinions, and prejudices, and, as far as in you lay, all the instincts which support government. Therefore the moment any difference arises between your national assembly and any part of the nation, you must have recourse to force. Nothing else is left to you; or rather you have left nothing else to yourselves. You see by the report of your war minister, that the distribution of the army is in a great measure made with a view of internal coercion.[675] You must rule by an army; and you have infused into that army by which you rule, as well as into the whole body of the nation, principles which after a time must disable you in the use you resolve to make of it. [321] The king is to call out troops to act against his people, when the world has been told, and the assertion[676] is still ringing in our ears, that troops ought not to fire on citizens. The colonies assert to themselves an independent constitution and a free trade. They must be constrained by troops. In what chapter of your code of the rights of men are they able to read, that it is a part of the rights of men to have their commerce monopolized and restrained for the benefit of others. As the colonists rise on you, the negroes rise on them. Troops again—Massacre, torture, hanging! These are your rights of men! These are the fruits of metaphysic declarations wantonly made, and shamefully retracted![677] It was but the other day that the farmers of land in one of your

_imp._
_out-_
_prelude_
_to_
_Haiti._

[675]Courier François, 30 July, 1790. Assemblée Nationale, Numero 210. [B] The *Courier Français* no. 210 (30 July 1790) printed the 'Memoire du ministre de la guerre sur l'état de nos frontieres' presented to the National Assembly on 29 July and the minister's introductory speech. Du Pin had explained the troop movements necessary to repress the disturbances in Lyon and Champagne: 'L'intérieur du royaume emporte, il est vrai, un plus grand nombre de troupes que de coutume. Mais vous connoissez parfaitement les troubles qui se sont élevés dans les départemens de la Correze, de la Niévre, de l'Allier & de l'Aube; la nécessité de conserver des détachemens dans ceux de la Seine & Marne, de la Seine & l'Oise, & du Loiret, dans la Normandie ...'

[676]Not identified.

[677]The *Déclaration des droits de l'homme* had unexpected effects in France's West Indian possessions. An attempt by the National Assembly in March 1790 to impose strictly controlled colonial assemblies provoked armed resistance from colonists who had already set up legislative assemblies of their own; these rebellions were suppressed by armed force. Negroes and mulattoes now began to make similar demands for human rights. The assemblies imposed by France had a franchise set by a property qualification, not mentioning race; this was changed to allow the vote only to negroes born of free parents, with the enfranchised in a second category, and slaves excluded entirely. On 24 September 1791 the National Assembly retreated further, depriving all blacks of the rights of citizens. This provoked a destructive civil war in the French West Indies. The Convention abolished slavery on 4 February 1794; Bonaparte reestablished it on 10 May 1802: Fierro and Liébert, pp. 755–6. See Mitchell B. Garrett, *The*

provinces refused to pay some sorts of rents to the lord of the soil. In consequence of this you decree, that the country people shall pay all rents and dues, except those which as grievances you have abolished;[678] and if they refuse, then you order the king to march troops against them. You lay down metaphysic propositions which infer universal consequences, and then you attempt to limit logic by despotism. The leaders of the present system tell them of their rights, as men, to take fortresses, to murder guards, to seize on kings without the least appearance of authority even from the assembly, whilst, as the sovereign legislative body, that assembly was sitting in the name of the nation—and yet these leaders presume to order out the troops, which have acted in these very disorders, to coerce those who shall judge on the [322] principles, and follow the examples, which have been guarantied by their own approbation.

The leaders teach the people to abhor and reject all feodality as the barbarism of tyranny, and they tell them afterwards how much of that barbarous tyranny they are to bear with patience. As they are prodigal of light with regard to grievances, so the people find them sparing in the extreme with regard to redress. They know that not only certain quit-rents and personal duties, which you have permitted them to redeem (but have furnished no money for the redemption) are as nothing to those burthens for which you have made no provision at all. They know, that almost the whole system of landed property in its origin is feudal; that it is the distribution of the possessions of the original proprietors, made by a barbarous conqueror to his barbarous instruments; and that the most grievous effects of the conquest are the land rents of every kind, as without question they are.

---

*French Colonial Question 1789–1791: Dealings of the Constituent Assembly With Problems Arising From the Revolution in the West Indies* (1916; repr. New York, 1970).

[678] On 4 August 1789 the National Assembly had abolished those seigneural claims against individuals which entailed personal service, but had reaffirmed seigneurial rights over property, to continue until they were redeemed. This pre-emptive concession, intended to render property rights secure, was aborted by the bonfire of other privileges it made that night, including tithes, and by the Assembly's announcement on 15 March 1790 that 'le régime féodal est entièrement détruit'. A 'feudal committee' of the National Assembly worked for almost a year to elaborate the redemption scheme, but its deliberations were irrelevant: direct action in the countryside in early 1789 had gone so far that the peasantry generally interpreted the concessions of 4 August as the abolition of all dues and charges, and ceased to pay them. The result was widespread financial ruin among the landowners, and violent action against them including the theft of property, the destruction of title deeds, and the burning of chateaux. See J. Q. C. Mackrell, *The Attack on 'Feudalism' in Eighteenth Century France* (London, 1973), pp. 174–5; Doyle, *Origins*, pp. 200–6; Roberts (ed.), *Documents*, pp. 236–8.

The peasants, in all probability, are the descendants of these antient proprietors, Romans or Gauls. But if they fail, in any degree, in the titles which they make on the principles of antiquaries and lawyers, they retreat into the citadel of the rights of men. There they find that men are equal; and the earth, the kind and equal mother of all, ought not to be monopolized to foster the pride and luxury of any men, who by nature are no better than themselves, and who, if they do not labour for their bread, are worse. They find, that by the laws of nature the occupant and subduer of the soil is the true proprietor; that there [323] is no prescription against nature; and that the agreements (where any there are) which have been made with their landlords, during the time of slavery, are only the effect of duresse and force; and that when the people re-entered into the rights of men, those agreements were made as void as every thing else which had been settled under the prevalence of the old feudal and aristocratic tyranny. They will tell you that they see no difference between an idler with a hat and a national cockade, and an idler in a cowl or in a rochet.[679] If you ground the title to rents on succession and prescription, they tell you, from the speech of Mr. *Camus*, published by the national assembly for their information,[680] that things ill begun cannot avail themselves of prescription; that the title of these lords was vicious in its origin; and that force is at least as bad as fraud. As to the title by succession, they will tell you, that the succession of those who have cultivated the soil is the true pedigree of property, and not rotten parchments and silly substitutions; that the lords have enjoyed their usurpation too long; and that if they allow to these lay monks any charitable pension, they ought to be thankful to the bounty of the true proprietor, who is so generous towards a false claimant to his goods.

When the peasants give you back that coin of sophistic reason, on which you have set your image and superscription,[681] you cry it down as base money, and tell them you will pay for the future with French guards, and dragoons, and hussars. You hold up, to chastise them, the second-hand authority of a king, [324] who is only the instrument of destroying, without any power of protecting either the people or his own person. Through him it seems you will make yourselves obeyed. They answer, You have taught us that there are no gentlemen; and which of your principles teach us to bow to kings whom we have not elected? We know, without your teaching, that lands were given for

---

[679]Cowl: 'A garment with a hood ... worn by monks'; rochet: 'A vestment of linen, of the nature of a surplice, usually worn by bishops and abbots': *OED*.

[680]See *Reflections*, p. [225].

[681]Cf. Luke 20.24–26: 'Shew me a penny. Whose image and superscription hath it? They answered and said, Caesar's. And he said unto them, Render therefore unto Caesar the things which be Caesar's, and unto God the things which be God's.'

the support of feudal dignities, feudal titles, and feudal offices. When you took down the cause as a grievance, why should the more grievous effect remain? As there are now no hereditary honours, and no distinguished families, why are we taxed to maintain what you tell us ought not to exist? You have sent down our old aristocratic landlords in no other character, and with no other title, but that of exactors under your authority. Have you endeavoured to make these your rent-gatherers respectable to us? No. You have sent them to us with their arms reversed, their shields broken, their impresses defaced;[682] and so displumed, degraded, and metamorphosed, such unfeathered two-legged things,[683] that we no longer know them. They are strangers to us. They do not even go by the names of our ancient lords. Physically they may be the same men; though we are not quite sure of that, on your new philosophic doctrines of personal identity.[684] In all other respects they are totally changed. We do not see why we have not as good a right to refuse them their rents, as you have to abrogate all their honours, titles, and distinctions. This we have never commissioned you to do; and it is one instance, among many indeed, of your assumption of undelegated power. [325] We see the burghers of Paris, through their clubs, their mobs, and their national guards, directing you at their pleasure, and giving that as law to you, which, under your authority, is transmitted as law to us. Through you, these burghers dispose of the lives and fortunes of us all. Why should not you attend as much to the desires of the laborious husbandman with regard to our rent, by which we are affected in the most serious manner, as you do to the demands of these insolent burghers, relative to distinctions and titles of honour, by which neither they nor we are affected at all? But we find you pay more regard to their fancies than to our necessities. Is it among the rights of man to pay tribute to his equals? Before this measure of yours, we might have thought we were not perfectly equal. We might have entertained some old, habitual, unmeaning prepossession in favour of those landlords; but we cannot conceive with what other view than

---

[682]The decree passed by the National Assembly on 20 June 1790 abolishing titles of nobility also prohibited the use of armorial bearings: Roberts (ed.), *Documents*, p. 240.

[683]Dryden had written of Achitophel [Shaftesbury]: 'Great Wits are sure to Madness near ally'd; / And thin Partitions do their Bounds divide: / Else, why should he, with Wealth and Honour blest, / Refuse his Age the needful hours of Rest? / Punish a Body which he could not please; / Bankrupt of Life, yet Prodigal of Ease? / And all to leave, what with his Toyl he won, / To that unfeather'd, two Leg'd thing, a Son': [John Dryden], *Absalom and Achitophel. A Poem* (London, 1681), p. 6, lines 18–25.

[684]For the wide reception of d'Holbach's materialism, see Darnton, *Forbidden Best-Sellers*, pp. 65–6.

that of destroying all respect to them, you could have made the law that degrades them. You have forbidden us to treat them with any of the old formalities of respect, and now you send troops to sabre and to bayonet us into a
submission to fear and force, which you did not suffer us to yield to the mild
authority of opinion.

The ground of some of these arguments is horrid and ridiculous to all rational ears; but to the politicians of metaphysics who have opened schools for
sophistry, and made establishments for anarchy, it is solid and conclusive. It is
obvious, that on a mere consideration of [326] the right, the leaders in the assembly would not in the least have scrupled to abrogate the rents along with
the titles and family ensigns. It would be only to follow up the principle of
their reasonings, and to complete the analogy of their conduct. But they had
newly possessed themselves of a great body of landed property by confiscation. They had this commodity at market; and the market would have been
wholly destroyed, if they were to permit the husbandmen to riot in the speculations with which they so freely intoxicated themselves. The only security
which property enjoys in any one of its descriptions, is from the interests of
their rapacity with regard to some other. They have left nothing but their own
arbitrary pleasure to determine what property is to be protected and what
subverted. Neither have they left any principle by which any of their municipalities can be bound to obedience; or even conscientiously obliged not to
separate from the whole, to become independent, or to connect itself with
some other state. The people of Lyons, it seems, have refused lately to pay
taxes.[685] Why should they not? What lawful authority is there left to exact
them? The king imposed some of them. The old states, methodised by orders,
settled the more ancient. They may say to the assembly, Who are you, that are
not our kings, nor the states we have elected, nor sit on the principles on
which we have elected you? And who are we, that when we see the gabelles[686]
which you have ordered to be paid, wholly shaken off, when we see the act of
disobedience afterwards ratified by yourselves, who are we, that we are [327]
not to judge what taxes we ought or ought not to pay, and who are not to
avail ourselves of the same powers, the validity of which you have approved
in others? To this the answer is, We will send troops. The last reason of kings,
is always the first with your assembly. This military aid may serve for a time,
whilst the impression of the increase of pay remains, and the vanity of being

---

[685]For the Lyon tax strike of July 1790, see W. D. Edmonds, *Jacobinism and the
Revolt of Lyon 1789–1793* (Oxford, 1990), pp. 56–62.
    [686]The *gabelle* was, specifically, a tax on salt; Burke used it as a synonym for taxes
in general.

umpires in all disputes is flattered. But this weapon will snap short, unfaithful to the hand that employs it. The assembly keep a school where, systematically, and with unremitting perseverance, they teach principles, and form regulations destructive to all spirit of subordination, civil and military—and then they expect that they shall hold in obedience an anarchic people by an anarchic army.

The municipal army, which, according to their new policy, is to balance this national army, if considered in itself only, is of a constitution much more simple, and in every respect less exceptionable. It is a mere democratic body, unconnected with the crown or the kingdom; armed, and trained, and officered at the pleasure of the districts to which the corps severally belong; and the personal service of the individuals, who compose, or the fine in lieu of personal service, are directed by the same authority.[687] Nothing is more uniform. If, however, considered in any relation to the crown, to [328] the national assembly, to the public tribunals, or to the other army, or considered in a view to any coherence or connection between its parts, it seems a monster, and can hardly fail to terminate its perplexed movements in some great national calamity.[688] It is a worse preservative of a general constitution, than the systasis of Crete,[689] or the confederation of Poland,[690] or any other ill-devised corrective which has yet been imagined, in the necessities produced by an ill-constructed system of government.

Having concluded my few remarks on the constitution of the supreme

[687]I see by Mr. Necker's account, that the national guards of Paris have received, over and above the money levied within their own city, about 145,000*l*. sterling out of the public treasure. Whether this be an actual payment for the nine months of their existence, or an estimate of their yearly charge, I do not clearly perceive. It is of no great importance, as certainly they may take whatever they please. [B] Necker's accounts, published in Le Moniteur of 3 June 1790, estimated the 'Garde militaire de Paris' at 4,000,000 *livres* 'au moins'.

[688]In June 1790 Mirabeau, too, predicted that although La Fayette seemed able to use his position as commander of the National Guard in Paris to seize dictatorial power, his position was fragile. La Fayette's dismissal on 17 July 1791, and the leading part thereafter taken by the National Guard in the unfolding tragedy of the Revolution, confirmed Burke's prediction.

[689]The union of hitherto-warring Cretan cities against an external enemy.

[690]Burke may have referred either to 'confederation' as a principle of Polish government (an armed movement in one or more provinces, organized in the name of the defence of the national interest or institutions against threatened innovation) or specifically to the Confederation of Bar (1768–72), an association of Polish Catholic nobility in 1767 to resist the toleration of Protestant and Orthodox minorities being imposed by Russia, which exercised a *de facto* protectorate over her neighbour. This led to war with Russia and the first partition of Poland.

power, the executive, the judicature, the military, and on the reciprocal relation of all these establishments, I shall say something of the ability shewed by
your legislators with regard to the revenue.

In their proceedings relative to this object, if possible, still fewer traces appear of political judgment or financial resource. When the states met, it
seemed to be the great object to improve the system of revenue, to enlarge its
collection, to cleanse it of oppression and vexation, and to establish it on the
most solid footing. Great were the expectations entertained on that head
throughout Europe. It was by this grand arrangement that France was to
stand or fall; and this became, in my opinion, very properly, the test by which
the skill and patriotism of those who ruled in that assembly would be tried.
The revenue of the state is the state. [329] In effect all depends upon it,
whether for support or for reformation. The dignity of every occupation
wholly depends upon the quantity and the kind of virtue that may be exerted
in it. As all great qualities of the mind which operate in public, and are not
merely suffering and passive, require force for their display, I had almost said
for their unequivocal existence, the revenue, which is the spring of all power,
becomes in its administration the sphere of every active virtue. Public virtue,
being of a nature magnificent and splendid, instituted for great things, and
conversant about great concerns, requires abundant scope and room, and
cannot spread and grow under confinement, and in circumstances straitened,
narrow, and sordid. Through the revenue alone the body politic can act in its
true genius and character, and therefore it will display just as much of its collective virtue, and as much of that virtue which may characterise those who
move it, and are, as it were, its life and guiding principle, as it is possessed of a
just revenue. For from hence, not only magnanimity, and liberality, and beneficence, and fortitude, and providence, and the tutelary protection of all
good arts, derive their food, and the growth of their organs, but continence,
and self-denial, and labour, and vigilance, and frugality, and whatever else
there is in which the mind shews itself above the appetite, are no where more
in their proper element than in the provision and distribution of the public
wealth. It is therefore not without reason that the science of speculative and
practical finance, which must take to its aid so many auxiliary branches of
knowledge, stands high in the estimation not only of [330] the ordinary sort,
but of the wisest and best men; and as this science has grown with the progress
of its object, the prosperity and improvement of nations has generally encreased with the encrease of their revenues; and they will both continue to
grow and flourish, as long as the balance between what is left to strengthen
the efforts of individuals, and what is collected for the common efforts of the
state, bear to each other a due reciprocal proportion, and are kept in a close

correspondence and communication. And perhaps it may be owing to the greatness of revenues, and to the urgency of state necessities, that old abuses in the constitution of finances are discovered, and their true nature and rational theory comes to be more perfectly understood; insomuch, that a smaller revenue might have been more distressing in one period than a far greater is found to be in another; the proportionate wealth even remaining the same. In this state of things, the French assembly found something in their revenues to preserve, to secure, and wisely to administer, as well as to abrogate and alter. Though their proud assumption might justify the severest tests, yet in trying their abilities on their financial proceedings, I would only consider what is the plain obvious duty of a common finance minister, and try them upon that, and not upon models of ideal perfection.

The objects of a financier are, then, to secure an ample revenue; to impose it with judgment and equality; to employ it œconomically; and when necessity obliges him to make use of credit, to secure its foundations in that instance, and for ever, [331] by the clearness and candour of his proceedings, the exactness of his calculations, and the solidity of his funds. On these heads we may take a short and distinct view of the merits and abilities of those in the national assembly, who have taken to themselves the management of this arduous concern. Far from any encrease of revenue in their hands, I find, by a report of M. Vernier, from the committee of finances, of the second of August last, that the amount of the national revenue, as compared with its produce before the revolution, was diminished by the sum of two hundred millions, or *eight millions sterling* of the annual income, considerably more than one-third of the whole![691]

If this be the result of great ability, never surely was ability displayed in a more distinguished manner, or with so powerful an effect. No common folly, no vulgar incapacity, no ordinary official negligence, even no official crime, no corruption, no peculation, hardly any direct hostility which we have seen in the modern world, could in so short a time have made so complete an overthrow of the finances, and with them, of the strength of a great kingdom.— *Cedò quî vestram rempublicam tantam amisistis tam cito?*[692]

[691]Théodore Vernier, comte de Monte-Orient (1731–1818). Burke may have misunderstood this part of his speech, as printed in *Le Moniteur* of 3 August 1790. Vernier had boasted of the tax burden having been lightened by 200 million *livres*, and of a corresponding reduction in the functions of government: Fierro and Liébert, p. 759.

[692]Cicero, *De Senectute*, VI, 20, quoted this line from the poet Naevius's play *The Wolf*, 'Tell me how you ruined your state so soon', and followed it with Naevius's answer, 'proveniebant oratores novi, stulti adulescentuli': 'new orators arose, foolish young men'.

The sophisters and declaimers, as soon as the assembly met, began with decrying the ancient constitution of the revenue in many of its most essential branches, such as the public monopoly of salt. They charged it, as truly as unwisely, with being ill-contrived, oppressive, and partial. This representation they were not satisfied to make use of in speeches preliminary to some [332] plan of reform; they declared it in a solemn resolution or public sentence, as it were judicially, passed upon it; and this they dispersed throughout the nation. At the time they passed the decree, with the same gravity they ordered this same absurd, oppressive, and partial tax to be paid, until they could find a revenue to replace it.[693] The consequence was inevitable. The provinces which had been always exempted from this salt monopoly, some of whom were charged with other contributions, perhaps equivalent, were totally disinclined to bear any part of the burthen, which by an equal distribution was to redeem the others. As to the assembly, occupied as it was with the declaration and violation of the rights of men, and with their arrangements for general confusion, it had neither leisure nor capacity to contrive, nor authority to enforce any plan of any kind relative to the replacing the tax or equalizing it, or compensating the provinces, or for conducting their minds to any scheme of accommodation with the other districts which were to be relieved.

The people of the salt provinces, impatient under taxes damned by the authority which had directed their payment, very soon found their patience exhausted. They thought themselves as skilful in demolishing as the assembly could be. They relieved themselves by throwing off the whole burthen. Animated by this example, each district, or part of a district, judging of its own grievance by its own feeling, and of its remedy by its own opinion, did as it pleased with other taxes. [333]

We are next to see how they have conducted themselves in contriving equal impositions, proportioned to the means of the citizens, and the least likely to lean heavy on the active capital employed in the generation of that private wealth, from whence the public fortune must be derived. By suffering the several districts, and several of the individuals in each district, to judge of

[693]The *gabelle* or salt tax was one of the symbolic grievances of the peasantry, made worse by being levied in some parts of France but not in others. Calonne had attempted to abolish it as part of the package of reforms obstructed by the Assembly of Notables. The problem was typically mishandled by the National Assembly, which in June 1789 abolished all existing duties, but decreed that provisionally, 'quoique illégalement établis et perçus', these would continue to be levied in the same way as before. The *gabelle* was abolished in 1790 under pressure of public opinion, though without the Assembly finding a substitute for the income it provided. Fierro and Liébert, pp. 759–60; Gail Bossenga, 'Taxes' in Furet and Ozouf, *Critical Dictionary*, pp. 582–90.

what part of the old revenue they might withhold, instead of better principles of equality, a new inequality was introduced of the most oppressive kind. Payments were regulated by dispositions. The parts of the kingdom which were the most submissive, the most orderly, or the most affectionate to the commonwealth, bore the whole burthen of the state. Nothing turns out to be so oppressive and unjust as a feeble government. To fill up all the deficiencies in the old impositions, and the new deficiencies of every kind which were to be expected, what remained to a state without authority? The national assembly called for a voluntary benevolence; for a fourth part of the income of all the citizens, to be estimated on the honour of those who were to pay.[694] They obtained something more than could be rationally calculated, but what was, far indeed, from answerable to their real necessities, and much less to their fond expectations. Rational people could have hoped for little from this their tax in the disguise of a benevolence; a tax, weak, ineffective, and unequal; a tax by which luxury, avarice, and selfishness were screened, and the load thrown upon productive capital, upon integrity, generosity, and public spirit—a tax [334] of regulation upon virtue. At length the mask is thrown off, and they are now trying means (with little success) of exacting their benevolence by force.

This benevolence, the ricketty offspring of weakness, was to be supported by another resource, the twin brother of the same prolific imbecility. The patriotic donations were to make good the failure of the patriotic contribution. John Doe was to become security for Richard Roe.[695] By this scheme they took things of much price from the giver, comparatively of small value to the receiver; they ruined several trades; they pillaged the crown of its ornaments, the churches of their plate, and the people of their personal decorations. The invention of these juvenile pretenders to liberty, was in reality nothing more than a servile imitation of one of the poorest resources of doting despotism. They took an old huge full-bottomed perriwig out of the wardrobe of the antiquated frippery of Louis XIV. to cover the premature baldness of the national assembly. They produced this old-fashioned formal folly, though it had been so abundantly exposed in the Memoirs of the Duke de St. Simon,[696] if to

[694]On 1 October 1789 the National Assembly voted to invite a *contribution extraordinare et patriotique* as a single 'voluntary' donation, assessed as one quarter of the annual income (payable in three instalments) by those with incomes over 400 *livres* per annum; poorer citizens were 'invited' to make *dons patriotiques*: *Le Moniteur*, 29 September–1 October 1789. See *Reflections*, p. [80].

[695]Fictitious characters in actions at English common law. See Maitland, *Forms of Action at Common Law*, pp. 57–9; Stephen, *Principles of Pleading*, pp. 45–58.

[696]Louis de Rouvroy, duc de Saint-Simon (1675–1755), denounced in his *Mémoires* the *dixième* introduced during the War of the Spanish Succession. Burke owned a copy

reasonable men it had wanted any arguments to display its mischief and insufficiency. A device of the same kind was tried in my memory by Louis XV. but it answered at no time.[697] However, the necessities of ruinous wars were some excuse for desperate projects. The deliberations of calamity are rarely wise. But here was a season for disposition and providence. It was in a time of profound [335] peace, then enjoyed for five years, and promising a much longer continuance, that they had recourse to this desperate trifling. They were sure to lose more reputation by sporting, in their serious situation, with these toys and playthings of finance, which have filled half their journals, than could possibly be compensated by the poor temporary supply which they afforded. It seemed as if those who adopted such projects were wholly ignorant of their circumstances, or wholly unequal to their necessities. Whatever virtue may be in these devices, it is obvious that neither the patriotic gifts, nor the patriotic contribution, can ever be resorted to again. The resources of public folly are soon exhausted. The whole indeed of their scheme of revenue is to make, by any artifice, an appearance of a full reservoir for the hour, whilst at the same time they cut off the springs and living fountains of perennial supply. The account not long since furnished by Mr. Necker[698] was meant, without question, to be favourable. He gives a flattering view of the means of getting through the year; but he expresses, as it is natural he should, some apprehension for that which was to succeed. On this last prognostic, instead of entering into the grounds of this apprehension, in order, by a proper foresight, to prevent the prognosticated evil, Mr. Necker receives a sort of friendly reprimand from the president of the assembly.[699]

---

of [J. L. Giraud Soulavie, ed.], *Mémoires de M. le Duc de Saint Simon* (7 vols., London, 1788–9): *LC*, p. 14; LC MS, fo. 4.

[697]Under Louis XIV and XV, a direct tax known as the *dixième* was imposed during wartime between 1710 and 1749. It was replaced by a five per cent tax, the *vingtième*, but this was doubled in 1756 and tripled in 1760–4 and 1782–6. After 1758, cities were compelled to pay *dons gratuits* that became, in effect, a permanent tax: Bossenga, 'Taxes' in Furet and Ozouf, *Critical Dictionary*, p. 583; Fierro and Liébert, p. 763; François Hincker, *Les Français devant l'impôt sous l'Ancien Régime* (Paris, 1971), p. 186.

[698]Necker's report, read to the National Assembly on 29 May 1790 and printed in *Le Moniteur*, 3 June 1790, Supplement. For the current year, he predicted a surplus of 11,400,000 *livres*, though with warnings of future uncertainties. This was not convincing, however, and on 29 September the Assembly voted another temporary expedient, the issue of a second tranche of 800 million *assignats*.

[699]*Le Moniteur* of 3 June 1790 reported the words of the President of the National Assembly in response to Necker's warning. M. de Beaumetz replied: 'On est toujours sûr de l'attention *bienveillante* de l'Assemblée, quand on lui parle de paix, de concorde,

As to their other schemes of taxation, it is impossible to say any thing of them with certainty; because they have not yet had their operation; but nobody [336] is so sanguine as to imagine they will fill up any perceptible part of the wide gaping breach which their incapacity has made in their revenues. At present the state of their treasury sinks every day more and more in cash, and swells more and more in fictitious representation. When so little within or without is now found but paper, the representative not of opulence but of want, the creature not of credit but of power, they imagine that our flourishing state in England is owing to that bank-paper, and not the bank-paper to the flourishing condition of our commerce, to the solidity of our credit, and to the total exclusion of all idea of power from any part of the transaction. They forget that, in England, not one shilling of paper-money of any description is received but of choice; that the whole has had its origin in cash actually deposited; and that it is convertible, at pleasure, in an instant, and without the smallest loss, into cash again. Our paper is of value in commerce, because in law it is of none. It is powerful on Change,[700] because in Westminster-hall[701] it is impotent. In payment of a debt of twenty shillings, a creditor may refuse all the paper of the bank of England. Nor is there amongst us a single public security, of any quality or nature whatsoever, that is enforced by authority. In fact it might be easily shewn, that our paper wealth, instead of lessening the real coin, has a tendency to increase it; instead of being a substitute for money, it only facilitates its entry, its exit, and its circulation; that it is the symbol of prosperity, and not the badge of distress. Never was a scarcity of cash, and an exuberance of paper, a subject of complaint in this nation.[702] [337]

Well! but a lessening of prodigal expences, and the œconomy which has been introduced by the virtuous and sapient assembly, makes amends for the

---

de fraternité, et des moyens d'accélerer la félicité de l'empire. Pourquoi mêler à ces idées consolantes la pensée affligeante de l'instant où vous pourriez cesser de coopérer à leur exécution? Il est des hommes qui ne devraient connaître de l'humanité que les affections douces qui unissent les êtres sensibles, et non pas les maux qui les affligent.'

[700]The Stock Exchange.

[701]The law courts. For Mirabeau's arguments in the debates of September 1790 that the new tranche of *assignats* would be more secure than English paper money because backed by church lands, see Bruguière, 'Assignats', in Furet and Ozouf, *Critical Dictionary*, p. 428.

[702]For the strength of British credit in the eighteenth century see J. E. D. Binney, *British Public Finance and Administration, 1774–92* (Oxford, 1958); P. K. O'Brien, 'The political economy of British taxation, 1660–1815', *Economic History Review* 41 (1988), 1–32. Burke's enemies in the 1790s like Price, Priestley and Paine, knowing little of public finance, predicted imminent ruin from the size of the national debt. In fact, the government was able to finance the war up to 1815 by ever-larger loans.

losses sustained in the receipt of revenue. In this at least they have fulfilled the duty of a financier. Have those, who say so, looked at the expences of the national assembly itself, of the municipalities, of the city of Paris, of the increased pay of the two armies, of the new police, of the new judicatures? Have they even carefully compared the present pension-list with the former? These politicians have been cruel, not œconomical. Comparing the expences of the former prodigal government and its relation to the then revenues with the expences of this new system as opposed to the state of its new treasury, I believe the present will be found beyond all comparison more chargeable.[703]

It remains only to consider the proofs of financial ability, furnished by the present French managers when they are to raise supplies on credit. Here I am a little at a stand; for credit, properly speaking, they have none. The credit of the antient government was not indeed the best: but they could always, on some terms, command money, not only at home, but from most of the countries of Europe where a surplus capital was accumulated; and the credit of that government improving daily.[704] The establishment of a system of liberty would of course be supposed to give it new strength; and so it would actually have done, if a system of liberty had been established. What offers has their government of pretended liberty had from Holland, from Hamburgh, from Switzerland, from [338] Genoa, from England, for a dealing in their paper? Why should these nations of commerce and œconomy enter into any pecuniary dealings with a people who attempt to reverse the very nature of things; amongst whom they see the debtor prescribing, at the point of the bayonet, the medium of his solvency to the creditor; discharging one of his engagements with another; turning his very penury into his resource; and paying his interest with his rags?

[703]Burke later added a footnote: 'The reader will observe, that I have but lightly touched (my plan demanded nothing more) on the condition of the French finances, as connected with the demands upon them. If I had intended to do otherwise, the materials in my hands for such a task are not altogether perfect. On this subject I refer the reader to M. de Calonne's work; and the tremendous display that he has made of the havock and devastation in the public estate, and in all the affairs of France, caused by the presumptuous good intentions of ignorance and incapacity. Such effects, those causes will always produce. Looking over that account with a pretty strict eye, and, with perhaps too much rigour, deducting every thing which may be placed to the account of a financier out of place, who might be supposed by his enemies desirous of making the most of his cause, I believe it will be found, that a more salutary lesson of caution against the daring spirit of innovators than what has been supplied at the expence of France, never was at any time furnished to mankind.'

[704]Burke was relatively well informed about French finances, given the evidence then available; it is only now that historians are able to show their serious weakness in the late 1780s, leading to the effective bankruptcy of August 1788.

Their fanatical confidence in the omnipotence of church plunder, has induced these philosophers to overlook all care of the public estate, just as the dream of the philosopher's stone induces dupes, under the more plausible delusion of the hermetic art, to neglect all rational means of improving their fortunes. With these philosophic financiers, this universal medicine made of church mummy[705] is to cure all the evils of the state. These gentlemen perhaps do not believe a great deal in the miracles of piety; but it cannot be questioned, that they have an undoubting faith in the prodigies of sacrilege. Is there a debt which presses them—Issue *assignats*.[706]—Are compensations to be made, or a maintenance decreed to those whom they have robbed of their freehold in their office, or expelled from their profession—*Assignats*. Is a fleet to be fitted out—*Assignats*. If sixteen millions sterling of these *assignats*, forced on the people, leave the wants of the state as urgent as ever—issue, says one, thirty millions sterling of *assignats*—says another, issue fourscore millions more of *assignats*. The only difference among their financial factions is on the greater or the lesser quantity of *assignats* to be imposed on the publick sufferance. [339] They are all professors of *assignats*. Even those, whose natural good sense and knowledge of commerce, not obliterated by philosophy, furnish decisive arguments against this delusion, conclude their arguments, by proposing the emission of *assignats*. I suppose they must talk of *assignats*, as no other language would be understood. All experience of their inefficacy does not in the least discourage them. Are the old *assignats* depreciated at market? What is the remedy? Issue new *assignats*.—*Mais si maladia, opiniatria, non vult se garire, quid illi facere? assignare—postea assignare; ensuita assignare.*[707] The word is a trifle altered. The Latin of your present doctors may be better than that of your old comedy; their wisdom, and the variety of their resources, are the same. They have not more notes in their song than the cuckow; though,

---

[705]Church mummy: 'A medicinal preparation of the substance of mummies; hence, an unctuous liquid or gum used medicinally': *OED*.

[706]For this system of finance see F. d'Ivernois, *A Cursory View of the Assignats* (London, 1795); Michel Bruguière, 'Assignats', in Furet and Ozouf, *Critical Dictionary*, pp. 426–36, and *Reflections*, p. [182]. It was pointed out that Burke had not before condemned paper money, although 'It was an expedient adopted in America, during her late struggle with the mother country': *Short Observations on the Right Hon. Edmund Burke's Reflections* (London, 1790), p. 31.

[707]'But if the disease in opinion does not wish to cure itself, what is to be done? Issue *assignats*—then more *assignats*; and afterwards more *assignats*'. Burke echoed the scene in Molière's *Le Malade Imaginaire* in which a candidate for the degree of Bachelor of Medicine is examined in dog Latin and continually repeats his remedy: *saignare*, draw blood. Burke owned a copy of Molière's *Oeuvres* (8 vols., Paris, 1760–70): *LC*, p. 14.

far from the softness of that harbinger of summer and plenty, their voice is as harsh and as ominous as that of the raven.

Who but the most desperate adventurers in philosophy and finance could at all have thought of destroying the settled revenue of the state, the sole security for the public credit, in the hope of rebuilding it with the materials of confiscated property? If, however, an excessive zeal for the state should have led a pious and venerable prelate[708] (by anticipation a father of the church[709]) to pillage his own order, and, for the good of the church and people, to take upon himself the place of grand financier of confiscation, and comptroller general of sacrilege, he and his coadjutors were, in my opinion, bound to shew, [340] by their subsequent conduct, that they knew something of the office they assumed. When they had resolved to appropriate to the *Fisc*, a certain portion of the landed property of their conquered country, it was their business to render their bank a real fund of credit; as far as such a bank was capable of becoming so.

To establish a current circulating credit upon any *Land-bank*, under any circumstances whatsoever, has hitherto proved difficult at the very least. The attempt has commonly ended in bankruptcy.[710] But when the assembly were led, through a contempt of moral, to a defiance of œconomical principles, it might at least have been expected, that nothing would be omitted on their part to lessen this difficulty, to prevent any aggravation of this bankruptcy. It might be expected that to render your *Land-bank* tolerable, every means would be adopted that could display openness and candour in the statement of the security; every thing which could aid the recovery of the demand. To take things in their most favourable point of view, your condition was that of a man of a large landed estate, which he wished to dispose of for the discharge of a debt, and the supply of certain services. Not being able instantly to sell, you wished to mortgage. What would a man of fair intentions, and a commonly clear understanding, do in such circumstances? Ought he not first to ascertain the gross value of the estate; the charges of its management and disposition; the encumbrances perpetual and temporary of all kinds that affect it; then, striking a net surplus, to calculate the just value of the security? When that surplus (the only security to [341] the creditor) had been clearly ascertained, and properly vested in the hands of trustees; then he would indicate

---

[708] An ironic allusion to Talleyrand, bishop of Autun.

[709] La Bruyere of Bossuet. [B] Jean de la Bruyère (1645–96) had, in these words, saluted the great Jacques-Bénigne Bossuet (1627–1704), bishop of Meaux. Burke again implied a contrast with Talleyrand's betrayal of the Church.

[710] An attempt to establish such a bank had failed in England in 1696.

the parcels to be sold, and the time, and conditions of sale; after this, he would admit the public creditor, if he chose it, to subscribe his stock into this new fund; or he might receive proposals for an *assignat* from those who would advance money to purchase this species of security.

This would be to proceed like men of business, methodically and rationally; and on the only principles of public and private credit that have an existence. The dealer would then know exactly what he purchased; and the only doubt which could hang upon his mind would be, the dread of the resumption of the spoil, which one day might be made (perhaps with an addition of punishment) from the sacrilegious gripe of those execrable wretches who could become purchasers at the auction of their innocent fellow-citizens.

An open and exact statement of the clear value of the property, and of the time, the circumstances, and the place of sale, were all necessary, to efface as much as possible the stigma that has hitherto been branded on every kind of Land-bank. It became necessary on another principle, that is, on account of a pledge of faith previously given on that subject, that their future fidelity in a slippery concern might be established by their adherence to their first engagement. When they had finally determined on a state resource from church booty, they came, on the 14th of April 1790, to a solemn resolution on the subject; and pledged themselves to their country, "that in the statement of the public charges for each year there should be brought to [342] account a sum sufficient for defraying the expences of the R.C.A. religion, the support of the ministers at the altars, the relief of the poor, the pensions to the ecclesiastics, secular as well as regular, of the one and of the other sex, *in order that the estates and goods which are at the disposal of the nation may be disengaged of all charges, and employed by the representatives, or the legislative body, to the great and most pressing exigencies of the state.*" They further engaged, on the same day, that the sum necessary for the year 1791 should be forthwith determined.[711]

In this resolution they admit it their duty to show distinctly the expence of the above objects, which, by other resolutions, they had before engaged should be first in the order of provision. They admit that they ought to shew the estate clear and disengaged of all charges, and that they should shew it immediately. Have they done this immediately, or at any time? Have they ever furnished a rent-roll of the immoveable estates, or given in an inventory of the moveable effects which they confiscate to their assignats? In what manner they can fulfil their engagements of holding out to public service "an estate disengaged of all charges," without authenticating the value of the estate, or

[711]For this debate see *Le Moniteur*, 15 April 1790. The italics were Burke's.

the quantum of the charges, I leave it to their English admirers to explain. Instantly upon this assurance, and previously to any one step towards making it good, they issue, on the credit of so handsome a declaration, sixteen millions sterling of their paper. This was manly. Who, after this masterly stroke, can doubt of their abilities in finance? But then, before any other emission of [343] these financial *indulgences*, they took care at least to make good their original promise. If such estimate, either of the value of the estate or the amount of the incumbrances, has been made, it has escaped me. I never heard of it. They have however done one thing, which in the gross is clear, obscure, as usual, in the detail.[712] They have thrown upon this fund, which was to shew a surplus, disengaged of all charges, a new charge; namely, the compensation to the whole body of the disbanded judicature; and of all suppressed offices and estates; a charge which I cannot ascertain, but which unquestionably amounts to many French millions. Another of the new charges, is an annuity of four hundred and eighty thousand pounds sterling, to be paid (if they choose to keep faith) by daily payments, for the interest of the first assignats. Have they ever given themselves the trouble to state fairly the expence of the management of the church lands in the hands of the municipalities, to whose care, skill, and diligence, and that of their legion of unknown under agents, they have chosen to commit the charge of the forfeited estates, and the consequence of which had been so ably pointed out by the bishop of Nancy?[713]

But it is unnecessary to dwell on these obvious heads of incumbrance. Have they made out any clear state of the grand incumbrance of all, I mean the whole of the general and municipal establishments of all sorts, and compared it with the regular income by revenue? Every deficiency in these becomes a charge on the confiscated estate, before the creditor can plant his cabbages on an acre of church property. There is [344] no other prop than this confiscation to keep the whole state from tumbling to the ground. In this situation they have purposely covered all that they ought industriously to have cleared, with a thick fog; and then, blindfold themselves, like bulls that shut their eyes when they push, they drive, by the point of the bayonets, their slaves, blindfolded indeed no worse than their lords, to take their fictions for currencies, and so swallow down paper pills by thirty-four millions sterling at a dose. Then they proudly lay in their claim to a future credit, on failure of all their past engagements, and at a time when (if in such a matter any thing can

[712]Burke subsequently omitted this sentence and inserted new text: see Appendix I.

[713]See Biographical Guide. The bishop spoke in the National Assembly on this subject on 21 December 1789; in October he had published *Considérations politiques sur les biens temporels du clergé* (Paris and Nancy, 1789).

be clear) it is clear that the surplus estates will never answer even the first of their mortgages, I mean that of the four hundred million (or sixteen millions sterling) of *assignats*. In all this procedure I can discern neither the solid sense of plain-dealing, nor the subtle dexterity of ingenious fraud. The objection within the assembly to pulling up the flood-gates for this inundation of fraud, are unanswered; but they are thoroughly refuted by an hundred thousand financiers in the street. These are the numbers by which the metaphysic arithmeticians compute. These are the grand calculations on which a philosophical public credit is founded in France. They cannot raise supplies; but they can raise mobs. Let them rejoice in the applauses of the club at Dundee,[714] for their wisdom and patriotism in having thus applied the plunder of the citizens to the service of the state. I hear of no address upon this subject from the directors of the Bank of England; though their approbation would be of a *little* more weight in the scale of credit than that of the club at Dundee. But, to do justice to [345] the club, I believe the gentlemen who compose it to be wiser than they appear; that they will be less liberal of their money than of their addresses; and that they would not give a dog's-ear of their most rumpled and ragged Scotch paper for twenty of your fairest assignats.

Early in this year the assembly issued paper to the amount of sixteen millions sterling: What must have been the state into which the assembly has brought your affairs, that the relief afforded by so vast a supply has been hardly perceptible? This paper also felt an almost immediate depreciation of five per cent. which in little time came to about seven. The effect of these assignats on the receipt of the revenue is remarkable. Mr. Necker found that the collectors of the revenue, who received in coin, paid the treasury in *assignats*. The collectors made seven per cent. by thus receiving in money, and accounting in depreciated paper. It was not very difficult to foresee, that this must be inevitable. It was, however, not the less embarrassing. Mr. Necker was obliged (I believe, for a considerable part, in the market of London) to buy gold and silver for the mint, which amounted to about twelve thousand pounds above the value of the commodity gained. That minister was of opinion, that whatever their secret nutritive virtue might be, the state could not

[714]The address of the 'Friends of Liberty' at Dundee dated 4 June 1790, read to the National Assembly on 31 July, was printed in *Le Moniteur* of 2 August 1790: 'Nous remarquons, pour l'honneur du siècle, et celui de votre Nation, que votre Révolution s'est faite sans guerre civile, et que ni les Domaines inutiles du Prince, ni les biens du Clergé n'ont été distribués à des mains avides, mais qu'ils ont été employés pour l'utilité de l'Etat dont ils sont la propriété. Nous prévoyons avec joie que cette flamme que vous avez allumée, consumera dans toute l'Europe les restes du despotisme et de la superstition'.

live upon *assignats* alone; that some real silver was necessary, particularly for the satisfaction of those, who having iron in their hands, were not likely to distinguish themselves for patience, when they should perceive that whilst an encrease of pay was held out to them in real money, it was again to be fraudulently [346] drawn back by depreciated paper. The minister, in this very natural distress, applied to the assembly,[715] that they should order the collectors to pay in specie what in specie they had received. It could not escape him, that if the treasury paid 3 per cent. for the use of a currency, which should be returned seven per cent. worse than the minister issued it, such a dealing could not very greatly tend to enrich the public. The assembly took no notice of his recommendation. They were in this dilemma—If they continued to receive the assignats, cash must become an alien to their treasury: If the treasury should refuse those paper *amulets*, or should discountenance them in any degree, they must destroy the credit of their sole resource. They seem then to have made their option; and to have given some sort of credit to their paper by taking it themselves; at the same time in their speeches they made a sort of swaggering declaration, something, I rather think, above legislative competence; that is, that there is no difference in value between metallic money and their assignats. This was a good stout proof article of faith, pronounced under an anathema, by the venerable fathers of this philosophic synod. *Credat* who will—certainly not *Judæus Apella*.[716]

A noble indignation rises in the minds of your popular leaders, on hearing the magic lanthorn in their shew of finance compared to the fraudulent exhibitions of Mr. Law.[717] They cannot bear to hear the sands of his Mississippi compared with the rock of the church, on which they build their system. Pray let them suppress this glorious spirit, until they shew to the world what piece of solid [347] ground there is for their assignats, which they have not pre-occupied by other charges. They do injustice to that great, mother fraud, to compare it with their degenerate imitation. It is not true, that Law built solely on a speculation concerning the Mississippi. He added the East India trade; he added the African trade; he added the farms of all the farmed revenue of France. All these together unquestionably could not support the structure which the public enthusiasm, not he, chose to build upon these bases. But these were, however, in comparison, generous delusions. They supposed, and they aimed at an increase of the commerce of France. They opened to it the

---

[715]Necker's memorandum was sent to the Assembly on 27 August 1790.

[716]'Apella, the Jew, may believe it, not I!': Horace, *Satires* Book I, v, 100–1. 'Iudaeus Apella' was a fictional character symbolising credulity.

[717]See Biographical Guide.

whole range of the two hemispheres. They did not think of feeding France from its own substance. A grand imagination found in this flight of commerce something to captivate. It was wherewithal to dazzle the eye of an eagle. It was not made to entice the smell of a mole, nuzzling and burying himself in his mother earth, as yours is. Men were not then quite shrunk from their natural dimensions by a degrading and sordid philosophy, and fitted for low and vulgar deceptions. Above all remember, that in imposing on the imagination, the then managers of the system made a compliment to the freedom of men. In their fraud there was no mixture of force. This was reserved to our time, to quench the little glimmerings of reason which might break in upon the solid darkness of this enlightened age.[718]

On recollection, I have said nothing of a scheme of finance which may be urged in favour of the abilities of these gentlemen, and which has been introduced with great pomp, though not yet finally [348] adopted in the national assembly. It comes with something solid in aid of the credit of the paper circulation; and much has been said of its utility and its elegance. I mean the project for coining into money the bells of the suppressed churches.[719] This is their alchymy. There are some follies which baffle argument; which go beyond ridicule; and which excite no feeling in us but disgust; and therefore I say no more upon it.

It is as little worth remarking any farther upon all their drawing and redrawing, on their circulation for putting off the evil day, on the play between the treasury and the *Caisse d'Escompte*, and on all these old exploded contrivances of mercantile fraud, now exalted into policy of state. The revenue will not be trifled with. The prattling about the rights of men will not be accepted in payment for a biscuit or a pound of gunpowder. Here then the metaphysicians descend from their airy speculations, and faithfully follow examples. What examples? the examples of bankrupts. But, defeated, baffled, disgraced, when their breath, their strength, their inventions, their fancies desert them, their confidence still maintains its ground. In the manifest failure of their abilities they take credit for their benevolence. When the revenue disappears in their hands, they have the presumption, in some of their late proceedings, to value *themselves* on the relief given to the people. They did not relieve the people. If they entertained such intentions, why did they order the

---

[718]'... for then a ray of Reason stole / Half thro' the solid darkness of his soul / But soon the Cloud return'd...': [Alexander Pope], *The Dunciad, Variorum. With the Prolegomena of Scriblerus* (London: A. Dod, 1729), Book III, Lines 223–4.

[719]Such a plan was proposed in the National Assembly on 28 and 29 August 1790: *Le Moniteur*, 29 and 30 August 1790. It was rejected only after advice that the alloy of which the bells were made was unsuitable for coining.

obnoxious taxes to be paid? The people relieved themselves in spite of the assembly.

But waving all discussion on the parties, who may claim the merit of this fallacious relief, has [349] there been, in effect, any relief to the people in any form? Mr. Bailly, one of the grand agents of paper circulation, lets you into the nature of this relief. His speech to the National Assembly[720] contained an high and laboured panegyric on the inhabitants of Paris for the constancy and unbroken resolution with which they have borne their distress and misery. A fine picture of public felicity! What! great courage and unconquerable firmness of mind to endure benefits, and sustain redress! One would think from the speech of this learned Lord Mayor, that the Parisians, for this twelve-month past, had been suffering the straits of some dreadful blockade; that Henry the Fourth had been stopping up the avenues to their supply, and Sully thundering with his ordnance at the gates of Paris; when in reality they are besieged by no other enemies than their own madness and folly, their own credulity and perverseness. But Mr. Bailly will sooner thaw the eternal ice of his atlantic regions,[721] than restore the central heat to Paris, whilst it remains "smitten with the cold, dry, petrifick mace"[722] of a false and unfeeling philosophy. Some time after this speech, that is, on the thirteenth of last August, the same magistrate, giving an account of his government at the bar of the same assembly, expresses himself as follows: "In the month of July 1789," [the period of everlasting commemoration] "the finances of the city of Paris were *yet* in good order; the expenditure was counterbalanced by the receipt, and she had at that time a million [forty thousand pounds sterling] in bank. The expences which she has been [350] constrained to incur, *subsequent to the revolution*, amount to 2,500,000 livres. From these expences, and the great falling off in the product of the *free gifts*, not only a momentary but a *total* want of money has taken place."[723] This is the Paris upon whose nourishment, in the course of the last year, such immense sums, drawn from the vitals of all France, has been expended. As long as Paris stands in the place of an-

---

[720]On 2 January 1790, reported in *Le Moniteur*, 4 and 5 January 1790: 'Nous inspirerons le respect au Peuple de la capitale qui a conquis la liberté par sa résolution ...'

[721]Bailly was an astronomer; the Atlantides was another name for the group of stars generally known as the Pleiades.

[722]'The aggregated Soyle / Death with his Mace petrific, cold and dry, / As with a Trident smote, and fix't as firm / As *Delos* floating once': John Milton, *Paradise Lost*, Book X, 293–6. For Delos see *Reflections*, p. [278].

[723]Burke quoted Bailly's speech to the National Assembly on 13 August 1790, summarised in *Le Moniteur* of 14 August 1790. The italics were Burke's. (The speech was not printed in the *Procès-verbal*.)

tient Rome, so long she will be maintained by the subject provinces. It is an evil inevitably attendant on the dominion of sovereign democratic republics. As it happened in Rome, it may survive that republican domination which gave rise to it. In that case despotism itself must submit to the vices of popularity. Rome, under her emperors, united the evils of both systems; and this unnatural combination was one great cause of her ruin.

To tell the people that they are relieved by the dilapidation of their public estate, is a cruel and insolent imposition. Statesmen, before they valued themselves on the relief given to the people, by the destruction of their revenue, ought first to have carefully attended to the solution of this problem:— Whether it be more advantageous to the people to pay considerably, and to gain in proportion; or to gain little or nothing, and to be disburthened of all contribution? My mind is made up to decide in favour of the first proposition. Experience is with me, and, I believe, the best opinions also. To keep a balance between the power of acquisition on the part of the subject, and the demands he is to answer on the part of the state, is a fundamental part of the skill of a true politician. [351] The means of acquisition are prior in time and in arrangement. Good order is the foundation of all good things. To be enabled to acquire, the people, without being servile, must be tractable and obedient. The magistrate must have his reverence, the laws their authority. The body of the people must not find the principles of natural subordination by art rooted out of their minds. They must respect that property of which they cannot partake. They must labour to obtain what by labour can be obtained; and when they find, as they commonly do, the success disproportioned to the endeavour, they must be taught their consolation in the final proportions of eternal justice. Of this consolation, whoever deprives them, deadens their industry, and strikes at the root of all acquisition as of all conservation. He that does this is the cruel oppressor, the merciless enemy of the poor and wretched; at the same time that by his wicked speculations he exposes the fruits of successful industry, and the accumulations of fortune, to the plunder of the negligent, the disappointed, and the unprosperous.

Too many of the financiers by profession are apt to see nothing in revenue, but banks, and circulations, and annuities on lives, and tontines,[724] and perpetual rents, and all the small wares of the shop. In a settled order of the state,

[724]Tontine: a system of life insurance proposed to Mazarin by Lorenzo Tonti in 1653. In return for a capital investment by a group of people, a fixed annual dividend would be shared equally among the survivors. The last survivor would draw the whole of the dividend. Louis XIV initiated such a scheme in 1689, but all state tontines in France were wound up in 1770. In Britain the system was regularly used in national finance between 1773 and 1789.

these things are not to be slighted, nor is the skill in them to be held of trivial estimation. They are good, but then only good, when they assume the effects of that settled order, and are built upon it. But when men think that these beggarly contrivances may supply a resource for the evils which result from breaking up the [352] foundations of public order, and from causing or suffering the principles of property to be subverted, they will, in the ruin of their country, leave a melancholy and lasting monument of the effect of preposterous politics, and presumptuous, short-sighted, narrow-minded wisdom.

The effects of the incapacity shewn by the popular in all the great members of the commonwealth are to be covered with the "all-atoning name"[725] of liberty. In some people I see great liberty indeed; in many, if not in the most, an oppressive degrading servitude. But what is liberty without wisdom, and without virtue? It is the greatest of all possible evils; for it is folly, vice, and madness, without tuition or restraint. Those who know what virtuous liberty is, cannot bear to see it disgraced by incapable heads, on account of their having high-sounding words in their mouths. Grand, swelling sentiments of liberty, I am sure I do not despise. They warm the heart; they enlarge and liberalise our minds; they animate our courage in a time of conflict. Old as I am, I read the fine raptures of Lucan and Corneille[726] with pleasure. Neither do I wholly condemn the little arts and devices of popularity. They facilitate the carrying of many points of moment; they keep the people together; they refresh the mind in its exertions; and they diffuse occasional gaiety over the severe brow of moral freedom. Every politician ought to sacrifice to the graces; and to join compliance with reason. But in such an undertaking as that in France, all these subsidiary sentiments and artifices are of little avail. To make a government requires no great prudence. Settle the seat of power; teach obedience: and the work is done. [353] To give freedom is still more easy. It is not necessary to guide; it only requires to let go the rein. But to form a *free government*; that is, to temper together these opposite elements of liberty and restraint in one consistent work, requires much thought, deep reflection, a saga-

---

[725]In Dryden's allegorical poem, 'Achitophel' represented Anthony Ashley Cooper, 1st earl of Shaftesbury (1621–83): 'In Friendship False, Implacable in Hate: / Resolv'd to Ruine or to Rule the State. / ... Then, seiz'd with Fear, yet still affecting Fame, / Assum'd a Patriott's All-attoning Name': [John Dryden], *Absalom and Achitophel. A Poem* (London, 1681), p. 6.

[726]Marcus Annaeus Lucanus (AD 39–65): Burke owned a copy of Nicholas Rowe (trans.), *Lucan's Pharsalia* (London, 1718). Pierre Corneille (1606–84): Burke also owned a copy of *Les Chef-d'oeuvres dramatiques de Messieurs Corneille, avec le jugement des sçavans à la fin de chaque pièce* (3 vols. [?Oxford], 1771): LC, pp. 5, 18; LC MS, fo. 3.

cious, powerful, and combining mind. This I do not find in those who take the lead in the national assembly. Perhaps they are not so miserably deficient as they appear. I rather believe it. It would put them below the common level of human understanding. But when the leaders choose to make themselves bidders at an auction of popularity, their talents, in the construction of the state, will be of no service. They will become flatterers instead of legislators; the instruments, not the guides of the people. If any of them should happen to propose a scheme of liberty, soberly limited, and defined with proper qualifications, he will be immediately outbid by his competitors, who will produce something more splendidly popular. Suspicions will be raised of his fidelity to his cause. Moderation will be stigmatized as the virtue of cowards; and compromise as the prudence of traitors; until, in hopes of preserving the credit which may enable him to temper and moderate on some occasions, the popular leader is obliged to become active in propagating doctrines, and establishing powers, that will afterwards defeat any sober purpose at which he ultimately might have aimed.

But am I so unreasonable as to see nothing at all that deserves commendation in the indefatigable labours of this assembly? I do not deny that among an infinite number of acts of violence and [354] folly, some good may have been done. They who destroy every thing certainly will remove some grievance. They who make every thing new, have a chance that they may establish something beneficial. To give them credit for what they have done in virtue of the authority they have usurped, or which can excuse them in the crimes by which that authority has been acquired, it must appear, that the same things could not have been accomplished without producing such a revolution. Most assuredly they might; because almost every one of the regulations made by them, which is not very equivocal, was either in the cession of the king, voluntarily made at the meeting of the states, or in the concurrent instructions to the orders. Some usages have been abolished on just grounds; but they were such that if they had stood as they were to all eternity, they would little detract from the happiness and prosperity of any state. The improvements of the national assembly are superficial, their errors fundamental.

Whatever they are, I wish my countrymen rather to recommend to our neighbours the example of the British constitution, than to take models from them for the improvement of our own. In the former they have got an invaluable treasure. They are not, I think, without some causes of apprehension and complaint; but these they do not owe to their constitution, but to their own conduct. I think our happy situation owing to our constitution; but owing to the whole of it; and not to any part singly; owing in a great measure to what we have left standing in our several reviews and reformations, as well as to what we have altered or superadded. Our [355] people will find employment enough for a truly patriotic, free, and independent spirit, in guarding what they possess, from violation. I would not exclude alteration neither; but even when I changed, it should be to preserve. I should be led to my remedy by a great grievance. In what I did, I should follow the example of our ancestors. I would make the reparation as nearly as possible in the style of the building. A politic caution, a guarded circumspection, a moral rather than a complexional timidity were among the ruling principles of our forefathers in their most decided conduct. Not being illuminated with the light of which the gentlemen of France tell us they have got so abundant a share, they acted under a strong impression of the ignorance and fallibility of mankind. He that had made them thus fallible, rewarded them for having in their conduct attended to their nature. Let us imitate their caution, if we wish to deserve their fortune, or to retain their bequests. Let us add, if we please, but let us preserve what they have left; and, standing on the firm ground of the British constitution, let us be satisfied to admire rather than attempt to follow in their desperate flights the aëronauts of France.

I have told you candidly my sentiments. I think they are not likely to alter yours. I do not know that they ought. You are young; you cannot guide, but must follow the fortune of your country. But hereafter they may be of some use to you, in some future form which your commonwealth may take. In the present it can hardly remain; but before its final settlement it may be obliged to pass, as one of our poets says, "through [356] great varieties of untried being,"[727] and in all its transmigrations to be purified by fire and blood.

I have little to recommend my opinions, but long observation and much impartiality. They come from one who has been no tool of power, no flatterer of greatness; and who in his last acts does not wish to belye the tenour of his life. They come from one, almost the whole of whose public exertion has been a struggle for the liberty of others;[728] from one in whose breast no anger dura-

---

[727]'Eternity! thou pleasing, dreadful Thought! / Through what Variety of untry'd Being, / Through what new Scenes and Changes must we pass! / The wide, th' unbounded Prospect, lie's before me; / But Shadows, Clouds, and Darkness, rest upon it': Joseph Addison, *Cato. A Tragedy* (London, 1713), Act V, Scene I, lines 10–14. *Cato* enjoyed lasting popularity among eighteenth-century Whigs. Burke had used this phrase in his letter to Depont of November 1789: Burke, *Correspondence*, VI, p. 46. Burke glossed those 'varieties' to mean 'chaos and darkness'.

[728]Burke's public life revolved around a series of crusades in defence of groups he regarded as unjustly treated, especially the Irish Catholics, the American colonists, and the Indians. His protest against the even more catastrophic injustices of the French Revolution is, in one view, consistent with his former commitments.

ble or vehement has ever been kindled, but by what he considered as tyranny; and who snatches from his share in the endeavours which are used by good men to discredit opulent oppression,[729] the hours he has employed on your affairs; and who in so doing persuades himself he has not departed from his usual office: they come from one who desires honours, distinctions, and emoluments, but little; and who expects them not at all; who has no contempt for fame, and no fear of obloquy; who shuns contention, though he will hazard an opinion: from one who wishes to preserve consistency; but who would preserve consistency by varying his means to secure the unity of his end; and, when the equipoise of the vessel in which he sails, may be endangered by overloading it upon one side, is desirous of carrying the small weight of his reasons to that which may preserve its equipoise.

## FINIS.

[729]I.e. the impeachment of Warren Hastings: his trial began on 13 February 1788, and ended in acquittal on 23 April 1795.

# Textual variations in subsequent editions

A Collation of Texts has been undertaken by W. B. Todd, and is published in the Oxford edition, pp. 525–9. Most of Burke's changes to later editions were confined to corrections of errors of the press. In some cases Burke added footnotes reflecting his reading of Calonne. In few places, Burke added text or made substantial revisions: these are given here. References are to the page numbers of the first (1790) edition.

*(1) Pp. [259–62]. Burke later amended these paragraphs to read:*

Now take it in the other point of view, and let us suppose their principle of representation according to contribution, that is according to riches, to be well imagined, and to be a necessary basis for their republic. In this their third basis they assume, that riches ought to be respected, and that justice and policy require that they should entitle men, in some mode or other, to a larger share in the administration of public affairs; it is now to be seen, how the assembly provides for the pre-eminence, or even for the security of the rich, by conferring, in virtue of their opulence, that larger measure of power to their district which is denied to them personally. I readily admit (indeed I should lay it down as a fundamental principle) that in a republican government, which has a democratic basis, the rich do require an additional security above what is necessary to them in monarchies. They are subject to envy, and through envy to oppression. On the present scheme, it is impossible to divine what advantage they derive from the aristocratic preference upon which the unequal representation of the masses is founded. The rich cannot feel it, either as a support to dignity, or as security to fortune: for the aristocratic mass is generated from purely democratic principles; and the prevalence given to it in the general representation has no sort of reference to or connexion with the persons, upon account of whose property this superiority of the mass is established. If the contrivers of this scheme meant any sort of favour to the rich in consequence of their contribution, they ought to have conferred the privilege either on the individual rich, or on some class formed of rich persons (as historians represent Servius Tullius to have done in the early constitution of Rome);[1] because the contest between the rich and the poor is not a struggle between corporation and corporation, but a contest between men and men; a competition not between districts but between descriptions. It would answer its purpose better if the scheme were inverted; that the votes of the masses were rendered equal; and that the votes within each mass were proportioned to property.

Let us suppose one man in a district (it is an easy supposition) to contribute as much as an hundred of his neighbours. Against these he has but one vote. If there were but one representative for the mass, his poor neighbours would outvote him by an hundred to one for that single representative. Bad enough. But amends are to be made him. How? The district, in virtue of his wealth, is to choose, say, ten members instead of one: that is to say, by paying a very large contribution he has the happiness of being outvoted, an hundred to one, by the poor for ten representatives, instead of being outvoted exactly in the same proportion for a single member. In truth, instead of benefitting by this superior quantity of representation, the rich man is subjected to an additional hardship. The encrease of representation within his province sets up nine persons more, and as many more than nine as there may be democratic candidates, to cabal and intrigue, and to flatter the people at his expence and to his oppression. An interest is by this means held out to multitudes of the inferior sort, in obtaining a salary of eighteen livres a day (to them a vast object) besides the pleasure of a residence in Paris and their share in the government of the kingdom. The more the objects of ambition are multiplied and become democratic, just in that proportion the rich are endangered.

Thus it must fare between the poor and the rich in the province deemed aristocratic, which in its internal relation is the very reverse of that character. In its external relation, that is, its relation to the other provinces, I cannot see how the unequal representation, which is given to masses on account of wealth, becomes the means of preserving the equipoise and the tranquillity of the commonwealth. For if it be one of the objects to secure the weak from be-

[1]Servius Tullius, King of Rome (578–543 BC), was credited with a new classification of the Roman people which prepared the way for the emancipation of the plebeians.

ing crushed by the strong (as in all society undoubtedly it is) how are the smaller and poorer of these masses to be saved from the tyranny of the more wealthy? Is it by adding to the wealthy further and more systematical means of oppressing them. When we come to a balance of representation between corporate bodies, provincial interests, emulations, and jealousies are full as likely to arise among them as among individuals; and their divisions are likely to produce a much hotter spirit of dissention, and something leading much more nearly to a war.

I see that these aristocratic masses are made upon what is called the principle of direct contribution. Nothing can be a more unequal standard than this. The indirect contribution, that which arises from duties on consumption, is in truth a better standard, and follows and discovers wealth more naturally than this of direct contribution. It is difficult indeed to fix a standard of local preference on account of the one, or of the other, or of both, because some provinces may pay the more of either or of both, on account of causes not intrinsic, but originating from those very districts over whom they have obtained a preference in consequence of their ostensible contribution. If the masses were independent sovereign bodies, who were to provide for a federative treasury by distinct contingents, and that the revenue had not (as it has) many impositions running through the whole, which affect men individually, and not corporately, and which, by their nature, confound all territorial limits, something might be said for the basis of contribution as founded on masses. But of all things, this representation, to be measured by contribution, is the most difficult to settle upon principles of equity in a country, which considers its districts as members of an whole. For a great city, such as Bourdeaux or Paris, appears to pay a vast body of duties, almost out of all assignable proportion to other places, and its mass is considered accordingly. But are these cities the true contributors in that proportion? No. The consumers of the commodities imported into Bourdeaux, who are scattered through all France, pay the import duties of Bourdeaux. The produce of the vintage in Guienne and Languedoc give to that city the means of its contribution growing out of an export commerce. The landholders who spend their estates in Paris, and are thereby the creators of that city, contribute for Paris from the provinces out of which their revenues arise. Very nearly the same arguments will apply to the representative share given on account of *direct* contribution: because the direct contribution must be assessed on wealth real or presumed; and that local wealth will itself arise from causes not local, and which therefore in equity ought not to produce a local preference.

It is very remarkable, that in this fundamental regulation, which settles the representation of the mass upon the direct contribution, they have not yet settled how that direct contribution shall be laid, and how apportioned. Perhaps there is some latent policy towards the continuance of the present assembly in this strange procedure. However, until they do this, they can have no certain constitution. It must depend at last upon the system of taxation, and must vary with every variation in that system. As they have contrived matters, their taxation does not so much depend on their constitution, as their constitution on their taxation. This must introduce great confusion among the masses; as the variable qualification for votes within the district must, if ever real contested elections take place, cause infinite internal controversies.

*(2) P. [268]. Burke later inserted:*

I wish, Sir, that you and my readers would give an attentive perusal to the work of M. de Calonne, on this subject.[2] It is indeed not only an eloquent but an able and instructive performance. I confine myself to what he says relative to the constitution of the new state, and to the condition of the revenue. As to the disputes of this minister with his rivals,[3] I do not wish to pronounce upon them. As little do I mean to hazard any opinion concerning his ways and means, financial or political, for taking his country out of its present disgraceful and deplorable situation of servitude, anarchy, bankruptcy, and beggary. I cannot speculate quite so sanguinely as he does: but he is a Frenchman, and has a closer duty relative to those objects, and better means of judging of them, than I can have. I wish that the formal avowal which he refers to, made by one of the principal leaders in the assembly, concerning the tendency of their scheme to bring France not only from a monarchy to a republic, but from a republic to a mere confederacy, may be very particularly attended to. It adds new force to my observations; and indeed M. de Calonne's work supplies my deficiencies by many new and striking arguments on most of the subjects of this Letter.[4]

[2]Charles-Alexandre de Calonne, *De l'état de la France, présent & à venir* (London and Paris, 1790).

[3]The subject of French national finances had become a subject of major controversy in the late 1780s, the major contenders being Necker, Loménie de Brienne and Calonne. Although now inclining away from Necker and towards Calonne, Burke's caution was justifiable.

[4]See L'Etat de la France, p. 363. [B] 'On chercheroit vainement, dans l'histoire du monde, l'exemple d'une organisation aussi monstreuse, à l'égard d'un empire indivis: elle seroit même insoutenable & mal conçue, dans la supposition qu'on voulût morceler la France en 83 souverainetés républicaines, par une suite de l'engouement qu'on a pris pour la Constitution trop peu connue, trop prématurément jugée, des Etats-Unis de l'Amérique. Ce déchirement de l'Empire François en autant d'Etats fédératifs qu'en pourroient produire les secousses convulsives qui le démembreroient, seroit-it donc le

*(3) P. [304]. Burke later inserted:*

This establishment of judges as yet wants something to its completion. It is to be crowned by a new tribunal.[5] This is to be a grand state judicature; and it is to judge of crimes committed against the nation, that is, against the power of the assembly. It seems as if they had something in their view of the nature of the high court of justice erected in England during the time of the great usurpation.[6] As they have not yet finished this part of the scheme, it is impossible to form a direct judgment upon it. However, if great care is not taken to form it in a spirit very different from that which has guided them in their proceedings relative to state offences, this tribunal, subservient to their inquisition, *the committee of research,*[7] will extinguish the last sparks of liberty in France, and settle most dreadful and arbitrary tyranny ever known in any nation. If they wish to give to this tribunal any appearance of liberty and justice, they must not evoke from, or send to it, the causes relative to their own members, at their pleasure. They must also remove the seat of that tribunal out of the republic of Paris.[8]

*(4) P. [343]. Burke later inserted:*

At length they have spoken out, and they have made a full discovery of their abominable fraud, in holding out the church lands as a security for any debts or any service whatsoever. They rob only to enable them to cheat; but in a very short time they defeat the ends both of the robbery and the fraud, by

---

but de toutes ces inexplicables manoeuvres? Il est du moins très-vraisemblable que c'en seroit le dernier résultat; & quoiqu'il soit hors de doute que ce seroit en même tems le tombeau où s'enseveliroit, après une longue suite de malheurs, toute la gloire & toute la puissance que s'est acquise la monarchie pendant 14 siècles, on a néamoins entendu un des Membres les plus clairvoyans de l'Assemblée annoncer froidement que le pouvoir donné aux corps administratifs, conduiroit & aboutiroit tôt ou tard aux Etats fédératifs. [footnote:] M. de Mirabeau l'aîné.' Burke's English critics seldom took proper account of Calonne's important work: their knowledge of French affairs was not all that they represented it to be.

[5]For the constitution of the court, and its eventual subordination to the legislature, see Roberts (ed.), *Documents*, p. 362. Established on 10 May 1791, it was swept away in March 1793 by the Revolutionary Tribunal, the body that presided over the Terror.

[6]A special 'court' had to be created to condemn Charles I in 1649.

[7]The *Comité des recherches* was created by the National Assembly on 28 July 1789 to investigate political conspiracies; 'c'est en pratique le ministère de la Police de la Constituante': Fierro and Liébert, p. 751.

[8]For further elucidations upon the subject of all these judicatures, and of the committee of research, see M. de Calonne's work. [B] See *De l'état de la France*, pp. 290–314; for the *Comité de recherches*, pp. 298–300.

making out accounts for other purposes, which blow up their whole apparatus of force and of deception. I am obliged to M. de Calonne for his reference
to the document which proves this extraordinary fact: it had, by some means,
escaped me. Indeed it was not necessary to make out my assertion as to the
breach of faith on the declaration of the 14th of April 1790.[9] By a report of
their Committee it now appears, that the charge of keeping up the reduced ecclesiastical establishments, and other expences attendant on religion, and
maintaining the religious of both sexes, retained or pensioned, and the other
concomitant expences of the same nature, which they have brought upon
themselves by this convulsion in property, exceeds the income of the estates
acquired by it in the enormous sum of two millions sterling annually; besides a
debt of seven millions and upwards. These are the calculating powers of im-
posture! This is the finance of philosophy! This is the result of all the delusions
held out to engage a miserable people in rebellion, murder, and sacrilege, and
to make them prompt and zealous instruments in the ruin of their country!
Never did a state, in any case, enrich itself by the confiscations of the citizens.[10] This new experiment has succeeded like all the rest. Every honest mind,
every true lover of liberty and humanity must rejoice to find that injustice is
not always good policy, nor rapine the high road to riches. I subjoin with
pleasure, in a note, the able and spirited observations of M. de Calonne on
this subject.[11]

[9] On 14 April 1790 the National Assembly voted a series of resolutions on tithes
and church goods to give effect to its general decision of 2 November 1789 that church
property was at the disposal of the nation. These resolutions promised that 'Dans l'état
des dépenses publiques de chaque année, il sera porté une somme suffisante pour
fournir aux frais du culte de la religion catholique, apostolique et romaine, et
l'entretien des ministres des autels, au soulagement des pauvres et aux pensions des ecclésiastiques ...': *Le Moniteur*, 15 April 1790.

[10] Burke overlooked the massive loss of loyalist property in the American Revolution, far greater in proportion to population and wealth than the losses of the French
royalists.

[11] "Ce n'est point à l'assemblée entière que je m'adresse ici; je ne parle qu'à ceux qui
l'égarent, en lui cachant sous des gazes séduisantes le but où ils l'entraînent. C'est à eux
que je dis: votre objet, vous n'en disconviendrez pas, c'est d'ôter tout espoir au clergé,
& de consommer sa ruine; c'est-la, en ne vous soupçonnant d'aucune combinaison de
cupidité, d'aucun regard sur le jeu des effets publics, c'est-là ce qu'on doit croire que
vous avez en vue dans la terrible opération que vous proposez; c'est ce qui doit en être
le fruit. Mais le peuple que vous y intéressez, quel avantage peut il y trouver? En vous
servant sans cesse de lui, que faites vous pour lui? Rien, absolument rien; &, au con-
traire, vous faites ce qui ne conduit qu'à l'accabler de nouvelles charges. Vous avez re-
jeté, à son prejudice, une offre de 400 millions, dont l'acceptation pouvoit devenir un
moyen de soulagement en sa faveur; & à cette ressource, aussi profitable que legitime,

In order to persuade the world of the bottomless resource of ecclesiastical confiscation, the assembly have proceeded to other confiscations of estates in offices, which could not be done with any common colour without being compensated out of this grand confiscation of landed property.

---

vous avez substitué une injustice ruineuse, qui, de votre propre aveu, charge le trésor public, & par conséquent le peuple, d'un surcroît de depense annuelle de 50 millions au moins, & d'un remboursement de 150 millions.

"Malheureux peuple, voilà ce que vous vaut en dernier résultat l'expropriation de l'Eglise, & la dureté des décrets taxateurs du traitement des ministres d'une religion bienfaisante; & desormais ils seront à votre charge: leurs charités soulageoient les pauvres; & vous allez être imposés pour subvenir à leur entretien!"—*De l'Etat de la France*, p. 81. See also p. 92, and the following pages. [B] The pagination of the London edition of Calonne was faulty at this point. Burke quoted pp. 95–96–81 *bis*.

# Richard Price's reply to Burke

[Burke's *Reflections*, published on 1 November 1790, was written as a reply to Price's *A Discourse on the Love of Our Country*, not as part of a controversy with Thomas Paine. Although the *Reflections* is now commonly compared with Paine's *Rights of Man*, Price's response to Burke is more revealing of Burke's immediate purposes. Price acted at once to rebut his critic: his reply took the form of a Preface to the fourth edition of Price's *Discourse*, published on 25 November 1790, and additions to its Appendix.[1] Although Price wrote nothing more in the controversy, he expressed satisfaction[2] at Priestley's defence of him, and Priestley's pamphlet[3] has been noticed in the footnotes to this edition of the *Reflections*.]

Preface to the Fourth Edition.

Since the former Editions of the following Discourse, many animadversions upon it have been published. Under the abuse with which some of them are accompanied, I have been comforted by finding myself joined to the City of PARIS, and the National Assembly of FRANCE. I cannot think of employing my time in making any replies. Knowing that it has been the labour of my life to promote those interests of liberty, peace, and virtue, which I reckon the best interests of mankind; and believing that I have not laboured quite in vain, I feel a satisfaction that no opposition can take from me, and shall submit my-

[1]There were other minor textual changes to the *Discourse* between the second edition and the third, and between the third and the fourth. They are not noted here.

[2]Price, *Correspondence*, III, pp. 334–40.

[3]Joseph Priestley, *Letters to the Right Hon Edmund Burke, Occasioned by his Reflections on the Revolution in France* (Birmingham, 1791).

self in silence to the judgement of the Public, without taking any other notice of the abuse I have met with, than by mentioning the following instance of it.

In p. 49,[4] I have adopted the words of Scripture, *Now lettest thou thy servant depart in peace*, and expressed my gratitude to God for having spared my life to see 'a diffusion of knowledge that has undermined superstition and error, a vast kingdom spurning at slavery, and an arbitrary Monarch led in triumph and surrendering himself to his subjects.' These words have occasioned a comparison of me (by Mr. BURKE, in his Reflections on the Revolution in France) to HUGH PETERS, attended with an intimation that, like him, *I may not die in peace*; and he has described me, p. 99, &c. as a barbarian delighted with blood, profaning Scripture, and exulting in the riot and slaughter at *Versailles* on the 6th of October last year. I hope I shall be credited when, in answer to this horrid misrepresentation and menace, I assure the public that the events to which I referred in these words were not those of the 6th of October, but those only of the 14th of July and the subsequent days; when, after the conquest of the BASTILLE, the King of FRANCE sought the protection of the National Assembly, and, by his own desire, was conducted, amidst acclamations never before heard in FRANCE, to PARIS, there to shew himself to his people as the restorer of their liberty.

I am indeed surprised that Mr. BURKE could want candour so much as to suppose that I had any other event in view. The letters quoted by him in p. 99 [*sc.* 97] and 128, were dated in *July* 1789, and might have shewn him that he was injuring both me and the writer of those letters.[5] But what candour or what moderation can be expected in a person so frantic with zeal for hereditary claims and aristocratical distinctions as to be capable of decrying popular rights and the aid of philosophy in forming governments; of lamenting that the age of Chivalry is gone; and of believing that the insults offered by a mob to the Queen of France have extinguished for ever the glory of Europe?

The Postscript in p. 4 [of the Appendix], and all in the Appendix after p. 34, have been added in this edition.

[4]I.e. of Price's *Discourse*.

[5]Price implied that both letters were written to him by the same author. The first letter has been identified as by Price's nephew George Cadogan Morgan: *Reflections*, p. [97].

Note intended for p. 34, &c.[6]

Mr. BURKE, in his Reflections on the Revolution in FRANCE, denies several of the principles which in these pages are said to be the principles of the Revolution. He asserts that our Kings do not derive their right to the Crown from the choice of their People, and that they are not responsible to them. And yet, with wonderful inconsistency, he intimates, p. 123, that a wicked King may be punished, provided it is done with dignity; and he is under the necessity of granting that King JAMES was justly deprived of his Crown for misconduct. In p. 19, he mentions the *legal conditions of the compact of sovereignty* by which our Kings are bound. The succession of the Crown he calls an *emanation from the common agreement and original compact of the State*, and the Constitution also he calls the *engagement and pact of Society*. In p. 26, he cites, as an authority against the right of the People to chuse their own Governors, the very Act for settling the crown on *William and Mary* which was an exercise of that right, and the words of which are: 'The Lords and Commons do in the name of all the people submit themselves, their heirs and posterities for ever,' &c. &c. This Act having been passed on purpose to establish a change in the succession for misconduct, it cannot be supposed that it was intended to deprive the nation for ever of the power of making again any such change, whatever reasons appearing to the nation sufficient might occur. That is, it cannot be supposed that it was the intention of the Act to subject the nation for ever to any tyrants that might happen to arise in the new line of succession. And yet this is the sense in which Mr. BURKE seems to understand it; and he grounds upon it his assertion in p. 27, 'that so far was the nation from acquiring by the Revolution a right to elect our Kings, that, if we had possessed it before, the *English* nation did then most solemnly renounce and abdicate it for themselves and for all their posterity for ever.' Mr. BURKE, before he published this assertion, should have attended to a subsequent Act, which has been recommended to my notice by the truly patriotic EARL STANHOPE. I mean the Act of the 6th of Anne, chap. 7th, by which it is enacted that, 'if any person shall by writing or printing maintain and affirm that the Kings or Queens of this realm, with and by the authority of Parliament, ARE NOT ABLE to make laws and statutes of sufficient validity to limit the Crown, and the descent, inheritance and government thereof, every such person shall be guilty of HIGH TREASON, &c.'

'Price intended this as a comment on p. 34 of his *Discourse*, where he had proposed, as 'the principles of the Revolution' of 1688, 'First; The right to liberty of conscience in religious matters. Secondly; The right to resist power when abused. And, Thirdly; The right to chuse our own governors; to cashier them for misconduct; and to frame a government for ourselves.'

[In the Appendix to his *Discourse*, Price added on p. 4 a paragraph, omitted here, headed 'Postscript' and containing a new calculation of the population of France. To the end of the Appendix he added the following additional material, making pp. 35–44, in an attempt to vindicate the conduct of the Revolution Society. It is not wholly persuasive. Neither his speech on 14 July 1790 nor the text of the speech that he intended to make on 4 November 1790 were evidence for the attitude to the French Revolution of the Society's other members. Other English and Scots Jacobins in the 1790s did call for a National Convention to bypass the Westminster Parliament in just the sense that Price here disavowed. The letter from Quimper may be read as containing an implicit threat, not appreciated by Price in his reply to it, of revolution exported by military force.]

ON the 14th of July [1790] a very respectable company, consisting of several hundreds of Gentlemen, met at the Crown and Anchor Tavern in the Strand, to celebrate the first Anniversary of the glorious Revolution in France, Earl STANHOPE in the Chair. At this meeting Dr. Price gave, as a toast,

An ALLIANCE between FRANCE and GREAT-BRITAIN, for perpetuating peace, and making the world happy.

This toast was introduced by the following Address to the company.

GENTLEMEN,

IN consequence of five wars in which we have been involved since the Revolution in 1688, the kingdom is now sinking under a load of debts, which render it incapable of meeting another war without the utmost danger. For certainly there is a limit, beyond which if we go in adding to our debts, ruin must follow; and one more war may bring us to that limit.

A long period of peace, therefore, to give us time for the redemption of our debts, is necessary to our security; and, perhaps, even to our existence.—In France there is a disposition to unite itself to us, by an alliance for maintaining and perpetuating peace. Such an alliance would be an union between the two first kingdoms in the world, for the noblest purpose. It would be an effect worthy of that union of philosophy to politics, which distinguishes the present aera of the world. It might save Britain. It would bless the world, and complete the hopes of all the friends of human liberty and happiness. I can say, from very respectable authority, that there has been a design formed, in the National Assembly of France, to make a proposal of such an alliance to this country:—'O heavenly philanthropists! well do you deserve the admiration not only of your own country, but of all countries. You have already determined to renounce, for ever, all views of conquest, and all *offensive* wars. This is an instance of wisdom and attention to human rights which has no example. But you will do more. You will invite Great-Britain to join you in this determination, and to enter into a compact with you for promoting *peace on earth and good-will among men.*'

GENTLEMEN,

SUCH are the fruits of the glorious Revolution which we are this day celebrating. It promises a new and better order in human affairs. The passions of Kings and their Ministers have too often and too long involved nations in the calamities of war. But now (thanks to the National Assembly of France) the axe is laid to the root of this cause of human misery, and the intrigues of Courts are likely to lose their power of embroiling the world.

In this kingdom we have been used to speak of the people of France as our *natural enemies*; and however absurd, as well as ungenerous and wicked, such language was, it admitted of some excuse while they consisted only of a monarch and his slaves. But now, with a spirit that astonishes mankind, and that makes tyrants tremble, they have broke their yoke, they have asserted their rights, and made themselves as free as ourselves. In doing this, we have been an example to THEM. THEY are now become an example to US; and we have reason to expect, that they will soon crown their glorious work by calling upon us to *meet* them (not as formerly in fields of blood at the command of a despot), but on the sacred ground of liberty, to embrace us as brethren, to exchange vows with us of eternal amity, and to settle the terms of a confederation for extending the blessings of peace and liberty through the world.— Thus united, the two kingdoms will be omnipotent. They will soon draw into their confederation HOLLAND, and other countries on this side the Globe, and the United States of AMERICA on the other; and, when alarms of war come, they will be able to say to contending nations, PEACE, and there will be PEACE.

I have therefore thought that it would be worthy of this respectable company on this most animating occasion, to express its wishes of success to the proposal I have mentioned, by drinking,

An Alliance between FRANCE and GREAT-BRITAIN for perpetuating Peace, and making the world happy. Amen and Amen!!

This address, together with a resolution proposed by *Mr. Sheridan,*[7] expressive of the joy of the company in the extension of liberty to *France*, and of its wishes of eternal amity between the two kingdoms, were conveyed to the National Assembly of FRANCE, and there received with applause—The sentiments in this address have also been echoed, with the warmest zeal, in letters

[7]See Biographical Guide.

from many different societies and districts in *France*. One of these letters has been selected for publication in this *Appendix*, because directed more particularly to the proposer of the toast just mentioned, and answered by him.

*Copy of a Letter from the District of* QUIMPER, *in the Department of* FINISTERRE, *conveyed by the Duke de la* ROCHEFOUCAULD, *and signed by M.* Francois Noel Bremaudiere, *President of the District, and the other principal Magistrates and Citizens.*
*Bretagne, Aug.* 4, 1790.

[The French text is omitted here]

TRANSLATION
*Of the foregoing Letter*

SIR,

We have been affected even to tears in reading the discourse which the love of mankind dictated to you at the meeting of the friends of the *British* Revolution. It is with an emotion which we cannot express that we see English Citizens developing those principles of liberty which the hearts of *Frenchmen* cherish with so much enthusiasm. You have observed, that when *Frenchmen* were debased by despotism, the two kingdoms could not unite; but now, since the love of liberty has raised us to your level, the two first kingdoms in the world ought to form only one family, encouraging by the union of its children all enslaved countries, and giving to unfeeling despots a lesson that may overwhelm them.

It has not been possible for us to believe that the people of England would prostitute their arms by opposing them to the rising liberty of FRANCE; but should any rash and daring ministers attempt this, we are persuaded that, at the first onset, the friends of liberty in the two countries would recognize one another, and, far from fighting, would cement by fraternal embraces that union which ought ever to subsist between two nations destined to exhibit to the astonished world an example of all the social virtues. We are happy in giving you this testimony of our admiration. Principles so excellent when professed by you, cannot fail to draw together, throughout the world, all the true friends of mankind.

THE CITIZENS OF THE DISTRICT
OF QUIMPER

## ANSWER

LONDON, *Oct.* 14, 1790.

GENTLEMEN,

THE letter which has been conveyed to me by your excellent fellow-citizen and co-patriot M. de *Rochefoucauld*, brought me a testimony of your approbation, on which I set a high value. Such notice confers a greater honour than any that titles can give or kings bestow. Accept my thanks for thus encouraging the attempts of a feeble individual to serve the best of all causes. The Discourse delivered on the 14th of July, at the feast in *London* for celebrating the Anniversary of the glorious Revolution in *France*, and which you have thus honoured, was indeed an emanation from a heart warm with zeal to promote peace and philanthropy among nations, and with an admiration of that disdain of slavery which now pervades your country, and which has produced there a Revolution unparalleled in history, to which philosophers and virtuous men are now looking as a noble burst of the human mind from the fetters of slavery and superstition, and the commencement of a general reformation in the governments of EUROPE. May Heaven prosper the great work, and grant that no adverse event may interrupt its progress, or prevent its happy completion!—Hitherto the world has groaned under despots; and the best interests of society have fallen a sacrifice to their passions and follies. We are now seeing the dawn of better times, and the example of France is likely to increase it into a glorious effulgence. From the instruction there given, the world will learn, that, as subjects of government and law, all men are equal; that in every State the Majesty of the People is the only Sacred Majesty; that all civil authority is a *trust* from them; that its end is not to take away, but to establish liberty, by protecting equally all honest citizens; and that the governing power in every nation ought to be, not the will of any man or classes of men pretending to hereditary rights, but the collected wisdom drawn from the general mass,[8] and concentrated in a NATIONAL AS-

---

[8]The Government of BRITAIN would be *nearly* such a Government as is here meant, and its constitution *all* that the writer of this letter can wish to see it, were the three States that compose it perfectly independent of one another, and the House of COMMONS in particular, an equal and fair representation of the kingdom, guarded against corruption by being frequently renewed, and the exclusion of placemen and pensioners. [Price's footnote. By 'the three States', he meant Estates, taken to be King, Lords and Commons. Price did not disclose that his understanding of equal and fair representation included universal suffrage. Paine's position was more candid: 'The right of reform is in the nation in its original character, and the constitutional method would be by a general convention elected for the purpose': *Rights of Man*, p. 56.]

SEMBLY, by such modes of election, and such an extension of its rights, as form a part of the new constitution of France.

I am, GENTLEMEN,

With the greatest respect,

Your most obedient and humble Servant,

RICHARD PRICE

On the 4th of November, in this year 1790, the Anniversary of the *British* Revolution was celebrated, as usual, at the LONDON TAVERN.

At this Feast Dr. Price gave, as a toast,

The Parliament of *Britain*—May it become a NATIONAL Assembly.

By this toast no more was meant than to express wishes of such a reform in the representation of the kingdom, as that the Parliament, consisting of Lords and Commons, might be justly deemed a *National* Assembly; that is, an assembly truly representing the nation, and speaking its voice.—But another sense having been given it, totally foreign to the intention of the proposer and of the company that applauded it, it becomes proper to publish the following introduction to it and explanation of it, which the proposer had prepared, but was not able to deliver.[9]

'It is a truth almost self-evident, that it is the collected wisdom and virtue of a nation that ought to govern it; and that, consequently, in order to constitute the best form of government, it is necessary to establish such modes of election, and such an extension of the rights of election, as shall best tend to collect into the legislative assembly of a nation the greatest quantity possible of the national wisdom and virtue.—There can scarcely be better arrangements for this purpose than those which have been lately adopted in FRANCE, and which form a part of its new constitution.

That kingdom has been divided into nine regions; and these regions have been subdivided into 83 departments. It has been further divided into 249 equal sections, called territories; and to each of these territories a right is given to one representative in the National Assembly. Its population is likewise to be divided into 249 equal parts, to each of which is in like manner annexed a right to one representative; and the same is true of the contributions to the revenue; so that the number of representatives constituting the legislative body will be hereafter three times 249, that is 747, or nine for each of the departments taking them one with another, some departments sending more

[9]Price did not explain why he was unable to deliver it. The assembled company were presumably therefore unaware of the more limited sense that Price claimed he placed on the phrase 'a *National* Assembly'.

than nine, and some fewer, according to the greater or smaller number of the equal parts just mentioned, of population and contributions which they contain. In consequence of these arrangements, France must continue always equally and fairly represented: and a body of constituents, equal in number and in their contributions, will always appoint an equal number of representatives.

But what deserves most to be attended to, is the manner in which these representatives are to be elected.

The mass of the people (not paupers, or minors, or in servitude), are entitled to votes. Their votes are to be delivered in the cantons where they reside; but the persons thus elected are not to be the representatives, but the *electors* of the representatives; that is, the body of the people are to select such persons in every department as they shall think fittest for the office of chusing them such persons as shall be best qualified to represent them in the National Assembly. This mode of appointing the members of a Legislative Assembly in a great kingdom was first suggested by Mr. HUME, in one of his political essays, entitled, 'An Idea of a perfect Commonwealth.' And perhaps a method better fitted to exclude corruption from elections, and to collect into a legislature as much as possible of the ability and wisdom of a kingdom, can scarcely be conceived.[10]

Compared with such a representation, What is ours?—The comparison is too humiliating.

The correction of the abuses in our representation ought to be the first object of the zeal of every Briton. While these abuses continue, our constitution cannot be considered as a free constitution, except in theory and form. It wants that counterpoise or independence of the three states on one another, in which its essence as a free constitution consists; and the boasts we make of it are ridiculous.

Equality of representation is the basis of public liberty. It is the *one thing needful* in our government. Let us then drink the Parliament of Britain—may it become a NATIONAL Assembly.'

[10]Price here betrayed exactly the attachment to geometric rationalism that Burke had seized on in the *Reflections*, published on 1 November.

# Index